BUILDING COMMUNITY IN HOUSTON

BUILDING COMMUNITY IN HOUSTON

ALICE BAKER, JULIA IDESON, AND IMA HOGG

KATE SAYEN KIRKLAND

Texas A&M University Press
College Station

First edition

♾ This paper meets the requirements of ANSI/NISO Z39.48-1992 (Permanence of Paper).
Binding materials have been chosen for durability.

Library of Congress Cataloging-in-Publication Data

Names: Kirkland, Kate Sayen, 1944– author.
Title: Building community in Houston : Alice Baker, Julia Ideson, and Ima Hogg / Kate Sayen Kirkland.
Description: First edition. | College Station : Texas A&M University Press, [2025] | Includes bibliographical references and index.
Identifiers: LCCN 2025020500 (print) | LCCN 2025020501 (ebook) | ISBN 9781648432620 (cloth) | ISBN 9781648432637 (ebook)
Subjects: LCSH: Baker, Alice, 1864–1932. | Ideson, Julia, 1880–1945. | Hogg, Ima. | Women civic leaders—Texas—Houston—Biography. | Civic leaders—Texas—Houston—Biography. | Women philanthropists—Texas—Houston—Biography. | Philanthropists—Texas—Houston—Biography. | Community development—Texas—Houston—History—20th century. | LCGFT: Biographies.
Classification: LCC F394.H853 K568 2025 (print) | LCC F394.H853 (ebook)
LC record available at https://lccn.loc.gov/2025020500
LC ebook record available at https://lccn.loc.gov/2025020501

FOR MY DAUGHTERS

Anne Conyers Leader Guether

and

Jennifer Barrett Leader,

multifaceted women of the twenty-first century

CONTENTS

BUILDING COMMUNITY IN HOUSTON

Prologue

Women are central to the peopling and civic life of the United States of America. Yet the significance of this centrality has been slow to enter the historical record. Only when twentieth-century analysts recognized the unintended consequences of industrial urbanization, massive immigration, and ethnic exploitation did stories of cultural and social change emerge as powerful explanations of the American experience and make visible heretofore unexamined female accomplishments. Countless diaries, letters, institutional documents, and works of art created over many generations reveal that women of all ethnicities in what is today the United States have long supported their families' economic well-being, expressed their personal political opinions, addressed the plight of their neighbors, and prompted change by promoting civic improvements in the public square. A steady stream of stories about women and the ways they have shaped the United States followed pioneering research of the 1970s and 1980s; today, women's, gender, and ethnic studies and archives proliferate on college campuses. Frequently these stories have been framed in adversarial terms—the war for individual freedom, the fight for voting rights, the crusade for legal justice, the battle for employment opportunities. Understanding these confrontational campaigns illuminates women's struggle to secure equality under the law in the workplace and at the ballot box, but it often neglects the associative efforts of women and men who collaborated to build viable communities and slowly bend the arc of history toward social justice for every citizen.

Alexis de Tocqueville was the first to explain how "Americans of all ages, all conditions, and all dispositions, constantly form associations . . . of a thousand . . . kinds." He noted that in democracies, "all the citizens are independent and feeble," but when they associate voluntarily, the bonds they forge empower broad civic accomplishment. Social work pioneer Sophonisba Breckenridge detailed "women's struggle to obtain larger freedom for themselves" in her 1933 compendium of female organizations, gainful employments, and government relationships. Her pathbreaking *Women in the Twentieth Century,* prepared for President Herbert Hoover's Research Committee on Social Trends, established women's critical role as sculptors of social change. In 1991 Anne Firor Scott reframed our historical portrait in her sweeping landmark study, *Natural Allies: Women's Associations in American History.* She reviewed two centuries of female associations and placed the natural allies of "organized womanhood" at the "heart of American social and political development." Scott demonstrated that voluntary female associations not only shifted the trajectories of individual lives but also reshaped America's story to reflect the concerns of women who organized to improve the lives and living conditions of all Americans. Before the franchise broadened to include women, female civic leaders defined the meaning of municipal duty through the associated actions of numerous civic groups. As early as 1778, women in North America organized to reveal community needs, build schools, create parks and open spaces, encourage artists and musicians, and craft an inclusive civil society. In the precarious settlements that stretched along the nation's ever-changing borderlands, survival rested on the ability of women and men to associate and cooperate.[1]

Women are also central to the saga of Texas, but only in the twenty-first century have historians revealed the importance of women to the peopling of Texas, turned their attention to the long-neglected Spanish presence in the region, charted the centuries of Native American dominance there, and recognized the roles of enslaved and freed women. Readers are now realizing that throughout Texas history women have participated in the uncertainties of settlement and the achievements of community building, have been artisans and businesswomen, and have spearheaded efforts to understand their neighbors, to improve the quality of daily life, and to introduce new solutions for long-festering social, economic, and political problems.

In the late nineteenth and early twentieth centuries, Houston's leading women and men imagined that a great city would rise at the confluence of White Oak and Buffalo bayous, where land, river, and sea transport converge. When announcing Houston's founding on August 30, 1836, the Allen family promoted the commercial attributes of the location and quickly persuaded officials of the nascent Republic of Texas to choose the aptly named site, then a cluster of stakes and tents, for the new nation's capital city by promising to build a capitol building and community amenities at their own expense. Within months, clever advertising and calls for skilled construction workers attracted nearly 1,500 adventurers. Congressmen who gathered in Houston at the end of April 1837 found a hastily erected Capitol building and a few cabins, boarding houses, and saloons. The republic's second president detested the muddy, muggy, cholera-prone town and decamped west to Austin when Congress finished business in 1839, but Houston's promoters were not discouraged.

The Allen brothers had already platted the town in the popular grid pattern, and Charlotte Baldwin Allen, whose inheritance made the settlement possible, had set aside plots for churches and a school and had donated a market square for the city's commercial center. By 1840 the town had organized a chamber of commerce to promote its shipping and port facilities and to attract ambitious settlers. Houstonians prospered after the republic joined the United States in 1845, and a growing railroad network connected Houston to New Orleans and expanded into the Texas interior by March 1861, when Texas declared for the Confederacy. Post-Civil War Houston housed the headquarters for Reconstruction activities west of the Mississippi, and businessmen continued to expand the railroad network, process cotton, and diversify the manufacturing sector in the last quarter of the century. By 1900, the vibrant town of 44,633 inhabitants had become a regional headquarters for several banks, law partnerships, and commercial enterprises, and the chamber of commerce, reconstituted after the Civil War, continued to promote Houston opportunities. A civil society of committed citizens was emerging when three events changed forever the trajectory of Houston's development.

On September 8, 1900, a lethal hurricane ripped across Galveston Island, decimating the population, destroying every church, and flattening thousands of buildings. Its port—the "lifeblood" of the state's most sophisticated city—was ruined. On September 23, 1900, a greedy valet, the tool of a devious lawyer, murdered William Marsh Rice in New York City. Immediately, over one hundred claimants sought access to Rice's multimillion-dollar fortune. On January 10, 1901, a gusher spewed sand, rocks, water, oil, and gas two hundred feet into the sky near Beaumont, eighty miles east of Houston. As Capt. Anthony F. Lucas had predicted, the salt dome called Spindletop covered a vast oil field. By May 1902 *Oil Investors' Journal* declared Texas "the Young Man's Empire," filled with "hustling young men."[2] As Galveston residents struggled to recover from the 1900 hurricane, Houston entrepreneurs sought public and private funding to dredge Buffalo Bayou and create a deepwater port, achieved in 1914 when civic leaders dedicated the Houston-Harris County ship channel. In 1891 William Marsh Rice established a trust that he hoped one day, after his death, would fund an institute for higher learning in Houston to train women and men for jobs in the manufacturing sector. He appointed his young attorney, James Addison Baker, to serve as chairman of the board that would oversee his project. Realizing the extent of Rice's fortune, Baker imagined an unrivaled research and teaching institution that would compare favorably to the most renowned seats of learning and would secure Houston's place among the great cities of the world. So was born today's Rice University and the city's commitment to high-quality education as a base for economic prosperity, political stability, and social justice. As oil discoveries in East Texas proliferated, producers turned to Houstonians for legal and banking advice and opened corporate offices in the city. The booming economy generated by wildcatting oil men made rapid growth inevitable. By 1910, 78,800 people lived in Houston, and civic-minded women and men were realizing that the city's newfound wealth could be used to raise the standard of living and create a beautiful urban landscape with educational facilities and cultural amenities that would match those in more established cities along the Eastern Seaboard.

The oil and gas discoveries that sustained Houston's emergence as an industrial giant in the early twentieth century occurred at a moment when many in the United States were beginning to understand the unintended consequences of rapid urbanization. Concerned citizens everywhere were recognizing that great discrepancies in wealth, unsafe workplaces, neglected neighborhoods, and sprawling development were undermining the ability of many to achieve the nation's founding ideals of life, liberty, and pursuit of happiness. Houstonians confronted rapid transformation—mature trees felled to make way for factories; skyscrapers invading downtown residential areas; impoverished farm families rushing to the city in search of jobs; desperate Mexicans fleeing revolution; aspiring African Americans stymied by newly enacted, exclusionary Jim Crow laws—and they responded with positive action. A spirit of progressivism defined public discourse in the years before World War I. Leading Houstonians saw their for-profit and nonprofit ventures as vehicles to build a magnificent modern metropolis shaped by strong democratic principles, common knowledge, and shared purpose. Magazine articles, newspaper editorials, and forum speakers noticed the "rise of social consciousness" and praised the cooperation, coordination, and efficiency espoused by businessmen, civic leaders, and clubwomen who advocated scientific city planning, volunteer association, urban improvement, and tolerant inclusion.[3]

Alice Baker, Julia Ideson, and Ima Hogg are three of Houston's many exceptional twentieth-century civic leaders. None of these women had been born in Houston, and they arrived in the regional city at a time of promise and change when enthusiasm for economic growth was tempered by fervor for social reform and dreams of cultural improvement. All began their visionary careers before women could vote; all built institutions that remain critical to the success of the community they loved; and all reached out to include every Houstonian in their collaborative efforts. Their lives were entwined in friendship and in a common perception of civic responsibility. As empathetic humanitarians, they recognized the community challenges that accompanied sudden economic prosperity and dynamic industrial growth; they were willing to advocate for change and to try new solutions when addressing civic issues; and they brought women and men together to solve problems. Central to their success was their shared perception that their lives became meaningful when embedded in community activity. They understood that strong individuals and families would build vibrant neighborhoods and communities; they believed that resilient communities would energize a great nation; and they wanted to harness the energy driving economic expansion to make it work for the common good. They believed the pursuit of happiness encompassed more than economic growth and unbridled consumption—it rested on social justice for all through access to education, healthcare, art and music, natural beauty, tolerance, and hope that life and liberty would be preserved for and revered by everyone. They understood that "the men and women of our community . . . are ready to give of themselves in service and . . . have steadfastness and integrity of purpose."[4] They identified aspects of Houston's urban life that demanded improvement and introduced coalitions of friends and colleagues to imaginative social and cultural solutions that had not yet been tried in Houston.

These philanthropic entrepreneurs defied categorization. Two never married; one was a happy wife and engaged mother; one controlled a considerable fortune. Like traditional conservatives, they valued the past, believed in the aspirational message of their country's founding documents, and worked within the sociopolitical structure of their time. Like optimistic progressives, they never doubted improvement was possible, had faith in incremental reform, and thought every citizen—regardless of race, creed, or gender—deserved social justice. Like compassionate liberals, they saw a role for government in their egalitarian enterprise to nurture the inalienable human rights of every individual. Like sensible pragmatists, they brought people together to achieve the possible, not the perfect, result. From 1893, when Alice Baker attended a meeting to discuss the plight of orphaned children, until 1975, when Ima Hogg died in London, these women used their social, financial, educational, and cultural capital to embolden all Houstonians to travel pathways toward just, happy, and wholesome lives. All three women displayed perseverance and passion when advancing their causes. All three defined what women's work meant in the twentieth century—to build a just society that guaranteed every citizen a safe home in a secure neighborhood; lifetime access to education and information; mental and physical healthcare; the joy of art, music, and reading; and the pleasure of gardens, parks, and recreational open spaces.

These women did not see themselves as heroines of a civic drama. Yet their legacies continue to shape Houston's story. When confronted in 1907 with the sad tale of an immigrant toddler asleep in a school doorway, Alice Baker rallied friends and introduced them to the settlement movement that had nurtured struggling populations in London, Chicago, and New York. For two decades, Alice oversaw the Houston Settlement Association and supported municipal parks and playgrounds for all her neighbors. Julia Ideson decided to forgo marriage and to devote her life to a career in the new discipline of library science. She completed the first library science program offered at the University of Texas, and in 1903 she was called to the newly formed Carnegie Public Library in Houston. Until her death forty-two years later, Julia worked with teachers and employers to ensure that all Houstonians had access to the public library and could find there the storehouse of books they needed to enrich their lives and stimulate their imaginations. Friends and admirers called Ima Hogg the "First Lady of Texas." For sixty-six years, her overarching vision encompassed advocacy for mental healthcare and the arts, service on the public Board of Education, and promotion of parks and historic preservation. Best known as a founder of the Houston Symphony and the creator of the Bayou Bend Collection and Gardens, Ima hoped that through the solace of music and the beauty of decorative arts she could build bridges between Texans and all Americans to appreciate the heritage that binds them to a common purpose.

Today, when the American family is fragmented and the democratic experiment is threatened, the accomplishments of these women suggest a cooperative, collaborative path to civic action. Their careers demonstrate that commitment to community is both altruistic and practical. These women recognized that poverty, illness, and ignorance in one part of town would hinder the prosperity and health of all. They saw that supporting parks, professional orchestras, and municipal museums would encourage newcomers to settle in Houston as well as provide personal pleasure. They knew that engaged citizens who understood their heritage would be good neighbors. And they believed that convening public-private partnerships would unite city government, commercial enterprise, private philanthropy, and individual neighborhoods in the common goal of building a city destined for greatness. In the words of Ima Hogg, they recognized that "responsibility is rewarding."[5]

Alice Baker, Julia Ideson, and Ima Hogg found personal fulfillment through community engagement. Their influence flowed not from the ballot box but from their yearning to build a great city whose assets would be shared by all. They were significant women, not because they sought fame or celebrity, but because they fought to brighten the lives of their neighbors and strengthen the core of their community. By insisting on inclusion and access in all their endeavors, these pioneering women quietly undermined the early twentieth-century status quo of exclusion and segregation, and they laid the groundwork for ongoing legal and political battles to expand access to the public square and to ensure civil, racial, and gender rights for all. By understanding their world, by appreciating what motivated them to move beyond the sheltered domestic scene to the perilous public stage, and by recognizing how they succeeded and what they left unfinished, perhaps we will find new pathways to a more civil and just world. Perhaps in the twenty-first century, remembering their actions will help us rebalance our national narrative and examine all the ways significant women and men have worked in association to build the United States of America. Perhaps, by understanding their lives, we will be able once again to swing the curve upward toward economic equity, political cooperation, cultural understanding, and social justice.[6]

Facing, Alice Graham Baker, circa 1909. MS 609, Woodson Research Center, Fondren Library, Rice University.

CHAPTER ONE

All Houstonians Are My Neighbors

Alice Graham Baker

OCTOBER 18, 1864–MAY 9, 1932

Prelude

One cold, rainy day in January 1907, Rusk School teacher Sybil Campbell discovered a little girl asleep on the doorstep at the school's entrance. The child was waiting for her older siblings to finish classes and take her home, where the young family would shelter until their mother returned from work. The school, located in a shabby wooden building on a slight bluff overlooking Buffalo Bayou, served a once-fashionable Second Ward neighborhood east of Main Street in Houston, Texas. By 1907 Jewish, German, Irish, and Mexican immigrants mingled with freedmen and Native Americans in crowded old boarding houses and crumbling tenements near Second Ward warehouses, cotton mills, docks, and railroad yards. Campbell immediately turned to esteemed volunteer Alice Graham Baker, explained the plight of this shivering child to her, and described the wretched living conditions along the bayou. The compassionate civic leader took quick action. She invited Campbell and ten friends to her handsome Main Street home on February 19 to discuss the distressing predicament of hardworking families who had no access to childcare, health facilities, recreation space, or training programs. Alice explained that many struggling neighbors needed safe streets, warm homes, parks, and playgrounds to build decent lives. In suggesting a path forward, she drew on her experiences with the Woman's Club of Houston and the First Presbyterian Church Ladies Association. Alice also adapted concepts that were introduced to London reformers by Arnold Toynbee in 1884 and reinforced by Jane Addams (1860–1935) when she established Chicago's Hull House settlement in 1889 and initiated a growing settlement movement in the United States.[1]

Waco Girlhood

The beautiful middle-aged woman who insisted all Houstonians were her neighbors was born Mary Alice Graham in Waco, Texas, on October 18, 1864, in the midst of civil strife. Her parents, Frank and Mary Augusta Graham, had settled near the Central Texas town in the 1850s. Waco sits atop a pre-Columbian agricultural village "nestled" in a "beautiful valley" that was tended by Waco tribal farmers until about 1830, when Cherokee competitors drove them from the rolling terrain where the Brazos and Bosque rivers converge. In the 1840s Anglo-American settlers discovered cornstalks and peach trees when they began moving into the river bottom "overlooked by an amphitheatre [*sic*] of hills." In 1846 blacksmith Jesse Sutton erected a log smithy in present-day East Waco, and within two years a consortium of investors had agreed to develop a two-league land grant and to plat a new town on the former tribal village site. By March 1, 1849, surveyor George B. Erath had separated the first block of Waco Village "town lots" from nearby "farming lots" and had reserved sites for the construction of male and female colleges.[2] Erath speculated that the "gushing spring" issuing from a limestone bluff was "a chief inducement" to the Native American and Anglo-American settlers.[3] State of Texas legislators created McLennan County in 1850 and named Waco Village the county seat when developers donated lots for a county courthouse and other public buildings. Waco attracted residents whose livelihood depended on the fast-growing cotton economy, which was expanding across the Brazos River Valley, and in 1855 city fathers incorporated Waco Village as the town of Waco. By 1859 Waco claimed 749 residents.

Francis Hugh (Frank) Graham, recently of Meade County, Kentucky, came to Texas's cotton country in the late 1850s, just as another former Kentuckian, Ranger Capt. Thomas Hudson Barron, was constructing Waco's first steam-powered textile mill.[4] Although Frank did not record his motives for settling in Waco, it is possible he knew of Barron's success and hoped to expand the Graham family's textile businesses during Waco's antebellum cotton boom. Incomplete census data list Frank as a slaveholder and farmer who owned livestock but make no mention of cotton or textile operations. While scouting the area, Frank met Mary Augusta Wilson (1839-1897), and on March 1, 1859, when not quite twenty-seven, he married the twenty-year-old Waco resident. The newlyweds settled north of town on the farm owned and managed by Mary Augusta's widowed mother, Ariana Abernathy Wilson (1797-1869). Ariana Abernathy was born in Greensville County, Virginia, on May 21, 1797, and married fellow Virginian David Wilson (1796-1850) in the mid-1820s, shortly before the couple migrated to Lawrence, Alabama, where their seven children were born. At age fifty-three, David Wilson died, and five years later, in 1855, his widow Ariana trekked to McLennan County with her son Robert (age twenty-nine), her married daughter Dionitia Elizabeth Fort (age twenty-four), and three surviving younger children, Virginia Ariana (age twenty-one), Philip Penn (age eighteen), and Mary Augusta (age sixteen). Ariana, Robert, and the Fort family established three successful, separately owned agricultural operations not far from Waco.

Frank Graham's family had been moving slowly southward and westward since John G. Graham emigrated from Londonderry, Ireland, to West Hanover Township in east-central Pennsylvania in the 1730s.[5] John's grandson Robert, born on May 4, 1791, in West Hanover, was an adventurous entrepreneur, who left home in his twenties to travel down the Ohio River to Louisville, Kentucky, founded in 1778 by explorer George Rogers Clark as a porterage site to circumvent the falls of the Ohio and to open river traffic from the Upper Ohio River Valley to the Gulf of Mexico. Robert's journey suggests he was well-versed in the steam-power technology transforming the region's river transport and textile production in the 1810s. While exploring textile manufacturing opportunities in Louisville, Robert met Roxana Winchell (1799-1886), a recent arrival from Ulster County, New York. The couple married on July 27, 1820, and seven of their eleven children grew to adulthood. Their sixth son, Frank, was born in Louisville on July 21, 1832.

By 1829, Robert Graham had amassed enough capital to build the first complete textile complex in Kentucky. With his partner, Graham constructed and, for eight years, operated Graham & Snead, a state-of-the-art steam-powered cotton mill. While coping with the vagaries of steam engines, Graham became intrigued by the possibilities of waterpower. He knew several gristmills had been flourishing along Otter Creek in nearby Meade County since the 1790s, and in 1835, Graham and a new partner, Thomas Anderson, built a large stone textile mill at a point where the rapidly flowing creek plunged over a falls.[6] The Graham and Anderson families moved to the wooded site, which they named Grahamton, and relocated the company headquarters to the new mill, renamed Graham, Anderson & Co. In 1847, Anderson and his sons took over the mill, while Graham moved to Rock Haven, Kentucky, to concentrate on shipping and marketing the mill's products. Robert Graham died there on August 20, 1862, and his widow Roxana returned to Louisville.

Their son Frank seems to have inherited the family's adventurous spirit that led him to Texas, but Civil War hostilities and martial enthusiasm drained manpower from the Brazos River Valley. Rebels from Waco and surrounding McLennan County provided six generals and raised seventeen companies for the Confederate Army. Frank Graham abandoned his business interests to serve with Company C of the Thirtieth Texas Cavalry, formed on August 18, 1862, by Col. Edward J. Gurley and known as the First Texas Partisan Rangers. Gurley's troop remained in the state for a year, protecting supply lines and defending the South Texas coast. In the summer of 1863, the Thirtieth transferred to Brig. Gen. Richard Montgomery Gano's brigade, which had been organized to protect Indian Territory. In the spring of 1864, the Thirtieth began disrupting movements of Union soldiers in Arkansas, but it returned to Indian Territory. The rebel unit fought Native American tribes and African American recruits loyal to the Union at the Second Battle of Cabin Creek on September

19 and later captured a wagon train carrying Union supplies worth about $1 million. Authorities disbanded the Thirtieth Texas Cavalry in May 1865, and Frank Graham returned to Waco, where he died in 1866 of unspecified causes.[7]

Before Frank Graham's premature death, he and Mary Augusta welcomed four daughters, who would remain lifelong friends, plant deep roots in Texas, and enjoy annual reunions in their homes. The first child, Anna Mae Graham, was born on May 23, 1860. Between deployments to Arkansas and Indian Territory, Frank returned to his family in Waco on furlough. His daughter Edwin Frances, known as Eddie, arrived in October 1863, and a third daughter Mary Alice, always called Alice, joined her sisters on October 18, 1864. The youngest child, Frances Malcolm Graham, nicknamed Frankie, completed the family on August 20, 1866, not quite two months before her father's death on October 14.[8] Mary Augusta's mother, Ariana Wilson, died three years later on July 22, 1869. Although Mary Augusta mourned her husband and her mother, she enjoyed her own siblings and was especially close to her widowed older sister Virginia Ariana Wilson Downs (1834-1906). However, a mystery shrouds Mary Augusta's marriage to Waco merchant James Taylor on February 27, 1871.

James may have been the brother of William A. Taylor (1832–1891), a successful Waco realtor and businessman, who married Virginia Downs on December 6, 1866. James is listed in the 1876-1877 *Waco City Directory*, but only his widow appears in the 1878-1879 volume. Perhaps Mary Augusta thought James had died while traveling but discovered otherwise, because from 1880 until her death in 1897, city directories and census records list her as the widow Graham (Mrs. Mary or M. A.). A James Taylor, brother of Waco's William A. Taylor, appears as the recipient of a $2,500 legacy in the 1911 will of his slightly younger sister Harriet Ellen Taylor Murphy. The bequest suggests that James was living in Maryland, where he had been born in 1838. In 1872, the mysterious James and his wife, Mary Augusta, became the parents of a daughter Harriet, known as Hattie, who was born in Waco that year. What happened to James Taylor and why Mary Augusta Graham Taylor resumed the Graham surname after a brief listing as the widow Taylor remain unsolved mysteries.[9]

Racial strife erupted periodically in the late 1860s, but Waco recovered from Civil War disorder relatively quickly during the Reconstruction era, in part because a spur of the Chisholm Trail cut through the town by 1868. By 1871 cowhands running nearly seven hundred thousand head of cattle to market had stopped in Waco for resupply and recreation. That year Waco was reincorporated as the "City of Waco" to celebrate the completion in January 1870 of a 475-foot suspension bridge across the Brazos River and the arrival in 1871 of

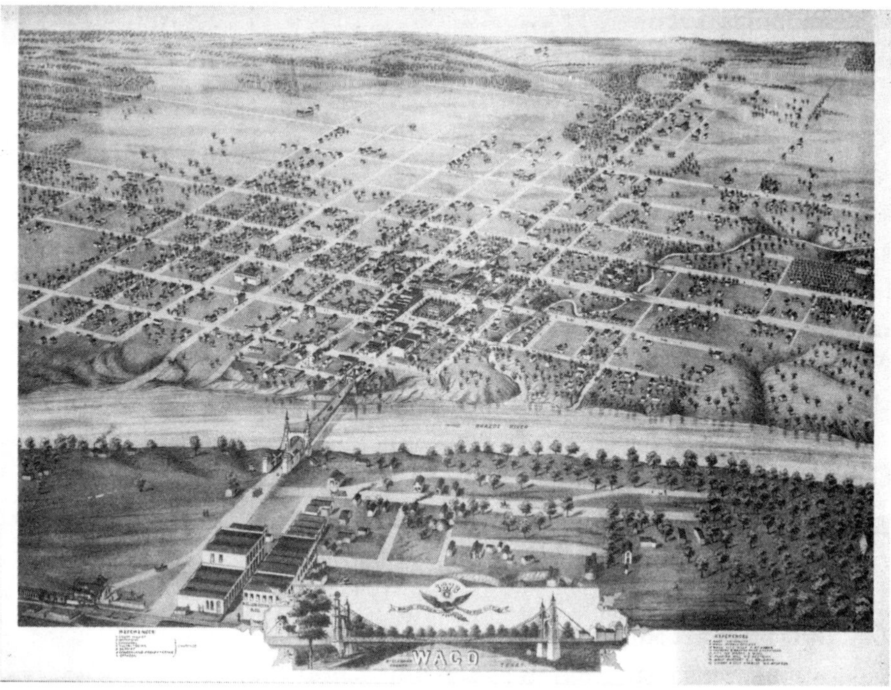

Bird's-eye view of the City of Waco, Texas, 1873. Texas Collection—Maps, Baylor University Library.

the Waco and Northwestern Railroad, the first of three rail lines that would connect the town to the rapidly expanding national network. Thousands of settlers heading west in the 1870s purchased provisions for their journeys in the bustling town. Some early chroniclers relished tales of "Six Shooter Junction," as Waco was called by those who frequented its rowdy saloons and gaming houses or visited the "Reservation," a red-light district where city authorities licensed and regulated prostitution until the early twentieth century. Other contemporary historians preferred to eulogize the city's beauty, its new brick houses and commercial establishments, its booming economy, and its numerous churches and educational institutions. When the Graham sisters reached adulthood in the 1880s, about twelve thousand people lived in Waco. From the cupola of the fashionable McClelland Hotel, a visitor could see streets "bordered on either side by the residences of citizens, many of whom have erected large and commodious mansions, . . . [or] tasteful cottages . . . surrounded by trees and ornamented by flowers."[10] Large cotton, woolen, cottonseed oil, and planing mills occupied industrial tracts along the river or the rail tracks and provided good jobs. Austin Street bisected a bustling commercial center of new brick buildings that offered a big-city array of consumer goods. By the 1890s, engineers had drilled artesian wells in the area, and Waco spas advertised their healing powers.

As the widowed mother of five daughters, Mary Augusta Graham was interested in the town's numerous churches and schools. She and her daughters attended the First Baptist Church at the corner of Fourth Street and Mary Avenue, within walking distance of their home at Second Street and Clay Avenue, where they lived in the 1870s, and of the frame house at 703 Washington Avenue, where they lived in the 1880s. Methodists were the first religious group to organize in Waco, forming a congregation in 1850 and erecting a small wooden church in 1851. On May 31, 1851, four charter members—three men and one woman—asked the well-known missionary and fellow Texan Elder Noah T. Byers to organize the "only Baptist church . . . that existed anywhere in the region" for several years. The founding committee offered Byers seventy-five dollars a year to serve as pastor to an initial flock of fifteen. The Baptists built a "primitive" structure of cedar poles and oak boards, which "was used as a preaching place in common" by the Methodists (est. 1850), Baptists (est. 1851), and Presbyterians (est. 1855).[11] The small Baptist congregation met formally in the First Methodist Church for a few years but in 1857 constructed the brick church where the Graham family worshipped until fire ravaged the building in 1877. Sabbath school and preaching activities continued in makeshift quarters until reconstructed facilities opened in 1883. By the 1880s the Roman Catholic Church of the Assumption, the Episcopal St. Paul's, and the German Methodist Episcopal Church also served the city.

During their teenage years, Alice and her sisters attended the flagship First Baptist Church, led by outspoken Pastor Benajah Harvey Carroll (1843–1914), whose vigorous preaching and widely read publications roiled Baptist theological debate. Carroll was the first pastor in Texas to enhance Sunday services with instrumental music and to ask women to serve as deacons. His stimulating tenure as pastor, which lasted from 1871 to 1899, made a lasting impression on the Graham family. Anna Mae's obituary recorded that Pastor Carroll baptized her in the Brazos River in 1876, following a well-publicized revival that summer, and that she remained an active member of the Waco congregation for seventy-eight years. Alice carried the lessons of her youth to Houston, where they shaped her personal and civic life. Remembered by her oldest grandchild as a woman "who never lost touch with the Lord," Alice took a leadership role in her church and gathered family and household staff around her piano to sing hymns on Sundays and special occasions.[12]

Waco's First Baptist Church parishioners were the earliest white citizens to bring educational institutions to the "Athens of Texas," as some optimists described their town. In the 1850s, "The people of Central Texas felt deeply the need of a great literary institution" and requested the Trinity River Baptist Association to determine an appropriate location for the Male High School. The association's committee recommended Waco as the site, purchased land for a campus, and began classes in 1857. In 1860 the school was reorganized as the Waco Classical School and the following year was renamed Waco University. Supervisors opened the Female Department in 1866 and developed the campus to accommodate coeducational preparatory and collegiate programs. Waco University competed so successfully with Baylor University, located in Independence, that the Baptist General Convention of Texas decided to merge the two schools in 1887, retaining the Waco University campus and the Baylor University name. Methodists chartered Waco Female College on February 11, 1860, as a nonsectarian women's school that offered preparatory and collegiate curricula. A handsome two-story brick building with a cupola rose on the site reserved for a female college on the original city plat, and in 1872 the addition of a boarding department and large dormitory enabled the school to accommodate out-of-town students. The Sisters of St. Mary of Namur came from Lockport, New York, in 1873 to establish a "complete and comprehensive" college-preparatory school "free from sectarianism." Their Academy of the Sacred Heart for female day and boarding students in grades one through twelve was "an imposing structure of brick," built in accordance with "the most approved rules of modern [Victorian] architecture." Catering primarily to female students, the academy accepted male day students in grades one through eight. In 1881 Waco welcomed the faculty, staff, and students of Paul Quinn College, founded in Austin in 1872 by the African Methodist Episcopal (AME) Church to educate newly freed African American men and women.[13]

Limited school records show the Graham sisters spent at least some of their academic hours at "highly esteemed" Waco University. The girls' ages during the years they were enrolled suggest that they completed both preparatory and college-level courses. Anna Mae attended Waco University from 1866 to 1871, when she would have been six to eleven years old; Alice was a member of the "Music Class-Piano" in 1879-1880, when she was fifteen; and Frankie went to Waco University from 1879 through 1884, when she was thirteen to eighteen years old. Possibly Eddie enrolled in 1872-1873, when she would have been nine or ten. Although teenaged Harriet (Hattie) Taylor is listed as a student in the 1890 census and *Waco City Directory,* her school affiliation is unknown.

According to the 1879-1880 Waco University catalog, a student could matriculate in the preparatory classes at any age, but a female had to be in her fourteenth (and a male in his fifteenth) year before entering the collegiate classes, unless the president gave special permission. All academic levels stressed penmanship, grammar, composition, history, geography, and written arithmetic. The collegiate bylaws mentioned roll call, recitation, and suspension—or worse—for playing "cards or any other game of hazard." Drinking alcohol was forbidden. Moral instruction was paramount, and teachers accompanied all female students to the Baptist Church for Sunday services (unless another church had been designated upon enrollment). Perhaps the vivacious sisters also attended Waco's female academies, but no alumnae records are available to verify the possibility.[14]

Anna Mae was the first sister to leave her mother's home, after she married William Douglas Herring (1858-1915) in the family's Clay Avenue parlor on May 20, 1879. Herring and his family lived across the street from the Grahams, and he became general claims agent for the transcontinental Southern Pacific Railroad. His death in 1915 left Anna Mae a widow for the thirty-nine remaining years of her life. Except for the last few years, Anna Mae lived in Waco, where she raised seven children and where she is buried in Oakwood Cemetery. Alice followed her oldest sister from the family hearth when she married James Addison Baker Jr. in 1883 and moved to Houston. Seven years later Frankie celebrated her marriage to Walter Preston Stewart (1862-1950) of Jacksboro. The Stewarts settled in Dallas and were the parents of three children. At age twenty-eight, Eddie married George William Pennock Coates (1857-1948) in 1891 and moved with him to Shackleford and then to Abilene, where their two sons—Francis Graham (Frank) and George Hunter—grew up. Frank Coates became a named partner at Baker, Botts, Shepherd & Coates, the law firm managed by his uncle James Addison Baker Jr.

Houston Connections

Railroads fostered romance in Texas in the 1880s, when Alice Graham, "one of Waco's fairest flowers," boarded a train on May 2, 1882, to travel to Houston for a visit. Exactly when she met a promising attorney and former Houston Light Guard captain is not recorded, but by the fall of 1882 James Addison (Jimmie) Baker Jr. had asked for her hand, and she had persuaded him to pose for an engagement portrait with three of her girlhood friends. Alice, barely eighteen at the time, is fashionably dressed in an elaborate bustled gown. She sits pensively, tilting her head on her left hand while holding her fiancé's broad-brimmed, light-colored hat in her lap. He sits to her left, formally dressed in a coat and vest with a gold watch and chain, holding her parasol against one knee. Behind them stand two young women, with a third seated on Jimmie's left.[15] The handsome young couple married on his twenty-sixth birthday, January 10, 1883. Nine months after her marriage and the ensuing honeymoon in St. Louis, Alice gave birth to Frank Graham Baker on her nineteenth birthday, October 18, 1883. Well-wishers could not have foreseen that this young couple, born in the shadow of the Civil War, was embarking on a loving partnership that would transform the way Houstonians experienced education, social service, civic responsibility, the arts, law, and banking.

Alice's new family traced its ancestry to the Anglo-Scots Presbyterian settlers of seventeenth-century Virginia. Jimmie's grandparents, Elijah Adam (1792-1845) and Jane Saxton Baker, migrated to North Carolina and moved on to northern Alabama about 1820, shortly before their first son, James Addison, was born near Huntsville, Texas, on March 3, 1821. The Bakers established a cotton plantation and a forge, worked by enslaved laborers, on a land grant in nearby Lauderdale County, where they raised five sons and a daughter. In the 1840s, James taught school for a year or two before he decided to read law with Samuel W. Probasco, a well-known frontier lawyer who practiced in Florence, Alabama. There, James met Caroline Hightower and married her on May 30, 1849. By January 1852, the pretty but frail young woman was dead, and her aging parents begged their grieving son-in-law to join them in Texas and take over their businesses, which included agricultural property in Walker County and Hightower & Co., a Huntsville general store that sold farm supplies and manufactured goods, made loans to its customers, and marketed area crops to commercial suppliers in Houston or Galveston. Within months of his arrival, James met Rowena Bland Crawford, the well-educated, lively principal of Huntsville's Female (Brick) Academy.[16]

Rowena was born in Alabama on April 8, 1828, to the Reverend Beverly Crawford (1790–1846) and his wife, Anna Bland McRobert (1800–1881). The McRobert and Crawford families had supported education and served Presbyterian churches in Virginia for four generations, and Rowena's Bland ancestors had settled along the colony's James River in 1654. In 1849 Rowena accompanied her aunt Elizabeth McRobert Baker (1795–1858) to Huntsville, Texas, where Elizabeth's husband Daniel S. Baker (1791–1857), a prominent Presbyterian evangelist, was organizing Austin College as the state's first institution of higher learning. By June 1853, a romance between the accomplished attorney and the clever teacher had blossomed, and James Baker and Rowena Crawford married on September 27. In keeping with the middle-class mores of her era, which considered household management and child-rearing essential full-time employment, Rowena resigned as principal of Brick Academy and devoted her considerable energies to managing her husband's properties and raising a family. As Walker County seat and home of the Texas state prison, Huntsville attracted many lawyers, but successful attorneys spent weeks away from home, riding horses for miles along poorly maintained trails to assist clients and to try cases in far-flung county courthouses. When apart, Rowena and James exchanged frequent letters that sparkle with humor, affection, and admiration.

In the early years of his marriage, James Baker served the community as an elder in Huntsville's First Presbyterian Church and as a trustee of Austin College, where he helped create the first degree-granting law department in the state. In 1860 he was elected to the Texas legislature and was soon embroiled in the secession debate. Now forty years old, James resigned his seat, and in October 1861, he enlisted as a private for a six-month tour of duty with the Confederate Army. Assigned to defend Galveston, under blockade since July 1861, James left Rowena to handle his business operations and care for their three small children—James Addison Jr. (Jimmie), born on January 10, 1857, Mary Susan (Minnie), born on May 13, 1858, and Anna Bland, who arrived on September 13, 1860. Rowena and James wrote to each other nearly every day while he was away. In her letters, Rowena described food shortages and high prices, dousing fires, and overseeing the planting and harvest seasons. She worried about childhood ailments and the illness of Silas, the family's resourceful, reliable enslaved foreman, because the doctor, who was sick himself, could not visit them. She eagerly awaited her husband's letters —"like good news . . . and green spots in a desert"— and sent the absent father messages dictated to her by the children.[17]

When James's six-month tour of duty ended, he decided to run for judge of the state's Seventh Judicial District (serving Galveston, Harris, Montgomery, Grimes, and Walker counties) to replace the incumbent, who had died suddenly. In a special election called by the governor for March 10, 1862, James outpolled two opponents, and he held the post until removed in June 1865, when all elected officials who had served during the Confederacy were replaced. Judge Baker, as he was known for the rest of his life, then returned to his family and duties in Huntsville. He resumed his law practice and became an expert on legal issues pertaining to the expanding interstate railroad industry. During the war, twins Jane and Jeanette (Nettie) were born on January 26, 1863, and three more children followed baby Jane's death: Rowena (1865-1866), Robert Lee (1867-1939), and Little Willie, a girl who lived a few weeks in 1869.

Huntsville, unlike Waco and Houston, did not flourish after the Civil War. The town suffered yellow fever epidemics, experienced racial strife leading to martial law, and shunned construction of a railroad through the city, citing its desire to protect the quiet beauty of a bygone era. The shortsighted decision hampered commercial development and made it difficult for students to travel to Austin College. The Presbyterian Synod decided to relocate the college to Sherman, Texas, in 1876, and Huntsville eventually had to finance an expensive spur to the north-south rail line it had previously spurned. In 1872 Judge Baker received a flattering offer from Peter Gray and Walter Browne Botts to join their prosperous partnership in Houston and form the law firm of Gray, Botts & Baker, which was renamed Baker & Botts three years later. Known as an effective advocate in the courtroom, Judge Baker—at age fifty-two—began his final and most successful adventure. Rowena Baker remained in Huntsville to dispose of family assets there, while James commuted by train and stagecoach between the two towns. Finally, in September 1876, Judge Baker could afford to purchase a home on San Jacinto Street for Rowena and the family, which included his mother, Jane Saxton Baker Croft Cobb, who died in 1884, and his mother-in-law, Anna McRobert Crawford, who died in July 1881. The family's relocation to Houston was complete in 1878, when they joined the First Presbyterian Church of Houston.

Like Alice Graham and her sisters, Jimmie Baker and his siblings grew up in a large family strengthened by firm Protestant principles. His parents worked hard and expected their children to take schoolwork seriously. Rowena Baker taught her children to read, write, learn their sums, and play the piano. An advocate of education for women, she enrolled Anna Bland and Nettie in the preparatory department of Mary Sharp College in Winchester, Tennessee, and later sent Minnie and Nettie to Notre Dame of Maryland Preparatory School and Collegiate Institute in Baltimore, Maryland.[18] Rowena prepared Jimmie to attend Judge A. C. Woodall's Academy in Huntsville before he entered the Preparatory Department of Austin College in 1873 and matriculated at Texas Military Institute (TMI) in the fall of 1874. Both parents wrote frequently to their absent children to share adventures and disappointments. Rowena admonished her daughters about their spelling and urged her son to forego "liquor and tobacco." Judge Baker described Houston's "unusual" Oktoberfest customs and explained how work crews were dredging Buffalo Bayou to create a ship channel. While glad his son considered expenses, the proud father warned the earnest teenager not to "acquire a reputation for penuriousness." Cadet Baker excelled in his studies and enjoyed "the entire esteem and confidence" of the TMI superintendent. His delighted parents and adoring sisters proudly watched Jimmie salute fellow graduates and their families at the TMI commencement on June 13, 1877. From their loving, but subtly ambitious, parents, the Baker children learned the importance of education, of striving for excellence, and of Christian morality as a basis for action.[19]

On December 1, 1877, the slim, athletic TMI graduate began reading law in his father's office. Baker & Botts occupied two rooms on the second floor of the three-story Gray's Opera House, which had been built by Peter W. Gray (1819-1874) on Courthouse Square across from the Harris County Courthouse. The well-regarded partnership was born when Col. William Fairfax Gray (1787-1841), formerly of Fredericksburg, Virginia, opened a law office on Travis Street in May 1837 and formed the firm of Scott & Gray in 1840 with his son Peter and friend Judge John Scott. In 1857 Peter's cousin Walter Browne Botts joined the practice.[20] Wounded while serving in the Confederate Army in Virginia, Colonel Botts returned to Houston to assist major clients until hostilities ended. Like all attorneys who had supported the rebel cause, Gray and Botts had to be reinstated as members of the Texas bar in November 1865 before they could resume their extensive legal practice, which included advising the city's first banker and representing entrepreneurs who were building the city's port facilities. Wealthy William Marsh Rice (1816–1900) was the firm's most important business client, and retainers from expanding railroad companies provided steady revenue. When Judge Baker arrived in 1872, he found his docket filled quickly, and by December 1877 he and Colonel Botts needed young Jimmie Baker's help organizing documents for trial, performing clerical duties, and running errands. After absorbing the legal knowledge found in the extensive law library owned by his father and Colonel Botts, Jimmie applied to the clerk of the Harris County Court for permission to practice in district and inferior state courts. A three-man panel, which included Colonel Botts, examined the young aspirant, who was welcomed to the practice of law in Texas on December 2, 1879, and joined the Houston Bar Association early the next year. On December 19, 1884, the rising attorney "filed the oath required by law" to practice before the Supreme Court of Texas.

During his legal apprenticeship, Jimmie Baker pursued a lively social life, centered on his membership in the Houston Light Guard, an influential volunteer militia unit organized on April 21, 1873, "to defend the city against its enemies." His fellow guardsmen included several graduates of TMI and seven men who would become mayor of Houston in the decades before World War I. Best known for its expert drill team and its lively dancing parties, the Light Guard occasionally maintained municipal order and heroically rescued victims of the 1900 hurricane that devastated Galveston. Jimmie Baker advanced to sergeant in May 1878 and served as captain from August 1879 to August 1880. He commanded the Light Guard during welcoming ceremonies for President Ulysses S. Grant when the war hero visited Houston in March 1880, and he trained the drill team for its first competition. By the fall of 1880, the captain's social life and his legal practice had expanded significantly. That year the three-man firm moved to two large rooms in the recently built Fox Building and in July 1881 changed the firm's name to Baker, Botts & Baker, indicating Jimmie's status as a junior partner with the two older men. At this point, friends and clients began to refer to the younger James A. Baker not as junior but as Captain Baker.[21] Perhaps association with a judge and a colonel, ranks acquired through service to the Confederacy, caused him to retain his Light Guard rank; perhaps he recognized the humor of these honorific titles. It is not surprising that he decided it was time to marry and begin a family.

Early Married Life

When Alice Graham married Jimmie Baker in 1883, she joined the large, lively household of family patriarch Judge James Addison Baker in his pillared Greek Revival-style home on a tree-lined corner at 204 San Jacinto and Lamar Avenue in Houston. A widower for four years, Judge Baker had lost his "beloved Row" on September 7, 1879, a few months before their son Jimmie was admitted to practice law in Texas courts. Living in the San Jacinto Street homestead were the judge's eighty-five-year-old mother, Jane Baker Cobb, his teenaged son Robert Lee Baker, and his nephew Andrew Morgan (Andy) Baker (1865–1912). Two daughters, Anna Bland (1860-1952) and Jeanette (Nettie, 1863-1920), also welcomed Alice to her new home, although both young women soon moved away. Anna Bland, who had been managing her father's household since the death of her mother, married George Washington Thompson (1857–1925) of Winchester, Tennessee, on November 27, 1885, and moved to Fort Worth. Nettie celebrated her wedding to Alexander Perry Duncan (1857–1912) at Houston's First Presbyterian Church on January 20, 1886, and settled in Waco. Assisting the multigenerational Houston household were ten freed men and women, who lived on the property with their eight children.[22] Alice would supervise this complex family home until Judge Baker's death in 1897.

In October 1883, the Baker clan welcomed Frank Graham Baker as enthusiastically as it had embraced Alice nine months earlier on her wedding day, and the hearty little boy formed a strong bond with his tender-hearted mother, whose October 18 birthday he shared. A month after his second birthday, Graham "wandered away" from home, "exciting great alarm." Search parties "went in all directions" to discover the child tearfully eating nuts and crackers with the city fire marshal. This incident coincided with another family crisis. While Graham was still a toddler, his young father contracted a nearly fatal disease, which frightened the family and necessitated a long period of convalescence. Although unnamed in any correspondence or documents, this ailment caused Captain Baker to rethink his responsibilities. "Had this illness proved fatal your grandmother would have been left alone with my son Graham . . . with practically no means of support," he later wrote to his grandchildren when providing each of them with an insurance policy that would mature on their sixty-fifth birthdays. Farsighted and prudent, the loving family man took great care throughout his life to set aside funds in interest-bearing bank accounts for each child and for his wife, Alice, and he balanced work and relaxation from an early age. A vigorous enthusiast of hunting, fishing, and hiking, the hard-working attorney began taking his family on long summer trips to Colorado with his sisters Anna Bland Thompson and Nettie Duncan and their families in the 1890s. No year passed without vacation time, frequently noted by local newspaper reporters. All his life Captain Baker suffered from a disorder he called sciatic rheumatism, and he and Alice often boarded the Houston Central Railway for Waco or San Antonio hot spring spas that promised to alleviate his chronic pain. There is no evidence that this condition, which he managed quietly, curtailed his multifaceted career or dampened his enthusiasm for his growing family. Alice's second child, daughter Alice Graham Baker, joined her brother Graham, not yet four, on May 13, 1887. Five and one-half half years later James Addison Baker Jr. arrived on November 3, 1892. Young Alice's attentive attitude toward Little Jim so pleased her father that he ordered a playhouse to be built for his daughter. Designed to replicate, in miniature, the family's pillared home on San Jacinto Street, this playhouse was treasured by three generations of Baker girls, who moved it from one home to another for seven decades.[23]

In the early years of their marriage, the Bakers established a conventional late nineteenth-century division of duties. Alice managed the household and garden, nurtured their children and relatives, and entertained their friends and colleagues; Jimmie expanded his legal practice and cemented his public reputation. Alice's household tasks were many and varied. The judge and his son

Alice Baker, circa 1894. MS 609, Woodson Research Center, Fondren Library, Rice University.

James Addison Baker Jr., age twelve. MS 40, Woodson Research Center, Fondren Library, Rice University.

walked to work and often returned home for lunch with colleagues or clients, so Alice, aided by her cook and domestic staff, prepared a daily menu suitable for guests. She trained her employees and set the daily work schedules. Wash tubs, clothes lines, brooms, and wood- or coal-burning stoves were the tools of late nineteenth-century household maintenance, although gaslight provided a soft glow in the evenings. Specified days for washing, ironing, and baking provided a rhythm for the week. An avid gardener whose floral arrangements won lavish praise from contemporaries and the press, Alice spent many hours planning and tending her garden.

As the 1880s wore on, Captain Baker gradually took over the firm's legal work related to William Marsh Rice's complex business affairs, and Rice trusted his energetic attorney to serve as director or officer of several companies he controlled. Baker also began advising local entrepreneurs and in 1886 helped found Commercial National Bank, becoming its president in 1897. Rice continued to employ Baker, Botts & Baker to handle his legal and business affairs, although he and his second wife spent most of each year in New York or New Jersey after their marriage in 1867. In the early spring of 1891, on one of his periodic visits to Houston, Rice consulted area educators about a project proposal. With their enthusiastic encouragement, he then asked Baker to prepare documents that would allow the millionaire to fund an Institute for the Advancement of Literature, Science, and Art in Houston after his death. By May 1891 Rice had organized a seven-man board, appointed Baker its chairman, provided a $200,000 endowment, and received a charter of incorporation from the State of Texas for his institute. Rice's friends and colleagues understood that his fortune would one day significantly expand this endowment. Captain Baker made protecting this trust and establishing the institute his central civic mission until his death in August 1941.

Judge Baker's railroad practice had expanded in the 1880s to include a network of associated attorneys throughout the state, and he decided to hire Robert Scott Lovett, a young man who had helped him with several clients. Lovett and his family moved to Houston in October 1892, and the firm was renamed Baker, Botts, Baker & Lovett on January 1, 1893. Major change came to the law firm in 1894 when Colonel Botts and his wife died, leaving Captain Baker to administer their estates and take charge of the colonel's business practice. That year Collis P. Huntington hired Baker, Botts, Baker & Lovett as attorneys in the trans-Mississippi region for his newly formed transcontinental Southern Pacific railroad system, and the Bakers and Lovett hired Edwin Brewington Parker as a firm associate to help with this major new client. A recent graduate of the University of Texas School of Law, Parker proved to be an organizational genius with a brilliant legal mind. By 1895 Judge Baker had transferred his practice to this triumvirate of younger men, who would transform the nineteenth-century partnership into one of the country's first modern law firms able to advise executives of the multifaceted corporations being spawned in the rapidly industrializing national economy. Their wives—Alice Graham Baker, Lavinia Abercrombie Lovett,[24] and Katherine (called Kate) Blunt Parker[25]—would become lifelong friends, and they would launch organizations that transformed the way Houstonians experienced social service, artistic expression, and music appreciation. Alice Baker reached out to struggling residents of Houston's Second Ward to establish the city's first social service neighborhood center. Lavinia Lovett held the founding meeting of the Houston Public School Art League, forerunner of the Museum of Fine Arts, Houston. Kate Parker, a well-trained pianist and choral performer, became a vital leader of Houston's music appreciation movement and was named founding president of the Houston Symphony Association.

Through fellowship with her husband's colleagues and their well-informed wives, Alice met serious women who were searching for ways to improve themselves and their community. In 1885 two well-connected middle-aged women, Adele Briscoe Looscan and Caroline Ennis Lombardi, introduced Houstonians to the women's club movement then sweeping the country when they formed the Ladies' History Class to formalize the social pleasure of discussing favorite books. Quickly rechristened the Ladies' Reading Club, their idea was imitated in 1890 when Louise Cohn Raphael established the Ladies' Shakespeare Club, with an appropriately theatrical focus. In 1891 the husbands of these enterprising women—Cesar Lombardi[26] and Emanuel Raphael—joined William Marsh Rice and Captain James A. Baker to sign the charter for Rice's proposed institute for literature, science, and art. In 1893 female reformers inaugurated the multifaceted Woman's Club to study a variety of civic issues. Three years later, women music lovers announced formation of their first musical club. Members of the Ladies' Singing Society, soon renamed the Treble Clef Club, hired a coach and began to provide concerts of "high artistic standard."[27] In the late nineteenth century, women formed these clubs to study literary, artistic, and civic subjects that would entertain and inform members. Almost immediately, club leaders expanded their goals to demand social reforms and cultural improvements that would elevate civic life for all Houstonians in the early twentieth century.

Club activities fascinated newspaper readers. Alice Baker did not record when she joined the Ladies' Reading Club, probably at Caroline Lombardi's suggestion, but in 1896, she participated in an afternoon meeting organized by Lombardi and Elizabeth Stevens MacGregor to discuss Lombardi's paper on "psychical research." MacGregor, wife of philanthropic real estate developer Henry F. MacGregor, read a story she had written; Alice sang for the group; and Adele Looscan wove a captivating tale of her own psychic experience. After a "cold collation," the group returned home by moonlight. Society columnists also described the entertainments, travels, and civic activities of attractive power couples like the Bakers. At a "spur of the moment" dance on a hot night in June 1899, the Bakers threw open the doors of their "perfectly charming" house to entertain a "sweet young guest" from Waco. A professionally trained young lady from Cuero delighted the guests with a violin solo before dancing began. The effusive reporter noted Alice's "gentle thoughtfulness" and the "courteous hospitality" of her husband.[28]

Although raised in Waco's First Baptist Church, Alice began to attend Houston's First Presbyterian Church with her husband and father-in-law when she came to Houston in 1883. On September 29, 1895, "on examination and profession of her faith," she was formally "received into membership" there. As the Baker children reached their early teens, each received baptism and became a member of the Presbyterian congregation.[29] Soon after her arrival in Houston, Alice joined the First Presbyterian Church Ladies' Association, formed under the guidance of the Reverend James McNelly by twenty female parishioners in 1879 to help finance a new manse. Like other late nineteenth-century church guilds, the Ladies' Association supported women as wives, mothers, and moral arbiters in the family and enabled women to expand their concerns beyond the fireside to the wider community. Through church-sponsored study groups and committees, association members used their domestic skills to improve community life and their organizational skills to raise money. Houston founder Charlotte Baldwin Allen served as an early Ladies' Association president and donated property to the growing congregation. In 1883 Ladies' Association members eager to support the manse published *The Texas Cook Book: A Thorough Treatise on the Art of Cookery*, the first fundraising cookbook produced in Texas and a statewide model for hundreds of church-sponsored recipe collections. In 1899, Alice expressed concern about continuing church indebtedness and formed the Little Club of Seven, girls and boys who performed musical arrangements and recited poetry in a series of evening fundraisers. Enlisting her children as actors, Alice announced a Friday, June 16, entertainment at her home, and the *Houston Post* provided publicity and extensive reviews. Graham Baker, then almost sixteen, "brought out the notes of his violin with purity and clearness," while his sister Alice, now twelve, "admirably accompanied" him on the piano, an effort rewarded by a "hearty burst of applause." James A. Baker Jr., not yet seven, was "too funny" dressed in clerical garb and assuming a "somber" posture as the main character in a tableau of *The Little Minister*, James M. Barrie's popular 1891 novel about the plight of overworked weavers in Scotland. Hostess Alice's imaginative efforts to defray church expenses continued for another three decades.[30]

Through their church affiliation, the young Bakers began a long association with one of Houston's most enduring service organizations, and Alice first demonstrated her empathy for the plight of struggling families. Houston was a small regional center of about twenty-eight thousand residents in the spring of 1892 when Kezia Payne DePelchin (1825–1893), matron of the Bayland Orphan Home[31] for boys and girls ages six to twelve, decided that she could no longer ignore the needs of infants and toddlers under age six. DePelchin prevailed upon her close friends Agnes Perry and Ruth House to provide a safe home "to care for friendless children."[32] DePelchin described the shelter, set in the 2500 block of Washington Avenue, as an adjunct to Bayland Orphan Home, located in the nearby Woodland Heights addition. She christened her new enterprise Faith Home, because she had faith that God and the kind people of Houston would support her efforts. DePelchin's trust was not misplaced. When this hardworking advocate for neglected children died on January 13, 1893, Ruth House invited the female leadership of Houston to attend a meeting at 4:00 p.m. on January 21 in the Shearn Methodist Church chapel to discuss the fate of Houston's most helpless children and to secure a permanent facility for their home.

Houston Post reporters publicized the meeting and explained the social need. Over one hundred civic-minded women, including Alice Baker, attended. They chose an all-female board of directors, elected Ruth House president, and named sixteen vice presidents. Then they called on the expert who had produced the documents for William Marsh Rice's educational institute to secure a charter of incorporation for the Kezia DePelchin Faith Home Association. Captain James Baker produced the charter on March 23, 1893, and organized a "male auxiliary" of six civic leaders to provide advice on legal and fiscal matters. Buoyed by the *Post*'s publication of weekly progress reports, the board and its volunteers organized seven committees to produce an outdoor fundraiser on April 4. With "tireless . . . zeal" and broad support, the association amassed sufficient funds by August 1893 to purchase a frame house in the Third Ward and to prepare it for occupancy by September 1. When that space proved inadequate, the association completed a second successful fund drive in 1898, securing $15,000 to build a three-story brick building with gray stone trimming and a slate roof on Chenevert and Pierce streets near downtown.[33]

Led by church women, the Kezia DePelchin Faith Home fundraising projects gained citywide support. Not only did the most prominent lawyers and bankers lend their professional expertise to a social service effort, but also labor unions provided manpower and materials to refurbish and construct the buildings. Butchers and bakers donated routinely to the kitchen; Raphael Brothers insured Faith Home for many years; Captain Baker underwrote printing of the constitution and bylaws; and in 1893 the fraternal Knights of Pythias decided to donate proceeds from the "anniversary hop, concert and drill at Turner Hall on August 28 as a benefit for the DePelchin faith home." Alice Baker and her friends organized chrysanthemum shows and other special events to raise money for the construction projects, and the faithful *Post* editors printed long lists of contributors to recognize generous benefactors and to spur further donations. When the employees of F. W. Heitmann & Co. won a fifty-dollar prize at the Fruit, Flower and Vegetable Festival, they donated it as a Christmas gift to all the children at Faith Home.[34]

The Baker family lost two beloved members in 1897, when Judge Baker and Mary Augusta Graham died. Judge Baker, who was often "lowspirited [*sic*] and despondent" after Rowena's death, fell ill in October 1896 while visiting friends in Tennessee. When the judge returned home, his symptoms of indigestion, weight loss, and fever did not abate, and he died at home on February 23, 1897. Captain Baker wrote to his sister Nettie Duncan that "everything [was] being done for him, yet by reason of his advanced age and failure to give his disease more prompt attention," the beloved father succumbed at age seventy-six, making his forty-year-old son senior man at the leading law firm in the Southwest.[35] A private railroad car carried the judge's coffin and mourning family and friends to Huntsville, where the patriarch joined his "dearest Row" and their four infant children in the family plot at Oakwood Cemetery.

A few months later, while visiting her daughter Eddie Graham Coates in Abilene, Mary Augusta Graham died unexpectedly of "congestion" on September 15, 1897, at the relatively youthful age of fifty-eight. She left behind five grieving daughters and property in Waco valued at $40,000 after probate, and she named her son-in-law, Captain James A. Baker, executor. Records show that

1416 Main Street, May 20, 1921. The fence and hanging baskets had been removed by 1921. (Baker Residence, 1898-1922). Private Collection, Courtesy of Virginia Meyers Chandler.

her youngest daughter, Hattie Taylor, never married and probably died in 1912. As executor, attorney Baker oversaw Hattie's share of her mother's property and paid his sister-in-law's expenses. After her mother's death, Hattie splurged on shopping sprees, visited her half-sister Alice in Houston, and took extravagant trips to New York and Newport. By 1900 Hattie was under a doctor's care, and for the next few years she spent time at hospitals in New York City, St. Louis, and Waco. Following settlement of a lawsuit with her sisters in 1905, she was taken by her brother-in-law William Douglas Herring to the Cincinnati Sanitarium on January 27, 1906. From that date through 1912, Captain Baker sent monthly payments to the sanitarium for her care. No medical diagnosis or death notice appear in family records.[36]

After Judge Baker died in February 1897, his son and daughter-in-law decided it was time to leave the San Jacinto Street homestead, and by late 1898 they had moved to the "grandest" Queen Anne-style house in Houston.[37] Designed and built in 1889 by prominent residential architect George Dickey for cotton broker Samuel K. Dick, the rambling, turreted villa and its gardens covered most of a city block at 1416 Main Street and boasted the asymmetry, steep-pitched roofs, and patterns of shingles and brickwork favored in the late nineteenth century. Alice Baker transformed the property by planting flower borders, trees, and shrubbery. Making use of the latest innovations in residential garden decoration, she installed an ornamental cast-iron fence around the perimeter and a Portland cement walkway from the street to the entrance. Her home was always filled with flowers and plants grown in her elaborate greenhouse, complete with sliding glass panels, and Alice placed hanging baskets of greenery in multiple bays of the wide porches that shielded the first and second stories from direct sunlight. Considered one of the city's most important residences when it was built, the house was frequently photographed while the Bakers lived there. This spacious building was now home to Captain and Mrs. Baker, Graham (age fifteen), Alice (age eleven), Jim (age six), and two Swedish servants. Alice continued to employ an African American cook and other household staff, and Captain Baker hired retired Southern Pacific Railroad workers to drive his family and work in the gardens, but the cohort of freedmen and women who accompanied Judge Baker and his family to Houston had been absorbed by the city's expanding African American community.

Houstonians had long enjoyed visiting friends on New Year's Day. Ladies would gather in several homes to welcome the gentlemen, who strolled from house to house in the tree-shaded fashionable neighborhoods. On January 1, 1899, the Bakers opened their elegant new home for a daylong reception that offered a midday luncheon and an evening dance. Reporters swooned over the crackling blaze in the entrance hall fireplace and the garlands, wreaths, red satin ribbons, and white damask dining table drapery, and they detailed the glassware, flowers, and refreshments with glowing enthusiasm. Twenty friends and several young ladies helped Alice receive guests during the gala event, ladling punch and pouring coffee to satisfy a steady stream of thirsty guests. Three years later, on January 1, 1902, reporters worried that the custom was fading away when only five houses were open, including the Bakers' residence. As many as fifty ladies welcomed visitors at each house, but the gentlemen had few stops to make. If flagging in 1902, the custom had revived by the time Ima Hogg and her brothers enjoyed paying calls on New Year's Day in the 1910s and 1920s.

Family Trials

The new century began joyfully for the Bakers, whose third son arrived on January 23, 1900. Walter Browne Baker, named to honor his father's former law partner Walter Browne Botts, joined sister Alice and brother Jim at 1416 Main Street. Graham, nearly grown at sixteen, was boarding at the Hill School, a

Alice Baker, circa. 1900. The Falk Studio, Waldorf Astoria, MS 609, Woodson Research Center, Fondren Library, Rice University.

prestigious college preparatory academy in Pottstown, Pennsylvania, founded by Presbyterian Matthew Meigs in 1856. Captain Baker, now a stocky middle-aged man of forty-three, oversaw a regional law firm that represented eight of the seventeen railroads running through Houston, two of the city's four banks, and the cutting-edge electric lighting and power utility. Alice, youthful and elegant at thirty-six, looked forward to enjoying her new baby for a few months before resuming her full schedule of church and social activities. Neither realized that the next decade would challenge their marriage, the law firm, and the city, bringing tragedy and triumph to the Baker family.

The hurricane that roared out of the Gulf of Mexico and razed a wide swath of Galveston Island on September 8, 1900, inflicted only minor harm to Houston's residential and commercial neighborhoods, although wind and rain damaged or demolished several manufacturing structures along Buffalo Bayou. On September 16 a fire attributed to storm debris destroyed much of the Merchants and Planters Oil Company cotton processing plant owned by William Marsh Rice. The company's on-site manager immediately telegraphed Rice for permission to rebuild quickly, and Rice discussed the situation with Robert S. Lovett, who was in New York working with Baker, Botts, Baker & Lovett clients. Under discussion were the rebuilding project and the ongoing lawsuits that developed when Rice contested his wife's will immediately after her death four years earlier on July 24, 1896. Unbeknownst to Rice, his second wife, Libbie Baldwin Rice, had signed a final testament in Houston on June 1, 1896. Her lawyer, Orren T. Holt, had persuaded her that as a resident of Texas (a community-property state), she could bequeath half of the Rice fortune to her choice of charities and relatives. William Marsh Rice, who planned to leave the entire estate to the trust he had established in 1891 to build an institution of higher learning, was furious and insisted the Rice domicile was in New Jersey or New York (not community-property states) during their entire marriage. Therefore, he argued, Libbie Rice had no legal right to distribute half of his estate, much of which had been established before he married her. Rice was still contesting the will on September 19 when he wrote a long letter to Captain Baker, outlining his detailed plan to rebuild the Merchants and Planters Oil plant and to finance the work with cash from his New York bank. Although Rice had been complaining of indigestion and a lingering cold, Lovett believed his client was in excellent health, given his nearly eighty-five years. Lovett endorsed the plan to transfer cash to the plant manager and returned to Houston. No one suspected the decision would hasten the old man's death.[38]

Since April 1897, Rice had employed an obsequious young man, Charles Freeman Jones, as a valet and clerk to assist him at his spacious Madison Avenue apartment. Jones's duties included helping Rice dress and exercise, cooking his meals, typing his correspondence, and preparing checks for his signature. During the summer of 1899, an unscrupulous lawyer with tenuous connections to Houston, Albert T. Patrick, had befriended Jones. Patrick was obsessed by tales of Rice's fortune, estimated to be $10 million by one Texas banker, and he hoped to gain Rice's favor and some of his wealth. Rice knew Patrick by reputation and refused to see him. Patrick then devised a complicated plot to swindle the old man by manipulating the greedy valet and securing a faked signature on a fraudulent will, which he drew up in May 1900. Not willing to await the natural death of an octogenarian, Patrick told Jones that Rice had poisoned his wife, an easily proved falsehood. Patrick then persuaded the gullible Jones to administer small doses of poison to weaken Rice and hasten the old man's demise. By September 1900 Rice, unwittingly, had been taking poison for several months, thinking he was treating minor ailments. Patrick did not know the amount of Rice's fortune, but when Jones told him about Rice's plan to rebuild a factory, the deceitful plotter decided he must act to ensure that no money was wasted on the project. On the night of September 22, Patrick ordered Jones to give Rice a stronger dose of the poison and to smother him with a cloth soaked in chloroform. The plot began unraveling the next day when Albert Patrick carelessly signed a $25,000 check, made out erroneously to "Abert" Patrick, with his correctly spelled name. A vigilant banker noticed the discrepancy, discovered Rice had died, and telegraphed Captain Baker in Houston; then he called the New York City police, who began to investigate the suspicious death.[39]

Appalled by events occurring in New York, Baker and Frederick Allyn Rice, William Marsh Rice's brother, wired associates in the city to secure all W. M. Rice's papers and property and to halt cremation proceedings. Then Baker and F. A. Rice caught the evening train to New Orleans and on to New York. Telegrams apprised the travelers of new revelations during their two-and-one-half-day journey. By the time Baker had reached the ferry pier at Jersey City, he had a clear picture of the crime. Thus began a ten-year struggle to convict Patrick of murder, to invalidate the 1900 will, and to safeguard William Marsh Rice's fortune so that Baker and his fellow trustees could develop Rice's Institute for the Advancement of Literature, Science and Art. Almost at once Baker realized the complexities of the case and knew he would be in New York for many months. On October 4 Patrick and Jones were arrested and charged with forgery; on October 6 Baker's secretary, Eula Gray, left for New York City, where she began to catalog Rice's vast estate; and on October 15, Alice Baker with Little Jim (age eight), Baby Browne, and a nurse followed. Captain Baker could not bear to be alone in New York without his family, but daughter Alice (age thirteen) remained at school in Houston, and Graham continued his studies at the Hill School in Pennsylvania. When the baby developed a cold, the harried attorney reluctantly bid goodbye to Alice and the boys as they boarded a train on November 22 for the long journey back to Houston. Captain Baker spent the rest of the year and most of 1901 traveling back and forth between his home and the developing murder investigation in New York City.

"The Murder of the Century," as the press dubbed Rice's death, created an international sensation. Press outlets across the country kept the story on page one with daily revelations, dramatic speculations, insinuating interviews, and lavish illustrations. Captain Baker spearheaded the criminal investigation and directed the legal strategy to secure Rice's fortune for the institute. He worked on the criminal prosecution to uncover the murder plot with Assistant District Attorney James Osborne, and he hired James Byrne of the prominent Manhattan law firm Hornblower, Byrne, Miller & Potter to defend against several civil cases related to the Rice estate. Baker and Osborne persuaded Jones to betray his accomplice in two sensational confessions, and Patrick was charged a second time on February 27, 1901, this time for murder in the first degree. Following a preliminary hearing in March and April, Patrick's trial on the charge was set for January 1902. Jones remained in protective custody as the star witness.

Lawyers and potential clients who followed press accounts of the court action applauded Captain Baker's calm, decisive demeanor and incisive reasoning, and they turned to him and his law firm to represent them in legal battles west of the Mississippi. This personal fame and national recognition came at a price. When the trials were over, Captain Baker noted he had spent seven months in New York City between September 1900 and December 1901 and another 170 days there between January 15 and July 19, 1902. Through 1904 he rented an office at 32 Broad Street with Hornblower, Byrne, Miller & Potter, where he put a brass plate on the door and conducted Baker, Botts, Baker & Lovett business while preparing the pending criminal and civil trials. When alone in New York, Captain Baker missed his wife and children. Meanwhile, Alice found the unwanted publicity unpleasant and frightening; the long separations and stressful drama of fraud, murder, and treachery made her uneasy and interrupted the rhythm of family life.

During the summer of 1901, the Bakers reunited for a holiday on Maryland's Eastern Shore, and in September 1901 everyone was in Houston preparing for the next school year. On Tuesday September 3, the Bakers chaperoned a "tacky party" for teenager Alice and twenty-six boys and girls, all "funnily dressed" in "tacky" costumes. The young guests gathered at the Bakers' home, climbed into wagonettes, and were driven to Angerhoefer's Garden for a "splendid supper" and moonlight ride home.[40] Graham Baker, just shy of his eighteenth birthday, accompanied the group before returning to the Hill School for his senior year. As the fall progressed and trial preparations intensified, Alice began to feel stressed and unwell, and Captain Baker told a friend she needed a change

Captain James Addison Baker, circa 1900. The Falk Studio, Waldorf Astoria, MS 609, Woodson Research Center, Fondren Library, Rice University.

of scene. On January 15, 1902, the couple said goodbye to their children and boarded a private car on the Southern Pacific Railroad for the journey to New York City, where Captain Baker was scheduled to testify at Patrick's criminal trial, due to begin on Monday morning, January 20. Reporters from around the world described developments in the Patrick case and printed illustrated accounts of Baker's lengthy testimony. In the trial's second week, for most of January 28 and 29, Baker explained his understanding of the murder and submitted to repetitive questions and a hostile cross-examination.

After three sleepless nights, the exhausted attorney finally collapsed for thirteen hours of sleep on January 30. Testimony of other witnesses had not concluded when the Bakers received a heart-stopping telegram. Their son Graham had pneumonia, and they were summoned to the Hill School by its devastated headmaster, John Meigs, son of the school's founder. Meigs had just attended the death of another student during the pneumonia epidemic that was raging through several boarding schools that winter. Since February 7, readers of the *Houston Chronicle* had been following front-page stories of Theodore Roosevelt Jr., who was stricken at the Groton School in Massachusetts. Soon ominous reports from Pennsylvania reached Houstonians. The Bakers had rushed through

Frank Graham Baker, circa 1894. MS 609, Woodson Research Center, Fondren Library, Rice University.

the wintry countryside from their New York hotel to their son's bedside, arriving at the Pottstown railroad depot forty miles northwest of Philadelphia on Sunday evening, February 9. Graham seemed to rally on Monday, but by Wednesday, February 12, "his condition became so hopeless" that Meigs sent the healthy students home for a fortnight "to avert . . . the shock of a second death." That afternoon, with his parents by his side, Graham succumbed. He was eighteen years, four months old and slated to matriculate at Princeton University in the fall. On February 13 Houston newspaper readers learned that young Teddy Roosevelt was "out of danger" but that "the idolized treasure of a happy household" in Houston had lost his battle with pneumonia.[41]

Dear friends Robert and Lavinia Lovett relayed the sorrowful news to the law firm, the press, and the family's wide acquaintance. As the Bakers began the sad journey to Houston with the body of their firstborn child, Robert Lovett made funeral arrangements for a service to be held at the Bakers' home on February 16. The Lovetts then escorted young Alice, Jim, and toddler Browne to New Orleans in the Southern Pacific Railroad's private car No. 45 to meet the travelers and bring the grief-stricken family home. The last leg of the journey was delayed, and the funeral service, led by the Reverend William Hayne

Leavell of the First Presbyterian Church, had to be postponed until 10:00 a.m. on February 17. Mourners listened to the church choir sing "Nearer, My God, to Thee" and followed the family to Glenwood Cemetery, where flowers covered Graham's gravesite. Eight boyhood friends carried his coffin from the house, and his Hill School classmates "most affectionately dedicated" their yearbook to his memory.[42]

Graham's parents were devastated by their son's death. Captain Baker wrote to James Byrne, who was attending the Patrick murder trial for him, that "there are reasons outside of business why I should prefer to remain here as long as possible. Mrs. Baker, while not confined to her bed is far from well, and I want to be with her as long as I can. She, however, realizes that it may be necessary for me to return to New York, and in that event she will be perfectly willing for me to do so." Alice was overcome and inconsolable. Graham shared her birthday and had been with her for the nineteen years of her marriage, a special bond time could not break. Decades later, descendants recalled the tragedy solemnly. One grandson described the loss of this gifted oldest son as "life-changing," while another felt that the Bakers' deep devotion to civic projects in some way mitigated the loss of their child. Friends rallied to support the family, and Byrne assured his colleague that the prosecution was going well. He suggested that Baker return about the middle of March for the closing argument, if possible.[43]

In the end, the entire family set out for New York on March 19. On March 26 the jury found Patrick guilty of first-degree murder. On April 7, the judge sentenced him to death, and that afternoon he arrived at Sing Sing Prison in Ossining, New York. Charlie Jones left jail in June 1902 and disappeared from public notice. Once the criminal trials were over, Alice and the children returned to Houston, and in August 1902, Robert and Lavinia Lovett invited young Alice to come with them to New York and join the family for a trip to Europe.

Patrick's sister, May Patrick Millikin, and her wealthy husband, John T. Millikin, believed in the convicted man's innocence and began a lengthy appeal. Every court effort failed, but on December 20, 1906, Governor Frank Higgins commuted the death sentence to life in prison. Six years later, on Thanksgiving eve, November 27, 1912, Governor John A. Dix granted Patrick a full pardon. Some felt bribes swayed these governors. For years after the murder conviction, Alice feared retribution and kept the doors of her home tightly secured at night, but Captain Baker lost track of both men. Patrick was disbarred and moved to Oklahoma, where he sold auto parts and cars until his death in 1940. Jones drifted aimlessly and shot himself in 1954. Neither man troubled the Bakers again.

Alice slowly resumed her domestic duties and turned her attention to her children, Alice, Jim, and Browne (known as Buster during his childhood). On September 9, 1904, she gave birth to Ruth Graham Baker, and seventeen months later the family welcomed Malcolm Graham Baker on February 18, 1906. While deeply concerned about his wife's happiness and overjoyed by the arrivals of Ruth and Malcolm (called Mac during his youth), Captain Baker was forced to turn his full attention to the numerous lawsuits arising from

Malcolm Baker and Ruth Baker, circa 1910. MS 609, Woodson Research Center, Fondren Library, Rice University.

claims on the Rice estate. Civil action had been delayed until the criminal trials could validate William Marsh Rice's 1896 will. By June 1902, however, over one hundred individuals and charities were seeking a share of the Rice millions as claimants under Mrs. Rice's disputed 1896 will, Albert Patrick's fraudulent 1900 draft, and William Marsh Rice's final testament of September 1896. Captain Baker and a battery of lawyers in Houston and New York struggled to preserve as much of the estate as possible for Rice's institute. Alice occasionally accompanied her husband on his trips to New York, and from 1903 to 1907, the fond father was able to visit his daughter Alice, who attended college-preparatory classes at Miss Spence's School for Girls in Manhattan during those years. Although he did not officially close the case until the last claimant's death in 1910, Captain Baker was able to settle with most of the heirs and their lawyers in 1905 and to announce an endowment fund of $4,631,259.08, which would be used to build the William Marsh Rice Institute for the Advancement of Literature, Science and Art. Fighting chicanery and fraud had depleted the estate by $1.8 million, nearly one-third of the fortune William Marsh Rice accumulated during his long business career.

The Settlement Association

In the years following the tragedy of Graham's death and the turbulent trials surrounding the murder of William Marsh Rice, the Bakers' commitment to civic life deepened. As a young lawyer and father, Captain Baker had been satisfied to build his law, banking, and business enterprises; he enjoyed an unblemished reputation as a man of integrity and assumed modest leadership in Houston's civil society. But as he grieved for his son and battled to save Rice's fortune, he began to see a larger purpose for his life. In the coming decades, Baker would use his business and legal resources to help transform Houston into a major American city; and he would deploy Rice's fortune to create a research and teaching institution of national significance. As a new bride and young mother, Alice Baker had directed her attention to domestic duties and seemed content to oversee her home and garden and to enjoy her children and friends. Like many fortunate women of her era, she was able to volunteer at her church and join women's clubs devoted to reading, music, and civic improvement, but after Graham's death, her focus, too, embraced a larger mission. Contemporaries knew her as a "woman of great charm and sweetness, but . . . strengthened by intelligence, vision, and a tenacity of purpose that refused to be stopped by obstacles."[44]

The Bakers left no diaries, documents, or book inventories to explain the origins of their civic commitment, and they destroyed most of their personal correspondence, so it is not easy to reconstruct their evolution as civic innovators. Both had been raised in financially secure households firmly rooted in the tenets of late nineteenth-century Protestant Christianity, and both believed that fortunate citizens, to whom much had been given, should serve their communities. Their actions suggest adherence to the post-Civil War social gospel mission—believers were called to apply to everyday life Jesus' revolutionary admonition to love all humankind; adherents united religion and social action to improve society and assuage the misery and squalor of millions whose lives had been disrupted by rapid social, economic, and demographic change. As her husband watched the walls of Rice Institute rise on a three hundred-acre campus south of downtown, Alice established the Houston Settlement Association in an old house adjacent to a dilapidated public school located in an industrial neighborhood.

At the turn of the twentieth century, women who belonged to Houston's religious congregations were the first to identify "victims in the struggle of life" in a bustling city, and they led early efforts to alleviate social needs through charitable "gifts of mercy and care." Christ Church (Episcopal) Ladies Parish Association founded Sheltering Arms in 1893 to protect "aged and needy" women who had lived in Harris County for at least six months. The association opened a facility for seven "inmates" three years later. In 1893 Shearn Methodist Church Women spearheaded the citywide effort of churches and synagogues to sustain the Kezia Payne DePelchin Faith Home for abandoned infants and toddlers. Eight Sisters of Charity of the Incarnate Word established St. Anthony's Home for the Aged in 1900 on a forty-five-acre campus, and they made its bucolic fields of grazing cows and pecking chickens available to indigent men and women over age sixty-five. The sisters received food contributions from local grocers and county allowances of forty dollars a month per client for those who had been referred to the home by the Harris County judge. In February 1904 eleven women activists founded United Charities to coordinate Houston's numerous charitable institutions, to ensure their causes were worthy of support, and to guide volunteers and donors who wished to help.[45]

These benevolent activities answered the age-old call to house and feed the downtrodden who could not care for themselves. But what of hardworking, often penniless, men and women who were newcomers to the rapidly urbanizing region? How could they confront crowded living conditions, impersonal industrial workplaces, and hostile suspicion without reassuring encouragement? When Alice Baker founded the Houston Settlement Association, she initiated an entirely different approach to securing social justice for underserved citizens. She did not see victims or inmates or clients; rather she recognized neighbors who, with support and education, could cooperate among themselves to develop civic resources for their neighborhoods. She was not a judgmental outsider, collecting data and dispensing charity or advice; rather Alice was a friend who listened and who shared with others the activities and ideas that brought joy to her life, including music, gardening, and maypole dances. Through cultural, social, and educational outreach, Alice and her co-workers hoped to weaken the class and ethnic barriers that kept Houstonians from understanding each other.

By 1907, when Alice heard Sybil Campbell's compelling story of the shivering child in a school doorway, she and other members of the Woman's Club had been working with young children for several years and had vowed to establish, fund, and staff a no-fee kindergarten in every Houston ward. The club opened its first free kindergarten and day care center in an abandoned store at Jackson and Magnolia streets in the Third Ward in October 1902. Its second experiment, in 1903, was a cooperative and free kindergarten that lasted only one year and was located in the former M. T. Jones home at 1215 Main Street. The third effort was housed in an unused building near the Second Ward's Rusk School in 1904. The first free kindergarten to be located in a public school building was scheduled to open with nineteen students on March 4, 1907, at the recently constructed Charlotte Allen School, located in the Third Ward at Elgin and Chenevert streets. Using these demonstration kindergartens to explain the importance of preparing students for elementary school in a formal academic setting, members of the Woman's Club lobbied Houston's school board to include free kindergarten classes in all elementary schools. Superintendent Professor Paul Whitefield Horn,[46] a well-known author of textbooks and articles on progressive education who introduced the junior high school concept and brought national recognition to Houston's schools, expressed interest in the clubwomen's advocacy, but the school board was unsupportive. Not until 1929 did free kindergartens become part of the curriculum in Houston's public elementary schools, but during the intervening decades Woman's Club members continued to lobby for free access to kindergarten for every Houston child.

During 1903 and 1904, Alice Baker had persuaded the First Presbyterian Church Ladies' Association, as part of its community outreach mission, to donate funds so that Sybil Campbell and Woman's Club volunteers organized by Mrs. M. M. Archer could hold a sewing class for immigrant women of the Second Ward. By 1907 Campbell managed several volunteer teachers; Annie Orem, professionally trained to teach manual arts, oversaw two classes of six to nine students each; and Alice had become the primary underwriter of the project. At first, the classes met in the kindergarten room of the Woman's Club, but by 1907 the First Presbyterian Church Ladies' Association was renting a small building "in a prettily shaded yard" at Runnels and Gabel streets to accommodate the popular classes. Alice studied settlement house concepts with Sybil Campbell and knew the young teacher aspired to provide more than sewing classes and kindergartens to the Rusk School neighborhood but needed financial and volunteer support to expand her programs. The image of a tiny child's suffering compelled both women to act.[47]

Houston reformers embraced social justice activism that winter. On January 26, 1907, the Women's Christian Temperance Union rallied a mass meeting of women at Houston City Hall to support a room in the three hundred block of Main Street where working women could rest and eat lunch and to promote Houston's first Young Women's Christian Association (YWCA). On February 19 Alice Baker began her meeting called in response to Sybil Campbell's plea of support for working families by explaining that "residents of every section of the city should have a fair chance at proper living conditions and moral surroundings." She suggested that the "educational work [of the sewing classes] so eagerly embraced by the girls of the [Rusk School] neighborhood" should be expanded to a full-service settlement. Alice and Sybil told the ten attendees about Arnold Toynbee's East End neighborhood center model that had opened in 1884 at Toynbee Hall in London. Settlements in New York, Boston, Chicago, and Dallas, they explained, were not palliative organizations dispensing charity. Rather, a settlement was a proactive experimental effort to help overcome social and industrial inequities created by modern urban conditions. Settlements nourished "friendships and social relations . . . between people who lived near each other but yet were strangers."[48] Volunteers settled near or visited with residents in underserved neighborhoods and introduced educational, recreational, and cultural programs they hoped would stimulate area residents to recognize neighborhood needs and find their own ways to improve living conditions and employment opportunities. Alice asked meeting participants to reach out to their peers, to explain the project, and to meet again on February 28.

During the intervening week, Alice asked her husband to help her write a constitution that described the purpose of the Houston Settlement Association she envisioned: to extend "educational, industrial, social, and friendly aid to all those within our reach."[49] Honored to be part of Alice's new project, Captain Baker performed the first of many tasks he would undertake for the Houston Settlement Association during the next three decades. He also encouraged his friends to offer legal and financial support to the nascent organization. Thirty-two charter members, including women respected for their civic activism and reforming zeal, attended the second meeting, adopted the constitution, and elected Alice president of a fifteen-member Houston Settlement Association board. The group recognized that its settlement should offer free kindergarten classes but did not want to infringe on the successful efforts of the Woman's Club to create kindergartens or manage the training class the club had initiated in 1903 to prepare teachers. Alice's newly constituted board appointed respected civic leader Estelle Sharp[50] to explain association goals to Woman's Club members. Sharp's reputation as a forceful fundraiser and advocate for the Dallas kindergarten movement preceded her move to Houston in 1904 when her brilliant inventor husband, Walter Benona Sharp,[51] relocated his oil tool and production interests to the city. Shortly after the Sharps' arrival, the founders of United Charities sought Estelle's advice and asked her to join their leadership council. Erect, elegant, and efficient, Sharp proved to be a talented administrator who helped the council define its mission and served as president several times between 1907 and 1914. She also became a powerful advocate for Settlement Association interests and remained on its board for five decades.

At the third meeting of the Settlement Association, Mrs. Frank B. King, wife of a prominent physician, announced that the Woman's Club would donate its Second Ward kindergarten building, located adjacent to Rusk School, to the newly organized association. Frustrated by the school board's indifference and persuaded by Sharp's advocacy, the Woman's Club had decided to support the Settlement Association initiative and to give its kindergarten books and supplies to the parents' association of the Charlotte Allen School. Renamed Rusk Settlement, the old building immediately became the center of social life for the surrounding area. Rusk School Principal J. W. Shepherd and his wife agreed to oversee the settlement building as part-time resident workers. Sybil Campbell continued to teach at Rusk School, served on the board of the Settlement Association, acted as head worker briefly, and became a part-time paid resident worker at Rusk Settlement.

Alice asked the board of the Houston Settlement Association to spend time during its initial year investigating Houston neighborhoods and learning about the nationwide settlement movement. She called on Campbell and leading Houston artist Emma Richardson Cherry to form a press committee and charged them with promoting the new organization and explaining its purpose. An enthusiastic report in *The Key to the City of Houston*, published by the Federation of Women's Clubs in 1908, suggests the press committee had been persuasive. City newspapers were eager to announce meetings and report board activities, and the volunteer group expanded quickly. The Ladies' Association of the First Presbyterian Church had pledged the first monetary gift to the new organization, and in one year Alice and the board had recruited nearly two hundred subscribers, as members were called, including twenty men. Many early supporters were people Alice had known well for years—her neighbor Roxalee Andrews (wife of lawyer Frank Andrews), her girlhood friend Marion Seward Holt, suffragette and businesswoman Annette B. Finnigan, and Katherine (Kate) Parker and Huberta (Hetty) Page Garwood, the wives of Captain Baker's law partners Edwin B. Parker and Judge Hiram M. Garwood. The association met on the first Wednesday of every month at the Baker home, and all members paid voluntary dues, "subscribing as his or her pleasure dictates," although bylaws stated that members who gave nothing for one year would be removed from the roster. Without assessing members, making public appeals, or holding fundraising events, the association raised enough money to repurpose the Woman's Club kindergarten building and to move the little house where sewing classes were first held to the settlement site.[52]

Sybil Campbell's story hour at Rusk Settlement, circa 1908. MS 609, Woodson Research Center, Fondren Library, Rice University.

Alice recognized the central role played by her friends who had organized women's clubs to marshal support for a public library, to provide classical music concerts, and to assist neighbors who could not help themselves. She believed that women and men in every neighborhood could organize similar clubs to improve their lives. During Rusk Settlement's first year, staff and volunteers helped residents develop clubs and activities to identify problems and to build trust among area neighbors. Under the expert guidance of paid workers Winifred Lyford and Annie Orem, thirty-five to fifty children attended the settlement kindergarten each week. Superintendent Professor P. W. Horn showed his support by handing out diplomas to the first class of kindergarten "graduates" in 1908. More than sixty-six girls registered for three popular sewing classes, and Rusk Settlement volunteers came to the campus to assist four cooking classes, a weekly story hour, boys' and girls' clubs, and an Alpha Club for young men. The Second Ward Citizens' Club, or Men's Club, organized in January 1908, and the Women's Club, founded the next month, met regularly to discuss how best to clean up the neighborhood and encourage neighbors to participate in settlement activities. In its first year, at least two hundred people used the settlement building each week for classes, dances, parties, and concerts.

Inaugural activities proved so successful that the Houston school board asked the Houston Settlement Association to equip a domestic science department at the Rusk School and promised to add sewing, cooking, and manual training classes to its curriculum. During the summer of 1908, the association purchased and installed equipment valued at $500, and classes began in the fall. Almost immediately the association persuaded the school to schedule a cooking class at night. Alice praised the first night classes—for eight girls studying domestic science under former Woman's Club president Mamie Gearing—as the association's greatest accomplishment, because she believed the collaboration brought the association "closely in touch with the public school, which is just where the Settlement belongs." Writers and citizens alike were beginning to understand the mission of Rusk Settlement. It "is not a charity, but rather a social center, and an educational institution, by which we hope to teach people . . . to help themselves to rise above heredity, environment and whatever would tend to discourage, and make the best of themselves and derive the greatest good and happiness from life." Alice also hoped to educate Houston's civic leaders and government officials about the needs of forgotten neighborhoods and the interdependence of all citizens.[53]

To celebrate its second birthday in February 1909, members of the Rusk Settlement Women's Club, neighborhood residents, and Settlement Association

Kindergarten building and Rusk Settlement house. MS 609, Woodson Research Center, Fondren Library, Rice University.

subscribers enjoyed a musical program and blew out two candles on a cake in the kindergarten room. On March 15, they rejoiced again when the association rented the old Settegast family homestead at Gable and Maple streets adjacent to Rusk School and began refurbishing the large southern-style house with its deep porches shading upper and lower floors. Alice furnished the parlor and kitchen, and her team decorated the other spaces in the "commodious" headquarters to provide club rooms, a pool room, two large game rooms, offices, a dispensary, and an apartment for the resident head worker. The original Rusk Settlement kindergarten house was moved onto the shady grounds, which provided a "delightful spot" for outdoor recreation and sturdy playground equipment. That May, the Settlement Association board hosted a housewarming at the house and grounds and welcomed "supporters from all parts of the city" to meet neighborhood residents.[54] Men of the Brazos Orchestra donated an afternoon concert while guests enjoyed punch, a maypole dance, and storytelling. The larger space, enthusiastic acceptance by area residents, and generous subscriber support allowed the association to open a dispensary and first aid room. In April 1909 Alice hired visiting nurse Elizabeth Norment to manage the health program. A graduate of the Johns Hopkins Training School, Norment had previously lived at Henry Street House in New York City. Her energy was staggering—during her eight-month tenure, she made 1,234 visits to homes of area families and dispensed 1,461 treatments to 127 patients, visiting patients several times during an illness. She also assisted physicians who volunteered to examine 249 students at Rusk School three times during the school year.

In the fall of 1909, Alice did not confine her efforts to the Rusk campus. She invited Dr. H. H. Hart, director of the Child-Helping Department of the recently formed Russell Sage Foundation in New York City,[55] to visit Houston and discuss the most effective ways to tackle the problems of delinquent boys. So impressive was Hart's analysis that the mayor, city commissioners, and county court consulted him after the lecture. With Hart's help, Harris County established the Seabrook School for Boys at Clear Lake in 1910. Alice had studied the work being done to build strong communities in other cities, and she wanted Houstonians to participate in and benefit from forward-looking national trends. In 1930, two years before Alice's death, the county spent $40,000 at the school to help forty or fifty "refractory" boys become "useful, upright, law-abiding citizens."[56]

In the summer of 1909, Alice left Rusk Settlement in the hands of resident workers and joined her family for a well-deserved vacation at Loon Lake in the Adirondacks. After the children returned to school, Alice and her husband joined Kate and Edwin B. Parker for a motor tour through New Hampshire's White Mountains in September. Yet, Rusk Settlement was never far from her mind. Alice and the board realized that their expanding programs demanded full-time professional management. When Alice returned to Houston in the late fall of 1909, she hired James P. Kranz to be full-time head worker at Rusk Settlement and to take charge of the professional staff and enthusiastic volunteers. Young and energetic, Kranz was a graduate of the University of Minnesota and had served as special agent for the Minneapolis Associated Charities while working in the Pillsbury and Unity House settlements. In 1907 he was a fellow at the New York School of Philanthropy and a resident of University Settlement. In 1908 Kranz went to Philadelphia to take charge of boys' programs at Southwark Neighborhood House. Alice explained to Kranz that the Houston Settlement Association board wanted to strengthen the current educational and social programs in 1910 and hoped to initiate an athletic program, a day nursery, a free dispensary, a Penny Provident Bank savings program, Sunday lectures, and legal aid services. With staff in place and a powerful story to share, Alice decided to publish a 1909 *Year Book* to review Houston Settlement Association activities, and she called upon the newly hired Kranz to help her compile and edit the information.[57]

Statement of Purpose, 1909–1914

Alice's masterful annual report revealed her deep understanding of social problems, her inspiring but firm leadership style, and her analytical approach to problem-solving. In thirty-two pages, she explained her vision and challenged Houston's leading women and men to address the needs of less fortunate neighbors. The association was issuing the *Year Book*, she wrote, "because . . . all social agencies relying on public contributions for support should make an annual statement" proving that the money raised had been spent in Houston by responsible individuals "for the purpose for which it is subscribed." Alice listed the association officers and directors, the 1907-1909 staff of eleven paid social workers and teachers who lived in the neighborhood, and the fourteen volunteer workers, who came to the settlement every week to assist with classes and clubs. Alice also explained social work as "practical social economy," or "community housekeeping," which she defined as the rights an individual resident can expect from its community. She affirmed a bill of social rights that reflected goals of Progressive Era urban reformers who wanted to provide healthy and safe working and living conditions for all citizens.[58]

"Everyone will concede," the report announced, "that a person has a right" to be born to a healthy mother in safe conditions; to enjoy a childhood protected from hunger and exploitation; to be "efficiently trained" for citizenship; to receive a living wage for "steady work, under sanitary conditions, . . . at reasonable hours"; to maintain a "decent standard of living" in a clean home with sufficient food, clothing, and "an insurance policy against sickness and death"; to be protected from "preventable diseases"; to drink pure water and breathe fresh air; to be safeguarded from "preventable crime"; and to enjoy a comfortable old age that ensures long-married couples remain together. More than one hundred years after these aspirational words were written, the Settlement Association goals have yet to be realized by every Houstonian. Alice understood that life could be hard, and she saw that a settlement center could alleviate many problems by offering protection for children, classes in nutrition and home care for young women, lessons in language and citizenship, cooperative action to improve the neighborhood, and a joyful, safe space where neighbors could discuss problems, absorb information, and have fun. She hoped that networking among volunteer workers, board members, and neighborhood residents would foster communication between affluent and underserved areas of town. Alice's report also revealed the need for government action—funding for public education, laws to monitor the workplace and public health, and municipal responsibility for clean water, sewage treatment, and police protection—at a time when governments at all levels were only beginning to recognize that private action could not meet all the needs of struggling citizens in densely populated, rapidly industrializing urban areas.[59]

Clubs lay at the heart of the settlement experience. They were organized by age and area of interest; club members set the rules, elected the officers, and conducted the meetings—providing lessons in the way democracy works. By late 1909 Rusk Settlement sponsored nine clubs that met regularly. Alice praised Second Ward Women's Club officers and members for assisting "in every way possible" and for equipping the kitchen from their meager resources. Club meetings combined educational and social goals and had become "neighborhood affairs." The Men's Club (Second Ward Citizens Club) had worked hard in its first two years to clean up debris and improve the "moral surroundings" by chasing prostitutes and troublemakers from the neighborhood. A club for kindergarten mothers met once a month with the teachers, who explained the children's curriculum. Dancing and sewing classes, open to girls and boys, met every week. The public Houston Lyceum and Carnegie Library chose Rusk Settlement for its first off-site outreach program and issued books every week at the settlement; a reading room furnished with magazines and picture books welcomed readers every day of the year; and on Tuesday afternoons about seventy-five children and parents attended story hour. The large yard was open every weekday for supervised play, and clubs hosted "concerts, entertainments and parties" on the lawn.[60]

In the report, Alice distinguished social from religious settlements by pointing out that the "social settlement works for the betterment of man regardless of creed." She explained that settlement efforts fell into three main areas. The work that took place at the settlement embraced clubs and classes to enrich members' educational, aesthetic, artistic, athletic, and social understanding. The second type of work comprised visits by the settlement staff to neighborhood homes to "learn the conditions with which the people are contending and then to aid them" in removing or improving these conditions. Alice called the third division of work "social betterment." By participating with settlement neighbors in classes and clubs and by visiting area homes, Rusk Settlement staff and volunteers came to understand the "adverse conditions" facing many families: children idling in the street or attending "highly suggestive performances" in poorly ventilated "death traps"; open sewers, impure water, and dirty shacks; school-age children at work; sickness and destitution; decrepit surroundings not alleviated by parks, playgrounds, or "desirable" social centers where families could enjoy a "wholesome break in the monotony of life." The settlement, Alice hoped, would help neighborhood residents focus on neighborhood needs and, with the aid of "enlightened public" support, reconstruct the social environment. She concluded her report with a financial statement and a record of the 192 Settlement Association subscribers. Alice Baker had achieved amazing success; her report inspired sponsors, board members, and staff to forge ahead.[61]

1910 proved to be an exciting year, the first under Head Worker Kranz's leadership. He kept the full program in operation through the entire summer, while the Baker family traveled for three months in Europe. To address the acute shortage of trained kindergarten teachers, Kranz opened a kindergarten college at the Cushman Private School. He provided most of the instruction, and program enrollees completed their practice training at Rusk Settlement. When Alice returned from her travels, she worked with Kranz and his staff to orchestrate the first Texas Conference of Charities and Corrections. Representatives from seven Texas cities conferred in Houston on November 27-29, 1910, and the Settlement Association defrayed all expenses and set the agenda. Before adjourning, the group agreed to call a second meeting in January 1911 in Austin under the auspices of the University of Texas. Twenty-two cities sent representatives, and with the help of A. Caswell Ellis,[62] well-known professor of pedagogy, and other experts, the conferees established a permanent state organization to coordinate the social agencies, to study community needs, and to meet regularly for progress reports.

The year ended dramatically when the old wooden Rusk School burned to the ground during the night of Thursday, December 15, 1910. Police suspected arson when the Southwestern Telephone and Telegraph Company revealed that wires in the vicinity had been cut and that a major cable had burned or been cut in two. Officers arrested a suspect who could not explain his presence near the building, but they could find no evidence to charge him. Superintendent Horn transferred some students to Austin School and found classroom space for the remaining pupils and staff in a portable building and in an old house near the school; classes for the second semester began on schedule on January 2, 1911.

When planning began for the building that rose from Rusk School's ruins, Alice Baker proposed an experiment. Armed with her cogent 1909 report and her ambition to link school and Settlement Association missions, she persuaded Houston's Board of Education to place Rusk Settlement headquarters in the school building itself and to create a "'socialized' school of the future" used after classes for play, study, evening lectures, and concerts.[63] Alice assured the school board that the Settlement Association would continue to manage and pay for its kindergarten, its dispensary, its after-school programs, and its adult classes and lectures. In January 1911 the city purchased three and one-half acres, including the Settegast property used by Rusk Settlement. The new school was sited to face Maple Street, and the Settegast building and kindergarten cottage were moved to the back of the property. The remaining acreage became a large playground and athletic space. Although the buildings and grounds now belonged to the school district, the Settlement Association continued to use them, free of charge, until 1951.

Alice encouraged the project architects to consult Professor A. Caswell Ellis when they designed the new Rusk School and its surrounding property to serve as a school, a community center, and a playground park. Alice was familiar with the detailed manual about safe school construction that Ellis had published in 1905, and his analysis strongly influenced the Rusk project. The modern building included sanitary water fountains, adjustable window shades, and steel lockers for each student. Cool fresh air could be pumped into the rooms and stale air drawn out by exhaust fans. The building—which was three-story, fireproof, and made of brick and cement—housed the Rusk Settlement community center on its first floor. All the rooms opened to the street, so adult visitors to the dispensary, the library, and the manual and domestic science classes could enter the building without interrupting school activities. The large dispensary allowed the settlement to hire more nurses and accommodate more residents. When the city developed a public health program during World War I, Rusk Settlement nurses became Houston's first visiting nurses, and citywide headquarters were placed in the former kindergarten cottage. The kitchens and lunchrooms, located on the first floor of the new building and staffed by the Rusk School Mothers' Club, were used for school lunches and for community center gatherings. The auditorium, reached by broad outside stairs at the rear of the building, was placed on the second floor with the kindergarten and some classrooms; more classrooms filled the third-floor space. Alice understood that placing the community center in the school strengthened both. The school building could be used all year; parents could send their children to school regularly and know they would be cared for all day; and Rusk Settlement could expand its programs. Teachers, social workers, residents, and civic supporters would learn from each other. Public education and municipal social justice would be firmly linked.

At the March 1911 annual meeting of the Settlement Association, Alice asked J. W. Shepherd, principal of Rusk School and former head worker at Rusk Settlement, to describe the cooperation between Rusk School and Rusk Settlement. Sybil Campbell "painted a vivid picture" of the "'socialized' school of the future" being introduced to Houstonians at the Rusk School/Settlement. Educators, she assured her audience, now realized that citizens had paid for public facilities that were largely wasted because school doors were locked as soon as classes ended. By combining educational and community center functions on one property, schools would become "true social centers of their neighborhoods," Campbell said. She noted that the Rusk buildings would be open for after-school and adult recreation and classes and that the auditorium would provide space for lectures, concerts, plays, dances, and parties. Excited meeting attendees, while wishing to maintain the "distinct individuality" of their association, pledged "to make Houston's first socialized school a complete success." Because of Alice's concern and foresight, Houston's public school officials had created a modern model school, attended by mostly immigrant students, in one of the city's poorest neighborhoods. In her 1913 compendium celebrating the Rice Institute, Julia Cameron Montgomery praised the "completion of Rusk school [as] a new era in scientific school building and equipment in Houston, and one to stimulate civic pride."[64] Alice's interest in and supervision of the Rusk Settlement never wavered, and her success brought the Rusk model statewide notice. Social service experts sought her advice, and Alice participated in contemporary discussion of best methods to solve social and industrial problems caused by modern urban conditions. In 1912, she joined Sybil Campbell, Dean J. L. Kester of Baylor University, Professor Frank Seay of Southwestern University, and Dan Jarvis of Fort Worth to represent the Texas Conference of Charities and Corrections at the Southern Sociological Congress, held in Nashville May 7–10.

Alice was a gentle but firm leader, whose steady hand inspired her friends and the hardworking settlement families to improve community life. During Rusk Settlement's early years, she established four traditions that were celebrated annually for decades. Board members launched the Alice G. Baker Baby Chest in her honor to provide clothing and supplies to each baby born in the neighborhood. At Easter, volunteers decorated the building, and neighborhood children enjoyed maypole dances. Neighborhood residents looked forward to the beautifully decorated "Tree of Light" that Alice provided Rusk Settlement every Christmas. The most popular activity occurred every year in the late spring when Alice welcomed members of the Second Ward Women's

Club, volunteers, and association supporters to her home for a day spent together. Alice encouraged Second Ward residents to plant gardens and at the receptions gave prizes for the best home garden and the best vacant-lot community garden. She also presented each guest with a "crusader" pin of daisies, collected from her own garden, to express her gratitude and appreciation for the year's work. The Bakers attended many events at Rusk Settlement, and their empathetic interest made a lasting impression. One young woman told a social worker about meeting the Bakers when she was a little girl: "We couldn't speak a word of English. . . . Captain and Mrs. Baker smiled at us and we knew we had found friends in a new country."[65]

Family and Civic Life

In 1907, the year Alice Baker persuaded her friends to establish the city's first full-fledged community center, Captain Baker's civic commitments reached a turning point when he completed preliminary plans for Rice Institute and launched a yearlong quest for a leader to take charge of the ambitious enterprise. In December, the Rice trustees announced that Edgar Odell Lovett, a promising young astronomy professor at Princeton University, would become the academic director of Rice Institute, effective in January1908. During this critical period of civic activity, the Bakers remained devoted and engaged parents. Their daughter Alice completed her studies at Miss Spence's School for Girls in the spring of 1907 and again toured Europe with Robert Lovett's family before returning home to enjoy her debutante season in Houston. From June to September 1907, the Bakers vacationed with the younger children on the Eastern Shore of Maryland before taking young Jim to the Hill School in Pennsylvania, where he would prepare for college until 1911. Walter Brown (Buster), now seven, three-year-old Ruth, and baby Malcolm, born in 1906, demanded Alice's attention that fall, but she found time to prepare for her older daughter's reign as queen of the No-Tsu-Oh Festival in November 1907 and to orchestrate two grand evening events to introduce twenty-year-old Alice to Houston society. As a leading Houston hostess, Alice Baker's social gatherings drew press attention. Always both meticulous and imaginative, Alice oversaw every detail, created dazzling floral and decorative displays, and maintained high standards. Invitees, even family, were expected to arrive on time, be appropriately dressed, and display good manners. An army of household employees assisted her efforts, so when her guests appeared, Alice always seemed serene, gracious, beautifully gowned, and "everywhere at once" attending to the comfort and enjoyment of the assemblage.[66]

Alice Baker (daughter), Queen of No-Tsu-Oh Festival, 1907. MS 609, Woodson Research Center, Fondren Library, Rice University.

Civic leaders devised No-Tsu-Oh (Houston reversed) in 1899 to update popular harvest festivals and promote Houston's industrial innovations. Old and young Houstonians reveled for fifteen years but did not revive the custom after a pause during World War I. For one week in November, citizens enjoyed parades, bands, balls, and commercial exhibitions to celebrate their allegiance to King Nottoc (Cotton), always one of the city's celebrated business or civic figures, and to salute his youthful queen, always the year's favored debutante. In 1907 Captain Baker's law partner, Judge Hiram M. Garwood, ruled as King Nottoc IX, while the Bakers' daughter Alice reigned as his queen. Two years later Captain Baker served as Nottoc XI, and in 1911, Rice Institute President Edgar Odell Lovett was crowned King Nottoc XIII. To honor their daughter and commemorate the November 1907 festival, the Bakers welcomed fifty-two guests to their home, where they served a five-course dinner to the king, queen, and royal party. Starry-eyed reporters described at length "every detail reflecting . . . the splendor of the scene," which was brilliant with gold or white chrysanthemums, flickering tapers, and damask-covered tables adorned with satin ribbons and delicate laces.[67]

Even more glamorous was the "Elegant Reception" the Bakers held for their daughter on December 1, 1907, from 8:00 p.m. until 11:00 p.m. Japanese, Indian, and Moorish themes decorated three entertainment rooms in the Baker home on Main Street. An "immense floral basket, several feet in height, overflowed with red chrysanthemums and asparagus fern," and Japanese umbrellas twinkled with incandescent lights. Carrying a bouquet of yellow chrysanthemums, Mrs. Baker wore an elegant gown of lace net, embroidered with gold chrysanthemums that shimmered over yellow chiffon. Young Alice, dressed demurely in white chiffon sprinkled with seed pearls and sequins, carried American Beauty roses while mother and daughter greeted their guests. Fifty-seven friends of the honoree and her parents helped the Bakers welcome the crowd. In March 1908, the Bakers chaperoned a private railcar carrying No-Tsu-Oh Queen Alice and five attendants to parties at the Mardi Gras Carnival in New Orleans.[68]

During these busy years, the Bakers began to enjoy two national pastimes recently introduced to Houston. Twenty women met at the First Presbyterian Church in October 1909 to form a Chautauqua Study Club that would "promote intellectual and social entertainment resulting in good fellowship" and follow the wide-ranging curriculum of the Chautauqua Literary and Scientific Circle.[69] Methodists had retreated to the shores of New York's Lake Chautauqua for several summers to train Methodist Sunday school teachers, and in 1878 they decided to staff a speakers' bureau and develop a study program that could be used by local Chautauqua clubs throughout the United States. The movement gained popularity and attracted a range of speakers, including several former US presidents. Alice joined Houston's group of thirty women for monthly meetings at the Carnegie Library. After several years in the library's modest boardroom, suffragist and civic leader Louise Masterson insisted the group gather in her handsome brick Colonial Revival residence at 3207 Burlington, one of the first homes and gardens constructed in the Westmoreland addition between downtown and Rice Institute. At these meetings, Alice, Ima Hogg, and other progressive women discussed Houston's many challenges, and they recruited Mary Lovett, the newly arrived wife of Rice Institute's founding leader Edgar Odell Lovett, to join the group.

Captain Baker was among the first to take up the newly popular sport of golf when he urged several businessmen to form the Houston Golf Club in March 1904. He and other duffers had been putting into tomato cans laid out on some "greens" near the Gun Club (soon to be developed as the Courtlandt Place enclave), but Captain Baker and Rice family members agreed to build a real golf course and small clubhouse on institute property along Buffalo Bayou. This experiment attracted international players traveling the US circuit, and in 1908 Captain Baker called on fellow golfers to build the city's first full-service country club on 150 tree-shaded acres along Brays Bayou, a twenty-minute streetcar ride east of downtown. Organized to promote and encourage "outdoor life, innocent sports and amusements, and . . . social intercourse and . . . higher ideals," the club provided a large reception room, a special ladies' "apartment," a men's locker room, and dining facilities. When Houston Country Club opened its spacious clubhouse in November 1909, its roster listed 507 members who had each paid one hundred dollars for a member share and pledged dues of $1.50 per month. Today the property with its grand old trees belongs to the City of Houston as the Gus Wortham Park Golf Course, which is conserved and administered for the public by the Houston Golf Association.[70]

After many years of service with the First Presbyterian Church Ladies' Association, Alice agreed in 1910 to become president of the group, which had been renamed the Westminster Guild. During her term, the guild sponsored nine service circles and a Bible study class. Alice's main project concerned the church's finances, and she asked guild members to spearhead a drive to pay off the $11,500 mortgage on the manse, held by South Texas Commercial National Bank. The guild promised to raise $300 a year for five years, and Alice made a gift of $115 to help fund this pledge. The women's offer to guarantee $1,500 prodded the First Presbyterian Church's all-male Board of Deacons to cover the balance and rid the property at Main and Gray of debt. Within a few days, three prominent deacons—attorney Joseph C. Hutcheson Jr.[71] and industrialists John F. Dickson and Edward A. Peden—promised $1,000 each, and the remaining board members also made multiyear pledges. Captain Baker, as a longtime church member, agreed to give one hundred dollars a year for five years. The guild challenge proved irresistible, and the debt was paid.[72]

Musical Contributions

Alice Baker loved performing and listening to music, whether classical, religious, or popular, and she quickly discovered fellow enthusiasts in her husband's law partner, Edwin B. Parker, and his talented wife Kate. Happily for these devotees, Houston boasted a strong musical tradition that had begun when German immigrants and their successful families hosted classical concert performances, open-air instrumental and vocal programs, and dancing parties. Pioneer Gustav Dresel described Houston's first musical event in 1837, and the town's German community built a *turnverein* on a city block defined by Prairie, Caroline, Texas, and Austin streets in 1854 to accommodate enthusiastic patrons. In May 1884 fervent German singers established a local *saengerbund* (singing choir), received a state charter in 1890, and began performing in statewide *saengerfests* (music festivals) that had been sponsored by the German-Texan Saengerbund for three decades. Before World War I, Houston hosted the statewide festival in 1885, 1894, and 1902, and in 1913 the Texas Saengerfest produced three days of unmatched entertainment in the City Auditorium, which had opened in 1910. During these years, Houston's local *saengerfests* included performances by the St. Louis Symphony Orchestra and by singers from New York's Metropolitan Opera.

Musical English-speaking Houstonians also sponsored men's, women's, and church choruses and applauded traveling groups who performed in Gray's Opera House on Courthouse Square. By the 1890s, Houston's reform-minded women had joined the national music club movement "to educate and improve the public taste by giving the best music only."[73] Members of the Ladies' Singing Society (later renamed the Treble Clef Club), formed in the 1890s, and the Woman's Choral Club, organized in 1901, arranged popular concerts that met professional standards. Reorganized in 1904, the Treble Clef Club grew to seventy-five singers and 672 associate members and attracted an audience of four thousand music mavens to the season-closing concert of 1911. Not to be outdone, musical English-speaking men organized the Houston Quartette Society in 1900. The popular group inaugurated the Federation of English Singing Societies of Texas in the fall of 1903, and in 1904 and 1905 it sponsored English singing festivals in Texas that attracted four hundred singers and featured performances by the New York and Pittsburgh symphony orchestras. In March 1907 Houston's music-loving civic leaders met with the manager of the Chicago Symphony Orchestra to discuss forming a local Music Festival Association so the city could participate in the nationwide effort to sponsor annual festivals in May. For four seasons from 1908 to 1911, Edwin B. Parker persuaded Houston's leading businessmen to guarantee local participation in the national pastime. The Chicago Symphony agreed to team with local choristers in 1908 and 1909, and in 1910 Walter Damrosch brought the New York Symphony to Houston on April 25. The performance featured Houston-born concert pianist Helena Lewyn, who was making her United States debut.[74] Delighted Houstonians presented a gold medal to the young artist. In May 1911, Damrosch returned and teamed with Hu T. Huffmaster, music director of the Woman's Choral Club, to direct a huge chorus of local singers. Performances drew overflow crowds and were important social events. The patrons' roster of five hundred listed music patron Ima Hogg, and the 1911 Music Festival Association board of directors included civic luminaries James A. Baker and Edgar Odell Lovett as well as Houston's first cultural critic, Wille Hutcheson,[75] member of a prominent Houston family, who wrote for the *Houston Post* and published music criticism in national journals.

Kate Parker was as impassioned about music as Alice Baker was about the settlement movement. For twenty years Parker labored to elevate Houston's taste by performing in concert and by holding musical lecture demonstrations at her home. From 1901 to 1909 she was musical director of the Woman's Choral Club, founded in 1901 by Wille Hutcheson to sponsor concerts by nationally acclaimed professional singers and to assist talented Houston women who aspired to professional careers. On May 25, 1908, Parker and several "leading professionals and best [female] amateurs" announced formation of the Thursday Morning Musical Club with the goal of creating a music conservatory. Candidates for club membership were asked to pass a stringent exam; members studied early and modern European, Slavonic, and American composers; and meetings featured the work of famous women musicians and composers. The assertively academic club chose Treble Clef Club musical director Margaret Cox as president, music teacher Mary Elizabeth Rouse as program chairwoman, and Woman's Choral Club musical director Kate Parker as overseer for the board of examiners. Parker undoubtedly urged her musical friend Alice Baker to join the new club. Both women enjoyed attending concerts when traveling and, during one scouting trip to New York in September 1906, had taken young Alice Baker to hear "the remarkably attractive baritone, Claude Cunningham," whom they immediately invited to sing in Houston while he was touring the South that November.[76]

Despite this array of choices, Alice Baker felt there should be a musical club for younger aspirants since all social entertainments depended on amateur local performers and most middle-class homes contained at least one musical instrument. Encouraged by Kate Parker, Alice and Galveston resident Corinne Abercrombie Waldo[77] inaugurated the Girls Musical Club "for the purpose of study and self-improvement along musical lines" to encourage younger women to practice and perform. Bylaws specified that "girls shall be given preference" as active members and officers, and for many years all officers were unmarried. Alice invited about forty young women, most of whom had been studying music since childhood, to her Main Street home on Wednesday morning, January 25, 1911, to inaugurate the club. Included among the guests was Woman's Choral Club member Ima Hogg, a professionally trained pianist who was teaching advanced piano students after spending fourteen months traveling and training in Europe. Girls Musical Club founders chose young Alice Baker to be president for the January–May 1911 season of the new enterprise, but they elected the more musically accomplished Ima Hogg to lead the 1911-1912 and 1912-1913 seasons. Membership, which rose to one hundred during Ima's tenure, meant serious commitment—annual club dues (three dollars), fines for tardiness, and expulsion after three unexcused absences. Active members included acclaimed artist Emma Richardson Cherry, librarian Julia Ideson, music critic Wille Hutcheson, talented musicians, and daughters of prominent families. Each member was expected to prepare lectures on composers or music genres and to perform at meetings held every other Tuesday from November through May. As club founder, Alice hosted the first bi-weekly meeting at her home on January 25, 1911. A year later at the meeting on Tuesday, January 9, 1912, which was open to guests, Rice Institute President Edgar Odell Lovett heard Ima Hogg and Wille Hutcheson interpret German composer Franz Schubert. Founding hostess Alice Baker and popular music teacher Florence (Bessie) Griffiths were named "privileged" members and were not required to meet the club's requirements, but their patronage was considered essential to the club's success. Until she moved to Washington, DC, during World War I, Kate Parker welcomed club members and friends at least twice a year to open meetings at her magnificent midtown home, which was known as The Oaks.[78]

Family Interludes

Houston's social and civic activity paused every summer when families who could afford to do so escaped the city's pulsating heat and traveled by rail or ship to cooler climates in the United States or Europe. While Captain Baker was untangling the William Marsh Rice murder and probate trials in New York City, the family vacationed along Maryland's Eastern Shore and at Loon Lake in the Adirondack Mountains of New York State. Every few years, the Bakers also made slow journeys around Europe. In 1910 young Alice, now twenty-three, photographed the group as it motored in open touring cars through England, Scotland, France, Germany, Switzerland, and Italy; flat tires and scenery

Rockhaven Cottage Bass Rocks, Gloucester, Massachusetts, Summer 1921. (Summer Home, c. 1911–c. 1932). Private Collection, Courtesy of Virginia Meyers Chandler.

amused the photographer. Not long after this memorable trip, the Bakers began spending their summers at Rockhaven Cottage, a rambling six-bedroom shingled house built in 1906 on a spit of land jutting into the Atlantic Ocean at Bass Rocks, Gloucester, Massachusetts. For two decades, the Bakers boarded a private railway car in Houston when Rice Institute's academic year ended and traveled with family, friends, and servants to spend three or four months at the comfortable retreat with its shady porches ideal for lazy outdoor living. The shore north of Boston became a summer playground as early as 1817, when Nahant attracted visitors. By the 1850s a railroad reached the fishing village of Gloucester on Cape Ann. Fifty years later, Bass Rocks was a haven for artists and for several Texas families. The Bakers clambered over the rocks and enjoyed the bracing sea breezes. Adults were caught on camera riding donkeys and eating watermelon. Captain Baker hired a secretary in Boston and made frequent trips to the city to deal with clients, visit medical specialists, and maintain contact with his law, banking, and institute colleagues in Houston. Alice filled the house with family and friends, spoiled her guests with gifts and sightseeing expeditions, and supplied guests with notepaper engraved with the Rockhaven Cottage letterhead and address.

During the summer of 1911, the family celebrated Jim's graduation from the Hill School and prepared for young Alice's autumn wedding to lawyer Murray Brashear Jones, member of an old Houston family who had finished the University of Texas in 1907, gained a bachelor of letters degree from Princeton the following year, and returned to his Texas alma mater to complete law studies in 1910. In the fall of 1911, Baker family friends toasted the coming nuptials with a flurry of events during a wedding week crammed with lavish luncheons, sumptuous dinners, and elaborate receptions honoring the bridal couple. Jim Baker returned from Princeton to serve as best man at the 8:30 p.m. ceremony on Wednesday, November 21, and Buster (age eleven), Ruth (age seven), and Mac (age five) assisted their sister. The mother of the bride filled the First Presbyterian Church with flowers, while violinist Marie Briscoe and pianist Kate Parker provided music throughout the service. When guests entered the Bakers' home for a champagne supper of pressed chicken, coffee, and cake, they found a "veritable garden of American Beauty roses." Following the reception, the bride, dressed in a blue gown trimmed with fur and pink roses, departed with her groom for a trip to California. When they returned to Houston, the newlyweds lived "temporarily" with her parents.[79]

Launching the Institute

The Bakers said farewell to their wedding guests and turned their attention to two significant events: Houston's largest bank merger, a victory for Captain Baker, and the opening ceremonies for Rice Institute, a team effort highlighting the talents of both Bakers. Since 1886 Captain Baker had balanced a dual career in law and banking while overseeing the creation of Rice Institute after 1891. By 1911 he recognized that Commercial National Bank—where he was director and shareholder—and South Texas National Bank—where Rice Institute held 640 shares—were facing stiff competition. Baker believed the banks needed to grow if they were to compete in a rapidly changing city, and he saw merger as the best route to expansion. Working with directors of both banks, he drew up a plan, secured agreement from the Rice Institute board on January 20, and completed negotiations on March 2, 1912, for what was at that time the city's largest bank merger. In 1914 he became president of the merged South Texas Commercial National Bank and in 1922 was named chairman, a post he held until his death in 1941.

The William Marsh Rice Institute for the Advancement of Literature, Science and Art dominated Captain Baker's civic life for fifty years and generated many responsibilities for Alice as well. Even as Baker was fighting to unmask murderers and save an immense fortune from wrongful claims, he was thinking about the institute's future. Having written the institute's charter in 1891, Baker knew well his client's ambition to provide some kind of higher learning to the white boys and girls of Texas free of charge, which was a remarkable, if incomplete, mission to extend advanced education to a broad pool of applicants. Over the years, William Marsh Rice had donated seven acres of land in downtown Houston and expressed interest in trade and design schools like Cooper Union, whose well-endowed campus at Astor Place was within walking distance of Rice's Wall Street office in New York City. However, the institute's charter left room for interpretation as to how higher learning could best be delivered. While embroiled in legal controversies, Baker began to canvass college presidents, political leaders, and educational experts about educational opportunity in the United States. He concluded that Rice's legacy could best be preserved by expanding the philanthropist's modest proposals. Houston, Baker foresaw, would benefit most by hosting a great center of learning to rival old institutions, like reform-minded Princeton and Harvard, and modern newcomers, like innovative Johns Hopkins and Stanford. In Baker's mind, Rice Institute should become a forceful engine to transmit learning, generate new knowledge, and propel Houston and the Southwest to greatness.[80]

By 1912 the institute's board had acquired nearly three hundred acres of land at the end of a muddy trail south of downtown; had hired the distinguished campus architects Cram, Goodhue, and Ferguson to transform the space; and had designated young Princeton University Professor Edgar Odell Lovett to guide the academic experiment. It was time to celebrate and announce Rice

Institute's arrival among the world's institutions of learning. In May, Chairman Baker and President Lovett agreed that the board of trustees would host the Academic Festival, a four-day event held October 10–13. They would invite renowned scholars, university representatives, and national leaders to mingle with Houstonians, Texans, and the fifty-three men and women who would matriculate on September 23 as the first class to attend Rice Institute. Baker received assurances from the architects in late May that buildings would be completed on schedule; then he and Alice departed for Bass Rocks, Massachusetts. Lovett sent his wife and three children to the cool mountains of Kentucky and turned his attention to the fall events. In July, he left Houston to confer with the vacationing Bakers for three days.

During the three years since Edgar Odell and Mary Lovett had moved to Houston, the Baker and Lovett families had grown close. The board chairman and the institute president shared a common overarching goal—to fulfill William Marsh Rice's trust by creating an outstanding center of learning—and they established clearly defined but complementary duties. Alice welcomed Mary and introduced her to civic organizations and to the women and men who would support and strengthen the fledgling institute. Like Alice, Mary had lost a child—her infant daughter, Ellen Kennedy Lovett (March 25, 1905–August 2, 1906)—but unlike Alice, Mary struggled to recover. She had contracted an illness shortly after the baby's birth and feared she was responsible for little Ellen's failure to thrive. For most of 1906 and 1907, Mary recuperated under a nurse's care at various convalescent homes. Although never robust after this long illness, Mary was well enough to accompany her husband on a 1908–1909 world tour of international educational institutions, a learning reconnaissance supported by the Rice trustees, who felt exposure to a broad range of educational options would strengthen the new institution, introduce Houston's academic aspirations to the world, and lure scholars to the Gulf Coast experiment. The Lovett's older son Malcolm and young Buster Baker were natural playmates, and they later recalled sitting on the Bakers' staircase on Friday evenings during one winter to watch their parents and a few other couples hone their dancing skills under the watchful eye of Miss Settle and an accompanist. By 1912 the two families were inseparable, and Alice often helped the Lovetts plan institute events.

In July 1912 President Lovett and the Bakers discussed every detail of the festival's complex agenda. The conferees agreed that Houston's religious and community leaders should form a reception committee for the more than 170 visitors expected to fill Houston's hotels. Alice studied each activity, suggested wording for invitations, and listed volunteers who could help with each event. She promised to oversee tea booths for a garden party in the Academic Court on Thursday at 5:00 p.m., to host a reception at the Baker's Main Street home at 9:30 on Thursday evening, and to marshal her friends to assist with all arrangements. She also offered to provide an appropriate invitation list for each event. The Bakers told Lovett they would ask friends to host a luncheon at the Thalian Club and would invite Baker, Botts, Parker & Garwood partner Edwin B. Parker and his wife, Kate, to sponsor a garden party at their seven-acre estate, The Oaks. Captain Baker said he would provide visitors with complimentary passes to the Houston Country Club and downtown Thalian and Houston clubs, although when visitors would have used these amenities—or changed their clothes between activities—remains a mystery.

The plan conceived at Bass Rocks was magnificent, befitting the roster of international celebrities invited to attend the inaugural festivities. Breakfast would begin at 8:30 a.m. on Thursday and Friday, with lectures, luncheons, concerts, receptions, dinners, and parties continuing until midnight. On Saturday, October 12, 1912, following the inaugural parade, presidential address, and celebratory luncheon, the Lovetts would honor the group at a farewell reception, and Captain Baker would hire a private train to take festival participants to the Hotel Galvez in Galveston for a relaxing shore supper and cooling sea breezes. On Sunday, travelers would board the return train to Houston in time for an 11:00 a.m. religious service in the City Auditorium, featuring choirs and leaders from several prominent Houston churches. Out-of-town guests would then depart, while Houstonians would crowd into every cranny of the First Presbyterian Church to hear famed Princeton University theologian and poet Henry Van Dyke preach a closing benediction at 7:30 p.m. Armed with a long list of tasks to be completed in the waning summer months, Lovett returned to Houston. The Bakers provided the promised lists and secured the required volunteers; then they left their children in Bass Rocks and departed for Germany to spend six weeks at a spa. Captain Baker continued to suffer from sciatic rheumatism, and around 1910 Alice developed high blood pressure, conditions about which doctors knew very little in the early twentieth century, but frequent spa treatments seemed to alleviate symptoms of both.

The Bakers sailed home on the *Kaiser Wilhelm*, arriving in New York on September 17. They went straight to Bass Rocks to close the house and prepare their children for the school year—Jim, a sophomore at Princeton, and Buster, Ruth, and Mac at Mrs. Kinkaid's School in Houston.[81] Many letters awaited them from President Lovett, posing numerous questions that had arisen during the Bakers' absence and apologizing to Alice for some of the enclosed invitations, which "reveal the absence of any feminine hand in their composition" but which had to be engraved without her approval and adjustments due to the fast-approaching events.[82] The Bakers and Lovett reviewed every detail to ensure that nothing had been overlooked for the comfort of speakers from Great Britain, Italy, Norway, Spain, and Germany and for the enjoyment of delegates representing an estimated 175 universities, colleges, societies, and academies, some from as far away as South Africa, Australia, and the Philippines.

Only days before Rice Institute's grand opening, the Bakers finally returned to Houston. The weather—although often topping ninety degrees—was described by observers as "perfect." *Houston Post* coverage of Rice Institute and its role in Houston's future began on October 6 with photographs and articles about the benefactor, the trustees, the faculty, the buildings, Dr. Lovett, the new students, and every inaugural activity. *Progressive Houston*, the monthly municipal "journal for the advancement of the city," devoted its entire nineteen-page issue to the new institute. Its editor praised the impressive ceremonies and earnest participants and quoted the *Post's* assessment: "The institute must necessarily become an important factor in the Houston of the future." Meticulous planning paid off. Alice and her army of volunteers enthusiastically welcomed curious Houstonians and honored guests. The Academic Festival that inaugurated Rice Institute was a triumph for the Bakers, for President Lovett, and for Houston. In the years to come, Rice Institute would be a catalyst for innovation and would indeed transform the city, while the Bakers would nurture town-gown interaction with unwavering support.[83]

Social Welfare in Houston, 1911–1918

As dreams for Rice Institute took concrete form, Rusk Settlement expanded its programs in the new school/settlement headquarters, and other neighborhoods and sponsors began to consider independent settlement experiments. Sometime about 1910, the Houston Industrial College, operated since the 1880s by the city's African American business and educational elite to train future employees, launched the Houston College Settlement Association. Led by Frederick W. Gross,[84] an influential Baptist organizer and college president, the college association housed its community settlement in a two-story building near the campus on San Felipe Road so teachers and students could mingle easily with neighborhood residents. The project was supported by the Woman's Baptist Home Mission Society, and after two years of steady but slow progress,

Gross appointed a teacher to collaborate full-time with volunteers, who conducted religious, social, and healthcare surveys and taught child-rearing classes to neighborhood residents in an effort to improve living conditions. An advocate of civic volunteering and community involvement, Gross held Negro Health Week every year and led annual College Settlement Association meetings to convene neighborhood stakeholders and sponsors. At the third annual meeting in April 1914, several Baptist pastors met with settlement neighbors and college personnel for Bible readings, prayer, and lectures on sanitation, agriculture, and vegetable gardening. President Gross urged participants to "use every effort" to improve "the social, religious and educational conditions of their children."[85] In response, neighbors planted community gardens, cleaned up streets and alleys, repaired houses and yards, suppressed gambling and loafing, and learned to decrease noise—all accomplishments praised by the anonymous authors of *The Red Book of Houston*. Sadly, there is no evidence that these programs continued after Gross's unexpected death in September 1915.

The Red Book of Houston, a unique compendium published only in 1915, used a format similar to Julia Cameron Montgomery's *Houston as a Setting of the Jewel: The Rice Institute,* released in 1913 to illuminate the progress of white Houstonians. Through essays and photographs, the *Red Book* recorded the business, cultural, religious, and educational accomplishments of successful African American citizens and featured leading men and women with their families as well as images of substantial buildings and grand houses owned or managed by well-to-do African Americans. While Montgomery features only men in her compendium, the *Red Book* pays homage to the important work of women and men in building a great city. Both books modeled their analyses on the pathbreaking 1908 *Key to the City of Houston,* published by the Federation of Women's Clubs to examine and extol the civic and cultural contributions of white women. In three slim volumes, contemporaries revealed and celebrated three separate but interdependent associative forces shaping social justice, educational growth, and cultural development in Houston during the years before World War I.[86]

In the spring of 1916, Alice searched for a new head worker at Rusk Settlement. She visited Corinne Fonde,[87] a social worker in the cotton mill district of New Orleans, and convinced the experienced candidate to accept the position. Soon after Fonde arrived in Houston, she spoke enthusiastically to the press. Fonde praised the Settlement Association board for its well-run committees that shared responsibilities for settlement activities. Association members, she noted, were "busy women" who still found time to meet at the settlement one day a week. She lauded the settlement's impressive classes for speech-impaired and deaf neighbors and praised Rusk's summer program that enabled children "whose lives are spent in the congested district of our city" to spend "two happy weeks" in the country. Fonde supported plans to form a council of club representatives, neighborhood residents, and Settlement Association board members to govern "all matters pertaining to the larger interests of the social center." The council's purpose, Fonde noted, would be nothing short of "true democracy—that sympathetic understanding which alone knits men together."[88]

While making changes at Rusk Settlement, Alice and her board were also overseeing expansion of Settlement Association responsibility. Brackenridge Neighborhood House (North Side Settlement), the first satellite organized by the Houston Settlement Association for white families, opened in 1916 and was connected to the Brackenridge School. Volunteers built a kindergarten and playground, planted a garden, and installed a library. By the early 1920s, supporters had left the association, moved the project to new quarters, and reopened the facility as the Saltus Street Day Nursery. Bethlehem Settlement, organized in 1917 by Jennie Belle Murphy Covington for African American citizens, was located on a steep rough road off Buffalo Drive (later Allen Parkway)

Bethlehem Settlement playground, 1920s. MS 609, Woodson Research Center, Fondren Library, Rice University.

at the edge of the San Felipe District, west of downtown. The old two-story house owned by the city sat between the city dump and a notorious vice district, but the settlement flourished. Bethlehem was supported by the Settlement Association and managed by the Bi-racial Settlement Committee—half-white and half-African American—that "functioned for years in remarkable harmony" under the leadership of Mrs. James Bethany. Like Rusk Settlement, Bethlehem maintained mothers' groups, a day nursery, a kindergarten, and numerous clubs, but the budget was small, and not until the 1930s did the Community Chest provide enough funds to fence the playground. The Ladies Missionary Society of the Pilgrim Congregational Church met at the settlement and provided financial support and dedicated volunteers to assist the small staff. In January 1918, the head worker praised the settlement's thirty-five–member community chorus and Sunday afternoon story hour, which usually attracted about fifty children. The city dump was removed when Jefferson Davis Hospital,[89] the first municipal medical facility for indigent patients, opened nearby on Elder Street in 1924, and the house was renovated and enlarged in 1938. Two years later in September 1940, the city demolished the building to create the publicly funded San Felipe Housing Project for low-income white families, a controversial move that displaced many African American households.[90]

When confronted by the social evils of a small child alone in a school doorway, Alice Baker had acted as a private citizen and had galvanized friends to support the settlement association movement in Houston. Her "splendid work" was admired by strong-minded women and men who were trying to coordinate charity work and social services. In February 1904, eleven women had organized United Charities to unmask imposters, oversee "the general charity work of the community, . . . aid the worthy poor," and "help people help themselves." Recognizing that "few people realize the condition that confronts us in Houston relative to child-rearing," directors hoped to improve underlying social conditions and strengthen families by finding employment for adults who could work and by helping children attend school and learn the lessons of good citizenship. As Settlement Association spokesperson, Alice served on the United Charites board from 1912 to 1914 with her friend Estelle Sharp, who had acted as the Settlement Association's liaison to the Woman's Club in 1907 and who was United Charities president for several one-year terms between 1907 and 1915. Spurred by Houston's women activists, the all-male Chamber of Commerce Charities Endorsement Committee also tried to manage social services by issuing donor cards to approved charities in 1910 to ensure donated funds supported "constructive social work." By 1913, the word "charity" was considered "offensive" by "people who need assistance" and by the volunteers who recognized these needs. To reinforce an emphasis on neighborly cooperation and civic responsibility, twenty-eight social service agencies—including the Federation of Women's Clubs, the YM-YWCA, the Houston Settlement Association, Jewish and Christian charities, the Mother Yates Emergency Home, and Colored United Churches—reorganized United Charities as the Houston Social Service Federation under Sharp's continued leadership. Directors of the new federation included Alice Baker, Harriet Levy,[91] and a committee of five who offered legal aid. Sharp challenged the group to root out the causes of poverty and social "illness," not just palliate symptoms.[92]

These private oversight efforts protected donors, distributed donations, and tried to centralize social service information and resources, but many Houstonians were beginning to believe that the municipal government should directly oversee the delivery of social services and protect women and children from exploitation. City commissioners were reluctant to interfere in privately funded charity work or to levy taxes to pay for social services, but they responded to public pressure and to the generosity of Houston Land and Trust Company founder Judge Edward Pinckney Hill (1838-1920). When municipal officials learned that the judge would bequeath $200,000 to the city as an endowment for social service purposes, Houston's commissioners created the Department of Charity, Benevolence, and Public Works on March 22, 1915, and established the Houston Foundation to administer his gift. A city ordinance authorized the foundation to receive bequests and donations, to investigate private charities, and to endorse those who followed foundation regulations. A seven-member Board of Public Trusts, which included Abraham M. (Abe) Levy as president and Estelle Sharp as second vice president, collected demographic statistics, oversaw activities to improve urban life, and assumed the functions filled for the past decade by United Charities/Houston Social Service Federation. While disbursing donated funds and receiving benevolent bequests remained the foundation's central function, the board agreed to focus on six problem areas: dependent and helpless children, temporary relief for destitute families, public health nursing, employment, humane treatment of children and animals, and the dissemination of social service information.

In its first year of operation, the Houston Foundation received $26,000 from the city to hire a professional social worker and establish the Council of Social Agencies, which would comprise representatives from all accredited organizations serving Houston's white population.[93] The foundation board also reached out to the Negro Social Service League to understand better the conditions in the African American community. In the segregated city of 1916, board members "planned our negro work on exactly the same lines as the work among the white population." The foundation board soon realized that gathering statistics was only a first step, and board members created the Social Service Bureau to be the operating arm of the foundation and the clearing house for all charity work. With reformist zeal, the board envisioned a centralized municipal agency overseeing all charitable activities to "promote and efficiently carry out constructive and preventive social welfare work."[94]

Two enthusiastic supporters of municipal government intervention, Will Hogg and Estelle Sharp, began urging independent benevolent organizations to join the Social Service Bureau, and they immediately approached Alice Baker. Hogg's diary reveals that through 1917 he consulted several times with Alice about social service programming, met with her Settlement Association board, and talked repeatedly with Captain Baker and Abe Levy about funding operations of the Social Service Bureau, which Hogg led from June 1917 until early 1918. After much deliberation, Alice decided to recommend to her board that the Settlement Association support this new municipal initiative and place its buildings and programs under the bureau's care. She would serve as chairwoman of the bureau's Social Service Committee, and her committee would oversee the Social Service Department, which would comprise Houston's settlements—Rusk, Brackenridge, and Bethlehem. The volunteer committee and its appointed chairwoman would replace the Settlement Association board and its elected president and would report to the executive committee of the bureau, which would coordinate financial support. While ceding oversight to municipal authorities and relying on Houston Foundation and city resources to cover the operating budget, the volunteers and paid staff of each settlement house would continue to manage daily programs. The Anti-Tuberculosis League, the Harris County Humane Society, the Kindergarten Association, and the PlayGround Association also joined the umbrella Social Service Bureau, and each was managed by its own committee and volunteer chair. This public-private partnership to deliver social services was an important experiment that forced municipal authorities to take responsibility for the social welfare of all Houstonians without devaluing the private-sector activism of volunteers and neighborhood leaders. For a decade, the system seemed to provide satisfactory solutions to social welfare needs in an era when municipal bureaucracies barely existed and when there were few professionally trained social workers.

When Alice Baker inaugurated the Houston Settlement Association in 1907, she also espoused the playground movement and its stated belief that "inasmuch as play under proper conditions is essential to the health and physical, social, and moral wellbeing of the child, playgrounds are a necessity for children as much as school," and she successfully placed Rusk Settlement in the Rusk School, with its spacious playground. In the late nineteenth and early twentieth centuries, concerned reformers across the United States developed volunteer associations to provide playgrounds, kindergartens, and settlements as "child-saving" solutions to the child-welfare challenges rampant in industrializing urban districts that were overcrowded by bewildered transplants. On April 12, 1906, vocal advocates from Washington, DC, and New York City founded the Playground Association of America (PAA) to help local volunteer playground associations work with school boards and city governments. Effective playground policy, the PAA believed, would train children to become healthy, good citizens. With PAA assistance, urban playgrounds grew from ninety in 1907 to 531 three years later. Alice shared an interest in playgrounds with her trend-setting husband, who served as a director of the Houston Play Ground Association in the 1910s. Baker's business partner William A. Wilson was Play Ground Association president at mid-decade, when the two men were developing Woodland Heights, an up-to-date streetcar suburb for the middle class located on 106 acres of wooded rural property north of Buffalo Bayou. Both men were acutely aware of popular calls for neighborhood parks and playgrounds to ensure "the safety of our democracy." Many Houstonians agreed with Russell Sage Foundation spokesman Clarence Arthur Perry, who used one of his public talks to explain why the "boy without a playground is father to the man without a job." Recognizing that "a properly conducted playground, with a supervisor, will do much to keep the children out of mischief," the Bakers urged their friends to support construction of playgrounds in crowded neighborhoods where children had no access to private gardens.[95]

The War Years

The Baker family was spending the summer of 1914 at Bass Rocks when the guns of August answered Europe's July crisis and shattered world peace. Until April 6, 1917, when the United States declared war on Germany, the Bakers carried on their usual pursuits. Young Jim finished Princeton in 1915 and began his studies at the University of Texas School of Law. Buster (age fourteen) followed his older brothers to the Hill School in Pottstown, Pennsylvania, while Ruth (age ten) and Mac (age eight) continued their educations at Mrs. Kinkaid's School in Houston. On September 30, 1915, the family joyously welcomed its first grandchild, Alice Baker Jones. Quickly nicknamed "Baby" (later Babe), the winsome little girl with golden curls and a laughing smile captivated the hearts of her grandparents and young uncles and aunts. During the war years, Alice, a youthful but white-haired grandmother in her early fifties, continued her advocacy for Houston's underserved citizens and families disrupted by war, and she joined home-front war councils to support troops stationed in the area.

While engrossed by new wartime responsibilities, Alice also anticipated another wedding. Jim had met Bonner Means, "an exceptionally pretty girl, of marked personal magnetism," when they were teenagers, and it was not long before the Bakers realized Bonner would one day marry their son. After Bonner had spent several weeks with the Bakers at Bass Rocks in July 1915, Alice wrote to thank the young guest for her visit and to assure her she had "greatly endeared" herself to everyone. Following the United States' declaration of war, Jim hastily completed his law school requirements, volunteered for the army, and came to an agreement with Bonner that they would marry before he was sent overseas. On May 8, 1917, the law school graduate reported to the First Officers Training Camp at Camp Funston—the old Fort Sam Houston in Leon Springs northeast of San Antonio—where Army regulars transformed raw recruits into officers in three months. On May 9, Bonner announced her plans for a winter wedding to twenty-four friends at an elegant six-course luncheon. Although Captain Baker wanted Jim and Bonner to wait until Jim completed his military service and Bonner finished her Rice Institute studies, he was overborn by the new recruit's ardent "love of country" and the couple's obvious devotion.[96]

Jim learned in July that he would be commissioned in August, and Bonner pushed the wedding forward to Saturday, August 4, allowing a mere month to prepare. Bonner wired Jim her promise for a "quiet" celebration, but full-page coverage by the "In Society" columnist confirmed that the prominent families who gathered at Christ Church (Episcopal) for an 8:30 p.m. service witnessed a splendid "marriage of widespread interest." The groom and his attendants, all attired in khaki uniforms, arrived directly from training on the day of the ceremony. "In keeping with the summer season and the strenuousness of the times," the wedding was considered "informal." Palms and ferns "filled the chancel," forming an "aisle of green" to the altar, where Dr. Robert E. Vinson, a Presbyterian pastor, and the Reverend Thomas J. Windham, an Episcopal priest, officiated. Bonner and her mother wore white, as did the bride's attendants—junior bridesmaid Ruth Baker, accompanied by junior groomsman Coulter Means, maid of honor Annie Wier Bonner, and matron of honor Alice Baker Jones. The mother of the groom wore gray tulle over gray satin. When vows had been exchanged, the bride's parents, Mr. and Mrs. John Coulter Means, received the bridal party and family members at their fashionable Rossonian apartment near downtown. The Edwin B. Parkers, in Washington on a wartime assignment, offered their well-staffed but empty home, The Oaks, to the newlyweds for two nights before duty called the groom back to Camp Funstan, where Jim received his commission on August 15. Ordered to report in ten days to the 90th Division at Camp Travis, near Leon Springs, Jim carried his bride off to Mackinac Island in Michigan for a quick wedding trip.[97]

Graham Baker's tragic death in 1902 haunted the senior Bakers' reaction to young Jim's voluntary military service, and they suppressed their constant worry that he might not return if dispatched to the front by throwing their energy into war work. When President Woodrow Wilson called on Americans to serve the war effort in April 1917, Houston's response was overwhelming, and each of five Liberty loan drives exceeded its quota. Sixty years old in 1917, Captain Baker shouldered several war-related duties while assuming many responsibilities of three law partners who accepted wartime appointments. In May 1917 he worked out the complex plan whereby Rice Institute and other owners of property north of Buffalo Bayou could lease their land to the federal government to build an emergency US Army training ground, named Camp Logan. In July 1917 Managing Partner Edwin B. Parker left Houston to become chairman of the War Industries Board and oversee restructuring of industrial plants to equip the armed forces. Ralph Feagin spent three years in Washington and New York with the national Red Cross, and top Baker, Botts, Parker & Garwood litigator Clarence Wharton served as executive chairman of Houston's War Service Commission. Created by the Chamber of Commerce and endorsed by Mayor Joseph Chappell Hutcheson Jr., the commission marshaled Houston's home-front response and oversaw activities sponsored by the YMCA, YWCA, Knights of Columbus, Jewish Board of Welfare, American Library Association, and other groups eager to support the trainees. Wharton also agreed to spearhead the local Red Cross Social Services Committee.[98]

Alice Baker's successful leadership of the Settlement Association and her diplomatic support of the nascent Social Service Bureau made her a local expert on welfare issues and volunteer mobilization. Clarence Wharton, who had known her for many years as the supportive wife of his partner James A. Baker, immediately enlisted her assistance for Houston's patriotic war work as a member of the Executive Committee of War Camp Community Service, the operating arm of his War Service Commission. Alice joined an executive committee that comprised Houston's most active civic leaders, including Estelle Sharp, YWCA advocate Louise Masterson, Mayor Joseph C. Hutcheson Jr., Houston Foundation President Abe Levy, and public schools Superintendent P. W. Horn. Alice also agreed to serve as chairwoman of the YWCA War Work Council, formed on June 1, 1917, to entertain soldiers and assist young women who had arrived in Houston to fill jobs in the city's exploding wartime industries. Alice quickly recruited a strong committee of twenty-four leading civic women to assist her and the vice-chairwoman, Huberta Page (Hetty) Garwood. For the next two years, Alice and her executive committee rallied two thousand young women and girls to volunteer for the Red Cross and to staff the YWCA Hostess House at Camp Logan, when the facility opened in 1917, and the YWCA Hostess House at Ellington Field, when air service training began there in 1918. YWCA volunteers decorated the light, airy rooms and large sunporches of these houses with wicker furnishings and cheerily patterned chintz, and they provided chaperoned lectures, concerts, and dances for soldiers and airmen who wished to entertain their wives, sweethearts, and family friends. In addition to their many hours of volunteer war work, the Bakers made several generous donations to the Red Cross Fund, the Patriotic League, and the YMCA and YWCA war chests. They also continued to make annual pledges to the Social Service Bureau and helped to underwrite the cost of building a YWCA building.

In August 1917, Alice Baker, Louise Masterson, and Agnese Carter Nelms were elected to the National War Work Council of the YWCA and attended its national conference in New York City. Because of this meeting and other business, the Bakers were not in Houston during the brief but notorious riot of August 23, 1917. That evening, African American soldiers of the 24th US Infantry—who had been sent from the Midwest to monitor civilian construction crews building Camp Logan—marched toward downtown Houston to protest police and civilian harassment of any infantryman who stepped away from base. Fueled by false rumors that a respected Black corporal had been killed and that white men had opened fire, over one hundred soldiers grabbed rifles from the supply tent and headed into town. In the chaos that followed, eleven civilians, five policemen, and four soldiers died before the soldiers retreated to base. Civil authorities imposed a curfew, the offending soldiers were hustled out of town to face courts-martial at an Army base in New Mexico, and volunteers fanned across the city to assure the populace that no neighborhood harbored rebellious soldiers. The riot was treated as a mutiny, and the convicted participants were hanged or imprisoned for life. Houston leaders, shocked by the disaster and the draconian punishments, tried to brush the incident aside and focus on the impending September 10 arrival of Camp Logan's first Army detachments—all from Illinois.

Attention turned to twenty War Camp Community Service subcommittees that were planning morale-boosting programs of music, food, and fun to introduce Camp Logan recruits to Houston during a festive hospitality week October 17-24, 1917. Volunteers from nearly every church, club, lodge, and civic society participated in the gala events. The Thalian Club and Press Club, renamed the Khaki Club, welcomed officers, and twenty-eight women's clubs affiliated with the Federation of Women's Clubs recruited members and their daughters to serve as canteen hostesses at numerous citywide activities. Alice Baker, Harriet Levy, Maud Abbie Sterling, and Mrs. R. C. Duff invited groups of one hundred men, and nearly as many hostesses, to their gardens, where watermelon carving was the central attraction. Six hundred soldiers feasted on watermelons in Hermann Park as guests of Rotary Club members and their families. Until returning soldiers marched in triumph down Main Street in the summer of 1919, special activities continued—the Public Library provided books to the camps; the Houston Symphony held concerts for the soldiers; and the clubs and volunteers produced constant entertainment.

While the senior Bakers enthusiastically supported Houston's home-front war effort, Jim and Bonner rented a "little bird-cage of a house" in San Antonio during the 90th Division's training period at Camp Travis (August 15, 1917-June 7, 1918). The newlyweds entertained the Bakers several times and corresponded with them frequently. Captain Baker's letters to his son were filled with advice about military etiquette, dress code, and posture. At the end of one admonitory epistle, the anxious parent admitted, "I expect you and Bonner will think that I am overflowing . . . with an abundance of advice, but the truth is that Mrs. Baker and I have been thinking and talking of you both very much . . . and wondering what the future holds. . . . I know you both realize that my advice is prompted by my love and devotion for both of you and my anxiety is to see you both well started on the road to success and happiness."[99] Alice and Captain Baker hoped their son's severe nearsightedness would keep the novice officer in the Quartermaster's Corps, where he was offered a posting, or in the Judge Advocate General's Corps, where their son-in-law Murray Jones served, but Jim was determined to see action with the infantrymen he was training.

On June 5, 1918, Jim and the 90th Division, commanded by veteran Maj. Gen. Henry Tureman Allen, began the long journey to the western front. Second Lieutenant Baker and his men served in the 359th Infantry, one of two

Texas infantries that comprised the 180th Brigade led by Brig. Gen. William H. Johnston. Alice, Bonner, and Jim's fourteen-year-old sister, Ruth Baker, traveled to Garden City, Long Island, to bid him farewell. Bonner's mother and Jim's father fretted in Houston. Mrs. Means sent him prayers, and on June 16, Captain Baker telegraphed his approval of Jim's decision to "give your precious life . . . for your home your loved ones and your country. . . . Your life has been a constant joy to your mother and me. I know you will be brave. . . . May God . . . watch over you and keep you from all harm and bring you back in safty [*sic*] shall be my constant prayer until I see your dear face again."[100] Jim and his division sailed from Brooklyn for England on June 20, were shipped across the channel to France for training in trench warfare, and by August 12 had begun marching across grim countryside devastated by four years of bombardment to relieve the 1st US Division along the front lines.

While on the twenty-six-day march from his training camp to the front, Jim wrote to Bonner and his parents from "Somewhere in France" and explained that he would write as often as he could. Correspondence was difficult; letters often arrived in bundles weeks after they had been written; and soldiers could not keep diaries because paper and pencil were forbidden on the front lines. Only when resting behind the lines could officers and their men bathe, eat decent meals, and find time to write home. Wartime stress deepened the love and respect shared by father and son. In August, Jim confided to Bonner that he wanted "no more" than "the approbation of you and Dad." On September 30, the self-controlled lawyer thanked his son for a recent letter and confessed, "You are in my thoughts day and night and the awful risks and dangers you are running almost overwhelm me." Bonner shared her letters with Jim's parents, and after reading an August letter that had arrived in October, the devoted father wrote three emotional pages to his "absolutely truthful, entirely reliable, . . . honest . . . and affectionate" son, assuring him that, "In every and all things you have been to me all that I could wish in the way of a dutiful and loving son." During the intense final months of the war, Jim's Company L was scheduled to attack on September 12 at St. Mihiel and on November 11 along the Meuse-Argonne line near Verdun. In September Jim was called back behind the lines for special officer training and was spared the fate of his fellow officers. All Company L officers were killed, wounded, or gassed. On November 11, in command of Company L since October 20 and poised to move forward, Jim received the order to stand down two hours before the 11 a.m. armistice brought an end to the slaughter; four soldiers in his company died that day during continuous shelling that began at 7 a.m. on that last morning of the war.[101]

Lt. James A. Baker Jr., standing, second from left, in Wehlin, Germany, November 1918–February 1919. MS 40, Woodson Research Center, Fondren Library, Rice University.

News of the armistice overjoyed the Baker family. Alice quickly agreed to assist Houston's Welcome Home Committee, which was planning celebrations and parades for the city's returning warriors. Captain Baker immediately began to exert his influence to speed his son's return. The 90th Division—nicknamed "the Pride of Every Texan"—embarked on a seventy-two-mile march across the Mosel and Rhine rivers into Germany as part of the allied occupying forces. Jim had been reassigned to Company I and was enjoying easy duty as aide-de-camp to Gen. Ulysses G. McAlexander. He confided to his sister Alice that he "was working every little string within my grasp to get home and hope to be successful before the month [January] is over." Meanwhile Jim's parents were exchanging letters with an old acquaintance, M. A. Mitaranga, whom they had known in Houston many years before the war and who was now a merchant in Marseilles. They commissioned him to prepare a "nice bountiful Christmas box" filled with jams, marmalades, cakes, chocolates, "and other similar things." Mitaranga obliged, but the box never reached its destination. Captain Baker also wired friends to ask where his son was located. Shamelessly stating he was "now advanced in years," the vigorous sixty-two-year-old wrote and telegraphed Gen. John J. Pershing on February 3, 1919, to ask the commander in chief to "approve his [son's] application for immediate discharge," because the younger man was needed to help with his father's law practice.[102]

Jim's early discharge was approved in February 1919, and General McAlexander recommended the returning lieutenant for "promotion to the grade of Captain" on February 24, 1919. On March 5 Jim began the slow journey toward Marseilles and a ship bound for New York. Late in March the Bakers traveled to Baltimore, where Alice was admitted to the Johns Hopkins Hospital for treatment of an unexplained illness. Captain Baker wired Bonner to join her in-laws in Baltimore so they could await Jim's arrival together. On April 4, when Jim's ship was expected at a Long Island dock, Bonner telegraphed the family hero, "Am in Baltimore . . . & Crazy to see you. Wire . . . when and where can I see you."[103] She rushed to Camp Mills on Long Island, where Jim received his promotion to captain and an honorable discharge. The happily reunited couple remained with his parents in Baltimore for six weeks while Mrs. Baker recovered satisfactorily from treatment. When Bonner and Jim returned to Texas, they spent several more weeks at her family's country retreat before settling in Houston.

Postwar Civic Action

War and separation deepened the Bakers' appreciation of family and friends and revealed how profoundly they loved—and feared for—their grown son and his "dear Sweet Bonner."[104] With peace reestablished in 1919, the family gladly returned to its prewar pursuits. Jim joined his father's legal and banking enterprises. Much to the senior Bakers' delight, Jim and Bonner moved into the family home on Main Street, where they remained for three years. During the 1920s, the younger children—Browne, Ruth, and Malcolm—finished their educations, married, and established their families. Yet the 1920s proved a challenging and unsettling decade. Houston's population exploded—from 78,800 citizens in 1910 to 138,276 in 1920. In 1930, Houston became the largest city in Texas with a population of 292,352. Houston's intense home-front support for the war effort forced local government to play a larger role in the lives of its citizens; oil discoveries drew newcomers and fueled unimagined economic prosperity; and a youthful materialism challenged social mores and prewar efforts to address the city's social welfare and cultural growth. How would civic leaders and municipal officials interact to balance material plenty for some with community well-being for all? How would they react to the city's new status as an industrial giant and population magnet?

Alice Baker remained chairwoman of the Social Service Committee within the city's Social Service Bureau until 1926. She continued to advocate "directly" for the "upbuilding of community life and the improvement of the environment" at the city's neighborhood settlements. At Rusk Settlement, she introduced legal aid services and citizenship instruction to meet the needs of a fast-growing Hispanic population fleeing the turbulent political situation in Mexico. To address "distressing" overcrowding and changing demographics, Rusk Settlement administrators Mary Ann Corbin, the head worker from 1919 to 1921, and Anita Jones, the head worker from 1921 to 1927, initiated a free bath program that provided showers and soap for a decade to households with no running water. Corbin and Jones also staffed a reading room on Sunday afternoons and offered night classes to teach fundamental English language skills to adults and children. During these years, Alice worked closely with the recreation and kindergarten departments of the Social Service Bureau; sponsored activity clubs in Jones, Hawthorne, and Dow elementary schools; and recruited Rice Institute students to work with the popular Settlement Association boys' and girls' clubs. She invited the wives of Rice Institute faculty members to serve on settlement committees and to collaborate with trained case workers, who encouraged families to keep their children in school and to find work. Alice's most successful recruit—Corrinne Tsanoff, the wife of Radoslav Tsanoff, a popular Rice Institute professor of philosophy—participated in Settlement Association activities for thirty years and wrote a history of the organization.[105]

By the late 1920s, supporters of the settlement movement had grown dissatisfied with Social Service Bureau policies, which had begun to emphasize palliative relief work at the expense of proactive neighborhood building. In 1926 Mrs. A. B. Prescott succeeded Alice Baker as chairwoman of the bureau's Social Service or Settlement Committee, as it was then called, and exerted her energetic diplomatic skills to explain that it was time for a change. The settlement houses, Prescott felt, received insufficient municipal funds and could better manage their neighborhood center programs if allowed to operate on their own without bureau oversight. To secure support for her viewpoint, she invited members of the original Houston Settlement Association board to tea at Rusk School. Some attendees had not seen the old campus in years, and afterward Alice wrote to former board members to request funds to buy a radio and pianos for the settlement. Prescott secured strong church support and recruited new volunteers to rejuvenate Settlement Association membership. Demand for settlement services continued to grow, and in 1928–1929 Prescott asked librarian Julia Ideson to reestablish the library substation at Rusk Elementary and to provide a Spanish-English dictionary and Spanish language reading materials. In May 1929 Rusk Settlement announced its first Mexican Fiesta featuring singing, dancing, and food. Citywide publicity attracted a crowd, and Prescott made the fiesta an annual event that raised significant funds during the 1930s. In the summer of 1929, the Settlement Association invited children and their mothers to the first postwar, weeklong summer camp sessions and programs at Camp Allen, run by the Episcopal Diocese on Trinity Bay. During this welcome respite from the heat, inner-city children explored the outdoors, and sleep-away summer camp programs expanded quickly in subsequent summers to include sessions at several campsites.

Prescott's leadership convinced the Settlement Committee it could operate independently under private management, and on February 19, 1932, committee members voted to withdraw from the Social Service Bureau. After haggling over money, the bureau granted the Settlement Committee's March 7 request for separation. On April 15, 1932, the Settlement Committee became once again the Houston Settlement Association, charged with operating three sites—Rusk Settlement, Bethlehem Settlement, and Saltus Street Day Nursery, the reorganized Brackenridge (North Side) Settlement, which had secured financial and volunteer support from the women of Palmer Memorial Chapel and the Down Town Club. The Community Chest, which began citywide fundraising in the 1920s, promised financial support.

Alice's war work reinforced her belief that children needed safe, stimulating places where they could play, daydream, and interact with others in the fresh air. She had seen how important it was to provide recreational outlets for young soldiers stationed in Houston, because many volunteers had not experienced exercise and play during their childhoods and were physically unfit for military service. In the fall of 1918, Alice hosted a meeting at her Main Street home to discuss plans for a Houston Recreation Department. For a decade, citizens had been demanding that the city establish tax-supported neighborhood parks where supervised recreation could strengthen the health of individuals and enrich the urban environment. During the war, citizens had spent tax dollars lavishly to provide recreation for soldiers encamped near Texas cities, and many playground enthusiasts felt the time was now right to demand tax-supported recreation for everyone. Corinne Fonde, Alice's protégé head worker at Rusk Settlement, urged supporters to "strike out of small corners for the larger goal, while war time makes demonstrations possible."[106]

Her earnest propaganda reflected the advice of city planning advocates, and Houston civic leaders agreed that municipal authorities should be involved with the development of citywide recreational facilities. In December 1918, city commissioners established the Department of Public Recreation and named Fonde its pioneering director. Immediately, Fonde undertook a two-year study of the city's recreation needs. Alice Baker agreed to serve as chairwoman of the department's first volunteer oversight board and shared leadership duties as vice-chairwoman or chairwoman for the next several years. Board members included P. W. Horn, superintendent of Houston schools; William A. Wilson, PlayGround Association President; Louise Masterson, a YWCA sponsor; and other prominent Houstonians. For the next decade, Houston journalists described neighborhood parks, playgrounds, and large city parks as "recreation for all ages" that was an "important factor in the life of [the] Nation."[107]

Corinne Fonde adapted many lessons learned from her years as a kindergarten teacher, social worker, and head of Rusk Settlement to develop Recreation Department programming. She had long believed that supervised recreation fostered good citizenship and prevented crime by filling spare hours with healthy activity, and on October 27-29, 1919, she represented the City of Houston at the Texas Conference of Social Welfare in Dallas, where she discussed the social benefits of recreation facilities. Although the sole Recreation Department employee in 1919, Fonde built a staff of forty by 1925, and in 1929 she trained thirty-six youthful volunteers to monitor over two hundred thousand young people between the ages of six and twenty at twenty-two playgrounds that year. Every year until the Department of Recreation merged with the Parks Department in 1943, Fonde explained the importance of her department to municipal authorities and fought for funds to operate her imaginative programs and to expand recreation amenities. She increased the number of available facilities by working with the public school system to share school playgrounds during the summer; she remodeled an abandoned incinerator on Buffalo Drive into a clubhouse and civic theater; and she explained the ever-present need for more swimming pools and safer playground equipment. Organized play for children and adults included baseball, swimming, track, volleyball, kite flying, a countywide "music meet"—and much more. In October 1924 Fonde's Recreation Department called for "vocalists of definite attainments" to join the nascent city-sponsored Harmonic Society for its first rehearsal at the City Auditorium banquet hall.[108] Alice Baker, Julia Ideson, and some fifty other patrons pledged their support for the municipal musical group. By 1930 Fonde's Recreation Department had become a major venue for local performing artists who entertained with recitals, dance revues, band performances, orchestra concerts, harmonica groups, whistlers, and glee clubs.

Despite public enthusiasm for recreation activities, municipal funds were always insufficient to meet demand. Lebert Howard Weir, a widely published expert on playgrounds, parks, and recreation, surveyed Houston's facilities in 1927. A consultant and early field secretary for the Playground Association of America, Weir lamented that, "practically the only playground for thousands of children in our great cities . . . is the street." His report to Houston's commissioners and members of the city's planning, park, school, and recreation boards recommended "more parks, more baseball diamonds, more tennis courts, more athletic fields, more swimming pools, more gymnasiums, more community centers, more indoor and outdoor theatres," more landscaped areas along the bayous, and more big parks throughout the city.[109] Weir suggested three-acre playgrounds every half mile and ten-acre playing fields every mile. Such facilities would have kept children off the streets, but their cost precluded full adoption of the scheme. Fonde continued to innovate and advocate until her retirement in 1946.

Beloved Leaders

In the 1920s, city bankers estimated Captain Baker's personal wealth to exceed $3 million. The putative millionaire continued to expand his law firm, oversee the South Texas Commercial National Bank and Guardian Trust, and develop his primary civic responsibility, the Rice Institute. Despite booming growth in Houston, Baker realized that providing a free education to one thousand undergraduates and twenty graduate students while improving the curriculum and expanding facilities would test the board's ingenuity and generosity. Alice Baker and Mary Lovett were particularly concerned about female students, who lived at home and could not eat on campus until the Episcopal Diocese of Texas built Autry House as a student center in 1921. The sympathetic older women invited the intrepid commuters to lunch or tea and tried to make their hours on campus enjoyable. At the annual meeting of the Rice Institute board on June 12, 1918, Captain Baker announced that he and Alice wished to remember their son Graham by endowing Rice Institute's first student scholarship—the Graham Baker Studentship—to be awarded each year to the student who maintained the highest grades. He also began asking philanthropic friends to underwrite programs and new buildings. Alumni raised funds for a classroom building, athletic facilities, and the memorial statue of William Marsh Rice. In

1926 George S. Cohen, president of Foley Brothers department store, honored his parents, Robert and Agnes Cohen of Galveston, by funding an elegant faculty club. William Ward Watkin,[110] founder of the Institute Architecture Department, designed the handsome structure to complement other campus buildings. During the 1920s and 1930s, the Bakers attended every commencement before decamping to Bass Rocks for their long summer vacation. They welcomed faculty, students, and alumni to their home and garden and invited Houstonians to luncheons and dinners honoring national academic leaders and visiting lecturers who were making guest appearances on the Rice campus. For two decades they sent their chauffeur to meet these dignitaries at the railroad station and provided guest rooms during their visits.[111]

Captain Baker maintained a full schedule during the 1920s, and both Bakers continued to assist and advise Houstonians who were spearheading a variety of civic causes, but Alice began to assume an advisory role and to encourage younger women to step into leadership posts. In 1919 and 1920 fundraising chairman Will Hogg asked Captain Baker to join other influential businessmen on the advisory finance committee that was raising money to expand the Young Women's Christian Association (YWCA) facilities for white women and to construct the Blue Triangle building for African American Houstonians. Alice Baker began supporting Houston's YWCA when it was founded in 1907 to operate boarding houses for young working women. She was helping Jennie Belle Covington develop Bethlehem Settlement when Covington organized the Blue Triangle in 1918 and secured its YWCA branch status two years later. Alice knew neither the YWCA nor the Blue Triangle branch had properly equipped buildings, and she endorsed her husband's efforts. In 1919, donors pledged $300,000 toward a $500,000 campaign that soon ballooned to $800,000, the goal officially announced in April 1920. Undeterred by skyrocketing construction costs, Will Hogg and his cochairman, the industrialist Edward Andrew Peden, secured enough pledges to provide the YWCA and the Blue Triangle branch with buildings and programs similar to those long enjoyed by Houston's white men. Will Hogg also secured a major pledge of $5,000 from the Bakers in April 1924 to support construction of the municipal Museum of Fine Arts, and he worked with Baker, Botts, Parker & Garwood that year to create Memorial Park and convey its land to the city.

The Bakers were among the first Houstonians to support the Community Chest, and their contributions were among the most generous pledges for nearly twenty years. Founders of Houston's Community Chest implemented a nationwide fundraising method, instituted after World War I to solve "the charity solicitation problem" and to organize civic philanthropy efficiently and effectively. An outgrowth of World War I War Chest bond drives, Community Chests no longer relied on wealthy philanthropists but instead called on all businesses and individuals to provide broad-based support for local service institutions. Seen as democratic, the Community Chest adopted current thinking that "privation is abnormal, temporary and remediable" and challenged all citizens "to care for members who are in need" and "enable them to live and grow." Houston's Community Chest was organized after the Chamber of Commerce formed a study group in 1921 to explore ways charitable organizations could regroup and resume fundraising activities interrupted during the war. Developer Jesse H. Jones and banker John T. Scott applied for a charter to establish the Houston branch, and Captain Baker's partner Clarence Wharton served as the new organization's first president. Wharton led a successful kick-off fund drive in 1923, and every year more organizations and more donors participated until by 1931 the annual campaign produced $600,000 for its approved agencies. The format of one brief citywide fundraising campaign met businesslike standards by cutting costs, avoided "the irritation" of repeat solicitations, and provided adequate funds for many organizations.[112]

Alice Baker's last major civic effort resulted from her years of service to the First Presbyterian Church. In 1929, Alice and two churchwomen asked Houston Foundation Director John Willis Slaughter and Captain Baker's nephew Alvis Parish, who was chairman of First Presbyterian Church's Board of Deacons, to speak to the Houston City Council on their behalf. The ladies of the First Presbyterian Church, Alice said, wished to finance construction of a unit for terminally ill patients at the Houston City Tubercular Hospital. Houston's fight to contain the spread of tuberculosis, a highly infectious and poorly understood public health hazard, had begun on November 11, 1911, when Dr. Elva Anis Wright (1868-1950) founded the Houston Anti-Tuberculosis League. Trained at Northwestern University Women's Medical College and Edinburgh University, Dr. Wright was a medical pioneer who moved to Houston on July 4, 1910. In 1912 she successfully persuaded Harris County officials and Houston commissioners to authorize a sanitarium to treat tuberculosis patients. When the project stalled due to insufficient funds, Dr. Wright opened a free clinic in 1913 at 806 Bagby, where patients received skin tests, diagnoses, and treatments until 1957. Efforts to build a sanitarium lagged until the fall of 1917, when the potential threat posed by soldiers assigned to Camp Logan forced Houston authorities to comply with Anti-Tuberculosis League agitators, Harris County Medical Society advice, Texas legislation, and federal War Department demands by providing separate hospital facilities for tubercular patients. During her tenure on Houston's War Service Commission, Alice saw how sorely tuberculosis patients suffered, and she was pleased when the city announced two important additions in 1923. Allie Belle Kinsloe Autry (1873-1935) had donated $60,000 to build the Autry Memorial Hospital School for children with tuberculosis, as a memorial to her son who had died at age twenty-three of appendicitis; and the city had allocated funds to create a wing in the Tubercular Hospital for treating African American patients. Surely, it was now time to help those who would not survive this terrible scourge.

Alice's petitioners before the city council successfully stated her case for a unit to serve the terminally ill, and she immediately formed a fundraising committee, hired an architect, and raised over $20,000 to develop space that included twenty-four beds, living and dining rooms, two treatment rooms, and bathrooms. The project and its initial pledges from the Ladies' Association were announced on Mother's Day 1929 at the First Presbyterian Church morning worship service, where the congregation was celebrating fifty years of "golden deeds" performed by church mothers. As always with Alice's fundraising efforts, she combined direct requests with hands-on activities. She and five friends updated previous church cookbooks with trendy ideas and raised $4,000 by selling *Old and New Cookery*. Alice also organized three events that netted $5,000 for the cause: she opened her home for two garden parties, which featured puppet shows, pony rides, and Native American dances performed by a Boy Scout troop; she persuaded Ellison Van Hoose, director of the First Presbyterian Church choir, to lead 250 singers and a fifty-piece orchestra in a fundraising concert of religious and patriotic music at the City Auditorium; and she staged a rummage sale. The new unit was dedicated on October 16, 1930. Alice's daughter, Alice Graham Baker Jones, and her teenaged granddaughter, Alice Baker Jones, furnished the living room and honored one of Houston's most beloved leaders by placing a tablet there, commending Alice Baker's "beautiful life and worthy example."[113]

Family Matters

When the Bakers purchased Rockhaven Cottage, they envisioned spending July and August in Massachusetts to escape Houston's heat, but as time passed, the family spent more and more time in the north. After their marriages, Alice Jones and Jim continued to visit with their spouses, and Browne, Ruth, and Malcolm began inviting friends for extended stays filled with sailing, tennis, and golf. In the 1920s, Alice and the girls gardened and scoured the countryside for antiques, while Captain Baker corresponded daily with his law partners and clients about ongoing business matters. The summer of 1922 began as usual when the Bakers departed early in June as soon as the Rice Institute commencement activities concluded. But the family was plagued by ill health for the next six months. Alice Jones and little Alice accompanied Murray Jones to Johns Hopkins, where he underwent an operation for undisclosed causes and spent most of the summer and fall recuperating in Baltimore. For several years it had been clear that Browne Baker's childhood friendship with Adelaide Lovett had blossomed into a strong attachment. Browne followed Adelaide to Paris when he finished Princeton in 1921, and during the fall of 1922, Adelaide recuperated from an ailment—perhaps extreme fatigue—at Rockhaven Cottage. Alice took her son's friend shopping, and Captain Baker read aloud to his guest in the evening. In a long letter to her future father-in-law, Adelaide exclaimed, "each Fall Day is ever more brilliant and charming. . . . Each day I become more grateful to you and Mrs. Baker for taking me in. . . . You are so . . . generous to those who have the good fortune to know you. . . . It is so refreshing to watch the ocean in its varying moods. Health seems to ride in on every wave."[114]

Unfortunately, health did not ride in for Captain Baker that summer. Sometime in the late 1910s he had been diagnosed with diabetes, and during the summer of 1922 the hard-driving lawyer was being treated in Boston for the troubling disease and other ailments. When it was time to close Rockhaven Cottage and accompany the children to school, he checked into Phillips House in Boston for continued treatment. Captain Baker was so worried about his health that he reviewed his will and wrote instructions to be opened at his death. In extensive correspondence with law partners and with Alice after she had returned to Houston, he complained of his "useless" arm, of avoiding an operation because he feared the effects of anesthesia on his diabetes, and of general discomfort, but neither his correspondence nor his ledgers reveal the names of doctors he consulted or explain his treatments. By late November he finally reported great progress and promised to leave for home on December 15.[115]

Meanwhile, Alice masterminded several momentous family events. Fortunately for posterity, Alice and her "darling" husband exchanged—and saved—letters that reveal the strength of their happy marriage, which had sustained the loving couple for nearly forty years. When Alice reluctantly closed Rockhaven Cottage and left her husband in Boston, she traveled to New York to place

Ruth in Miss Spence's School for Girls and to Pottstown to leave Mac at the Hill. She also visited friends, attended the theater, and went shopping before continuing on to Houston in late October. There, two mammoth tasks awaited her—a move from their home on Main Street, where the family had lived for nearly twenty-three years, and the wedding of son Browne to Adelaide Lovett, scheduled for December 23.[116]

Late in the summer, the family in Bass Rocks had learned that Edwin B. Parker might wish to rent his home, The Oaks, to the Bakers. Parker had now been in Washington, DC, since 1917, and he realized he would not be returning to Houston; Captain Baker had been enamored of the property for years. The Oaks was a splendid Frank Lloyd Wright-inspired house designed by fashionable Fort Worth architects Sanguinet and Staats for the Parkers in 1908. Nearly seven acres of gardens surrounded the main house, servants' quarters, and carriage house in a pleasant residential area just beyond the bustling commercial development moving relentlessly out Main Street and making the Baker home less desirable. Telegrams and letters among the Parkers, the Bakers, and son Jim—busy with projects in Houston—secured the rental agreement, but settling into a new home in time for wedding visitors and celebratory parties would challenge Alice's organizational skills. Alice kept her husband apprised of progress and praised the excellent condition of the house. Mrs. Parker, Alice wrote, was being "so helpful," and Jim and Browne were "so considerate" and doing everything for her in his absence.[117]

In letters typed by his secretary because writing at the hospital proved difficult, Captain Baker responded warmly to his daughter-in-law Bonner and to Adelaide Lovett about their thoughtful assurances that they missed him very much, and he offered advice to Alice about the children. The lonely patient must have also sent more personal missives to his busy wife, because Alice responded with loving affection to one letter just before Thanksgiving.

> *My Darling,*
> It makes me extremely happy to know that you do love me and miss me and but for my duty here at home I would be with you every minute of the time.... I have wanted you oh so much—but for your sake ... it is well that you are not here in this ... house leaving period.... We have so much to be thankful for in our children & the boys in particular and then when I think of our great and abiding love for each other my gratitude knows no bounds & I feel very lowly for I do not deserve all that has come to me.... With more love than I can ever express—*Your own Alice*

Adelaide Lovett and Walter Browne Baker, December 23, 1922.
Private Collection.

On moving day, November 22, Alice's sister Anna Mae sent her congratulations and noted, "You are always happiest when you have some big & great plan to work out. I am so glad your dreams are coming true." Alice reassured her husband that she had moved "enough of 1416 Main to make us feel at home" and had blended new and old décor so efficiently that Jim could hold an important business dinner in early December, Browne could host his stag revels on December 22, and Alice would be ready to welcome the bridal party on Christmas Eve.[118]

Admonished by Alice to stop in New York City to procure "a dress suit . . . and everything to go with it" and to escort Ruth and Mac home, Captain Baker arrived with his son and daughter just in time to attend the festivities. The wedding between W. Browne Baker and Adelaide Lovett cemented the long friendship of the Baker and Lovett families. Captain Baker and President Lovett had worked amicably for nearly two decades. If not always in agreement on details, each trusted the other's judgment and recognized the individual talents that had enabled them to steer the fledgling institute through its challenging early years. Alice Baker and Mary Lovett remained compatible teammates who supported each other. Most recently, when Mary Lovett chaperoned her daughter in Paris during Adelaide's two years of study at the Sorbonne, Alice wrote to her friend frequently about Houston activities and stepped in as hostess for several Rice events. The small Lovett-Baker wedding took place in the paneled faculty chamber of the administration building at Rice Institute. Mary Lovett transformed the space with large jars of calla lilies and garlands of smilax. Cathedral candles shed "luminous rays" on an altar constructed for the occasion. Adelaide chose her parents' twenty-fifth wedding anniversary for her own ceremony, wore her mother's wedding gown, and carried the prayer book her maternal grandmother had used for her 1865 marriage. Adelaide's brother Alexander (age eleven) managed his sister's delicate train, and Alice Baker Jones (age seven) held the ring for her uncle. Holiday greens decked the chamber, and guests enjoyed a six-foot tiered tower "decorated with gold and silver leaves, doves, bridal blossoms and woven ribbons and topped with a home scene." Following a wintry January wedding trip, the couple settled in Houston, where Browne began his business career at Guardian Trust, chartered in 1917 under Captain Baker's supervision.[119]

Soon after Captain Baker rented The Oaks, he created Graham Realty as a family corporation to hold the Main Street block and other downtown properties he had acquired through the years. He handed management of these disparate commercial investments to his son Jim, who was already involved in another real estate project. After World War I, speculators were developing residential neighborhoods in the area north of Rice Institute and west of property reserved for a museum of fine arts. In the summer of 1922, Jim and his father began discussing plans to design a residential enclave they named Broadacres on vacant land Captain Baker had purchased near Rice in 1908. Like other enclaves being built in cities across the United States, Broadacres was imagined as a carefully planned, handsomely landscaped, limited-access neighborhood, discreetly protected by deed requirements to avoid commercial development. By December 1922 Jim had gathered seventeen investors to support the scheme. On January 31, 1923, Captain Baker transferred the property to the Broadacres consortium, and in February 1924, City Engineer Herbert Kipp produced the formal site plan showing two long boulevards, two shorter cross avenues, twenty-five large lots, and underground utilities. Rice Institute architect William Ward Watkin designed and installed pairs of brick posts for each of the four points of entry. Jim Baker became chairman of the supervisory management committee and encouraged lot owners to hire well-known architects and maintain high construction standards. His wife, Bonner, created a landscaping plan for trees and shrubberies along the boulevards.

Although three lots were set aside for Baker family members, no Baker ever lived in Broadacres. In late 1922 Captain Baker had signed a two-year lease on The Oaks, but in June 1923, Edwin B. Parker told his longtime partner he was ready to sell his home. For some time, the Bakers had talked about moving permanently to land farther from commercial congestion. Joseph Cullinan invited them to invest in Shadyside, the residential enclave adjacent to Rice Institute that he had been developing for several years. While planning Broadacres, Captain Baker asked William Ward Watkin to design a Spanish-Mediterranean villa on oversized lot nine, but when the Parkers decided to sell, the Bakers abandoned their search and acquired their dream home and garden. On July 12, 1923, Alice had settled at Bass Rocks for the season when she received a telegram from her elated husband, who was still in Houston. "Believe I can get the Oaks for $125,000, which is cheap," he wrote, if Alice could make suitable changes and if she approved the price. Two days later, Alice received final word. "I have bought and now tender you the Oaks with my hearts best love. I wish you may be as happy in its possession and enjoyment as I expect and hope to be all well and send love Jimmie."[120] Captain Baker's boyish excitement did not deflect him from hiring a surveyor to check the 6.73-acre parcel. Nor was he pleased with well-known builder Christian J. Miller's cost-plus contract figures for interior renovations. Popular architect John F. Staub,[121] who designed Alice's changes, had to remind the eagle-eyed investor that remodeling always exceeded the cost of new construction, on a square-foot basis.

The Parkers had called their property The Oaks for the eighty oaks and specimen trees that grew there. The grounds also featured a Japanese teahouse, a large rose garden, several sunken flower beds, and a vegetable garden and chicken yard. Alice added planter boxes under the windows and a breezeway

The Oaks, Baker family home, 1922–1941. MS 609, Woodson Research Center, Fondren Library, Rice University.

covered with sweet honeysuckle. A greenhouse protected seedlings for the gardens and provided plants and flowers all year for her peerless floral displays. From 1924 until her death, Alice proudly opened her home for Rice Institute receptions and for "garden-visiting afternoons" sponsored by the Garden Club of Houston to raise funds for the club's civic projects. She also continued to invite Settlement Association women's clubs for annual outings at her home and garden.

Alice retained much of the heavy furniture favored in the late nineteenth century when she decorated the handsome dining room and library. The Bakers' grandsons never forgot how their grandfather promised them a nickel or dime if they could walk around the dining table in the darkened room without bumping into chairs—or running away in fright. The library housed the Bakers' extensive, well-ordered book collection, with each volume assigned a case, section, and shelf number, written neatly on the flyleaf. Alice placed her piano in the music room and the results of her antiquing adventures in the drawing room, brightened by Chippendale-style furnishings and elegant fabrics in the Colonial Revival decorative taste favored by Americana collector Ima Hogg and the proprietors of handsome homes being built in fashionable

The Oaks, drawing room, 1922–1941. MS 609, Woodson Research Center, Fondren Library, Rice University.

Shadyside, Broadacres, and River Oaks. Galleries, a breakfast room, and a large kitchen completed the downstairs. Upstairs, screened sleeping porches off the bedrooms and baths brought relief during Houston's long hot season. A large game room in the basement contained a pool table and enough comfortable upholstered armchairs to accommodate Captain Baker's law partners, who had been meeting there on Thursday evenings since 1908 to discuss firm business, first at E. B. Parker's invitation, and then, until his death in 1941, at Captain Baker's. The basement also housed the heating system, the laundry room, and a wine cellar.

As his children married, Captain Baker helped each young couple purchase a home. In 1915 he turned over property on Courtlandt Place to his daughter Alice, where she and Murray Jones lived with their daughter in a house designed by architect Birdsall Briscoe[122] and completed in 1917. Jim and Browne thought Broadacres lots were too expensive and instead built homes in their father's less expensive Turner Addition adjacent to Broadacres on its east side. In 1926-1927, Sam Dixon designed and built a "temporary" house that fronted rural Poor Farm Road (now Bissonnet Street), where Jim and Bonner lived for the rest of their lives. Browne and Adelaide built a house that shared a back-garden hedge with Jim and Bonner but faced Berthea Street. Adelaide's brother Malcolm Lovett and family friends also built homes on the Berthea cul-de-sac in the late 1920s and 1930s.

The fall of 1924 found the Bakers on another voyage to Europe. Their daughter Ruth had been spending the year traveling in "France, Germany, Switzerland, Italy and other countries on the continent" after she finished her studies at Miss Spence's School for Girls. Alice joined Ruth in Paris for a ladies' sightseeing and shopping frolic with friends. Captain Baker met his longtime comrade and former law partner Robert S. Lovett, and the two men began a tour of western front battlefields, trying to understand what their sons had experienced in 1918. Toward the end of the tour, Captain Baker was so moved by the scene that he wrote to his daughter-in-law Bonner Baker, explaining the "marvelous and wonderful trip. . . . Today we were at Verdun and in the Argone [*sic*] Forest, and all day the sweet face of dear Jim has been before me. I wish I knew where he was in the Argone, so that I might see the very things his eyes saw. . . . The beauty of this poppy plucked from the battle scarred field of Verdun recalled sweet thoughts of you, my dear child, and I enclose it with my hearts devotion to you & Jim. Lovingly, Mr. Baker." Of course, neither he nor Robert Lovett could ever see the "endless waves" of men facing "another hell," or feel the "knife-edge wind of November," or hear the shrill scream of endless daily bombardments, or smell the fear of death in mud-filled trenches—a generational barrier that would not be crossed.[123]

Ruth, now twenty, returned to Houston in December 1924 and stepped into a whirl of social activity when her parents introduced her to their friends at two debutant presentations linked to the Baker family. Alice Baker Jones and Mary Lovett founded The Assembly in 1920, and Ruth's brothers, Jim and Browne, helped establish the Allegro Club in 1925, just in time for Ruth and seven friends to make their bows at the club's inaugural Cinderella Ball. During this busy year, Ruth fell in love with Preston Moore, a graduate of Princeton University, described by one admiring friend as the nicest man he had ever met. The "In Society" reporter was delighted to recount the details of another Baker wedding, when Ruth and Preston were married on October 24, 1926, at 7:30 in the evening. The awed columnist described the "impressive and stately" candlelight ceremony at the First Presbyterian Church and the bride's bouquet of "white orchids with a shower of lilies of the valley falling to the hemline of her skirt." Roses filled every reception room at The Oaks for the splendid celebration hosted by Ruth's parents. Following a honeymoon trip to New Orleans, Havana, and New Haven—where the bride and groom attended the Yale-Princeton football game—Ruth and Preston began married life in a "picturesque home" on The Oaks property at 207 Bremond, which Captain Baker had refurbished for his daughter.[124]

Alice could turn proudly from Ruth's activities to a project organized by her daughter-in-law Adelaide Lovett Baker. On January 22, 1925, Adelaide and eleven friends who were "anxious to make a difference"—most of them the daughters of Houston's prewar progressive civic leaders—announced a volunteer group that became the Junior League of Houston.[125] While visiting in New York before her marriage, Adelaide had been impressed by the Junior League mission to channel the talents and energy of privileged young women and develop them as civic leaders. Founded in New York in 1901, the Junior League set goals followed by volunteers in cities across the country. Local league branches helped young women identify social issues, assigned them to projects where the service could change lives, and raised funds to support league-sponsored programs. Adelaide and two daughters of philanthropic oil man Joseph Cullinan—Mary Cullinan Cravens and Margaret Cullinan Wray—persuaded their friends to open a luncheon club in the basement of the Gibraltar Savings and Loan building so they could raise funds to establish a well-baby clinic for children with no access to healthcare services. Volunteers managed the lunchroom and assumed administrative and nonmedical support duties for the doctors and nurses in the clinic. Adelaide became the first Junior League president, and like her mother-in-law, began a lifetime of advocacy for civic involvement that enabled volunteers and the people they served to enrich their lives. While immersed in this new enterprise, Adelaide also became a mother when her first child, Walter Browne Baker Jr., arrived on November 13, 1925, much to the delight of his grandparents—a first grandchild for Adelaide's parents and a long-awaited companion for ten-year-old Alice Baker Jones.

In the winter of 1925-1926, the Bakers rushed to Princeton, where their son Malcolm was stricken with flu. Remembering son Graham's fate in 1902, the frightened parents brought their youngest child home and nursed him back to health. When fully recovered, young Mac finished his studies with the class of

1929 at Rice Institute, under his parents' watchful eyes. While at the Hill from 1920 to 1923, Mac had carried on a witty correspondence with his mother, and until Alice's death, he was buoyed by a tender mother-son relationship. Toward his father, a formal figure in his mid-sixties during this youngest child's teenage years, the playful Mac felt deep respect but less rapport. Like his older brothers, he followed his father's path as a banker, working at South Texas Commercial National Bank until after Captain Baker's death, when he pursued other business interests.[126]

While at Rice Institute, Mac met beautiful Anita Dee Stewart, daughter of the widowed Anita Bolmes Stewart and the late John Stewart. Anita was crowned Queen of the May at Rice Institute during her senior year, and after a college courtship, the couple married at 5:00 p.m. on November 15, 1929. According to the ever-present "In Society" reporter, the "impressive service" at Palmer Memorial Chapel was of "statewide interest." The bride, given in marriage by her brother John, dazzled in "an exquisite costume of ivory satin." An enormous bouquet of orchids and lilies of the valley "cascaded along the length of her skirt." The night before the wedding, Mac's parents entertained the wedding party at The Oaks, where "flowers of the Southland" decorated the house. Following a wedding trip to New Orleans, Havana, and Florida, Mac and Anita moved into another house abutting The Oaks, near Ruth and Preston Moore. During the early summers of their marriage, they spent many weeks at Bass Rocks, delightful times with Baker family members that they remembered fondly in later years.[127]

Alice Baker's last years brought joy and sorrow. High blood pressure continued to trouble her despite longer and longer stays in the refreshing, relaxing atmosphere of Bass Rocks, and by 1931 her eyesight was beginning to fail. While happily watching her younger children marry and establish their families, she also sustained her daughter Alice, whose marriage to Murray Jones was dissolved, a bitter event that occurred just as the worried mother's health was fading. Alice Jones rented the Courtlandt Place home her father had given to her fifteen years earlier and moved to The Oaks with her teenage daughter Alice (Babe). The Bakers were delighted to have new companions, and Alice Jones began to manage her parents' household. Granddaughter Alice completed the course at Mrs. Kinkaid's School in June 1931 and spent the next two school years in New York City, where she finished high school at Miss Spence's School for Girls. In 1930–1931, grandchildren Babe and Brownie were joined in an eighteen-month period by five additions to the Baker family. After years of waiting, Jim and Bonner welcomed James A. Baker III (Jimmy) on April 28, 1930, and his sister Bonner on November 6, 1931. Between these two longed-for

Captain Baker and Alice Baker with grandchildren Alice Jones and Brownie Baker, circa 1930. MS 609, Woodson Research Center, Fondren Library, Rice University.

children, came Adelaide and Browne's second son, Lovett, on September 21, 1930; Malcolm and Anita's first child, Shirley, on January 18, 1931; and Ruth and Preston's first son, Preston Jr., on August 7, 1931. These youngsters would become mischievous companions and lifelong friends.[128]

A Quiet Farewell

In September 1931, the Bakers were entertaining Robert S. Lovett at Rockhaven Cottage. Lovett had lost his wife, Lavinia, on November 18, 1928, and was fond of relaxing with his former law partner and longtime business associate. On September 23 the old friends were sitting on the porch while Captain

Baker read President Edgar Odell Lovett's annual matriculation address "about the hour you were delivering it." In a congratulatory letter, the board chairman thanked the Rice Institute president for sending him the speech and mused about the perfect fall weather, the recent visit of President Lovett's son Alexander to Bass Rocks, and his own plans to meander for ten days through New England, New York, and Quebec with Robert Lovett. The Bakers returned to Houston early in November that year, and Alice spent the next few months enjoying the five babies born during the previous two years. In May 1932 it was her turn to invite Anna Mae Herring, Eddie Coates, and Frankie Stewart to her home for the Graham sisters' reunion, held every spring or summer since the Bakers' marriage forty-nine years before. During the afternoon of May 9, Alice "appeared to be in the best of health" as she entertained her family in the garden. About 5:30 p.m. she rose to go inside, where she was stricken a few minutes later by a cerebral hemorrhage caused by "hypertension." She died at home at 9:15 p.m., with her beloved husband, children, and sisters gathered at her bedside. A month later, Captain Baker lost his dearest friend, Robert S. Lovett, on June 20, 1932.[129]

Family, friends, and the thousands of Houstonians whose lives Alice Baker had changed expressed sorrow, shock, and sadness that this "great civic leader . . . and inspiration to all who knew her" as "the embodiment of Southern hospitality and graciousness" was no more. On Thursday afternoon, Charles L. King, pastor of the First Presbyterian Church, officiated at the funeral service for the kind, loving woman who had opened her home and her heart to all Houstonians and knew them as her neighbors. Alice's nephews—Hunter Coates of San Antonio, Baker Duncan, and J. Bruce Duncan of Waco; George Thompson Jr., Beverly V. Thompson, and Bert Honea of Fort Worth; and Francis G. Coates, Frank Duncan, and W. Alvis Parish of Houston—bore her casket from The Oaks and laid her body to rest in Glenwood Cemetery beside her son Graham. Baker, Botts, Andrews & Wharton and Rice Institute closed for the day "as a mark of respect to Captain Baker during his bereavement." On her grave marker, Alice's "dearest" husband chose the beloved words of seventeenth-century English Bishop Jeremy Taylor to express his feelings: "A good wife is Heaven's last best gift to man—his gem of many virtues, his casket of jewels, her voice his sweet music, her smile his brightest day, her industry his surest wealth, her lips his faithful counselor." The Bakers had treasured their strong marriage based on mutual affection and respect and nourished by shared goals; with love and high expectations, they had built a strong family and had brought light and understanding to the community that had welcomed them. In all their activities, Alice counted on her husband's business expertise, and Captain Baker relied on his wife's civic dedication. Each appreciated how hard the other worked to promote the family's happiness and their city's prosperity.[130]

Captain Baker took great pride in Alice's commitment to the community and continued to support her causes until his death. To commemorate Alice's life, he donated funds to landscape a garden at the Museum of Fine Arts of Houston and provided copies of six old master paintings for an art gallery at Sam Houston State Teachers College in Huntsville. To recall her presence, he carried on family customs she had cherished for the rest of his life. To memorialize her legacy and benefit the Settlement Association, he urged his daughter Alice Baker Jones to join the association board and to serve as cochairwoman of Friendship House, a Settlement Association branch opened in 1934 on Navigation Boulevard east of downtown. Alice Jones and volunteers from Palmer Memorial Chapel organized clubs for mothers, children, and teenagers and provided Thanksgiving and Christmas dinner for area residents. Alice Jones recruited Houston Symphony musicians to develop a Friendship House music program, and she persuaded her father to host a gala at The Oaks on May 15, 1935, to benefit Settlement Association projects. As a final effort to perpetuate Alice's life work, Captain Baker guided his longtime client and family friend Edith Ripley to establish the Daniel and Edith Ripley Foundation, funded by the nearly $2 million legacy of her husband, a humanitarian, cotton exporter, and banker. The foundation charter stipulated that, after Edith Ripley's death, which occurred in 1934, foundation trustees would build a memorial benefitting women and children. In 1938 Ripley Foundation trustees approached Settlement Association President Corrinne Tsanoff about a cooperative effort to expand community-building outreach in Houston. The resulting alliance led participants in 1939 to construct a $200,000 state-of-the art recreation and health center east of downtown on Loving Street; income from remaining funds would defray operating costs. Ripley House, dedicated on April 14, 1940, became the Settlement Association headquarters and transformed the association's ability to deliver social services throughout the Houston area. On August 3,1941, after a simple service of song and prayer, Captain Baker joined Alice and their son Graham in the Glenwood plot guarded by a marble angel representing the virtue of faith, who stands on three steps that support a rusticated granite Latin Cross.[131]

CHAPTER TWO

A Storehouse of Knowledge for All of Us

Julia Bedford Ideson

JULY 15, 1880–JULY 15, 1945

Portrait of Julia Bedford Ideson by Julian Muench, 1936–1937. Presented to the Houston Public Library after Ideson's death by a group of friends. MSS0032–095, Julia Ideson Collection, Houston Public Library, Houston Metropolitan Research Center.

Prelude

Five thousand Houstonians gathered in Martha Hermann Memorial Square on Monday evening, October 18, 1926, to launch the "South's Finest Library," recently completed on the city block bounded by McKinney, Smith, Lamar, and Bagby streets. The First High School band entertained the crowd. William A. Vinson, president of the public library's board of trustees, presided over the 7:30 p.m. program and afterward swung wide the structure's handsome double doors and invited the curious guests inside. For several years, press accounts had detailed construction plans, funding efforts, and civic purposes for a new, much expanded central library. A September 29 notice in the *Houston Chronicle* invited "every Houston citizen" to attend the library's "coming out party," and announced that Rice Institute President Edgar Odell Lovett would deliver the principal address.[1]

Central to the evening's success was tall, elegant Julia Bedford Ideson, for two decades the person most closely associated with the Houston Public Library as its founding librarian and constant inspiration. It was she who had called attention to library needs, she who had persuaded Houstonians to endorse two bond elections for construction, she who had worked daily with the building committee and architectural team, and she who had overseen every detail of the celebratory events. Contemporaries revered their librarian, whose life of dedication to reading and education was "a bright page in the history of the city . . . that explains in large measure the growth and intellectual development of Houston." For Julia, the evening celebration was the culmination of her dream to place the public library at the heart of Houston's vibrant civic life. The new building's iconic architecture embodied her personal aspirations: the edifice would endure and be useful; it would enable excellence and future growth; and it would make reading for knowledge and pleasure available to everyone.[2]

Nebraska Childhood: 1880–1892

Julia Bedford Ideson was born to John and Rose Baseman Ideson on July 15, 1880, in Hastings, Nebraska, eleven days after a "terrific wind" ripped through the town, pushing buildings off their foundations, blowing away roofs, and shifting houses as much as twenty-four inches without waking sleeping residents.[3] Five years after Nebraska became the thirty-seventh state, pioneers founded Hastings in 1872 on fertile farmland between the Platte and Little Blue rivers at a point where the Burlington and Missouri River Railroad crossed the

St. Joseph and Denver City Railroad. The settlement prospered when railroad company advertisements that promised good jobs and cheap land lured homesteaders from Liverpool, England, Ireland, Germany, Denmark, and Russia to a frontier huddle of hastily built wooden shanties, shops, and saloons. Despite scorching summer heat, arctic winter blizzards, destructive fires, and sudden windstorms, the town had attracted 2,817 settlers and a newspaper publisher by 1878, the year Hastings organized a baseball club, formed a brass band, and became county seat of rural Adams County. Hastings continued to flourish through the 1880s and reached a population high of 13,584 by 1890.

New Yorker Alison Baptiste Ideson (1851–1934) was the first member of his family to settle in Hastings. A. B. Ideson began his career in the lumber business in New York City at age eighteen. In his early twenties, he joined C. N. Paine & Co. in Oshkosh, Wisconsin, and moved to Hastings in September 1877 to manage its subsidiary Badger Lumber and Coal Yard, established by the Oshkosh corporation in 1873 to sell lumber, cement, stucco, and "the celebrated Rock Springs and Wyoming coal as well as 4 other brands" to Nebraskans.[4] Before A. B. Ideson returned to Oshkosh in the early 1890s, he opened and managed several affiliated lumber yards in the fast-growing state. In 1878 his wife, Sophia Eleanor Roehrig (1853–1909), joined her husband in Hastings, where their daughters Ethel (1879-1956) and Dione (1881-1935) were born.

Impressed by the area's agricultural and commercial promise, A. B. Ideson encouraged his older brother, John Castree Ideson (1847-1906), to bring his family to Hastings. At age nineteen, John began traveling for a nursery in New York State, but from 1872 to 1877, he helped George W. Baldwin run a stationery and book business in Houston, Texas. From 1870 to about 1899, Baldwin's storehouses on Main Street also held a subscription library of several thousand volumes, mainly light fiction written in English or German. John Ideson returned to the East Coast in 1877, where he met and married Rosalie E. (Rose) Baseman (1855-1937) of Baltimore. On October 12, 1878, their daughter Margaret was born in Reisterstown, near Baltimore. By the end of the year, John, his wife, and infant daughter had joined A. B. Ideson in Hastings. John purchased six hundred acres in Hamilton County, abutting the northeast corner of Adams County, where he developed a stock-breeding operation worked by local farmers. In February 1879, John and his brother incorporated J. C. Ideson & Co. to furnish stationery and books to the area.[5]

The Ideson brothers had barely established their businesses and planned their homes when catastrophe struck the bustling town. After fire destroyed many buildings in October 1878, city fathers had spent $3,300 on up-to-date

Hastings, Nebraska, 1890s. Courtesy of Adams County (Nebraska) Historical Society.

equipment for the newly incorporated fire department, but on September 14, 1879, an uncontrollable blaze broke out in the Allison Drug Store. Before volunteers could contain the flames, paint supplies exploded, the hand pump on the new engine broke, and a wooden windmill with its arms spinning caught fire, spraying sparks wildly. Thirty-three downtown buildings burned to the ground, an estimated loss of $100,000. Citizens quickly passed a building code demanding that builders use fireproof materials in the future. The town's first professionally trained architect, Charles C. Rittenhouse, who practiced in Hastings from 1877 until 1895, transformed the commercial center with handsome late-nineteenth-century brick and stone structures and a new Adams County Courthouse, which was completed in 1889. Framing, finishing, and heating these buildings required the lumber and coal sold by A. B. Ideson at the Badger Lumber Yard, and ambitious businessmen demanded John Ideson's stationery services and supplies. The Ideson brothers' future in the attractive town seemed assured, and the two families quickly emerged as leading citizens.

From his arrival in September 1877 until his departure nine years later, A. B. Ideson actively promoted Hastings's development. In January 1879 he built the town's first brick commercial building, planted trees on the residential lot where he planned to construct a home, and fenced his cemetery plot. In February 1879 local businessmen appointed A. B. to the executive committee tasked with establishing a college in the town, a goal accomplished when Hastings College offered classes in rented space in September 1882 and moved into the first campus hall two years later. While building a large statewide business, A. B. joined several investors in the fall of 1879 to establish Hansen, the first railroad depot north of Hastings on the St. Joseph and Grand Island Railway He surveyed the town, which would serve as a grain and livestock shipping station, and opened a Badger Lumber Yard branch to provide building materials for the quick construction of a depot, hotel, post office, and general store. In December 1879 A. B. also helped organize the Business Men's Association, renamed the Hastings Board of Trade in 1887. In 1880 A. B. was named secretary of the Hastings Fair Ground Association (1880-1882) and secretary of the Adams County Agricultural Society (1880-1881). That year he moved his family into the "elegant two-story [clapboard] residence" he had built at 606 West Fourth Street "in accordance with the latest and most approved" architectural designs. Two years later, the *Gazette Journal* noted that fashion-conscious A. B. was "having the whole interior of his residence papered with some of the handsomest wallpaper brought to the city." In 1881 A. B. joined four other men to introduce a telephone system to forty subscribers. He served as vice president and general manager of the Hastings Telephone Exchange from 1882 until Bell family interests purchased the local company in 1886 and merged it with the national network. On May 7, 1883, A. B. became vice-chancellor and charter member of Pioneer Lodge No. 28 of the Knights of Pythias, a nationwide fraternal order devoted to "friendship, charity, and benevolence." When C. N. Paine & Company sold its Hastings lumber interests to the Howard Brothers of Denver and Omaha in September 1886, the town lost one of its most enthusiastic boosters. A. B. and his family moved to nearby Deep Well in Hamilton County, where he established and managed another Paine-sponsored lumber yard.[6]

In 1880 John Ideson joined his gregarious brother and six other Hastings men to launch St. Mark's Episcopal Church. A. B. accepted the duty of warden, and John became treasurer. The founders selected a site on Fifth Street and in 1881 built a Gothic-style church measuring twenty-eight by sixty feet, with tall, slim windows piercing the wooden siding, a deep-pitched roof, and a modern furnace. By 1880 John had become the "popular" proprietor of the "largest and best selected stocks [of books, stationery, sheet music, and musical instruments] in Western Nebraska." Shoppers gathered at his centrally located store, just north of the Post Office, to browse and discuss books while examining the "fancy" goods, "papeteries" (writing materials), toys, dolls, and "notions" displayed there. From 1881 through 1887, John expanded his store and acted as agent for the Wells Fargo Express, and from 1888 until he left Hastings in 1892, he also sold general insurance with P. H. Passy and G. F. Wilkin in offices near the bookstore. John was considered benevolent on June 15, 1882, when he signed an agreement with thirty-nine Hastings merchants to close their shops at 8:30 p.m. so clerks and proprietors would have "some time for recreation." So important was the family that a few days later, the *Gazette Journal* reported that "Mr. John Ideson's little girl rolled out of bed" but "was doing as well as could be expected." John's wife, Rose, a student of literature, was among the respected Hastings women who gathered in 1885 to form a Chautauqua reading circle that provided stimulating enjoyment until it was disbanded about 1900, because many families had moved away.[7]

Books surrounded Julia Ideson from birth and shaped her earliest memories. In later years, she recalled that she dreamed of being a librarian when she was a little girl. Her father collected a large home library and purchased *Andersen's Fairy Tales, Swedish Fairy Tales, Pussy Willow and Other Child Songs,* as well as *Grammar School Geography* and other textbooks for his daughters.[8] Occasionally a circus came to town, and after the Kerr Opera House was constructed in 1884, it sponsored traveling and local entertainment, but the Ideson girls relied on books to imagine a wider world. Adams County organized the Hastings school district in July 1872 and built a two-story frame building where classes were taught from 1873 until 1892. The four Ideson cousins would have attended this school, which accommodated 350 pupils. Margaret (age twelve) and Julia (age ten) were probably considered too young to attend the Academy of the Visitation, a girls' day and boarding school operated by the Chicago-based Sisters of the Visitation, which offered classes for grades nine through twelve plus two years of college after it opened in January 1890. Unfortunately, there are no extant enrollment records to confirm attendees.

Sadly, this comfortable Nebraska childhood did not last. Three destructive fires and one devastating windstorm battered the town and caused John Ideson to rebuild or relocate his store twice in eight years. Low commodity prices in 1890, as well as high property taxes, inflated freight rates, scant rainfall, soaring temperatures, and political agitation, warned Adams County residents that tough days lay ahead. By 1894 several businesses in Hastings had failed, and desperate farmers had hired rainmakers from Iowa to alleviate the drought and halt the agricultural depression sweeping the state. By 1900 Hastings had lost nearly half its population. John was the first Ideson to abandon Nebraska's harsh climate when he closed his store and moved to Texas in 1892. In 1894 A. B. returned to the Paine company headquarters in Oshkosh, where he prospered and was promoted. He spent the last three decades of his life in Norwood, Ohio, serving as the town's mayor and ending his long career as corporate secretary of the Paine Lumber Company. After his death in Ohio on December 27, 1934, his body was returned to Oshkosh for burial. Although the Ideson families left Hastings, Ethel and Dione continued to exchange visits with their cousins Margaret and Julia. Several Oshkosh newspaper accounts recorded the whirl of activities organized in Julia's honor during her lengthy visit to the A. B. Ideson family in July and August 1901. Ethel and Dione hosted a "crazy" party for thirty guests and chartered a "ride" on Lake Winnebago that ended in a moonlit return home after 11 p.m. By the time of this visit, Julia and her family had resettled in Houston.[9]

Houston Home: 1892–1899

John Castree Ideson brought his family to Houston by 1892 and worked at the G. W. Baldwin Bookstore until George Baldwin's death in the late 1890s. During these years, the Idesons changed residences several times, joined Christ Church (Episcopal), and belonged to a circle of friends whose travel, social, and civic activities appeared occasionally in local society columns and business pages. In addition to his bookstore interests, John Ideson developed a commercial, residential, and agricultural real estate business headquartered in the modern five-story Kiam Building, constructed in 1893 by clothier Ed Kiam to house his retail store at street level. The building's contractor installed electric lighting and the city's first electric elevator, which took businessmen and lawyers to offices on the upper floors. John Ideson's realty advertisements included purchase opportunities for a "new dairy, all in perfect order" with livestock and equipment; a "modern 5-room house on the car line" nine blocks from the Capitol Hotel at Main Street and Texas Avenue; and ten thousand acres of rice land "cheap" and "improved." For several years, Ideson acted as agent for the Missouri Pacific Railroad system's immigration bureau, established by Gould family interests to encourage settlement along its rail lines west of the Mississippi. Ideson and the bureau's three other Houston agents hosted the February 1905 annual convention of the Missouri Pacific system's land and immigration agents, taking advantage of the "delightful conditions of mid-winter in South Texas" to entertain and impress the national throng.[10]

Only six months before his death, Ideson completed a multi-state deal between prominent Houston attorney Capt. Joseph C. Hutcheson and wealthy Illinois manufacturer George Postel (1852–1915).[11] Hutcheson and his syndicate of local investors had recently spent $36,000 for a large parcel of land between Buffalo Bayou and the Galveston, Houston, and Northern Railroad tracks, where they planned to develop rice farms and a pleasure resort. George Postel offered $50,000 to the group and announced he would create the manufacturing suburb of Deer Park for Houston instead. John Ideson and W. C. Hurtell of East St. Louis handled the deal and agreed to act as local representatives for the Postel interests. This much-publicized sale suggested that comfortable times lay ahead for the family, but Ideson apparently did not enjoy good health. While his wife, Rose, was visiting relatives in Maryland, John traveled to a spa in Mineral Wells, hoping its waters would "benefit" an unnamed chronic condition. He died there on August 23, 1906, attended by his daughter Julia.[12]

At the University of Texas: 1899–1903

In the 1890s Margaret and Julia Ideson attended Houston's public schools and were often guests at the well-chaperoned "merry" parties "of young folks" so popular with society reporters. Both young women were graduates of Houston High School and studied at the University of Texas. Newspaper articles provide glimpses of Julia's high school years; she was popular with her peers, an amateur thespian, and a serious student. As secretary of her junior class, she was one of four officers who oversaw the "scene of mirth and brilliancy" at the annual "hop" given by the juniors for the graduating class. At her senior Class Day on May 31, 1899, Julia performed the role of Cordelia during a "morning with Shakespeare" that featured music and recitation.[13] Houston Mayor Samuel H. Brashear handed Julia her diploma at 5:00 p.m. June 1, 1899. That fall, the new graduate followed her sister Margaret to the University of Texas with plans to study pedagogy in the Department of Literature, Science, and Arts.

Encouraging two daughters to attend a four-year, degree-granting college or university was unusual in an era when only one in four Americans finished high school, but the Idesons urged their daughters to read, to study foreign languages, and to take college-preparatory courses during high school. While many parents feared that a daughter who attended college would be unsuitable for marriage, seen as the safest life path for women in the 1890s, the Idesons supported their daughters' musical, athletic, theatrical, and academic pursuits. Perhaps their father's struggle to find prosperity in frontier Nebraska and preindustrial Houston suggested that the girls should be able to support themselves. While Margaret did combine marriage with a modest theater career, Julia seems to have remained single so she could dedicate her life to education and reading. Slim and athletic, Julia grew from a pretty girl to a handsome woman with large, compelling brown eyes, a good sense of humor, and a clearly stated ambition to become one of the finest librarians in the United States.

When Margaret and Julia Ideson boarded the train for Austin in the late 1890s, they left the busy commercial city of Houston (population 44,633 in 1900) for a town of about 20,000 people whose main sources of income were the state government and the public University of Texas. Like most Texas towns in the 1890s, Austin attracted little industry, approved weak local government, and had no developed public parks or playgrounds, but the city did boast underground sanitary sewers, electric streetcars and lighting, and the multipurpose Millett Opera House. Texans had recognized the need for a state-supported university in 1839, when the congress of the Republic of Texas set aside a site for a university and allocated fifty leagues (241,400 acres) of land to support the imagined enterprise. The 1876 state constitution stipulated a "university of the first class," and finally, in 1881 Texas voters authorized placing the university's main campus on a hilly forty-acre tract in Austin and the medical department in the prosperous port of Galveston. On November 17, 1882, the University of Texas Board of Regents, including newly named chairman, Ashbel Smith, laid the cornerstone for the west wing of the original Main Building on the Austin campus. Classes began in September 1883, but construction of the $250,000 project continued for sixteen years. The west wing was fully operational in January 1884; the center portion opened in 1889; and the east wing was finally ready in 1899. Main served all purposes until 1908—when university regents authorized a second building—and housed a two thousand-seat auditorium, a chapel, a library, nine large lecture halls, and thirty classrooms. Law classes met in the lowly basement, a cause of much amusement to student comedians.

Margaret in 1897 and Julia in 1899 entered the Department of Literature, Science, and Arts after taking entrance exams in English, history, mathematics, Latin, and Greek. Other departments comprised engineering, mines, law, medicine, pharmacy, and nursing. Class requirements to complete a bachelor of arts degree included English, mathematics, Latin, Greek, and physical culture in the freshman year and English and Greek in the sophomore. Bachelor of literature aspirants took required classes in English, mathematics, Latin, a modern language or a science, and physical culture as freshmen and English and the chosen modern language as sophomores. Margaret matriculated at the university in the fall of 1897. A popular athlete, she joined the Young Ladies Tennis Club and captained the Cardinall Basket Ball Team in 1899–1900. She was a member of the Ashbel Smith Literary Society, served as class secretary in 1898, and was class vice president in 1899–1900. Margaret and about fifty classmates received BA degrees in 1901,[14] and on June 26, she married middle-aged Henry W. Ladd (1851–1916) at St. David's Church in Austin. The Ladds remained in Austin while Julia completed her studies and welcomed Julia's college friends and other young Austinites to their home for ping-pong contests and receptions. Margaret performed in theatricals during her undergraduate years, and when the Ladds moved to Manhattan, she began an acting and dancing career there, at the time an unconventional step for a middle-class, married woman. After Henry Ladd's death in May 1916, Margaret pursued her theater career in Mexico City for two years but returned to New York City, where she married chemical engineer Frank Alfred Swertz on August 18, 1923.[15] Rose Ideson remained in Houston after her husband's death in 1906 and kept house for herself and her professional daughter Julia. She made frequent long visits to Margaret's New York home and died there on January 8, 1937. Margaret never had children and died at her Rockaway Beach, Long Island, home on November 4, 1949, outliving her sister.

Julia's academic path was more complicated than her sister's. She enjoyed college life and attended dances at Austin's fashionable Driskill Hotel. She also contributed to the Ashbel Smith Literary Society, where she became associate editor for the organization founded by and for women in 1888 to recognize excellence in English and to publish student essays. Julia was initiated "into the mysteries of Kappa Kappa Gamma" sorority at a "beautifully decorated" banquet in January 1903. Most memorably, she met her lifelong friend Ima Hogg when both women enjoyed social gatherings as members of the undergraduate Blue Bonnet Club. While she enjoyed these activities, Julia's constant ambition was to qualify as a professional librarian. When she enrolled as a candidate for the BA degree in 1899, Julia assumed the best credential for a career as librarian would be a good general education with special training in pedagogy.[16]

Melvil Dewey, the charismatic originator of decimal classification that standardized library organization, founded the first library school in the United States at Columbia University in 1887. Although demand for professionally trained librarians was growing in the late nineteenth century, few colleges and universities followed Dewey's pioneering example. Women's colleges and the Association of Collegiate Alumnae proactively scoffed at library training classes, claiming they provided technical rather than academic expertise. Julia was delighted to learn during her freshman year that the University of Texas had realized "the profession of librarian requires some technical training as well as a good education" and would offer "a one-year library science class

Julia Ideson at the University of Texas, circa 1900. MSS0032–099, Julia Ideson Collection, Houston Public Library, Houston Metropolitan Research Center.

conducted along the lines employed in its library." While the course required "a good general education" that met university admission standards, completion of the program would not count towards a bachelor's degree. Eight hours of lecture and laboratory work each week would cover "order and accession work; classification; cataloguing; reference work and bibliography; loan systems; binding; and care of pamphlets and documents."[17] Students would also complete practical apprenticeships in the various library departments. With the prospect of officially sanctioned library training, Julia rethought her education plan.

After her freshman year, Julia spent a year in Houston but returned to Austin in the fall of 1901 to complete the sophomore requirements for the bachelor of literature degree—classes in English, Latin, history, mathematics, and Spanish. Viewed by teachers as amiable, intelligent, and diligent, Julia continued degree-qualifying courses in English, mathematics, Spanish, and zoology during her junior year, but she also joined six students as a member of the second library science training class. University librarian Benjamin Wyche and library cataloguer Caroline Wandel taught library economy in the fall and reference and bibliography that spring. Later in life, Julia recalled being a mediocre student unable to conquer the mysteries of mathematics, but she mastered library science enthusiastically and became the second assistant cataloguer at the University of Texas library in February 1903 when she received her certificate of program completion. She never completed the bachelor's degree, but she did acquire sufficient practical experience to secure accolades and excellent references. When a search committee from Houston sought a leader for its first public library, Julia was ready to answer the call to service.[18]

Like most civic-minded Houstonians, Julia followed publicity about plans for a public library building funded by a gift from Andrew Carnegie. Before construction was complete, she wrote to attorney and Houston Library Association board member Edgar Watkins on June 2, 1902, to apply for the job as librarian, noting that she had fulfilled the required work for a university degree, had completed the library course classes, and was "getting considerable practical training" while working in the university library. Two enthusiastic letters of recommendation supported her application. University librarian Benjamin Wyche described his junior cataloguer as "unusually energetic and intelligent." Wyche quoted a history professor who had praised the "unusually able student" for her "uncommonly keen intellect and quick perception" and her "careful and faithful . . . performance of class duties." The university's assistant librarian opined that Julia's "aimiable [*sic*] and obliging disposition" would be "of great value to her in Library work." On February 27, 1903, Julia learned "unofficially" that the Houston position would be hers in the fall, when the contract of the temporary librarian was due to expire. On May 14, 1903, Julia returned to Houston armed with a letter from the head cataloguer at the University of Texas stating that since February Julia had been "regularly employed as an assistant" and that her work "has been . . . most satisfactory." On August 4, library board member Elizabeth Ring[19] notified Julia that the persistent aspirant had been "unanimously elected" librarian, to be announced officially in the fall. Ring assured her new hire that the board "would do what is right about your remuneration" and predicted that "with you for permanent librarian our library will be one of the most attractive and best managed in the state." Publication of this news produced a gratifying letter from University of Texas President William L. Prather; he was proud that Julia had been chosen from "among many candidates," noting that her recognition demonstrated the importance of university training for young women.[20]

Campaign for a Public Library: 1836–1903

Attorney and diarist William Fairfax Gray (1787-1841) carried his personal and law libraries from Virginia to Texas when he settled in Houston and opened his law office on Travis Avenue in May 1837. A few months later on December 5, the well-known bibliophile joined Mirabeau B. Lamar and twenty-five other men to adopt the constitution of the Philosophical Society of Texas, formed in part to encourage scientific and literary attainments, collect geological and natural history specimens, and form "a public library in embryo."[21] Gray's vivid record of Anglo-Texan settlement and separation from Mexico has endeared him to Texana enthusiasts, but his law library—including the volume that first records the seminal 1803 US Supreme Court decision *Marbury v. Madison*—enabled arriving settlers to prepare for legal careers. Among those legal aspirants was Gray's son Peter W. Gray (1819-1874), who began practicing law with his father in 1840. Peter Gray built a flourishing law practice, held several public offices, and was named to the Texas Supreme Court shortly before his death in 1874. An early civic leader, Peter Gray helped organize Houston's first Episcopal congregation at Christ Church in 1839 and supported two short-lived efforts to establish circulating libraries—the 892 volumes made available by Henry F. Byrne & Company at 7 Long Row in 1839–40, and Postmaster Capt. Martin Kingsley Snell's Circulating Library and Reading Room, opened near the post office in 1844. When both efforts failed, Peter Gray founded the Houston Lyceum in 1848 as a free public reading room and book repository. His modest efforts to share books and to encourage reading for pleasure and education would inspire a prolonged civic campaign that finally secured a public library building for Houston five decades later.

Since antiquity, great public libraries have distinguished developed societies. Episcopal clergyman, the Reverend Dr. Thomas Bray, opened the Library of Charles Towne in South Carolina in 1698 and secured funding from the provincial government to purchase books, maintain a catalogue, and devise rules for library users. Although the first publicly funded library in North America lasted only a few years, the South Carolina experiment established a precedent of government support for "the promotion of so Good and Necessary a Work" as the provision of books "to encourage Religion and Learning" in the colony. Benjamin Franklin and a group of friends declared Philadelphia's sophistication when they formed the Library Company of Philadelphia in 1731. These founders of the first subscription library to be organized in the British colonies offered to share books deposited in a public space with any free male readers who could afford a small subscription fee. In 1748 seventeen men founded the Charles Town Library Society as the first subscription library in the Carolinas. When Peter Gray and five other men signed a charter from the State of Texas on March 20, 1848, they hoped to introduce the tradition of subscription libraries to frontier Texas. The Houston Lyceum was conceived as a public library and debating society "to diffuse knowledge among its members," "elicit useful information," and "produce improvement in the art of public speaking." Any free white male who wished to pay a minimal user fee and abide by library rules would be welcome. Unfortunately, the initial burst of enthusiasm waned, and on May 27, 1854, a small group of Houstonians adopted the constitution and bylaws of a reorganized second Houston Lyceum Society, which soon merged with the Young Men's Christian Literary Society to form the Houston Lyceum. The second lyceum opened its official headquarters in the courthouse, drew up strict operating rules, and assertively sought new members and donations of money and books. A lyceum committee began planning the city's first night school in 1855, and in 1856 the *Telegraph and Texas Register* refuted rumors that "nothing of a literary nature" would survive in Houston by insisting that the "flourishing condition of our Lyceum is a source of pride to every Houstonian."[22] In June 1857, Editor Edward Hopkins Cushing[23] donated the "nearly complete" first ten volumes of the *Telegraph*, on condition the lyceum have them bound. After his death in 1879, the lyceum purchased the avid horticulturist's 140-volume personal library.

From June 1860 until 1877, lyceum members met infrequently, but in August 1877 seventeen men gathered to revive the Houston Lyceum, accept the library of a private school that had closed, and retrieve antebellum books and records. Supporters successfully petitioned the city council for space in the banqueting hall of the new market house, and in 1878 the group moved its books and furnishings from the courthouse to the banqueting hall and reopened a members' reading room. Eager to expand participation, members formed the

Apollo Club in October 1881 to sponsor musical and literary entertainments, and they invited "several ladies" to become honorary Houston Lyceum members and help organize Apollo events, a move that successfully attracted attention and provided funds. Although members defeated an 1882 recommendation to catalogue the library's property "to insure against loss," in January 1883 banker and landowner B. A. Shepherd donated a large newspaper collection to the lyceum, and the US Patent Office began sending its *Official Gazette* to the lyceum the following year. In March 1884, with support from Houston Congressman Charles Stewart, the lyceum was named the depository for United States government documents for the First Congressional District of Texas.[24]

If men led Houston's first efforts to provide a public reading room, it was women who brought a full-service public library to Houston fifty years later. Female bibliophiles dissatisfied with honorary lyceum membership and desultory male oversight of the reading room wanted full membership and a professionally managed library—with staff, catalogue, regular hours, and support from the city. Finding male civic leaders unresponsive to these aspirations, Adele Briscoe Looscan[25] invited her close friend Caroline Ennis Lombardi and six other women to her home at 620 Crawford on February 26, 1885, to discuss forming a Ladies' History Class for self-improvement. By April 5, Looscan and Lombardi had gathered twenty-four members and transformed their original idea into the first woman's literary club organized in Texas. The Ladies' Reading Club constitution and bylaws capped membership at fifty, specified meetings every Tuesday afternoon from October to June at the Parish House of Christ Church, and quickly shifted the organization's goal from self-education to civic reform. Monthly dues of ten cents per member paid for magazine subscriptions and books. In an early report to her members, Looscan recognized that "club life was a novel experience and, at times, a difficult undertaking" for women who had previously focused on home and church activities, but she understood the power well-informed women would exert when working together for community improvement. In 1890 Louise Cohn Raphael initiated Houston's second women's club, the Ladies' Shakespeare Club, and on December 8, 1893, eight founders who wanted to "create solidarity of feeling among women on a basis of common interest" met at the home of Estelle Jenkins (Mrs. John T.) Brady to form the Woman's Club, dedicated "to literary culture, education, art, and philanthropy." Members of these clubs made building a public library their primary civic mission.[26]

Women had long been pressing their husbands for admittance to full membership in the Houston Lyceum, a goal they finally achieved in 1887. Female participation increased lyceum membership and improved its precarious financial position. At last members could afford to pay a librarian twenty-five dollars a month, could keep the reading room open from 3 p.m. to 6 p.m. and from 7 p.m. to 10 p.m., and could expand the book collection. These improvements made library advocates more determined to build a permanent, properly funded facility. Learning in 1891 that William Marsh Rice had donated $200,000 to establish a public library and institution of higher learning in Houston, lyceum members approached trustees about cooperating but were told that no plans for Rice's gift would be made during the donor's lifetime. In 1892 a delegation of women from the Ladies' Reading and Shakespeare clubs prepared a petition to the mayor, asking the city government to take over management of the lyceum and convert the member-only organization to a free public library supported by tax dollars. Municipal authorities were not interested.

Although petitions to Rice trustees and city officials failed, clubwomen were not discouraged and instead began campaigning to promote lyceum use and build a full-fledged public library. In October 1892, Ladies' Reading Club members rented their first meeting room in the market house ballroom, and the lyceum expanded its reading room hours to include Sundays. In 1894, Adele Looscan and a phalanx of clubwomen pressured lyceum members to extend use of the lyceum reading room to the general public. In response to the lobbying, a lyceum committee, appointed at the January 1895 annual meeting, recommended issuing a "book check" (or library card) for the annual fee of three dollars to any white adult citizen who wished to use the reading room and lyceum collection. In August lyceum officers began issuing three-month book checks to white high school students for one dollar, provided parents or guardians assumed responsibility for loss or damage. The Houston Lyceum also hired its first female librarian, former Ladies' Reading Club member Margaret Hadley Foster. Foster inaugurated "ladies' day" at the reading room and explained lyceum needs to clubwomen. In 1897, the Ladies' Reading Club voted to request annual dues of five dollars per member to purchase books for the lyceum.

Women also advocated moving the lyceum from the bustling commercial market house to a home more congenial to female members. In her 1895 annual report, President Adele Looscan suggested the Ladies' Reading Club ask members of all women's and teachers' associations to co-sign a petition to the officers of the lyceum. Looscan proposed that each female guarantor pledge to pay lyceum dues of three dollars per year, and each club promise to purchase books worth five dollars every month, if the lyceum would approve moving to better quarters. Lyceum leaders agreed, and in September 1897, the lyceum, under the efficient guidance of new librarian Kate Shaifer, moved its collections to three rooms on the top floor of the four-story Mason Building, located at the corner of Main Street and Rusk Avenue. In these new surroundings, the lyceum shared rooms and rental fees with the Ladies' Reading and Shakespeare clubs. The Ladies' Reading Club then donated 150 volumes and its magazine files to the lyceum collection.

Reform-minded Houston women took an unprecedented step in 1897 when a delegation of ladies ventured to city hall to petition the municipal government for a city park. The presence of women in the council chamber stunned the all-male governing body, but the ladies prevailed, and the resultant Sam Houston Park emboldened female advocates to pursue other civic projects during visits to city hall. Library promoters asked themselves why their efforts should not be similarly successful. By 1898 female library advocates had found an ally in Cesar Maurice Lombardi, president of the lyceum, trustee of the Rice Institute, and chairman of Houston's Board of Education from 1886 to 1898. Lombardi wanted to investigate the viability of a municipal library for Houston, and he persuaded lyceum members and clubwomen advocates to write three hundred mayors nationwide to gather information about facilities in their cities. Responses to the queries showed that rival Galveston maintained the only municipal, tax-funded library in Texas and was already allocating $2,000 per year to its public library. Armed with data, Lombardi called a meeting to draft an appeal to the city council and secure endorsements from the Ladies' Reading Club, the Shakespeare Club, and the Woman's Club. Houston officials acknowledged the petitioners and referred them to the finance committee, which recommended that the 1899 budget include an appropriation to support the lyceum. Mayor Samuel H. Brashear told the women's groups that he, too, supported the library project.

To ensure passage of this appropriation, indomitable Ladies' Reading Club member Elizabeth Fitzsimmons Ring formed a women's committee and conceived a hands-on approach; the group braved city hall on January 2, 1899, carrying invitations to the mayor and councilmen to visit the lyceum clubrooms for a reception, guided tour, and presentation. On January 23, 1899, Ring and her fellow hostesses welcomed the seven officials to the lyceum headquarters and feted them with an elegant repast of chicken salad, hot biscuits, and coffee. As the gentlemen ate, the tenacious clubwomen entertained their guests with music and recitations and explained their concerns. To serve Houston's reading public properly, they reasoned, the club room needed more staff, more reading materials to fill the empty bookshelves, and more equipment to process the books. Most of all, the lyceum needed municipal financial support. Lyceum President John H. Ruby praised the women as the library's "chief supporters," and Mayor Brashear said "frankly and sincerely" that his administration would "cheerfully" help the Houston Lyceum. Swayed by the women's convincing arguments, on March 13 the mayor and his council approved an appropriation of $200 per month to support a free public library, on condition that $150 a month be spent for new books. The lyceum accepted these terms and agreed to "furnish a library and free public reading room for all citizens."[27]

With these assurances, library advocates redoubled their efforts to recruit new lyceum subscribers and planned their campaign to erect a library building. In October 1899, Woman's Club President Belle Sherman Kendall[28] and Secretary Mamie Gearing petitioned Andrew Carnegie for the funds needed to build a municipal library. From Carnegie's first library gift in 1886 until World War I, the great Pittsburgh, Pennsylvania, industrialist, philanthropist, and pacifist funded 2,509 public libraries, including 1,679 in the United States. Camp County coal miners were the first Texas recipients of Carnegie's benevolence when the coal and steel magnate donated $5,000 in 1898 to match local funding for a library building that also housed the opera house, city hall, and social center in the tiny but aptly named Pittsburg, Texas. In 1899, Dallas, Fort Worth, and Houston received three of the thirty-four grants made to Texas municipalities to initiate thirty-two public library systems. Totaling $645,000, these Carnegie gifts were often made in response to requests from local women's clubs, which were sponsoring subscription libraries in their towns. On October 28, 1899, Carnegie's secretary, James Bertram, wrote to Belle Kendall from the millionaire's residence at Skibo Castle, Ardgay, Nova Scotia: "Mr. Carnegie thinks that Houston should have a free library, and he would be disposed to help it to obtain this if the city were to provide a proper site and agree to maintain it at a cost of say $4,000.00 per annum. Mr. Carnegie would be glad to give $50,000.00 to erect a suitable building." At last Houston would have its public library. The letter was promptly "placed in the hands of the Mayor" for deliberation.[29]

While municipal officials discussed the Carnegie challenge, library advocates acted. On January 9, 1900, Adele Looscan and Elizabeth Ring invited representatives from the Ladies' Reading Club, the Shakespeare Club, the Woman's Club, the Current Literature Club, and the Mansfield Dramatic Club to establish the City Federation of Women's Clubs. The new federation would use its womanpower to fulfill Carnegie's requirements; together, these clubwomen would choose an appropriate site and raise funds for the land purchase.

At the first convention of the Texas Federation of Women's Clubs in 1899, Ring had been asked to lead the organization's critical library committee, tasked with establishing public libraries throughout the state and creating a Texas Library Commission. A lifelong advocate of cooperative action, Ring made Houston's library her first success story. On June 11, 1900, City Federation members met with lyceum officers to coordinate work on the library project and to establish the Houston Lyceum and Carnegie Library Association with authority to accept "all the property and effects of the Houston Lyceum," to take title to property for the library building, and to manage the enterprise. Original association officers included Mayor Samuel H. Brashear, ex officio, Elizabeth Ring, Belle Kendall, four other men, and generous donor Norman S. Meldrum. Industrialist Henry H. Dickson was named first president. With combined City Federation-lyceum leadership in place, the mayor and council passed an ordinance on June 18, 1900, to accept the Carnegie gift and to promise the annual appropriation. Once the Library Association had received its state charter in August, its officers met with city officials. The association agreed to provide a free public library while the city agreed to appropriate $4,000 each year to maintain the library. The agreement was ratified by city ordinance on September 24, 1900.[30]

Ring and her female enthusiasts asked Houston philanthropists, businessmen, and the federated literary clubs to sponsor the construction project. They held fundraising lectures and entertainments until by 1901 they had raised the $7,880 needed to purchase a vacant half block, located at McKinney and Travis, from the First Presbyterian Church. On December 13, 1900, the Houston Lyceum and Carnegie Library Association received its first endowment gift when Norman S. Meldrum and his wife donated $6,000 to establish the Norma Meldrum Children's Library Fund in memory of their daughter, who had died on November 23, 1899, a month before her tenth birthday. The bequest included $1,000 to buy books and furniture for the children's room in the new building and a perpetual trust of $5,000 to provide income for the purchase of children's books.[31] The Library Association board asked esteemed San Antonio architect James Riely Gordon[32] to provide a design in the classical or Beaux-Arts mode that would reflect the city's forward-looking, progressive aspirations. The board also hired Martin and Moodie Company to interpret the design and build the library. Known for constructing courthouses and jails, the company, founded in Comanche, Texas, by William Martin and Peter Moodie, excelled at adapting the revival styles popular in nineteenth-century America. Although Carnegie did not specify a design preference, most of the libraries he funded were two-story rectangular structures with pillared central entrances built above a basement. Exuberant Houstonians, however, authorized one of the grandest library structures in Texas.

Construction on the building began in 1901. On March 2, 1902, Belle Kendall accepted the ceremonial trowel used that day to lay the library's cornerstone and promptly presented it to her fellow Woman's Club members. On October 1, 1903, Julia Ideson was named first permanent librarian, to begin work on November 1. The Ladies' Reading Club voted to furnish the trustees' boardroom, which would also serve as a meeting space for Federation of Women's Clubs member groups, and in late October club members gave a party to mark completion of construction. On March 2, 1904, Elizabeth Ring and the Federation of Women's Clubs welcomed a "Great Crowd" to an "elaborate" dedication ceremony and reception. "Amid a Blaze of Light," proud Houstonians listened to "felicitous" speeches and watched artist Emma Richardson Cherry unveil a replica of Venus de Milo, a gift from the Art League of Houston to adorn the new building's central rotunda.[33] Association President Henry Dickson[34] introduced Julia Ideson and her assistant, Ethel P. Jones, praised Houston's hardworking women, and announced that the new building housed ten thousand volumes and four thousand government documents. Mayor Orren T. Holt accepted the building and its contents on behalf of the people of Houston.

The Carnegie Library: 1904

Houstonians praised their ornate library building enthusiastically. The edifice embodied their aspirations for the great city they imagined rising along Buffalo Bayou. Although described as "Italian Renaissance" in contemporary reports, the plethora of pediments, columns, and statues suggested a temple of learning that bound Houston dreams to the glory of Greek art and philosophy and the grandeur of Roman power and wealth. Library patrons could enter by one of two "main" entrances, whose broad stone steps led to domed, marble-floored colonnades; heavy double doors opened to entry vestibules and then to the "imposing" rotunda surmounted by a "magnificent" dome, its roof embellished by the figure of an angel reading a scroll. Three "massive" stone pediments supported by stone Corinthian columns and surmounted by bronzed American eagles faced Travis Street, McKinney Avenue, and the First Presbyterian Church. Across the back of the building was a rectangular wing devoted to utilitarian workrooms, stack space, and an auditorium. The entire building was faced in gray pressed brick and trimmed in Bedford limestone. Windows

Carnegie Lyceum and Library and First Presbyterian Church. MSS0187–0105, Postcard Collection, Houston Public Library, Houston Metropolitan Research Center.

on the first floor were spaced between the columns and finished with carved stone pediments.[35]

Although the public area inside was handsomely articulated by Ionic columns, the floor plan was clear and practical. From the vestibules, visitors entered a two-story rotunda. On the first floor, three "commodious alcoves," which corresponded to the exterior pedimented colonnades, housed the Norma Meldrum Children's Room (between the two vestibules), the Reference Room (on the left) for reference books, bound periodicals, and indexes, and the Reading Room (on the right) for current periodicals and newspapers. Behind the richly paneled delivery desk, stood the Venus de Milo statue, and beyond her, an alcove workspace and offices for the librarian and the cataloguer. From the workspace, formidable double doors allowed staff access to the large stack room, constructed like a fireproof bank vault to accommodate thirty-five thousand books. Marble stairs to the left and right of the delivery desk led to the second floor, which also comprised three alcoves that opened to a broad balcony encircling the space. These alcoves contained government documents, the arts and architecture collection, and a meeting room for the Library Association board and Federation of Women's Clubs member organizations. An auditorium with a vaulted ceiling occupied the space above the stack room. Interior walls were finished in "rough" plaster, and the rooms were "brilliantly" lighted by gas and electricity and heated by steam. A basement, reached by iron stairs, provided "abundant" space to unpack books and file newspapers and to house a boiler room, fuel bins, and the janitor's closet. The slate-roofed building was "absolutely" fireproof. City council members authorized an extra $10,000 to ensure that Houston's "expensive" architectural jewel was the only Texas building of its size whose floors, ceiling, roof, and dome were constructed with fireproof materials to withstand the periodic blazes that plagued urban areas. The project cost nearly $71,000, but city fathers proved as willing as ladies' reading clubs to support additional costs.[36]

Julia Ideson arrived at the Houston Lyceum and Carnegie Library at a moment of expanding opportunity for the city and changing attitudes within the library profession. Fueled by Spindletop oil wealth, industry investors had begun to move their headquarters to the friendly city. Trustees of William Marsh Rice's estate had unraveled a murder plot and quelled demands from over one hundred claimants to the dead man's fortune; in 1904 they opened administrative offices and began to plan the nationally significant Institute for the Advancement of Literature, Science and Art. Houston had recovered quickly from the 1900 hurricane and was poised to replace Galveston as Texas's major port. Libraries, too, were changing. No longer viewed as repositories of documents for the educated few, they were becoming workshops for citizens seeking self-improvement and catalysts for civic cooperation. In Houston, the public library was "now recognized as an important factor in the life of the town." Julia flourished in this energetic atmosphere. Her initial actions revealed the "frank integrity and great courage," the "grace and charm," and "the force of character" and "perseverance" that would guide and sustain her during her career. Her deep "seriousness of purpose" and ambition never wavered. Julia wanted to place Houston's public library prominently at the center of civic life; in this library every citizen could continue his or her education, and all children would be taught to love reading for pleasure and for information. Julia began her tenure supported by assistant Ethel Jones, an errand boy, a janitor, a limited budget, and a small group of determined library devotees. She remembered years later how her team had spent "hectic" days preparing the collections. Just "a young girl in the midst of a deluge of books," she had "to do all the cataloguing, plating, mending of books, ordering . . . everything" herself, but she "loved" the "endless routine work." With tireless organizing she would labor relentlessly to build collections and to guide reluctant readers toward the truth and beauty of well-expressed ideas she believed awaited them in books.[37]

Julia Ideson, circa 1903. MSS0032–0085, Julia Ideson Collection, Houston Public Library, Houston Metropolitan Research Center.

Ideson Takes Charge

The new librarian recognized three immediate tasks: to survey current collections and process new donations; to reassure library supporters and reading enthusiasts; and to encourage all Houstonians to make trips to the library an everyday routine. Before the library's opening reception on March 3, 1904, Julia Ideson and her assistant carefully prepared displays of the juvenile collection in the Norma Meldrum Children's Room. This large, prominent space emphasized Julia's ambition to place children at the center of her efforts to nourish lifetime reading habits. By catering to the special needs of young readers, she hoped to make them fall in love with books. Julia also began cataloguing what was known for thirty years as the "Circle M Collection." When Houston native John Ephraim Thomas Milsaps (1852–1932) realized there would be a public library in Houston, he told Library Association trustees that he would begin making anonymous gifts to the new institution from his four thousand-volume collection of books, diaries, scrapbooks, antislavery documents, and religious pamphlets and sermons. Until his death in 1932, Milsaps made periodic donations of documents, valuable Bibles, paintings, mineral and zoological specimens, and many curios from the Philippine Islands. An officer in the Salvation Army from 1883 until his retirement, Milsaps traveled widely and represented the organization in Hawaii and the Philippines. His meticulous diary ran to seventy-three volumes. His generosity enabled the public library to offer a rare archive, but maintenance of this unorthodox collection proved an ongoing challenge to the staff, even after assistant librarian Martha Schnitzer was hired to catalogue the collection. During her first year, Julia also welcomed more conventional additions. Baker, Botts, Parker & Garwood, the successor law firm to Houston Lyceum founder Peter Gray's practice, gave the library fifty-three bound volumes of the *Houston Post* (1901–June 1904) and *Galveston News* (1881–June 1904), and Ira P. Jones donated his bound files of the *Houston Post*. Viewed by citizens as "indispensable to a well-equipped public library," these volumes described "local progress" for posterity. Julia's efforts resulted in "rapid but substantial growth" in stock and equipment during her first year.[38]

Preparing these varied gifts and choosing new volumes for the collection tested the technical skills of the library staff, but reassuring her supporters and library users required Julia's ability to work with the enthusiastic clubwomen who had made development of a public library their primary mission. Julia was a strong-willed woman with a keen understanding of what she wished to accomplish. So were the knowledgeable women who had worked tirelessly to secure the public library. Houston's reform-minded clubwomen were the wives, sisters, and mothers of the men building Houston's law firms, banks, and industries.

Early library supporters Alice Baker, founder of the Houston Settlement Association, and music enthusiast Katherine (Kate) Parker were married to the senior men at Baker, Botts, Parker & Garwood, whose 1904 gift inaugurated Julia's successful collection-building campaign. Three of the Library Association officers in 1904 were literary club founders Adele Looscan, Elizabeth Ring, and Louise Cohn Raphael, who remained lifelong library backers. These women knew everyone who could help the young librarian work with city government, raise money, and publicize the library, and like Julia, they wanted to enrich the lives of all Houstonians. Julia quickly realized that working with these women and supporting their advocacy for parks and playgrounds, social services, good schools, safe roads and public utilities, art displays, musical performances, and appropriate protections for children and immigrants paralleled her fight to place the library at the center of civic life. She listened to them and gained their respect; she joined their club circles; and she relied on them to organize fundraising and special events and to proselytize the library among potential readers.

While depending on the steadfast patronage of Houston's clubwomen, Julia also reached out to businessmen and teachers, asking both groups what materials would be useful to them and to their employees and students. She told industry leaders that she wanted the library to reflect Houston's commercial and industrial life, and she wanted Houston workers to find information in the library's books, periodicals, and newspapers that would help them retool their trade and professional skills. She met with teachers to discuss ways the children's collections could enhance classroom learning and expand curricula, and she soon began to help public school teachers develop libraries in their schools. In the early years of her leadership, Julia's budget to purchase books was limited, and she relied on in-kind and monetary donations. She used her social capital brilliantly to guide supportive men and women toward donations that would help her create library collections of lasting value to Houston readers.

Explaining the library's function and possibilities to her supporters and civic leaders proved much easier than promoting the building's widespread use. Houston's library, like libraries everywhere, had originated for the convenience and pleasure of educated men. Many early patrons were lawyers or teachers who needed advanced reading skills to earn a living. Nineteenth-century Houston Lyceum members engaged in debates, prepared orations, and read aloud to each other. A typical evening meeting in 1880 included thirteen readings, recitations, debates, and musical offerings. The new library no longer sponsored these long evenings, but the elegant building, the hushed atmosphere of its quiet reading rooms, and the "good" manners demanded by the

Carnegie Library interior, circa 1914. Beach Photo. MSS0114–0677, Library Collection, Houston Public Library, Houston Metropolitan Research Center.

professionally dressed librarians discouraged working men and women, who had little leisure time to spare and no interest in a formal, forbidding environment. Many Houstonians had not completed eighth grade and had difficulty reading for pleasure or understanding a complex text. Many did not see how reading would improve their ability to earn a living. Addressing these problems and bringing all groups into the library family consumed much of Julia's time and imagination for the next four decades. By placing an invitation to the library's opening ceremonies in newspapers and by welcoming all Houstonians to the debut reception, Julia established her open-door approach. She made sure every annual report was printed in the local newspapers, and she turned every library activity into a news story that occupied columns of print. Lists of new books, reading contests for children, information about Houston's latest improvements, stories of her travels on library business, tales from the publishing world—all were subjects for Julia's clever pen. Publicity was a critical factor in attracting attention to the library, but Julia also began to keep records—who came to the library, what did they read, what did they check out to take home, what did children do at the library? Julia used the statistics gathered from answers to these and other questions to create new programs and to gain support from donors and city councilmen for her work. Julia believed that public libraries must cater to the needs of all the voters who were paying for the collections and programs through taxation. While it was the librarian's responsibility to introduce standards of excellence, it was also her duty to respond to public requests. At the end of her first year, Julia was pleased to note a "marked increase in patronage and popularity" that brought "scores of people" into the building every day and was a "measure of pride to the people of this city."[39]

Good publicity helped Julia build local support, but she also sought state and national affirmation. In the four decades before World War I, professionals, businessmen, farmers, and artisans organized thousands of local, state, and national associations in the United States to gain political influence and social standing through their respective occupations. Julia immediately joined the American Library Association (ALA) and the Texas Library Association (TLA) so she could make Houston's library known to the profession and enrich her service to Houston by introducing the latest information about library practice. In October 1876, ninety men and thirteen women who were visiting the Centennial Exposition in Philadelphia gathered to form the American Library Association to discuss problems confronting the country's two hundred librarians and to hear Melvil Dewey explain his new decimal-system method of classification that would standardize organization of library holdings. On June 9, 1902, thirty-eight library advocates founded the Texas Library Association. Promoted by the Texas Federation of Women's Clubs and the University of Texas, the group established ambitious goals and chose University of Texas President William Prather to serve as its first president.[40]

Julia's lifelong support for the TLA began on November 18, 1904, when she welcomed attendees at the association's third annual meeting to the Carnegie Library for the 3:30 p.m. concluding session. While in Houston, librarians from Fort Worth, San Antonio, Galveston, Waco, and the University of Texas met Julia and fellow library leaders Elizabeth Ring and Ethel Jones, as well as clubwomen who were members of the association. Session participants discussed proposals for a state library commission, elected officers for the coming year, and heard "several papers on library topics." Attendees at the fourth TLA meeting, held in Waco in May 1906, elected Julia secretary (1907–1909). Important topics of the year mirrored problems facing the Houston library: professional training, lifetime education through public lectures, the role of libraries in the lives and education of children, and technical problems of library management. After the sixth TLA meeting in June 1908, held in Fort Worth, Julia spent meaningful time at the Dallas and Fort Worth public libraries. That year she produced the first edition of *The Handbook of Texas Libraries,* a compendium of all the libraries in the state with descriptions of their programs and holdings. Julia also lobbied to establish the Texas State Library and Archives Commission, a goal achieved in 1909. In 1910 the TLA met in Houston during the first week of May. Louise Raphael led a committee of five to entertain delegates, and visitors enjoyed a puppet show and lawn party at a private home and a trip to Galveston's Rosenberg Library after their business sessions. Librarians reported receiving "much useful information," and Houstonians were delighted when their librarian was elected president of the organization by delegates "who regard her as possessed of unusual qualifications for library work."[41]

In her capacity as president (1910–1911), Julia represented the Texas Library Association at the New York State Library Association meeting at Lake George that October. She spent "a week long to be remembered" and met "the leading lights" of the library profession. In a report to the Houston Library Association board, Julia described the "lovely body of sapphire water that lies in the midst of beautiful tree-covered hills" just tinged with fall color. Colleagues had received her with "great cordiality," she wrote, and she was particularly impressed by the presidential address, which outlined a "revolution in education" affecting both teachers and librarians. Other lectures during the week touched on matters affecting Houston's library: selecting books, appealing to the public, working with teachers, using photographs and lantern slides to enhance lectures, and the need to "open the eyes and ears to the poetry about us in nature and life." For five more weeks, Julia enjoyed her vacation and traveled home via Louisville, Memphis, and New Orleans so she could visit the libraries in those cities.[42]

Reaching Out: 1905–1914

Julia Ideson's second year as librarian brought exciting news. Houston businessman Teolin Pillot, who had purchased the property and extensive book collections amassed by bookseller George Baldwin in the late 1890s, now donated one thousand volumes to the Houston Lyceum and Carnegie Library. Public announcement of this gift allowed Julia to establish management procedures for the library's growing collections and to define collaboration between the

Library Association board and the City of Houston.[43] Julia was fast becoming the public face and guiding hand of Houston's public library, but the library's chain of command was unusual. In July 1905 Houstonians adopted an elective commission form of governance overseen by a mayor and four commissioners, who supervised a small professional staff and cooperated with volunteer boards tasked with overseeing public schools, property appraisals, public health, and the public library. Touted as management "on business principles" with clear lines of responsibility, in practice, the new system was weak.[44] Although the mayor and commissioners allocated funding, authorized expenditures, and named the slate of Library Association board members and officers, they recoiled from asserting their taxing authority and were happy to turn over management of the library to its volunteer board and capable librarian.

The Library Association board during the years before World War I comprised seven to nine members who were fully engaged with committee work. The mayor and public school superintendent were ex officio members. Superintendent Professor Paul Whitfield Horn attended meetings regularly and worked closely with Librarian Ideson on school, library, and civic initiatives. The volunteer board president gaveled monthly meetings to order, and members expressed their opinions strongly, but the central focus of each meeting was Julia's meticulous report, outlining every expenditure and enumerating book circulation and patron attendance. Julia regularly brought concerns before the board, and many issues were referred to the Administrative, Finance, Building, Book, or Rules and Regulations committees for further action. The board appointed other committees, some having only one participant, to examine specific issues, and delegations, again often with only one or two delegates, carried board proposals to the mayor's office when official authorization was required. Julia sat on every committee as a full or ex officio member.

Board members recognized that the librarians worked long hours, and as early as 1905, they granted Julia a six-week vacation. During her first extended leave the observant librarian visited Harvard University Library in Cambridge, the nation's oldest public library in Boston, several libraries in New York City, the Dana Library in Newark, New Jersey, and the Library of Congress in Washington, DC. While sincerely impressed by the superb collections housed in these established institutions, Julia also proved a gracious ambassador for Houston's library collections and programs. For forty years, she used her annual vacation time to exchange ideas with librarians from towns and cities of many states and several European countries, and she happily incorporated successful programs and policies from other libraries in her own planning.

Julia Ideson with fellow librarians at the American Library Association Annual Meeting, Asheville, North Carolina, 1907. Left to right: Julia Ideson, W. H. Brett, unidentified, Miss S. Askew, and W. S. Burns. Courtesy of the American Library Association Archives.

The board also provided a stipend for Julia to attend the American Library Association annual meetings in May or June. She and other Texas librarians reported continuous growth in their state's use of libraries, and after World War I, Julia assumed leadership positions in the national organization. Sometimes the meetings coincided with her annual vacation, and she always included visits to local or regional libraries on her itinerary.

Julia emphasized programming for children. Loan statistics from these years show that juvenile circulation held steady at around 2,200 books per month. Norman Meldrum continued to support the beautifully furnished

Norma Meldrum Children's Room with donations to the Norma Meldrum Children's Library Fund. In 1910 he authorized his banker W. B. Chew, president of Commercial National Bank, to "honor all checks and drafts" drawn against the fund by his wife, Edith, or by Julia Ideson, enabling both women to enjoy mutually pleasurable searches for the expanding collection. Julia's Saturday morning ten o'clock story hour for young children quickly outgrew the Meldrum alcove and by 1906 had moved to the lecture hall. On December 29, the *Houston Post* announced that popular storyteller, poet, and humorist Judd Mortimer Lewis[45] would delight Houston youngsters with the tale of "Solomon Crow's Christmas Pockets" that morning. Three years later, on September 1, 1909, children's poet Eugene Field[46] drew a crowd of three hundred, and everyone had to move next door to the First Presbyterian Church. The *Houston Post* columnist who reported the event commended Julia's "unqualified" success and hard work and praised the volunteer teachers and citizens who willingly entertained the "several thousand" children who had attended story hour during the past year.[47] In October 1908, the Library Association board voted to hire an assistant librarian to manage the Children's Department, and in March 1911, staff moved the children's room upstairs to make more space for children's activities and provide an office for the specialist who successfully supervised programs and book purchases for Houston's youngest readers. Always proud to advertise her activities, Julia agreed to organize a display at the *Child Welfare Exhibit* of the Texas State Fair in Dallas in October 1912 to show how Texas libraries could benefit children.

School Superintendent P. W. Horn assumed leadership of Houston's public schools just as Julia was introducing her plans for the Carnegie Library. The two professionals were kindred spirits who believed in the efficacy of education and reading to improve, even rebuild, society. American Library Association policy outlined school reforms to "bring teachers and librarians into . . . mutually helpful relations," and by 1900 many school systems welcomed library books in their classrooms. Horn inaugurated regular "teacher institutes" to discuss practical issues confronting his teaching staff. As guest speaker at a teacher institute on Saturday, January 20, 1906, Julia noted she had already begun to work with teachers in some of the schools. In her "significant" remarks, she laid out a cooperative plan, explaining that librarians were also educators who enhanced classroom curricula by lending books to public schools, and she asked teachers to encourage students and their families to visit the library. Julia expressed empathy for teachers who tackled the "reading question" that plagued state and national librarians for decades: how could libraries, as extensions of educational systems, encourage their patrons to read the literary canon or practical nonfiction rather than popular novels? Within months of Julia's talk at the institute, teachers were clamoring for her advice and for loans from the library.[48]

Two requests in the fall of 1907 promised to expand library patronage further and to address one of Julia's critical problems—how to reach out to Houstonians who could not easily visit the Carnegie Library. The first request came in October, when a delegation from the Settlement Association, organized that February by Alice Baker and a group of civic-minded women, petitioned the Library Association for books to place in a reading room at the Rusk School neighborhood settlement; the women also requested the room be considered a branch of the library. Although the group did not expect "material aid," it hoped to borrow library books to help the area's predominantly immigrant population learn English and understand US history and culture. On November 23 Miss Peck, supervisor of primary education in the public school system, made the second request when she told the Library Association board that parents would be "very much interested" in having regular deposit stations placed in their schools to make it "more convenient" for residents to enjoy library books. Volunteers, she promised, would help administer the book exchanges. If hardworking men and women could not come to the library, then perhaps the library should go to them. On December 10, 1907, the Library Association board unanimously adopted a motion to open delivery stations in ward schools, on condition an adult volunteer, "preferably a teacher," would act as custodian of the books and oversee their distribution.[49] By 1910, the library maintained deposit stations at Rusk Settlement, Reagan School, Sherman School, and Lubbock School. Julia reported to the Board on November 1, 1910, that the Woman's Club of Woodland Heights had volunteered to furnish a library room in the streetcar suburb northwest of downtown and would oversee distribution twice a week, if the library could send them fifty volumes. In 1911, deposit stations at the McKee Street Methodist Church and the Washington Avenue Methodist Church joined the locations at Woodland Heights, Rusk Settlement, and four schools. Julia regularly reported on these outreach programs at board meetings. She and her assistants visited the stations, introduced story hour, and in 1913 even addressed a night school class sponsored by Rusk Settlement in the German language spoken by many neighborhood residents.

While Julia explored ways to encourage every Houstonian to read and supported requests to help the immigrant population served by Rusk Settlement, she also considered proposals to bring library services to Houston's African

American community at a time when Jim Crow laws mandating segregated school systems and restricting use of public transportation and public facilities were replacing de facto separation of black and white Texans. Noting the effectiveness of Houston's white clubwomen, Houston's African American female leaders formed the Married Ladies Social, Art and Charity Club in 1902. Open to seventy "respectable married women living with their husbands in Harris County," the club rallied support for causes affecting its membership and inspired formation of several other civic clubs.[50] These civic-minded women were among the first to imagine a public library for their community. When Hollywood School Principal Professor Edward Ollington Smith[51] was refused service at the Carnegie Library in 1906, he discovered that these clubwomen and many of their husbands were ready to organize a Colored Library Association and request library service under the aegis of the Houston Library Association. Smith immediately found two powerful allies in Julia Ideson and his boss, P. W. Horn.

After his snub at the circulation desk, Smith accepted leadership of the drive to build a "Colored Branch" and wrote to Julia to request a meeting with the Library Association board. The librarian welcomed Smith's actions because she realized his advocacy would enable the Houston Library Association to serve the African American community. The association board first discussed the prospect of a "colored branch" on June 9, 1908, and authorized Superintendent Horn and the Reverend Harris Masterson to meet with Smith's committee. On Aug. 1, 1908, Smith submitted a plan to the association board, "asking assistance" to "establish a colored branch." Six weeks later on September 15, the Library Association board unanimously approved Smith's plan for a library book deposit station as a first step: "if the colored people would secure the use of suitable rooms and attendants, the library would donat [*sic*] one hundred dollars, and such duplicates as could be spared." Julia promised to train a librarian and to help Smith's group secure funding for a library branch building. Following an October meeting, Houston Library Association officers finally spoke to the press. E. O. Smith, the *Houston Post* reporter explained, had "called attention to the fact that there is no public reading room or depository of books in Houston available to the colored people." Smith's request for a book deposit station was "favorably received," and Julia told reporters the plan as outlined by the board was "feasible."[52] She and her staff immediately found 270 duplicate books and helped Smith's committee select and catalogue 264 new books, purchased with $200 donated by friends of the Houston Library Association board. The Houston Board of Education authorized placing a library station at Colored High School for three years. Emma Meyers took up her duties as librarian on May 5, 1909, and began making monthly reports of station activities to the Library Association board; she noted 356 loans in her June 8 report and 375 on November 18. Smith's Colored Library Association board of five volunteers managed the station's programs, but Julia integrated the station expenses into her planning and annual budget. In 1910 the Houston Library Association allocated $500 a year for Librarian Emma Meyers's salary and approved her request for two weeks leave and two weeks of vacation that summer, provided she could find a substitute.

While the deposit station at the corner of San Felipe and Frederick streets provided library books for Houston's African American population, Smith continued his quest for a full-fledged library branch. In 1910, he enlarged the Colored Library Association board by four members, whose sole job was to raise money for a new building. At the Houston Library Association board meeting on November 8, 1910, members read a communication from Smith stating that this fundraising committee had successfully held a variety of events. The committee had paid $500 down to purchase a lot from the United Brothers of Friendship Lodge on the corner of Frederick and Robin streets in the Fourth Ward, and J. B. Bell had assumed the balance due of $1,000. Smith had also written to Booker T. Washington, whose secretary was native Houstonian Emmott J. Scott; Washington and Scott agreed to help the Houston group apply to Andrew Carnegie for a construction grant. Although Carnegie had turned down a 1909 request from the Houston Library Association for funds to build an addition to the original library, he happily provided funds to build the new branch library, adding his usual stipulation that the library be incorporated and the city defray maintenance costs. On April 28, 1911, the state granted a charter, and the city signed a contract with Carnegie and the Colored Library Association: Carnegie would provide $15,000 to cover construction, and the city would pay $150 per year for upkeep. To celebrate and support the library, fifty leading citizens paid fifty dollars apiece to dine with Booker T. Washington at the handsome home of influential Houston physician Benjamin J. Covington and his civic-minded wife, Jennie, on September 27, 1911.

Smith's committee immediately hired William Sidney Pittman,[53] the best known African American architect in the United States, to design and build the community's long-desired temple of learning. The son-in-law of Booker T. Washington, Pittman had studied at Tuskegee Institute for a year before being offered a scholarship to the all-white Drexel Institute in Philadelphia. A talented designer and draftsman, he completed Drexel's five-year program in

Carnegie Colored Library dedication, April 11, 1913. MSS0114–1115, Library Collection, Houston Public Library, Houston Metropolitan Research Center.

three years and established a practice in Washington, DC, where he worked on other Carnegie-funded projects. Pittman moved to Dallas in 1913 and became the first practicing black architect in Texas. The well-built structure Pittman designed for Houston incorporated the expected elements for Carnegie libraries. The main rooms occupied a one-story rectangle set above a full-story raised basement. Wide entry steps led from the sidewalk to a central entrance framed by two pillars that supported a handsome pediment. The building housed an auditorium, a children's reading room, and an adult reading room. Like the central library, this branch sponsored children's story hours and reading clubs, and adult patrons could choose from an array of newspapers and periodicals. Houston Colored Carnegie Library, dedicated on April 11, 1913, continued to operate under Smith's volunteer board until 1921, when the city charter was amended for funding purposes to place the branch permanently under the direction of the Houston Library Association board. Houston Colored Carnegie patrons strongly objected to the decision because the association board had no black members at that time, but the monetary advantages overcame opposition.

Julia Ideson also supported a 1909 initiative to establish a library at the Baptist Temple in Houston Heights, then an independent suburb of Houston connected to the city by an electric railway line. The privately funded library opened with one thousand volumes of literary classics, historical works, and biblical literature, all housed at the Baptist Temple in cabinets boasting "handsome shelves with glass doors." Librarian Julia Spencer, an experienced teacher "well informed in the world of literature," supervised the collections and managed a department for children. Enthusiastic supporters and several local pastors gathered at the library's dedication to hear a "splendid address" on the life and philosophy of Leo Tolstoy by theologian Benajah Harvey Carroll, former Waco pastor and then president of Southwestern Baptist Theological Seminary. In her brief congratulatory remarks, Julia Ideson noted there were "entirely too few libraries in this part of the state." She explained that only about 10 percent of Houston residents could easily access the city's Carnegie Library, and she believed the Baptist Temple library "was the greatest thing" its supporters "could do for their part of the city."[54]

Programming Challenges: 1907–1914

Julia Ideson agreed with many members of the Texas and American library associations who saw librarians as crusaders in the quest to improve popular taste and enrich school curricula. She was determined to introduce all Houston's children to the pleasures and values of reading, and she worked tirelessly to make library offerings available to every area of the city, but she did not forget the lawyers, doctors, businessmen, and sophisticated readers who wanted self-improvement and civic reform and who hoped to continue their educations through reading, discussion, and lectures. The lyceum tradition of readings and debate had waned during the last years of the nineteenth century, but clubwomen and other civic groups began to hold their meetings in the library boardroom as soon as the Carnegie building opened. Julia frequently spoke to these groups, as a member or guest, to explain her plans for the library, to introduce topics of civic interest, and to review new acquisitions. Patrons also requested that she highlight library holdings relating to civic and health issues in her frequent press releases and newspaper articles, and she stoutly defended the "several interesting books on civic improvement and kindred subjects" in the library collections.[55] When Julia's book list suggestions proved popular, Southern Printing Company proposed publishing a bulletin listing new library acquisitions and other information in February 1911. The board accepted the plan, and the company distributed periodic printed reminders of library collections during the years before World War I.

The interest in formal lectures generated by these meetings, talks, and published lists led to the idea that the lyceum lecture tradition could be reshaped for the new era. At the Library Association board meeting on October 8, 1907, Julia reported that she had recently attended the founding meeting of the Houston Lecture Association, "although not officially instructed" to do so, because the Library Association board president was out of town. As she often did, Julia took the initiative because she knew "the Board would be willing to co-operate in a movement of this kind."[56] The new lecture association would demand no dues, but members were required to sell tickets and advertise the lectures. Superintendent P. W. Horn was particularly interested in this group and in January 1909 requested that the Library Association board donate twenty-five dollars to help defray expenses for the winter lecture. By November 14, 1911, Horn's discussions with Ideson and interested Library Association board members led him to advocate a more elaborate proposal. Horn gave the committee a list of nationally known lecturers who would be touring Texas in 1912. He suggested the Library Association and the public school Board of Education cooperate with the Lecture Association as co-presenters for lectures in Houston. Horn, Ideson, Louise Raphael, and Mrs. E. N. Gray agreed to investigate the matter and report in January.

In Houston's small leadership circle, matters could be addressed quickly. At the meeting on January 9, 1912, Raphael announced that Rice Institute would like to provide "financial aid" for the lectures, and Gray reported that the mayor had agreed to allocate $250 in city funds. Louise Raphael's husband, Emanuel, since 1891 the secretary of the Rice Institute Board of Trustees, knew the institute, still under construction, hoped to develop a series of public lectures. Cooperating with the library and lecture associations seemed an ideal first step. Excited by this firm support, the Library Association board agreed that if Rice Institute and the city could provide $500, and the school and library boards could each provide $100, the total of $700 would enable the sponsoring organizations to offer three lectures each year at no charge to the public. By February 13, 1912, donations of $500 from Rice Institute and $250 from the city were in the bank, and the first presentation—lectures on Arabia, Turkey, and India—had been held at Beach Auditorium over three days before increasingly large audiences. The cosponsors announced a roster of nationally acclaimed guest speakers, including Dr. George Pierce Baker of Harvard, who gave a talk on April 16, 1912, about "The Drama as a Social Force."[57]

Successful programs, steadily growing reader participation, and enthusiastic community support ensured Julia's popularity and board respect. She was making the library essential to all Houstonians. However, almost from the first board meeting, three persistent problems plagued library progress: building maintenance and space for collections and activities, retention of trained personnel, and sufficient funds from municipal and private sources. As early as September 1907, the trustees learned that the building's "modern" heating apparatus needed to be "thoroughly overhauled" and that the electrical lighting needed to be updated with fixtures that were cheaper to operate. That fall, Julia also announced plans to allocate more space for reference materials and expressed her wish that patrons be allowed to browse among open stacks. She explained that displaying popular fiction and nonfiction of general interest in accessible, or "open," stacks had become common procedure "in many of our best libraries." The board approved the necessary repairs and Julia's proposals, and on November 23, 1907, the librarian announced the public would have free access to "readable books of all classes," displayed on bookshelves in the alcove originally allocated to reference works. Two years later, in December 1909, Julia again tried to accommodate library patrons; the reading room was moved upstairs to the former public documents room, leaving more room downstairs for reference materials and open shelves.[58]

In December 1910, Julia learned that the area set aside for a law library in the recently built Harris County Courthouse could be made available to the public library for storage of materials that could no longer be accommodated in the reading alcoves or book vault containing thirty-five thousand volumes. Julia accepted the offer enthusiastically and obtained funds to finish the courthouse space as a library annex. Her staff moved bound volumes of newspapers, government documents, Circle M curios and uncatalogued items, and duplicate or rarely used books to this annex in 1911. The next year, Julia also placed newly acquired volumes of important county census records from the 1850s and 1860s in the courthouse space. In December 1912, Julia announced a major reorganization of the library building's interior space. The room originally designated for club and board meetings would become the children's room, and the rest of the space upstairs would become the adult reading room and would house magazines, periodicals, and current government pamphlets. Downstairs, patrons would browse in expanded open stacks, which included a wide assortment of popular reference works. No longer did Mr. Carnegie's elegant temple provide adequate space for the library's growing collections and the public's increasing demand for reading materials and educational activities.

Building a strong professional staff also proved challenging due to limited funds. Julia quickly became widely known as a superb mentor, and by 1907 graduates of library programs were writing her for permission to serve as free apprentices for four to six months. Some of these applicants, mostly young women, remained as paid staff, while others carried the lessons of Houston's librarian to small towns across Texas. Pay was low; after four years of service, Julia received $1,200 a year, while her five staffers were paid thirty-five to fifty dollars per month. In 1910 Julia's salary was raised to $1,500 a year, and when Martha Schnitzer, originally hired to catalogue the Circle M Collection, added library bookkeeping to her duties in the summer of 1911, she received a twenty-five-dollar raise to seventy-five dollars a month. To accommodate patrons and avoid the hot midday hours, librarians often worked from 8:30 a.m. until 10:00 p.m., with a long break in the middle of the day. Debilitating illness and unexpected resignations seemed to plague the staff; overwork and fatigue were often cited as causes for both. From December 4, 1908, until February 23, 1909, Julia herself fought typhoid fever. Early in her prolonged ordeal, she received a letter from Louise Raphael, the Library Association board's corresponding secretary, who wrote on January 13, 1909, to commiserate about the "trying illness" and tell her she "must not worry a moment over the library administration as it is going along evenly and is well attended to, owing to your excellent management."[59] Despite personnel turnover and budget restraints that made hiring inexperienced apprentices necessary, by May 1913, Julia oversaw six professionally trained employees.

Julia's ability to develop programs, maintain the building, and retain staff depended on city funding. At first the original municipal allotment of $4,000 per year seemed sufficient, if not generous, support, but by April 1908 demands for higher salaries and expensive repairs caused the board to ask city commissioners to increase the library appropriation to $5,000 in 1909. Officials agreed to consider the increase, but only if assistant librarians were paid on the same basis as public school teachers. The board accepted this condition and promptly granted raises to its four assistant librarians, effective March 1. In 1909, for the first time, the board felt its finances were "sufficiently strong" to authorize spending $200 per month for new books, and in March 1910 the mayor supported another increase of $1,000 for the 1910–1911 fiscal year. In 1911 the commissioners rebuffed a March request to raise the annual stipend by another $1,000, claiming additional sums would be "impossible" due to the city's deficit.[60] However, in 1912 demands for space and pay raises were so urgent that the board requested $12,000 for the March 1912–February 1913 fiscal year, and in January 1913, the board lobbied the mayor for a $15,000 grant, including a tenfold raise to $1,500 for the recently opened Colored Carnegie Library. Annual donation lists showed that numerous citizens and companies made small monetary gifts and in-kind donations to help defray expenses. Rental fees from the many civic groups that held events in the auditorium or met in the boardroom also provided funds, even though the board only allowed groups that did not charge fees for their activities to use library space. No resolution of funding issues had been reached in 1913, when Julia accepted an unusual offer.

As the tenth anniversary of Julia Ideson's tenure as Houston's public librarian approached, she could look back on the decade with pride. She had made many friends for the library and had established herself as the revered voice of an institution beloved throughout the city. Her success had come at a price—long hours, intermittent serious illness, ongoing and unresolved struggles over money, and tensions between library board members and the mayor had all taken their toll. Even while on vacation, Julia explored local libraries wherever she went. On September 14, 1912, the San Antonio Carnegie Library offered her a job as head librarian. She was tempted, and Houston Library Association board members expressed alarm. The board reassured her but realized that perhaps it was time for a sabbatical. When the American Art Students' Club in Paris invited Julia to join them for a year as club secretary from December 1, 1913, to December 1, 1914, she accepted. Martha Schnitzer, the well-qualified assistant librarian, stepped up to serve as acting librarian. Board and staff members regretted "losing [Julia] as a personal and official member" for the year but praised her accomplishments. "We count it a very happy privilege thus to express the high value we place upon your ten years of service, . . . a service marked by rare wisdom, personal faithfulness and intelligent effectiveness." In a letter written on behalf of the board, Elizabeth Ring presented the beloved librarian a platinum wristwatch. Ring noted she was the only current member who had been on the board ten years earlier when some felt the job might be "too big a task for such a young girl," but, Ring continued, "From the first you have put your whole soul into your work. . . . You have kept the board in touch with library work all over the country. You have succeeded in making this the most efficient library in the State of Texas. Whatever you may do in the future you will have the satisfaction of knowing that your work in Houston has been a great success." Houstonians celebrated Julia's Parisian adventure with elegant bon voyage events. The College Women's Club entertained its departing founder at a "farewell compliment" reception from four until six on Tuesday evening, November 23. Artist Emma Richardson Cherry and her husband, Dillon, welcomed "a few friends very delightfully" at an evening party on November 27. On the Tuesday afternoon before Julia left Houston, the Woman's Political Union invited the public to say farewell to the woman who had "endeared herself to a wide circle of friends." Union directors Louise Masterson, Mrs. J. W. Parker, Mrs. Lockhart Wallis, and Annette Finnigan organized tea at the Thalian Club ballroom from 4:00 p.m. to 6:00 p.m. Houston's leading women, including Alice Baker and Ima Hogg, assisted as hostesses. With these happy memories, Julia Ideson departed for Paris.[61]

Friends and Colleagues

Blessed with kindness, tact, and good humor, Julia Ideson had endeared herself to Houston's civic leaders, society hostesses, and library patrons during her first decade as director of Houston Lyceum and Carnegie Library. Admired for her "deep seriousness of purpose," Julia "maintained an air of light-heartedness" that produced an "unusual quality of leadership" and made friends for the library and for herself. Society columnists recorded her social success and personal popularity. In May 1905, Julia helped the mother of a bride serve "distinguished" guests at a magnificent, rose-bedecked wedding, described by the "Houston Society" columnist in minute detail. Julia and a bevy of Houston's younger "set" supported chairwoman Kate (Mrs. E. B.) Parker as hostesses for an evening reception and dancing party at the Thalian Club when Sidney Edward Mezes, fifth president of the University of Texas, visited Houston alumni on November 9, 1908, with faculty and students in tow. In late February 1909, Louise (Mrs. Harris) Masterson invited Julia and fifty-five women and young ladies to help her entertain the wife of Harvard President Charles William Eliot, when the venerable educational reformer traveled to Houston during the last year of his four-decade tenure transforming the New England college into a renowned research university. Throwing wide the doors of her grand home from 4:00 p.m. to 6:00 p.m., Masterson offered the "ladies of Houston" an opportunity to meet Mrs. Eliot "personally" during her brief stay in the city. When Kate Friend from Waco presented a Shakespearean lecture, illustrated by stereopticon pictures taken under her supervision while she traveled in Europe, Julia was listed among Houston's most significant women as a patroness for the public event, held at the Young Men's Christian Association building on Wednesday evening, February 16, 1910. In 1913 she joined her dear friends Ima Hogg, Annette Finnigan, Emma Richardson Cherry, and a roster of leading women in the Cherry home to honor Cherry's debutante daughter at an afternoon open house that preceded an evening dance.[62]

Press reports noted Julia's travels to conferences and meetings to visit friends and to spend long summers in Mexico, New England, Colorado, or Europe. During a visit to Mexico in the fall of 1908, Julia flattered one *Houston Post* reporter by explaining that the home paper was a "daily necessity even in Mexico." A lucid writer and lively lecturer, Julia described her trips in long newspaper articles. After her first four-month adventure in Europe, Julia illuminated the glories of Milan Cathedral and Italian paintings to the Ladies Reading Club, of which she was an honorary member. She supported early efforts to expand the city's professional music scene and worked with Houston's first music critic, Wille Hutcheson, the Reverend Peter Gray Sears, and Rabbi Henry Barnstein to form the Public School March Music Board, self-appointed to collect sheet music of patriotic and classical march compositions and to distribute bound copies to public school pianists and music teachers. In May 1909, Julia joined dozens of Houston music lovers to support the May Music Festival choral and symphony concert at the Prince Theatre, featuring soloists from the Chicago Symphony Orchestra. Asked in June 1913 to play Miss Prossy (Secretary Proserpine Garnett) in an amateur performance of George Bernard Shaw's 1894 *Candida*, Julia revealed her keen sense of humor and "kept things lively with a sharp and apparently practiced tongue," a contrast to her public persona of "quiet courtesy."[63]

During her first decade as librarian, Julia helped inaugurate two important civic organizations, the Houston Museum and Scientific Society in 1909 and the College Women's Club in 1910. For several years Julia had hoped to find an appropriate home for the many objects collected by John E. T. Milsaps on his travels in the Pacific, and in June 1909 she hosted a planning meeting at the Carnegie Library to consider establishing a scientific society and a museum of natural science. On Friday evening, October 1, she and other sponsors approved a charter application to state officials to establish the Houston Museum and Scientific Society for the study of specimens from the natural world. Also present at these meetings were Superintendent P. W. Horn, who believed the society and a future museum would benefit the Houston school curriculum, and J. H. G. Becker, a "prominent" naturalist and expert in cotton cultivation who had assembled "probably one of the most complete" collections of rare East African plant, mineral, and animal specimens. In June 1910 the society received its state charter, and Mayor Horace Baldwin Rice agreed to provide space in the new City Auditorium for storage and display of the Milsaps and other collections stored in the library basement. The new society also persuaded Professor Henry Philemon Attwater to catalogue his extensive collection of Texas specimens, including a mighty bison, and place the objects on loan in the auditorium museum "indefinitely." It would be five decades before a museum of natural science building began to rise on the edge of Hermann Park, but Julia had solved her Milsaps problem. The generous, if eccentric, donor had unexpectedly sent twenty-six cases of books to the library in November 1910 and visited Julia a few days later. Librarian Ideson reported to the board in December that Mr. Milsaps "expressed satisfaction at the manner of caring for the collection" and would be happy to place his curios with the Houston Museum and Scientific Society. While enthusiastically supporting the creation of a museum and society devoted to the natural world, Julia also "issued a call to the college women of Houston" to form a club that would investigate the living and working "conditions of women in Houston" and "provide an efficient corps of leaders" to serve female needs. The original group of thirty-five young women elected Julia president for the inaugural 1910–1911 year and announced that "active work" of the Women's College Club would start at once. Among Julia's last actions before she left for her year in France was her effort to help the club sponsor a consumers league to protect unwary shoppers.[64]

Julia Ideson shared her love of the arts with her college friend, Ima Hogg, who had moved to Houston in 1909 to join brother Will after a long period of study and travel in Europe. The college friendship deepened in the next decades as both women worked tirelessly to nurture Houston's cultural life and bring social justice to all residents. Julia and Ima joined the Girls' Musical Club when it was formed at Alice Baker's home in 1912 and in later years enjoyed motoring around the country together. The two women exchanged personal news in long letters when apart, and Ima illustrated her travels with postcard mementos from favorite touring destinations. When former Houston resident Annette Finnigan[65] returned to the city in 1903 to help manage her father's business interests, she discovered common bonds with the new librarian. Julia later praised Finnigan for having "the most thorough and brilliant mind of any-one I know," and others believed them to be "best friends." Both women were "charming and intelligent," both were college graduates, and both forcefully fought for their beliefs. The battle to enfranchise women drew them together; a mutual love of books cemented their alliance.[66]

Suffrage Advocate: 1903–1914

Women's suffrage in Texas briefly found champions in Dallas, when forty women and ten men organized the Texas Equal Rights Association (1893–1896) as a branch of the National American Woman Suffrage Association (NAWSA). Annette Finnigan and her father, John, expressed enthusiasm for the suffrage cause while living in New York City, and in 1901 they attended a conference of the New York Equal Suffrage League. Annette served as corresponding secretary of the league and in 1902 joined NAWSA's executive committee, capably led by President Carrie Chapman Catt. When Annette and her sisters Elizabeth Finnigan and Katherine Anderson resettled in Houston, they decided to revive the suffrage question. In February 1903 they invited men and women who supported votes for women to meet in their home, where the group formed the Houston Equal Suffrage League and voted to ask NAWSA President Catt to visit Houston in March 1903. The Finnigan sisters then helped women in Galveston organize a league that summer. At a Houston convention in December the two groups met to form the Texas Equal Suffrage Association (TESA) and hear NAWSA Vice President Dr. Anna Howard Shaw inspire the crowd. Described by one admiring reporter as young, buoyant, and full of hope, Annette served as TESA president from 1903 until 1906 and brought newsworthy national suffragists to public meetings in Houston. John Finnigan supported his daughters' efforts eagerly and urged his business friends to advocate for equal suffrage.

When the Finnigans returned to New York City in 1906, enthusiasm for the suffrage cause flagged. Julia Ideson had joined the Equal Suffrage League when she returned to Houston in 1903, and she tried to carry on Finnigan's work. On Sunday, April 30, 1906, at 3:30 p.m., she addressed the league meeting in the reception rooms of the *Houston Post*. Julia analyzed the liberal philosopher and naturalist John Stuart Mill's autobiography, while Catherine Emmott (1862–1949) discussed the influential philosopher's writings on "The Subjection of Women" and the need for women's suffrage. The *Houston Post* and newspapers across Texas proved faithful to the cause of votes for women and kept the issue alive by covering local meetings and the 1908 Texas tour of recently elected NAWSA President Anna Howard Shaw. Although militant British suffragette Emmeline Pankhurst and her daughter Christabel did not travel to Texas in 1909, their national tour created a statewide sensation when press photographs and banner headlines announced that the recently jailed agitators would help their American sisters. Texas readers were spellbound by heroic tales of marches, hunger strikes, and other disruptive actions, but most American suffrage leaders found the aggressive Pankhurst tactics alarming.

John Finnigan died in 1909, and Annette took control of his business interests, dividing her time between New York City and Houston. In 1912 the suffrage issue again claimed her attention when Shaw made a second tour of Texas. In January 1912 Finnigan established the Woman's Political Union in Houston to revive the aspirations of the earlier Houston Equal Suffrage League. Supporters of women's suffrage met at 10:00 a.m. on January 28 to elect officers for the year and to announce plans for increasing membership and "bringing noted speakers in the suffrage cause" to Houston.[67] Annette Finnigan was named president, Louise Masterson first vice president, and Julia Ideson treasurer. A few days later, prominent clubwoman Mary Eleanor Brackenridge[68] formed the Equal Franchise Society in San Antonio to provide lectures and educate the public about woman suffrage. In April 1913 Brackenridge persuaded the San Antonio Equal Franchise Society to host a suffrage convention. One hundred people from seven local pro-suffrage organizations met in San Antonio to hold the first state convention since 1904 and to reestablish the Texas Equal Suffrage Association (TESA). Finnigan served as honorary chairwoman of the convention, and Brackenridge was named president for the 1913 term, while Finnigan served as president in 1914 and 1915. Brackenridge set up a suffrage clipping bureau and asked members to send articles to TESA headquarters in San Antonio. On May 19, 1913, Emmeline Pankhurst rallied Houston supporters at the City Auditorium during her second US tour, and Julia helped arrange a reception in her honor. In late June local leaders decided to convene an outdoor rally featuring Finnigan and Ideson as speakers. Although many patrons were discouraged from attending by bad weather, latecomers were able to talk informally with both women after the meeting was postponed one week.

When Annette Finnigan turned her attention to statewide activities, "witty" and "experienced" NAWSA organizer Perle Penfield became president of the Woman's Political Union of Houston. Ignoring the city's sultry summer temperatures, Penfield announced an ambitious campaign to rally support for equal suffrage at a series of outdoor evening meetings in every ward of the city. The first four meetings, scheduled for the week of July 14, were held at the Hawthorne School playground, Elizabeth Baldwin Park, Settegast Park, and on the lawn of suffrage spokeswoman Catherine Emmott's home in Brunner, three miles west of downtown. Each meeting was organized by volunteer hostesses and managed by a presiding chairwoman. At each meeting, Penfield spoke forcefully, reviewing the worldwide fight to secure votes for women and explaining the recent biennial convention of the International Woman Suffrage Alliance, whose attendees in Budapest included representatives from some of the twenty-five nations where women had secured the vote. Julia Ideson managed the Baldwin Park meeting on Tuesday night, "one of the largest and most enthusiastic yet held," and joined Penfield as featured speaker on Thursday evening.[69] Press coverage was consistently positive but failed to sway everyone. In November, dissenting males held a mock suffragette parade downtown, complete with banners, speechifying, and ridicule. Julia's departure for France came at a moment of heightened interest in equal suffrage, and when she returned she joined the final campaign for a constitutional amendment.

War, Peace, and Politics: 1914–1919

Julia Ideson's sojourn in Paris began as she had expected with opportunities to make new friends and to visit places she had only imagined through reading. Just as her 1911 travels in Italy had awakened a love for Italian paintings, so her 1914 sabbatical in the heart of Paris stimulated a curiosity about French culture. Her duties for the American Art Students' Club were easily managed and left ample time to explore Paris and its environs with the Houston friends who visited the city during her stay. That summer she and her sister Margaret Ladd planned to take a walking trip into the Black Forest, with a preliminary trip to Belgium, but the assassination of Austrian Archduke Franz Ferdinand and his wife, Sophie, on June 28, followed by five weeks of tense negotiation and rumbles of war, threatened this adventure. Friends and officials told Julia not to travel in the Low Countries, but she and Margaret left for Liège, Belgium, which was "peaceful and quiet" when they arrived on August 1. Discovering that train service into Germany "had been suspended," the sisters set out on foot the next day for a nearby town. They got no further than the frontier when "a rush of Germans back to their own country" forced them to return to Liège. They found the city "in a panic, for rumors" of an approaching German army were "rife." The Ideson sisters jumped on a troop train headed west to Brussels, where the "pitiable sight" of weeping women greeted them. Twenty-four hours after they escaped Liège, the charming city "was a mass of ruins." The train from Brussels stranded the sisters at the Belgian border fifteen miles from Lille, but after the long walk across the border into France, they managed to obtain seats from Lille to Paris on a train "jammed to its utmost capacity with people hurrying to their families and men going to enlist."[70]

In Paris Julia found that in one week, the city "had become an entirely different place from the glittering capital we had left." In a dispatch to the *Houston Post* that she sent from England, Julia described the scene. The city was "in mourning" and its citizens were "under siege." Buses had been commandeered, the metro was closed, and there was "not one" taxi at the station. The sisters set off on foot, lugging their bags, but finally just stopped and waited for an available cab. At their pension, all was gloom, and the men had gone. Cafés were deserted and museums closed. Most shops were shuttered, although one had a sign announcing, "This shop will be reopened on my return from Berlin." Angry crowds attacked anyone suspected of being German, raged at the "perfidy of the military party," and showed "an air of hatred for an emperor who for the sake of national aggrandizement will plunge nations into a terrible war." Urged by the United States ambassador, "paralysed [*sic*] compatriots" at the American Express office prepared to flee the city. It took the Ideson sisters nearly one full day to travel the four-hour trip to the coast, where they "secured passage to England on a merchant steamer loaded with vegetables and fowl." In London, searchlights flared across the sky, scanning for German zeppelins. From London, Julia and Margaret traveled to Liverpool, where Julia found passage on the SS *Arabic*, sailing for Boston on September 22. A train to New York City and a sleeper to Houston ended the intrepid traveler's aborted adventure. Free-spirited Margaret remained until September 17, 1916, when she sailed for New York from Bordeaux; her adventures while in war-torn Europe remain unrecorded. As Julia told a reporter later, "I think the best sight I enjoyed, however, was the outline of the city of Houston as it appeared when the train pulled into the station. After all there is no place like home, and I am happy to be back."[71] The beloved librarian returned to her duties on Monday, November 2, 1914.

Despite headlines recounting tragic events abroad as European empires aimed powerful artillery at each other along the eastern and western fronts, Julia's routine seemed quite normal for the next two years. Under Martha Schnitzer's capable management, all library programs had continued to grow in 1914, but the issues Julia had left behind—crowded conditions, overworked staff, and insufficient funds to pay new staff and purchase new books—remained glaringly apparent. Well-dressed children and their parents crowded around reading tables in the Norma Meldrum Room, while serious high school students pored over volumes in the busy research and reference department. When librarians arrived at the Rusk School Settlement and other deposit stations, they could hardly manage the numerous children eager to borrow books. At the monthly meeting of city department heads in March 1915, Julia reported that the Houston library was the most heavily patronized in the state with 20,203 white borrowers and 12,000 patrons of the Colored Carnegie Library that month. She noted that a mere six employees served as many as one thousand visitors on busy days. More money, Julia said, was needed or the library would "go backward."[72] Julia requested an allocation of $1,000 a month, remarking that $7,800 for the Central Library and $1,500 for the Colored Branch barely covered the cost of personnel, with little left to buy books. When the city budgeted $12,000 for the library in 1916, Ideson produced an illustrated report on January 1, 1917, to explain how she had allocated the city appropriation. With six staffers, Julia had helped readers borrow 134,600 books, periodicals, and pamphlets; she had purchased 2,728 adult books and 1,013 children's books; she had managed twenty-three deposit stations, sixteen of them in public schools; over one thousand encyclopedias and dictionaries tempted curious patrons; and the main library stack room, designed for thirty-five thousand volumes, was now crammed with 47,357 books. Like Mayor Ben Campbell, whose 1916 annual report extolled Houston's economic power and scholastic attainments, Julia projected enthusiasm for Houston's future.

Following riveting tales of her flight from Paris and escape back to Houston, Julia discovered that her movements continued to intrigue the newspaper-reading public. Journalists recorded her social engagements—including a "prettily appointed reception" for a bride and groom and their families—her summer travels to Colorado, and a head-on car collision that caused her minor injuries. Julia had left for Paris before her dear friend Ima Hogg joined music clubwoman Kate Parker and cellist Julien Paul Blitz to introduce the state's first professional symphony orchestra at a twilight concert on December 19, 1913, but when the second Symphony Association season opened in November 1914,

Julia was present in Ima Hogg's box, a custom that reporters would record faithfully for three more decades. As library representative, Julia asked each year that the library be allowed to provide a float in the city's Fourth of July parade, an event given wide publicity. In 1915, she presented "a tableaux [*sic*] representing the pleasure the children derive from the library."[73]

In April 1915, Mrs. J. L. Walker revealed that the recently organized Texas Woman's Fair Association would "open its first fair in Houston in October." Critical of the No-Tsu-Oh festival, which celebrated businessmen, cotton, and commerce, Walker and her team intended their annual event to validate female abilities and interests. Organizers obtained a charter in August and marshaled their forces under a twenty-five-member executive board. As a star attraction, they invited Julia Ideson to serve as toastmistress for the College Women's Luncheon at the Bender Hotel. Nearly two hundred college women from around the state reserved tickets to celebrate the finale of a "whole week devoted to women and their activities." The Texas Woman's Fair attracted representatives from eighty-five institutions and celebrated women as homemakers and mothers, farmers and gardeners, teachers and nurses, professionals and businesswomen, and college graduates. A Monday parade of prominent club and professional women riding in automobiles opened the weeklong event, which included programs and activities for girls' clubs and "brilliant musical programs" of a female orchestra conducted by Laura Stevens Boone. On "Farm Women's Day," state and federal farm bureau spokesmen addressed attendees, and Julia spoke about the need to provide county traveling libraries throughout the state. *Post* reporter Harry T. Warner declared the fair "from many standpoints one of the greatest successes Houston has seen." It was "not a society event, . . . not a part of any other movement," it was "for the glorification of the women who are the home makers of Houston and of Texas." The 1916 fair appealed to "all men and women who admired pluck and progressiveness," and the November 1917 fair applauded voluntary war work, patriotism, and women's suffrage. The governor of Illinois reviewed twenty thousand troops sent recently from his state to Camp Logan, and organizers asked clubwoman Anna Pennybacker and suffragist Minnie Fisher Cunningham to address the crowd. This exuberant event was not revived after World War I.[74]

Through her civic work and friendship with Ima Hogg, Julia Ideson became friendly with Estelle Sharp, the sophisticated, wealthy widow of inventor Walter Benona Sharp, whose drilling tools revolutionized the oil industry. The Sharp family had moved to Houston early in 1904, and Estelle immediately turned her attention to social justice issues, serving several times as president of United Charities, a group that changed its name to Social Service Federation in 1912. On September 29, 1916, Sharp incorporated the Texas School of Civics and Philanthropy to secure properly trained men and women for "public social service; for professional positions in voluntary, civic and social agencies; and for effective work as directors, members of committees, friendly visitors, contributors, or in the independent use of time and money for charitable purposes." Sharp was familiar with the Chicago School of Civics and Philanthropy,[75] a pathbreaking effort to research community conditions and train enrollees for community work, and she probably knew that Sophonisba Breckenridge[76] and Edith Adams had interviewed 1,562 families in 1909 to gather statistical evidence of "demoralizing" social conditions.[77] She asked Judge Henry J. Dannenbaum, Houston Foundation Manager M. A. Turner, librarian Julia Ideson, recreation specialist and Rice Institute Professor Charles F. Ward, Houston Foundation Acting Director Martha Gano, and civic leader Mrs. W. F. Wilson to serve as incorporating trustees. In the second year of operation, Sharp replaced Martha Gano and M. A. Turner with Houston Settlement Association founder Alice Baker and public school Superintendent P. W. Horn.

For two years Sharp's School of Civics and Philanthropy met at the YMCA building and generated much interest in social work as an academic discipline and a professional career. Director Stuart A. Queen, a sociologist trained at the University of Chicago, and four Rice Institute professors, supported by a long roster of national and local guest lecturers, covered social work, domestic economy, public health, sanitation, delinquency, settlement work, religion, labor problems, ethics, and local government. Sharp's ambitious experiment to examine the supportive pillars of a just society proved hard to administer independently, but the excitement generated by the school's program led her in 1918 to endow the Sharp Lectureship in Civics and Philanthropy at Rice Institute—the first endowed lectureship at the new university—and to provide four annual student scholarships to train "social workers for social welfare work" in the region.[78] Sharp's initiative, guaranteed by Will Hogg, Joseph Cullinan, Abe Levy, and banker John T. Scott, allowed Rice Institute to create a sociology department and name sociologist John Willis Slaughter its resident lecturer. In February 1918, interest generated by the school's courses encouraged area social workers to form the Social Workers Club of Houston, which met for lunch twice a month to discuss the many social issues challenging its members. The club elected Social Service Bureau Superintendent Lucy J. Collins as president; Harris County School for Girls Superintendent Ethel Claxton as vice president; B'nai B'rith field worker B. Freefield as treasurer; and Librarian Julia Ideson as secretary.

Julia meshed these new civic projects with continued support for the Woman's Political Union of Houston and votes for women. While Julia was in Paris, Annette Finnigan oversaw the Texas Woman Suffrage Association (TWSA) from its Houston headquarters at the Hotel Brazos. Reform-minded clubwomen, especially supporters of the women's temperance movement, had been the first to speak in favor of suffrage for women, and they saw education of the public as their primary goal. In the movement's second phase and final march toward equal suffrage, professional women like publisher and businesswoman Florence Sterling, attorney Hortense Ward, and Women's Trade Union leader and seamstress Eva Goldsmith broadened the base of support and led efforts to organize and politicize the movement through increasingly efficient lobbying of the Texas legislature. Businesswoman Finnigan recruited Minnie Cunningham, founding member and president of the Galveston Equal Suffrage Association, to serve as a statewide field organizer and lobbyist and to establish local pro-suffrage organizations in every senatorial district. In July 1914 Finnigan wrote letters to every legislative candidate to determine if he supported a woman suffrage amendment to the Texas Constitution. Then she asked Woman's Political Union of Houston President Perle Penfield to help her send letters, prepare petitions, and lobby for a voters' referendum calling for the constitutional amendment.

When the legislature met in January 1915, Finnigan knew each legislator's suffrage views. She and her sister Elizabeth, now married to suffrage supporter William H. Fain, decamped to Austin for the session. Although "unaccustomed to the political atmosphere of Austin," Finnigan felt the hard work had been worthwhile, even though no suffrage legislation passed. Julia Ideson and five members of the Woman's Political Union organized a banquet to celebrate Finnigan's leadership of the state effort. Female and male suffrage supporters gathered at Houston's Bender Hotel on Wednesday, March 24, to hear nine speakers laud Finnigan and extol the suffrage cause. Mrs. Eckhart Wallis presided and explained her "conversion to suffrage" after hearing Finnigan speak several years earlier. Julia glowingly described her friend as a woman of "poise, great courage, fine intelligence and remarkable tenacity," who more than anyone had "given herself to the cause of progress." Mayor Ben Campbell recognized the "perfect wave going over the country in reference to civic improvement" because of female influence. Minnie Cunningham brought messages from Galveston and challenged the audience to "dedicate" itself to the cause of suffrage "as never before." Newspaper editor Marcellus E. Foster reminded female guests, "You are classed with paupers, insane and criminals" in being disfranchised; he assured the audience he was "with the movement." When Finnigan rose to respond, she briefly spoke of the 1915 campaign and declared, "We have not been defeated. Victory is only delayed."[79]

In the spring of 1915, Julia continued to endorse equal suffrage at open-air forums sponsored by the Woman's Political Union of Houston, but she also wrestled with issues of war and peace. In early April, she took charge of arrangements at the City Auditorium's banquet hall for the visit of public speaker Bertha Kunz Baker (1864–1943), who was traveling across the United States under the auspices of the Woman's Peace Party. Well-known to Houston clubwomen who had sponsored her lecture tours several times, on this occasion the impassioned orator promoted "the movement for permanent peace among the nations of the world" by creating a world organization to settle disputes and by ending hostilities "on such terms of settlement as will prevent this war from being but the prelude to new wars." On May 18, Julia herself spoke at a program backed by the Daughters of the American Revolution (DAR), one of "many similar meetings held throughout our broad land in the interest of peace." Convened in the "restful quiet" of the Central Christian Church, which was "filled with mellow light filtering through the stained glass," the meeting featured four participants: Mrs. W. A. Rowan explained the purposes of the DAR to conserve early national history; Mrs. J. W. Lockett provided a "scholarly" overview of women's pleas for peace; Julia Ideson discussed the Nobel Peace Prize, noting the irony that a man whose inventions made possible "limitless destruction" should have endowed rewards to celebrate those "who do the most to promote peace and build up the arts and sciences"; and poet and *Post* contributor Judd Mortimer Lewis closed with a "few lines" he had penned to celebrate the benefits of peace.[80]

Between these two appearances in support of world peace, Julia attended the May 12–14, 1915, state convention of the Texas Woman Suffrage Association in Galveston. Outgoing President Annette Finnigan served as convention chairwoman and oversaw the election of her close associate, the energetic Minnie Fisher Cunningham, as the organization's new leader. Finnigan asked Julia to coordinate the roster of speeches at the Galveston Opera House. Cunningham revealed ambitious plans to make the "voice of the Suffragist . . . heard in the land" during the coming year: a name change to Texas Equal Suffrage Association (TESA); advocacy for a state bill to allow female suffrage in primary elections; strong lobbying; expanding membership from the current 2,500 to

10,000 by the 1916 convention; and a demanding statewide program of lectures, forums, debates, essay contests, event appearances, and parades. In a "brilliant and beautiful finale" to the convention and to her tenure, Finnigan entertained delegates and friends at Houston's Brazos Court Hotel, where the "ivy hung walls . . . shrubbery and flowering plants" formed "an ideal setting for the hospitality." Immense baskets filled with flowers decorated the court, a five-piece orchestra played at the reception from 8:00 until 9:00 p.m., and then amateur actors presented *How the Vote Was Won*, starring Julia Ideson, six other women, and two good-natured men. Finnigan asked her friends Julia Ideson and Ima Hogg and several other Houston women to help greet guests at the elegant gala. The play was such a hit that the Woman's Political Union of Houston held a garden party two weeks later on the roof of the downtown Carter building to reprise the "clever farce" and entertain guests with music, dancing, and refreshments. Deemed "one of the most successful social and financial events of the year," the evening cloaked a serious bid for equal suffrage support with the familiar trappings of Houston's society receptions. Finnigan certainly expected to continue her fight for equal rights when Carrie Chapman Catt called on all state and local organizations to support a national amendment in 1916, but that year she suffered a debilitating disease and crippling paralysis that forced her to withdraw from all civic and commercial responsibilities. She returned to New York City, and once again local political activity lagged for several months. Houston women attended the 1916 state suffrage convention but focused on educational work, not political action. Woodrow Wilson promised to keep Americans out of the war raging in Europe and won reelection.[81]

Resolved to push for equal suffrage when the January 1917 legislative session convened, Texas women approached legislators willing to introduce resolutions to support primary suffrage. Governor James E. Ferguson's unswerving opposition scuttled these efforts, but by summer he discovered the wrath and power of the suffrage voices he had ignored. Texas Equal Suffrage Association leaders provided their statewide contact list to Will Hogg, and hundreds of pro-suffrage women joined formidable temperance crusaders to lobby with Hogg and secure the "corrupt liquor" governor's impeachment and departure from office.[82] Pro-suffrage Lieutenant Governor William P. Hobby replaced the disgraced Ferguson. Reinvigorated by statewide agitation, the Houston Political Union asked Julia to explain "The History of Woman's Suffrage" at afternoon and evening sessions of its suffrage school. Held at the Rice Hotel in February and at the Kress building in March, suffrage school classes trained campaign volunteers in the mysteries of public relations, fundraising, and effective meeting procedure. In April the Union sponsored a rally for NAWSA President Anna Howard Shaw to inspire local interest. Threat of war united suffrage supporters, reformers of all kinds, and patriotic citizens in common purpose and brought new press and personal endorsements for the suffrage cause. When the seventh Texas Equal Suffrage Association convention opened on May 15 in Waco, hundreds of Texas women endorsed the national effort to demand an amendment to the US Constitution, and conventioneers wired Woodrow Wilson to express their support for federal action.

Germany resumed submarine warfare on February 1, 1917, thereby provoking the United States to sever relations and declare war on April 6. When Wilson went to war, Houstonians mobilized. Several civic leaders entrained for Washington, DC, to lead the national war effort, and industrialist and library supporter Edward A. Peden accepted state responsibility for food conservation and distribution as federal food administrator for Texas's eight districts. Peden turned to Julia Ideson to serve as publicity director, and they both sought advice from a price-interpreting committee that included local grocers William D. Cleveland and Joe Weingarten and former teacher Ethel Reed Coop. In November, Julia became state library director under the US Food Administration and used her post to address home-front conditions across the state. Julia responded enthusiastically when Alice Baker, chairwoman of the local YWCA War Work Council and member of the executive committee for War Camp Community Service, called on members of twenty-eight women's clubs to muster two thousand women and girls to support soldiers who were training at Camp Logan and Ellington Field and to mentor young women who were working in local wartime industries. Julia helped Alice welcome the first Camp Logan recruits during Hospitality Week October 17–24, 1917, and counseled Malcolm G. Wyer,[83] who was hired by the American Library Association to establish the camp's library facilities. The camp's one-story library building held ten thousand to fifteen thousand books on loan from libraries and patriotic citizens around the country. Wyer described in detail his five-month mission to organize the Camp Logan library for its official opening on January 29, noting he ate in the mess hall for enlisted men for two weeks before joining the officers' mess for another two weeks to understand what soldiers wanted to read. Wyer applauded Julia's wise counsel and assistance. When she learned a training camp was planned for Houston, she began soliciting donations and had amassed two thousand "first-class" volumes for the ALA organizers. She suggested Wyer use an automated numbering machine, and she arranged "very popular and enjoyable" story hours and musical programs for patients at the camp hospital. Julia also allowed members of her staff to work at Camp Logan one morning and one afternoon each week. These staff volunteers monitored soldiers who manned the library building as well as numerous substations and mess hall book exchanges throughout the encampment. Following ALA guidelines, Julia welcomed soldiers to the downtown library and issued library cards to soldiers and their families. "The khaki uniform was a common sight in the library at all times," she reported.[84]

War fervor stimulated suffrage agitation. In mid-December 1917 Julia asked members of the Houston Equal Suffrage Association (the former Houston Political Union) to authorize a resolution that supported a federal equal suffrage amendment. At a well-attended lunch meeting, several speakers argued that "if the women were left at home during the war to run a man's world they should be given a man's equipment for the work." Persuaded by the oratory, the group seized "a wonderfully opportune moment" to adopt Julia's resolution and send it to Houston's congressional delegation. Julia's message read, in part: "The suffrage amendment should be passed by congress at its earliest opportunity as a war measure. The splendid democracy and loyalty of the American women demand this recognition. The government needs the vote. The women need the protection of the vote." Attorney Hortense Ward, "a woman of very keen political perception" who had successfully gained suffrage endorsements from prominent Houston businessmen Will Hogg, Joseph S. Cullinan, Jesse Jones, and banker John Scott, took over as president of the Houston Equal Suffrage Association in January 1918. She and Minnie Cunningham, president of the Texas Equal Suffrage Association president, carried Julia's resolution supporting a constitutional amendment to Washington, DC.[85]

In Texas Ward and Cunningham lobbied for a primary suffrage bill, which passed and was signed by Governor Hobby on March 26, 1918. By June, ninety-eight woman suffrage organizations had formed in Texas, and between June 26 and July 11, activists registered 386,000 women voters, including 14,750 in Harris County. TESA lobbying spurred 223 Democratic county conventions to endorse women's suffrage, and in September the Texas Democratic Party sanctioned a pro-suffrage plank at its state convention. That fall NAWSA called Cunningham to Washington to lobby full-time for passage of the Nineteenth Amendment to the US Constitution, which would secure the substance of Julia's resolution and extend national voting rights to women. Cunningham triumphed in June 1919 when Congress submitted the amendment to the states. She returned to Austin for a final blitz that secured Texas's ratification on June

28, making Texas the ninth state to accept federal woman suffrage and the first in the South to do so. A Victory Convention in October 1919 celebrated TESA success and transformed the activist group into the League of Women Voters under the continuing leadership of Minnie Cunningham. Tragically, this leap forward for women's rights preceded a devastating blow to the black population in 1923 when the Texas legislature rescinded the right of black citizens to vote in Democratic primary elections, the only state elections of significance at a time when the Democratic party dominated Texas politics.

While solidly behind the suffrage activity, Julia found her hours filled with local oversight duties at the Houston public library and with statewide administrative decisions for the US Food Administration. By 1918, Julia's library management, patriotic activities, and suffrage support became inseparably entwined. When she expanded library service and welcomed servicemen, she secured the library's place at the heart of Houston's civic culture. When she called on voluntary associations and clubs to support home-front war efforts, she made converts to the suffrage cause and demonstrated to doubters that women were valuable citizens capable of patriotic sacrifice. Julia enlisted volunteers throughout the state to survey libraries for information about local food needs and to distribute books and information pamphlets that educated Texans about the importance of planting victory gardens at home or in neighborhood vacant lots. She emphasized family participation and shared sacrifice. She admonished mothers to be soldiers in the kitchen and provided healthy recipes so households could support the troops by having days each week without meat or wheat or pork. She distributed seed packets and asked children to pledge they would not waste food. She displayed US Food Administration posters that declared "Food Will Win the War" and urged everyone to "Sow the Seeds of Victory."[86]

In March 1918 Julia asked the library board to participate in a nationwide fund drive that urged all Americans to raise $5 million and collect ten million books and magazines for soldiers at home and abroad. "Splendid" Houston men and women contributed 5,165 books; newspapers advertised the drive; donors dropped off books at schools and moving picture houses; and laundry wagon drivers picked up books with the contributors' dirty clothes. The library staff sorted and prepared the books for distribution—mostly to lonely soldiers stationed along border points served by Fort Bliss, near El Paso. On the final Monday of Julia's push, a battalion of women who had "volunteered their cars and their own services" made door-to-door collections. In her final report,

World War I poster, US Food Administration, 1918. MSS0032–051, Julia Ideson Collection, Houston Public Library, Houston Metropolitan Research Center.

World War I presentation, US Food Administration, 1918. MSS0032–008, Julia Ideson Collection, Houston Public Library, Houston Metropolitan Research Center.

Julia thanked a long list of workers and contributors, praised her hardworking library staff, and urged Houstonians to "form the habit" of bringing books to the library "as soon as they have read them," to ensure a steady stream of reading material for soldiers.[87]

Julia was one of Houston's top sellers of Liberty loan bonds. She helped Harris County Judge Chester H. Bryan and Harris County Liberty Loan Women's Committee Chairwoman Elizabeth Ring raise over $45 million to exceed the quota for each of five major Liberty loan drives, making Houston the only major Texas city to outstrip expectations. In April 1918 Julia set off with fellow suffragists Hortense Ward, Lavinia Engle, and "official chauffeur" Mrs. R. L. Young on a triumphant tour of southern Texas counties to help local committees sell Liberty bonds. Mrs. Young drove over one thousand miles "with little or no trouble, making the last lap of the journey, 247 miles, in one day."

Their car, dubbed the "Liberty loan limited" and decorated with streamers and banners, "was greeted everywhere with patriotic applause." Enthusiasts in Victoria fired a cannon, and other towns held street parades to advertise Liberty loan meetings. Citizens entertained the quartet "with cordiality" and purchased far more bonds than the promoters expected.[88]

Like many women who watched their brothers and friends leave for the front, Julia yearned for overseas duty. She had supported homesick soldiers, had raised millions for the war effort, and had fought for political recognition of women. At last, in early 1919, the American Library Association invited Julia to join its Library War Service in Europe, where she would be paid seventy-five dollars a month plus "necessary" expenses, board, lodging, and travel, effective February 10. Julia received a leave of absence from the Houston Library Association and placed library supervision in the capable hands of Assistant Librarian—and Texas Library Association President-elect—Martha Schnitzer. On February 9, with the community's blessing, Julia left Houston for New York City, and on February 21 she sailed on the SS *Pocahontas* for Le Havre, France. Following a weeklong delay because she had not brought enough photographs for all the necessary documents, Julia arrived in Brest to work at the Camp Pontanezen library, which served American soldiers waiting to be demobilized and sent home. The camp stretched across flat land near the port three miles from Brest and had been used by the French military since Napoleonic days. In World War I, American soldiers debarked there for orientation before marching to the front. During the months of fighting, the camp of field tents joined by board walkways was home to thousands of soldiers who had contracted infectious diseases. By 1919 Pontanezen covered one thousand acres and could process eighty thousand soldiers a week for their journeys home. A telegram to her mother, announcing Julia's safe arrival after a ten-day voyage, and infrequent letters to friends found their way into local newspapers and provided a vivid glimpse of immediate postwar life.[89]

Julia's service from March through September "promise[d] to be wonderful if we get enough books." She arrived in Brest to discover that everything was "rather dirty" and that it rained constantly. In a letter to American Library Association colleagues, she recommended the next group of recruits bring plenty of photographs, invaluable numbering stamps, sugar, and ink for the fountain pens. Soldiers were finishing the library, which opened officially on March 21, so she shopped for supplies at the naval stores and settled into the Continental, Brest's "leading" hotel. The lodging was also rather dirty but offered central

Julia Ideson, second on right, and library staff in Brest, France, 1919. MSS0032–0114, Julia Ideson Collection, Houston Public Library, Houston Metropolitan Research Center.

heat—"when it works"—and "quite gay" dances with two American bands. The city was "unruly"—"port cities always have the scum of all countries"—and military police escorted women around town, to "lovely" parties for visiting generals, and from the hotel to the camp. ALA volunteers joined Y "girls" and Red Cross personnel doing vital work for the army and navy. There were "unlimited" work possibilities, and the staff "expected to be swamped."[90]

Julia loved the "cheery looking" library, warmed by a big open fireplace and finished with rough-hewn rafters. The building could accommodate two hundred men but by closing time at 9:00 p.m. "was usually jammed to the hatches." Eleven men, including "an Irishman, a Scotchman, an Italian, an Alsatian, a plumber, a machinist and various other Americans [who are] all good friends," preferred helping the library staff to standing guard. From beginning to end of her stay, Julia and other Texas librarians assigned to Brest wrote home

Soldiers checking out books at the American library in Brest, France, 1919. MSS0032–021, Julia Ideson Collection, Houston Public Library. Houston Metropolitan Research Center.

begging for urgently needed books to satisfy "some 70,000 men" forced to share "considerably less than 7,000 volumes." One returning soldier described "oft-repeated calls for books" to fill his "many lonesome hours" and confessed he "snitched" as many as he could from shipments slated for bases south of Brest. Julia's exhilarating and hectic tour of duty ended in the fall, leaving her worn down by overwork and ill health. Always courageous, she boarded one of the first international airplane passenger flights from Paris to London and sailed from England to New York on the *Pocahontas* on October 21, arriving ten days later.[91]

Postwar Expansion: 1920–1921

During sixteen years as Houston's librarian, Julia Ideson strengthened library holdings and secured the institution's popularity throughout the community. As a resolute leader, she listened and brought people together with quiet persistence to advance the library's mission. As an effective manager, she mentored inexperienced staffers and used her limited resources carefully to achieve goals. As a tenacious fundraiser, she rallied municipal officials, courted public opinion, and coaxed private donors to expand collections and services. As an eloquent communicator, she produced lucid reports, wrote lively newspaper stories, and spoke ardently to explain how the library could benefit every Houston family. As an ambitious visionary, she used her many talents to pursue her overarching dream—that Houston's public library aspire to excellence and stand at the center of urban civic life. When she returned from France, Julia knew her greatest challenge lay before her. She would need all her hard-earned social capital to marshal public support and to address the long-simmering issues that hampered expansion. It was time to attack the library's financial problems with imaginative solutions, and it was necessary to replace the Carnegie Library jewel box with a structure capable of meeting current needs and anticipated future growth. The town of 44,633, which had joyfully welcomed the Houston Lyceum and Carnegie Library in 1903, had become a major city of 138,276 by 1920. Optimistic as its business leaders, industrialists, and bankers may have been when the new decade dawned, few could have foreseen that the Bayou City would more than double in size by 1930, when the sprawling metropolis reached 292,352 residents.

Julia began her postwar campaign to improve the city library by helping Harris County build resources of its own. For many years, Harris County residents had used Houston's public library, but Julia believed every county should support a library responsive to rural communities. She had orchestrated legislation authorizing state support for county libraries in 1915, and, with peace assured, she felt it was time to push for libraries in every county. According to American Library Association sources, only 14.7 percent of Texans had easy access to free public libraries, and Julia noted that 197 of the 252 counties in Texas had no library supported by and serving the whole county. At the insistence of Texas State Librarian Elizabeth H. West, Julia agreed in February 1920 to serve as state director of the Books for Everybody fundraising effort launched by the ALA to raise $2 million to make "public library service a vital influence in every American community." At the ALA annual meeting, held in Colorado Springs that June, delegates elected the ALA's first female president—Alice S. Tyler, director of the Western Reserve University Library School in Cleveland, Ohio. The association also named Julia Ideson to the council. Members unanimously adopted a resolution affirming the nationwide Books for Everybody plan to expand library service through county libraries. When Julia returned to Houston, she "asked all librarians of the state to put the movement across" by backing the drive to secure the $25,000 promised to Texas from the ALA campaign and by forming library committees in every Texas county. She also invited Houston Art League President Florence Fall and library board member Elizabeth F. Ring to serve as her advisers on a state fundraising committee.[92]

Julia then spearheaded the effort to create a Harris County library system and to explain the advantages a county library would bring to rural communities. She told directors of the Harris County Dairy Association that county libraries could be established under the 1915 law, amended two years later to permit county commissioners to pay for a library by levying a tax of not more than five cents per one hundred dollars property value in the unincorporated areas of the county. The library would be headquartered in the county courthouse, and books would be circulated to all county communities and schools. Julia noted that Dallam and Cooke counties already had inaugurated systems and that the Texas plan included ideas from the successful California system, which "brings the world's best literature to the farms and rural communities." The city library, she assured the group, would loan books to the county and would "co-operate with the county library in every way possible." Other meeting speakers noted that a county library at a cost of about $6,000 a year would provide educational opportunities for the young and keep them from moving into the city. County facilities would also deliver special resources to the foreign population "flocking" to rural areas. A committee of dairy association members promised to discuss the proposal with the county judge and commissioners.[93]

On October 18, 1920, Julia helped the superintendent of county schools, the publicity manager for the chamber of commerce, three YWCA officials, and Harris County Judge Chester Bryan establish the Harris County Library Association to campaign for a Harris County library system. Julia told the association that it could hire a competent librarian to direct the county system if each community would promise to furnish a suitable place to keep books and would provide a trained individual to oversee their distribution. Judge Bryan confirmed his support for the proposed library system but asked association members to "gather petitions from rural districts desiring free books" and present them to the commissioners. Success would depend on demand. In December, with ample proof of enthusiastic demand, Julia published a long article in the *Houston Post,* thanking Judge Bryan and the commissioners for their "forward-looking attitude" and for their willingness to authorize the county library system. Julia explained that libraries would be located in county schools "as rapidly as possible," giving students access to thousands of county and city library books. In small communities, she wrote, a circulating library for adults might be combined with the school library; but in larger towns, the school and circulating libraries might be separated. The Harris County Library would be the first for South Texas. At the final meeting of the commissioners court before the 1921 budget was announced, the association proposed a $9,000 appropriation, but Julia admitted, "Whatever amount you give will make us happy." Meeting attendees understood that an appropriation would be made and that the Harris County Library would begin operation in 1921.[94]

The county library promised to alleviate overcrowding at Houston's downtown library and to make books available to the city's surrounding communities. Having resolved one long-standing problem, Julia and the Houston Library Association board believed "the time was ripe" at last to demand stable funding for the city library. On Wednesday, January 5, 1921, Julia and the library board met with the city council and requested that an ordinance authorizing tax-based funding for the city library be placed before the public on February 9 during the primary balloting. Park advocates sponsored by the Young Men's Business League had already applied for an ordinance election on that day, asking that funds be allocated for park development and improvement. Councilmen explained that they could not authorize two ordinance elections within six months of each other unless the people of Houston petitioned for them. To place the library request on the February 9 ballot, the city secretary would have to receive petitions with at least 1,673 names by the following Monday afternoon. At the Wednesday meeting, Julia assured the library board and city council she would have petitions "calling for the submission of a charter amendment to voters" ready to sign on Thursday morning. Reporters and editors of the *Post, Chronicle, Press,* and *Labor Journal* enthusiastically demanded action. Editorials supported the funding request, and news articles advertised the need for "all friends of the library and citizens interested" to sign petitions at the library on Thursday, Friday, or Saturday. An army of volunteers rushed into action to track down supporters in their homes and workplaces. Female participation was vital. According to city officials, signatures of Houston's women could be submitted without being checked by the city secretary because all Harris County women had the right to vote without paying the registration or poll tax required of male voters. Julia secured nearly two thousand signatures well before the deadline. On February 9 voters by a margin of 8,102 to 4,312 authorized the city in 1921 and "each year thereafter" to levy an ad valorem tax of not less than $.025 per $100 valuation on all "real, personal, or mixed" property of any individual or corporation within the Houston city limits. With funds to maintain city library programs assured, Julia could address the crying need for more space.[95]

Julia later described 1921 as a year of "substantial progress" for libraries in Houston and Harris County. The Harris County library system was in place, with its headquarters in the Harris County Courthouse and book exchange stations in several rural communities. To bring library service to more city neighborhoods, the Houston Library Association focused on construction of branch libraries. The Houston School Board allowed the Library Association to build temporary one-story frame structures on the campuses of Houston Heights High School and North Side Junior High School. Each building provided a reading room, built-in shelving, a librarian's office, a lavatory, and heaters. A photograph of the Heights Branch, supervised by Elise Wilkinson, shows the home-like library sitting behind the large brick school, surrounded by tall pine trees and covered with latticework to support the vines planted around the building by the parent-teacher association, which had advocated strongly for the branch. The popular Carnegie (North) Branch, under Louise Franklin's able direction, had been operating successfully for eight months when members of the Sherman School Mothers' Club organized a formal opening of its two thousand-book collection on November 7. The committee invited "the public and friends of the library" to enjoy a reception and several speeches, including remarks by Julia Ideson. In April Houston Library Association trustees assumed full management and financial responsibility for the Colored Carnegie Library branch, capably led by Bessie Osborne. In September they renamed the system—which included the central library, the three branch libraries, and satellites at fifteen schools and six deposit stations—the Houston Public Library. That October, assistant librarian Martha Schnitzer and cataloguer Anabel Norwood moved several collections and the administrative, ordering, and cataloguing functions and staff members to remodeled space on the fifth floor of the Harris County Courthouse, where books, newspapers, and government documents had been stored for a decade in space originally set aside for a law library. For the next four years, the original library and its courthouse annex became the Carnegie and Courthouse Branch. Julia concluded her 1921 annual report by noting that the new facilities and stable funding plan would provide "more adequate service" to everyone.[96]

Building the House of Books: 1922–1926

Julia Ideson made building a new central facility her top priority in 1922. She had long argued that the downtown building was inadequate and had made clear that only a larger building on a more commodious lot would accommodate Houston's rapidly expanding population. Press reports voiced strong support for library expansion and carried long articles about library activities. As early as 1919, Mayor A. Earl Amerman had suggested building a new library to memorialize Harris County soldiers who had perished in World War I. On September 1, 1920, Ammerman named a committee to consider purchasing a new site for a larger library that would include enough land for a downtown park. He asked Rice Institute architect William Ward Watkin to provide plans, and he challenged committee members to decide whether money to pay for the improvements should be raised by a bond issue or by public subscription. Watkin sketched a long, two-story Italianate building that was printed in the *Post* and *Chronicle* in September 1920; the Kiwanis Club pledged its full support; and William States Jacobs, pastor of First Presbyterian Church, made known the church's interest in reacquiring the Carnegie Library property. After eighteen months of discussion, the mayor's library committee, noting the increasing success of bond issues to fund local projects in the post-World War I years, proposed a bond issue of $200,000 in May 1922 to get the library expansion project started.

In the months before the May election, Julia explained the "urgent need" to pass the proposed bond issue to men's luncheon groups, the Federation of Women's Clubs, the League of Women Voters, and the Kiwanis club. Conditions in the current quarters, she assured reporters, were "almost intolerable." Bookshelves had expanded to "parts of the library where shelves were not intended," making workspaces "stuffy" and so crowded "everyone gets in the way of everyone else." Her earnest pleas led her audiences to pledge support for construction funding. On the evening of Thursday, April 27, ten days before the election, the Woman's City Club held an open forum to explain city needs. The library bond issue faced serious competition. The mayor, the president of the school board, a commissioner, and Julia Ideson lobbied voters to support a new school tax and bond issues for street and bridge improvements, for the city/county hospital, and for the public library. Their entreaties succeeded. Houstonians recognized the city was growing in population and wealth, the government was expanding, and the citizens were demanding improvements in the quality of urban life. Voters believed in the city's future, and every initiative passed on May 6, 1922. Immediately, library trustees formed a building committee to develop plans for a new building. Chaired by civic reformer Rev. Harris Masterson Jr., the committee of volunteers included library board President Henry H. Dickson, library trustee and stalwart supporter Elizabeth Ring, attorney William A. Vinson, accountant R. H. Byers, Baptist minister Rev. E. P. West, Librarian Ideson, and city officials.[97]

With the first round of funds assured and a building committee in place, Julia began to consider a location for the new building and plans for its construction. Later admirers remarked that Julia had been the driving force behind the new library, but she always gave credit to others; indeed, building the library proved the value of meshing public and private-sector support for any major civic enterprise. Masterson and his committee opened negotiations with Oscar F. Holcombe, the new mayor, and requested that the city purchase a building site with money from the general funds so all bond funds could be used for construction. After some deliberation, Holcombe agreed to this plan, and discussions began regarding the precise location. Holcombe demurred about the first choice, which turned out to be fortunate because the committee settled on the block bounded by McKinney and Lamar avenues and Smith and Brazos streets. The so-called Bagby block included the former home of banker and early lyceum supporter Thomas Bagby and faced Martha Hermann Square, a park donated to the city in 1913 by philanthropist George Hermann to memorialize his wife. The city council approved purchase of the property in September and concluded the $92,500 deal.

While the building committee was deliberating, Julia traveled to Detroit to attend the ALA annual meeting from June 26 to July 1. She was promoted to the national association's executive committee and admired Detroit's handsome new municipal library, headquarters for ALA activities. She praised the "very splendid" exterior architecture of renowned library architect Cass Gilbert but felt the "inside [was] an architect's rather than a librarian's plan." The building committee wanted to consider Gilbert for the Houston project but was resolved that if a nationally known architect were given the commission, he would be required to work in association with W. A. Dowdy, the city's official architect. Library association trustees asked Julia to meet with Gilbert while she stopped in New York City during a July and August tour of eleven libraries she had planned for her summer working vacation. The short and frequently interrupted meeting did not go well. Julia telegraphed that Gilbert was not interested in collaboration, an opinion confirmed by Gilbert in a letter to Chairman Masterson the next day. Julia talked to Edward L. Tilton, another well-known New York architect, who had designed the libraries Julia visited in Wilmington and Providence. Tilton was willing to collaborate with the city architect and even promised to help with fundraising efforts, but no offer from the committee followed his preliminary meeting with Julia. Mindful of the interior inadequacies of the externally elegant Carnegie Library, Julia told the committee she wanted a practical plan that would "fit into . . . daily life and be part of it," as Newark Public Library head John Cotton Dana recommended. As she traveled, Julia quizzed library heads about what worked and what did not, and she used observation notes and the comments of colleagues to frame her own plans for Houston.[98]

Julia was still corresponding by telegram, when the committee invited local architects William Ward Watkin, Maurice J. Sullivan, and Birdsall P. Briscoe to prepare library designs in consultation with the city architect, but this competitive in-city approach failed. Julia returned with many ideas she wanted to include in the new library, and in November Masterson met with the mayor and library trustees. The group decided to invite Ralph Adams Cram, whose firm had successfully executed plans for Rice Institute, to take on the new Houston commission; Masterson stipulated that Cram must design the building. The group also proposed that Watkin and his partner Louis A. Glover be named associate architects to prepare working drawings and oversee construction; city architect Dowdy was asked to help as needed. The board made a formal offer to Cram on November 9, and his firm accepted the commission eight days later, pending an explicit understanding of duties and compensation. Cram, as design architect, wished to review and approve all working drawings prepared by Watkin and Glover from his designs. On December 11, Mayor Holcombe appointed the firms of Cram and Ferguson and Watkin and Glover as the associated architects for Houston's library project. The delicate division of architectural duties and the need to accommodate Librarian Ideson's strong ideas and Chairman Masterson's deep interest challenged everyone's diplomatic skills for the next four years.

For two decades Julia had visited libraries and accumulated information about successful buildings. When she returned from her summer 1922 travels, which included exploration of recently completed projects, she was ready to explain her goals to the committee. In early December she outlined an explicit program that Chairman Masterson carried with him when he left for Boston in mid-December to discuss the project with Cram, who had recently returned from six months in Spain. Julia stressed practicality, flexibility, and utility. Above all, the new building should embody current American Library Association aspirations to make public libraries community social centers; like Houston's parks, the new library should, Julia believed, offer "hospitality to visitors." Julia explained that she wanted a practical building of three stories over a full basement that would accommodate 250,000 books and was "adapted to the needs of the community." The ground level would provide space for a children's department, newspaper reading room, five hundred-seat auditorium, and administrative offices; the second floor would serve as the "main level" and central delivery hall with a large reference room, reading room, and study areas; the third floor would hold special collections and more staff offices; the mezzanine between the first and second levels would house the librarian's office; and the basement would accommodate storage and utilities. Julia also demanded flexible, "fluid planning" with few permanent walls so space could be easily modified to meet changing community needs with relatively little expense. Finally, she stressed the building's usefulness; not only should reading areas provide ample natural lighting and good cross ventilation, but also books should "meet the demands and requirements of this part of the country," be used, and be accessible. Julia's new library required classrooms, clubrooms, space for a natural history museum (not yet constructed elsewhere), and a "special room to display collections of letters, manuscripts, photographs, and souvenirs [that would] form a . . . historical museum" of Texana. The final plans adhered closely to her vision.[99]

Masterson presented these ideas to Cram, who had been imagining the Houston project during his recent travels. The architect immediately suggested adapting the "style of exceeding beauty" he found in Spanish Renaissance buildings, a genre suited to the Southern climate, well-adapted to Texas's historical ties to Spain and Mexico, and appropriate for a public building dedicated to the transmission of culture and learning. By January Cram had produced two plans —A and B—for the Houston committee to review. The committee preferred the L-shaped plan B, which Watkin described as "thoroughly Spanish," to the U-shaped plan A and made several suggestions, which became plan C.[100] Another round of changes produced plan D in April. Mayor Holcombe accepted this plan, with one change: he suggested rotating the building by ninety degrees. The *Houston Chronicle* published plan D, generating renewed interest in the project. Cram then produced sketches, which caused another round of changes, but on August 10 Cram sent plan E to the library board for approval. The mayor and city council adopted the board-sanctioned plan on September 24. Houston would build a library designed with a central register flanked by east and west wings—an L wing attached to the west front wall, and another L jutted off the east wing's back wall. These sections, which incorporated all Julia's wishes, could be built one at a time to accommodate funding constraints. Watkin and Glover used plan E as the basis for their working drawings, and the board prepared promotional material.

During the design phase, architects and board members recognized the need for another bond election because projected costs far exceeded earlier expectations; the architects resisted suggestions to build one unit at a time, and major cuts seemed unbearable. Cram left Boston in mid-February to meet with Ideson and Masterson in Houston and to formulate a strategy to convince the mayor to spend more money. Bearing the drawings and a compelling argument, library advocates persuaded Holcombe to approve a bond issue to cover construction of the central register, the east and west wings, and the L wing on the front that would house the auditorium. By mid-March Holcombe had authorized a bond election in late April. Julia and her team eagerly explained the urgent need for an additional $300,000 to cover construction costs, which had surged 80 percent in the previous two years. Unfortunately, five of the six scheduled bond issues, including the library's petition, failed. The mayor blamed indifference caused by lack of publicity and resubmitted the petitions for another try on June 10. This time Julia and her team mounted a feverish campaign. Library staff distributed handbills and bookmarks to all library visitors and placed a large sign outside the building, urging pedestrians to "Vote Yes for the Library." Civic leaders found form letters in their mailboxes. Boy Scouts carried placards to forty stores and other public places and put posters in schools. Volunteer speakers besieged clubs and organizations "unremittingly and unendingly" until voters demonstrated by 7,208 to 3,864 that they wanted more funding for their library and "couldn't bear to have Miss Ideson disappointed." So determined was the building committee that its members signed a contract with low bidder Southwestern Construction Company and broke ground eight days before the June 10 election to begin work on the central register and east and west wings. The committee signed a second contract with Southwestern in the fall to complete the L wing, but Houstonians had to wait eighty-five years for the rear wing's appearance. Watkin, Glover, and Southwestern Construction inspected the project on November 27, 1925, and accepted the work. The final phase of furnishing the new building then began. Once again, the mayor came to the library's aid; in 1925 he authorized money from the general fund to equip the handsome structure.[101]

While focusing attention on the central library construction project, the Library Association did not neglect its branch libraries. In 1923 trustees decided proceeds from the sale of the Carnegie property would be used to build permanent facilities for the North and Heights branches, and each library was allotted $50,000. Residents of the high-density, low-income northside area had responded enthusiastically to the temporary Carnegie (North) Branch building, and the permanent facility for this underserved area was the first to be completed. A committee of northside citizens selected a site with "many beautiful trees" at Henry and Common streets, near the neighborhood's junior and senior high schools.[102] The city purchased the lot for $23,000 in January 1924, and W. A. Dowdy, the city architect, designed a Colonial Revival-style redbrick building with a two-story central section flanked by one-story wings. A two-story portico supported by four white pillars framed the entrance. M. C. Parker & Company made the low bid; construction began in July and was completed in January 1925 at a cost of $50,730. Structural issues delayed the official opening until November 10, 1925, when Elizabeth Ring, the mayor, and project Chairman Harris Masterson led the roster of speakers, who congratulated North Branch Librarian Louise Franklin. The next Saturday, 350 children celebrated: popular children's author Mary Hazelton Wade[103] spoke, and book tableaus presented by Houston's Department of Recreation entertained the crowd. When the original central library closed, North Branch was renamed Carnegie Branch to commemorate Andrew Carnegie's "generous gift" to construct Houston's first public library building.

Library trustees and the Heights Branch Committee finally agreed on May 20, 1924, to spend $7,000 for a lot with beautiful shade trees on Heights Boulevard at Thirteenth Street. Louis A. Glover agreed to design a building and presented his plans to the library board on December 9. The board quickly gave its approval and advertised for bids six days later. On February 11, 1925, Universal Construction Company won the low-bid contract and completed the work by November 6, 1925. The handsome one-story Spanish Renaissance revival-style building finished in soft rose stucco won immediate admiration; neighbors and friends landscaped the grounds enclosed by a wrought iron fence; and the city celebrated on March 18, 1926, after delayed equipment had finally been installed. The northside Carnegie Branch, remodeled and enlarged in 1949, was razed in 1980 to make way for the Carnegie Neighborhood Library and Center for Learning. Dedicated on December 5, 1982, the new center was supported by the Houston Public Library, the Houston Independent School District, and the Houston Community College system. The Houston Public Library renovated and expanded the Heights Branch building in the 1970s.

Branch libraries addressed Julia's wish to make library books easily accessible to every Houstonian, but the final stage of construction on the new Central Library building absorbed most of the librarian's time. Her annual report for 1925 described the "splendid" edifice as "perhaps one of the most beautiful library buildings in the country." In preopening publicity, she extoled the building's capacity to expand service in the future well beyond the current 38,631 cardholders and 100,000 volumes. In November 1925, Julia saw only

Houston Public Library staff, circa 1925, with Julia Ideson (labeled 12) at the center of the second row. MSS0032–125, Julia Ideson Collection, Houston Public Library, Houston Metropolitan Research Center.

"bright prospects" for Houston's public library system. With uncharacteristic pride, the usually modest librarian closed an article in the *Houston Chronicle* with her enthusiastic assessment: "A central library perfectly planned, two new branches and the colored branch . . . make it possible for every part of the city to be in reach of books. The writer does not wish to be boastful, yet she must say that no city in the South surpasses and few equal the library development here as a tribute to the citizenship that has made this possible. In no mean city could such libraries . . . be."[104]

For nearly a year prior to the October 18 "coming out party" organized to highlight the new building, Julia and members of her staff held "Reading with a Purpose" radio talks at noon every Thursday to advertise library resources and "acquaint" the audiences with "reading opportunities," including over one hundred Reading with a Purpose courses sponsored by the American Library

Association. Librarians Dickson, Hicks, and Franklin spoke to clubs and organizations and to the Mid-Winter Conference of the YWCA. On the evening of November 17, 1925, members of the Texas Library Association, in Houston for their annual convention, marched up the sidewalk that had been finished that afternoon to satisfy their curiosity with a surprise tour of the unfinished building—the first visitors to Houston's latest civic amenity. The next day, Martha Schnitzer and her helpers began moving departments from the county courthouse, where several staff members had spent four years in crowded "exile." Working when courthouse elevators could be used from seven to eight in the morning, after five in the evening, and on Saturdays, they resettled office furniture and several thousand volumes by January 1926. For the next eight months, Julia and all library employees, inspired by the "exhilarating feeling" of working in the beautiful new space, "labored long hours" to move everything from the 1903 library building to its expanded headquarters. The original library structure finally closed on October 16, when staffers removed the few remaining books and furnishings. The press tantalized readers with long descriptions of the new building's handsome interiors and modern lighting fixtures. Articles reprised the lyceum and library histories, gave a "major part of the credit" to their librarian, and outlined plans for the opening celebration in minute detail.[105]

At 7:30 p.m. on Monday, October 18, 1926, five thousand library enthusiasts listened to remarks by Library Association board President William A. Vinson, Mayor Oscar Holcombe, Julia Ideson, architect William Ward Watkin, and President of the Houston Federation of Women's Clubs Mrs. A. K. Newby before absorbing the formal address of Rice Institute President Edgar Odell Lovett. With gracious thanks and polished oratory, Lovett declared, "Books and houses of books were among the earliest products of established civilizations, and in turn books and houses of books are indispensable to the institutions of our own civilization." He explained, "to the City its public circulating library is quite as important as are water supply, lighting system, and telephone exchange, for are not the objects of a public library instantaneous contact with ideas or information, illuminating guidance in finding one's way to truth, and health and help in the enjoyment and endurance of life?" Lovett praised the "forward-looking men and women" who conceived, designed, and built the "monumental building, striking alike in dignity and beauty." He lauded the librarians' "inestimable service to their own and future generations" and acclaimed the library as an "active agency in the liberating of the mind . . . from ignorance,

Houston Public Library, south view, 1926. RGA0005–1844b-001, Houston Press Photo Collection, Houston Public Library, Houston Metropolitan Research Center.

prejudice, superstition, and intolerance." The eminent Rice Institute leader closed with a poem composed for the occasion to celebrate Houston and its "House of Books in Hermann Square."[106]

New Horizons: 1926–1929

Curious visitors who approached the portals of Houston's new "House of Books" were not disappointed. An impressive building and surrounding gardens covered the city block. Graceful windows and wrought iron grillwork pierced the plain exterior. The central entrance—with its "collar of lace" carved on the upper parapet, its front doors and second-story window framed by marble columns, and its three shallow marble steps—suggested the grandeur within. Spacious high-ceilinged rooms—eighteen feet on the first and third floors and twenty-two on the second floor—enriched by carved oak woodwork and built-in bookcases provided well-lighted spaces for reading, research, and meetings. On the first floor, patrons could return books, peruse daily papers at the newsstand, or chat in the west wing "whispering gallery" as they walked to the auditorium wing, which accommodated three hundred performance or lecture patrons on the first floor and housed special collections and clubrooms on the second and third floors.[107] They could also escort children to the east wing Norma Meldrum Children's Room and adjacent story-hour space, each furnished with small tables and chairs carved with fairy tale scenes. Visitors could also ascend the broad staircase to the elaborate two-story central delivery hall on the second, or main, floor of the building. There patrons could peruse books in the adjacent east wing principal reading room, which accommodated two hundred readers and housed thirty thousand volumes; or they could avail themselves of the smaller west wing reference room; or they could search the card catalogue and request books at the busy central desk. Richly carved oak columns marked the entrance to the space and to the reading rooms, while four marble columns supported the third-floor gallery and the clerestory finished with an ornate oak entablature painted in blue, gold, and red and covered by an ornamented coffered ceiling. Librarians sat behind carved desks in the central hall and reference room to help guests order books or to answer questions on every imaginable topic. Stairs led patrons to the third floor west wing classroom, music department, and cataloguing department and east wing collections of medicine, local history, and genealogy. The kitchen, dining, and sitting rooms were reserved for the staff.

Stimulated by the handsome surroundings, Julia Ideson planned an array of programs for the new building. Even without the rear wing, there was ample space for activities. To assist her in program planning and book selection and to emphasize the library's importance to Houstonians, Julia continued to keep her meticulous circulation statistics and began recording the professional affiliations of borrowers so she could build the specialty collections she thought essential to a top-ranked urban library. In 1929 she counted 2,319 guests who specified ninety-two occupations, with clerks, teachers, and stenographers topping a list that included one weather observer, eighteen decorators, and sixty-four machinists. She recorded the number of reference questions posed, the number of cardholders, the number of novels taken home, the number of children who attended story hour, and the number of special events that occurred every month—forty in October 1929 alone.

Book circulation grew steadily from 509,666 volumes in 1927 to 621,795 in 1929. Julia had always relied on book donations from library supporters, and friends of the library donated books and collections related to the arts, gardens, natural history, and technical and scientific subjects. Donors also gave books and pamphlets on favorite topics like childcare and bibliographies for

Houston Public Library's central delivery hall, circa 1926. RGA0013–2965, Houston Public Library Collection, Houston Public Library, Houston Metropolitan Research Center.

the women's reading clubs. In a thank you note to Adele Looscan, Julia assured her friend that she had read her book, which was a "boon" to the library, and asked her to please "send two more copies."[108] In 1928 the cataloguing department processed 9,552 books for the main library and three branches, and that year Julia completed the first inventory taken since 1904, a four-year effort that disclosed a loss of 7,366 books over two decades, "not bad considering the open shelves, lack of supervision, and large use of the old library," concluded the careful librarian.[109] The next year Julia noted a circulation downturn in the children's department, but her careful statistics showed that this change was caused by a happy coincidence: Houston high schools had opened good libraries that year to handle research needs of the high school population.

Every year the library staff mounted exhibits with museum artifacts or with material on loan from Houston collectors. Local lore was always popular with library visitors, and for many years, Julia gratefully accepted collections of documents or books related to the "gallant history" of Texas. In June 1925, the library board authorized its librarian to cooperate with the Harris County Historical Society to create a "historical museum" at the Central Library to preserve documents, papers, and objects for posterity. Even though Julia believed museum exhibits "were not properly the field of the public library," she promised to bring the past to life until Houston could build its own historical museum. In 1929 Julia recommended that the large room on the third floor be used to display the Milsaps Circle M, Texana, and map collections and to house the index file of newspapers and local publications. That year Julia exhibited letters, papers, and artifacts loaned by descendants of Republic of Texas presidents Mirabeau B. Lamar and Anson Jones, which revealed the "calibre [*sic*] of early statesmen of Texas," who "at the inception of the Republic [were] laying the foundation for the institutions of higher education in Texas."[110]

Julia always reported cooperation with city departments. Public works landscaped library building properties , which then were maintained by parks department employees. When the street department needed help naming new streets in the fast-growing city, the librarians provided a list of Texas heroes whose names might be appropriate. Julia also worked with the city planning commission, chaired by her friend Will Hogg, whose Hogg Brothers Inc. donated 272 pamphlets and periodicals on the subject. From July 26 to 28, 1928, the Democratic National Convention met next door to the Central Library in the quickly constructed Sam Houston Hall, and Julia ordered "as many books and pamphlets on political questions" as she could find to help Houstonians understand the convention process.[111] The platform and resolutions committee deliberated in the library auditorium, and many important visitors signed the library guest book and perused the shelves. With so many guests in town, Julia introduced postcard views of the library, made in color and in sepia tones, to sell as souvenirs of time spent in one of Houston's most magnificent buildings. The liberal policy adopted by the library board regarding use by outside groups—to make library facilities available free of charge to organizations who sponsored cultural or civic programs—had paid off. In 1929, the library hosted over two hundred meetings. New programs for children that year included "Vacation Reading," an activity "with emphasis on world friendship." All branches participated in the annual "Book Week," when children exhibited dolls, posters, and artistic projects, and every year fifth graders visited the Central Library "to establish one sure contact between school and library" and to learn proper library etiquette.[112]

In 1929 the library budget was approaching $80,000 a year, and a staff of forty—eighteen professional librarians, sixteen untrained workers, and six janitors—administered programs at the Central Library, the handsomely constructed Carnegie (North), Heights, and Colored Carnegie branches, and at five year-round delivery stations at Council House, Foley Brothers, Harrisburg, Park Place, and West End. The Rusk Settlement station had struggled to maintain staff in the 1920s but reopened as a library branch in 1928. Julia frequently expressed gratitude to donors, praise for staff, and excitement about programs, but every day she recognized new demands as Houston's economy expanded, technology changed, and people relocated to the booming town. Julia realized that city officials and library trustees had put every available resource into the new building, but plans for the rear wing, as yet unbuilt, haunted her because she knew just how she would use the space.

As early as 1927, she reported that "many visitors have expressed a pleasure and delight in the beautiful building mingled with a disappointment in the fact that their hopes of a book collection equally fine had not materialized."[113] By 1929, Julia "deplored the lack of funds" in the library budget for book acquisition.[114] She explained that twice the number of books were needed to maintain the American Library Association standard of five books per resident if the library were to keep up with Houston's explosive growth. Julia wanted to provide service to new parts of the city; she wanted to bring books to hospital patients and convalescents; she wanted to expand Braille editions; and she wanted to increase reference resources. She knew the delivery stations in Harrisburg, Park Place, and the West End should be converted to full branches. She wanted to build out the unoccupied room on the east wing's third floor for the historical department and to place rare books under appropriate archival supervision. She knew she could finish the space and add a capable librarian to the staff for only $3,000. Julia also wanted to hire a librarian whose sole task would be supervising the technical and industrial materials, and she believed the new Dumble Collection should form the nucleus for a special geological library. Finally, she wanted to double the seating capacity in the periodicals room by the simple expedient of adding more chairs. As she looked ahead, Julia wondered how she could find funding to overcome the book deficit and implement her other dreams.

Torchbearer: 1929

During the 1920s Julia Ideson often seemed to devote every hour to planning and building the grand Central Library, but she continued to pursue her many professional, civic, and personal interests. She attended annual meetings of the

Julia Ideson and her mother, Rose Baseman Ideson. MSS0032–119, Julia Ideson Collection, Houston Public Library, Houston Metropolitan Research Center.

American Library Association and the Texas Library Association and biannual conferences of the Southwestern Library Association, which was founded at the TLA annual meeting on October 26, 1922, to promote library growth in Arizona, Arkansas, Louisiana, New Mexico, Oklahoma, Texas, and Mexico. She valued staff camaraderie and was photographed walking with colleagues along the tree-shaded sidewalks of Forest Hill, a community of curving streets laid out by city planners Hare & Hare in 1910 between the Houston Country Club and Bray's Bayou. Julia and her mother shared their apartment home for many years with assistant librarian Louise Franklin.

Like Alice Baker and her husband, Ima Hogg and her brothers, and Houston's other civic leaders, Julia donated to the Community Chest. Founded in 1922 "to care for [citizens] who are in need," its annual campaign raised funds to support a list of approved social service agencies.[115] Julia remained active in the League of Women Voters, often addressing the group or serving as toastmistress for regularly scheduled citizenship luncheons at the Rice Hotel. She occasionally hosted monthly meetings of the Kappa Kappa Gamma alumnae association, and she maintained her membership in the Girls' Musical Club, entertaining them in 1920 with a talk about her trip to Naples, Italy. In June 1924, at a club meeting attended by Ima Hogg, Julia asked members to help her select a comprehensive musical library for the music room she planned to install in the new library building. When eleven men organized an outing club near Seabrook, twenty-five miles from Houston on Clear Lake, they invited Julia and two other women to serve as fellow directors of Oaksmere Lodge, which celebrated its opening in May 1921 with an "elaborate" program of music, dinner, and dancing throughout a day and evening open house. The large, two-story clubhouse, set "in the midst of a smooth sloping lawn, dotted with cedars and palms," overlooked the lake and provided the athletic librarian an escape from the city.[116]

When not attending symphony concerts and operas with Ima Hogg and other musical friends, Julia indulged her love for the theater. In November 1919 Julia and fellow College Women's Club members who had appeared in amateur theatricals organized the Green Mask Players to bring the new experience of "little theater" to Houston. Little theaters objected to early cinema and theatrical commercialism but instead encouraged experimentation and produced one-act plays specifically written for them by professional playwrights. The Green Mask Players attracted leadership support from Stockton Axson, chairman of the Rice Institute English department, John Clark Tidden, head of the Institute's art department, and prominent architect Birdsall P. Briscoe, who designed the group's elaborate sets and costumes. Backed by fifty influential Houstonians who guaranteed twenty-five dollars each, the Players produced a successful debut season at the South End High School Auditorium in Spring 1920. For the next two seasons they offered three bills, each with three one-act plays. In October 1921 the Players announced a contest for local playwrights. One hundred dollars would be awarded to the best one-act play "of sufficient merit to warrant its production by the Green Mask Players."[117] Julia occasionally performed, served as secretary, and oversaw subscriptions. Despite good press for the mixed amateur and professional company, the Green Mask Players could not compete with popular productions developed by the Rice Dramatic Club, which John Clark Tidden organized in November 1921. In 1925 the Green Mask Players gave their curtains to the public library for its new auditorium, and in 1928 they donated the balance of their funds, $94.74, to the library to purchase theater books.

More long-lasting was Julia's leadership of the Open Forum, a "voluntary association of citizens," founded in 1926 to preserve First Amendment rights and to bring distinguished, independent thinkers to Houston to provoke discussion on topics that were usually seen as both liberal and controversial. In its first seasons, Julia welcomed speakers to the library auditorium, but soon the crowds moved to the City Auditorium, where audiences for an evening in November 1929 with British analytic philosopher, essayist, and social critic Bertrand Russell overflowed into the second balcony. Other speakers that year included Max Eastman, an editor, scientist, and "restless profit of the new era," and Norman Thomas, a Presbyterian minister, Princeton University graduate, and perennial Socialist Party candidate described as "far and away the best speaker to have graced [the Open Forum's] platform—in two years" and "one of the strongest and most significant figures in American public life." Until the Open Forum's demise in 1938, Julia suggested speakers, urged participation, and advocated for the group's efforts to challenge Houstonians. For twelve years, forum organizers attracted financial support and audience participation from leading citizens Ima Hogg, Will Clayton, Oveta Culp Hobby, and public schools Superintendent E. E. Oberholzer; from important professional women including city planner Ethel Brosius and journalist Ramona Brady; from progressive institutions Rice Institute and the League of Women Voters; and from members of women's and men's civic clubs.[118]

Members of the Women's Advertising Club of Houston recognized Julia's lifetime of civic service when they passed the "torch of civic-mindedness, high principle, public service, [and] constructive purpose" to her on April 30, 1929, at a testimonial banquet in her honor hosted by the Knife and Fork Club at the Rice Hotel. The club's torch had first been bestowed on Edna W. Saunders in 1927 to honor the empresario who "has brought the music of the world" to City Auditorium since 1910. From Saunders, the torch had passed to builder and businesswoman Mellie Esperson Stewart, whose thirty-two-story Niels Esperson tower pierced the city skyline in 1927. Now the "slim, busy hands of Librarian Julia Ideson" would hold the torch and retain the engraved tablet enshrining the "innate ability, untiring devotion to her work, and interest in the welfare of the public, [which] has created a center of educational literary facilities in Houston." A large host committee of notable Houstonians included Captain James A. Baker, Judge Hiram M. Garwood, and Ima Hogg. William States Jacobs served as toastmaster, and Mayor Walter Monteith made the principal address. Symphony supporter Maurice Hirsch, Reverend Peter Gray Sears, library maven Elizabeth Ring, and Women's Advertising Club President Mrs. M. L. Gill made remarks and presentations to the woman who had "held aloft the torch of learning" since 1903. Julia Ideson, a "distinguished figure in

Julia Ideson, 1930s. MSS0032–087, Julia Ideson Collection, Houston Public Library, Houston Metropolitan Research Center.

white georgette, a rose silk cape thrown gracefully back from her shoulders," received the award graciously and entertained her friends with witty remarks about her long career.[119]

Books for the Great Depression: 1930–1939

Julia Ideson moved the growing library collections to their new home with great expectations to expand services and diversify collections. As Houston's 1929 "torchbearer," the beloved librarian remained optimistic about future prospects, but events that fall ended elaborate dreams as 1920s speculation spiraled into the decade-long Depression. Before the selling frenzy of October 28–29, farmers were struggling, manufacturing was slowing, and oil prices began to dip, leaving thousands of investors with overvalued portfolios. By 1932 stocks had lost 80 percent of their value. By 1933 half the banks had failed, and fifteen million US workers were unemployed. Houston did not suffer as badly as many areas of the country—bankers cooperated to save local banks, and oil revenues, while low, continued to bolster the economy—but gone was the boosterism that foresaw endless grand projects for the city. Nevertheless, on November 24, 1931, Houstonians celebrated the fifth anniversary of the Central Library designed by Cram and Watkin. Flower arrangements and exhibits on every floor greeted visitors, who also enjoyed a "program of music and talks" in the auditorium. Library board members, former trustees, donors, and staff formed a reception committee to welcome honored guests—the president of the Texas Federation of Women's Clubs, the president of the Houston Federation of Women's Clubs, and all the clubwomen of Houston whose "pioneer efforts" established a modern, publicly funded library and secured Andrew Carnegie's enabling gift. At the time of the celebration, Houston's public library system comprised the Central Library, the Colored Carnegie, Carnegie (North), and Heights branches, and eight delivery stations, including Rusk Settlement, Council House, Foley Brothers (for Foley employees), Young Women's Cooperative House, Thomas Jefferson School (staffed by the PTA in the summer), Florence Crittenton Rescue Home, and the Harrisburg and Park Place county library outlets, which transferred to the city system when those areas of town were absorbed within Houston city limits in 1928.[120]

As Houstonians tightened their belts in the 1930s, the population continued to grow, and Julia was forced to do much more with less money and fewer professional staffers. Librarians everywhere realized they were "fighting social bankruptcy" and "promoting human welfare" by expanding library services. "Throngs entered the Main Building each day," noted Library Association President William A. Vinson in 1934, and "the search for information seemed to be more intensive than ever . . . in a period of extreme anxiety." Julia and the Houston Library Association faced old problems and new challenges. Lack of money had plagued Julia from the beginning of her tenure; now tax revenues plateaued and then shrank during the 1930s as property values dipped. Library use surged as books became "the chief recreation in many families" and cheered "many worried minds." Novels borrowed at no charge took the place of costly moving pictures and assuaged personal woes, while job seekers sought information that might lead to new employment. Finally, changing demographics forced Julia to reorder priorities, expand service to new residential areas, and adapt space to new use.[121]

Julia's 1930 annual report began with the staggering figures of the 1930 census (292,352 Houstonians), which, she believed, explained the "library's great problem of making both ends meet." Per capita expenditures of twenty-nine cents per resident placed Houston well below American Library Association standards and far behind thirteen of the fifteen cities of Houston's size. Nor did the financial picture improve during the remaining years of Julia's tenure. Despite the Depression, Houston grew steadily, demand for library services surged, and the rate of levy for the library remained $.025 per $100 valuation. During the five-year period from 1931 to 1936, when tax collections and the library's income were "greatly reduced," Julia performed miracles of "economy and adjustment." In 1932 she noted the library had the "busiest year of its life," but the "retrenchment did not interfere with the basic services of the library." She often reminded her board of the ALA resolution adopted in December 1931. The Depression, the ALA declared, "offers a challenge to the public libraries of America," and "economic insecurity breeds intellectual unrest"; library trustees must "champion the cause of the library before appropriating bodies, pointing out the necessity of maintaining in spite of all obstacles, these essential services which promote intelligent thinking and vocational education or re-education and which help to keep up the public morale." Not until 1937 was there a slight uptick in revenue and an improvement in the budget. Yet the 1940 census revealed a 35 percent gain in population; with stagnant income, the per capita library expenditure sank to twenty-three cents per citizen.[122]

By 1930 Julia had to make expensive repairs on the new building, fight termites in the Heights Branch, and order a new metal roof for the Colored Carnegie Library, leaving few funds to meet rising demands for new books. With shrinking city revenues, Julia relied heavily on her numerous friends, on Houston organizations and businesses, and on the generosity of library patrons to supplement her small acquisition budget. In 1930 donors provided over six thousand books, pamphlets, magazines, pictures, and maps for several collections. Every year through 1945, societies like the Daughters of the American Revolution and the Daughters of the Republic of Texas gave books about American and Texas history to the library, while the Tuesday Musical Club (the Girls' Musical Club until 1930) donated annually to the music collection. In 1931 Bessie T. Hill donated $1,000 to establish a fund in memory of her mother for "books the library could not otherwise purchase," and 186 donors raised money for a "Lindbergh Globe" set in a handsome, carved walnut stand—the same type presented to Charles Lindbergh after his pathbreaking transatlantic flight. Patrons continued to provide in-kind donations of books, maps, pamphlets, and other materials—7,537 items in 1935, 8,769 in 1936, and a banner donation year of 13,298 items in 1939 that included 4,690 books and 1,957 maps. In March 1936 the library received a major bequest, the library of Adele Briscoe Looscan, whose extensive collection included three generations of books from a Texas "family of bookloving [*sic*] pioneers."[123]

Annette Finnigan had recovered enough from her debilitating illness to spend two decades traveling with a companion and collecting art for Houston's museum and books for her dear friend's library. In 1931 Finnigan made her first major gift to the library, sixty-five "volumes of unusual beauty and value" rarely seen except in Europe or in major American collections. The gift included medieval manuscripts, early printed books, and seventeen works "of Oriental calligraphy and illumination," including editions of the Koran and "a quaint life of Mohammed from the fourteenth century." In 1935, 1936, and 1937 Finnigan made annual donations of $1,000 to purchase books about Texas, Mexico, and the Southwest, and in 1937 she presented a piece of antique Spanish majolica purchased in Malaga to be placed in one of the library walls. After Finnigan died on Wednesday, July 18, 1940, following a long fight with cancer, her will established the Annette Finnigan Endowment Fund of $25,000 "to purchase books and maps of special interest" and to provide "a permanent source of enrichment for the Library's resources." Like the Meldrum endowment, interest income from the fund would defray book purchases in perpetuity. In 1942 Julia used the first income from Finnigan's fund to purchase "the lithographed edition of the Catalog of the Library of Congress," which was being issued over three years and slated to reach 160 volumes.[124]

Julia also stretched her limited budget by finding new kinds of support. The Southern Garden Club cared for the grounds of the main building and each year donated specimen trees and other shrubs and plants to enhance the beauty of the campus. Radio station KPRC provided free advertising when its broadcasters interviewed the librarian, sponsored library programing, and in 1940 introduced *The Golden Key*, a fifteen-minute children's program of readings from classic children's literature. To supplement the meager acquisition budget in 1933, the local Federation of Women's Clubs organized a book drive for the library in late November. Publicity produced by the children's librarian for posters, radio announcements, and newspaper articles told Houstonians that "Hoarding is out-of-date" and admonished them to "Share your books" and "Put your idle books to work." In ten days, volunteer women gathered 6,002 books, "the majority of which were . . . satisfactory titles for library use."[125]

Exhibit funding was severely curtailed, but Julia drew on library collections and loans from friends to create small exhibits in the central building. In 1930 she displayed valuable rare books from the Circle M Collection, including a 1717 printing of Roman poet Virgil's *P. Virgilii Maronis Opera*, illustrated with wood carvings, and she asked Sam Houston High School Latin teacher Pearl Penn to share maps and mementoes from her summer cruise celebrating the poet's two thousandth birthday. In 1932 Ima Hogg loaned picture books she had purchased while visiting the Soviet Union three years earlier, and Julia mounted a large display of the art books Annette Finnigan had recently donated. That year the Colored Carnegie Library initiated what became a popular annual juried art exhibit of works by Houston's African American artists. Judges in 1936 submitted the best works to the Texas Centennial Exposition in Dallas. In 1937 the Carnegie Corporation donated 101 costly illustrated art books and 865 color photographs of paintings, sculptures, and architectural masterpieces to the library. The Tuesday Musical Club held several recitals to raise money for contributions of sheet music to the library branches and in 1941 presented nineteen record albums to the Central Library to inaugurate a phonograph record collection. In 1940 the library received a pledge of $15,000 to build an eastside branch library at Central Park in honor of Monroe D. Anderson. The library association acquired a lot in 1942 but decided to defer construction until World War II ended.

Although revenues for Julia's budget shrank and alternative funding became mandatory, use of library facilities grew steadily during the uncertain years of the Depression and the Second World War that followed. Book circulation rose 15 percent to 612,158 in 1930 and spiked to 900,078 in 1932 at the panic's nadir. It slumped to 716,741 in 1936, when the economy was finally beginning to recover and then rose every year thereafter as the population exploded. Unhappily, money from city taxes remained steady at about $75,000 to $78,000 per year. While salaries stagnated and workloads increased, Julia maintained services through economy and adjustments that included closing libraries on Sundays and holidays, reducing hours in the children's room and branches, and seeking help from volunteer workers. She even installed a modern self-charging system, first used in Detroit. After several months of deliberation, Julia placed an announcement in local newspapers explaining how patrons would charge their own books. "Write your own card number on the book card in the back of the book on the first unfilled space. Just as you are leaving the library, hand the books open with your card to the assistant to check. Your library card becomes your identification card. It will not be dated." Responses varied from amusing to cynical to threatening, but most people complied with the time-saving measure that made "rush hours pass more smoothly."[126]

The Great Depression introduced a source of revenue unknown to most Americans in 1929—federal emergency assistance. For the first time, federal funds helped maintain library buildings, support new programs, embellish the interior, and build collections. Shortly after the crash, Julia "was given the privilege" of a work crew sponsored by Herbert Hoover's emergency relief efforts; workers paid with government funds moved book collections, built shelves, laid drainpipes, and performed janitorial duties over a three-month period. Houston began to feel the full impact of federal assistance when President Hoover named banker, builder, and *Houston Chronicle* Publisher Jesse H. Jones chairman of the Reconstruction Finance Corporation (RFC), which was charged on January 22, 1932, with mobilizing the country for economic recovery. Jones remained with the RFC through 1939, becoming secretary of commerce in 1940, and his largesse included securing federal funds to build Houston's City Hall and the Sam Houston Coliseum.

Franklin Roosevelt's New Deal developed what some laughingly described as an alphabet soup of federal agencies authorized to employ people and make grants to civic projects. By 1934–1935 Julia was partnering with Washington bureaucrats as the library paid for materials while federal programs defrayed labor costs. Workers paid by the Works Progress Administration (WPA), Federal Emergency Relief Administration (FERA), Public Works Administration (PWA), Civil Works Administration (CWA), and National Youth Administration (NYA) "practically made over" the Carnegie Colored Branch, repaired all library buildings, cleaned windows, built shelving, and treated over five thousand leather-bound government documents with leather preservative—jobs that probably would have been left undone without the 259 work days assigned between May 29 and August 15, 1935. FERA financed eight workers from the Rice Institute who provided 935 hours during the school year to type memoranda and reports, assist the catalogue department, and prepare books for shelving. Julia particularly favored the self-named "Uncle Sam's daughters," ninety-five young women from the NYA working under Frederica Killgore, who was on loan to the NYA from her post as children's librarian. They mended books, clipped newspapers, mounted pictures, typed catalogues, and cleaned soiled books. This clever team invented and produced swivel newspaper stands to handle oversized newspaper volumes. To celebrate the Texas centennial,

NYA workers compiled twenty-two scrapbooks for the reference and historical departments to record frontier settlements and the lives of people whose everyday deeds were overlooked in most history books. While the librarians agreed that "the training of these many young people is laborious and sometimes discouraging, requiring persistence and patience," the more capable recruits relieved staff members of desk routine and mechanical work and allowed the librarians to focus on "real library service." Projects sponsored by these agencies continued through 1939, when the WPA also provided a grant of $3,071 to the Park Place Branch building fund. Federal funds paid for valuable work, and many young men and women received training, discipline, and much-needed income that helped them survive economic hardship; some even returned to the library for additional assignments.[127]

Julia Ideson applied to the Public Works Administration for funds to build out the west wing service area and a small garage proposed in the original plan, but her request failed. Instead, the administration sponsored an art project of eight murals for the Central Library, executed by three Houston artists. Galveston native Angela McDonnell (1876–1946), who had studied at the Art Institute of Chicago and spent nearly two years painting in Spain, recounted Houston's Spanish heritage in three murals installed in the lunettes along the west-wing corridor leading to the auditorium wing: *Avila, the Excuses for Conquest*; *La Rabida, Cradle of the New World*; and *Toledo, Art and Literature of Spain*. Her work was the first to be completed, following the installation of *Toledo* in September 1935. Ruth Pershing Uhler (1898–1967) moved to Houston as a child but earned a degree from the Philadelphia School of Design for Women and received a fellowship that enabled her to paint and exhibit in Philadelphia for eleven years before she returned to Houston in 1925. For a decade Uhler painted and exhibited in Texas before becoming a teacher at Houston's Museum of Fine Arts and in 1941 the first curator of education, a position she held until her death twenty-six years later. Her large mural, installed in May 1936, fills the east wall of the staircase landing. Titled *The First Subscription Committee, 1854*, the mural recounts efforts to solicit money and books for a public library from the banker Thomas Bagby and his family. Well-known artist and cultural leader Emma Richardson Cherry (1859–1954) painted oil on canvas images of four historic buildings to hang on the east and west walls of the delivery hall on the main (or second) floor: *Arlington*, the home of Robert E. Lee; *Beauvoir*, the home of Jefferson Davis; the *Republic of Texas Capitol*, located in Houston from 1836 to 1838; and the *President's House* occupied by Sam Houston, when he was president of the Republic of Texas from 1836 to 1838. The PWA paid for two of the images, while two were gifts to the library from Cherry, who embellished the scenes with Texas plant life.

Houston's downtown changed dramatically in the 1930s. For more than a decade, residents had been moving away from downtown; trolley service carried middle-class homeowners to the Heights north of Buffalo Bayou; two interurban electric railways brought workers to manufacturing plants east of town or took beachgoers to Galveston; and new parkways along the bayous joined downtown offices to prime residential land west of town where the Hogg family was building River Oaks as a planned community. Handsome Victorian mansions near downtown succumbed to the wrecking ball as office buildings began to crowd the skyline. City Planning Commission Chairman Will Hogg envisioned the 1926 Cram-Watkin library as the first structure along a mall of civic buildings that would include a post office, city and county courts, and at the west end an imposing city-county administrative building, all to be designed in the Spanish Renaissance style of the library. City officials shelved plans for further civic center development after the 1929 crash, but in 1936, with encouragement from Jesse Jones, Houston officials secured funding from the Public Works Administration for an imposing city hall tower and capacious coliseum to house conventions, performing arts, and civic gatherings on a grand scale. Construction of the buildings, street paving, and mall landscaping in 1937–1939 brought turmoil to the area. In addition to budgetary constraints and demographic changes, Julia now faced building debris that blocked street access to the library and to nearby parking spaces. As war clouds gathered, library patronage had shifted; the Central Library still provided strong resources for research, but branches now offered many programs for children and expanded their lending collections so nearby residents could enjoy reading at home.

The beautiful Meldrum Room was the first space to feel the effects of changing residential patterns. Every year Harriet Dickson, the children's librarian, sponsored Book Week to advertise new publications and encourage family visits to the library. She also introduced new programs like the series of nature talks where naturalists and zookeepers discussed snakes, stars, and trees with youthful enthusiasts. In these years when families rarely traveled, participants in the Vacation Reading Club took imaginary journeys, stamping their passports with the names of books they had read or placing stars for each book on a map of the world. One year the SS *Libraria* carried readers to friends around the world; another year, participants were "book gypsies," exploring a trail of adventures. In 1938 members of the Flying Carpet Club "visualized books as magic mediums of travel," and in 1939 the library celebrated a weeklong Mexican Fiesta in May and a Mexican Trails summer reading club. Dickson gained a national reputation, attended ALA conventions, and was named official examiner for the Boy Scouts merit badge in reading, an honor she felt would enable her to "work the library into the boy life of Houston." Despite the "well-filled bookshelves and attractive atmosphere" of the Meldrum Room, children's circulation at the Central Library declined as families moved away from downtown, and the room's use changed. Elementary school classes still visited the downtown library every year, but the room added a parents' resource center, offering special seminars for parents and housing a collection of books and pamphlets about parenting and parent-child relationships. The Meldrum Room also stocked books on child training and psychology recommended by the parent education classes taught in the Houston public schools.[128]

Although hampered by budget constraints, Julia and her staff believed the library "feels the pulse of a growing city" and recognized that reading trends paralleled local and national events. Following the 1929 crash, patrons requested books on finance, new ways to make money, and escapist fiction. Julia continued to build the popular genealogy, history, business, arts, and sciences collections, but she also responded to new requests for books about the oil and synthetic rubber industries, about technological change, and about flood control following several devastating floods in the 1928–1939 period. As menacing actions in Europe and Asia threatened another world cataclysm, patrons began to request books about World War I, the Versailles Treaty, aviation, shipbuilding, and military preparedness. Adolf Hitler's *Mein Kampf* topped circulation lists as Houstonians tried to understand what was happening in Germany and "comprehend the purport of the European mischance." Librarians in the research department experienced a surge of requests and began to address hundreds of questions over the telephone. Although working long hours, these dedicated professionals found "the sheer joy of contributing" to the knowledge of each inquirer made the busy hours "exhilarating."[129]

In 1935 the Houston Public Library was one of ten systems chosen by the American Library Association to participate in a nationwide effort to measure reference services. For the week of October 14, the participating libraries kept a record of all reference questions in four categories: "questions about persons and places in the city, about the library, and about the catalog"; fact-finding questions; questions that needed additional research; and queries about reading suggestions. In the one-week period, librarians fielded 5,691 questions, which Julia projected would mean that the library handled an "almost unbelievable" three hundred thousand queries every year. While some questions took thirty to forty-five minutes to research, "a far larger number took thirty seconds." By 1939 four special reference librarians responded to questions on everything from "the manufacturing process of various forms of synthetic rubber" to correct etiquette. That year a twelve-day survey revealed that librarians at the Central Library had answered fifty questions by telephone each day, an increase over telephone use in previous years. Julia's carefully kept statistics repeatedly showed that library usage was increasing and that most of the increase was in branches located in residential areas.[130]

For years the library's Extension Department staffers had worked closely with the Houston public schools, the parent-teacher associations, and other neighborhood groups to open reading rooms in local schools and to transform school stations into branch libraries. Although total Houston Public Library staff shrank from fifty-two in 1933 to forty-one in 1938, Julia continued to expand the Extension Department, and by 1937, when funding began to improve, the Houston Public Library provided reading materials to 121 agencies, including the Central Library, the three branches, fours sub-branches (Eastwood, West End, Harrisburg, and Park Place), twelve stations (including a new station for Central Park in a small frame building on the campus of Edison High School and two stations at summer camps run by the Girl Scouts and the YWCA), and more than one hundred classroom libraries. In 1938 Julia launched the library's most popular outreach effort when the Traveling Branch began biweekly stops at parks, a factory, an orphans' home, and several schools and community centers; a district post office, a grocery store, and a fire station allowed curbside service. "It's Christmas once a week," exclaimed one patron. The Traveling Branch bookmobile, with its shelves of books, reached hundreds of Houstonians without adding new staffers and was as "convenient as the corner drugstore and as friendly as one's own club." At long last, the bookmobile brought library service to everyone.[131]

Colored Carnegie Branch Librarian Florence Bandy's thorough annual reports to the board illuminated the importance of Julia's extension programs. In 1938, Bandy explained, the library's most important role was to make "the reader feel welcome" and to help "the laboring classes from all parts of the city" find the books they needed. That year the Colored Carnegie Branch provided a bibliography of books for teachers and lists of career-building resources to adults. The library was "definitely useful to the Houston College for Negroes" because its collections supplemented college resources. At the request of Howard University and Julia Ideson, Bandy and her staff prepared bibliography cards describing the 525 Houston Public Library holdings "by and about the Negro." Bandy kept records of patron attendance and book circulation—Margaret Mitchell's *Gone with the Wind* was the most requested novel that year—and welcomed patrons to Saturday morning story hours and meetings of the Negro Art Guild of Houston, the Cullen Booklovers Club, and the Wednesday Morning Study Club. Despite Bandy's enthusiastic pride in her branch's accomplishments, *Houston Informer* critics were skeptical and year after year noted persistent underfunding at the Colored Carnegie Branch, which was only 4 to 5 percent of library expenditures. "It would be a joke . . . to compare . . . opportunities for intellectual and cultural development" at the Colored Carnegie Branch with those at the municipal libraries, "which Negroes are taxed to support, but from which they are excluded" was the editor's acid conclusion.[132]

In 1939 Julia happily reported a year of "special accomplishments." The Central Library opened a room on the second floor to house the geological collection and special technical books. In April Julia organized the "Childhood Favorites" exhibit "of much interest" to children of all ages. Over eighty librarians and Houston pacesetters shared the books they most enjoyed as children. Contributors included Mayor Oscar Holcombe; library patrons Captain James A. Baker, Elizabeth Ring, Professor Radoslav Tsanoff, and William A. Vinson; cultural leaders James Chillman, Edgar Odell Lovett, and art historian Stella Shurtleff; children's poet Judd Mortimer Lewis; and Julia's dear friend and generous philanthropist Ima Hogg. On May 5 about 250 guests, including seven of the ten founders, gathered at the Colored Carnegie Library to celebrate thirty years of service. Elizabeth Ring represented the library board, and Judge Joseph C. Hutcheson Jr. gave the principal address, "The Negro Library Movement in Houston Comes of Age." On July 10 "friendly citizens of the Heights" dedicated a reading patio and memorial fountain at Heights Branch. The following week, on July 17 the "enthusiastic and determined" citizens of Park Place dedicated their long-awaited branch; the building was underwritten by the Park Place Library Association, which matched government funds from the PWA. On October 25 supporters celebrated expanded library access for the African American community at the opening of Emancipation Park Branch, an "attractively furnished" space in the popular park's new recreation house. Speakers at the event included Recreation Department Director Corinne Fonde, Assistant Librarian Martha Schnitzer, library board member Mrs. Roy Arterbury, and Mrs. M. O. Sledge, chairwoman of the Emancipation Park Improvement Club. To expand services further, the library installed a well-stocked delivery station at Ripley House when the East End neighborhood center opened in

1940. The next year the library board, spurred to action by the West End Civic Improvement Club, opened West End Branch on February 4, 1941. As war clouds loomed, the Houston Public Library had helped readers in every part of the city discover the pleasure and value of reading.[133]

Beloved Citizen: The 1930s

During the tumultuous Depression years, Julia Ideson remained a beloved citizen and continued to support civic organizations she had long admired. As one of the city's public intellectuals, she frequently submitted articles to the press, expressed opinions on the radio, and addressed gatherings on festive occasions. When "Heck," a contributor to the *Houston Labor Journal*, "challenged the technique of the American Public Library" in 1930 by suggesting Houston's library should advertise more, print a catalogue of its holdings, and dispense with the "card index system," Julia requested "public space" to respond since his point of view was not unusual. In a masterful, five-page analysis, printed in full, Julia noted that, although she would be delighted to have more publicity and more patrons, during that year alone, the library had benefitted from 175 articles, ten editorials, and one illustrated tribute spread across two pages. Julia then carefully explained the card catalogue system and why it was practical, helpful, and efficient. In closing, she expressed gratitude to the *Journal* for its longtime support and for the "opportunity to explain the library's workings." In 1932 Julia became the first Houston woman to list her accomplishments in *Who's Who in America*, and in 1933 she strongly opposed a bill proposed in the Texas legislature that would have abolished the state library. In 1936 she and fellow College Women's Club members—then numbering three hundred—celebrated the club's twentieth anniversary with a tea at the Junior League. Julia helped the League of Women Voters conduct Houston's first "Voters School" in the library auditorium in 1930, and on the eve of war in November 1941, Julia told a League of Women Voters-sponsored "defense breakfast" that the "Public Library is the bastion of democracy, and every new project of national defense is reflected in the requests at the library." Until it ceased operation in 1938, Julia remained on the Open Forum board and promoted its lectures. She entertained speakers and produced handouts of works by or about each participant to enrich audience understanding.[134]

Annual trips to regional, state, and national library association meetings continued to highlight Julia's year. She served as president of the Southwestern Library Association from 1932 to 1934, and on October 21–24, 1936, she and her staff welcomed members of the group to Houston for the organization's first meeting in the city since its founding in 1922. On April 25–27, 1935, Julia and fifteen members of her staff attended the Texas Library Association meeting in Austin. She and Frederica Killgore, children's librarian at the Houston library, joined the Penitentiary Book Selection Committee, a new initiative to develop library resources in prisons that was supported by the Texas Federation of Women's Clubs and the League of Women Voters. These reform-minded women were examining prison conditions and demanding changes; books for inmates were a top priority. In the mid-1930s Julia also served as library consultant to the Texas State Penitentiary in Huntsville. In 1935 Julia edited the centennial edition of the *Handbook of Texas Libraries,* the fourth handbook iteration and the second under her skillful direction. Claiming she worked on the project in her "spare time," Julia gave much credit to her Houston staff. Praised at the American Library Association convention in Denver as the "most detailed and thorough of any handbook ever published," the new edition established "a pattern for the future" and covered the past and present history of the field in 150 pages with forty pages of illustrations. Julia enthusiastically traveled to ALA conferences during the 1930s. As a member of the executive committee, she formulated policy and shared the latest library trends with the Houston library board. She extolled the June 23–28, 1930, trip to Los Angeles, praising the "crisp and cool" weather, the California hospitality, and the "outstanding" visit to the treasures of the Huntington library and art gallery. Three years later Julia loaded two automobiles with staff and headed to Chicago from October 16 to 21, 1933, for the annual ALA meeting, where she was promoted to first vice president and chaired the October 20 third general session devoted to new trends in education and the place of books and reading in modern society. Killgore also gained wide recognition as treasurer of the ALA section for library work with children in 1935–1937, as a member of the Newbery Medal Committee in 1935 and 1936, and as the compiler of a directory of children's librarians in America.[135]

In the 1930s the friendship between Julia Ideson and Ima Hogg deepened. They worked on several projects together and discovered a mutual love for Mexico. Ima frequently traveled to Mexico in the summer, and Julia attended at least five seminars sponsored by the Committee on Cultural Relations with Latin America. From July 13 to August 3, 1929, she visited Mexico City for the committee's fourth seminar. Two years later, she returned to Mexico City from July 4 to July 24, 1931, to absorb the wisdom of honorary chairman and philosopher John Dewey. The thirteenth seminar, which took place from July

Julia Ideson, far right, and Ima Hogg, center, at Varner Plantation, 1924. camh-dob-012143, Ima Hogg Photographs, Dolph Briscoe Center for American History, The University of Texas at Austin.

13 to August 1, 1938, was also held in Mexico City. The next year participants met from July 7 to July 27 in Cuernavaca—a daily train journey from San Antonio—and benefitted from the musical talents of composer and symphony director Carlos Chavez.[136] In 1938 the former University of Texas classmates were inducted into the Philosophical Society of Texas, one hundred years after its founding to stimulate learning and public discourse. Julia and Ima joined the three pioneering women who had been inducted the year before—poet and University of Chicago graduate Karle Wilson Baker, American Federation of Women's Clubs President Mrs. Percy V. Pennybacker (Anna Hardwicke), and former state librarian and renowned archivist Elizabeth Howard West. Julia served as Philosophical Society recording secretary in 1940, and Ima was elected the first woman president in 1948. In March 1939 Texas Chairwoman Oveta Culp Hobby, executive vice president of the *Houston Post*, invited Julia Ideson, Ima Hogg, Emma Richardson Cherry, and seventeen other Houston women to serve on her advisory committee to oversee women's participation in the 1939 New York World's Fair. Hobby also named Adelaide Lovett Baker to chair Texas's subcommittee for art. The daughter of Rice Institute President

Inchcape, the home built by Julia Ideson on Buffalo Bayou, 1930s. MSS0032–91, Julia Ideson Collection, Houston Public Library, Houston Metropolitan Research Center.

Edgar O. Lovett and daughter-in-law of Settlement Association founder Alice Baker, Adelaide had established the Junior League of Houston and represented the next generation of civic leadership. In 1940 Julia Ideson, Ima Hogg, Estelle Sharp, Huberta Garwood, and Settlement Association President Corrinne Tsanoff joined sixteen other women leaders to found the Pan American Round Table to discuss problems affecting the Western Hemisphere and to promote amicable relations between countries in North and South America.

From time to time, Julia followed her father's example and invested in real estate, but for most of her life she lived in an apartment in Houston. In 1928 she decided to build a house for her mother and herself. She found a densely wooded six-acre plot of undeveloped land overlooking Buffalo Bayou at the end of Logan Lane, a quiet spot off Memorial Drive, but plans to build were delayed by hurricane flooding in 1929. Work began in 1930 on an "airplane bungalow"—so called because the one-story building included a "pop-up" second story of one or two rooms, with many windows that created a pleasant airflow in summer. Julia chose "Inchcape" as the name for her "lovely little country place" allegedly because the sloping site reminded her of a poem by Robert Southey, a moral tale of poetic justice set on a rock off the south coast of Scotland. She lived in this house until her death, although in 1935 the property suffered severe flood damage that destroyed most of her personal papers and many of her books. She enjoyed frequent garden suppers on a wide porch that overlooked the bayou and was surrounded by trees and shrubs. At one memorable twilight repast with lifelong friends Ima Hogg and Austinite Dorothy Thornton and several others, the guests dined comfortably at a table facing the ravine "above whose banks stretched an immense canopy of azure" as the sun sank into the west.[137] Julia and Ima loved to share driving duties on long summer automobile trips to the Grand Canyon and Hollywood, in New England, and through the Old South. Both were inveterate postcard collectors, memorializing their travels in thousands of images. The two intrepid travelers sailed to Europe in 1937 for an adventure Julia chronicled for Houstonians.

Late in May, nearly five months after her mother's death on January 8, Julia entrained for New York City to visit her sister Margaret for a few days before embarking on a six-month paid leave of absence from Houston, in part a journey to study great European libraries and report back to the board. In New York she met traveling companions Ima Hogg and Ethel Robinson Brown of Austin and joined Houston friend Huberta Garwood, who accompanied the three sojourners for a voyage on the *Vulcania*, an Italian passenger ship sailing to the Azores, Lisbon, Gibraltar, and a cruise of Mediterranean ports. The ladies enjoyed first class accommodations and were honored by a farewell ship dinner of green turtle soup, chicken, turbot, crawfish, lamb, beef sirloin, capon, asparagus, spumoni, and pastries—a memorable menu saved by the librarian. On June 16 they debarked in Venice, where Julia visited the state library founded by the doges in the tenth century. Saying farewell to Huberta Garwood, the three friends traveled to Florence, where Ima purchased three statues to adorn her gardens in Houston and Julia explored several libraries "of the museum type." A motor trip through the hill country allowed them to stop in Siena for the Palio festival, "which had been held ever since the middle ages," and for a visit to the Piccolomini Library, a "gem" housed in the Siena Cathedral. Somewhere en route, the group posed for a photograph on a rocky outcrop before proceeding to Rome, where the Vatican revealed "all sorts of rare book treasures." In Rome they boarded a train for the journey to Salzburg, where they arrived for the July 29 opening of the annual music festival and three weeks of "heavenly music." Julia reported they "were . . . entertained with a close up view of the Duke and Duchess of Windsor" and were proud to hear young Houstonian Victor Alessandro ably conduct an orchestra concert. They left the Salzburg festival in time to catch the final performances of the Munich festival and enjoy four weeks of library tours and rest. Julia visited several libraries but made a special effort to study the original Codex Aureus of St. Emmeram, preserved in the Munich City Museum. Considered one of the finest Carolingian illuminated manuscripts, the four gospels are bound in a covering encrusted with jewels and gold. Annette Finnigan had entrusted a rare facsimile to the Houston Public Library a few years earlier, and Julia could now report she had stood in awe before the "most beautiful book in the world." While in Munich, where buildings and music programs were emblazoned with Nazi swastikas, the women also spent three "interesting" days at the annual Nuremburg Rally, described by Julia as the "Hitler festival." In Paris, although Julia caught the flu, the travelers visited the American Library before boarding the boat train for Le Havre and the voyage home on the *Ile de France*. Julia sailed on September 29, arrived in New York City on October 5, and wrote a long report for her Houston friends and an article, "A Fleeting Look at European Libraries," for the *Bulletin* of the Texas Library Association. She returned to her desk on December 11.[138]

The War Years: 1940–1945

By 1940, Houstonians understood that the protection of two oceans would not save the United States from war. Soon the nation would have to do more than bolster Great Britain and its empire, whose embattled soldiers, sailors, and airmen were fighting Hitler in Europe and combatting Japan in Asia. Although the library still received PWA and NYA assistance, Houston's economy was "riding a tidal wave of wartime production" as workers poured into manufacturing plants.[139] Skyrocketing wages lured young library employees to abandon the profession, while newcomers to the expanding city demanded more services than ever. The shift of patrons from the Central Library to its branches was clear in Julia Ideson's abundant 1940 statistics. While 324,472 books circulated from the Central Library, 488,410 were borrowed from the branches; 487 lectures and meetings took place in branches, while 188 occurred downtown; and teachers brought 1,483 school children to the main library and 3,843 to neighborhood branches. Most critical, reference librarians addressed 37,023 questions at the branch libraries, and only 31,621 downtown, indicating the importance of providing research materials and staff throughout the system. Looking forward, Julia planned to continue centralizing administrative tasks—professionally staffed departments for ordering, cataloguing, and book preparation and care would serve all library agencies; the Extension Department head would supervise all branches and delivery stations; the children's librarian would oversee all programming for young readers; and, Julia hoped, soon she would hire one person to oversee care of all the buildings and their grounds. To keep her overworked and shrinking staff happy, Julia inaugurated a pension plan in 1943 and simplified book circulation by introducing a photographic charging system at each library's checkout and return desk.

Early in 1942, while December 7, 1941, still "filled our hearts with dismay," Julia and the board realized they must protect irreplaceable objects in their collection, especially the fragile early newspapers. If Japan could bomb Pearl Harbor, almost anything might happen. In 1938 the San Jacinto Museum had been created to maintain a museum of Texas history at the newly constructed San Jacinto Battlefield Monument. At the time, Julia and the library board decided to stop collecting Texas documents and memorabilia and instead to divert donors of those items to the new museum. They also began to transfer to the San Jacinto site the Texana "manuscripts and souvenirs" long stored in the library as a courtesy. Following Pearl Harbor, the director and board of the San Jacinto Museum offered "unlimited storage space" in the monument vault for rare documents owned by the Houston Public Library.[140] Julia accepted their offer of temporary asylum for precious records and transferred twenty thousand pounds of old newspapers and valuable manuscripts to safe harbor at the monument for the duration of the war, or for as long as the Houston Public Library wished to "share the burden of maintaining the community records" with the San Jacinto Museum. She made space on the library's third floor available to the San Jacinto Museum curator and WPA assistants so the team could prepare objects for the move.

To meet wartime demands, help men prepare for overseas duty, and support the home front, Julia ordered more books related to shipbuilding, war industries, and civil defense, and stocked a variety of foreign language dictionaries. Because there was no longer much demand for formal lecture space, she remodeled the auditorium as a large reading room to house the library's fifty-nine newspapers and 697 periodicals. She created a Nutrition Center at the Central Library and stocked it with materials to support health and nutrition classes taught by public schools and the Red Cross. The Heights Branch opened a Consumer Information Center where visitors could pick up free literature about food rationing, vegetable gardening, ways to repair household appliances, and care of well-worn clothing. Even as new patrons were besieging established and new library branches, the Extension Department experienced terrific staff turnover and loss of employees to war industries and the armed services. When PWA funding stopped in 1943, the library system lost nineteen workers. Despite these staff cuts, Julia welcomed soldiers and their families to every library outlet, and she encouraged anyone engaged in war work of any kind to take advantage of library programs and resources.

Julia also found new ways to promote library activities. She spoke several times on the radio talk show *Look & Listen*, sponsored by the Museum of Fine Arts. In one program she talked about the book as a work of art and described the treasures donated to the library by Museum of Fine Arts patron Annette Finnigan. Another time she discussed a gift from the Carnegie Corporation to support adult education. In a long interview on April 10, 1942, she told her audience about the "Victory Book Campaign," a national drive to collect ten million books and send them to soldiers, sailors, and marines serving on battlefronts around the world. Julia explained that campaign cosponsors—the American Library Association, Red Cross, and USO— were asking everyone "to share books from your bookcase with men in the barracks." She noted that Houston's quota was ten thousand books and that more than eight thousand had been received in "a steady stream . . . pouring into the central library and its branches and into the Harris County Public Library."[141] Julia urged everyone to participate. Faculty and students at Rice Institute and the University of Houston would find deposit boxes on campus; students could take books to their schools; and housewives could drop off books at Weingarten or Henke & Pillot grocery stores. The manager of Loew's State Theatre offered a month's movie pass for two guests to the person attending *The Bugle Sound* who brought the largest number of usable books to the theater drop box. Julia's 1942 annual report revealed that Harris County donors had given twenty thousand volumes, which were sorted by the Houston Public Library reference staff; the library shipped 16,600 books to Ellington Field, to Texas military camps, and to ships being built in Houston. The library processed another twenty thousand books in 1943. Julia directed the Houston Victory Book Campaign advisory committee from 1942 until her death.

Although preoccupied with the challenge to keep up-to-date with changing technology and "provide war-weary people . . . books to help them forget the war," for the first time in a decade Julia began to turn her attention to the future. What would postwar Houston and its library look like? What steps should she take to prepare? As early as 1941 Houston leaders began to consider these questions, and in 1942–1943 Julia served on the Houston Chamber of Commerce Educational Committee. She attended the War and Post War Problems Institute for Texas and Oklahoma at the University of Texas, where she spoke on panels discussing the future of libraries and other educational issues. When the Houston Federation of Women's Clubs began to hold its annual fall Institute of Government in 1941, Julia distributed lists of books relating to agenda topics, and each year thereafter she and her department heads shared views about the library and its role in Houston's civic life.[142]

In the 1920s Julia began supporting the activities of Houston's Commission on Inter-Racial Cooperation, a local branch of the state commission. Georgians had introduced the first commission in 1920 to alleviate racial strife during demobilization after World War I, and Texans followed their example. Julia was particularly interested in Will Hogg's housing survey, made while he was preparing his "City Plan for Houston" in 1929, and she supported his proposals to build a planned community similar to his River Oaks subdivision in an African American neighborhood as a means of providing better housing. Interracial cooperation floundered after Will Hogg's unexpected death in 1930, but during the war years, Julia participated in activities of the reorganized Texas Commission on Interracial Cooperation and its Houston branch. Although the commission's success was debated at the time, cooperative efforts caused the police department to hire black patrolmen, improve city services in black neighborhoods, and support the Houston Negro Hospital, funded by commission member Joseph S. Cullinan. Soon after the Hogg Foundation for Mental Hygiene began operations at the University of Texas in February 1941, Julia attended a course on race, where Hogg Foundation Director Robert L. Sutherland discussed the psychological basis for racial attitudes, and other speakers examined social, legal, economic, political, and religious issues related to race. Julia received the newsletter published by the Texas commission, including an issue reprising comments by leading African American journalists calling for racial cooperation to defeat the Axis powers. Houston's *Negro Labor News* urged "unity of our war efforts" and noted in capital letters: "The two races working together must face the danger of the situation realistically and must outsmart the Axis in their scheme to divide and conquer the American people. . . . As I see it only Hitler and the Japs will be benefitted if the American people stop fighting the enemy to start squabbling over the race question, whether about the Negro, the Jew, the Italian or the German. As Americans we must hang together during the crisis or hang separately."[143] Would unity in wartime, Julia wondered, bring reconciliation in peacetime?

In her 1944 annual report, Julia noted "the successes of our forces in every field" and the "return of interest to the world of books." Circulation had risen again with renewed enthusiasm for children's books. Readers requested material about peace and postwar planning; they wanted to study the fate of Germany, the issue of economic stability in a postwar world and President Roosevelt's four freedoms—of speech and religion, and from want and fear—famously articulated in his January 6, 1941, State of the Union address. On November 7, 1944, Houston voters authorized $26,250,000 for postwar municipal improvements, and Julia used her report to explain her plans for the $150,000 library allocation. She wanted to complete the stack build-out and finish the west wing of the Central Library; to air condition all buildings; and to build the Monroe Anderson Branch. At the Houston Library Association annual meeting, she expressed deep gratitude to her staff who had survived three years of tumultuous personnel changes. Nine members, including Librarian Julia Ideson and Assistant Librarian Martha Schnitzer, received pins recognizing at least twenty years of service to the city. With five endowment funds and a "shower of gifts" from 352 donors, the balance sheet looked stable, and the future beckoned with promise.[144]

During the previous decade, the library had lost many friends. John Ephraim Thomas Milsaps, whose Circle M Collection proved a boon to researchers but a headache for the cataloguing department, died November 29, 1932. The Meldrums passed from the scene with her death in 1933 and his three years later, but their legacy of annual gifts and a $25,000 bequest provided a living memorial. Lifetime library advocate and founder Adele Briscoe Looscan and building chairman Rev. Harris Masterson Jr. also died in 1936. In 1940 Julia mourned the loss of her close friend and library enthusiast Annette Finnigan, whose many gifts and $25,000 endowment greatly enriched Houston's understanding of ancient cultures and the arts. In 1941 Captain James A. Baker, who had set up the Norma Meldrum Children's Library Fund and overseen its growth for forty years, died in August, and the "valiant" Elizabeth Fitzsimmons Ring, who served the library "with pride" until her death, followed that September. In January 1942, the library family lost the Reverend Peter Gray Sears, president of the Houston Library Association board from 1913 to 1917, as the founding generation made way for new leadership.[145]

The last known photograph of Julia Ideson, 1945. MSS0032–098, Julia Ideson Collection, Houston Public Library. Houston Metropolitan Research Center.

Unexpected Ending

Early in July 1945, Julia Ideson held a staff meeting. She was "as vibrant, charming, fascinating" as ever, although she was not feeling well. The next day, the librarian flew to New York for a summer vacation on Long Island with her sister, Margaret Ladd Swertz. The sisters decided to visit friends who lived on the Delaware River near New Hope, Pennsylvania. While there Julia suffered a fatal heart attack on Sunday evening, July 15, 1945, her sixty-fifth birthday. Margaret accompanied her sister's casket to Houston a few days later, and mourners encircled the Central Library building to pay their respects to the generous, adventurous, beloved librarian before her burial in Houston's Hollywood Cemetery with her parents. William A. Vinson, president of the Houston Public Library Association board, expressed the "deep sense of personal loss" felt by "those of us who have been associated with her for more than thirty years" and the sorrow her death "brings . . . to the people of Houston." She was a "grand person," and "we have consolation in the fact that the library system of Houston will stand as her monument." Staff members had "lost a friend and counsellor [*sic*]. Her interest in building the Houston Public Library according to the highest standards of the Library profession was her constant thought. Her lofty ideals . . . were an inspiration. . . . Her untiring efforts to bring to the citizens of Houston the best books in every field . . . set an example. . . . The Houston Public Library is so essentially hers that any future growth in institution or staff will be but the lengthening of the shadow of one outstanding woman." Colleagues at the Texas Philosophical Society noted Julia's "force of character, her perseverance, her intelligent planning and her unswerving devotion" to the library that absorbed "all the overtones of her being," although "few people possessed a wider, more varied and more devoted circle of friends." A *Houston Chronicle* editorial affirmed that the library, under her guidance, had become "nationally known as one of the best-run libraries in the country." Julia's friend and fellow humanitarian Rabbi Henry Barnston cited the book of Proverbs to describe her as "a valiant woman who shall find her price is above rubies." Julia, he said, felt "the library was as dear to her as life itself. She tended it and nursed it . . . and stood ready to further the sacred cause of reading and education" everywhere.[146]

Trustees of Houston's public library association were stunned by Julia's unexpected death. They turned to Martha Schnitzer, as they had done during Julia's sabbaticals, and asked the assistant librarian to serve as acting librarian. In May 1948, after forty years with the library, the board named Schnitzer librarian, but she held the post for a mere ten months before retiring. Harriet Dickson, the children's librarian since 1924, then assumed Julia's mantle as librarian and completed one of her predecessor's long-desired goals by finally building out the stacks as they had been planned in 1926 by the Cram-Watkin architectural team. In December 1946 beloved friends Ima Hogg, Rabbi Henry Barnston, artist Emma Richardson Cherry, and architect William Ward Watkin unveiled a portrait of the former librarian, painted during her lifetime by Houston artist Julian Muench. Over one hundred friends contributed to the gift and paid tribute to Julia's "kindliness, firmness and tenacity in holding to her ideal." In 1951 the Central Library building was renamed the Julia Ideson Building, and Houstonians recalled the librarian's "quiet dignity" and her lifetime of service to reading. In 1952, following the death of Margaret Ladd Swertz in 1949, the assets of Julia Ideson's estate, valued at $25,000, were used to establish the Julia Ideson Staff Benefit Fund. As Julia had requested in her will, half the income was reserved for pensions, and half was used for sick benefits to active or retired staff or for emergency loans to current staff. In 1977 the Julia Ideson Building was placed on the National Register of Historic Places, and in 1979 respected Houston architect S. I. Morris lovingly restored the building—with funding from federal grants, municipal bond drives, and Friends of the Houston Public Library—as the new home for the Houston Metropolitan Research Center archives and special collections. In January 2004 the building received a Texas historical marker, and it has also been designated a City of Houston Historic Landmark. In 2006, with a $10 million promise of support from Mayor Bill White, philanthropist Phoebe Tudor, development expert Margaret Skidmore, and library supporter Minette Boesel formed Julia Ideson Library Preservation Partners and raised $32 million by October 2010 to construct the south wing and loggia and to restore the building's interior. Since 2011 the building has been open for events. It perpetuates Julia's legacy, houses the city's rare books and archive collections, and welcomes visitors to two large reading rooms and the restored Norma Meldrum Children's Room.[147]

In 1903 Julia Ideson dedicated her life to making the Houston Public Library one of the finest in the country. For forty-two years she built partnerships with civic leaders, clubwomen, politicians, businessmen, professional librarians, and readers of every age. Her Philosophical Society of Texas peers understood her importance, noting that Ideson "made a continuous study of the city and its developments and lent herself to anything that was for its betterment. . . . [H]er knowledge of books was comprehensive and her judgments liberal."[148] By 1945 Julia had fulfilled her dream to place Houston's public library at the center of civic life as a symbol of the city—handsome, well-designed buildings improved neighborhoods and served as social gathering places; imaginative, innovative programs revealed new worlds and stimulated curious readers; and welcoming librarians enriched the lives of questing Houstonians by guiding them to reading resources. As librarian, Julia Ideson wanted to show how reading could reveal and explain challenges facing every Houstonian, yet she understood that sometimes people preferred an amusing novel or play to help them relax for a few hours. She wanted to build research collections that illuminated the past and stirred aspirations, yet she knew that often patrons needed the definition of a word or more facts about bicycles. As a citizen, Julia Ideson understood the power of words to change lives. She fought for a woman's right to vote; she spoke out for inclusivity, racial understanding, cooperation, and world peace; and she introduced Houstonians to world leaders and cultural pacesetters. She loved music and theater and promoted the city's municipal art museum. She loved her country and traveled widely to explore its diverse communities. She loved her friends, her garden, and the birds that sang outside her home on Buffalo Bayou. To Houstonians, Julia Ideson became a beloved figure who stood tall at the very heart of their vibrant city and fought every day to bring social justice to all who entered the storehouse of knowledge she created.

CHAPTER THREE

The Bridges That Unite Us

Ima Hogg

JULY 10, 1882–AUGUST 19, 1975

Ima Hogg as Gibson Girl, circa 1900. The Elliotts, Austin, Texas. MS 21–039, Ima Hogg Papers, Museum of Fine Arts, Houston Archives.

Prelude

"The weekend belonged to Miss Ima Hogg." On Friday and Saturday, March 4 and 5, 1966, Houston's visionary civic leader conveyed Bayou Bend Collection and Gardens, the consummation of a "long-cherished dream" conceived in 1920, to Houston's Museum of Fine Arts. Fellow collectors Katharine Prentis Murphy, Henry and Helen Flynt, and Ralph and Cynthia Carpenter; trusted dealers Albert Sack and Bernard Levy; and noted scholars Charles Van Ravenswaay and John M. Graham II flew to Houston from the East Coast. Renowned author Meyric Rogers and his wife boarded a train from Chicago, while college friend Dot Thornton and other admiring Texans traveled to Houston to celebrate with "the twinkling-eyed octogenarian." On Friday evening admirers enjoyed a formal "dinner of welcome and appreciation" hosted by the weekend's honoree. Saturday dawned cool and breezy as guests gathered under a tent for the 10:30 a.m. dedication. The Right Reverend J. Milton Richardson, bishop of the Episcopal Diocese of Texas, offered the invocation, and Edward Rotan, president of the Museum of Fine Arts Board of Trustees and master of ceremonies, recognized the committee who had "primary responsibility" for the weekend's "essential arrangements." He then addressed the honoree.

> Many Museums have been given important collections. Others have been given handsome buildings, while still others have been given generous endowments. Few if any have been as fortunate as the Museum of Fine Arts . . . in receiving a composite of all three in Bayou Bend. All the beauty we see around us . . . is the creation of one dedicated person. It represents the culmination . . . of study, imagination, courage, knowledge and resources all pointed to this particular day.[1]

Swathed in furs and wearing a fashionable hat, Ima rose to address her "many, many dear friends and visitors." With habitual modesty, she declared herself "in a state of shock" from the outpouring of affirmation. The "first lady of Texas" then acknowledged a litany of people who had helped her: the day's participants, her forbears, the grandfather and father who had taught her to love history, her brothers, museum colleagues, "ever-responsive and loyal" River Oaks Garden Club members, devoted employees, "wonderful girls" serving as "essential volunteer docents," and her beloved personal friends. "Deeply touched" by the crowd, she spoke of the purpose for her unique gift: "Texas, an empire in itself, . . . seems . . . remote and alien to the rest of our nation. I hope in a modest way Bayou Bend may serve as a bridge to bring us closer to the heart of an American heritage which unites us." In closing, she noted she "would be

Ima Hogg speaking at the dedication of Bayou Bend, March 5, 1966. Gittings Photography. MS 21–184, Ima Hogg Papers, Museum of Fine Arts, Houston Archives.

free to pursue my other projects and . . . watch the sunsets from my high-rise apartment." While she would "continue to love Bayou Bend, . . . in one sense I have always considered I was holding [it] in trust for this day. Now Bayou Bend is truly yours." Museum Director James Johnson Sweeney responded, "You, Miss Hogg, . . . have given not only a work of art, but an example of fuller living and an incentive to a fuller life. . . . Bayou Bend . . . is your 'poem,' which you have turned over to us for safe keeping and enjoyment." Houston Mayor Louie

Welch thanked the generous donor "in behalf of all the unborn generations . . . who are to enjoy the richness of this great legacy." Texas Governor John Connally, Winterthur Museum Senior Research Fellow Charles F. Montgomery, and University of Texas Chancellor Harry Ransom praised "her good works of genius and devotion." Participants and guests then gathered in the Sterling Gallery at the museum, where Director Sweeney, his wife, and members of the board helped the farsighted philanthropist, clad in "an orchid, rose and black print dress, a black ensemble coat, and an orchid hat," receive her well-wishers. On Saturday evening, close friends entertained dedication participants at small, elegant dinner parties in their homes.[2]

Family Roots

Guests visiting the Bayou Bend Collection and Gardens often challenge their docents to explain two troubling issues—why did loving parents choose such a peculiar name for their daughter, and why did such a pretty girl never marry? "Our cup of joy is now overflowing!" wrote happy father James Stephen Hogg to his brother John. "We have a daughter . . . of as angelic mien as ever gracious nature favor a man with, and her name is Ima!"[3] The blue-eyed bearer of this name often explained that her father had revered his older brother Thomas Elisha, a multitalented mentor who had penned *The Fate of Marvin*, an epic romance, shortly after the Civil War; to honor this beloved brother's memory, the ecstatic father called his daughter Ima, after the poem's beautiful, blue-eyed heroine. This explanation failed to impress the baby's maternal grandfather, James Alexander Stinson, who galloped to her side when he heard the news of his grandchild's birth on July 10, 1882. His efforts to change the name failed. She had been christened, and Ima Hogg she would remain. The story stands, as there is no evidence to refute the claim. There also is no evidence to explain why Ima never married, although there is much speculation. The trajectory of her amazing life, the generosity of her civic commitment, and the complexity of her sweeping vision suggest that the burden of her surprising name and the singularity of her unmarried state did not prevent her from forming a strong personality and building a life of significant purpose.

Unwavering love for her parents motivated and strengthened Ima. Although public figures, James Stephen and Sarah Ann Stinson Hogg cherished their children. The mother Ima remembered was gentle, "fastidious," and imbued with a "discriminating sense of beauty." Only five feet, two inches tall, "her tiny hands" and "little feet," which "never gave her enough support," belied a stoic

Sarah Stinson Hogg, circa 1885. H. R. Marks, Austin, Texas. 3T240/3T241, Ima Hogg Photographs, Dolph Briscoe Center for American History, University of Texas at Austin.

determination that impressed her daughter. An accomplished needlewoman and frugal housekeeper, Sallie stretched a small salary by fashioning stylish gowns for herself and sewing "the most exquisite hand-made creations made of the finest muslin, dimity or swiss [*sic*]" for her daughter and by supervising private parties and government receptions closely. A devout Methodist and accomplished pianist, Sallie hoped her oldest son would become a minister and began teaching her only daughter to play the piano soon after her third birthday. Despite frail health, Sallie raised four lively children, supported her ambitious husband's career as "Father's confidante and advisor in all questions," and took an active interest in her flower borders and vegetable gardens to make her homes attractive and welcoming havens. The principled, activist father Ima recalled was "a foe of greed and graft" who "won many battles for the people" and "was fond of prophesying the splendor of the future." A giant who stood well over six feet and weighed well over two hundred pounds, Ima's father was a fun-loving man who took his children on political jaunts and gathered neighborhood friends for buggy rides around Austin or games in the back

James Stephen Hogg with his youngest child, Thomas Elijah Hogg, 1887. Yancey and Ramberg, Austin, Texas. Di_08341, Ima Hogg Photographs, Dolph Briscoe Center for American History, University of Texas at Austin.

yard. Jim Hogg loved pets, walked home for lunch every day, and spent many evenings reading history books in the parlor. He invited his children to meet dignitaries who visited the governor's mansion and taught his sons and daughter that public service was every Texan's civic duty. An "avid student of history and biography . . . he tried to indoctrinate [his children] with the heritage of our country."[4] The lessons Ima learned from her compassionate parents shaped her life and philanthropy. Her immovable affection caused her to protect her father's legacy and to bristle when enemies and cartoonists fumed against his policies or depicted him as a demagogic buffoon.

Ima was proud of her Hogg family heritage. The name Hogg, variously spelled Hogge and Hoag, derives from Viking settlers along the east coast of Scotland and means "careful" or "prudent," two qualities she admired. Hogg families began settling in Virginia by the 1650s, and John Lindsey Hogg, the progenitor of Ima's family, was born in Winchester, Frederick County, in 1732. He joined Revolutionary War forces in Virginia and South Carolina, and his son Thomas Blair Hogg (1768–1849) married Margaret Chandler in 1795 in

South Carolina, attained the rank of major with the Georgia volunteers during the War of 1812, established a plantation in Alabama, and migrated to Mississippi, where he grew cotton and was a state legislator. In 1848 Thomas and Margaret followed their son Joseph Lewis Hogg to Rusk, Texas, where Thomas died in 1849 and Margaret in 1853. Born in Morgan County, Georgia, Joseph Lewis Hogg (1806–1862) continued the family's pursuit of agricultural prosperity. At the urging of Sam Houston, he escaped the 1839 depression by establishing a plantation near Nacogdoches in East Texas with his wife, Lucanda McMath, and two daughters, Martha Frances (1834–1920) and the infant Julia (1839–1896). Trained as a lawyer, Joseph Lewis Hogg nurtured his friendship with Houston, joined the local militia, and served in the Eighth Congress of the Republic of Texas, where he supported union with the United States. Named chairman of the Judiciary Committee of the Texas State Constitutional Convention, he framed the laws of the new state. Following a tour with the Texas Mounted Volunteers in the Mexican-American War, Joseph Lewis purchased about 2,500 acres near Rusk in Cherokee County, where he built Mountain Home, raised seven children, five of them born in Texas, and ran a cotton and lumber operation with the labor of about twenty enslaved people. In 1860 Joseph Lewis Hogg affirmed secession and split with his old friend, Unionist Governor Sam Houston, who was forced to resign. In 1861 the new governor appointed Hogg colonel in charge of recruitment in Texas, and a few months later Confederate President Jefferson Davis named the aging warrior a brigadier in the Confederate Army. Hogg contracted dysentery during the siege of Corinth, Mississippi, and was moved to a private home in the care of his manservant, only to die on May 16, 1862; his wife, Lucanda, and youngest son, Richard, died the following year.

James (Jim) Stephen Hogg was born at Mountain Home on March 24, 1851, the fifth child and third son of Joseph Lewis and Lucanda McMath Hogg. His father prospered during young Jim's childhood, and his older sister, the family storyteller and "compulsive writer of verse" Martha Frances (Fannie) Hogg, recalled with nostalgia the lavish hospitality of her parents. Years later when framing his political platform, Jim Hogg paid tribute to "Home! The Center of Civilization: The pivot of constitutional government: The ark of safety. . . . The haven of rest in old age," and he declared, "Every man should have a home!"[5] Joseph Lewis hired a music master and tutor for his children because there were no schools in Rusk, and he made each child study a musical instrument—Fannie and Tom played the violin and Julia the piano. Even as a child, Jim was encouraged to develop his voice, and Ima remembered he sang in all registers, including a humorous falsetto. War interrupted Jim's formal education, and peace brought unending struggle to save Mountain Home. At sixteen, Jim hired on as a printer's devil for the *Rusk Observer*, sleeping in the office and eating with the editor's family. In 1868 he worked at the *Quitman Clipper* and tried farming. In 1869 Jim helped save the Wood County sheriff from a band of outlaws and was nearly killed late that year when one of the vengeful ruffians shot him in the back. Appalled by postwar disorder and encouraged by Martha Frances and Tom, Jim returned to journalism and began reading law. After a brief stint with the *Tyler Democrat-Reporter*, Jim sold some family land and started the *Longview News* before moving his operation to Wood County as publisher of the *Quitman News*. He wrote strong editorials that favored rights of the people and fought the sale of county bonds to subsidize Texas and Pacific Railway expansion into Wood County. As a result of his animosity, the railroad located its depot ten miles south in Mineola, founded in 1873 to accommodate traffic from the Texas and Pacific and the International and Great Northern railways. At age twenty-two, Hogg won the contest for Wood County Justice of the Peace and the next year married Sarah Ann Stinson (Sallie).

Ima cherished her mother's family, whose forbears settled in Virginia, North Carolina, and Georgia. She remembered her grandfather James Alexander Stinson (1828–1907) as a gentle, jolly, even-tempered man. Born in Troup County, Georgia, he and his first wife, Sarah Ann West (1830–1856), were the parents of John (1853–1888), Sarah Ann (Sallie), and James (1856–1926). Sarah Ann West died when her daughter was two, following the birth of baby James, and in 1860 Stinson moved his family to Speer in Wood County, Texas, near its county seat Quitman. On November 1, 1860, Stinson married Sarah Ann Moreland Jones (1831–1863), the widowed mother of two surviving children (John and Penelope Jane, or "Pink"). Sadly, Sarah Ann Jones died not long after the birth of her son Benjamin Sidney Stinson (1861–1875). Responsible for the welfare of six young children, in 1866 Colonel Stinson married Mary Anne Johnston (1835–1907), the woman Ima knew as a loving grandmother and mother of two musical daughters, Lillian (Lillie) and Clifford (Cliffie) Stinson,[6] who adored their older half-sister Sallie. Stinson was promoted to colonel in the Confederate Army and prospered after the war. He joined the local grange and practiced modern farming on his lumber and cotton plantation, where he ran a gristmill and sawmill. In 1869, when Sallie was fourteen, her father enrolled her in Professor Morgan H. Looney's private school near Gilmer, where she met eighteen-year-old Jim Hogg, who was taking a course at Mr. Bagget's pay school near Quitman. Stinson discouraged this friendship, believing Sallie was too young for romance and should complete her education. Five years later, as the more settled justice of the peace, Jim began courting in earnest. The cautious father was finally convinced of the couple's devotion, and the persistent suitor married his petite bride in the Stinson parlor on April 22, 1874. Ima attributed her love of old things, flowers, and country life to summer sojourns at Grandfather Stinson's comfortable farmhouse in Speer, where she delighted in outdoors adventures, explored dusty trunks in the attic, romped around the gardens, and played piano duets with her aunts.[7]

Felicitous Childhood

As newlyweds, Jim and Sally Hogg moved to the clapboard four-room "Honeymoon Cottage" in Quitman, where their first child, William Clifford Hogg, was born on January 31, 1875. For more than six years, young Will received his parents' full attention, and the little boy grew close to his mother, accompanying her on shopping trips, sharing her love for beautiful things, and helping her with household chores. Jim was elected Wood County attorney in 1878, and in 1880 he ran successfully for district attorney of Texas's old Seventh District. Shortly after the election, he moved the family to Mineola, where railroad connections carried him to district courthouses and where Ima delighted her family on July 10, 1882. Although not yet three when the Hoggs left Mineola, Ima always remembered a dogwood tree that grew outside her bedroom window. Michael Hogg arrived on October 28, 1885, while the family was living in Tyler, an antebellum shipping and commercial center and county seat of Smith County, whose economy revived in the 1880s after two railroads built machine shops there. In 1886 Jim Hogg campaigned successfully for Texas attorney general and moved to Austin in January 1887, while his family spent a few months with the Stinsons in Speer. In the late spring, the family reunited at their new Austin home, a two-story wooden house at 500 West Fourteenth Street, located on a large westside lot with space for gardens, horses, and their favorite Tyler-bred cow; a cistern in the backyard supplied water. Will at twelve was now a serious schoolboy; Ima attended kindergarten nearby and began formal piano lessons, leaving toddler Mike at home. Soon after the family had settled in its new home, Thomas Elijah arrived on August 20, 1887.[8]

After the first railroad reached Austin in 1871, the population more than doubled;[9] by 1887 four railroads connected passengers with the national rail network. Masons laid the cornerstone for Old Main on the University of Texas campus in 1882, and by 1887 classes met in the completed West Wing. Attorney

General Hogg walked to his temporary headquarters in the Land Office Building at Brazos and Eleventh streets until the grand new Texas Capitol, rising from the ruins of an 1881 fire, was officially dedicated in May 1888. Most roads were unpaved, and mule-drawn streetcars clopped up and down the central district. A dirt road led from the Capitol construction site to the forty-acre University of Texas campus, linking the two main sources of employment in the city. Although municipal authorities did not install underground sewers, a city waterworks, or electric lighting until 1891, performing artists began entertaining Austinites in 1878 at lumber merchant Charles Millett's Opera House, where twenty-four-inch limestone walls protected up to eight hundred patrons during Austin's long hot spells. Ima remembered attending a concert with her parents and dancing in the aisles. Newcomers built handsome homes on the west side of town, and the grand sixty-room Driskill Hotel—promoted by its cattle baron owner, Col. Jesse Lincoln Driskill, as the finest hotel south of St. Louis—opened in 1886 to lodge politicians and visitors in comfort. Austinites loved the outdoors and explored the surrounding landscape on horseback or went boating on the Colorado River or Barton Creek.

Sallie could not enjoy Austin's civic life at first. Tom's birth was difficult and her recuperation slow. The baby spent most of his first year with a local African American wet nurse, while Will lived in Speer with his Stinson grandparents for several months. During her long recovery, Sallie suffered a relapse in the fall of 1888, when her beloved half-sister Cliffie Stinson, only seventeen years old, succumbed unexpectedly to black jaundice and her brother John Stinson died at age thirty-five after a long period of ill health. Six-year-old Ima began her formal schooling at Hood Seminary on Seventh Street and remembered her Aunt Cliffie's death as the "earliest tragedy of our family," noting that Cliffie was "very beautiful and a gifted musician . . . cherished by the whole family." The Stinson clan had also lost John Jones in 1886 but had welcomed Colonel Stinson's sister Lizzie Phillips after her husband died in September 1888. Sallie's health was never robust after Tom's birth, and she frequently packed "a big basket lunch" and took her children to Speer for long sojourns. Ima later recalled the all-day train journey from Austin to Troup, Texas, where the Hoggs arrived in time to spend the night with friends before catching another train for Mineola. Weather permitting, Grandfather Stinson sent someone to Mineola early in the morning to meet the family with a wagon large enough to carry several people and their luggage across "many creeks and sloughs," sometimes "frightening" and "impassable." The tired travelers usually arrived at the Stinson farm by four o'clock, but the trek was worth the trouble. Ima played piano duets with Aunt Lillie and shared a room with her Great-Aunt Lizzie Stinson Philips.[10] The elderly aunt explained that the old bureau in the bedroom was a family heirloom, which one day would belong to the little girl, and she described an "enchanting world of romantic and classical literature" peopled by Greek and Roman heroes. "Grandfather's home was a little paradise to us," Ima recalled. "It was on the slope of a hillside which went gently down to a swift, flowing shallow creek. The house was commodious and was a lovely cool place in the summer."[11] Her grandfather liked to peel peaches and apples for snacks and to split watermelons on the back porch to eat before breakfasts of beaten biscuits, ham, grits, and eggs.

Jim Hogg completed two terms as attorney general, ran successfully for governor in 1890, and moved his family into the governor's mansion early in 1891. On January 20, 1891, Sallie, Will, and Ima watched proudly as "Father took the oath of office in the Senate Chamber of the great pink Capitol." In the evening, "Mother wore an exquisite lavender brocade gown with deep lavender metallic orchids outlined with silver thread" to the "crowded" inaugural ball. Ima continued at Hood Seminary until 1891, when she matriculated at Miss Carrington's University Preparatory School, run by spinster sisters Mignonette (Minnie) and Lillian Carrington at Tenth and Guadalupe streets, where she had "time for my piano" and studied French, German, and Latin. She began serious piano training at the Conservatory of Music under Austin's leading musician, Edmund Ludwig, a Russian émigré who claimed he had been taught by the great pianists of his youth. Ima's family and teachers noted her perfect pitch and considered her a prodigy. She began to accompany her father's hymn singing on Sunday evenings and was rewarded when she turned ten—a beautiful square rosewood piano arrived at the mansion for her sole use, and her proud father provided a volume of songs that she always treasured. She also mastered the banjo and guitar and enjoyed serenading friends in the evenings. Brother Will began boarding in Omen, Texas, at the Summer Hill Select School, established in 1879 by Professor A. W. Orr. Ima thought her brother received "very fine training" for college, and she recalled the "lonesome" governor, in "need of [Will's] company," wrote his son on June 1, 1891, "I am really proud of the good reports of your course and conduct at school. . . . With your high sense of honor, self-respect and industrious habits, I feel perfectly assured of your success in life."[12] Will was an apt pupil and in September 1892 entered Southwestern University in Georgetown, Texas.

Contemporaries of the governor and his children believed that no family had enjoyed life in the governor's mansion more. Ima's lively memoirs depict

William Clifford Hogg, 1895. Journeay, Austin, Texas. MS 21–038, Ima Hogg Papers, Museum of Fine Arts, Houston Archives.

the mansion as the center of Austin's social life, and the "grounds were a neighborhood playground." Energetic Ima "was allowed to compete with the boys," and although Mike and Tom "seemed very much younger to me, we were great playmates." Will, at sixteen, was "dignified and not often conspicuous." He did not wrestle, play marbles, or slide down the curving banister of the center hall stairway, as his siblings did until "Father took tacks and hammered them all the way down the railing of the stairs" to end the practice. Governor Hogg "always found time" to take his children and their friends to the circus—where his party always had the "most advantageous seats." A white picket fence enclosed the city block surrounding the mansion and protected the work horses and cows and a growing menagerie of pets, including a large cage for cockatoos and "other beautiful plumed birds, some lovely songsters." Every morning, Ima recalled, her father "had a little visit with the animals and birds" before walking to his office. Ima loved their black Newfoundland and a pony named Dainty, but her father preferred Jane the parrot, who flew about the mansion at will and shrieked "Papa, Papa" when the governor returned home.[13]

While the children loved their new surroundings, Sallie Hogg struggled to overcome the deficiencies of the governor's residence, designed and built by architect-contractor Abner Hugh Cook[14] and first occupied by Governor

Elisha Marshall Pease on June 10, 1856. Later governors added gas lighting in the 1870s and installed telephones and indoor plumbing in the 1880s, but by January 1891, when the Hoggs took possession, the house was dilapidated and scantily furnished. Ima recalled, "We were prepared for a most hospitable home but I shall never forget our consternation on first seeing the interior. It was in dreadful disrepair." Before the family moved in, Sallie had the house "entirely papered and painted immediately at my Father's expense"—although he was later reimbursed—and "many days were spent scraping hardened chewing gum from under the tables and chair arms. There were literally buckets of old chewing gum scraped, even from the door moldings." Ima noted there was only one large bathroom, containing "an enormous tin tub, said to have been made for Sam Houston." Ima remembered the "Southwest bedroom had the famous Sam Houston four-poster bed" while her parents' "Southeast bedroom . . . had very attractive, late Victorian walnut furniture." Ima's reminiscences provide a detailed description of every room and record that heat came from fireplaces, "except in the bathroom which had a good wood stove." She described a "very large range, which burned wood," and running water to the kitchen sink and to a washroom between two parlors on the main floor. Sallie managed the large house, four children, and many parties with a small staff: a cook, a German-speaking housemaid—the "beautiful Grace Bauer . . . devoted to my Mother"—a laundress, and a "white man to care for the gardens, horses and cows and do the driving." Tom also remembered a "negro man 'George' who attended the horses and cows and did the milking." Sallie purchased supplies wholesale and supervised cooking, baking, and housework, including the spring "ordeal" when everything was taken outside for a thorough cleaning. Her daughter concluded, "Housekeeping was a rugged occupation."[15]

Once the Hoggs had refurbished and modestly furnished the house, Ima observed elaborate dinners, dances for young people on Saturday nights, Sunday hymn singing, and lengthy political receptions. The governor lavishly praised his wife's hard work and supported her recuperative visits to the Stinson clan in Speer. He recognized that she tired easily and never asked her to accompany him on campaign trips. He wrote frequently to family and associates, optimistically explaining that Sallie was feeling better or doing well, but from 1887 on her health slowly declined. By June 1889, Sallie and her seven-year-old daughter had begun the first of several trips to mineral water spas. The little girl and her exhausted mother jolted along 130 miles of rail from Austin to Bremond in Central Texas and then hailed the mule-drawn carriage that bumped along a narrow rail line for three miles to Wooten Wells. Doctors in this era knew little

Ima Hogg, 1894. Journeay, Austin, Texas. MS21–036, Ima Hogg Papers, Museum of Fine Arts, Houston Archives.

about the causes of disease and often prescribed rest for maladies as severe as pancreatitis, as infectious as measles, or as annoying as a broken leg. Diaries and letters mention frequent visits to a spa where imbibing or bathing in the soothing, hot mineral waters were said to cure all afflictions. Any benefit from the Wooten Wells trip was temporary, and in July 1890 Ima and her mother traveled to Sour Lake, near Beaumont, where the mineral waters had been restoring health since the 1850s. While Jim Hogg campaigned to become the state's youngest and first native-born governor, Ima noted that Sour Lake "had a terrible old hotel but after two weeks there my mother was always greatly improved." The worried little girl also despaired, "No one seemed to know what was the root of my Mother's great physical disability." By 1891 Sallie "was often ill," and "frequently gave her orders [for grand occasions] from her bed. Her maid, Grace, was thoroughly capable . . . and could supervise almost as well as Mother." That May, Ima and Sallie trekked all the way to Hot Springs, Arkansas, where Ima was "not greatly impressed with the benefits [of forty-seven thermal springs], although it was a very beautiful place. Mother did not seem to gain anything." In 1893 Sallie took the children to the Stinsons for the summer, and Ima reported to her father that "Mamma has been very ill." Despite warnings and fervent pleas from his daughter to come to Speer for her eleventh birthday, the governor remained in sweltering Austin, eating at a nearby boardinghouse and attending to government business. That September Ima accompanied Sallie to San Antonio for a medical consultation.[16]

When Sallie was unable to accompany her husband on trips around the state to visit prisons, insane asylums, and schools, or to campaign for office, the governor asked Will and Ima to join him. In 1892, during Hogg's political campaign for reelection, Ima attended several of the eighty-nine speeches her father delivered during a three-month statewide tour. Ima remembered "a great deal of rain" and the "greatest inconveniences making train connections, laying off for hours at junctions at midnight and arriving at any hour at some destination." Rally attendees frequently asked about the governor's children and their names, and press reports speculated with varying degrees of jocularity that pained young Ima. One friendly journalist retold the family explanation about Ima's name and described her as "a bright little miss of 7 or 8 years, a perfect blonde, with golden hair and blue eyes and of willowy form. She is quiet and rather timid in a crowd, but when alone on a car seat with her papa she prattles away in childish innocence and . . . inquisitiveness."[17]

In his final term of office, Jim Hogg became Texas's elder statesman and popular spokesman, but he also began to think of his future. In June 1894, the governor left his wife and younger sons in Speer while Will worked in San Antonio, and he invited twenty-three prominent Texas executives, lawyers, and journalists to board several private railroad cars for a ten-city goodwill tour that began in Chicago, Albany, and New York and included Washington, DC, Cincinnati, and St. Louis on the way home. Ima, now twelve, was the group's only female companion. At every stop, the delegation promoted Texas investment opportunities. Despite great railroad activity supported by out-of-state capital, despite Hogg's reform agenda, and despite a growing population, Texans had not yet generated the surplus capital required to modernize the economy. They needed investors' money from Boston, New York, Philadelphia, and other financial centers to establish new industries in the huge state. An astute observer, Ima wrote long letters to her mother. "It was a very amazing and enlightening experience and Father seemed to believe that anything in which he took part was becoming for me also," including poker games, heavy imbibing, and late nights, although she was "usually put to bed by ten o'clock." Having heard tall tales of New York from "the colored cook at the Mansion," the city's skyscrapers and two million residents were "a great disappointment to me! Broadway was not as wide as Congress Avenue. Macy's was not as stylish as Hatzfeld; but the Fifth Avenue Hotel and Delmonico's were glorious enough"—especially the hotel elevator and the ice cream service. Ima told her mother about the "lovely things" she saw in New York, including a "piano that played by electricity," a "cat as white as snow," a "simply grand" theater, and fabulous flowers everywhere. At one florist shop, she explored a "refrigerator as large as a room" for flower storage. Demonstrating a firm sense of ladylike behavior, she told her father she did not want to be photographed "alone with a pack of men." She enjoyed the visit to Providence, Rhode Island, best because Governor Daniel Russell Brown and his "charming family and a daughter my own age" entertained them, and "it was a great relief to find a little companion."[18]

While Governor Hogg was traveling, poor health continued to plague Sallie and to worry her two older children. On July 11, 1894, Will warned his father, "Mother seems—in every letter she writes to me—blue and morose on account of her ill health. Write her and brace her up into a more happy mood." Despite this warning, the governor attended the state Democratic Party convention in August where he oversaw the nomination of his attorney general to replace him. He then set off on his last campaign tour, writing Sallie "my engagements are thick and fast . . . so you will be a 'widow' until after the election." On November 28, 1894, the day before Thanksgiving, Jim Hogg performed one of his last official acts. After three years of study and deliberation, he pardoned Ben Krebs and James Preston, falsely accused of murder eighteen years earlier and condemned in a great miscarriage of frontier justice. On December 20, 1894, the retiring governor wrote to his beloved older sister Martha Francis Davis in Pueblo, Colorado, "in the quiet solitude of the night" while his wife and children slept. Listing his many political accomplishments, he noted, "My period of public life is therefore 'well-rounded' and my cup of ambition is full. . . . I am so glad that I am able to leave office honorably and fully satisfied that I must tell <u>somebody</u> of it—who better than yourself? . . . My Sister, to whom I could always go for a smile, for help and encouragement in the struggling days of my blundering youth?"[19]

Charles Culberson succeeded the satisfied "people's governor" on January 15, 1895, and the Hoggs moved first to the Driskill Hotel and then to Mary Begley's boardinghouse at 206 West Ninth Street. During a freezing winter,

Mike and Tom Hogg, circa 1892. H. R. Marks, Austin Texas. Camh-dob-012137, Ima Hogg Photographs, Dolph Briscoe Center for American History, University of Texas at Austin.

Will studied at the University of Texas School of Law and boarded near the campus with widow Addie Robinson. Former Governor Hogg and former District Judge James Harvey Robertson established Hogg & Robertson, a law partnership at 105 West Eighth Street. Now forty-four, the retired officeholder became agent for several Texas companies and legal counsel for local rail lines. With the March thaw, he set off for St. Louis, Chicago, New York, and Boston on a four-month search for investors. While traveling, he wrote optimistic letters to his "Darling Sallie" but confessed, "While I have made a great many valuable acquaintances and have done much to remove the bitter prejudice against Texas I have done nothing definite in procuring the financial aid for the railways." On their April 22 wedding anniversary, he exclaimed, "Twenty two years ago to-day we were married! Do you remember? Time has dealt gently, kindly, with us both since then. We have always had plenty and have been allowed by our Great Father our share of happiness. But few days have passed without my returning thanks to Him for it all." Sadly, time had not been kind to Sallie since her husband's departure a few weeks earlier, and her illness had flared once more, although she tried to write cheerfully. By April, Mike and Tom were living with their Stinson grandparents, while Will and Ima stayed with their mother to finish the school year.[20]

In response to her husband's happy anniversary letter, Sallie finally revealed she was not feeling well. On May 1 Jim Hogg wrote from Boston, enclosing drafts for $150. He suggested she see local doctors and then travel to Pueblo, Colorado, to consult his cousin Dr. William Davis and to remain there for a rest in the cool, soothing climate. "Wherever you go take Ima with you. Make her your help and associate. Stop her from staying all night with other girls so that she will be constantly with you. I know if she knew how lonesome you are without her she would never leave you for anybody." Poor Ima, not yet thirteen, remembered, "I was with Mother all the time when she was ill, and my mind was filled with horror." Sallie visited her neighbor and friend Dr. Thomas D. Wooten on May 7, and the kindly medic told her that she suffered from "bronchitis and catarrhal affection [but] that [her] lungs [were] all right." The discomfort increased and within three days Sallie and Ima had visited specialist Adolph Herff in San Antonio, received the dire diagnosis of tuberculosis, and departed for Pueblo. Although disconsolate, Will forced his mother and sister to leave and made all the arrangements. The worried travelers sped to Fort Worth, where they spent the night with friends; then they boarded a Pullman sleeper for the overnight journey to Pueblo. Composing a reassuring letter to her husband from a "car so rough that it's almost impossible to write," Sallie told her traveling spouse she had not been sick on the trip and selflessly admonished him not to order anything for her that "you can't financially afford." She hoped that Ima, who "has not been looking well," would benefit from a stay in the mountains even if her own health did not improve.[21]

Anxious Adolescence

Happy childhood for Ima and her brothers died that summer. Jim Hogg and his children finally recognized their beloved wife and mother would not regain her fragile health. In July 1895, the former governor returned from his travels in the Northeast, brought Mike and Tom home from Speer, and moved with them to rooms in widow Sophronia (Mrs. John W.) Robertson's large, Southern Colonial home at 900 West Seventeenth Street. Letters that month relayed mixed messages. Having received word from cousin and physician William

Davis that "Sallie is getting along well," the upbeat husband replied on July 11 that he planned to visit in August. Jim wrote cheery missives to Sallie about his trip to Speer and his first days back at the office, apparently unaware that Sallie had written her "dear son Willie" on July 8 that she had been ill for two weeks and had written "to Papa Saturday that I wanted him to come up." On July 10, Ima's birthday, the poorly informed governor happily felicitated "My Dear Ima" on the "pleasure" he had received when "the Great God . . . presented to my humble household my dear and only daughter." Always, he told the thirteen-year-old, "my confidence in the purity of your nature, . . . firmly . . . justifies my hope that in no act of your life shall I ever find cause for disappointment or regret. God bless you my worthy daughter." While these flattering words might have buoyed an adult, they placed a burden to make proper choices on a little girl who pleaded with her father two weeks later on July 25 to come quickly to her mother's bedside. "I am going to write for Mamma as she is sick and can't . . . . When are you coming? . . . Mamma has been sick in bed for two weeks." In response, Jim announced on July 27 that he planned to visit "about the 7th or 8th of August"; and on July 31, he wrote that he and all three boys would be there soon, as both Mike and Tom had begged to visit their Mamma. On August 1 William Davis telegraphed that Sallie's illness was desperate; the family must set out at once. The boys and their stunned father left Austin the next day. By September 6, Will wrote a friend, "Mother does not seem to improve nor to grow worse. . . . She would suffer very much unless kept under partial influence of opiates." Tom turned eight on August 20, and one month later, at midnight on September 20, Sarah Ann Stinson Hogg, age forty-one, was released from further suffering. Texans mourned their beloved recent first lady. To honor her, a special train carried the casket and grieving family back to Austin. A "committee of citizens" met the travelers early in the morning on September 24 and escorted them to the governor's mansion for the funeral service at ten o'clock and the subsequent burial in Oakwood Cemetery. In a show of respect for the former first family, state offices remained closed that day until two o'clock in the afternoon.[22]

Years later, Ima described her father as "bereft," and recalled Sallie's death left deep scars in the hearts of her children, husband, and father. Young Will, feeling responsible for the pending disaster, began to grieve when he put his mother and little sister on the train for Colorado in May. "You are gone," he wrote his mother, "so has the larger part of my self. You hated to go—I hated to see you go; but all is well. Be calm and content; everything else will seem so." To his sister Julia, Jim Hogg confided on October 14.

> In all the storms of an eventful life the severest shock that I ever received was the death of poor Sallie. Indeed, since Mother's death when I was twelve, I had never been called to witness the death of a relative. It is all over, except now and then—almost hourly—when memory recalls the past and with it my wife's suffering and death compared to her gentleness and virtue. Then my feelings overcome me. She never spoke an unkind word to me in her life and never had I to account to others for a word or act of hers. God knows if all men were so blessed the earth would be more like heaven. My ambition is to raise my children after her model. If I succeed the world will be much better for it.

Grandfather Stinson expressed his sadness more stoically: "Yours of the 16th inst bringing me the intelligence of daughter's precarious and dangerous condition was not altogether a surprise only that her disease had advanced more rapidly than we anticipated. . . . That her preparation has been made for a triumphant death I have no question. She was always good."[23]

For Ima, adolescence proved a challenging period of tension between emotional intensity and forlorn separation. Her father expected his daughter to fill the role of his adored wife and to abide by the era's image of idealized womanhood while he traveled constantly to promote Texas business interests. In an attempt to continue normal family life, the former governor began to look for a house in Austin and turned to his older sister Fannie (Martha Frances Hogg) Davis, who had raised him when their mother died. Ima later described the household.

> Our Aunt Fannie evidently was not prepared by experience or nature to have charge of such undisciplined children as she found us to be. While Father was away . . . during the day, she was using all her strength of will and ingenuity to train the two younger boys and myself. She believed in giving us chores and filling every idle moment . . . with some duties. . . . Her efforts served mainly to make the children unhappy.

Jim and Sallie Hogg had encouraged play and exploration, and they had enjoyed including the children in their lives. Aunt Fannie believed in discipline and punished bewildered little Tom for everything, causing him to hide under his bed. His older sister worried "no end" about "the most outgoing, sweet child you ever knew" and feared for his future development and happiness.[24]

Although the governor relied on his sister, he decided that until he had found a permanent home, Ima, Mike, and Tom would benefit from time at the

Martha Frances Hogg Davis. Camh-dob-012142, Ima Hogg Photographs, Dolph Briscoe Center for American History, University of Texas at Austin.

Coronal Institute, a private boarding school in the Texas Hill Country near San Marcos, where about three hundred girls and boys in all grades received a traditional education. The governor invited his cousin William's daughter Pearl Davis to accompany Ima during the November 1895 to summer 1896 sojourn. While Mike and Tom studied basic reading and arithmetic, Ima and

Pearl pursued advanced piano, and Ima produced ink and pencil sketches in studio art. When world-renowned pianist Ignacy Jan Paderewski performed in San Antonio in 1896, the girls attended his "electrifying" performance, and Ima recalled she tried "to imitate the way he played each phrase" of a Schubert "Impromptu" ballet she was studying. While consoling each other in San Marcos, the Hogg cousins learned their Aunt Julia had died on February 22, 1896, at age fifty-six.[25]

The widowed governor had not amassed enough capital to purchase a house, but his lifelong friend Thomas Mitchell (Tom) Campbell[26] urged him to buy prime property on Rio Grande and West Nineteenth streets—and loaned him $6,500 to close the deal in May 1896. Delighted by the furnished, "very comfortable home," located "in an excellent neighborhood" with "plenty of ground for a small orchard" of fig and fruit trees and "a great barnyard full of chickens, ducks, turkeys and geese," the jovial governor urged his siblings and friends "to spend awhile with us." Will moved into two rooms on the partial third floor, where he lived until he finished law school in June 1897. Ima recalled that her father was proud of his flower borders and vegetable garden and found Jack and Jill, his two ornery "very large" ostriches, amusing. No one could go near the birds penned in their special lot, but her father loved to "sit on the porch and interpret their conclaves and chatter." With sisterly tolerance, Ima noted that Mike and Tom "at one time or another, had a pet bear and fawn, but these became troublesome and had to be sent away." Softhearted Mike saved wounded baby animals, and the family kept cows and horses. Ima preferred Joe, an elegant white horse provided to the retiring governor by Tennessee Governor Robert Love Taylor, and she began taking "long rides up to Mount Bonnell in West Austin," a round trip of nearly eight miles. In March 1897 the governor sent Ima a "photograph of our new pony and trap, . . . a fine outfit" for the ladies to drive; Mike and Tom named the latest pet Daisy. Aunt Fannie "did her best to keep house—but that was not her forte" noted Ima; instead, the aging widow tended "a number of canary birds . . . religiously," continued her unpopular role as "disciplinarian," and "pinched pennies in her effort to help Father get on his feet financially."[27]

By the fall of 1896, the family had established new patterns. Governor Hogg took the recently installed electric streetcar or hitched Joe to his buggy and trotted to the office; Will studied avidly in his third-story aerie; and Mike and Tom attended public school. Ima returned to Miss Carrington's University Preparatory School and resumed piano study with Professor Edmund Ludwig. She began a lifetime habit of saving programs from concerts she attended and from her recital performances. On December 10, 1897, she played a Franz Schubert piano solo and variations at the 8:30 p.m. joint recital of Ludwig's piano class and Louise Pfaefflin's voice class; on May 17, 1898, Ima presented *Fantaisie Polonaise* by German-Swiss pianist and composer Joachim Raff (1822–1882); and in late January 1899, she helped celebrate Charles Culberson's election to the US Senate by performing *Kammenoi Ostrow*, a tone poem by renowned Russian pianist, conductor, and composer Anton Rubinstein (1829–1894). With the solace of her music, Ima suppressed the heartbreak of her mother's death, but she continued to worry about her little brothers and to find Aunt Fannie's strict approach to child-rearing unpleasant. More troubling was her aunt's unsolicited and incorrect medical prognostication that the Hogg children would inherit their mother's tuberculosis and, therefore, they should never marry—a fear predicated on Fannie's own experience. Her husband had died of the disease, and her tubercular son suppressed his illness by practicing medicine in Colorado.[28]

Ima recalled her father browsing "a good deal" at Gammel's Book Store, adding volumes to his "very good collection of Texiana," and sitting at home in the evening reading, but in fact, the beloved parent spent more and more time traveling. The former governor continued to attend the state Democratic Party conventions, backed candidates he believed would carry on his reforms, and campaigned strenuously for presidential nominee William Jennings Bryan in 1896 and 1900. Fifteen-year-old Mike was "by [his father's] side from start to finish" in Waco at the rancorous August 1900 Texas Democratic Convention, where the governor fought for party support of several constitutional amendments. "Men were amazed at his courage," Mike reported to Ima. While juggling political commitments, Jim Hogg pursued investors for Texas companies and developed his law practice. He relied on Will to exercise fatherly influence over the three younger children and turned to Ima for companionship, placing responsibilities of adulthood on the two older children before they were prepared to handle them.[29]

By October 1897 Will had moved to San Antonio to establish a solo law practice. He boasted to Ima that he had received "four invitations to eat turkey" and was watching a painter complete "a sign on a certain bay window" reading "Law Office, Will C. Hogg." The novice attorney exclaimed, "That sign denotes all that is beautiful in the world to me—truth, simplicity, sincerity, and modesty." The governor praised Will warmly: "You have never drawn a draft on me. . . . You have never been drunk. You have never gambled. You have never idled away your time on street corners nor at vulgar resorts. You have never forced the blood of shame to my cheeks from a wounded heart by a single disreputable act." Jim Hogg suggested his firstborn, now called "Brother" by his siblings, could "wield a marked influence over Mike by gaining his confidence." While Will should not tease Mike, he could "indulge in . . . jokes, tricks or diplomacy" with Tom. Unfortunately, toward Ima, Will adopted a sarcastic banter that verged on insensitivity. In December 1895, after twitting his sister about her failure to write, he administered a blow to her fledgling efforts at self-definition. "So, you are going to take art, are you when you finish your music? That's nice—but don't you think 'cooking' and 'house-keeping' class would pay your bills with better results?" In subsequent letters, Will criticized her behavior and suggested books she should read. Although Will began to imagine a "jolly good time" when "you and I, together . . . will read good books; you will play for me a little bit; and we will devote a whole week to good fellowship as sister and brother," he constantly pressured his sister to "do your duty" to family members. It is little wonder that this talented young woman was reluctant to respond.[30]

Ima's father, while far more affectionate to his "dear little Ima," placed a further burden on her slim shoulders; he began to see the image of his dead wife in his lovely daughter. On her seventeenth birthday, the doting widower wrote from New York, "You are seventeen years old! If on this account you are weaned I am sorry for it. But I am not weaned from you. In every feature of your face, in every movement of your hand I can see your Mother! Perhaps this . . . accounts for my partiality for you. . . . She was honorable, truthful, gentle, faithful, generous, faultless. In her I confided with absolute safety all my professional, political and business movements, intentions and acts. In you I look for a friend and counsellor as wise, as faithful, as true. Lovingly, Your Father." In the last weeks with her mother, Sallie, too, had confided in Ima. Her dear, conscientious daughter, she explained, must take care of Papa and the boys. How was Ima to please all these important people; how could she serve as a surrogate wife and mother to this beloved but grieving quartet when she was brokenhearted herself? In the years prior to her father's death, Ima worked diligently to make her father and her brothers happy at the same time that she tried to build friendships with peers, pursue her music studies with professional determination, and fill her dance cards with the names of possible suitors. In later years, her friends believed these insistent expectations caused Ima to place family demands before personal needs and to husband her fortune for the people of Texas with perfectionist zeal.[31]

Despite the emotional pressure placed on her, Ima did have fun during visits with the daughters of her uncle John Hogg and on trips with her father. In 1897 her cousin Velma, five years Ima's senior, visited Austin, and Ima accompanied the young woman home to Decatur that March. When Ima returned to Austin a month later, she brought her cousin Maud, her own age, with her for the first of many visits. Late that summer Ima joined her father and his traveling companions in the "pleasantly . . . cool climate" along the Saint Lawrence River before spending a week each in Boston and New York City. Ima and a friend had a "gay time," changing their dress "about four times a day" and recording the trip with Ima's Kodak camera. In February 1898 Ima and her father toured Mexico with "about twenty Northern people," who had been invited the previous October to explore business opportunities. Ima recalled the special train allotted the travelers and noted, "Father's connections were most cordial. . . . President [José de la Cruz Porfirio] Diaz gave a reception at Chapultepec to which I went and a banquet where I was not included." The Mexican trip was a great success, despite news of the ominous February 15 explosion and sinking of the battleship *Maine*, which killed 260 American sailors stationed in Havana Harbor and inaugurated the Spanish-American War (April–December 1898).[32]

A few months later, following a fishing trip with Mike and Tom, the peripatetic former governor and his daughter set off for California and Hawaii on July 31, 1898. Nineteen days earlier, Congress had passed a joint resolution to annex the Hawaiian Islands as a defensive United States presence in the Pacific Ocean and had invited Jim Hogg and other dignitaries to witness formal ceremonies in Honolulu. The Hoggs' voyage aboard the troopship *Arizona* took eight days, including a mid-ocean halt to repair one of the rudders, which delayed their arrival until after the ceremonies. The governor dubbed Honolulu "a gem by the sea," and told friends he "never enjoyed a trip more." Ima celebrated her sixteenth birthday, recorded the voyage in "My Freak Book," signed by the *Arizona*'s officers, and adored her stay at the Hawaiian Palace Hotel. "We were invited," she noted, "to Queen Liliuokalani's birthday party celebration with music and native dancing outdoors which was lovely. The [Iolani] palace she lived in was not elegant and she was a large unattractive woman." Years later, Ima surprised Hawaiian visitors to Bayou Bend by confiding she had met their queen. Ima also told the story of her return voyage many times. Her father booked passage to the mainland by way of Seattle, where he had never been. When he and Ima boarded the vessel, a "terrible feeling" came over Ima, and she burst into tears; she was sure something was wrong. The governor changed his travel plans, and when their ship reached San Francisco, the Hoggs learned that the Honolulu to Seattle steamer and everyone on board had been lost off the coast of Oregon during a terrible storm. In a letter to Will on August 16, the proud father described his daughter as "a great traveller," but "she's a little lazy about getting up." In the fall, however, Ima attacked her studies. On December 18, 1898, the governor reported that she was "studying very hard" so she could finish Miss Carrington's and matriculate at the University of Texas in the fall of 1899.[33]

University Years

Ima completed her studies at Miss Carrington's, visited her cousins in Decatur, and spent July and August 1899 in Manitou, Colorado, with her Davis relatives. Now thirteen and eleven, Mike and Tom, laden with "guns, and bat and ball, and clothes, and luncheon for six" made their first solo journey from Austin to Speer to spend June alone with their Stinson grandparents. Awaiting them in July was a plan concocted by their father and Llano rancher R. H. Moseley to hire Mike and Tom as summer hands so they could earn wages and learn "to labor and be independent." Of course, the former governor defrayed all expenses. The experiment was cut short when Mike succumbed to fever and chills, and the boys returned home in August to the care of their father and Aunt Fannie. Jim Hogg soon departed for Mexico, where he wrote Ima that he had "no objections" if she desired "to enter the University. . . . I should like for you to take such courses as may not interfere with your study and practice of music. . . . I know that you will do right, do the best, and act the lady under all conditions." Although Ima described herself as immature, unprepared, and frightened, she happily entered the freshman class in September. For two years she successfully balanced academic requirements, new friendships, and social gaiety.[34]

In 1899 University of Texas professors instructed several hundred students in the recently completed Main Building. Male students lived off campus in boardinghouses or fraternities, while females lived at home or boarded with friends to ensure proper chaperonage. Congress Avenue was still unpaved, and Ima walked to class from her home. Although Will now managed his siblings' expenditures for their father, Ima felt a new sense of freedom. Music study brought her to the university, but she was fascinated by the "inspiring courses" and educational beliefs of youthful Professor Alexander Caswell Ellis. Ellis strove to understand how children learned; he brought the parent-teacher association movement to Austin and worked for years with women's organizations and suffragists to improve the lives of Texans. To Ima, he was an "ideal educator" whose "warm interest in people . . . gave him insight into human behavior."[35] His farsighted reform work profoundly influenced her adult pursuits, and she consulted him for many years. Music study consumed most of Ima's time. She performed occasionally, playing an Edvard Grieg piano solo to honor the Derthick Club[36] on February 12, 1900. She heard the "always great" Paderewski on March 3, 1900, in Austin and treasured the "red-letter evening" when a "beautiful" small orchestra from Mexico presented a classical repertoire on campus. Years later she recalled, "From that night I never rested until we had a symphony orchestra in Texas."[37]

There were no official sororities during Ima's two years at the university, but she made lasting friendships, acquired the nicknames "Imie" and "Irmie," and had lots of fun at fraternity-sponsored parties. Through her memberships in the Ashbel Smith Literary Society and the Blue Bonnet Club, Ima met Houstonian Julia Ideson, who became a lifelong companion and supportive colleague when the classmates settled in Houston a few years later. Ima also enjoyed the Valentine Club and four dear friends, known always as "The Girls"—Vivian Brenizer (later Caswell), Dorothy "Dot" Thornton, Ethel Robinson Brown, and Bess Evans. After Ima had left the university, Vivien and other Valentine Club members organized a Pi Beta Phi chapter on February 29, 1902. The university disciplinary committee accepted their petition, stipulating only that the Pi Beta Phi group prove that women's fraternities were not undemocratic, demoralizing, or purely social. A few years later Ima became an honorary member of the University of Texas chapter and received a pin. Classmates recalled a "really charming" and "most conscientious student," who was "unaffected in manner" and often invited them to study in her family's "cosy [*sic*] library." On one occasion, Ima introduced her friends to the famous orator William Jennings Bryan. "Every Saturday night [Ima's friends] went to [an elegant] German or [casual] hop, usually held over one of the fire-stations. . . . Nobody drank alcoholic beverages at a dance—nor did a boy smoke without asking the girl's permission." In her second year, Ima attended "some five or six" fraternity balls at the Driskill Hotel that lasted "until the wee hours. Some dancers even went to a restaurant for breakfast. I usually arrived home near daylight ready for a nap." No one commented on the hours, but the governor offered paternal advice, concluding one letter: "I have all along known you to be sensible, prudent, and well-poised. It cannot be amiss however to present these general suggestions for your own reflection in the light of the well known axiom that a woman's character is her capital." Once Ima was "old enough to have young men callers," her father established a routine: "Promptly at ten o'clock he went up to his bedroom, and a heavy dropping of shoes would be a signal for the caller's departure."[38]

Just as events in September 1900—the ferocious hurricane that flattened Galveston and the murder of William Marsh Rice—dramatically altered the lives of Alice and James A. Baker, so the gusher that erupted at Spindletop at 10:30 a.m. on January 10, 1901, changed forever the fortunes of James Stephen Hogg and his children. During Ima's years at the University of Texas, her father's business prospects began to pay off. His law practice was busy; he purchased additional property on Nineteenth Street; and he took advantage of Capt. Anthony F. Lucas's prediction that oil lay beneath a salt dome near Beaumont. The governor partnered with Fort Worth lawyer and legislator James W. Swayne (1855–1929) to form the powerful political-business Hogg-Swayne Syndicate with Judge Robert Brooks, A. S. Fisher, and Thomas M. (Tom) Campbell and to purchase fifteen acres at Spindletop, so the syndicate could drill and swap oil leases. After Hogg-Swayne asked oil industrialist Joseph S. Cullinan[39] to manage its properties, the consortium prospered, added new investors, and became the Texas Company in 1902.

With prosperity assured, the former governor decided to make some changes. He confessed to his nephew William Davis that "Sister Fanny" had "been in feeble health for several months" and could no longer manage the household. Although William's mother had "always been a diligent, faithful hard-worker," the governor had been "unable to check her . . . in her efforts to do everything on the place."[40] It was time for Fannie to retire and for the Hoggs to employ a housekeeper. Jim Hogg had long wanted a "homeplace" where he could indulge his interest in experimental agriculture and reestablish the Mountain Home retreat of childhood memory, and in 1899 he and his law partner bought the Gaines Plantation in West Columbia, Brazoria County. By 1901 the governor was spending time on The Estrada, a farm near Austin, but that spring, after the Spindletop bonanza, he purchased 4,100 acres near the Gaines Plantation property, which included the old Patton Place homestead and a salt dome similar to the Beaumont formation. Now, Jim Hogg could create a family plantation on land once owned by pioneer Martin Varner, who had been one of Stephen F. Austin's original colonists.[41] He also hoped to make an oil discovery of his own one day. Within a year he proudly announced to Will that he had made his last payment on the property.

Basking in his new prosperity, the former governor focused attention on his children. He realized Mike and Tom needed serious, concentrated preparation for college work. Ima had completed "two joyous years" at the University of Texas, but she now wanted to pursue professional piano study in a great metropolis. With expanding business interests, the governor urged Will to return to Austin as his law partner. After months of deliberation, "Will has his shingle out with us at last," Jim wrote happily to his daughter on January 26, 1902, "Hogg, Robertson & Hogg!"[42] The former governor turned to an old friend when he chose schools for Mike and Tom. During campaign trips, Jim Hogg had met James McCoy Carlisle (1851–1922), a Tennessee native who had migrated to Grayson County, Texas, to teach school. Carlisle had founded a private school and served as superintendent of public schools in Whitesboro, Corsicana, and Fort Worth when Governor Hogg named him superintendent of Texas public instruction, a post he held from 1891 to 1899. In 1900 Carlisle opened a private school in Hillsboro, which two years later he reorganized as Carlisle Military Academy, chartered by the state to provide "literary, military, and manual training" for boys and a few girls. Carlisle's plan to balance intellectual growth with military training, to instill discipline, and to prepare students for college was considered progressive and suited Jim Hogg's needs. In the fall of 1901, the former governor put Mike to work at his Spindletop operation for twenty-three days in September and then enrolled him at Carlisle's Hillsboro school. He placed Tom at another boarding school in Salado, but when the teenager complained of homesickness, his father allowed him to transfer to Carlisle's school after Christmas. The brothers remained at the academy until the fall of 1903.

New York Interlude

With her father's warm approval, Ima Hogg selected New York City's National Conservatory of Music, considered the "outstanding institution for professional musical preparation in the United States" from its founding in 1885 until the First World War. Ima, now nineteen, became a "special boarder" at the Montpelier School for Young Ladies, just off Riverside Drive at 311 West Eighty-Second Street, a long trolley-car trip from the conservatory, located at 126–128 East Seventeenth Street. Named for James Madison's plantation and operated by Mrs. Frederick Greene, a daughter of impoverished Virginia planters, the school provided an urban experience to a dozen girls from the South. Ima took few courses there but benefitted from Greene's chaperonage at society balls and on weekend train excursions to the US Military Academy at West Point. Greene organized visits to New York museums and art galleries, where Ima discovered the work of contemporary European artists and responded with interest to Claude Monet paintings exhibited in February 1902 at the Durand-Ruel Galleries, 12 East Fifty-Seventh Street. That summer Greene died from "distressing heart trouble," and Ima moved to the "quite different and more convenient" Comstock School, run by the "delightful and cultured" Lydia Day at 38 West Fortieth Street. An experienced teacher introduced Ima to European literary giants Henrik Ibsen, Gerhard Hauptmann, and Feodor Dostoyevsky, and the vivacious Day arranged frequent evenings at plays and operas. Ima noted, "I really was a hard student of music, in spite of some dissipation. A strong constitution made it possible for me to work and attend concert after concert, opera after opera, with theater thrown in, almost every night." Annotated programs show her maturing comprehension of technique and deepening appreciation of "sympathetic" interpretation. She enjoyed two Metropolitan Opera seasons—and condemned one *Lohengrin* chorus as "horrid." She saw her first performance of Charles Gounod's internationally acclaimed *Faust* in February 1902, relished the sixth and seventh seasons of the New York Philharmonic Orchestra, and heard the Boston Symphony on its New York tour. She described the "unsurpassed" technique exhibited by Polish pianist Josef Hofmann,[43] and she extolled two "never to be forgotten" concerts given by Paderewski in March.[44]

At the National Conservatory, Ima met its visionary founder Jeanette Meyer Thurber (1850–1946). Unusual among late nineteenth-century music schools, Thurber's conservatory encouraged women students, hired female teachers, and championed African American and immigrant aspirants to musical careers. Jeanette Meyer, a "strikingly" beautiful brunette with "dark eloquent eyes" was the daughter of cultured parents who loved music. She studied at the Paris Conservatory and when only nineteen married Francis Beattie Thurber, a successful New York businessman who shared his bride's idealism and passion for music. At a time when classical music was considered a luxury for the wealthy, Thurber wanted to make works by acclaimed composers available to everyone. She promoted American musicians; sponsored a cross-country tour that introduced the work of German virtuoso Richard Wagner to United States audiences; and was the first patron to sponsor "a professional stock company with the avowedly democratic intent of bringing world-class opera to a broad spectrum of the American public at affordable prices."[45] Although her American Opera Company flopped after two tours, her National Conservatory introduced the precepts of postsecondary music education; became the only arts institution awarded a congressional operating charter; and through

Adele Margulies, beloved mentor to Ima Hogg. Camh-dob-012137, Ima Hogg Photographs, Dolph Briscoe Center for American History, University of Texas at Austin.

the diaspora of its graduates from 1885 to 1930, nurtured the national climate for music study and appreciation. Thurber's personal papers and the records of her American Opera Company and National Conservatory have disappeared, but her obsessive desire to introduce great music to all Americans made a lasting impression on a petite pianist from Texas. The dreams composed by Jeannette Thurber found voice in Ima Hogg's quest to share classical music with everyone.

Thurber developed an outstanding faculty, and it was among these musicians that Ima met her teacher and lifelong friend Adele Margulies,[46] a Frédéric Chopin and Franz Liszt specialist. Born in Vienna, Margulies took first prize at the Vienna Conservatory for three straight years. She made her New York City recital debut on November 3, 1881, and became the first professor of piano at the National Conservatory in 1887. In 1890 Thurber sent Margulies to Europe to persuade Czech genius and composer Antonín Dvořák (1841–1904) to visit New York, where he directed Thurber's conservatory for three seasons from 1892 to 1895 and composed some of his finest works before returning to Prague. Margulies inspired and encouraged her pupil from Texas, although Ima recalled that her first audition, with "the great [Hungarian] master pianist and teacher, Rafael Joseffy,"[47] had been a "complete failure. . . . My teachers in Austin had greatly exaggerated my talent and status as a performer. . . . When [Joseffy] heard me play he patted me on the back and suggested another preparatory teacher." Ima soon heard "Adele Margulies play with her trio and I knew at once she had what I wanted. She was an amazing pedagogue, who knew how to impart what she knew to others. . . . Under her I felt transformed and . . . I progressed rapidly."[48] Ima continued to study with Margulies and made special trips to attend concerts when her trio performed from 1904 to 1925. In later years, Ima introduced Margulies to Houston audiences at several master classes and supported her retirement. Shortly before the beloved mentor's death in June 1949, Ima wrote her frail friend that she had placed the extensive Adele Margulies Library of Chamber Music at Houston's Central Library in her honor.

In February 1902, former governor Hogg and his business partner Thomas M. Campbell sailed to England for a three-month campaign to raise capital for their oil venture. Although they failed to attract investors, the governor wrote long letters to Ima, discussing his religious convictions, praising his hosts' warm hospitality that "vibrate[s] with wit and humor," and describing his feelings about "queer" Old London with its gloomy fog, elaborate dinners, and outmoded court customs. While Jim Hogg recounted new impressions,

Ima began to search for life's meaning by considering a change in her religious affiliation from the Methodist to the Episcopal church, and she revealed her quest in letters to her father. In May, her father replied: "As to the Episcopal Church: If it is your choice and you so desire I could have no objection to your joining it. Tom is thinking of joining the Methodist Church. Your Mother and her people all belonged to it. Mine were of the Baptist persuasion. Let your own conscience and better judgment be gratified in this question and I shall be satisfied."[49] A decade later, on April 12, 1912, Ima took the momentous step she had pondered for so long and was received by Christ Church (Episcopal) in Houston.

Shortly before Christmas 1902, Will alerted his sister to a change in her circumstances. Writing from the Hot Sulphur Wells Hotel in San Antonio, where the young attorney was visiting his ailing father, Will warned, "Prepare to become a comfortably rich woman. Your land at Columbia [Varner] has healthy prospects of proving gusher territory. Drilling . . . is progressing rapidly and James Stephen 'would not be surprised to see 'em gush by Christmas.' Don't begin to spend money on your prospects just now." Former governor Hogg gathered his children and his sister Fannie at Varner for a lavish holiday that December. Equipped with new guns, saddles, and ponies, Mike and Tom accompanied their father on a short hunt. Fannie described the house as "a massive pile of bricks" with many windows, and she praised the enormous vegetable production. Her brother, she noted, gave the "twenty-five negroes at work here" and their families Christmas dinner and a barn dance. Following this festive interlude, Mike and Tom returned to Hillsboro, and Ima traveled back to New York. To recognize her diligent study, Ima's teachers asked her to participate in the conservatory's March 1903 public recital, and she chose a nocturne by Frédéric Chopin and a work by Robert Schumann, two of her favorite composers. As the semester drew to a close, Ima seemed unsure about her future. Should she continue piano studies, or should she return to Texas to make a home for her father and brothers? Friends thought her letters sounded "so sad, forlorn and in the dumps," and they worried about her health. She made no decision about the fall semester and spent the summer at Varner with Aunt Fannie, Mike, and Tom, where events occurred that ended her New York interlude.[50]

Ima soon realized that her brothers were not receiving the rigorous academic instruction needed to prepare them for college. Mike aspired to a place at the United States Naval Academy in Annapolis, and Tom needed greater challenge and discipline, so Ima wrote to friends and to Yale University President Arthur Twining Hadley for suggestions about college preparatory schools in the Northeast. While pondering her brothers' futures, Ima stuck a needle in her knee early in July. The cartilage became infected. Antibiotics were still unknown, and Ima was very ill. Nursed by Aunt Fannie and her brothers, she could not walk, even with crutches, for several weeks. In early August her friend Pearl Coburn wrote to inquire about Ima's health and to suggest St. Paul's School in Concord, New Hampshire, or Lawrenceville School, located in a New Jersey village of the same name near Princeton University. Anson Phelps Stokes Jr., secretary of the Yale Corporation, responded for President Hadley with a list of schools.

By September 1903 Ima had moved to the Austin Sanatorium at Congress and Fourteenth streets to continue rehabilitation, while Will accompanied his younger brothers to the Hotel Joyce in Baltimore and "rigged them out" for school. Mike, nearly eighteen, took the train to Annapolis, where he spent a semester cramming for the Naval Academy entrance exams with "Prof. Wilmer . . . the most competent instructor" of hopeful applicants. Tom, sixteen, began the first form (eighth grade) at Lawrenceville, boarding in Griswold House. Ima's brothers, father, and friends wrote newsy letters to cheer her recovery. Her physical ailment caused an emotional sadness, or "blue mood," we would call depression, but which was not identified or effectively treated in the early years of the twentieth century. By Christmas, Ima had joined her father at the Driskill Hotel, but not until January 4, 1904, could she report, "At last I walk without crutches, though I limp a good deal at times, and can't walk very far." She confessed to "Dearest Mickie" that she had danced a little—though "Papa was frantic when he heard about it." Mike failed the Naval Academy entrance exam and instead transferred to Lawrenceville, where he entered the lower third form (tenth grade) in February 1904.[51]

Mike made friends quickly at Lawrenceville and, despite spending two weeks in the infirmary with pink eye, was elected president of Griswold House and captain of the house baseball team. Tom, on the other hand, was "lagging behind his class in English and Elocution." Will did not reveal Tom's poor grades to his father but instead blamed Tom for "backwardness . . . due to pure negligence on your part." Will wrote harshly to Headmaster Dr. Simon J. McPherson, announcing, "Tom is old enough, healthy enough and intelligent enough to begin to do some studying, . . . and . . . if he can't keep up with his mates without extra tutoring, he should be degraded; after he reaches the lowest form, if he does not show some zeal, we will take him out of school." As the family began to make plans for the summer, Jim Hogg sat down to write a long letter to Mike on June 3. He explained he was "trying to shift some of the cares of life to Will and Ima," who "perform them well." He expected that soon Mike and Tom "will be able also to relieve me" and complimented the way "you boys get along so well together." Other correspondence confirms that Ima had assumed a motherly role toward her younger brothers—arranging their vacations, buying their clothes, and decorating their rooms at school.[52]

Ima and her friend Betty Greene left Austin in the summer of 1904 for the long trip to New England. When they changed trains in St. Louis, they made a quick visit to the World's Fair. The journey continued to Trenton, New Jersey, to meet Mike and Tom, and on to Holyoke, Massachusetts, where the girls stayed for a few days with Pearl Coburn. The boys, followed a few days later by their sister, made the final trek to Larkhurst, a resort hotel in the Berkshire highlands of western Massachusetts. Ima described the region as beautiful but "unexpectedly inconvenient." Mike hiked, fished, and golfed, while Tom began "courting" two sisters "to the extent of his prodigious energy," playing golf with them and escorting them to church. Ima's knee bothered her again, a year after the original injury, and she went to New York City for a miserable treatment of "red hot iron—on my knee and spinal column." She wrote her father the day before her twenty-second birthday that while strolling, on the doctor's orders, she had seen "a magnificent necklace" in an antique shop; the governor responded quickly with a check for eighty dollars to purchase the gold and opal bauble. A few days later Ima returned to the mountains, where she and her brothers remained happily for the rest of the summer.[53]

Fall 1904 brought many changes to the Hogg family. When school began in September, Tom had progressed to the second form (ninth grade), but Mike repeated tenth grade. Ima furnished her brothers' Lawrenceville rooms before she and her father proceeded to the World's Fair in St. Louis. The Hoggs joined other "distinguished visitors from the Lone Star State" at a reception held in the Texans' honor, and on September 28, "Miss Ima Hogg of Austin gave an impromptu piano recital at the Texas Building."[54] In November Ima and her father began to spend more time in Houston. The former governor lived at the Rice Hotel and explored transferring his legal practice to Houston. As the houseguest of her cousin Dr. Baylor Hogg and his wife, Ima attended the No-Tsu-Oh festival and the Thanksgiving Eve ball for King Nottoc and his debutante queen. Will had been traveling regularly to St. Louis on business and decided in December to become corporate attorney for the St. Louis Mercantile Bank and Trust.

Will received a report in November 1904 that Tom needed to "develop backbone and application" to his studies, but Ima and her father were startled just before Christmas to learn that Tom's "very bad cold" had turned into pneumonia. They left immediately for Lawrenceville. Although the *Houston Post* reported that Miss Ima Hogg was "attending her brother," she remembered that "Father took charge with the nurse to follow orders. . . . Hot poultices were constantly applied to chest back and sides. All parts were greased with lard." Right after New Year's Day 1905, the former governor, Ima, and Tom left Mike behind to begin the spring term and took a train for St. Louis to visit Will. When they returned to Austin for the January gubernatorial inauguration festivities, Ima and Tom began boarding at Burleson House, run like a private home by Mary Dial, who took charge of Tom's convalescence. No longer forced to "nag him so much," Ima enjoyed "a good many receptions."[55]

End of an Era

On a wintry January 26, 1905, Jim Hogg boarded the morning train at West Columbia to commute from his country haven at Varner Plantation to his new office in Houston, sixty-five miles to the north. While stopped at a station, a railroad coupling of "three or four freight cars" to the passenger train, "made with more force than usual," jolted the passengers in Hogg's car but did not "throw any persons . . . out of their seats." The grossly overweight former governor, who had developed a chronic heart condition, had a bad cold and sore throat. He continued his journey but complained of a chill and fever when he reached Houston's Rice Hotel. An abscess formed at the back of his neck, but on February 1 Hogg distributed the card formally announcing Hogg, Watkins and Jones, his Houston partnership with Edgar Watkins and Frank Jones. Four days later, he was seriously ill. A telegram to Ima, in Austin enjoying the social scene, explained that her father needed surgery. The sufferer later recalled that to reach the abscess the surgeon "had to cut it from five different places in my mouth." Ima rushed to her father's side and nursed him tenderly while he was bedridden for the next six weeks with a badly swollen neck. In mid-March, Ima "bundled [him] up and brought" him to the Reinhardt Ranch near Boerne, Texas, northwest of San Antonio. "I am . . . an invalid under rigid surveillance," he complained to Will but assured his worried son that "Ima is rosy and fine. I am yet very weak but slowly improving," and "Tom got a job" on Walter Schreiner's Kerrville ranch, about forty miles further north, "and is . . . probably roping cattle—the ambition and joy of his exuberant life." By April 5 the governor had improved enough to make a brief speech in Dallas at a dinner honoring President Theodore Roosevelt, but that month the family was worrying about

Mike, confined to a hospital in Trenton with measles, and Tom, still in Kerrville, because he was not fully recovered from his earlier bout of pneumonia. By late April, the governor, his daughter—"My running mate—my Mascot!"—and her favorite horse Napoleon, nicknamed "Nap," were "boarding" at the Rice Hotel, and the ailing man had filed suit for $100,000 damages against the International and Great Northern Railroad to compensate for injuries suffered during the harsh railroad coupling.[56]

The governor's recovery did not last long. Mike came home from Lawrenceville for the last time in June and settled in Austin with a private tutor to prepare for the University of Texas entrance exams. Summer heat drove Ima and her father to Varner, where the governor again felt unwell. In August, Ima and her father joined Tom in Kerrville, but the trio soon moved to Cliff House, at the foot of Pike's Peak in Manitou Springs, Colorado. The picturesque, high-altitude resort, founded by doctors in 1872, was popular with Texans, and Ima had a "dandy gay time" for ten days until "everybody I know" left. Happily, Mike passed his exams and enrolled at the University of Texas, and Ima persuaded Tom to enter Colorado College in Colorado Springs for the fall semester. Although the family enjoyed the cool mountain air, the injured governor developed breathing problems. In late September Ima begged Will to come from his job in St. Louis to help her bring their father back to Varner, where his health improved slightly.[57]

With renewed confidence, the perennial politician accepted an early November speaking engagement to address a political conclave that included four candidates for governor. In late October Ima and her father set out for Dallas via a brief respite in Mineral Wells. On the final leg of this journey, the governor became so weak they could go no further than Fort Worth. Quick-witted Ima recognized that her father could participate in the Dallas meeting from afar; she arranged for him to use Edison's talking machine to record the speech, which she then sent to Dallas, where the startled audience heard the governor's familiar voice. Press accounts flooded towns across Texas, and Jim Hogg fans wrote to Ima to express their concern about her father's health. As was her lifelong habit, Ima responded thoughtfully to each well-wisher. After a month in Fort Worth, the governor regained enough strength to take the train to Austin. He remained for a few weeks at the Driskill Hotel before going to Varner with Will, who was terminating his short-lived business affiliation in St. Louis and forming the law partnership of Carlton & Hogg in Houston. Letters to Ima show she remained in Austin for several parties while her father continued "to improve under the skillful treatment of your Brother Will and our servant Richard Davis." On December 9, the former governor reported, "Each day I take plenty of exercise, either walking, talking or horse-back riding."[58] The family gathered for a jolly Christmas and long discussions about the future. Before Will returned to his law practice, he and Ima persuaded their father to undergo a complete medical examination at the Battle Creek Sanitarium in Michigan. They arranged to meet in March for the journey.

On Friday, March 2, 1906, Ima and her father left Varner Plantation for Battle Creek. They stopped in Houston to have dinner and spend the night with the governor's law partner Frank Jones. Cheerful and chatty, still "in the vigor of his mental strength," the governor finally retired to his bedroom at midnight. The next morning at about eleven o'clock, Ima knocked on his bedroom door and called out to him; hearing no response, she entered the room to rouse the late sleeper. The "Great Texas Commoner," not yet fifty-five years old, "fell peacefully to sleep" and suffered a fatal heart attack in the night. Only twenty-three, Ima had now been present at the deathbeds of both parents. Houston's *Chronicle* and *Post* reported she was "stricken by the burden of her grief" and "under the care of a physician." The governor's former partner Judge James Robertson and his friend Col. Edward M. House made funeral arrangements in Austin. At ten o'clock Monday morning, undertakers moved the casket to the train station and loaded it into the baggage car, which was "literally covered with floral decorations from Houston friends." At 10:30 a.m., "Miss Ima Hogg, gowned in black and leaning on the arm of her brother Will, walked to a carriage which waited in front of the [Frank] Jones home." Three carriages proceeded to the station, where a crowd "stood back in silent respect." At the family's request, there was no special train; instead, two cars were added to the regularly scheduled Houston-to-Austin passenger train. A private car, "Teche," served the Hoggs and the governor's two law partners, and an extra Pullman accommodated several Houston "committees of escort"—from the Houston Bar Association, Houston Cotton Exchange, Houston Business League, and Houston Labor Council. The train, including its regular cars crammed with mourners, pulled away from the platform at 11:00 a.m. and arrived in Austin at 4:50 that afternoon.[59]

Bearers transported the casket from the train to the reception room at the state capitol. Early Tuesday morning, March 6, guards moved the former governor's body to the Senate Chamber, where it lay in state surrounded by elaborate flower arrangements as hundreds of mourners remembered Hogg's "distinguished service to the State and his quiet acts of love and aid for those whom he befriended." Observers noted the "sincere sorrow and grief" of the "cosmopolitan throng" that included "rich and poor," delegations from other states, and a "large number of colored people" for whom Governor Hogg "had used his best efforts to defend . . . and protect . . . from violence." Obeying the "special request of his bereaved children," there was "no display of ostentation" but rather a simple thirty-minute service of prayer, scripture, and beloved songs, led by the Reverend J. A. French and the Reverend B. H. Werlein, who noted Jim Hogg's "one object in life was to live close to the people. He was more than a statesman, more than a lawyer, he was a good man." Fourteen pallbearers and ten honorary pallbearers escorted the casket to Oakwood Cemetery, where the "rugged and strong-natured man" was laid to rest next to his gentle and beloved Sallie. Perhaps mindful of his place in history, the "people's governor" asked his children to "plant at the head of my grave a pecan tree and at my feet an old-fashioned walnut tree." When these trees, rooted firmly in the past, "shall bear, let the pecans and the walnuts be given out among the plain people so that they may plant them and make Texas a land of trees"—a place of prosperity in the future. The governor's last will, signed on October 16, 1905, when he was so ill in Fort Worth, made a special bequest of Austin property to his daughter. The rest of the property, wherever situated, was to be divided "share and share alike" among his four children; Mike and Tom were to be given a "liberal and practical education such as will fit them for any profession or vocation they may choose to pursue"; and "if it be found practicable," Varner and the surrounding acreage were to be held for fifteen years after his death in hopes that a major oil strike would occur there during the interval. Will, Henry Marsh of Tyler, and Judge James Robertson were named executors; Marsh declined to serve, and Ima was appointed executrix. Will, Ima, and the judge filed the will for probate in May, whereupon Robertson also declined to act, leaving Ima and Will to share settlement duties.[60]

When Ima returned to Austin following her music studies in New York, she became her father's steady companion and helpmate, "the sunlight" of his household. For the final year of the governor's life, she "scarcely left" his side and was seen by his worried public as the "guardian angel—the only one who could control him," the devoted daughter who accompanied him on visits to the doctors, heard their advice, and nursed him through episodic periods of improvement and decline. Since her mother's death in 1895, "Dear Darling Ima" had provided emotional balance and social connection for her father. Although he was often physically absent and psychologically obtuse, thinking more of his own loneliness than of his daughter's awakening sensitivity, deep bonds of love tightened between the flamboyant father and the dainty daughter. It was hard to resist his praise. Did he really "respect [her] opinion more than [he] did [his] own"; did "the influence [she] wield" over the brothers "amount to a great deal"; did she "grow more like her dear Mother"; did she have a thoughtful, "splendid character, . . . sweet disposition, . . . and charming manners," and would he "proudly take [her] anywhere"? Since childhood, the governor had traveled with Ima, introduced her to his friends, and urged her to play the piano. As a young woman, he encouraged her to take an interest in politics, explained his oil business to her, told her to make her own decisions, and, in death, bequeathed her and her brothers equal shares in his legacy. But the doting father never understood that this overwhelming trust and love seemed to lead only in one direction—to a domestic life of companionship with her father and brothers. What if she chose a traditional path of marriage and her own family? What if she preferred the exciting but unsure life of a pianist in a great city far from domestic duties? Even when she was studying in New York, her father seemed to assume she would come back to Texas. "I think of you—the best friend I have this side of Heaven! I shall look with much solicitude and pleasure for your return home," he wrote in April 1902.[61]

Ima resisted this plea for over a year, but by the time of her father's accident, she had acquiesced to his plan. Now death had snapped the bonds that had seemed unbreakable. An uncertain future loomed ominously. For several months, grief and illness precluded commitment, while Ima continued to fight the tension she had long felt between fulfilling the conventional expectations of her family and satisfying her yearnings for personal independence as a professional musician. Left alone to make a choice, she saw no clear path ahead, but shortly after the funeral she sought refuge in rural Lampasas with close friend Sarah (Sadie) Campbell,[62] daughter of Jim Hogg's Texas Company partner Thomas M. Campbell. During the month with her friend, Ima responded to the outpouring of letters sent to assuage her loss, and she regained her physical strength. By April Will reassured Mike and Tom that "Sister . . . seems in very good spirits." She was now back in Houston, was "riding out every day in the phaeton," and was "so much better" than she had been before her trip to Lampasas.[63]

During Ima's student years, several eligible suitors braved the chaperonage of her formidable father and protective brothers to invite her to parties, place their names on her dance cards, and write letters expressing their affection. The spirited young lady loved to dance and attend parties; she participated in the flower parades and civic functions popular in her youth; and she energetically played games, rode horseback, and climbed mountains. In 1902 she mentioned an interest in house decoration and rushed back to New York after Christmas, ignoring the 1903 gubernatorial inauguration ball in Austin but accepting invitations in New York, actions that made friends suspect a serious beau. During her 1904 summer in the Berkshires, Ima corresponded with Harry Taylor, whom she had met at Pearl Coburn's Holyoke home, and with Wilbur P. Allen, a youthful lawyer from Austin who called her "my pedestal lady" and "my dear, incorrigible, impossible friend," suggesting that Ima flirted but did not encourage his ardent two-year pursuit. During her August 1905 stay in Manitou supervising her father's recuperation, Ima corresponded lightheartedly with Houston admirers Walter Betz Renn and Will Harris. Only a spring 1905 letter from "Sweetheart" suggests a serious relationship— "Most heartily do I agree with you, sweetheart, that Fate could not be so unkind as to keep long separated two such loving and trusting hearts. I think only that I love you and that you are mine and that no power on earth can separate us." The identity of "Sweetheart" and the resolution of this romance remain unknown, although it might have been young Harvard graduate Renn, who was living at the Rice Hotel in 1905–1906, during the time Ima and her father boarded there. Her most persistent suitor was Marcus Aurelius Weems, a doctor practicing near Varner who was fifteen years her senior. Weems began to visit Ima and send her flowers in 1903 when she injured her knee at Varner, and his enduring courtship continued after her father's death, but unwillingness to commit marked all Ima's romances. Did none of these men compare to her splendid father; or, having watched her mother's hard work, difficult pregnancy, and poor health, did the thought of domestic drudgery repel her? By 1906 her dear friends Dot Thornton and Julia Ideson had chosen the maverick path of professional spinsterhood—Thornton as a teacher and Ideson as a librarian. Would music bring Ima a lifetime of satisfaction?[64]

In March 1906 Will assumed his father's paternal, legal, and business activities, and he moved the family headquarters to Houston, a fateful decision for his siblings and for their adopted city. Tom and Mike stayed in Austin, but by April, Will, Ima, and her horse Napoleon were living with Will's partner Oswald Carlton and his family at 1602 Travis Street. Ima recalled her older brother as a large man, who "went through so many periods of change. . . . His heart was as big as Father's and his devotion as deep." As a child he was shy and studious, much attached to his gentle mother and determined Aunt Fannie; at the university he was a "hermit" and introvert whose friends were young faculty members "or other intellectuals," but when he went to San Antonio, Will "blossomed into an outgoing extrovert." Toward his siblings, he remained the stuffy, censorious overseer of their behavior and checkbook, christened "Podsnap" by Mike, after a pompous character in Charles Dickens's *Our Mutual Friend*. Formidable Aunt Fannie described Mike at age three "as perfect as inborn manhood can make a boy. Naturally refined from babyhood he must be innately a gentleman always." Shy and quiet in society, Mike romped and wrestled with Tom and teased Ima. A mediocre student, Mike would remain at the University of Texas as an undergraduate and law student from September 1906 until the summer of 1911. Tom, called a "blunderbuss" as a toddler, performed poorly in school. Sports, hunting, fishing, wrangling cows, and trying one activity and then another reflected a restless temperament and inability to focus that boded ill for the future. On March 26, 1906, Will warned Ima, "Tom is spending about as much time downtown now as he did a month ago; this is a bad sign and he will surely drift into his former habits of extravagance and shiftlessness." That May, in a letter to Tom laced with sarcasm, Will noted that his brother had endorsed a check to the owner of a pool room and wanted to know if he planned to pursue that career at the Rice Hotel while the two brothers shared living quarters there during the summer. Will hoped Tom would work in his office for the summer, but instead Tom and Ima, who was "still quite nervous and restless, especially of nights," departed for Mineral Wells in June to improve their health.[65]

Decisive Journeys: New York and Europe

Mineral Wells did not provide a cure for the grieving brother and sister. Tom fell ill, and Ima decided she needed a change of scene. Since her father's death, Ima had hoped to visit her former chaperone Lydia Day and her music teacher Adele Margulies in New York, because she felt the solace of music would help her find a way forward. In early September 1906, Will accompanied Tom and Ima to New York City, where she checked into the Hotel Martha Washington, which opened at 30 West Thirtieth Street in 1903 as the first New York accommodation that catered to women who were traveling alone and was managed and staffed entirely by women. Before returning to Houston, Will took his siblings to the races at Sheepshead Bay in Brooklyn. The Hoggs were among a crowd driven to the racetrack in "over 500 autos, each with its cargo of stunningly gowned men and women . . . who had the joy of seeing . . . Texas horse, Temaceo, win the first race." Ima reconnected with friends and began daily visits to museums and galleries and nightly outings to concerts and plays. Will wrote his sister about business matters and reported in November that crews had installed the first derrick at Varner; he "confidently expect[ed] to hear the hiss of steam from the throat of a drill" by December 14. Ima and Tom sailed from New York on the *Lampasas* and reached Galveston on the evening of December 9. Will met the travelers the next day, and that evening Mike, following a hint from his brother, called Ima "over the long distance phone." The weeks in New York revived Ima's spirits, and she began planning a lengthy journey through Europe. Tom decided to find clearer purpose in his life by enlisting in the Marine Corps for three years; by July 1907, the new recruit was writing from the Marine Barracks in Norfolk, Virginia.[66]

During the first months of 1907, Ima enjoyed social events, visited Varner, and returned to her piano. She also renewed her reticent romance with the tenacious Dr. Marcus Aurelius Weems, who called on her again and sent her affectionate letters and flowers from his garden. Despite his devotion, and her "real esteem" for him, Ima continued to organize an extended stay in Europe. She offered to send Weems her beloved black stallion, if Weems was "in earnest" about caring for Napoleon, but the courtly doctor's efforts to spend time alone with her before she left Houston were thwarted by bouts of sickness or attentive chaperones. In mid-June Weems followed Ima and her friend Helen (Mrs. Lewis) Thompson[67] to New York, where the ladies purchased travel wardrobes before sailing on the Hamburg-American passenger ship *President Lincoln*. Again, Weems failed to contrive a meeting alone with elusive Ima, but when she reached her stateroom on June 27, she discovered the persistent suitor had sent her flowers and a letter to be opened after she sailed. Several days at sea passed before Ima read and replied to the letter. She tried to discourage Weems gently: "Your letter made me feel quite sad. . . . I do appreciate though I do feel so utterly unworthy. . . . I am really so unlike anything that you . . . imagine . . . for I am quite ignorant as to any real feeling of more than friendship for anyone. . . . Love is a thing . . . absolutely ungoverned by reason or will." She promised postcards and closed with a formal "kindest regards and my best wishes."[68]

Flowers, gifts, books, bon voyage messages, steamer trunks (two apiece), and several suitcases filled the first-class stateroom Ima shared with Lucy (Mrs. Ben) Thompson of Nacogdoches, Texas. Bands played, whistles blew, streamers billowed, and the stateside crowd cheered as the giant liner was pulled slowly away from its berth at New York's westside docks to begin its maiden voyage to Plymouth. Ima could not remember "being more run down or weary than before getting on board," but while at sea, she regained her health, played shuffleboard and cards, read books, and met new friends. With Lucy and Ima were Houstonians Helen and Lewis Thompson, their sons Ben, age four, and Lewis, age three, with their governess Magdalena; Ben Foster and his sister

Ione of Kansas City; and Charles Scott, a chemistry professor from Austin College. Ima began a diary and recorded the "temperate" weather until the last two "stormy and very cold" days, the "never ceasing fascination of the sea," and the "moonlit nights." Like most Americans abroad, Ima was an avid tourist; she rated hotels and rustic inns, tracked expenses, recorded journeys from town to town, and purchased postcards of paintings, architecture, stained glass windows, and scenery at every stop. Her "delight with rural England" never waned, and when a "small boy" passed her train window, she could not resist a "tiny paper basket with at least 1½ doz. tremendous [straw]berries all daintily nested in fresh green leaves."[69]

Salisbury, Ima's "first great" cathedral, "overwhelmed" her "by its symmetry and beauty of exterior, though even the quiet bare interior is most uplifting & inspiring." The group moved on from Salisbury to Winchester, where Ima "felt like a barbarian to find [she had] walked over the resting place of Jane Austen. . . . I believe for the first time I know what History means!" Then on to London where the travelers had box seats for the opera their first night. She attended Parliament on Saturday and after church at St. Paul's went to Hyde Park to watch the "Church Parade" of "very beautiful women, magnificently gowned," strolling to and from church accompanied by "Eng. men in their top hats." Taking one suitcase each, Ima and her friends left their trunks in London while they sped from place to place by horse-drawn coach and coal-fired train. Between July 10 and 27, the group explored Windsor Castle, where Ima spent her twenty-fifth birthday; Oxford; Warwick; Stratford; Chester; Liverpool; the English Lakes, with "scenery as fine as I've ever seen"; Belfast; Glasgow; the Scottish Lake District, "vaster & wilder than Eng. Lakes, only very hazy"; Stirling Castle; and Edinburgh before returning to London. Ima wrote enthusiastic letters to family, friends, and the Texas press, detailing her fast-paced tour.[70]

Following four days of relative inactivity and rest in London, the group boarded the boat train for Dover at 9:00 a.m. and arrived at Ostend in Belgium after a "horrid little trip" of three hours. Once again, the touring pace was intense. They passed through the "rich farming country" from Ostend to Bruges, where they went to St. John Hospital to see the works of Hans Memling. "These masterpieces are truly worth our trip to Bruges—only it should take longer than the two hours we gave them." On August 2 they spent the morning at the Waterloo battlefield, "caught 1:15 train for Brussels," and visited the museum there all afternoon. The next morning Ima shopped all morning at "Rue de la Madeleine," which was the "most fascinating shopping district I ever saw." She then took the train to Antwerp, where she admired a "fine bronze statue" by Flemish Baroque artist Peter Paul Rubens before rushing on to the Hague, where "so many speak Eng. we have little trouble." During three days in Holland, Ima heard the Berlin Philharmonic Orchestra, took an excursion "on a little steam boat full of Americans," watched peasants "driving in small carts pulled by dogs," inspected cheese making, and visited the Rijks Gallery in Amsterdam to see Dutch artist Rembrandt van Rijn's *Night Watch*, "magnificently hung in a perfectly lighted room all by itself," before taking the train to Cologne.[71]

Once in Germany, Ima and her friends floated down the Rhine to Coblenz, where they "took our first German beer" before traveling on to Wiesbaden, "a beautiful town," where Ima finally rested "completely." In the "bright warm days," she listened to music all day. Germany, she wrote, "is adorable. Germans kindly and homely." The group continued on to Frankfurt and Heidelberg, where the travelers saw a "floor covered in blood stains" from a century of student dueling. They viewed the ruined castle and then walked "along the quaint narrow streets." Although caught in the rain, Ima declared the day "one of the most satisfying I can imagine." The group spent a long day traveling to Munich on a railroad route that "went through tunneled mountains—and the Black Forest." Ima remarked how well the German government cared for and replenished its "lovely forests," quipping, "Would that our own Texas had some laws to protect our poor trees." After four train changes, the weary travelers arrived in Munich on August 18. Ima, who described herself as "physically, mentally, morally, spiritually and nerve exhausted" from "improving" her mind, remained there for fifteen "glorious" days, skipping a visit to Vienna so she could attend Richard Wagner's *Ring* cycle, where she purchased a souvenir fan covered with images of star performers from the year's festival. Her lifetime love affair with Wagnerian opera and with Germany had begun. Ima moved to the Quisisana Pension, where Helen Thompson's "delightful friend" Mrs. Mary J. Cooper[72] took her "in full charge." Ima "dared to play on the piano a little" and listened to the "discussion of various scientific and everyday subjects" among pension guests. Ima and Cooper strolled in the English Garden and sat on "the banks of the Isis reading to each other" from the *Rheingold* libretto. Much refreshed by her interlude, Ima discovered the benefits of independence. On Tuesday, September 3, she traveled second class to Innsbruck to rejoin her friends for a tour of Switzerland and Italy. Her compartment companion was "the cook . . . of some Frau Grafin who was herself 1st class . . . and I carried on an animated dialogue in German—most enlightening."[73]

Souvenir fan from Richard Wagner Opera Festival, 1907. MS 21, Ima Hogg Papers, Museum of Fine Arts, Houston Archives.

In Switzerland, Ima and her friends hiked through "woodsy places." Boats on the lakes, cogwheel climbs "through unsurpassed scenery," and "the impression of heavenly beauty" filled her diary. On the all-day trip to Montreux, the travelers "came into sight of Lake Geneva—the dim & misty atmosphere over the mountains, the bluish cast over the lake gave a Turneresque picture to the scene from our high mountain road." Just as memorable was the "Palace Hotel, the scene of a lively fashionable crowd of drinking & smoking women." Friday, September 13, found the group in Milan, where Ima and her friends visited the cathedral. Ima noted an "immediate change of conditions" in Italy, "warmer, unkempt lands, rundown looking houses—poverty." Early Saturday morning, the travelers left Milan for Venice. Like all tourists, they quickly found a gondola to glide under the Bridge of Sighs and experienced the "Piazza at 5:30 P.M.! The glorified façade at this hour of St. Mark's was a most perfect moment. . . . Venice is far beyond my expectation. Nothing could be more enchanting." The Americans departed for the all-day trip through "pretty mountain scenery" to Florence, where the ladies shopped on Thursday, but only the cathedral was open on Friday because of a national holiday. After a "hard trip" to Naples, the adventurers took a boat to Capri to explore the Blue Grotto. They "stooped . . . flat & slid into a cavern big enough to hold some 20 boats—and the sight quite took away my breath as satiated with lovely things as I am now." Ima was too hot and tired the next day to note much at Pompeii but traveled on to Rome, where she occasionally explored ancient ruins by herself during a five-day visit. On October 3 the group left Rome and stopped in Pisa to change trains and view the "lovely" cathedral before returning to Florence for several days. There she received a letter on October 4 from Leola Fisher that cemented plans to spend several months in Berlin.[74]

It is not clear when Ima decided to study in Germany. She might have thought about it in the early summer when she and Leola Fisher, a friend from her Houston social circle, discovered each would be traveling abroad. Leola and her family left Houston on July 16, and in the fall Leola and her brother Henry (age eighteen) settled in Berlin for an extended period of study under the supervision of their grandmother Selma White. Ima remembered a chance meeting in Florence with Alice MacFarland, a young musical friend from Houston, and encouragement from Will as the "direct" causes of her decision. Alice urged her to live with a German family, learn to speak German, and study her music seriously. Will told her to "stay awhile in Germany" and suggested she "study languages" and keep up the walking exercises. He promised to forward money through the American Express Company and have the *Houston Post* sent to her every day. Ima's new self-confidence, her immersion in German culture and music, the availability of agreeable companions, and Will's insistence "at the final moment . . . that I take any opportunity to improve myself" convinced her to extend her adventure abroad.[75]

For the second time, Ima left her friends; she "started out on [her] journey all alone and awfully lonesome, too," but arrived safely in Berlin on October 10. Leola Fisher, her fun-loving, violin-playing brother Henry, and their easygoing grandmother welcomed Ima warmly to their apartment at 5 Savignyplatz in Berlin. Ima had barely unpacked before the Fishers whisked her to an opera, and she saved programs from sixteen events in the two months before Christmas. By November, Ima had sublet a room in the "snuggest, sweetest" apartment rented by Selma White for Leola and Henry at 22 Mommensenstrasse in the new suburb of Charlottenburg, west of the city. Her "tiny" room, which had to accommodate "a Bechstein to practice on" and a "tiny" furniture suite of white wardrobe, washstand, vanity, table, and two chairs "made to order," was "very cheerful looking, and I love to be in it." On New Year's Day 1908, Charles Scott, the chemistry professor from Austin College who had been traveling with Ima's group during the summer, unexpectedly appeared. Police had been troubling Ima about her passport, and Scott promised to handle the matter for her. He visited Ima every day, secured the passport, and on January 4 "came and spent the time making himself miserable again." Although Ima had not mentioned his romantic intentions in previous diary entries, she now revealed that she had "hoped he had understood [her] after what I told him last summer. I acted like a cold-blooded vampire, he told me I was heartless." She was upset by the encounter, and once again she repulsed the advances of a besotted beau. The disappointed professor left for Heidelberg the next morning.[76]

Ima found Fraulein Liese to teach her German and began private piano lessons "at his home" with Xaver Scharwenka (1850–1924), a Bohemian-Polish pianist, composer, teacher, and director of the renowned Klindworth-Scharwenka Conservatory. Scharwenka specialized in the work of Frédéric Chopin and introduced Hector Berlioz and Franz Liszt to German audiences. Ima's diary is full of references to Mrs. Cranberry and Mrs. Merchant, her nicknames for Leola, and to playful Buddy and Hiawatha, her monikers for Henry, who, apparently, could be very frank and sometimes hurt her feelings. On most days, the trio would consume breakfast, lunch, and tea at the apartment, then attend a concert, and sit up very late—sometimes until three in the morning—talking, eating, and playing games or duets. Through cold, snowy weather in January, the fraulein frequently failed to appear for the language lesson, and Ima had trouble practicing for three to four hours each day. Although she thought Scharwenka was "nice" and "too clever and funny for words," she began to find his praise "outrageous" and his teaching not "deep enough." Instead of practicing, she took advantage of the heavy snow to enjoy a sleigh ride with Leola and Mrs. White on January 10. In her diary she noted, "I can't think any of us had ever been sleighing and the novelty was intoxicating, the cold, cold air in the face, the nice warm rugs tucked around you, soft furs to snuggle up in and the merry people in the streets. Nothing . . . could have made a lovelier scene." The next day she felt "wicked" and by January 14 confided to the diary: "I am absolutely no-account, good-for-nothing, and if I don't bestir myself, I shall never get anything into my head. Really, I feel hopeless. . . . I am homesick and stupid and lonesome and utterly miserable." Her cathartic confession seems to have helped; Ima began to practice more, chased "the blues" away after receiving "several letters" from "those 'old sweethearts of mine,'" and on January 29 wrote "to Xaver, telling him I couldn't take any more lessons."[77]

Ima decided to approach Dr. Martin Krause (1853–1918), a German pianist, teacher, music critic, and writer, who had studied under Franz Liszt after he met the Hungarian virtuoso in 1882. On February 15, Ima had her first lesson with Krause, who "encouraged me a great deal by telling me at once that he saw I had unusual talent." At her second lesson, Krause assigned Bach and insisted she practice four hours every day—"real work," Ima noted. Ima also hired a "fine" German teacher, and her productive, busy schedule made her tired but strong enough to cope with "sad news" from Will: Grandfather Stinson had died and brother Tom had been deployed to Cuba. Ima confided her grief to her diary, where she recalled the last few days with her father. This written release allowed her to focus on her German lessons and mastering Bach. She was even able to accept Krause's dictum that she lacked patience and must use more discipline in her practicing, in part because his critiques were laced with compliments. After her lesson on February 29, she told her diary that the admiring mentor said "he was 'astonished at my talent'—I hesitate to write this, but I do like to remember it." Ima continued her studies through May 1908. In June Ima, Leola, and the Fisher family traveled to the Hartz Mountains, where they strolled "through fresh paths along the verdure clad slopes and banks of brooks whose borders are brightened by real blue forget-me-nots."[78]

When the young women returned to Berlin in September, Ima attended a few concerts before packing to go home. On October 6, 1908, she telegraphed Will in Houston to meet her in New York City on October 13 and sailed from Bremerhaven on the *Kaiser Wilhelm der Grosse*. Ima's diary ended abruptly, and her departure seemed unexpected since the piano and language lessons had been going well before the summer break. Ima did not explain her return home, but many decades later she told an intimate friend that she "fell in love while studying in Germany"—whether with an individual or with the country is unclear. Apparently, she did not discuss a serious relationship, but the possibility may help explain why she never married and instead formed a household with her bachelor brothers. It is more likely, however, that her unsatisfactory romances and reluctance to marry stemmed from family circumstances following her mother's death. Aunt Fannie's unfounded warnings about tuberculosis; the assumption of adult roles as her father's companion and mentor to her younger brothers; her overbearing older brother; bouts of "blue" feelings; and her growing desire to accomplish something significant weighed against forming a loving relationship that would lead to conventional marriage.[79]

Ima returned to Texas in an uncertain frame of mind. Friends greeted her with delight, and she plunged into a round of card parties, weekend football games with Will, and theater evenings. Following a trip to the Texas State Fair in late October, Ima went to Austin in November to visit friends. In December she stayed with her European traveling companion Helen Thompson in Houston until she joined Will and Mike at Varner for Christmas. In January 1909 Ima attended a local concert before going to New York for several weeks of music and a reunion with the Fishers, even though Leola and Henry remained in Germany with their grandmother. On February 25, Will told Mike he was thinking about buying property in Houston for a family home, because he was tired of his bachelor quarters. He explained to Tom a few days later that he was "contemplating establishing a home" for the four siblings, because Ima "is all we have left to tie us together, and we owe it to her to fix her up just as happily as possible." To begin the home-building process, Will and Ima settled briefly in the Warrington Apartments on Fannin Street but by October 1909 had secured number two in the elegant, newly constructed, three-story Oxford Apartments at Fannin and Clay, where they remained for several years.[80]

The year 1909 proved pivotal. Despite her many social engagements, Ima realized important decisions lay before her, as she began her life of civic commitment while establishing herself as a professional woman. While in Berlin, Ima was surrounded by women and men training for or pursuing careers as professional musicians. Her teachers had praised her talent, but she realized that her impatience, her unwillingness to practice for hours every day, and her wide-ranging interests were incompatible with the unsettled yet focused life of a concert pianist. She believed she could find fulfillment by sharing what she had learned with aspiring pianists in Houston and by supporting musical culture in her adopted city. After hearing members perform in January, Ima joined the Woman's Choral Club, and she attended the Houston Music Festival performance of the Chicago Symphony in May. That October, after a summer trip to Lake Chautauqua, Ima met with twenty-eight reform-minded women in a First Presbyterian Church Sunday School room to organize the Houston Chautauqua Study Club, dedicated to continuing education and presentation of research papers. She served as the group's first recording secretary, venturing downtown every Friday for the ten o'clock meeting. Ima also accepted her first advanced piano students—Florence (Bessie) Griffiths, Eloise Helbig, and Marie Louise Hogg, the daughter of her cousin Dr. Baylor Hogg. She performed professionally on December 8 at a musicale, where she accompanied Mrs. J. M. Cary's violin solo while cellist Julien Paul Blitz[81] supported three vocalists. She took a quick trip to New York to hear Sergei Rachmaninoff at Carnegie Hall on January 16, 1910, and to watch the Adele Margulies Trio two days later, before returning home to prepare her pupils for their first recital at her Oxford Apartments home in February.

In June 1910 Ima and Mike sailed from Galveston to Bremen on the North German Lloyd liner *Hanover* for a three-week ocean voyage and a European tour that introduced Mike to the glorious places and people his sister had enjoyed in 1907–1908. Mike reported their safe passage to Will, noting that Ima was "a good sailor," but he was not. The travelers worried about Tom, but Will reassured them their youngest brother had "cut out his foolishness," although this foolishness included excessive drinking, untrustworthy friends, and quarrels with his oldest brother. From Bremen, Mike and Ima sped to Berlin, where Ima reunited with Leola Fisher, who had married Siegfried Goetze, son of the Fishers' neighbor and landlord, on March 10. Both young women mourned the death of Selma White when Leola's ailing grandmother died on July 23, but Ima and Mike walked for "four or five miles" through alpine scenery every day and attended several musical evenings before leaving for Cologne on July 31. A brief stop in Brussels and the loss of Ima's fourth umbrella brought the pair to Bruges, where Mike marveled at "the exquisite workmanship and the beauty of Memling's pictures." They crossed to Dover, stopped at Canterbury to visit the cathedral, and continued to London before returning to the cathedral city later in the week for a cricket match. A short stay in Windsor and a "not to be missed" steam trip up the Thames to Henley took them past beautiful estates "profuse" and "gay" with flowers. They continued to Oxford, Warwick Castle, and romantic Kenilworth, before admiring the rugged beauty of the Peak District and the magnificent collections at Chatsworth. After a month in Scotland, they returned to Houston in October.[82]

Mike finished law school in 1911 and joined Will and Ima in Houston, where he practiced law with Gill, Jones, and Stone for three years. Ima made a month-long musical pilgrimage to Bayreuth that year for Wagner's *Ring* cycle and to Munich for the summer festivals. In the summer of 1912, she sailed from Galveston to LeHavre with music-loving friends Mary Elizabeth Rouse, owner of a Houston music studio, and Laura Franklin, who had crossed the Atlantic with the Hoggs in 1910. Ima and her friends made Munich their headquarters for several weeks, while they attended the *Ring* cycle in Bayreuth and the Saengerfest in Nuremberg, before departing for a visit to Paris and the journey home. Mike surprised Ima in July with news that Tom had married Marie Willett, "a very fine and pretty girl," at a "great wedding." Mike noted that he and Will thought their young brother "a lucky dog" to find someone so "sensible and one of the most popular girls in Tyler."[83]

Houston, circa 1913, looking west from Buffalo Bayou on Main Street with the courthouse at upper left. MSS0114–0688, Library Collection, Houston Public Library, Houston Metropolitan Research Center.

Music, a Civic Force for Houston

Music was Ima Hogg's first love and lifetime passion. Music provided a "fortress of refuge" in her darkest moments and brought "inspiring" joy to her brightest hours. Through music Ima discovered who she was, formed deep friendships, and achieved civic fulfillment. Ima returned to a fast-growing city of seventy-eight thousand ambitious residents in 1909 determined to participate in Houston's musical culture. Music mavens eager to learn about the international concert circuit received her warmly, and she quickly assumed leadership roles by virtue of her knowledge and enthusiasm. By the end of 1909, Ima was serving on a committee of the Woman's Choral Club and was named an officer and member of the executive committee the following year. In 1911 she attended the founding meeting of the Girls' Musical Club, inaugurated at Alice Baker's home on January 25, 1911, and agreed to chair the executive committee in 1911 and to be president for the 1911–1912 season. She was unanimously reelected for the 1912–1913 year, and she was followed from 1913 to 1915 by her close friend Mary Fuller, who guided the club to membership in the Texas Federation of Music Clubs. During Ima's first year as president, the club studied the "Romantic Movement in Music," and during her second year, the club addressed the classical periods in music and their representative composers. Ima presided at the meetings on February 11 and 25, 1913, for two of four sessions devoted to Johann Sebastian Bach and George Frideric Handel. On February 25, Ima discussed "Bach's Perfected Fugue Form" and played the "Well-Tempered Clavichord" (Fugue in G-minor, no. 6) and the Prelude in B-minor, no. 22, choices she reprised at Kate Parker's open meeting on March 18. The next year, on November 17, 1914, Ima prepared a paper on Russian folk songs illustrated with a piano duet of the "Volga Boat Song." She compared Russian, German, and English folk songs by including a Sergei Rachmaninoff piano solo and Russian dances for the violin in her program.[84]

Ima never forgot the promise she made to herself while studying at the University of Texas; her desire to form a professional symphony for Texas grew during her years in New York and her travels in Europe. When she returned to Houston and began teaching advanced music students in 1909, she discovered a lively music scene, a number of professional ensembles that played in theaters and restaurants, and an enthusiastic public. Ima was impressed by the cooperation between Walter Damrosch's professional New York Symphony Orchestra and Hu Huffmaster's highly trained volunteer chorus, whose combined efforts brought great pleasure and success to the May 1911 Houston Music Festival. She applauded the outpouring of interest during the inaugural Academic Festival that introduced Rice Institute to the world stage in October 1912. Guests from around the world heard the Kneisel Quartet of New York perform twice, and Hu Huffmaster led the Houston Quartette Society and talented singers from several Houston churches in three choral tributes. Touring programs broke national records in 1912 and 1913; even the elegant Majestic Theatre and the $235,000 City Auditorium—which hired Edna Saunders[85] as its full-time booking agent—could not satisfy Houston's demands for musical entertainment. When Modeste Altschuler, conductor of a Russian symphony orchestra, abandoned his musicians in Houston in 1912, music sponsors recognized an opportunity to build a resident professional symphony orchestra in Houston.

Belgian cellist Julian Paul Blitz, conductor of a popular group that played in Gus Sauter's Viennese-themed restaurant and musical director of the Treble Clef Club, decided to approach members of the club about his wish to create a symphony orchestra for Houston. Repeatedly, he was referred to Ima Hogg. In the spring of 1913, Blitz met with Ima, Kate Parker, Alice Baker, *Houston Post* theater and music critic Wille Hutcheson, and several other women to establish a ladies' committee and plan a concert of classical music that would use local talent and attract an audience. Ima and her friends in the Girls' Musical and Woman's Choral clubs agreed to secure 125 guarantors at twenty-five dollars each, while Blitz promised the women he would choose and rehearse thirty-five musicians who played in local cafes and hotels. On a blazing June 21, 1913, at five in the afternoon, the ladies' committee waited nervously in the ornate lobby of the Majestic Theatre, a lavishly decorated vaudeville and moving picture house that had dazzled the 1,500 attendees at its opening night in 1910. Theater owner Karl Hoblizelle donated two hours between vaudeville shows; Ima's volunteer posse corralled the audience; and Blitz provided the "ebullient" Amadeus Mozart Symphony no. 39 in E-flat major, the fantasia from Georges Bizet's *Carmen*, and the "Waltz of the Flowers" from Peter Tchaikovsky's *Nutcracker Suite*. Houstonian Blanche Foley sang Christoph Gluck's "Divinités du Styx" from *Alceste* with "purity" and "clarity." Rabbi Henry Barnstein enumerated the objectives of civic leaders to bring great music to Houston, and "Dixie" concluded the afternoon. Wille Hutcheson, who promoted appreciation of the classical canon in her news columns and in music journal articles, noted the evening was "intensely warm," the "concert was in many ways a revelation" to the socially prominent men and women who filled the theater, and the musical effort offered "far more to enjoy and admire than to condemn or sharply criticize." Buoyed by the "cordially enthusiastic" response, Ima now believed her dream could be realized, and the volunteer committee decided to continue its efforts after the summer heat had subsided. Most potential sponsors then departed for vacations in cooler climates. The Hoggs spent July in Franconia, New Hampshire, with Estelle Sharp, her sons, and the Cullinan family, and on August 1 Ima and Julia Ideson left Houston for a trip to the west that included hiking in Yosemite National Park and a visit to Hollywood.[86]

In the fall, Wille Hutcheson continued to publicize the concept of a resident professional symphony orchestra as an important step toward transforming Houston into a sophisticated metropolis. In a long November article, Hutcheson explained that organizers foresaw a three-concert season of selections with widespread appeal; local musicians would live in the community; prices would be low "so that the orchestra may be really claimed as a people's orchestra"; and the organizing committee would marry musical appreciation with social prestige by offering box seats, hosting festive underwriting parties, and encouraging formal attire. While Hutcheson prepared the public, Katherine Parker hosted Houston's leading civic women and helped Corinne Abercrombie Waldo organize a committee to devise an action plan. The committee invited potential guarantors to the Houston Chamber of Commerce offices, where they elected officers and named Julien Paul Blitz conductor. The women sought support from leading businessmen to ensure firm financial footing and argued that a city where fine music thrived would be a city where business prospered. Although not convinced that a resident orchestra would succeed, Parker agreed to serve as the organization's first president. As Ima pointed out, Parker symbolized the music movement in the city through her affiliation with the Woman's Choral Club, the Thursday Morning Musical Club, and the Girls' Musical Club, and through her husband's association with the Houston Music Festival. Ima became first vice president; Frantz Brogniez, an amateur composer of oratorical and orchestral works, was named second vice president; and a "galaxy" of business leaders, bankers, and lawyers consented to serve on the twenty-eight-member board, while seven respected religious and civic figures formed an advisory committee.[87] Blitz and Girls' Musical Club members Katherine Parker, Ima Hogg, Mary Abbey, and Corinne Waldo signed the Houston Symphony Association's charter of incorporation and confirmed that the first season of three twilight concerts would open at the Majestic Theatre on December 19, 1913, followed by two performances in the spring of 1914.

Then the work began. Ima remembered paging through the telephone book, calling everyone she knew to secure sponsors at twenty-five dollars each. Half the call recipients did not know what a symphony orchestra was, and many who did thought such a venture would never thrive in Houston. Abe Levy used his Levy Brothers Dry Goods advertisements to urge customers to "do something 'For the good of Houston'" and pack the audience. Ima put her brother Will to work. He wrote friends, explaining that his sister, "whom I dare not refuse," wanted him to secure sponsors; Will asked donors to sign the enclosed pledge form and return it to his office. Ima, Will, and the volunteer committee persuaded 138 leading Houstonians to underwrite the first season and sold individual tickets for twenty-five cents to one dollar apiece. On Friday afternoon, December 19, 1913, Ima listened with pride as baritone Arturo Lugaro and Conductor Julien Paul Blitz inaugurated the twilight season before a capacity audience. Houston's social leaders, guided by boxholder Alice Baker, attended in force. Theater critics praised the musicians, the founders, and the attendees. Ima had brought a municipal orchestra to Texas, had added Houston to the list of musically progressive cities, and had given her fellow citizens a unique Christmas present—their own symphony orchestra. Season two established Thanksgiving afternoon as appropriate for the opening concert. In later years, Ima was often called the founder of the Houston Symphony, but she demurred. Her approach to her first major civic action presaged future behavior. Always modest, she encouraged diverse groups to cooperate in a unifying enterprise and shared founding honors with other enthusiasts. Ever tenacious, she worked hard until the goal was achieved. A clear-sighted visionary, she recognized that small steps would ensure success. Acutely political, she knew she needed help from prominent citizens and deferred leadership to the musically brilliant and socially connected Kate Parker. For sixty-two years, Ima was the symphony's guardian angel, engaging a large chorus of supporters to realize her dreams.[88]

The War Years

The Houston Symphony's first season ended, and Ima Hogg began to plan for the summer of 1914. Her friend Julia Ideson was in Paris, and her brothers Will and Mike were busy developing Hogg, Dickson & Hogg, a cotton brokerage they had launched in June with partner Raymond Dickson. Ima tussled with the decision—traveling in Europe was her first choice, but she "suffered unreasoning fear of a kind I never knew possible. I . . . wanted to come to Europe . . . but could never make myself plan for it . . . and something in me feared and cried out against it."[89] Only on her thirty-second birthday, July 10, 1914, did Ima explain her decision to Will and pack her steamer trunk for a sojourn abroad. The next day she and Will took the Galveston-Houston Electric Interurban to the Galveston pier so she could sail to Bremerhaven on the *Chemnitz* with her music-loving friends Mary Elizabeth Rouse and Ruth Curtin,[90] who had already booked passage on the North German Lloyd liner. Ima knew a Serbian anarchist had assassinated the Austro-Hungarian Empire's heir apparent, Archduke Franz Ferdinand, and his wife, Sophie, on June 28, and her misgivings were confirmed when word of war between Austria and Serbia reached her during the voyage. In retrospect, Ima recalled that the *Chemnitz* had dallied in Baltimore to load an unusually large supply of coal. Two days before landing, the ship "was painted dark gray," and "seventeen men of war were lined up" along the route through the English Channel, giving the waterway a "frowning expression." Ima remembered extraordinary sunsets on the last two evenings at sea: "With the news of probable war on our minds, the sunset . . . looked like a half eclipse, blood-red, sinking behind a long stretch of thick black cloud. All the rest of the sky was clear and the water was smooth enough to reflect a long streak of blood red." Germany declared war against Russia on August 1, the day *Chemnitz* passengers debarked in Bremerhaven.[91]

As soon as she arrived, Ima repeatedly cabled Will to report that she was safe. On August 3 she began a stirring daily diary describing the tense situation.

War between England, whose "liberal government" and literary heritage she admired, and Germany, whose "beauty and culture" she adored, was abhorrent, and her "sympathies [were] torn in such . . . waste of precious things." Surrounded by friends, caught up in stirring events, and challenged by her inability to find quick passage home, Ima responded proactively; she expressed her opinions and conflicted feelings in her diary and used the writing process to work through her fears. Instead of "heading for Munich" and then to Switzerland and Germany, Ima made her way from Bremerhaven to England and wrote to Will from the Imperial Hotel in Russell Square on August 4 to reassure her brother she had arrived safely in London with several other Americans. She had already been to an antiwar demonstration led by "brilliant" women speakers. Will responded on August 17 that he had received her first two letters, but no cables had gone through. "You depict the European situation as I imagined it was. The conflict will be terrible and its cost to civilization will be immeasurable. You are in a position now to get a first-hand view of the distress of war in its effect on the public heart and mind." Other letters and cables reflect Will's concern for Ima's safety and efforts to bring her home, including letters with family friend William Jennings Bryan to thank the secretary of state for securing his sister's return passage on the SS *New York*.[92]

Ima's diary is packed with vivid detail about her journey to England and her unexpected visit there. Authorities hustled *Chemnitz* passengers onto a boat train to Bremen, thirty-five miles south of the port. Ima wrote enthusiastically about her trip through Germany: "My eyes were rejoiced . . . by the beautiful fields and the rosy faced toilers. . . . Germany has never looked lovelier to my eyes or the Germans sturdier and finer." They "love their families and their beautiful land more than they do their government." In Bremen, Ima discovered all foreigners were making plans to leave, while "Germans [were] walking about in a dazed way with such serious, anxious faces"; banks were closed; money was tight; and a "panic for food was abroad." Ruth Curtin and Ima spent almost a day at the American consul getting certificates of exit for themselves and Mary Rouse. The three Texans abandoned their trunks at their hotel and crammed a few belongings into bags. They joined a "big crowd" of *Chemnitz* passengers taking trains through Holland to exit ports. Everyone "seemed rattled," by "one succession of shocks and strain" during the three days Ima rode on a "hard" third-class bench from Bremen to Hook of Holland before boarding the *St. Petersburg*, which would carry her to Harwich, England. At every stop, rumors of German atrocities greeted them, while at Rotterdam "flocks of Germans came in on trains going back at the call of their country." The boat for England "left at midnight packed and jammed." After her "terrible" trip, Ima wrote Will that "the tragedy is like nothing I can imagine," and President Woodrow Wilson must help Americans return home because Europeans "are in the deepest distress of heart and mind with their own to think of."[93]

Despite constant effort, it took six weeks to rescue the stranded travelers because all commercial shipping ceased when Great Britain and its global empire faced off against Germany and its allies at midnight on August 4. Americans relied on the American Express Company for cash—"forty dollars was the limit to each person"—and everyone registered at the Savoy Hotel, the United States headquarters for dispensing information and assistance. Will cabled money, and Ima repeatedly assured him she was fine and could take care of herself. Ima spent the anxious days shopping, having clothes made, attending concerts and plays, visiting London's museums, and riding on double-decker buses. She was fascinated by the Speakers' Corner at Hyde Park and joined crowds for band concerts and vigils outside Buckingham Palace, where throngs waited every day, hoping to glimpse King George V. After ten days in London, Ima and her friends went to Cambridge, where they spent a week in rooms usually rented to students and where she occupied a suite usually reserved for the brother of the empress of Japan. While there, the young women attended services at King's Chapel and heard the "melting beauty of that choral singing." They enjoyed the "lovely" English twilights, and Ima terrified Ruth and Mary, who "sat very stiffly in their seats" while she punted them on the River Cam. Back in London, the three women took rooms at 9 Porchester Terrace near Hyde Park, where they felt "calmer and restful." Late in August, Ima's friend Rowena Teagle "came in her car" and took Ima "through beautiful country" to her rented house that seemed "typical of the comfortable, elegant country life you imagine. The gardens particularly fascinated me. . . . Flowers are planted here and there among the vegetables." Sadly for Ima, Rowena left for New York two days later.[94]

Although most German music had been banned, Ima attended concerts at Queen's Hall and visited art galleries. On Sunday, August 30, she reflected on the horrors of war, noting "papers are livid with German atrocities." Appalled that "the most refined of the English desire to see Germany 'wiped off the face of the earth,'" still she recognized that "the case against the ruling powers in Germany does seem convicting." To maintain her equilibrium, Ima attended promenade concerts and enjoyed lectures at the National Gallery. She began to "poke around" antique shops and "fell to the allurements of a silver goblet." On September 10 she succumbed to the charms of a silver tea set, "really a dream, and such a bargain I couldn't resist it—persuading myself to do without the dressy winter suit I was planning.... The shop man was so excited... and ready to bargain." For the first time, in the midst of war's turmoil, Ima recorded the excitement of collecting that would engulf her when she discovered American decorative arts in 1920. Shortly before she left London, Ima joined a huge crowd ("almost no women") at the Guildhall. The "memorable event" featured brass bands and speeches by London's lord mayor and by four noted politicians—Prime Minister H. H. Asquith (who "talked so indistinctly and with very little charm or magnetism"), Conservative party leader Andrew Bonar Law (who was frank and firm), former Prime Minister Arthur Balfour (who was "fine"), and First Lord of the Admiralty Winston Churchill (who looked like mercurial Mr. Micawber from Charles Dickens's *David Copperfield*). Ima concluded, "Nothing impressed us like the police," who were handsome, well-dressed, and helpful. Ima also described the "thrilling occasion, . . . the hall itself so beautiful" when she wrote Will on September 3 to tell him she had booked her return passage.[95]

The Guildhall meeting, followed immediately by a visit to Hyde Park Corner, led Ima to ponder the "silly" tradition of divine right of kings, the "idea of mixing God and Christ in such a war of jealousy and hatred," and the free speech permitted at Hyde Park. One speaker was a socialist who virulently condemned the war, although he insisted he was not pro-German. Ima was "frightened all the time for fear there'd be a riot." Her fears were realized on her last Sunday, September 13, when the immense "mob" gathered at Hyde Park "was so violent, the police came to escort the speaker out of the park." Ima mused in the lengthy final entry of her diary that "the whole world seems in ferment. Why should we yet dream of peace as a reality when there is not an establishment of any sort of justice or equality." She summarized her feelings dispassionately about "the network of international diplomacy... spun during the past decade." Germany "wants expansion... for the sake of concentrating vitality.... England has satiated herself in the glory of conquest.... France has had her day.... Russia is murmuring in her sleep, and we in America are self sufficient, at least—so I hope." Despite its parliamentary government, England had failed to give "the same self-respect and decency to her working classes that Germany has." Ima concluded, "The charm and excitement of these epoch making days... told too greatly on my mind.... We were in a fever of inquiring ... a state of bewilderment.... But... it has been a wonderful experience.... I really am very grateful for the shelter and hospitality of the world's greatest and in many ways most admirable city—London. She has opened her arms to everyone like a big mother. And they have rushed to her for protection . . . and in my heart I love her and her people!"[96]

Ima sailed from Liverpool on the New York-American Line's SS *New York* on September 16, while Ruth Curtin left Liverpool for New York on the SS *St Louis* on October 24. Mary Elizabeth Rouse remained in England until 1916. In cables exchanged by Will and Ima, she said she would arrive in New York on September 23, and he planned to be there on October 5. As soon as Ima checked into the Hotel Majestic at West Seventy-Second Street on September 23, she penned a letter to "My dear Mr. Podsnap" to tell him she had arrived and was "glad to be home so I can speak freely." Respect for "the country which was housing and feeding me made me very circumspect and confused too. . . . Have been so well and strong. Hastily, Missima."[97] Anxious to see her brothers, she quickly debriefed friends in New York and boarded a train for Houston, arriving at the Oxford Apartments on October 2. The next day she and Will went riding.

Ima quickly resumed her interrupted activities. While she was stranded in London, the Symphony Association board reelected her first vice president and Kate Parker president. On Thanksgiving afternoon 1914, Ima attended the opening night concert for the second full season. The family remained in Houston through Christmas, and Ima enjoyed shopping and attending parties with her brothers. On December 19, she was hostess at the Houston Country Club for a "very prettily appointed" dinner dance honoring two debutantes.[98] Despite disturbing headlines describing daily disasters in Europe and the dreadful U-boat sinking of the neutral passenger liner *Lusitania* on May 7, 1915, Ima's life in 1915 and 1916 followed a busy pattern of civic activities, parties, and occasional trips. In 1915 Ima moved to the Marie Louise Apartments and spent the summer in Lisbon, New Hampshire, where she took piano lessons in July and August. That October she helped organize the Texas Federation of Music Clubs and agreed to serve as vice president (1915–1917). She spent November in New York City, attending concerts and recitals, and met her brother Will, Rice Institute President Edgar Odell Lovett, and Joseph Cullinan's children Craig and Nina for Thanksgiving there. In Houston, she attended meetings of the Chautauqua, Girls' Musical, Women's Choral, and College Women's clubs. Society reporters assiduously reported the guests she invited to share her box at every symphony concert—Julia Ideson, her piano students, and prominent female civic leaders.

Ima's teaching career began in 1909 and ceased in the summer of 1918. Bessie Griffiths and Eloise Helbig, who were never charged for their lessons, continued to be her star music students. Despite a general ban on German composers, the two girls played works by Johannes Sebastian Bach at a recital on June 12, 1915. Griffiths's progress was recognized when she performed Amadeus Mozart's Piano Concerto no. 20 in D Minor with the Houston Symphony Orchestra on February 22, 1917. A few of Ima's protégés later taught music themselves, and Jacques Abram (1915–1988), who always recalled his Houston teachers Ima Hogg and Ruth Burr, built a successful concert career. Abram began improvising when he was three and performed in public at the age of six. He went on to the Curtis Institute and at age thirteen transferred to the Juilliard School. Ima had begun piano lessons at age three, and she must have decided to take this prodigy as one of her last students. In later years, Ima's pupil returned six times to perform with the Houston Symphony while his childhood teacher listened attentively in the audience.[99]

The first three symphony seasons under popular Conductor Julian Blitz attracted steady sponsors, a growing audience, and good reviews. At the end of the second season, Blitz, who also led the Blitz Orchestra at the Rice Hotel, wanted to expand symphony offerings and asked patrons to fund additional evening concerts to accommodate working men and women, but the board felt it could not absorb the added expense and refused his request. Despite sold-out crowds, Blitz decided to step down in June 1916, and Ima's peers asked her to organize her first of many searches for a new conductor. Limited by a small budget, Ima hired local violinist Paul Bergé (1881–1970) to conduct the three-concert November 1916–April 1917 season at the Majestic Theatre. Bergé, from Louisiana, had studied violin in Europe and had recently moved to Houston to direct the Brazos Hotel café orchestra. His tenure would last only two seasons.

War abroad did not silence Houston's vibrant musical community. In 1916–1917 *Houston Chronicle* publisher Marcellus Elliot (Mefo) Foster[100] sponsored visits from Diaghileff's Ballet Russe, the Minneapolis Symphony Orchestra, and Metropolitan Opera tenor Giovanni Martinelli. In February and March 1917 Edwin B. Parker, chairman of the Grand Opera Committee, corralled the Houston Symphony Association, the Treble Clef Club, and the Woman's Choral Club to sponsor performances of *Aida* and two other operas produced by Boston's National Grand Opera. The year 1917 challenged Ima Hogg's capacity for hard work and fractured her loyalties as it became untenable to speak favorably about German culture or to hope the United States would remain neutral. In late January, after a ten-month hiatus, Kaiser Wilhelm resumed U-boat bombardments against all shipping, and on February 3, the United States retaliated by severing relations with Germany. The Houston Symphony's fifth season ended in April 1917, just after the United States declared war against the Axis powers on April 6 and two days before Easter. To close the season, Ima organized an Easter week *soirée d'art* that featured Franz Liszt's Concerto in E Flat Scherzo finale. Ima played the orchestral accompaniment; cellist Julien Blitz and violinist Rosetta Hirsch provided solos; and Henry Stude gave a reading. Seeking consolation in music at this tragic moment, Ima accepted leadership of the Houston Symphony Association and began to plan the 1917–1918 three-concert season. She also agreed to continue as vice president of the Texas Federation of Music Clubs and to serve as chairwoman of its committee to investigate "the possibilities of a Texas Symphony Orchestra."[101]

While preoccupied in 1917 by her search for musical excellence, Ima also volunteered for war work with Houston's War Camp Community Services Committee and faced a number of family challenges. Will had been mulling the notion of building a house in the Shadyside enclave being developed by his business partner and friend Joseph Cullinan. He took an option on lot Q, but the uncertainty of war militated against such a complex project. Instead, Will decided to rent—and later purchase—the family's first house at 4410 Rossmoyne Boulevard in a new enclave north of Hermann Park, being developed as "Houston's most beautiful address" by oilman Ross Stirling. Ima spent a few days in New Orleans in March 1917, shopping for furnishings, after Will delegated oversight of the move from her apartment and her brothers' bachelor quarters to his capable sister. On May 6, Mike Hogg, now thirty-two, volunteered for service in the army and left for officers' training at Camp Funston near San Antonio. On May 13, W. C. Hogg no. 1 produced a deep sand well at West Columbia that presaged more riches to come. In June Will returned to Texas from Washington, DC, where he had been exploring ways to help the war effort. He moved to the Driskill Hotel in Austin for four months to marshal the forces that would successfully impeach and convict Governor James E. Ferguson of several improprieties, including an attempt to wrest power from the University of Texas Board of Regents by overseeing and then firing professors. Ferguson had appointed Will a regent in 1913, but the university enthusiast quarreled with the governor and resigned early in 1917 to lead the coalition seeking to rid Texas of its errant governor.[102]

Ima was able to visit Mike in San Antonio three times during his training period, which ended August 15, when the newly minted Lieutenant Hogg spent his leave in Houston before returning August 28 to Camp Travis to train the raw recruits that began to arrive in San Antonio a few days later. Quickly promoted to captain, Mike served in the 360th Infantry, 90th Division of the

Mike Hogg in World War I uniform, 1918. Camh-dob-012144, Ima Hogg Collection, Dolph Briscoe Center for American History, University of Texas at Austin.

American Expeditionary Force and Army of Occupation. While Mike was at Camp Travis and Will was fighting Governor Ferguson, Ima traveled to New York with fellow civic leaders Estelle Sharp and Florence Fall to enjoy a month of music, museums, and sightseeing. When Ima returned in November, she hosted a musical event at her Rossmoyne Boulevard home. Two artists stationed at Houston's Camp Logan, a pianist and a gifted singer, gave a recital to members and guests of the Girls' Musical Club during Thanksgiving week. Then the Hogg family gathered in San Antonio to celebrate Christmas 1917.

The pace of activities intensified in 1918. Tyndall-Wyoming Company's Hogg no. 2 strike on January 4 and gushers from January 15 to January 23 produced a giant oil discovery in West Columbia and catapulted the Hoggs into the firmament of successful oil producers; within weeks Varner Plantation grew a forest of derricks that dwarfed the family's country retreat. Music, like Alice Baker's hospitality houses and Julia Ideson's book drives, proved an important outlet and entertainment for thousands of army recruits being trained in Texas. As vice president of the Texas Federation of Music Clubs and president of the Houston Symphony Association, Ima worked night and day to find musicians for concerts, recitals, band performances, and dances. European musicians had been returning to their home countries since 1914, and now young Texas performers were being drafted for the US forces. On April 3, 1918, Ima opened the third annual three-day meeting of the Texas Federation of Music Clubs and invited meeting participants to be her guests at the final performance of the Houston Symphony season. When the fifth season ended, Ima counseled with her board, and the group sadly decided not to plan a 1918–19 season. They could not imagine the long conflict would be over by Thanksgiving 1918, now the season's traditional opening day. Meanwhile Will had begun the liquidation of Hogg, Dickson & Hogg in March and had taken an apartment in Washington, DC, where he volunteered for several assignments with US Army Intelligence and the US Food Administration.[103]

Not realizing the pressure his sister was under, on May 3, 1918, Will ordered her to get the furnace fixed and arrange to have the car painted "now" (double underlined) before she left Houston for the summer. On June 11 Ima boarded the train for New York so she could congratulate Mike, who had received top grades in officers' school. On April 14 Ima gave her beloved younger brother a "'lamb's wool' comfort" and bid him farewell as he embarked for France from Camp Mills, Long Island. Shortly afterward, completely exhausted, Ima joined Estelle Sharp and Helen Thompson at Delaware Water Gap. Events of the previous months had devastated Ima; her blessed homeland at war with her beloved

Germany; her brother Will fighting the governor of Texas and then absent in Washington; and her brother Mike off to the trenches on the western front, where "it has been impossible to write at times."[104] Worst of all, her dreams for acclaimed professional symphony orchestras in Houston and in Texas were suspended. Ima had worked tirelessly, and her physical and emotional energies had drained away. Fearing the future, blaming herself for failing the symphony, and wondering how she could rebuild Houston's musical culture, she fell ill and collapsed on her thirty-sixth birthday.

Recovery and Rejuvenation: 1919–1924

On July 11, 1918, Dr. Gavin Hamilton wired Will Hogg to notify him Ima was "suffering from a marked degree of anaemia" and "was much run down . . . particularly her nervous system." Hamilton recommended the popular "rest cure" and its diet of milk and eggs, made famous in the 1880s by Silas Wier Mitchell, an influential Philadelphia neurologist whose solution to middle- and upper-class female neurasthenia, or inability to cope, was total bed rest, isolation from family and friends, massage, and the dubious diet. Ima and her friends left Delaware Water Gap on July 19 and joined Will in New York, where he was looking for a permanent apartment. Will begged his sister to place herself under a doctor's care and frantically sought medical advice. Instead, Ima and Estelle Sharp left for the cool mountain air of Lake Placid on August 10 and then went to Spinney's camp on Moosehead Lake in Rockwood, Maine, for a month. Ima wrote frequently to Mike but apparently heard little from him, although he assured her that he had written at least one letter every week since leaving for France. Mike's lighthearted, lengthy letters downplayed the danger and destruction everywhere and instead described the countryside "alive with flowers," Fourth of July at a "wonderful" chateau, and a visit with family friend Raymond Dickson. Ima's experiment in self-cure ended in illness, and by mid-September, she and Estelle had returned to New York. Although Ima had "positively refused to go to a sanitarium" in July, by October 1, 1918, Will erroneously directed mail to his sister care of Dr. G. W. Ford in Kerhonkson, New York—undoubtedly Dr. Andrew G. Foord of Kerhonkson, who ran the Foord Sanitarium, a timber mill, and a reforesting plantation in Ulster County, seventy-four miles north of New York City. On October 27, Will himself fell ill, underwent an operation, and spent the next month recuperating in a New York City hospital. Looking out her Kerhonkson window at the rural scene, Ima began to "see some benefit" from her rest cure and left the sanitarium on

December 4. She and Will went Christmas shopping in New York and returned to Houston on Christmas Eve, in time to call on their friends the next day. Mike wrote several letters to Sis and Brother in November and December but never mentioned a slight wound he had received during a charge on November 2, only days before hostilities ended on November 11. Instead, Mike described Wehlen, Germany, "a beautiful little town on the Moselle River," where the 90th was stationed after the armistice and where he was "lounging" in the large, elegantly furnished home of a "rich wine-merchant," suggesting to Ima that the beautiful country she loved might still remain.[105]

Ima again fell ill following a motor trip with friends in March 1919. Her Houston physician Judson Taylor suggested she consult Jefferson Medical College Professor Dr. Francis X. Dercum,[106] who was well-known for his writings on nervous and mental disorders. Shortly after Ima heard Metropolitan Opera soprano Alma Gluck at Houston's City Auditorium on March 24, she traveled with Will and a nurse to Philadelphia, where she entered a "rest house" at 1939 Wallace Street on May 3, 1919. A dreadful mastoid abscess in her right ear, which Ima later described as a searing pain and knocking sound, required surgery. Buoyed by Mike's safe return from France and his comforting visit to her in Philadelphia after her June 14 operation, Ima made a "splendid surgical recovery," but she suffered a great deal of exhausting pain and finally succumbed to pneumonia. That Christmas, Will visited his sister at the rest house, where Ima remained until March 26, 1920, when she and a nurse moved to a "pretty house in Ardmore" (Merion), outside Philadelphia, her home until March 1921. During her year of recuperation, Ima accepted the death of Aunt Fannie (Martha Frances Davis) on May 12, 1920, corresponded with friends and former students, and took summer trips to Atlantic City and Lake Placid with a nurse. In the fall, feeling much stronger, she proudly "sailed forth in the beauteous new car to the matinee" concert in Philadelphia and began planning a theater and shopping trip to visit Will in New York City from October 7 to October 25.[107] That November Mike and Will each visited their sister in Merion and escorted her to several concerts, always Ima's surest solace when haunted by depression. A true fan, she heard her favorite virtuoso Italian Arturo Toscanini conduct Milan's La Scala Orchestra at New York's Metropolitan Opera House on December 28, 1920, and again at the Philadelphia Academy of Music on January 15, 1921.

In the 1920s Will and Ima lived in New York City almost as much as they lived in Houston, first on the West Side at Forty-Fourth Street, and after October 4, 1921, on the more fashionable East Side, where their large apartment at 290 Park Avenue, between Forty-Eighth and Forty-Ninth streets, provided housekeeping help, rooms for family servants, and dining service from the Pierre Restaurant, located on the first floor. In Houston, Will and Mike organized Hogg Brothers, Inc., effective May 1, 1920, as a family corporation created to manage the numerous business ventures of the four siblings. They built a penthouse office headquarters and roof garden atop a multipurpose building that also housed the three-story Armor Auto Company showcase. Ima was improving in September 1920 when Will sent her a list of landscape paintings by George Inness (1825–1894) and William Keith (1838–1911) to consider for their home on Rossmoyne. Grateful he had asked her opinion, Ima revealed that she wanted "things" for their home "above all to be genuine of their kind." She hoped to find "a few (2) lovely pictures which are large to give the [drawing] room a . . . restful feeling." Because she had "thought often and looked often" at great collections, Ima hoped her brother would wait to make any purchases until they could "look together and decide together."[108] On October 7, 1920, when Ima joined Will in New York City, her brother made a confession—she must visit Levy's Galleries and view several works by Frederic Remington that he had purchased for the new offices. During September shopping sprees, Will bought one bronze statue and twenty-five paintings by the New York artist to form the first corporate art collection in Houston. Ima approved her brother's purchases, and until Mike's death in 1941, the Hogg Brothers' beautifully appointed offices were "a showplace of business maneuvering," entertaining, and civic planning for Houston's most progressive citizens.[109]

Ima and her energetic brother haunted antique stores that October, and Ima agreed to sit for her portrait by Wayman Adams. Inspired by a chair she saw in Adams's studio, Ima purchased a similar New England maple armchair (1735–1790) a few days later from Collings and Collings, where Will had found an elegant Hepplewhite-style card table (1800–1820). Ima was amazed by the well-stocked emporium of "all kinds of furniture quite new and strange to me," housed in a four-story brownstone at 805 Madison Avenue. She told Will she would like to form a collection of American furniture to be placed in a Texas museum one day—four years before the innovative Metropolitan Museum of Art in New York opened its American Wing or the future collector Henry Francis duPont purchased his first example of American furniture. Ima sent Will a proposal on January 21, 1921, saying she had "been thinking about the large room at the office. . . . As I have my own ideas about antiques and furniture and am fond of collecting them," would he let her "buy the furniture for myself," with the proviso that the "firm may use it as long as it likes"? Will enthusiastically encouraged her musings; at last his sister was thinking of the future. He told Ima to furnish the office living room "just as you want it," charge her purchases to Hogg Brothers, and ship everything to Houston. Now eager to return home, Ima departed for Houston alone because Will was "unavoidably detained" by the Louis Guerineau Myers (1874–1932) auction at the American Art Association Rooms on February 25, 1921. The new enthusiast acquired a "mass of stuff, particularly sixteen varieties of Windsor chairs" from the well-known scholar-connoisseur's collection. Will described his "first experience at an auction" to Ima and made three purchases in her name—a New York armchair (1785–1825), a lolling chair (1785–1820), and a rare transitional New York sofa (1785–1820). Until Will's death in 1930, the petite, ladylike Missima and the tall, outspoken Podsnap remained friendly coconspirators as they collected Americana for the office, for Varner Plantation, for the New York apartment, and for their home in Houston.[110]

In April 1921 Ima spent a few days in Austin with her college friend Dot Thornton before participating in the Hogg Brothers annual meeting as a full partner, and she anticipated a happy summer. Alas, while Tom and his wife, Marie, enjoyed a motor tour in New England and Canada and Mike sailed to Europe, Ima found herself consulting Dr. Dercum once again, this time for appendicitis—"too disgusting to start the summer career."[111] After several attacks, Ima was put on a liquid diet and underwent an operation on June 24, 1921; fortunately, brother Tom came to Philadelphia to console her. Between visits to his ailing sister, Will bought two barrels of glassware and historical flasks, which he shipped from New York to the Hogg Brothers offices in July. Ima remained in the hospital until July 14, when she, Will, and Tom took a five-day trip to Atlantic City. On July 19, Ima and a nurse traveled to New York City and on to Lake Placid, where they remained until the end of August. Ima was forced to consult Dr. Dercum again in September. She underwent another operation in late November and began another period of recuperation in Philadelphia that lasted until February 1922, when she returned to Houston for a few months. During this second recuperative period, Ima and her brother splurged again. Will attended the January 1922 sale of Jacob Paxson Temple (1880–1924) treasures at Anderson Galleries in New York, where on January 23 he bid successfully for hard-paste porcelain fruit baskets and vases from William Ellis Tucker's Philadelphia factory (1827–1838). He also acquired an oil painting—*Penn's Treaty with the Indians*—by an unnamed artist, which was later identified as an important work by Edward Hicks (1780–1849), a Quaker from Bucks County, Pennsylvania. Ima asked artist Wayman Adams to bid for her at the Temple auction, and he successfully acquired large and small Windsor settees for the Hogg Brothers offices. In January or February 1922, Ima discovered William B. Montague, an antiques collector and dealer in Norristown, Pennsylvania, and motored from nearby Philadelphia to his shop, where she purchased thirty-seven Tucker porcelain items, which she had shipped to Houston to inaugurate her ceramics collection. Although Will thrived on auction competition, Ima did not enjoy the public exposure, and when she bought twenty-seven glass objects from the second Temple collection sale in 1923, she again asked Wayman Adams to serve as her agent.

Excited by her successful antiquing in 1922, Ima returned to Houston in good spirits. That April she attended a dinner hosted by Rice Institute President Edgar Odell Lovett to honor the Godwin Lecture series speaker, one of only two endowed activities at the institute in 1922. The conversation and company—including Alice Baker, Estelle Sharp, and Huberta Garwood, Ima's successor as president of the Houston Symphony Association—must have stimulated Ima's imagination, because by late May 1922, she had embarked on a musical adventure to fund, anonymously, a "Lectureship in Music" that would "stimulate an intellectual interest in music among the students of the university" and "elevate the taste of all of us."[112] President Lovett was delighted by her interest, because two years earlier, he had approached Will about funding an endowed music lecture series as a testimonial to Ima's civic service. Lovett and Ima worked out details of her support—$1,500 a year for four years to bring acclaimed musicians to Houston for performances and lectures. The programs of John Powell on April 5 and 6, 1923, were typical. The visiting pianist and composer performed an evening concert at the City Auditorium and provided two 4:30 p.m. lecture/recitals at the Palace Theatre; press critics applauded; the Hoggs entertained performers and music lovers; and Houston's political, academic, and social leaders filled the seats of thirty-five boxes. Two years later, Ima attended the lecture/concert series of multitalented French composer, organist, and teacher Nadia Boulanger[113] at the Scottish Rite Cathedral January 27–29, 1925. Ima continued to support the lectureship until its formal termination in 1928, and her gift inspired the institute to develop a music department.

In July 1922 Ima vacationed at the Lake Placid Club but fell victim to another ailment in September that demanded another operation in November. This time Ima decided to recuperate in Houston, but before leaving her Philadelphia physician on December 13, she purchased an oak table and a chair for her bedroom. Ima declared she had recovered by April 1923 when she sailed with Mike and Estelle Sharp for a four-month visit to Switzerland, Austria, and

Hungary. When the group returned to Quebec on August 1, Ima and Sharp visited Lake Placid for six weeks and then met Will in New York on September 16. Although the trip restored Ima's spirits, insomnia plagued her in Lake Placid, and on November 11 she consulted Dr. Austen Fox Riggs,[114] a popular author and pioneering therapist who ran a clinic in Stockbridge, Massachusetts. The nearly four months she stayed there changed her life. By February 1924 Ima had learned to control her fitful sleeping with a regimen of exercise and purposeful rest, and she had acquired a mentor who reawakened her childhood interest in mental health care and showed her that everyone "must have a purpose which you believe in and which you will give yourself to." In later life, when awakened in the night, Ima would jot down her thoughts, relax, and sleep. After a busy spring in Houston, during which she resumed her clubwoman affiliations, Ima joined her Chautauqua friend Ruby Blake (Mrs. Turner) Williamson for several weeks in England and Ireland. Ima continued to Vienna "for a period of study," while Ruby Williamson hunted for antiques and art in France, Belgium, and Holland. In September and October, Ima joined Will and Estelle Sharp for more European touring. When they returned, Ima entertained Estelle Sharp at the Hoggs' Park Avenue apartment and went to Stockbridge on November 17 for a fortifying ten-day session with Austen Riggs. Refreshed and inspired, she traveled to Houston for Christmas 1924.[115]

Redefining Purpose: 1922–1924

Ima Hogg had been a dutiful and loving daughter: she cared for her dying mother; she provided companionship to her grieving father; and she mentored and loved her complicated brothers. In her mid-twenties, Ima redefined herself as a professional musician: she studied in music capitals; she taught aspiring piano students; and she teamed with Houston's music mavens to establish the first professional symphony orchestra in Texas. Now middle-aged, Ima's world had been transformed, and it was time to discover a new purpose for her life. She had survived the crucibles of world war and debilitating physical and mental illness, and her family had been blessed with unimaginable wealth. The task before Ima, Will, and Mike was the immediate need to manage their wealth responsibly so they could use their bounty to build balanced personal lives while strengthening the humanitarian and democratic values in their community. Unlike Andrew Carnegie, who explained his gospel of wealth at length, the Hoggs did not write about their philanthropic vision, but the institutions they built revealed their commitment to inclusive civic philanthropy as a vocation and addressed Carnegie's central precept: "The problem of our age is the proper administration of Wealth, so that the ties of brotherhood may still bind the rich and poor in harmonious relationship." Jim and Sallie Hogg had taught their children three foundational lessons—that a happy home and morally grounded family formed the basis for a strong community and nation; that public service was the highest responsibility of every citizen; and that they should love Texas and their fellow Texans. Will and Ima had spent hours at Varner with their father, talking about how best to improve the lives of all Texans. The governor's words lingered as his children developed a long-range strategy to share their good fortune.[116]

As they realized the extent of the West Columbia oil strike, the Hogg siblings held numerus discussions and formulated grand schemes that affected every sphere of modern life, but they always articulated one central conviction: the oil discovered under family land was a natural resource, not the product of their invention or labor, and the proceeds from its production should, therefore, be used to benefit all Texans. Will is reputed to have said, "The government made a mistake originally in not reserving for its own use all the wealth below the soil. What I don't pay back in taxes on the oil which should not have been mine, I'm glad to give away for the public welfare." Influenced by the teachings of Austen Riggs, Ima insisted that communities and families would prosper only if each individual acquired the intellectual, emotional, and physical tools to lead a "wholesome life." As institution builders, these philanthropic entrepreneurs used their money proactively to affect social change through preventive rather than palliative approaches to urban challenges. They discussed common goals for their civic enterprises, used their ties to political and business leaders to bring people together in public-private partnerships, and leveraged their wealth by convincing others to support their vision of social justice for every citizen. The siblings made a formidable team, cemented by numerous affectionate nicknames that reveal mutual support and playful affection as Brother, Missima, and Mickey defended their civic causes. Buoyed by new wealth and redefined goals, the twenties proved a productive decade for the Hogg family.[117]

By 1924 Will Hogg had been a mainstay of Houston's business and civic culture for nearly two decades. As a lawyer, cotton factor, oil man, and land investor, he participated in all sectors of Houston's economy and became one of Houston's richest men. His strong-armed fundraising techniques were famous—he canvassed his friends to subscribe to worthy causes by placing their names and monetary pledges in black or blue bound books, and he assured each subscriber no one would pay unless the stated goal could be reached, but he covered "shortfalls" by making up the difference himself. "Vivid, dynamic, rough," but never "deliberately malicious,"[118] Will endeared himself to satiric newspaper columnists O. O. (Odd) McIntyre and Irvin Cobb,[119] who dubbed him Houston's leading man and chronicled his escapades in their nationally syndicated reports. Will belonged to the Houston Chamber of Commerce after it reorganized in 1910, discussed early city improvement plans with his partner Joseph Cullinan in 1912–1913, raised money for the Boy Scouts as vice president and finance committee chairman in 1914–1916, and supported the Emma R. Newsboys Association, which was founded in 1910 by social reformer and publisher Ferdinand (Ferdie) Trichelle.[120] Trichelle created the association to honor her mother and to "harbor and guide homeless, neglected, and destitute boys" by providing meals or a place to live for hundreds of "little rascals" who hawked newspapers across town in the mid-1910s.[121] From 1915 to 1918 Will served the Houston Foundation and its Social Service Bureau. Although Will never ran for public office, he flaunted his famous surname when he crisscrossed the state on behalf of the University of Texas. In 1911 he created the university's Ex-Students' Association[122] to promote school spirit, to make the public understand the need for a great state university, and to generate financial support. He demonstrated his devotion to the University of Texas as a regent from 1913 to 1917, in his famous fight to unseat Governor James Ferguson in 1917, and with his financial support for buildings and programs in the 1920s. In 1919 Will asked Mike to help him raise over $300,000 for a Young Women's Christian Association (YWCA) building as a tribute to the "splendid spirit of service" of Houston women, and he gave an additional $15,000 the next year to cover cost overruns. Mike spent the prewar years establishing a legal and business career. After the war he became a generous supporter of the University of Texas and built his reputation as the "brilliant manager of the financial affairs of the Hogg Family." It was "level-headed" Mike who "acted as a brake to the impulsive . . . outbursts of his dynamic and dominating elder brother," and who guided the enthusiasms of his visionary sister.[123]

When the family's oil revenues skyrocketed in the early 1920s, Will and Mike began quietly acquiring properties they held in reserve for future development. Through their San Rodrigo Land and Cattle Company, in 1920 they purchased 160,000 acres in northern Mexico, where they took Irvin Cobb and other friends on hunting forays until Mexico expropriated the land in 1924. Mike and law school friend Hugh Potter scouted land north and south of Buffalo Bayou suitable for a civic center, public parks, and residential neighborhoods, while Will demonstrated the commercial viability and civic value of well-built, planned improvements. In November 1921 the Hoggs received a charter for Varner Company, created as a Hogg Brothers subsidiary to hold real estate in San Antonio and Houston. In 1921 and 1922 Varner Company acquired a majority interest in Stude Holding Association property north of White Oak Bayou and west of downtown and subdivided the area into four connected sections—Norhill, North Norhill, East Norhill, and Norhill Park. The Hoggs set aside land for a school and public parks, platted modest homesites on a traditional grid pattern, paved streets, installed sewer facilities, and built a parkway along White Oak Bayou to link new homes to the downtown business district. Within four years, more than 90 percent of the lots had been sold to middle-income residents, and the Hoggs had shown that developers could make a profit while providing affordable housing to modest customers.[124]

The year 1924 proved pivotal for the family and for the city of Houston. Will completed the lagging fund drive for the Museum of Fine Arts of Houston building; Hogg Brothers began to convey 1,500 acres north of Buffalo Bayou to the city for a nature park; and Mike suggested that the Hogg family take over Country Club Estates and develop its properties. When the fundraising campaign sponsored by the Houston art league to support a permanent municipal art museum building flagged after construction began in February 1923, desperate supporters turned to Will Hogg, whose family had already donated $10,000 to the project, and requested another gift. Will rudely refused to comply, but a few days later he expressed remorse for his conduct and said he would find the needed money himself. Between March 24 and April 12, 1924, Will pressured thirty-one friends and associates to pledge at least $5,000 each. Will guaranteed an additional $30,000, and on April 11, he wrote subscribers to announce that more than $200,000 had been raised by "a coterie of businessmen of Houston to discharge the deficit and complete the two wings as planned. . . . The spontaneous and community-loving response . . . speaks volumes for the future of Houston. One is fortunate to have his home and to work and to die in a town as fine in heart and soul as is Houston." Will left town to avoid gushing expressions of gratitude at the opening-day ceremonies on April 12. To celebrate the new museum, Hogg Brothers placed several paintings from its Remington Collection on display in the handsome but unfurnished galleries. The Hoggs made only two demands: admission to the municipal facility must be free, and hours must be established when African American visitors were welcome. Their ultimatum launched an inclusive policy in keeping with the museum's official motto, "Erected by the people for the use of the people."[125]

While solving Houston Art League's fundraising problems, the Hoggs were also expanding their holdings along Buffalo Bayou. In March 1923 Mike purchased 118 acres south of the bayou in a wooded area he called "Tall Timbers" to use as a bachelor retreat for hunting, riding, and entertaining. Later that year Varner Company, through Varner Realty Inc., a subsidiary created for the purpose, bought 875 acres north of the bayou where Camp Logan had been home to thousands of army trainees during World War I, and in the spring of 1924 purchased another 630 acres adjacent to Camp Logan. Journalists were stirring public curiosity about the camp's fate, and civic activist Catherine Emmott[126] formed a committee to lobby at city hall and to insist the camp land be preserved as a municipal park "in memory of the boys." Emmott's advocacy appealed to Ima, Will, and Mike. In April the Hoggs made a proposal: Varner Realty would acquire and hold the land until the city could raise funds to take title; the sales price to the city would be the original cost plus accrued interest or property taxes. To begin developing "Memorial Park," on July 1 Varner Realty sold the city undivided title to 174 acres "for park purposes only" and granted an option to acquire more land each July 1 until the entire 1,503 acres amassed by the Hoggs would belong to the city. To underwrite the first purchase, the siblings made a gift of $50,000 for the 1924 down payment. The Hoggs commissioned Sid Hare and his son S. Herbert Hare of Kansas City to design an eighteen-hole golf course and other park improvements.[127]

Meanwhile, Mike Hogg and Hugh Potter had approached Will about buying out a group of investors who were building a new country club and developing Country Club Estates as a residential area abutting club property. Potter always claimed Will laughed at their limited proposal. "Why buy only 200 acres?" he asked. "Why not buy 1,000 acres more? Why not make this something really big, something the city can be proud of?" Will next convinced Potter to retire from his law practice, "take charge of this thing," and develop the land "with the entire resources of the Hogg estate behind it."[128] In May and June 1924, Will, Mike, and Hugh Potter secured controlling interest of Country Club Estates Inc., purchased an additional seven hundred acres of farmland between Shepherd's Dam Road and Mike's Tall Timbers retreat, and incorporated Mike's property in the project. In July, Will and Mike invited potential investors to dinner at the chic Rice Hotel, where Will introduced Hugh Potter and explained his visionary scheme to build a planned community called River Oaks.

For Will, River Oaks was "simply an intelligently planned community woven from the best threads of land planning practice." He imagined the project as an aspirational model for residential development in Houston that suggested a new "way of living" for its homeowners.[129] Houses of various sizes designed by reputable architects would sit within gardens along landscaped, often curving, streets lined with specimen trees. Sidewalks would invite strolling among pocket parks filled with rose bushes, past the handsome elementary school, and on to the welcoming country club, where membership was an enticement to prospective buyers. Small shopping centers would sit discreetly along the perimeter; the Forum of Civics community center would nurture companionship and connection among city reformers; handsome entrances to the development would alert passersby to the promise within; and stands of old trees would link the Hoggs' modern plan to Houston's past. This idyll of country life, removed from urban decay, unfettered sprawl, and noisy traffic, expressed the Hoggs' ambitious goal, which was illustrated in the elegant advertisements of architect-artist Edward Muegge "Buck" Schiwetz[130] and announced through a sophisticated marketing campaign in Houston's *Gargoyle* and other media.

The Hoggs cut broad River Oaks Boulevard through scrubby brush to connect the country club entrance with Westheimer Road in July 1924. By 1930 Hogg Brothers had spent $1.8 million on the project; the company had installed utilities; planted hundreds of crape myrtles, rose bushes, and oak trees in common areas; and attracted affluent customers. River Oaks struggled at first to find buyers for the undeveloped west side of downtown, which had been annexed in 1927. The promised parkway from the business district to the Kirby Drive gates had to be constructed, and there was strong competition from developments south of downtown near Rice Institute. The Hoggs protected their planned community against commercial intrusion with deed restrictions and construction limitations. They offered "private showings" of fifteen "completely furnished" model homes designed by noteworthy local architects and urged potential buyers to hire staff architect Charles W. Oliver or landscape architect Henry Hutchinson, who had trained in London and Berlin, to design each property.[131] The siblings worked together. Will oversaw the marketing plan and wrote letters to friends and business associates inviting them to purchase fourteen large properties platted in the exclusive ninety-acre Homewoods enclave that abutted the River Oaks development. Mike, as vice president of the corporation, collaborated with Hugh Potter to oversee on-site management. Ima planned Homewoods and created a model home for River Oaks, and she consulted Houston Independent School District personnel in 1929 to build and landscape the progressive elementary school for residents.

The Hoggs chose Homewoods plot C, an irregularly shaped 14.5-acre parcel on a bend in the bayou, and began, at last, to design the home they had dreamed about for so long.

Designing Their Dream House

The ark of safety, known today as Bayou Bend Collection and Gardens, reflects the vision, values, and sophisticated taste of its cosmopolitan, well-read, middle-aged creators. When Will, Ima, and Mike moved into Bayou Bend, they were fifty-three, forty-six, and forty-three, respectively. Fueled by his father's assertion that "Home!" was "the Center of Civilization . . . the ark of safety . . . and the haven of rest in old age," Will, as head of the family, had long imagined a domestic haven. While pursuing lucrative business ventures and developing oil reserves in West Columbia, Will decided to refurbish the old Patton Place farmhouse at Varner Plantation as a weekend refuge for entertaining investors and friends, and in 1916 he asked his university classmate and longtime family friend Birdsall Parmenas (Bert) Briscoe to develop plans for a major modernization. War intervened; gushers produced millions of barrels of oil each month; and in 1919 Will decided to "fix up the old place as George Washington would do if he had a bank roll." He told Briscoe to create an elegant Colonial Revival exterior that linked Varner Plantation to Mount Vernon and Jim Hogg's retirement from public life to George Washington's retreat to the "simpler" life of a farmer after his long service to the nation.[132] While the Varner project was under way, Will told Briscoe that he and Ima would soon build a Houston home and would want him to draw up the plans—possibly for the Shadyside option on lot Q, which lapsed that summer. Sadly, Ima's long illness cut short the discussion. Tom and Marie Hogg, also flush with proceeds from the West Columbia oil wells, were the first family members to build—a grand Spanish-Mediterranean-style country house at 202 Bushnell Avenue in San Antonio, designed for them by architects Atlee B. and Robert M. Ayres in 1923–1924.

The 1927 design for the Hoggs' dream house modeled high-quality residential construction that adapted historic styles to modern use. Architects John Staub and Birdsall Briscoe fused the Georgian Palladian floorplan—so popular among European colonists in the eighteenth century and Colonial Revival enthusiasts in the early twentieth—with Spanish Colonial elements from the Southwest, Greek Revival details that recalled the independent Texas republic, and a columned façade to evoke the Old South. Christened "Latin Colonial"[133] by Ima, the eclectic style and stucco exterior suited the humid climate and tied the house to venerable building traditions. Conceived as a private residence, the house was secluded from public view by a winding, wooded drive that leads to Lazy Lane, the meandering byway through Homewoods. The east wing, dubbed the "Fat Men's Wing" in Will's correspondence, provided a separate outside entrance and a staircase to the brothers' bedrooms, sleeping porch, dressing and bathrooms, and exercise space on the second floor. Downstairs, a paneled parlor and informal "tap room" with adjacent small kitchen provided space for the brothers to entertain their guests. The west wing housed the housekeeper's domain and kitchen downstairs and an elegant guest suite on the second floor. Its windows overlooked a two-story dependency that comprised a three-car garage below rooms for live-in domestic staff and an attached house for the gardener. Ima reigned over the central portion of the house. Upstairs she created a public/private space—a handsome sitting room with a paneled fireplace wall and, behind double wall-pocket doors, a bedroom with a dressing room and bath. Two other bed/bath suites completed the second-floor midsection. The downstairs space in the central block served domestic and civic purposes. A central hall leading from the south entrance to the north terrace welcomed guests and was flanked by a dining room on the west and a drawing room on the east. A library bridged the quasi-public world of the central block with the brothers' east wing retreat. The elegant, large spaces of the center hall, dining and drawing rooms, and library accommodated family parties but were also planned as public spaces with a civic purpose. In these rooms, for many years Ima entertained guests at musicales and receptions and held meetings with troops of volunteers who supported her philanthropic causes. A finished basement ran the length of the house and provided a lavatory and a secret door to the wine cellar (an apt hiding place during Prohibition). For several decades, the trunk line for telephone service ran from the cellar to eight Lazy Lane homesteads. Architectural historian Stephen Fox notes that the estate itself served a commercial purpose for the Hoggs. Visitors would see the beauty before them, and some, the developers hoped, would try to emulate the ambition of the professionally designed project by purchasing adjacent lots; others would be drawn to homes in close proximity to such elegance and buy property in River Oaks.

John Staub was long named the architect of Bayou Bend, and his close friendship with Ima lends credence to the claim, but correspondence with "Mssrs. Briscoe and Staub" and equal payments to both architects during the design and construction phases of the project imply shared responsibility. Both

Briscoe and Staub had designed model houses for River Oaks Corporation, and in February 1926 Ima wrote to Will: "Mr. Briscoe and Mr. Staub are working very congenially together, and I am delighted over having made this double choice." The architect of record may be less important than the vision forged by Will and Ima. Mike wisely remained a silent observer of the battle between his older siblings, but housekeeper Gertrude Anderson Vaughn (a member of the household since 1917) remembered that Will and Ima fought over every detail from location of the building to placement of the ironing board. Will was often out of town, but he scrutinized every expenditure and demanded written reports every week.[134]

As early as 1916 Ima revealed her aesthetic preferences when she urged Joseph S. Cullinan to adapt the Mediterranean style of Rice Institute for homes in his Shadyside enclave. When considering plans for River Oaks' model homes, Ima suggested John Staub study the creole buildings of New Orleans's French Quarter. In February 1926, as she planned her new home, Ima told Will that she and the architects were working for "maximum comfort" in "minimum space," and she praised the "stunning" elevations for their "character of old Charleston . . . houses, which has always been much my idea." In March she met Staub and Briscoe in New Orleans to search for vintage cast ironwork to use on the house. She then traveled to New York City, where she joined family friends Col. and Mrs. Edward M. House for three soothing months that included a Mediterranean cruise, camel riding in Egypt, postcard collecting in Italy, and ballet in Paris. By June 1927 the arguments were resolved, and Will confided, "The more I look at the plans of this house and visualize this house, the more I am entranced by the simplicity and practicality and what, I think, will be the comforting loveliness of it." That summer, the siblings approved plans for the "Residence of Miss Ima Hogg, Houston, Texas" and signed a contract with Christian J. Miller to build one of Houston's most expensive residential projects of the 1920s, a home and outbuilding costing $217,164.[135]

Ima's impact on the interior build-out of Bayou Bend proved as powerful as her influence on the exterior plan. An early visitor to the American Wing at New York's Metropolitan Museum of Art after its 1924 opening, she was intrigued by the use of period woodwork in the reconstructed rooms and pleased when John Staub introduced her to the wing's overseer, Charles O. Cornelius.[136] The Americana expert and Staub had been classmates, and Ima consulted Cornelius several times about her interiors before his premature death in 1937. On May 15, 1927, she attended the piano recital of her former pupil Eloise Helbig, now Chalmers, who had been studying with Adele Margulies in

Ima Hogg riding a camel in Egypt, 1926. MS 21–046–001, Ima Hogg Papers, Museum of Fine Arts, Houston Archives.

New York. Ima and Eloise then visited Sadie Campbell Blaffer at Bass Rocks, on Boston's North Shore, where they went to concerts in Gloucester and Boston and met the legendary interior designer Henry Davis Sleeper (1878–1934), whose sumptuous summer home, Beauport, sat atop a large rock overlooking Gloucester Harbor. Sleeper's forty-room house, each lavish space featuring a decorative or historic theme, influenced many contemporary collectors and homeowners and introduced the concept of displaying colored American glass in window embrasures to catch the sunlight. Inspired by what she had seen in New York and Gloucester, Ima began searching New England for period woodwork, paneling, beams, floorboards, and bricks to adorn Bayou Bend.

Although Ima followed Sleeper's example when she installed her glass collection, she found very few architectural details she could use—old paneling and mantels and some wide pine floorboards from Ipswich for her bedroom suite and a few beams for the tap room. Instead, she relied on contractor Miller and his talented artisans to craft most of the millwork and flooring for the house on site. Their sophisticated ability to recreate period detail continues to awe visitors, who admire the library decor, based on paneling in Newport, Rhode Island's historic Metcalf Bowler House; the drawing room fireplace, inspired by the parlor fireplace at Shirley Plantation in Virginia; the graceful, curving stairway, similar to stairs installed at the Texas Governor's Mansion; and the front door, reminiscent of Charleston's Nathaniel Russell House. Ima also influenced the elegant canvas wall coverings in the dining room, working directly with New York mural painter William Andrew Mackay.[137] In April 1928 she suggested gold dogwood on white background, and he replied that her scheme "would be handsome and distinguished," but proposed the "reverse, the soft warm, pinkish white dogwood . . . on a background of gold." When Ima saw drawings for both schemes, she agreed with Mackay's discerning judgment. He later asked to "correct one error"—the dining room wall coverings, he wrote in 1930, were "painted by William Andrew Mackay, designed by Miss Ima Hogg."[138] That year she also chose exotic French wallpaper depicting "The Banks of the Bosphorus," made from wood blocks by Dufour et Le Roi about 1812, for the sitting room in the guest suite.

As Bayou Bend's construction phase neared completion, Will and Ima acquired several outstanding examples of Americana to furnish the handsome rooms. Collings and Collings remained their primary source, providing several treasures during shopping sprees in 1927 and 1928—a settee with eight matching side chairs and a handsome mahogany bedstead, both from Massachusetts (1750–1800), a black walnut Rhode Island desk with burl veneer (1700–1730), a pair of mahogany New York card tables with saber legs (1805–1819), and a rare ladies' writing desk with the era's fashionable tambour doors (1794–1810) from Boston. In 1928 Ima also made her first purchase from the renowned New York firm of Ginsburg and Levy—a cherry tea table (1735–1782) and a cherry high chest (1750–1782) from Wethersfield, Connecticut. With their earliest treasures finally in place, Will, Ima, and Mike enjoyed their first meal in the new house, a breakfast with their friend and business partner Raymond Dickson on election day November 6, 1928. They sat down for their first family dinner when Tom and Marie Hogg visited on November 13. These meals, and the people who served them—Gertrude Anderson (later Vaughn), Ben Mouton, Della Jones, and Charles Rhodes Jr.—were recorded in an embossed guest book labeled "Bayou Banks." Ima discussed a name for the new house with Julia Ideson, writing she wanted to suggest rural "contentment," the name used in early correspondence. By 1929 a new guest book reflected the change from "Bayou Banks" to "Bayou Bend," referring to the home's location at a bend in the bayou. Family friend Estelle Sharp purchased 4410 Rossmoyne, and on November 22, she invited the Hoggs to celebrate her first meal at their former home. By 1931 two national publications had featured Bayou Bend, the first of many to praise the Hoggs' contributions to architecture and to their city's civic life.

Projects Fulfilled: 1925–1929

During the 1920s, Will Hogg advocated strongly for city planning and zoning as mechanisms to ensure urban beauty and efficiency, and he gained a reputation as the city's most outspoken enthusiast for a municipal department of planning empowered to carry out a formal city plan that would control future development by separating commercial and industrial zones from residential and recreational spaces. From January through March 1927, Will lobbied for legislation pending in the Texas legislature that would allow cities to authorize planning commissions with enforcement powers, while Mike Hogg campaigned successfully to fill a recently vacated seat in the Texas House. Noted as a "student of public affairs" with a "retiring disposition," Mike gained the endorsement of Houston's establishment, including Julia Ideson, former governor William P. Hobby, and numerous lawyers. After a "landslide victory" in February 1927, Mike left for Austin, where he helped enact laws in March that enabled cities to authorize zoning ordinances, control subdivision platting, levy money for parks, require building setbacks, and allow municipal assessments for street widening and improvements. Will's "characteristic energy" and his advocacy for "proper zoning and for beautification" made him the best candidate to lead Houston's planning process.[139]

Will became chairman of the seven-member Houston Planning Commission on April 15, 1927, and applauded the June 29 city ordinance that created a Department of Planning and authorized a major city plan. At their first meeting on July 9, Will and his fellow commissioners hired city planning consultant S. Herbert Hare as commission consultant and named city engineer Lewis B. Ryon Jr. as secretary. Journalists strongly supported urban planning and beautification during Will's twenty-seven months as commission chairman, and Will expanded his advocacy. From 1926 through 1930 Will paid nurseryman Edward Teas to plant thousands of rose bushes, flowering trees, and his father's favorite pecan trees at schools, hospitals, parks, and commercial sites. Will asked River Oaks Corporation employee Ethel Brosius, River Oaks resident Blanche Sewall, and friend Mary Elliot to write *A Garden Book for Houston* as a "practical guide book" for the region, and he paid for its publication in 1929. The "simple and clear volume" provided information to gardeners in Harris

County, forty-five surrounding counties, and lower Louisiana. On May 15, 1926, Will announced the Forum of Civics, "an organization designed to stimulate civic pride and to combine many and varied forces for betterment and beautification of our city and county." He hired Birdsall Briscoe and Joseph Northrup Jr. to renovate the 1910 John Smith county school on Westheimer and Kirby as the forum headquarters and library and invited three hundred civic associations, professional societies, and public officials to use the space for meetings so members could cooperate, discuss urban issues, and hear national experts speak about municipal challenges. In 1928 Will began publishing the weekly magazine *Civics for Houston* as the forum's mouthpiece to offer "practical ideas about your city, your home and your garden." Edited by former *Condé Nast* employee Hester Scott, the publication covered everything from gardening and design to the "Dark Side of Houston," where degraded neighborhoods lacked city services.[140] Unhappily, Will and his editor disagreed about presentation and content. Scott was appalled by Will's angry reaction to her professional comments. He considered her criticism insufferable, lost his temper, fired his editor, and closed the magazine after one year. The progressive messages found in *Civics for Houston* were adopted by the *Houston Gargoyle*, a slick weekly journal founded in 1928 by Estelle Sharp, which advocated urgently for social justice and building safe communities.

Will's overbearing attitude undermined the planning commission's success. Although he mirrored his father's populist affection for the people and wanted Houstonians to be informed, Will held meetings in secret to protect the experts, left most of the work to consultants, and ignored the claque of developers who opposed zoning and government supervision of their lucrative activities. He also devoted time to unrelated projects and was absent from the city for long periods. In January 1928 Will and Mike joined the host committee responsible for funding and producing the Democratic National Convention, held that June in downtown Houston. Will took many short trips to Los Angeles, where investment in moving pictures intrigued him, and he spent July to October 1928 in Europe and December 1928 to April 1929 in South America. The elegant city plan, beautifully prepared and presented by S. Herbert Hare, called for "adequate, comprehensive" recreation spaces and parks; imagined a handsome civic center inspired by City Beautiful concepts that would place municipal and cultural institutions around a plaza centered on the Spanish Renaissance-style public library; and advocated zoning to protect property values and rationalize planning. Will submitted a final report on October 30, 1929, resigned as commission chairman on November 1, and left town the next day for a tour of the globe. Former Mayor A. Earl Amerman took over as chairman and released the plan to the public on December 12, 1929. A storm of protest, led by powerful opponents of zoning, scuttled the zoning proposals and weakened the planning commission. Supporters of the plan had failed to explain that planning was an ongoing process enabling all private interests to state their positions. Zoning as an option for rational use of space has always met strong resistance in Houston, but Will's failure to stay in town and defend his ideas ensured the plan would be widely ignored.[141]

When Ima Hogg emerged from her long battle with physical ailments and mental depression, she joined the Museum of Fine Arts, Houston Board of Trustees from 1925 to 1933, and served on its Entertainment Committee in 1926, but music remained her enduring interest. During the 1923–1924 season of the Girls' Musical Club, Ima hosted the club's three open meetings at her Rossmoyne home, and in the spring of 1925, she suggested that the club create a "Trustees' Musicians' Fund" to provide "special benefits for [needy] Club members" and to support local women who wished to pursue professional music careers.[142] To demonstrate the value of professional training and raise money for the fund, Ima asked soprano Blanche Foley and music columnist and club president Mary Elizabeth Rouse to help her organize a gala concert at the Main Street Auditorium on the evening of April 16, 1925. Ima understood the importance of endowment income as a permanent source of funding, and she recognized that gala events would draw potential donors to the cause. Ima supported the club for the rest of her life but agreed with supporters in 1930 when they conceded that most active Girls' Musical Club members were neither young nor unmarried and voted to change the club's name to Tuesday Musical Club.

Efforts to revive a local professional symphony orchestra flagged in the 1920s, when Houston audiences cheered Chicago's "King of Jazz" Isham Jones and his fourteen-piece orchestra or danced until dawn on the Rice Hotel Roof. Ima agreed to continue as president of the Houston Symphony Association in 1919, but by 1921 her illness and long absence from Houston called for change. Huberta Garwood, wife of Houston Music Festival patron Judge Hiram M. Garwood, became association president from 1921 to 1931. Her board maintained a membership roster and sponsored chamber orchestra recitals but could not generate support for symphonic programs. Music critics bemoaned the small audiences at presentations by local performers and national artists, and Edna Saunders began promoting international ballet troupes, New York's

Metropolitan Opera soloists, and a season of Chicago Civic Opera performances in March and April 1927. Yet, Ima sensed a latent love for classical music among her friends. The lecture/recitals she sponsored at Rice Institute drew respectable audiences, and on March 20–23, 1927, the Texas Federation of Music Clubs filled hotel rooms when nearly three hundred delegates arrived during Houston's azalea season for musical meetings, concerts and recitals, social engagements, and a reception at the Museum of Fine Arts. Past presidents of the Girls' Musical Club hosted federation participants at a grand breakfast, and choir director Ellison Van Hoose amassed a chorus of convention delegates for a songfest on Tuesday evening. On March 1,1928, local violinist Josephine Boudreaux[143] caused a sensation when she displayed her talent at the Scottish Rite Cathedral. Following this success, Boudreaux formed the Houston String Quartet, renamed the Boudreaux Quartet in 1929. The Houston Symphony Association invited her to perform a series of chamber concerts at member homes for a 1929–1930 season. Two hundred tickets sold immediately, and Ima opened Bayou Bend for the season finale—four quartets by Felix Mendelssohn and Alexander Borodin. Music enthusiasts began to imagine a rejuvenated Houston Symphony Orchestra, and in 1929 Ima discreetly initiated a survey of orchestras around the country to learn about problems facing municipal orchestras and to discover conductors who might be willing to settle in Houston.

Temporarily stymied by Symphony Association problems and spurred by conversations with Austen Riggs, Ima turned her imagination to the much-discussed problem of the "maladapted" child and to the many challenges of youthful delinquency. Riggs had invited Ima to visit a demonstration child guidance clinic he was organizing in Pittsfield, Massachusetts. His clinic and one in Dallas were two of seven demonstration clinics participating in a pilot program from 1922 to 1927 to help "normal" children overcome temporary problems.[144] In an attempt to identify children at risk, for whom early intervention and counseling might assure a productive life, the Commonwealth Fund[145] had teamed with the National Committee for Mental Hygiene to train psychiatric social workers, examine "unadjusted" children, and set up clinics to show how communities could cooperate with teachers and social service agencies to help children and families. Riggs suggested that Ima might find purpose in her own life if she could bring this idea to philanthropic leaders in Houston. Ima accepted Riggs's suggestion immediately and began to devour the limited literature relating to demonstration clinics, mental health care, and child development. She discussed her ideas with Estelle Sharp, who was working with the Houston Settlement Association and other service providers. She invited Dr. George Stevenson, director of the Division of Community Clinics for the Commonwealth Fund, to visit Houston, meet with civic leaders, and critique the city's social service organizations. In 1926 Ima and her friends persuaded the Houston Community Chest to authorize $7,500 for a child guidance clinic, but Dr. Stevenson thought municipal awareness was insufficient to support a clinic. Three years later, Stevenson changed his mind. He now believed Houston's social service infrastructure had matured and would benefit from a child guidance clinic component.

In 1929 Estelle Sharp's *Houston Gargoyle* devoted several articles to "child-saving" problems and explained that local advocates had formed a steering committee to "make the public fully aware of the powerful influence of mental hygiene in erasing crime, insanity, and disease" and to establish a "Mental Hygiene Clinic."[146] On April 23, 1929, at 7:00 p.m., Ima greeted supporters at Bayou Bend and called the founding meeting of the Houston Child Guidance Clinic to order. Her neighbor John E. Green Jr. read the steering committee report that proposed allocating $25,000 per year for a clinic. Rice Institute sociologist John Willis Slaughter, who served as executive secretary of the Community Chest and head of the Houston Foundation, recommended thirty-three candidates for the board, including representatives from Faith Home, the Houston Family Service Bureau, the Houston Board of Education, the Junior League, and the Parent-Teacher Association. In later interviews, Ima said she believed the difficulties she and her brother Tom had experienced might have been prevented if there had been trained experts at a child guidance clinic for her father to consult after their mother died.

Ima returned from four months in Europe in time to attend the October 16 meeting where the board voted to name Dr. James Cunningham as director, to hire two social workers, to rent a headquarters house at 703 Gray Street at Louisiana Street, and to raise $10,000. Ima pledged $2,500 to support a clinic that "protects and conserves human material." On November 1, 1929—only days after the Wall Street financial crash—the Houston Child Guidance Clinic opened and pledged to fulfill the mission stated in its state charter: "The diagnosis, treatment and guidance of problem children. The study of the principles of mental hygiene, and the application of these principles to problem children and other persons connected with or related to such children." With the creation of Bayou Bend and the birth of the Child Guidance Clinic, Ima began a new phase of her life as chatelaine of a lovely estate and spokesperson for civic mental health care.[147]

Summer Travels and New Collections: 1928–1930

Houston was hot in June 1928. Temperatures soared; politicians descended on the city to attend the Democratic National Convention; reporters slept in hotel hallways; and sweating delegates sought refuge in "Hospitality House," a giant, temporary, tent-like structure next to the main—also temporary—convention center building. Funded, constructed, and staffed by volunteers corralled by Will, Mike, and Ima Hogg and their friends, Hospitality House provided ceiling fans, refreshments, relaxation, reading and writing materials, telephones, and smiling committees of women to provide respite from the noise on the convention floor. Newspaper publisher and developer Jesse Holman Jones pulled strings in Washington and brought the convention to Houston; a consortium of Houston businessmen, including Will and Mike Hogg, underwrote the event; and citizens enjoyed the excitement, despite the heat. In his usual spirit of impetuous fairness, Will resented Jones's effort to take sole credit for this important civic enterprise and wrote a scathing, widely distributed letter to Governor Dan Moody to oppose any effort by Jones to "allow" himself to be nominated as a favorite son candidate. Do not "proffer as President this ill-fitted pseudo-statesman who . . . is always using the other fellow's chips to his own advantage," Will advised, adding Jones will "make yourself and your friends ridiculous."[148] Ima supported her brothers' effort by joining the museum committee of volunteer art lovers to staff a four-hour Hospitality House shift on June 25. Shortly after the convention ended, she and Estelle Sharp fled the heat to relax at Sharp's ranch in Alpine, Texas, before proceeding on a tour of New Mexico, where Ima attended the Gallup Inter-Tribal Indian Ceremonial, which was first organized in 1922 to celebrate Native American rituals and crafts. While there, she indulged her acquisitive habit by purchasing an array of articles related to pueblo life.

As with many of Ima's enterprises, it is hard to know when the inspiration to build a collection of Native American artifacts arose. The Hoggs had long been intrigued by Southwestern history and culture, and their library contained volumes about the conflict between Anglo settlers and their Mexican overlords that produced the Republic of Texas. Ima may have attended the exhibit of North American crafts sponsored by the Fred Harvey Company at the 1904 World's Fair to promote travel to the Southwest; or she may have visited the Museum of the American Indian, established by collector George Gustav Heye in New York City.[149] In 1926 Ima purchased a five-color woodcut of Gustave Baumann's *Corn Dance, Santa Clara* from a selection of works depicting Native American rituals on display in the Museum of Fine Arts of Houston's galleries. In the summer of 1928, she bought her first pueblo object at Fred Harvey's outlet in Albuquerque; once ensconced at La Fonda Hotel in Santa Fe, she began to splurge.

Early in September 1928, Ima bought two important "prehistoric pots"—probably small Mimbres ollas, dated circa AD 1000—at the Santa Fe Trading Post, conveniently located in La Fonda. Later that month she was tempted by two Zuni rings, a bracelet, and a bridle at the Fred Harvey trading post. She also purchased a watercolor landscape and three lithographs—*Juan*, *A Bit of Walipi*, and *Santiago*—from artist/lithographer Gerald Cassidy, a graduate of the Art Students League in New York who had moved to Arizona to recover from pneumonia and had settled in Santa Fe in 1912, where he worked and collected Native American artifacts until his death in 1934. Ima returned to Houston with trinkets, jewelry, more than one hundred pots, and awakened enthusiasm. She realized these well-crafted objects, representative of a fast-disappearing culture, rivaled in importance the furnishings she had purchased for Bayou Bend. She placed several pots in the Bayou Bend library, which displayed Windsor chairs and hooked rugs, and asked James H. Chillman Jr., director of the Museum of Fine Arts of Houston, to store most of her purchases in the museum. Probably following discussions with Chillman, Ima began corresponding with Buton Staplie, of Coolidge, New Mexico, about a necklace, an exhibit, and a lecture. The result delighted Ima and provided Chillman a *Loan Exhibition of Houston-Owned Indian Handcrafts from Crafts del Navajo of Coolidge*. On display February 2–23, 1930, these objects introduced a new art genre to Houstonians and reminded Texans of the important role pueblo culture played in United States history. While the exhibit was in place, Hogg family friend Dorothy Hoskins used her column in the *Gargoyle* to discuss "American Indian Pottery" in terms that echoed Ima's beliefs. Native American ceramics, Hoskins pointed out, represented the superb craftsmanship of pueblo culture, married design with function, and were often created by women.

In the summer of 1929, Ima Hogg left the fledgling Child Guidance Clinic and her new home in capable hands and invited her frequent traveling companion Eloise Helbig Chalmers to accompany her on a life-changing adventure—a trip organized by New Educational Fellowship through its Open Road program, which enabled westerners to visit the Soviet Union.[150] The intrepid women sailed on June 21 from New York to Oslo on the Scandinavian America liner *Hellig Olav*. At stops in Oslo and Stockholm, they visited folk museums with open-air concepts that would resurface years later in Ima's imagination when she conceived her final project—restoration of the German-centered village of Winedale in Fayette County. At Oslo's beautifully executed Folks Museum, organizers had brought old houses and churches together to create an outdoor village museum that explored traditional Norse culture through architecture and objects in an effort to shape national identity for the relatively young country, which had been independent since 1814. Ima was charmed by what seemed to her a daring idea and a new way to comprehend ethnic differences, and she compared Stockholm's skimpier Nordske Museum unfavorably. Confusion at the border between Finland and Russia, when the promised Open Road escort failed to appear, caused Ima, as she had done on several previous foreign trips, to leave her purse on the train; despite her anxiety, she was soundly scolded by a man in uniform for losing her purse and for trying to tip the kind soul who retrieved it. Train travel in Russia opened her eyes to the contrasting poverty and sadness of people in the streets and the magnificent luxury of old czarist palaces—one turned into a nursing clinic for local peasants and another housing splendid art collections. Neither the Hotel Europa in Leningrad nor the Hotel Select in Moscow met her meticulous standards, but Ima wrote the well-traveled Julia Ideson that "the Russian experience was the richest I ever had."[151] With earnest curiosity she viewed paintings by avant-garde Russian artists and explored the magnificent fine art collections of Sergei Shchukin and Ivan Morozov, confiscated by Vladimir Lenin and hung together in Morosov's former mansion, renamed the State Museum of New Western Art. These experiences inspired Ima to splurge when she reached the art galleries of Munich and Paris that fall.

While reveling in new experiences, Ima received startling news: Mike had married. Lovely Alice Nicholson Fraser entered Hogg family records in a diary entry showing that Will, Mike, and Alice ate a Mexican supper in San Antonio on June 16. Will continued to Los Angeles, where he rented a house at 801 Bedford Drive for the summer, and Ima had reached Russia when Mike and Alice wed secretly at a friend's home in Galveston on July 20. Ima later suggested that Will was devastated by Mike's marriage, which the Hoggs' secretary, H. E. Brigham, admitted was "quite a shock," but brother Will recovered enough to entertain the newlyweds in Los Angeles and to present a watch to the bride on her birthday. By the time Brigham wrote to Ima in Paris, "Mr. Will was so charmed with the bride that he is claiming the credit for making the match." Mike feared to confide in his siblings, but when the family gathered that fall, Alice's kindness and Mike's obvious happiness reassured everyone.[152]

The surprise wedding did not hamper Ima's latest enthusiasm—forming a collection of works on paper by the titans of contemporary European art. By 1929 Ima had traveled and studied several times in Europe; she had lived for long periods in Philadelphia and New York City; and she had visited numerous historic sites, museums, and art galleries. She might have browsed in galleries of the four dealers who offered cubist, surrealist, and German expressionist works to New York shoppers, and she probably purchased her small oil *Portrait of Lorette (Meditation)* by Henri Matisse from King-Parker Gallery in May 1928. New York collectors and critics largely ignored modernist artists in the 1920s, but Ima was fascinated by every kind of aesthetic expression she encountered, and she embraced contemporary art. She now realized she could build specific personal collections to enjoy at home and then place in Houston's collection-starved, young municipal art museum for public pleasure and education.[153]

Ima may have decided that she wanted to form a collection of works on paper for Houston's museum by the time she arrived in Munich, because while there in late August, she asked bibliophile and gallery owner Hans Golz to send six drawings and eight prints by nine well-known artists—including Jean-Baptiste-Camille Corot, Camille Pissarro, Paul Cezanne, Edouard Manet, and four by Pablo Picasso—directly to Houston Museum of Fine Arts Director James Chillman. Although her brothers often called their sister "Miss Titewadd," and although she frequently requested "museum discounts" when she was bargaining with sellers, the pure exhilaration of collecting overwhelmed her that fall. When Ima reached Paris, she continued shopping at the Paul Guillaume Gallery, where she purchased a sketch by Amadeo Modigliani, an André Derain lithograph, and two etchings and one drypoint by Henri Matisse. From Paul Rosenberg, exclusive Paris agent for Pablo Picasso and Marie Laurencin, Ima acquired two Picasso colored stencils and two pastels on wove paper—*Head of a Woman*, which she later traded, and the great *Three Women at the Fountain* (1921), which she displayed in her home until the 1960s. The Paris purchases were shipped to Bayou Bend and paid for from her Hogg Brothers account through banking arrangements with a Paris representative of her Houston bank. Ima framed few of her works on paper because she liked to store them in her upstairs sitting room and take them out occasionally for quiet reflection.

Before Will left Houston to begin his world tour on November 1, 1929, he and Ima made plans to travel in Europe during the summer of 1930. Will detailed his journey and recorded concerns about his health in his diary. Long overweight, Will had worried about his diet and his receding hairline for years, but his travel journal suggests serious medical problems, and a photograph, probably taken

Will Hogg with Gilley in Berlin, 1930. Di_05909, Ima Hogg Photographs, Dolph Briscoe Center for American History, University of Texas at Austin.

while in Germany, depicts a slim, dapper boulevardier, an excessive weight loss that often signals illness. Ima met Will in Paris, where he had been for some time, entertaining his close friend O. O. (Odd) McIntyre, making a Cairn terrier named Gilley his constant companion, and acquiring a lavish collection of perfumes in exquisite bottles for his sister-in-law Alice. Missima and Podsnap immediately began to haunt art galleries and concert halls, as Ima tried, unsuccessfully, to persuade her reluctant companion to take an interest in contemporary art. July and August found the pair at the Leipzig Bach Festival, adding to Ima's art collection in Berlin, where she bought her first works on paper by Lyonel Feininger and Paul Klee, and purchasing several German modernist works in Munich, where she bought Oskar Kokoschka's *Wanderer in a Storm*, a lithograph from his Bach-Cantata series. Years later, Ima confided that she particularly liked works of art linked to music. In Bayreuth, Will indulged Ima's passion for Richard Wagner's epic operas, and both travelers mourned the death of longtime Bayreuth Festival organizer Siegfried Wagner on August 4, when black flags draped civic buildings.[154]

By the time the couple reached Baden-Baden, Will was very ill. Ima cabled Mike and Alice, who set out at once, but the "devastatingly vivid personality" died on September 12, eight days after an emergency gall bladder operation and just before Mike and Alice arrived to comfort Ima, who was exhausted by the ordeal. The grieving travelers accompanied their brother's body home on the North German Lloyd liner *Bremen*. Although the failed operation was accepted as cause of death, Will's tremendous weight loss and nagging ailments suggest that cancer was the culprit. O. O. McIntyre and Irvin Cobb met the family in New York City and accompanied their friends back to Houston, where they remained as pallbearers for the funeral held at Bayou Bend on September 26, 1930. Honorary pallbearers included a roster of University of Texas leaders, journalists, political figures, theater producers, portrait artist Wayman Adams, and quipster movie star Will Rogers of Beverly Hills. Mourners, "ranging from the most successful business men of the nation to the youngest newsboys of Houston," followed the nationally recognized figure to Oakwood Cemetery in Austin. He was buried beside his parents under the pecan trees—"rustling in the first northern wind of winter"—which the Hogg children had planted in 1906 to fulfill their father's last wishes. Journalist Marcellus Elliot (Mefo) Foster, who had planned to meet Will in Paris in September, led the chorus of praise for the "great city builder, . . . who built for beauty and posterity rather than for any personal gain." Admirers praised Will's unrivaled generosity, his humble kindness "to the lowliest of people," his shyness, his exuberance, and his insistence on fair play. This "valuable and public-spirited citizen," one wrote, "defended the highest ideals of citizenship" and "recognized and appreciated the noble and the beautiful." McIntyre stated that "few men met death so valiantly. . . . His chief concern during his final hours was for his beloved sister and his two equally beloved brothers."[155]

For Ima, Mike, and Tom, Will had been a perplexing and "fascinating character . . . full of contradictions and complexes." He shunned the limelight and was a steadfast friend to many, but he also dominated his siblings while depending on their attention for emotional support. A tall, imposing man with thinning brownish blond hair and a "big heart" who could not resist a hard-luck story, Will dreamed that one day Houston would be a beautiful cultural beacon, and he helped hundreds of college students anonymously with thousands of dollars from his private account. As his most enduring legacy, he established student loan funds at every college and university in Texas to give deserving students a head start. Yet he could be overbearing, and everyone avoided his explosive temper; he was awkward around strangers and often lashed out at subordinates. His colorful language was legendary, as Governor Jim Ferguson discovered when Will harangued him for putting his "putrid paw of patronage" in university affairs. Will loved his siblings, but he never relinquished the paterfamilias role thrust on him at a young age.[156]

Ima had been desolated by the loss of each parent, and when Will died she was exhausted and distressed for a few weeks, but she soon rallied, perhaps because civic duties demanded attention, or because Mike and Alice provided loving support. Will's terrier Gilley became her new companion.[157] To celebrate their brother's life, Ima and Mike placed the entire Hogg Brothers Remington Collection at the Museum of Fine Arts, Houston January 3–18, 1931. The loan was a major exhibit at that time and included twenty-three paintings, forty-two "illustrations in black and white," four pen-and-ink, and one sculpture of a bronco buster. Never before had the entire collection been exhibited, and to ensure the public's enjoyment, Ima invited teams of volunteers to serve as hosts and hostesses every afternoon and evening. The exhibition opened on January 3 with a special event, and on Sunday afternoon, January 4, the museum's Founders Society joined museum officers and trustees to serve as the first exhibit guides; that evening the Houston Friends of Art welcomed visitors. Forty-five professional, business, religious, and civic clubs—including Ima's Chautauqua, Down Town, Tuesday Musical, College Women's, and Houston Garden clubs—shared host duties during the next two weeks.

New Responsibilities: 1930–1939

In the 1930s, Mike Hogg became primary manager of Hogg family interests, while Ima Hogg focused on two important causes—the Houston Child Guidance Clinic and the Houston Symphony. Ima returned from her 1929 European sojourn in time to support hiring youthful psychiatrist James Morrow Cunningham as founding director of the Child Guidance Clinic, effective November 1. The "keen, earnest, hopeful" Dr. Cunningham had recently completed a

Columnist O. O. McIntyre and Mike Hogg on vacation, 1930s. MS 21–091, Ima Hogg Papers, Museum of Fine Arts, Houston Archives.

fellowship at the Institute for Child Guidance in New York, where he earned praise for his ability to talk to juveniles and for his eagerness to attack the "problem of correcting bad habits."[158] He was joined by three highly qualified associates with strong child guidance experience—psychologist Mary Lasater, a former Commonwealth Fund fellow at the New York Institute; head social worker Charlotte Henry, a graduate of the Family Service Course at Western

Reserve University; and social worker Lucretia Brewer, who had trained at the Cleveland Child Guidance Clinic. From November 1, 1929, until she left on May 31, 1930, to meet Will in Europe, Ima worked tirelessly with Kenneth Womack, a cotton broker who was board chairman, with Leopold Meyer, a department store executive who served as treasurer,[159] and with devoted supporters Estelle Sharp and Nina Cullinan[160] to stabilize finances, to educate Houstonians about mental health issues, and to show how the clinic could address family problems. On January 20, 1930, the board invited three hundred Houstonians to visit the clinic, meet the staff, partake of tea and sandwiches, and learn about the mission of this new community agency—"designed to act as a bureau for mental health work for children . . . [through] the study, treatment and prevention of childhood behavior problems, which may be forerunners of chronic physical illness, . . . mental disorders, delinquency, crime and other social problems."[161] On November 17, 1930, the board held its inaugural open casework conference to demonstrate clinic procedures to professionals and donors, and on December 12, Ima attended the clinic's first annual meeting and received the first printed annual report.

Ima soon discovered that explaining and funding the clinic's complex, and often contested, mission was difficult, especially after the Wall Street panic when she could not "get through to monied people." From 1929 until 1932, Ima guaranteed $10,000 per year, and records show she was the primary benefactor. She wrote dozens of letters, spoke to many civic organizations, and brought potential donors to the clinic. She secured the professional support of public schools Superintendent Edison E. Oberholtzer,[162] who pledged to recommend the clinic to worried parents and teachers. She wrote to George Stevenson, director of the National Committee on Mental Hygiene, to outline funding needs, noting that "a new welfare work . . . is not so readily understood," and she supported the board's decision to approach the Houston Community Chest for funding.[163] In 1931, Leopold Meyer explained clinic needs, noting he was not sure Ima would continue her level of support indefinitely, and in 1932 the Child Guidance Clinic became a Community Chest client when the fundraising group agreed to meet $15,000 of the $18,000 budget for the coming year; Ima and Mike underwrote the shortfall. By 1941, the Community Chest financed the entire operating budget.

Although Ima never served as the president, she exerted leadership through three important committees and supported the work of the Doctors' Committee—a group of Houston doctors who served on the board and voluntarily monitored the mental health program. In 1931, 1932, 1937, and 1944, Ima was chairwoman of the Nominating Committee to recruit new board members and select board leaders. From 1930 through 1933 and again in 1937, Ima directed the Mental Health Education Committee, where she developed reading lists and pamphlets to inform board members and the public about current research and therapeutic programs. She promoted public lectures, brought visiting speakers to Houston, and argued for her belief that the clinic should focus attention on community service, rather than on the research projects favored by much of the medical staff. The board was forced to cut salaries by 10 percent in 1931 and to cut staff in 1932. When Dr. Cunningham resigned, effective January 1, 1935, Ima chaired the Selection Committee to find his replacement, a role she played again in 1938 and in 1943. After an exhaustive and frustrating five-month national search, Ima checked into New York's Clifton Springs Sanitorium for a long rest before spending July through September 1935 enjoying music festivals in Europe. With her blessing, the board named Chicago resident J. P. Molloy, MD, the second clinic director, effective August 16, 1935.

Ima solicited contributions for Houston's inaugural four-day performance of Wagner's Ring cycle in March 1930. Although the experiment thrilled enthusiastic audiences, she sailed to Europe on May 30 somewhat despondent about support for a civic symphony in Houston. She returned four months later to discover backers of one opera company and three symphonic groups creating a furor of musical speculation. In August 1930, First Methodist Church Choir Director Noma (Mrs. John Wesley) Graham, known fondly as Ma Graham, decided to establish a music school and municipal opera company in Houston. She traveled to Italy where she met opera maestro Uriel Nespoli in Milan and persuaded him to lead her new enterprise. After struggles with customs, the "short, stout, nervous" conductor, prone to pacing and "flinging his arms in Italian outbursts," occupied Graham's "new and elaborate studio" on Westmoreland Boulevard in January 1931 and began training singers to perform *Aida*.[164]

While Noma Graham pursued her opera dreams, Victor Alessandro, music director of public school bands and orchestras, began rehearsing forty dues-paying musicians to form the Houston Philharmonic Orchestra, a quasi-professional (unpaid) group backed by cotton and real estate broker N. D. Naman and his associate W. H. Hogue. In the fall of 1930, Alessandro and Naman announced plans for a free concert series on Sunday afternoons, beginning on March 15, 1931. Horrified that a group "not heretofore associated with the symphony movement at all," had planned a concert series, Ima, now second vice president, and other Symphony Association supporters met in the Houston Chamber of Commerce offices with Philharmonic Orchestra sponsors

Naman and Hogue and local empresario Edna Saunders, who had worked with the Symphony Association in the 1920s to bring orchestral and chamber music groups to Houston. Ima and her friends asked everyone to work together under the well-recognized Symphony Association leadership to build a "truly representative" orchestra for the city. Naman and Hogue felt that a group organized by the musicians themselves was sufficiently representative and declined to participate. Saunders, perhaps concerned about competition from a revived resident orchestra, marched out of the meeting and began working with her close friend Ellison Van Hoose, former director of the Treble Clef Club and at the time choir director for the First Presbyterian Church, to create a "strictly commercial" Little Symphony of twenty-two musicians that would present concerts highlighting vocal artists. The group announced a debut performance on April 28, 1931, at the Palace Theatre (previously the Majestic Theatre). Spurred by the competition, the Houston Symphony Association reorganized. Knowing Noma Graham had been unable to fund her opera plans, in February 1931 they invited Uriel Nespoli to conduct a revived symphony orchestra, and he quickly auditioned seventy-five professional (paid) musicians. The Symphony Association board named new leadership under "wise" and dignified Dr. Joseph A. Mullen as president, with Huberta Garwood and Ima Hogg as first and second vice presidents, and it announced that the Houston Symphony Orchestra would perform two free concerts on May 6 and 7 at the Palace Theatre.[165]

In March, April, and May 1931, the concerts sponsored by all three groups took place as promised. The Houston Philharmonic's offerings on March 15 and May 3 found favor with music critic Hubert Roussel; Van Hoose's Little Symphony efforts were well attended; and the May 6 and 7 programs of the reconstituted Houston Symphony Association musicians, though "hastily gathered and quickly trained" by Nespoli, received warm praise. Adding luster to the association's opening program was the debut of popular violinist Josephine Boudreaux as concertmaster. Critic Roussel noted that "she played with a fine fury all evening," and she served in the orchestra's top leadership position through 1937. President Mullen later reflected, "the verdict of the press, the musicians and the public was so unanimously and insistently favorable" that the board decided "Houston wants and needs this Symphony Orchestra."[166]

In May the three groups announced full seasons for 1931–1932, and Houston patrons departed for the summer. The Houston Philharmonic and the Little Symphony launched advertising and sales campaigns, but only the Symphony Association could boast Ima Hogg's oversight. She and the board negotiated contracts with Nespoli and with the local American Federation of Musicians. Following a refreshing two-month trip to Mexico in August and September, Ima set to work. She collected advertisements for the concert programs, organized a membership drive, and gathered a volunteer force that sold six hundred season subscriptions. As an anonymous "friend of the orchestra," she purchased hundreds of tickets for public school teachers, "meritorious" pupils, and others who might find the cost of a ticket beyond their reach in the flagging economy.[167] She found new board members and suggested programs and musicians for the reorganized orchestra. The Symphony Association was impossible to beat. The three orchestras shared performers, but only the association paid its sixty musicians. Houston's civic and business leaders backed the Symphony Association, and the faltering economy left many music enthusiasts unable to support the challengers. There was room in Houston for only one symphonic society. In November 1931 the Symphony Association invited Florence Hogue, wife of philharmonic supporter W. H. Hogue, to serve as board secretary.

In the fall of 1931, Ima and Mary Fuller invited their beloved teacher Adele Margulies to Houston to teach an eight-month master class for pianists and teachers, the first held in the Southwest. The experiment proved so successful that her students persuaded Margulies to return the next year. Ima performed in several highly praised musicales at Bayou Bend during Margulies's visits, and on January 14, 1933, she played in concert with Margulies's students at the Houston Public Library, adding the strain of practicing several hours a day to her advocacy for the Symphony Association. While enjoying her former mentor's company, Ima searched for talented musicians and watched Nespoli's progress carefully. His spirited performances often featured local talent. At his first concert in November 1931, Drusilla Virginia Huffmaster,[168] not quite fourteen, made her professional debut with Edvard Grieg's Concerto for Pianoforte in A Minor, op. 16. Ima was impressed and urged Huffmaster to train with Margulies in New York and to study abroad; she underwrote this instruction and took her protégé to music festivals in Europe during the summer of 1935. Concertmaster Josephine Boudreaux delighted the audience at Nespoli's second program in December with Beethoven's Concerto for Violin, op. 61, while Houstonian Card Elliott, by popular request, followed the scheduled Prologue from *Pagliacci* with a popular ballad in January 1932. The *Houston Press* praised the symphony for hiring unemployed musicians, providing low-priced tickets, and running only a small deficit ($300), but the board was not pleased with its flamboyant Italian conductor.

Nespoli's programs were poorly rehearsed and too long; key sponsors did not like him; and the executive committee voted to fire him. The aggrieved conductor aired his complaints in the press and filed suit for breach of contract, but he finally accepted the decision and pursued an opera career in New York. Search committee members Ima Hogg, President Mullen, Huberta Garwood, Florence Hogue, and Treasurer Bernard Epstein accepted Epstein's recommendation to hire Frank St. Leger, the "charming and cultured" junior conductor of the Chicago Opera Company. St. Leger and his delightful wife, Kay, impressed female music mavens and well-heeled businessmen. He signed a three-year contract on June 8, 1932, and the couple moved into the Gardener's Cottage at Bayou Bend that September. With symphony matters settled, Ima and her friends Dot Thornton and Hallie Bryan Perry departed for New Mexico, where Ima attended her second Gallup Inter-Tribal Indian Ceremonial and purchased pottery for the collection of Native American artifacts she had begun to assemble in 1928. Musical Houston expectantly awaited St. Leger's debut on November 7, 1932; Ima renewed her subscription to box six; and early press reports applauded the improved performance that resulted from disciplined rehearsing. Recognizing the precarious economic times, board leaders reprinted an endorsement by Houston Chamber of Commerce President Hugh Potter in the first program: "The primary purpose of the Houston Symphony Orchestra Association is to make good music available to every man, woman and child in the community. . . . Beauty, art, science survive regardless of the severity of business and financial upheavals; in fact, at such a time they are of most service to mankind."[169]

When the symphony's 1932–1933 season ended, Ima's two beloved interests—the Child Guidance Clinic and the Symphony Association—seemed stable. However, the dedicated benefactor was denied a restful summer. After nearly four years of strenuous civic work, sharpened by financial worries and the loss of brother Will, Ima was physically and emotionally exhausted. Early in July she and Estelle Sharp set out for Rochester, Minnesota, to consult doctors at the Mayo Clinic about persistent back pain. Ima underwent orthopedic surgery on July 8 and was recuperating when she was diagnosed with phlebitis. This painful setback made her realize recuperation would be a long, slow process, and she wrote the Symphony Association board to suggest she resign. Her proposal caused panic and produced a spate of letters. Dr. Mullen explained that return of the "hepatic function" was "lazy" and could produce a blue mood, but he was sure she would "beat old man depression." Florence

Hogue, exclaimed, "The symphony . . . never would have developed had it not been for your optimism generosity and genius" and resignation "would disturb the confidence of the public and delay subscription." In September members tried to convince Ima to accept the presidency, but she adamantly refused any official responsibility and insisted, successfully, that her name be removed from programs for the November concerts, although it returned to the board roster a month later.[170]

In October Ima relocated to the Wyatt Clinic in Tucson and remained there as an outpatient living at the Arizona Inn until February 1934. Despite the painful illness, Ima stayed engaged with her Houston activities, and she asked Hogg Brothers' Office Manager H. E. Brigham to ship her beloved terrier Gilley, some music books, and her "dumb piano"—a dummy keyboard she used to exercise her fingers—to Arizona. Her extensive correspondence with friends continued, and brother Tom was able to spend time with her. On November 8 Mike shared news of "a long confab with brother St. Leger" about the "intrigues of your Symphony Orchestra." The "ins and outs," he said, "are the usual things that will happen when you have to run an organization . . . on a shoestring." St. Leger sent her a cheery letter in late November about Drusilla Huffmaster's talent and his hopes for the season. Julia Ideson admonished her valued friend to "stand up to a little loneliness." Knowing Ima's self-deprecating tendencies well, the librarian continued, "How can you be such poor company for yourself when you are such good company for others? . . . Oh Ima win some happiness from the experience. Don't let it hurt you." Estelle Sharp joined the invalid for Christmas, and Alice wished her sister-in-law a "happy Christmas" and assured her that "Mickey says he is giving you his heart." In January Ima's trusted housekeeper Gertrude Vaughn wrote to say she had attended the symphony concert, and the crowd was the "largest of the season." It was time to go home, and Ima's recuperative exile ended in February when she returned, refreshed, to her busy civic life.[171]

Ima discovered that St. Leger's musicians sounded better, but his unchallenging programs bored the orchestra's most ardent supporters. When St. Leger's contract expired at the end of his third season, Symphony Association President Joseph Smith, who held the post from 1934 to 1936, did not immediately opt to renew. An advertisement in the April 15, 1935, concert program contained an ominous announcement from competitor Edna Saunders, who would be bringing star violinist Fritz Kreisler, acclaimed pianist Josef Hofmann, and the eighty-man St. Louis Symphony Orchestra to Houston during the 1935–1936 season; it was clearly time for the Symphony Association to find a

Gertrude Anderson Vaughn, housekeeper for Ima Hogg. Camh-dob-012141m Ima Hogg Photographs, Dolph Briscoe Center for American History, University of Texas at Austin.

conductor who would push the orchestra to a higher level of excellence. While in New York with Symphony Association Music Committee members Mary Fuller, Joseph Mullen, and Mrs. Herbert Roberts, Ima had "already taken steps" to find a replacement. St. Leger, sensing a lack of support, secured a position with the Metropolitan Opera Company and moved to New York. Ima and the Music Committee studied twenty-three applications and recommended hiring three well-regarded guest conductors—Vittorio Verse, Modeste Alloo, and Alfred Hertz—while actively continuing the search during the 1935–1936 season. Critics acclaimed the "significant step forward"; large, curious audiences relished programs that raised the level of play; and musicians rose to the challenge of three demanding directorial styles. The experiment reassured doubters, who had complained about rising operational costs—from $12,000 in 1930 to $16,000 in 1936.[172]

In May and June 1936 Ima conducted a one-woman reorganization of the Symphony Association when Joseph Smith announced he wished to retire as president. As chairwoman of the board nominating committee, she invited several prominent Houston men to Bayou Bend one afternoon in May. Upon entering the house, each guest received a cup of Ima's well-laced fish house punch and a note stating he had been named the new association president. After several rounds of punch and persuasion and much laughter, Baker, Botts, Andrews & Wharton lawyer Walter Walne accepted the post of president, which he held until 1942; oilman Harry Wiess and Ima agreed to serve as vice presidents. To secure business support, the new team asked Walne's partner Jesse Andrews to serve as chairman of the search committee for a new conductor and announced that cotton broker William L. Clayton would form a committee of powerful businessmen to fund the projected $30,000 budget. On June 14 Ima entertained a membership group at Bayou Bend to announce results of a whirlwind subscription campaign, and on June 30 she hosted the search committee deliberations that named Ernst Hoffmann as new conductor. Ima's check for $1,000 led the July 4 donation list, one of only fifteen gifts of one hundred dollars or more. In November President Walne summarized his appreciation for Ima's impact: "The orchestra is obviously the child of your imagination and without your vision . . . judgment . . . and loyal support . . . Houston would have no orchestra today."[173]

Described as handsome, businesslike, and analytical, Hoffman had studied at Harvard University and the Berlin Conservatory for Music and was the son of a German violinist. Hoffman's German connections and commitment to high standards appealed to Ima. His willingness to do anything to help musicians endeared him to longtime Concertmaster Raphael Fliegel, who remembered the maestro as a "fine man" and "great conductor." The appointments of Walne and Hoffman heralded a decade of stability, and to celebrate the symphony's new leadership, the board rechristened its association the Houston Symphony Society. Ima worked closely with Hoffman to build the audience and supported his introduction of pop concerts, made popular in Boston "to indoctrinate young people with the critical importance of fine music." She continued to purchase tickets for public school teachers, deserving students, and charitable groups in an effort to ensure that everyone could experience symphonic music. By 1937 Ima had gained association approval for a tiered pricing structure, special matinee concerts for children at twenty-five cents a ticket, and auditorium sections reserved "for negroes at popular prices." Walne told the mayor in 1938 that the symphony was a major civic asset and an ambassador for Houston because it sponsored six regular concerts, six low-priced pop concerts, four school concerts, and four engagements in Beaumont and Galveston.[174]

Ima had long cajoled businessmen to underwrite the symphony with significant financial gifts, but from her first efforts in 1913, she relied heavily on women volunteers to do the hard work—canvassing subscribers, researching potential donors, planning fundraisers, finding instruments, entertaining musicians, working with children, and serving as ambassadors to the wider community. With Walter Walne's approbation, Ima formed the Women's Committee (renamed the Houston Symphony League in 1978), whose multifaceted mission would ensure financial stability, organize Houston's energetic women, and recognize their years of unsung service. In April 1937, now a mature fifty-five, Ima invited younger women to her home and asked them to help her "build an ever greater Orchestra." A veteran of twenty years' service credited Ima with the committee's success, recalling, "Like the conductor of her own orchestra . . . and with the greatest of artistic perfection [she] was able to evoke the best possible performance from each of the players." Ima kindled allegiance by holding meetings at Bayou Bend or other interesting places and by offering her friendship and guidance, and she wrote leaders of numerous women's organizations, seeking their affirmation for her new project. As the committee's first president from 1937 to 1939, she established subcommittees to handle each function of the committee; she made meetings fun; and she garnered lots of publicity. Under her aegis, the committee adopted bylaws, assumed responsibility for the subscription drive, introduced a gala fundraiser, and initiated a Children's Committee to supervise special activities for young Houstonians. As she passed the gavel to her successor, Ima announced that the Women's

Committee would inaugurate a maintenance fund drive to provide another source of revenue for the musicians.[175]

Houston newspaper editorials praised the symphony as a valuable cultural force, while reporters covered work sessions at Bayou Bend and devoted columns to the gala. During the 1937 subscription campaign, journalists noted that more than three hundred volunteers formed teams to canvas clubs, businesses, churches, schools, and residential areas. In 1938, the first year the orchestra performed in the spacious new Music Hall, a columnist opined that women working for three weeks at Bayou Bend checked twenty-two thousand names in seven hundred hours of labor while Ima's terriers Gilley and Bonney greeted and "bid a canine Godspeed" to every volunteer. Ima rewarded deserving volunteers with orchid corsages from her hothouse, and she was named "First Friend of the Symphony" in 1938. In 1939 the Women's Committee held a Viennese Ball at the Houston Country Club that netted $1,057. Ima closed a decade of visionary support for Houston's musical culture by inviting Tuesday Musical Club members and their friends to a musical tea at Bayou Bend on November 8, 1939, at 3:30 in the afternoon.[176]

Ima, Mike, and Alice: The Gardens

"A love affair with nature is a rewarding experience. It gladdens the eye and replenishes the spirit," wrote Ima Hogg near the end of her life. Ima's love affair began when she collected wildflowers as a child, and it never ended. When traveling, Ima hiked up mountains, tramped through forest glades, and strolled in flower-filled parks; as soon as she had a house of her own on Rossmoyne, she planted a garden. Even as the Hoggs planned their dream home, they thought about its garden and were careful to preserve trees where possible. After the site was staked in 1926, Will asked civil engineer Herbert Kipp to prepare a topographical plan and lay out the driveway, and he advised Ima to plant regional natives—magnolias, holly, wild peach, yaupon—and the Asian import, crepe myrtle, along the fringes of the property. The Hoggs hired Blume System Tree Experts in December 1926 to oversee the trees after arborist Dr. Conway Blume inventoried 128 hardwoods, including four kinds of oak and a rare paper birch. When imagining the Bayou Bend gardens, Ima recalled the dogwood near her window in Mineola, the irises that grew at Mountain Home and were transplanted to her father's gardens, the colorful borders her mother cultivated at the Texas Governor's Mansion, her grandfather's formal brick-edged beds filled with spring bulbs and roses, and her father's experiments with fruit trees and vegetables at Varner. She pictured her own rejuvenating paradise of repose—a Southern sanctuary reflecting family tradition and tenets of the country-house architects who used porches, loggias, and terraces to connect freestanding houses with surrounding garden rooms, stretches of lawn, and woodsy retreats. She began transforming the property by adding dogwood along the driveway, which curved gently from Lazy Lane through a wooded area to the south facade.[177]

In 1928 the Hoggs asked landscape architects Hare and Hare to prepare a garden plan. The grandiose, expensive design for extensive formal areas north and south of the house misinterpreted the Hoggs' intention to preserve the natural landscape and was never executed, although Ima did adopt the Hares' suggestions to extend a garden room east of the house and to terrace the area sweeping from the house to the bayou. The Hoggs also talked to landscape architect William H. Caldwell, president of Houston Landscaping Company, the firm employed by River Oaks Corporation. Caldwell produced plans for an east side garden, which influenced Ima's instructions to her three-man gardening team, but from 1929 until 1948 Ima kept meticulous garden books containing sketches and lists of plants that reveal she actually visualized the gardens. By May 17, 1929, Ima had installed two experimental gardens, and she decided to introduce them at a garden party. In the East Garden abutting the brothers' wing, the guests found multicolored annuals, perennials, and bulbs set in long, lateral strips, terminating in a crescent, with grass pathways separating the borders. On the north side, down the hill by the gardener's cottage, lay the second garden, shown in Ima's sketch as a formal parterre of brick walks and brick-edged beds in concentric circles around a central garden, all planted with annuals and perennials in Ima's favorite blue, white, and pink palette; later correspondence revealed her struggle to grow roses there. Two weeks after the gardens' debut, Bayou Bend suffered a terrible flood as heavy rainfall caused the bayou to overflow its banks on May 31 and undo Ima's handiwork. In August 1932 Bayou Bend withstood severe tree damage when a category four hurricane struck Freeport. In December 1935, runoff from heavy rain in the Hill Country and a deluge in Houston engulfed downtown, ruined the municipal water plant, and left the city with no water for drinking or fighting fires. At Bayou Bend, water rose waist-high in the downstairs and left marks visible until remodeling in the 1970s. Ima took refuge with Mike and Alice at Dogwoods and described the "great disaster" at her home, "completely swamped by a rushing stream of water." Undaunted, Ima reworked her gardens again and again, each time improving their beauty.[178]

To repair damage from the 1929 flood, Ima hired crews that summer to clean up debris and replace topsoil. In the winter and spring of 1930, Ima oversaw the addition of white spirea, bridal wreath, and cape jasmine gardenias to the woodlands, and that spring she experimented with seven azaleas, but her focus was the installation and nurturing of 210 rosebushes representing fifty varieties, many recommended by American Rose Society experts in the *American Rose Annual*, which she first ordered in 1930. That year Ima began adding plant material each spring and fall. Her library of garden books grew steadily as she educated herself about the demands of Gulf Coast horticulture. She placed orders herself, specifying every detail, including which blue pansy she preferred; and she wrote to engineers at the Agricultural and Mechanical College of Texas in College Station about the problems of Houston's truculent alkaline clay. Her first azaleas did not thrive. After trial and error with material supplied by Louisiana growers, Ima finally demanded vendors send dirt with the plants so she could have it analyzed. In mid-September 1930, Ima learned that Alvin Wheeler would begin work at Bayou Bend. For a decade Ima and Wheeler gradually developed the mix in which azaleas and camellias flourish, and Wheeler served as Ima's horticulture consultant for thirty years.

Early in 1931 Mike and Alice purchased Judge Proctor's Lazy Lane house, which they named Dogwoods, and the three Hoggs began talks with landscape architect Ruth London, who had recently joined Studio Gardens (1930–1937), a collaborative of artists and horticulturalists managed by Estelle Sharp and her partner Vera Baker Chinn.[179] For their adjoining properties, divided only by a shared driveway, the Hoggs chose plantings that became standard in Houston gardens—azaleas, camellias, bulbs to flower in the spring, and wax-leafed evergreen shrubs and trees to provide shady canopies year-round. In October 1931 Ima purchased Harold Hume's book *Azaleas and Camellias* and decided to try her first sweep of azaleas on the gentle slope north of the East Garden; she added another 250 azalea plants in December. In March and April 1932, Ima and Mike ordered their first camellias from Louisiana grower Clovis Chargois and famous horticulturalist Edward Avery McIlhenny[180] of Avery Island. A severe hurricane in August 1932 demanded major repairs and halted garden development, but Ima must have been satisfied by cleanup after the storm, because she entertained the College Women's Club at a late afternoon garden party on October 14 to honor the senior girls at Rice Institute and new club members.

While ill in 1933 and 1934, Ima maintained a lively correspondence about the gardens with H. E. Brigham. Shortly before her operation at the Mayo Clinic, Ima instigated the firing of her old German gardener, Fritz, and ordered twenty-nine loads of dirt and one ton of charcoal to rework all the beds. While recuperating, she remembered, "It is time for Wheeler to be sowing seeds for the fall garden. Enclosed is a list of seeds." In November 1933 she sent Brigham a drawing about where to plant camelias she had ordered through the River Oaks Corporation. In February 1934 Ima returned to Houston, rejuvenated and eager to work on her garden. She was pleased to learn that McIlhenny was now supplying azaleas and camellias to several Houston gardens and had opened a subsidiary of his Avery Island Jungle Gardens operation at the corner of River Oaks Boulevard and Westheimer, where it remained for several years. In March, Ima traveled to New Orleans, New Iberia, Baton Rouge, and Natchez to bask in beautiful weather and visit several outstanding gardens. Inspired by the trip, she decided to improve the East Garden and asked Ruth London to develop a plan, dated July 24, 1934, for what was to become the "Azalea Garden of Miss Ima Hogg" after a two-year period of construction.[181]

London incorporated the original lateral borders but created a formal room enclosed by evergreen hedges and marked by brick terraces and edging. The long rectangle terminated in an octagonal pool and fountain with terraces on either side. London also introduced small sculptures to the left and right of the central lawn, purchased a "Grecian settee" and other iron garden furniture from Weber Iron Works in New Orleans, and placed an iron gate in the hedge "wall" to separate the garden from the ravine below. Outside the hedges, London placed parallel allées of camellias; inside, she filled the borders with "wide banks of pink azaleas shading from pale to deep tones, beds of blue pansies and Dutch irises all blend[ed] in a harmony of exquisite loveliness." By August the garden had been staked and awaited Ima's approval so work could begin. Ima returned from summer travels and began ordering plant materials while London supervised construction, which continued for several months. While working on the East Garden, Ima transformed part of the woodland area into the distinct but still natural White Garden filled with dogwood and white-flowering shrubs. Alas, this hard work was nearly destroyed by the flood of December 1935, which so damaged the house that workmen were still "completing the new floors and painting the woodwork" a year later. With dogged tenacity, Ima, Mike, and Alice restored their gardens enough to join their Lazy Lane neighbors Katherine Bel and Harry Hanszen on March 22, 1936, for a special two-day house and garden pilgrimage preceding the River Oaks Garden Club's annual Azalea Trail. Ima introduced Houstonians to her East Garden, to her revamped White Garden, and to the unplanned Waterfall Garden, created when the East Garden fountain began to leak. Finding an unusual but simple solution, Ima revealed the beauty of natural drainage by allowing water to spill down a hill of ferns and greenery into a rocky tarn. She repeated this technique several times along the bayou fingers that edged the property.[182]

Ima's delight in her garden was enhanced by the knowledge that Mike and Alice were developing gardens next door, were experimenting with plant materials and designs, and had joined her in garden club activities. In 1924 seven friends had formed the Garden Club of Houston "to stimulate an interest in home gardening; to promote the knowledge and love of gardening among amateurs; to assist in the conservation of our native plants; to protect our native birds, and to encourage civic planting."[183] Not long after its founding, Ima joined the club, and three years later in the fall of 1927, she helped twenty-six residents organize the River Oaks Garden Club to study flowers and cultivation, to beautify backyards, to conserve wildflowers, and to sponsor garden shows and competitions. When Alice married Mike, Ima introduced her sister-in-law to both clubs. While Ima was always supportive and opened her home for tours and meetings, she never took a leadership role in either club and became an associate of the Garden Club of Houston in the early 1930s. Alice was twice chosen president of the River Oaks Garden Club (1931–1932 and 1938–1939) and frequently participated on important projects. Ima, Alice, and Mike all won prizes for horticulture and flower arrangements at club shows.

In 1931 the Garden Club of Houston became the first Southwestern club to join the Garden Club of America (GCA), founded by Philadelphia-area friends in 1913 as the first national association of garden clubs. In 1935 the Garden Club of Houston sponsored the River Oaks Garden Club for GCA membership. Following the spring 1937 GCA annual meeting, several GCA members stopped in Houston on their way to Mexico. The travelers were welcomed warmly and feted lavishly. Houston's homes and gardens, with their spacious lawns, masses of azaleas, and baskets of semitropical bougainvillea impressed some of America's most fastidious horticulturalists. After this visit, officers invited the Garden Club of Houston to host the GCA annual meeting in 1939, which was a great honor, since annual meetings had traditionally rotated among Philadelphia, Wilmington, New York, New Jersey, and once or twice New England. The Garden Club of Houston renewed its efforts to secure River Oaks Garden Club's membership in the national organization and asked its sister club to cosponsor the event. The prospect of entertaining the nation's most discerning gardeners caused a frenzy of garden design and replanting among the thirty-seven property owners who agreed to open their homes for touring every afternoon or for dinner parties, luncheons, and teas during the four-day event. Active members of both clubs tackled transportation and program planning, and Alice, River Oaks Garden Club president during the event itself, joined Ima on the entertainment committee.

Garden journalists, then as now, were widely read in the 1930s, and Houston gardeners and their clubs received warm praise for their civic stewardship—they aided clean-up weeks, supported garbage container drives, fought billboard proliferation, promoted legislation for bird and wildflower sanctuaries, and valued natural surroundings. The press and the chamber of commerce recognized that the annual meeting of the GCA was an honor to be prized and advertised. On October 3, 1938, reporters announced that the chamber of commerce had assured club planners that the chamber would help make the event a success. In January 1939 newspapers printed long articles explaining the program, listing the hostesses of lunches and dinners, and naming the officers of the GCA and the two host clubs.

Houstonians enjoyed a cascade of gardening activities during the first quarter of 1939. On January 27 and 28 the River Oaks Garden Club hosted its second annual camellia show in the River Oaks Country Club ballroom, where 150,000 camellias were displayed for public viewing. Ima Hogg received the GCA Sarah Todd medal, the first time it was awarded to someone who lived south of Atlanta. Her "most beautiful" exhibit was a dining table adorned at one end with an enthroned Madonna decorated with camellias and at the other end and along each side with Venetian glass figurines holding gleaming gold tapers. Runners of golden ivy and camellias completed the award-winning arrangement.[184] On February 12, Libbie Masterson opened the National Flower Show at Sam Houston Coliseum and welcomed exhibits from forty-six Houston, Texas, and out-of-state garden clubs. The River Oaks Garden Club held its third annual Azalea Trail on February 25–26 and previewed four new gardens, including Ima's Diana Garden and the Woodland Garden created by Mike and Alice along the bayou edge of their property.

By the time nearly three hundred GCA annual meeting attendees checked into the Rice Hotel on Tuesday, February 28, 1939, the city's premier hostesses and their gardens were ready. Each attendee received a program book listing the officers of the GCA and the two host clubs; the organizers and hostesses for the event; the daily programs; and a one-page photograph and description of each garden to be visited. For four days members attended lectures and meetings in the morning and toured houses and gardens in the afternoon; the evenings were reserved for dinners in private homes and two spectacular early evening tea events. The meeting closed with an optional trip down the ship channel and afternoon tea at The Oaks, the much-admired seven-acre formal garden surrounded by specimen trees that was home to widower Captain James A. Baker and his daughter and Garden Club of Houston member Alice Baker Jones.

Ima began thinking about developing Bayou Bend's north lawn in the mid-1930s. From the window of her upstairs sitting room, where she spent many hours listening to radio concerts, examining things she loved, or playing her piano with musical friends, Ima could look toward the bayou and imagine a beautiful garden in the space. In the spring of 1937, with the GCA meeting only two years away, Ima attended a camellia show in Lafayette, Louisiana, and visited E. A. McIlhenny on Avery Island. Brimming with ideas, she ordered several mature azaleas and eight camellias for November delivery. She had bought several grafted camellias from McIlhenny before her trip, and during her visit she discussed the special white-pink "Missima" camellia he was developing for her. When she returned to Houston, Ima focused on plans for the central sweep of the north lawn. By the time she departed for her summer trip to Europe with Julia Ideson, Ima had overseen recontouring of the lawn and had designed shallow, grassy steps from the terrace toward the bayou. Her work crew had raised the wall separating the garage area from the main lawn by three feet to obscure the dependency, and Ima had ordered new hedges between the west garden and a new garden room planned for the end of the lawn.

As usual when traveling, Ima corresponded with H. E. Brigham about ongoing work in Houston and about her discoveries abroad. In Florence, Ima visited the studio of sculptor Antonio Frilli, who produced garden statuary, benches, and urns, and she confided to Brigham that she was considering life-size garden statues, provided she could bargain a good price. While Julia Ideson reveled in old manuscripts and libraries, Ima browsed at competing studios, trying to decide whether to buy one or three statues. When the friends returned in September, Ima ordered a replica of *Diana of Versailles* with a green marble plinth, several Roman-style urns, and garden benches from the Frilli studio, sending the sculptor a check for $384.10 as a down payment and securing his promise the statue would be completed before the 1939 GCA meeting. *Diana* arrived at Bayou Bend in December 1937. By the time Ima decided she would also like replicas of Clio and Euterpe, she placed the order too late for delivery before the GCA event.[185]

Although Ima had worked amicably with Ruth London on the East Garden (or Azalea Garden), she does not seem to have consulted her after 1937. Ima was acquainted with the doyenne of garden design—New York landscape architect Ellen Biddle Shipman—and had heard her lecture in Houston in 1935. Ima knew that Shipman had previously installed life-size statues with reflecting pools and was currently designing gardens for Lottie and Stephen P. Farish in River Oaks and for Laura Rice Neff on South Boulevard. Coincidentally, Shipman was speaking in Houston, and on January 15 Ima and Shipman met to discuss the *Diana* project. A single consultation fee payment suggests that Ima took Shipman's advice about placement of the statue in relation to a reflecting pool. On January 22 Ima met with C. C. "Pat" Fleming, a young landscape architect who had recently opened offices with Albert Sheppard. Ensuing appointments and a rough sketch show that Fleming and Sheppard oversaw installation of the Diana Garden, while they also helped Alice and Mike Hogg and three other participants prepare for the GCA Annual Meeting. As always, Ima was intensely engaged in the project; her ideas controlled the garden's design; she fretted over the removal of a tree; and she placed large orders for mature plants with several growers. She also decided where she would locate the Clio and Euterpe statues—the former at the center of her West Garden, and the latter directly opposite Clio in a less formal garden niche created by a hedge of Japanese yew and shaded by a magnificent loblolly pine and a towering American sycamore. As was her custom, Ima left completion of the project to Fleming and Sheppard while she was away for the summer. On July 12, 1938, Ima and Dot Thornton sailed on the *Deutschland* for two months of music and travel in a Europe trembling on the brink of war. Ima returned in September to be with Mike and Alice in Baltimore, where Mike was recuperating from an August 10 operation. October found all three Hoggs back in Houston, where final preparations for the GCA visit were well under way.[186]

Ima Hogg and Olga Wiess were scheduled to entertain GCA attendees for late afternoon tea on the second evening of the GCA conclave, and they wanted to astonish their guests by installing little-tested outdoor lighting in their reflecting pools and surrounding landscape. No one in Houston had experienced outdoor lighting, and there is no report of the Wiess attempt, but years later Albert Sheppard described a month of nighttime trial and error under Ima's critical eye as he and Pat Fleming experimented with unreliable lighting technology. Soft rain fell on Wednesday as GCA delegates arrived at their assigned gardens. Bayou Bend guests entered from Lazy Lane and remained in the house, admiring their hostess's handsome interiors and beautiful floral displays. Ima waited patiently until a few ventured outside into the misty twilight and discovered the garden was "magical in the silvery rain." Delighted cries drew everyone onto the north terrace under its protective portico to experience the "miracle of a very subtle and complete scheme of illumination"—a brightly lit *Diana,* dramatically floodlit trees, and arching jets of water spraying from either side of a lighted rectangular reflecting pool.[187]

While perhaps the most theatrical moment of the week, Ima's tea shared praise with other remarkable events. Alice and Mike Hogg's woodland garden "of exquisite beauty" had transformed a ravine into "an extensive Azalea Trail [that] winds toward rock-ledged pools and waterfalls" banked with azaleas, dogwood, and wisteria. On Thursday guests arrived for high tea and lingered into the evening hours at the extensive gardens of Azalea Court, the grand home and gardens created by John Staub for Lillie and Hugh Roy Cullen. Burning tapers protected by hurricane lamps lit the scene as guests strolled from garden to garden, serenaded by a woodwind ensemble from the Houston Symphony. The July 1939 *Architecture Magazine* reported that not a single garden illustrated in the article was older than fifteen years; the greatest lesson from the visit, in the writer's opinion, was "the accomplishment that can be wrought with the quick and lush growth possible in a semitropical region." Houston pacesetters viewed the results differently. Houston was not well known to most of the country in 1939, but after four days spent with the city's most respected gardeners, GCA delegates realized that Houstonians were hiring nationally recognized city planners, garden designers, and architects to reinvent their sultry bayou city as a sophisticated, livable metropolis. A businessman told one reporter, "In Houston garden clubs are behind every movement for the betterment of the city and bring great value to civic life."[188]

Following the GCA meeting triumph, Ima continued to make her gardens accessible to the public for musicales, dramatic presentations, and garden tours. She supported local garden club activities and began to attend GCA meetings. On June 5, 1940, Ima told garden club members about shrubs and plants she had seen at GCA events in Virginia and Maryland that might flourish in Houston. From 1943 through 1946, she served as a director of the GCA, working on the admissions and board nominating committees. While attending GCA events, Ima met renowned gardener and GCA official Louise du Pont Crowninshield,[189] who introduced her new Texas friend to her brother, the voracious collector Henry Francis du Pont. In 1941 and 1942, Ima added one more garden to the series of rooms and surprises she had created in the 1930s. On a stretch of lawn east of the driveway at the edge of the woods, she placed a modest but charming blaze of color in the shape of a butterfly, its wings, antennae, and body outlined in brick laid by Fred Eckert, the mason who built the Diana Garden pool and made pedestals for Clio and Euterpe. In the wings, Ima first planted blue pansies and annuals of various colors, but after a few seasons she changed

Performance in the Diana Garden at Bayou Bend, 1940s. Henry Southerland. Camh-dob-012146, Ima Hogg Photographs, Dolph Briscoe Center for American History, University of Texas at Austin

to Kurume azaleas in several shades of pink, framed by boxwood borders. For the next two decades, Ima maintained the beauty of these gardens. In March 1955 the Garden Club of America again held its annual meeting in Houston, and Ima welcomed delegates to Bayou Bend as the event's hospitality chairwoman.

Memorializing Will: The Hogg Foundation

Will's death did not diminish the Hogg family's presence in Texas; instead, memorializing their brother opened new avenues of philanthropy to Ima and Mike. After Will died, friends and colleagues praised his exceptional generosity, soaring vision, and resourceful personality. In 1933 the Museum of Fine Arts installed a plaque near the 1924 entrance to recognize Will's relentless fundraising campaigns, his constant advocacy for a people's museum, and his many endearing virtues. In 1940 Will's admiring friend, the pathbreaking Texas musicologist and folklorist John Avery Lomax (1867–1948), wrote a glowing biography for the *Atlantic Monthly,* which filled Ima with last-minute foreboding but was fully vetted by Mike. Will's final testament made bequests to friends, relatives, and domestic employees; it established student loan funds at every college and university in Texas; it funded six scholarships at the University of Texas; and it stipulated that Ima and Mike could use his personal belongings, pictures, and furniture during their lifetimes, after which everything would be given to Houston's Museum of Fine Arts or to a "proper" department at the University of Texas. Most important, Will requested his executors, Ima and Mike, to use the "rest and residue" of his estate in one of three ways: to launch a vocational school for poor boys and girls in Brazoria County as a memorial to James and Sarah Stinson Hogg; to create a lecture foundation at the University of Texas to attract scholars of "proved learning"; or to support a foundation "for the common good of all or any part of Texas" to which his siblings would later contribute a part of their estates.[190]

While traveling with her brother that fateful summer of 1930, Ima shared her concerns about mental health care, a topic that recalled their father's interest. She renewed these discussions with Mike, stressing that her "own field of special interest in which I knew that . . . Will concurred, was that of mental health." Remembering Will's devotion to the University of Texas and anxious to secure funding for mental health care on a broad scale, Ima urged Mike to choose option three—the creation of a foundation for the "common good" of all Texans—and place it under University of Texas supervision. This foundation would also address option two by attracting scholars of "proved learning." Mike agreed with his sister and for the next decade used his business skills to wrest maximum value from Will's estate. The Great Depression and Will's far-flung business investments, which included moviemaking in Hollywood, the Findex filing system, a deepwater port in Corpus Christi, seventy-nine properties, coal mines in Kentucky and Tennessee, and options on gold mines in Mexico, challenged Mike's ingenuity, but by 1938 he had fulfilled Will's testamentary obligations and had sold the family share of River Oaks to Hugh Potter for "about $1,250,000." The siblings then dissolved Hogg Brothers and distributed its assets among Will's estate, Ima, Mike, and Tom.[191]

Ima, too, needed time to refine her vision and to persuade University of Texas President Homer Rainey, the board of regents, and administration officials that her plan would add value to the university. She wrote foundation experts for advice, and she benefitted from her experience with the Houston Child Guidance Clinic. Ima relied on the teaching of two significant mentors: Dr. Austen Riggs, who asserted that every person must have purpose in his or her life; and Dr. William C. Menninger, who believed "no one is perfectly balanced in life—everyone needs help."[192] As a result of her deliberations, Ima, with Mike's enthusiastic approval, established a unique institution, the first foundation in the United States devoted solely to positive mental health care for families. To guarantee effective professional management, Ima placed the foundation under the board of regents; and to safeguard her primary purpose—to educate Texans in the art of better living by nurturing positive mental health through social justice, education, and community participation—she embedded the Hogg Foundation for Mental Hygiene within the academic structure of the University of Texas. Ima promised that she and her brothers would support the foundation financially, that family members would serve only as advisers, and that the foundation director and his team would have free rein to develop the institution within the broad parameters of the family's gift.

"Whispers From the State Capitol" columnist D. B. Hardeman was among the first to embrace the "social significance" of a press release to the nation announcing the Hoggs' gift in July 1939. Hardeman praised the "first important move in Texas to study the prevention, rather than the cure and treatment, of mental diseases," and he noted that the Hogg Foundation for Mental Hygiene (renamed the Hogg Foundation for Mental Health in December 1957) was "expected to prevent a great deal of human loss" and "bring the university closer to the people and . . . make it a vital force in the life of the state." Stephen Pinckney, lawyer for Will Hogg's estate, presented more than $1.8 million to form a private foundation administered by the public university and controlled by the publicly appointed board of regents. Letters of praise flooded Ima's mailbox. Leopold Meyer, who shared board duties with Ima at the Houston Child Guidance Clinic, was "really stunned with joy" by the announcement. Ima believed that the unique structure would secure funds for controversial work, would force the public sector to consider mental health issues, and would enable community leaders, university scholars, and government officials to cooperate. For thirty-five years, Ima periodically restated her thinking and highlighted the foundation's central purposes: to assist those in need; to address a broad public constituency; and to provide a public platform for advocacy and reform. The foundation would create programs of its own, would make grants to communities and individuals, and would favor pilot programs matched by community funds. The pioneering effort to stress positive mental health, rather than mental illness or insanity, lay at the core of the foundation's mission; and its focus included isolated rural communities, small towns, African American and Hispanic Texans, and all those who struggled to build a wholesome life.

The foundation would accomplish its goals through consultation, integration, and cooperation at the local level.[193]

In the fall of 1939, Homer Rainey conferred with the Commonwealth Fund's George Stevenson and with Ima, who was on vacation in Mexico, before he organized an advisory search committee to find a director. The committee comprised Ima, several doctors, Houston Child Guidance Clinic Director J. P. Malloy, Irene Conrad of the Houston Community Chest, Gaynell Hawkins of the Dallas Civic Federation, and three influential experts Ima suggested—Austen Riggs, Johns Hopkins Hospital psychiatrist-in-chief Adolf Meyer, and University of Texas home economics Professor Mary Deering. After six months of meetings, the committee recommended Robert Lee Sutherland (1903–1976) to the regents, who offered Sutherland the position on June 15, effective September 1, 1940. Colleagues described Sutherland as a man of "compassion, empathy, and modesty" whose "remarkable capacity for detecting common ground, . . . regardless of background and political persuasion" enabled him to build lasting relationships. President Rainey knew the nominee well and recommended him highly. A native Iowan who was educated at Knox College (BA), Oberlin University (MA), and the University of Chicago (PhD), Sutherland was former associate director of the American Youth Commission and professor of sociology, dean of men, and chairman of counseling at Bucknell University. A college debater, Sutherland had written an "outstanding" dissertation that analyzed African American life in Chicago, and he specialized in social ethics. The new director and Ima discovered many mutual interests and immediate rapport. As soon as Sutherland arrived in Texas, Ima invited him and his "lovely family" to meet with her on October 5 at Bayou Bend, the first of many visits that nurtured a mutual enthusiasm for exploring visionary objectives. Ima and Sutherland discussed mental hygiene work in Texas, and Ima proposed he attend a conference of social workers that Ima, Mike, and Alice were hosting in Houston on November 19. The Hoggs introduced the newly appointed director of their new Hogg Foundation to "about two hundred social workers, educators, and others" at a conference and dinner held at the River Oaks Country Club. Sutherland outlined his plans for the foundation, explained its goal to help individuals "get complete enjoyment out of community life," and invited all guests to attend an inaugural Hogg Foundation conference, scheduled for February 1941. Ima in turn asked Sutherland to stay at Bayou Bend whenever he came to Houston.[194]

The inaugural Home and Family Life Conference, held February 11–13 in the Hogg Memorial Auditorium, demonstrated the convening model on which future work would be based. Social service providers, academics, political figures,

Robert Lee Sutherland, director of the Hogg Foundation for Mental Health, 1940–1971, with a photograph of William C. Hogg. Camh-dob-013492, Dolph Briscoe Center for American History, University of Texas at Austin.

and civic leaders met in discussion groups to explore mental health strategies. At the official inauguration on Wednesday evening, February 12, President Rainey affirmed the Hoggs' vision for a positive, preventive, therapeutic approach to issues. Echoing Hogg family beliefs, Rainey explained, "The home lays the foundation for the whole of American democracy in its individual, group, and institutional relations." The foundation will recognize family problems, he said, an approach that will "play the most important role in the redirection of education in the next 20 years—mental health for the normal man." In 1941 Texas ranked last among states for mental health care, and the Hogg

Foundation's convening mechanism provided a novel way to resolve the inherent conflict between local participation and expert management. By working in communities, foundation staffers hoped to expand services, inform citizens, and reorganize the state system of mental health care delivery. Sutherland announced that during its first year the foundation would make no project grants; instead, he and his assistant would travel about the state holding seminars, learning from local leaders, and explaining how sound mental hygiene would enhance all phases of community life. Ima attended the inaugural conference and exclaimed, "It was a joy to me to have the opportunity of listening in on the able talks and discussions." Sutherland won her trust when he "so graciously made me feel a part of this splendid work." During the next three decades, the ardent director discovered "the daring and breadth of [Ima's] ideas" and her "wisdom and skill in thinking through practical methods" for attaining her goals. She introduced him to potential supporters and defended his actions to regents and university presidents who wondered why a community service foundation was managed by an academic institution. He kept her informed and sought her advice because she provided wise guidance. She invited the Sutherlands to attend symphony concerts and sent his family books, flowers, and grapefruit.[195]

Sadly, Mike did not live to see the flowering of the foundation he had worked so hard to create. His August 1938 operation at Johns Hopkins was a harbinger of declining health, but Mike remained busy. In 1939 he joined the Museum of Fine Arts, Houston Board of Trustees, while Ima served on the Endowment Committee. In 1939 and 1940 he served on a state commission charged with creating a Jim Hogg Memorial Park, a project he turned over to Ima for later completion. In January 1940 Mike visited his grandfather Hogg's property where Mountain Home had provided a happy childhood for Mike's father. Although the house had been demolished years before, the property was for sale. Mike persuaded Ima and Tom to help him purchase what remained of the property, and the siblings conveyed the land to Cherokee County for a nature park. Deeply concerned about Franklin D. Roosevelt's precedent-breaking campaign to seek a third term, Mike launched the "No-Third-Term" movement in Texas on August 30, 1940, at Fair Park Auditorium in Dallas. He urged the crowd to "assure the preservation of the Republic" and to support Republican Wendell L. Willkie, "who will lead us out of chaos and back into the democratic way." Mike agreed to be advisory chairman for the Texas Democrats-For-Willkie committee. He canvassed hundreds of donors, campaigned vigorously all over the state, and convinced his sister to make her "maiden and farewell political" talk on KTRH radio. On October 10, 1940, Ima called on fellow Democrats to support the "Democratic-Republican candidate for President" and restore the two-term rotation in office so important to her father. Ima's speech was a hit, and she confessed, "I got a kick out of expressing myself over the radio." When Willkie lost, Mike graciously urged everyone to support President Roosevelt, and he pledged "wholehearted allegiance to a re-united America." The intense two-month campaign exhausted Mike, and following the November 19 dinner for Robert Sutherland, he left for Baltimore and a complete checkup at Johns Hopkins Hospital.[196]

The results were not favorable, although Mike told friends he felt fine. He could not attend the February 1941 Family Life Conference at the Hogg Foundation, but he continued to consult with Sutherland. On May 1, 1941, his long-time hunting companion Irvin Cobb, not in good health himself, wrote sadly to "Alice Honey" that he was "distressed that dear old Mickie doesn't get better any faster." A medical consultation that summer showed the malignancy identified in November had spread and was inoperable. Mike had been running a fever for some time and had not improved on August 11, when Robert Sutherland wrote, "knowing that you were not feeling too well," to bring him up to date about Hogg Foundation activities. Confined to his bed for the last weeks of his life, Mike prepared his final testament on September 18, and on October 10, he succumbed to the long struggle with cancer, attended by his beautiful wife and loving sister. A quiet funeral at Dogwoods followed, with the Reverend Charles Sumners of St. David's Episcopal Church in Austin officiating. Mourners accompanied the casket on Mike's final journey to Austin, where he was buried with his parents and brother in Oakwood Cemetery. Writing to Mike's "oldest and dearest friend" Raymond Dickson, Irvin Cobb expressed sorrow that his wife Laura's illness prevented him from being in Houston to celebrate their dear mutual friend, who "died as he had lived—with courage, with unselfishness, with fortitude." An admiring public remembered Mike as a "quiet man, actuated by the highest ideals," while close friends recalled a loveable extrovert with a great sense of humor who gave "untiring" service to business and "invariably cheerful and optimistic" inspiration to others. Mike took a keen interest in public affairs and found "a distinct resemblance between the life and practices of a family and the life and practices of a nation." He named Alice sole executrix of a will that framed the future of Hogg family holdings. His interest in the Remington Collection went to Ima, and then to the Museum of Fine Arts, Houston; his share of Varner Plantation was divided between Ima and Tom during their lives, and then conveyed to the State of Texas; and the residue of his estate was reserved to his wife for her lifetime, and then given to the University of Texas Board of Regents to establish a "Department of Municipal Government" to train women and men for service. Brother Tom, "ill and on the move," wrote Ima on November 5 that his thoughts for her and Alice were "ever present." He was "deeply grateful" for their "Christian fortitude and courage during this trying episode . . . [which were] an inspiration not only to me but to those around you." Ima and Alice made gifts to a Mike Hogg Memorial Fund to train visiting teachers through the Hogg Foundation.[197]

On Her Own: The 1940s

With Mike Hogg's death, Ima Hogg became president of the Hogg family interests, and in November she wrote Alice, Tom Hogg, and staff members of Hogg Brothers and its affiliated companies that there would be changes, although she could never "fill the place occupied by my dear departed brothers." She closed the letter as her father had concluded many of his, "May a wise Providence guide us in our course." Ima had spent many hours talking to her father and brothers about the family businesses, and Mike had explained his activities to Alice shortly before his death, but neither woman was an entrepreneur, and Tom had always been a passive partner. Ima hoped to manage the family's assets effectively but not engage in new ventures. She replaced the in-house legal staff of three lawyers, a secretary, and a treasurer with one executive and outside counsel. Loyal business manager H. E. Brigham wished to retire and was given livestock and a lifetime occupancy of the Oil Cottage at Varner as rewards for long service. Ima, Alice, and Tom employed William Booker Ferguson, Hogg Brothers treasurer and comptroller since 1921, as executive vice president of Varner Company and Hogg Oil and as general manager of joint properties held by Hogg family members. Alice retained Baker, Botts, Andrews & Wharton attorneys to probate Mike's will, handle his estate, and assist her with ongoing legal business.[198]

Tom spent more time with his siblings in the 1930s. In February 1935, H. E. Brigham told Mike that Tom wanted to run Varner Plantation, noting he believed Tom could "render quite a service" because he was always happiest when working with horses and livestock. Brigham foresaw that Tom would spend more money than Brigham would but felt the occupation might keep the youngest brother from "running up bills" and "taking up with the wrong kind of person." The experiment worked briefly, but in September 1936 Mike wrote Ima, who was in Munich, that Tom was "in one of his periodical tail-spins" and

"Marie was getting very peculiar notions." He reported that Tom and Marie, with two doctors and their wives, were taking a rest cure in Canada. Perhaps the respite helped because Tom, who was now separated from Marie, wrote Ima on Thanksgiving eve 1936 that he had much to be thankful for and was eagerly awaiting his visit with her, Mike, and Alice after many years. Following his divorce, Tom continued to struggle with alcohol, smoked incessantly, and was never able to manage money. In 1939 he overcame an attack of congestive heart failure and swollen ankles, but after a bout of pneumonia in March 1942, he surprised his sister on May 21, when he telegraphed word of his noonday marriage in Quincy, Illinois, to Margaret Wells. Hoping that Tom had found a strong companion, Ima welcomed her new sister-in-law warmly, sent her a "most gorgeously beautiful coffee service," and began a cheerful correspondence that boded well for the future.[199]

Thinking about ways to celebrate Will's life and fulfill his wishes had made Ima consider the fate of her works on paper and her Native American artifacts. During her tenure as chairwoman of the Houston museum's accessions committee (1927–1928 and 1930–1931) Ima realized the challenges and expense of acquiring works of art for a municipal museum, and now she hoped to diversify museum holdings by donating her collections. Ima bought works on paper in spurts, making about forty purchases during her 1929 European adventure and her 1930 trip with Will. In the fall of 1931, while touring in Mexico City, she added her first watercolors by Mexican artist Roberto Montenegro. That winter in New York City, Ima procured a dozen works by German expressionists from visiting Dresden dealer L. W. Gutbier, including color lithographs by Wassily Kandinsky, watercolors by Ernst Ludwig Kirchner and Max Pechstein, woodcuts by Franz Marc and Karl Schmidt-Rottluff, and etchings by Käthe Kollwitz and Emil Nolde. On interwar trips to Mexico, Ima added works by José Clemente Orozco and Diego Rivera, as well as several more Montenegro watercolors and drawings. She also acquired four lithographs by American icon Rockwell Kent and three woodcuts by German Renaissance genius Albrecht Dürer (1471–1528), whose work influenced early twentieth-century German artists. Ima's purchase of three lithographs by prominent Japanese American artist Yasuo Kuniyoshi and one lithograph by acclaimed American realist painter George Bellows introduced Houstonians to these artists. By 1937 Ima felt her collection, which included three Ina O. Cassidy lithographs of Native American life and the first John Singer Sargent work in Houston, represented a broad introduction to works on paper in several media, and she offered to transfer to the Museum of Fine Arts, Houston all but the great Picasso pastel

Three Women at the Fountain (1921), which she retained until 1969, when she moved this beloved work to the museum . Following necessary cataloguing and curatorial work, Ima placed her works on paper at the museum on June 14, 1939. Director James Chillman told his patron that her donation "enriched the collections many fold" while individual items embodied "high artistic value."[200]

The transfer of her works on paper had been so seamless that Ima decided to donate her "North American Indian Collection." Except for a few objects on view in the Bayou Bend library, Ima's Native American artifacts acquired in the late 1920s had been placed on long-term loan at the museum—some pieces purchased with a "museum discount" and shipped directly to the museum from the vendor. During a three-month visit to Santa Fe in 1934, Ima bought silver and turquoise jewelry and ceramics at the Old Santa Fe Trading Post and visited Ina Sizer Cassidy, who sold her sixty-one Hopi kachina figures, four musical instruments, and one large jar collected by Cassidy between 1912 and 1933. When Ima discovered the kachinas had been stolen, she tried to return them. However, the Hopi believed these sacred messengers to the spirit world were desecrated when taken from the pueblo and would not accept them. Reminded of the pitfalls of collecting, Ima wrote to experts at the School of American Research in Santa Fe and to state agencies in Albuquerque to discover the ethnography of nineteenth-century examples and to gather information about contemporary artists, in particular the Martinez family of potters from Pueblo San Ildefonso, whose work she admired and purchased. Ima continued collecting on trips in 1935 and 1942 and participated in two summer exhibits at the museum: a 1936 exhibit of thirty-five paintings and a 1942 exhibit of 129 objects that was expanded in the fall to a show of four hundred artifacts by pueblo artists. In 1941 Ima told Director James Chillman she wished to make the loans permanent. In August and November 1943 Ima corresponded with John Bullington, chairman of the museum board, to make final arrangements for the transfer, effective January 20, 1944. Ima reserved the right to borrow items of jewelry—which she did several times. She made her gift anonymously and stipulated that it go to another museum if Houston's Museum of Fine Arts could not use the contents. She wished the objects to be labeled "Bayou Bend Collection," despite the anonymity request, and she provided $1,200 to construct exhibit cases. Ima's transfer method—loan exhibitions, convenient timing, verified value, and additional funding—generated public interest and allowed Ima to take advantage of tax laws. Her gift launched the museum's Department of Southwest Art and presaged the Art of the Americas Collection.[201]

Family members always assumed the Hogg Brothers' Remington Collection would be placed at the Museum of Fine Arts. After his two major shopping sprees in 1920, Will made a few more purchases, and until the final transfer, Hogg Brothers continued its generous loan program to museum exhibits. When Ima reduced the number of Hogg Brothers employees and closed the roof garden offices after Mike's death, she hired Dallas Art Museum Conservator Charles Muskovitch in January 1942 to analyze conservation needs of the family's collection. Satisfied that the paintings, drawings, and sculptures were in museum-worthy condition, Ima negotiated an agreement, effective May 18, 1943, whereby she and Tom conveyed the entire collection to the Museum of Fine Arts, Houston. She stipulated that the collection be installed as a unit, that it not be loaned, and that it be given to the University of Texas or some other museum in Texas if the Houston museum could no longer exhibit the works. Ima made one exception: in 1973 when the collection was reinstalled in the recently completed Brown Pavilion, she allowed works of "inferior quality" to be sold so the acquisitions committee could add *Cotopaxi* by Frederick Edwin Church (1826–1900) to the museum's holdings of works by American artists.[202]

In 1942 Ima bought a brass candlestick, the first object of Americana she had purchased since 1928. After Mike's death, when she was considering the future of her collections, she worried that the number of objects at Bayou Bend might overwhelm a museum setting. She and Ray L. Dudley, Museum of Fine Arts board president from 1941 to 1943, began discussing the future of Bayou Bend and its amazing assemblage of American decorative arts dating from 1650 to 1850. Dudley gently "urged" her to place the property and its furnishings under the museum's appreciative and expert guidance. At first, "seemingly insurmountable obstacles" made her uneasy, but she allowed the seed Dudley planted to take root, and she began formulating the message she wished to convey through her gift. Her works on paper brought examples of great European, Mexican, and American masters to Houston; her Southwest Collection conserved the vanishing pueblo culture of Western states; the Hogg Brothers Remington Collection explored cowboy culture of the Old West. Ima and Will were prescient, even rebel, collectors. They recognized new genres and redefined "art" to include sophisticated painting and sculpture; decorative furniture, ceramics, and metal wares; and pueblo artifacts and domestic quilts. They refused to prioritize the importance of any artistic expression. They were among the first collectors to see the importance of material culture as a tool to explain the past. Now Ima would be able to show that art made in America was as "fine" as art made anywhere, but how could the objects at Bayou Bend be arranged to explain her insights and illuminate America's story? She had not articulated her answer when she began once more to collect systematically.[203]

Ima turned to New York's foremost dealers to find new treasures. At first, she depended on their discerning judgment, but after closely studying rich woods, graceful curves, and superior craftsmanship, she "soon learned to recognize value[her]self" and "to know [what] was genuine." In 1943 she purchased a pair of New York Chippendale-style side chairs from Ginsburg and Levy to enlarge her colonial period holdings. That year she made her first purchases of early nineteenth-century furniture for the collection—two pairs of Grecian chairs, one with a lyre back from Israel Sack and one with an eagle back from Ginsburg and Levy, choices that reflected Ima's love of music and her patriotism. In 1944 Ima bought a nine-piece Rococo Revival parlor set from New York dealer Carll Chace for the Blue Room, her brothers' former sitting room. The prescient collector recognized that the set, manufactured and carved by New York master John Henry Belter (1804–1865), a German-American artist ignored by most collectors for another thirty years, represented important antebellum craftsmanship and taste. In January 1946, she wrote Joseph Downs, curator of the American Wing at the Metropolitan Museum of Art in New York, to say she felt "rusty" and isolated, but her purchases seem self-assured, and she asked Museum of Fine Arts, Houston Director James H. Chillman Jr. to authenticate objects "for a museum collection." That fall, after a summer of treasure hunting in New England, Ima felt sure she would give her property to the museum, and her quest to obtain the finest examples of American craftsmanship accelerated. In 1948 the magazine *Antiques* featured her collection, and by 1950 Ima had added nineteen significant, often rare, pieces from New York dealers Israel Sack, Ginsburg and Levy, and Charles Woolsey Lyon and from Pennsylvania dealers Joe Kindig Jr. of York and David Stockwell of Philadelphia. At this time, Ima made a list of objects she needed to fulfill the plan forming in her imagination and began to take advantage of tax laws that allowed her to transfer ownership of objects to the museum while retaining them in her home.[204]

Response to War: 1942–1946

Ima embarked on her tenure as custodian of the Hogg family fortune at a precarious moment. Warlords held sway over much of the world, and within two months of Mike's death, the United States joined the struggle to suppress tyranny. As she had twenty-five years earlier, Ima found solace in music and led efforts to assist the war effort through civic action. Once again, symphony sponsors questioned whether the orchestra could continue, and after six years Walter Walne wanted to retire from his position as board chairman. When the executive committee, under Ima's deft guidance, asked Hugh Roy Cullen to form a search committee to replace Walne, the legendary wildcatter whose wife, Lillie, adored symphonic music, knew his civic duty and said he would serve for the duration of hostilities and would underwrite annual operations—$125,000 by 1944–1945. Cullen saw the symphony as a morale builder for civilians and for military personnel stationed in East Texas, and he was determined to broaden the orchestra's appeal. He prodded Conductor Ernst Hoffman to expand the touring season and to invite famous guest artists to perform with the orchestra, and he persuaded the Houston City Council to budget $5,000 to underwrite free summer concerts in Houston neighborhoods plagued by youthful delinquency. Every symphony experience began with "The Star-Spangled Banner," and in 1945 Hoffman produced seventy-four events: ten subscription concerts, one gala, four operas, eight student performances, twenty-eight tour stops statewide, and twenty-three visits to military bases and USO halls. The symphony offered free admission to men in uniform at Sunday afternoon pop concerts and began to broadcast concerts statewide with underwriting from Texas Gulf Sulphur Corporation. Cullen told friends Hoffman "worked like a dog" during the war, and Ima praised Cullen's "leadership, guidance, and very generous contributions." Ima herself directed a long-range planning committee that met three times during Christmas week in 1943, and that year Women's Committee subscription sales and annual fund gifts surpassed previous goals.[205]

Ima also remained busy with the Houston Child Guidance Clinic during the war, serving on the finance, planning, and nominating committees. She coordinated the 1943 search for Director John H. Waterman, who led the clinic from 1944 to 1948, and in June 1944 began eighteen months of meetings at Bayou Bend with a committee to review mission and programs. She recommended new bylaws and a name change to Guidance Center of the Bureau of Mental Hygiene of Houston—shortened to Guidance Center of Houston in 1949 and to Child Guidance Center of Houston in 1956. The name changes and the purpose of Ima's committee highlighted the unresolved struggle to clarify the center's mission. Should the center operate a psychiatric clinic to treat children and adults, the goal favored by its medical doctors; or should it maintain a community-wide mental hygiene program, the goal Ima imagined? War dislocations increased juvenile delinquency, often caused by family disruption. To help families in trouble, Ima convened a meeting on November 4, 1945, among representatives of the juvenile court, probation department, police department's crime prevention bureau, and Child Guidance Center board and staff. She described a cooperative Baltimore program funded by that city's guidance center, county government, and Johns Hopkins University Hospital. The group decided to try the Baltimore model and to hire a psychiatrist to work full-time with Houston's probation and crime prevention bureaus, all expenses shared by the Child Guidance Center and the city's police and probation departments.

Despite her busy schedule, Ima felt she could do more to allay the trauma of war. When several women formed the Citizens' Educational Committee in 1943 to secure female candidates for the Houston Board of Education positions three and four, Ima answered their call. Now sixty-one, Ima was well known for her social justice advocacy and had long affirmed the Hogg family belief that high-quality public education created good citizens and made viable a strong democracy. Her father had believed that supporting public schools was every citizen's obligation, and a seat on the seven-member school board, organized in 1923 to oversee the newly formed Houston Independent School District (HISD), would enable Ima to perform a civic duty and to shape policy for future generations of Houston children. Ima worked with innovative Superintendent Edison E. Oberholtzer, who led the district from 1924 to 1945, to create the progressive River Oaks Elementary School in the late 1920s and to bring Child Guidance Center programs to the attention of Houston school teachers. She was also aware of wartime problems: a staggering jump in population—from 384,000 to 600,000 during the war decade—a need for more school buildings and more staff, inequities in teacher salaries, mothers rushing to good-paying war-related jobs, and tensions between progressive academic planner Oberholtzer and conservative financial overseer Hubert L. Mills.

In a brief campaign before the April 3 election, Ima attended coffees and meetings and gained the support of prominent Houstonians, of three major white-owned newspapers, and of labor unions and their leaders. Although Ima endorsed equal pay for equal work without regard to sex or race, she received mixed support from African American newspapers. Ima prepared statements for the press and made an election-eve radio appeal on KPRC. She promised to represent "all citizens of Houston, regardless of class, color, or creed" and to "go on the Board of Education without commitments and bound by no preconceived ideas." She told voters that the school board should have at least two female members to represent the female point of view, that she was qualified after a lifetime of advocacy for public schools, and that it was her wartime duty to serve Houston's children. Fewer than 10 percent of Houstonians voted in the contest that pitted her against popular dentist Dr. C. M. Taylor. Taylor also supported pay raises and better conditions for teachers, and the Hogg-Taylor race was businesslike and cordial. Longtime board member Dr. Ray Karchmer Daily, who served on the board from 1928 to 1952, a "lively, brilliant little woman, whose charm and . . . merry smiles have won her legions of friends," faced chief opponent Mrs. Sam Davis, who attacked Daily's record and insinuated her study in Europe was antidemocratic. Daily and Hogg saved an anonymous leaflet impugning Ima for being "very old, very rich—no children," while smearing Daily as a "Russian born Red Jewess" being investigated by the FBI. The scurrilous attacks backfired when Daily trounced her opponent, 5,097 to 1,959, while Ima outpolled Taylor by 4,369 to 3,034. On April 5, 1943, Dr. Daily introduced her elegantly dressed colleague to the school board. Ima thanked the group and remarked that before her term began officially in May, she would meet with each board member, the superintendent, and the business manager "to get the benefit of their council [*sic*]" and be "better prepared."[206]

Ima was well aware of the inequities suffered by African American families in the segregated school system. Although two high schools and the Houston Colored Junior College (later called the Houston College for Negroes and now Texas Southern University) had been built in the 1920s, these facilities lacked advanced classes, extracurricular activities, swimming pools, and sufficient supplies or textbooks. Starting pay for black teachers was $675, and for whites it was $1,125. While Ima's campaign was in progress, three actions converged to force school board action on April 12. First, that spring Dallas teachers had sued and won equal pay for black and white teachers, thereby establishing a trailblazing precedent. Then, on April 6 after six years of struggle, black employees at Hughes Tool accepted a labor contract with the colorblind Steel Workers Organizing Committee that theoretically ended wage and job segregation and promised equal pay for equal work. Finally, *Houston Informer* publisher and attorney Carter Wesley galvanized African Americans to form a citizens' committee, raise funds, hire black attorney F. S. K. Whittaker, and petition the school board on April 5, the day Ima was introduced. The following week, school board attorney Melvin E. Kurth reported to the April 12 board meeting that he had met with Whittaker, and the lawyers had agreed that African American salaries would rise slowly to reach parity with white salaries in September 1945, retroactive to pay scales on March 1, 1943—a decision that Wesley called "the most inspiring example of racial cooperation and democracy at work." With Ima's election to the board, supporters of equal pay gained a majority, and legal opposition crumbled. For the rest of her term, Ima joined Daily and the equal-pay sponsors to pressure adherence to the schedule and to address the steadily rising budget challenge as black, white, male, and female pay scales inched toward parity. To secure the best teachers possible in a tight labor market where new earning opportunities were opening for women, the board raised starting wages dramatically during Ima's tenure—from $1,125 in 1943 to $2,300 in 1947–1948. With the board's actions, Houston became the first large Southern city to equalize pay scales without a court fight. On May 3, 1943, James H. Law, president of the Colored Classroom Teachers and Principals Association, spoke for 445 teachers when he thanked the school board for a "second emancipation."[207]

While advocacy for equity was Ima's most lasting contribution to the school system, she also brought remarkable energy to several committees. Board of Education service was no sinecure; members were expected to visit schools, to attend two full board meetings a month, to serve on two committees, and to rotate among the officer positions each year. During a typical work week in February 1945, Ima attended the board meeting, visited nine schools, spent a day on Hogg family business, and fulfilled six other obligations. Ima was first assigned to the New School Properties Committee and was made chairwoman of the Lunch Room Committee for 1943–1945. Despite her modesty, Ima was a local celebrity whose activities had been followed by the press for years. When she visited schools, reporters and cameramen followed, and the public was able to understand the deplorable classroom conditions through her eyes—standing water on sidewalks and playgrounds, plaster falling from walls, cooks and teachers sharing space. Ima found the conditions "baffling" and failed to see how the aging and overcrowded schools would survive the population explosion. To address the problems, she campaigned for construction bond issues, explaining "the city has literally outgrown its public school plant."[208] Managing the Lunch Room Committee meant running a small business, and Ima was supposed to break even while providing healthy meals to forty thousand students each day at a low price. The task appealed to her bargaining instincts, and she used her term to educate her young audience about the benefits of good nutrition and the importance of drinking milk, which she procured at rock-bottom prices. No detail—from meat contracts to health regulations to favorite brands—escaped her attention, and she ran a budget surplus, which allowed her to improve equipment and raise salaries.

Ima's experience as a mental health advocate influenced her school board attitude toward juvenile delinquency, nursery school and daycare for working mothers, children with special needs, and visiting teachers. At board meetings she urged her colleagues to cooperate with Houston Parks and Recreation Department personnel so schoolchildren would have access to supervised recreation at city parks and school playgrounds whenever school was not in session. During the war years, Ima and her sister-in-law Alice often discussed the struggles of nearly nineteen thousand mothers who worked in Houston's war industries. Alice served as chairwoman of the Working Mothers Advice Center, which oversaw private-sector initiatives to care for unsupervised children. In 1943 the city asked the Houston ISD Board of Education to administer the city's first Lanham Act nurseries, created by the federal government to underwrite local childcare facilities for children ages two to five. When school board members had to approve extension of the program in 1944, Ima and Ray Daily successfully defended the use of federal funds to provide unmet social service needs during wartime. After federal funding ceased in 1945, private agencies supported by the Working Mothers Advice Center opened nursery, after-school, and summer camp programs and lobbied for kindergarten classes in every public school. In 1949, as Ima's term drew to a close, she and Daily, her frequent ally, pushed the school board to authorize six free kindergartens in black elementary schools for the 1949–1950 school year.

Ima and Alice also joined forces to help disabled children whose programs had been reduced or closed in the mid-1930s. In June 1943 Ima met with specialist Margaret Caillet about starting a school for children with special needs. Ima shared Caillet's plans with Superintendent Oberholtzer and persuaded her friend Susan Vaughan Clayton to donate $1,000 to the Board of Education to equip a pilot program. In September, classes opened at the one-story Eastwood School with Caillet, an assistant, and a nurse on staff. Ima asked Alice to organize a support group of prominent women to educate the public about problems confronting the disabled. When the state began funding special-needs education in September 1945, the program developed swiftly, and the school board adopted recommendations made in Ima's final report. Through these public-private programs, Ima identified unmet needs, provided solutions, and strengthened cooperation between philanthropic and municipal institutions seeking social justice for young Houstonians.

Ima believed firmly in public access to parks, playgrounds, and special school programs, and she understood that money could build and furnish classrooms and attract better teachers, but she also wanted the school board to study the issues underlying student problems. She pressed citizen groups to petition the school board to reinstate a visiting teacher program that had been used successfully in Houston from 1929 until 1934, when it lapsed for lack of funding. On October 9, 1944, a coalition of school, civic, church, and social welfare groups that included school principals and parent-teacher association representatives petitioned the board to reinstate visiting teachers. Board members learned, to their chagrin, that 14 percent of children age ten to seventeen were "known to the police department," and they appointed Ima to form a committee and examine visiting teacher programs. Ima presented a long bibliography of materials on the subject to her colleagues and invited Carmelita Janvier, nationally known director of special services for Orleans Parish, Louisiana, to visit Houston. Ima arranged dinners and meetings with community leaders, public school staff, and black principals to ensure all constituencies heard Janvier. Ima also held a meeting for classroom teachers where she spoke at length to reassure doubters who feared outside interference. She explained that visiting teachers were trained social workers who only "aid and supplement" other personnel in a preventive program to identify problems, visit homes, and guide families toward effective social services. Ima told her audience that the program worked best when social service staff and teachers cooperated. She consulted Superintendent Oberholtzer and made a long formal report of her findings to the school board on November 27, 1944. Impressed by her zealous diligence, the school board approved the superintendent's recommendation that a coordinator be hired to launch a visiting teacher program. Ima relentlessly pushed district administrators to hire staff and proudly reported that Eleanor Craighill, a recruit from New Orleans, would supervise six visiting teachers, three black and three white, beginning in September 1945.[209]

Ima believed that reinstating the visiting teacher program was her primary achievement as a member of the Board of Education, but she knew from her work with the Houston Child Guidance Clinic that the city lacked trained teachers, social workers, and mental health care specialists. In 1944 Ima asked Robert Sutherland, executive director of the Hogg Foundation, to develop a plan for the foundation to partner with the Child Guidance Clinic, the University of Houston, and the University of Texas to create and fund a professional training program. She studied a report on welfare and training issues provided by Sutherland, applauded the "galaxy of stars" who agreed to be instructors for the inaugural 1945–1946 course, and praised the mutually beneficial partnership. The next year, Eleanor Craighill proposed establishing scholarships for teachers to be trained as social workers and mental health-care specialists, and HISD principals praised the critical impact of the district's visiting teacher program. Ima donated $1,500 to the Hogg Foundation to support scholarships at the University of Texas and the University of Houston. The Hogg Foundation also provided money to the HISD Visiting Teacher Department for summer in-service sessions. Ima's concern for the city's public schools continued after her term ended. She reported to Sutherland in September 1949 that she had attended "a joint meeting white and colored" with the visiting teachers, who thanked the foundation "for the scholarships which have made it possible to develop their work."[210]

To meet local demands for further education, in 1927 Superintendent Edison E. Oberholzer introduced a segregated junior college system managed by the school superintendent and the Board of Education. In 1933, the Texas legislature authorized the change to a four-year system, still managed by the school board and run by Oberholzer as president. By 1945 it was clear that the demands of an expanding public school system and a growing public university could not be handled effectively by one board of trustees and one person serving as both school superintendent and university president. During Ima's term, she participated in the complex debate leading to separation of the university system from the Board of Education. She agreed to the formation of an advisory board of fifteen civic leaders led by multimillionaire school dropout Hugh Roy Cullen, and she supported efforts by the new advisors to secure legislative approval for the split. Quite a fight ensued, but on March 12, 1945, the legislature passed the law that established a freestanding University of Houston and a College for Negroes. Governor Coke Stevenson promptly signed the measure. The next day, Oberholtzer became the first president of the University of Houston. On March 3, 1947, the legislature granted autonomy to the Texas State University for Negroes, renamed Texas Southern University in 1951.

Numerous other matters came before the Houston Board of Education, including the hiring of a new superintendent, and Ima handled endless questions dealing with budgets, bond issues, property condemnations, athletic programs, staff vacations, and typewriter purchases. She also placed reproductions of art masterpieces in all the schools, advocated for a district-wide music program, and insisted art programs be included in African American schools. In February 1949 Ima announced formally that she would not stand for reelection to the school board, stating she had fulfilled her wartime commitment and hoped a woman would be elected to replace her in the April election. Her friend Dr. Margaret Patrick, who directed physical education for HISD, wrote to thank her for bringing "a unique talent" to the "solution of problems." Ima demurred, "I don't think I am particularly fitted for many phases of school board membership . . . [but] I shall miss . . . the activity, for education in all its phases has always been of prime interest to me." For six years, she had used her unique talents to build partnerships among the Board of Education, the Child Guidance Center, the Hogg Foundation, and Houston's civic leaders to improve the academic experience for all Houston's children.[211]

During the last year of her term on the school board, Ima assumed several other responsibilities. In December 1947, the Philosophical Society of Texas elected her to be its first female president. The venerable institution—created on December 5, 1837, by leaders of the new Republic of Texas to collect information and diffuse knowledge about Texas—had been reorganized on January 18, 1936, as an educational, nonprofit corporation. In 1937 the society invited three women to join the all-male institution—poet and scholar Karle Wilson Baker (1878–1960); suffragist and clubwoman Mrs. Percy V. Pennybaker (1861–1938); and Texas State Librarian and twice president of the Texas Library Association Elizabeth Howard West (1878–1945). West was named fourth vice president of the society, and in 1938 beloved librarian Julia Ideson and visionary civic leader Ima Hogg joined the female roster. As president, Ima convened the 1948 annual meeting at the Ramada Club in Houston and addressed the members on December 11. While the "significant honor" of her election had been "a complete surprise," she welcomed the chance to select a speaker and topic for the annual meeting. She was concerned that discussion in Texas "over-emphasizes our material resources . . . to the neglect of our cultural attainments," so she had invited society member Dr. Radislav Andrea Tsanoff to consider "The Creative Arts in Texas." A popular, much-published professor of philosophy at Rice Institute since 1914, Tsanoff displayed a "broad knowledge and deep affection for all the arts" and provided "inspiring leadership" to civic life. In 1948 Ima was also asked to serve on the search committee for a new Houston Child Guidance Center director, and she helped hire Dr. Harry Little, who held the position from 1948 to 1966. In December, with the search successfully completed, Ima told the center's board she intended to retire; instead she bowed to board pressure and assumed lifetime honorary active status, with ex officio privileges on all committees. Two months before, in October 1948, the Museum of Fine Arts had named Ima its "honorary curator of Early American Art," and for the next twenty-five years she focused energy on her primary passions of art and music while continuing to advocate for mental health care and public education.[212]

The 1940s ended as they began, with the death of a beloved brother. Tom Hogg's second marriage to Margaret Wells had been happy, and they had spent much of each year at his ranch in Yuma, Arizona, where Ima visited them with pleasure. Tom's long history of restless enthusiasms, his debilitating battle with alcohol, and his inability to manage money abated, and a San Antonio pastor who had befriended the undisciplined young Tom remembered how the questing youth empathized with the downtrodden and dispossessed. Others recalled Tom's love for sports, dogs, and horses. As he aged, Tom continued to smoke and developed a chronic heart condition, but his last letter to Ima cheerily discussed his decision to invest in registered Tennessee walking horses. A week later, Tom, aged sixty-one, suffered a fatal heart attack at his Yuma Ranch early in the evening of March 8, 1949. Tom was buried with his parents and brothers at Oakwood Cemetery in Austin. Ima and Margaret were named executors of his last testament, and Margaret received a life interest in Tom's large estate, which passed to the Hogg Foundation after her death. As restorative measures, Margaret spent a few weeks at Mineral Wells, and in June Ima sailed for a trip to Italy, Paris, and London with a promise to return in time for the Houston Symphony Society's annual maintenance drive in September.

Ima Saves the Symphony: 1946–1956

Hugh Roy Cullen fulfilled his promise to retire when peace was assured and announced he would leave his position as activist wartime president of the Houston Symphony Society by the end of 1945. The executive committee, influenced by Ima Hogg's wish, asked Cullen to accept the semi-honorary position of chairman and named Joseph S. Smith to a second term as president; Ima agreed to continue as vice president, the post she had accepted in 1944. Symphony devotees knew that Conductor Ernst Hoffman was beloved by musicians, popular with the audience, and supported by donors, but Houston's businesses, manufacturing capacity, and population had surged during the war, and powerful symphony patrons felt the orchestra should keep pace and move from regional to national acclaim. When Cullen discovered that Smith, probably at Ima's instigation, did not plan to renew Hoffman's contract, he was furious. Cullen resigned on April 23 and sent a blistering letter to the *Houston Post,* praising Hoffman for his superlative dedication during the war and daring Smith to find $100,000 to cover annual costs. He shunned further board meetings and telegraphed Ima, who was on vacation in Mexico. The irate former president complained about the situation to insurance magnate Gus Wortham and begged Hoffman not to announce his resignation at the next concert. Ima rushed back from Mexico to mediate, but Smith, realizing he could not succeed without Cullen's support, resigned as president-elect on May 8, and the executive committee insisted Ima take over. She agreed, but only if Wortham would serve as chairman and assure the vital backing of business leaders. Ima then met with Cullen, who was "shocked" to understand that she wanted to fire Hoffman and give him $10,000 severance. Gently but persistently, Ima assuaged her major donor, who continued to support his wife's favorite organization financially but turned his full attention to building the newly independent University of Houston. Ima had the "painful" task of explaining to the popular, but humble, conductor that the 1946–1947 season would be his last. Later she told critic Hubert Roussel that Hoffman was "very sweet" and "always so reasonable." Press drama and board member correspondence suggest Hoffman was harshly treated, but Ima and the conductor remained friends until a fatal car crash ended Hofman's life in 1955. In February 1947, with harmony restored among board members, the search for a new conductor began.[213]

Ima and her executive committee never did discover a graceful way to move from one level of performance to the next in their quest for excellence and recognition, but most board members applauded Ima's drive to enhance the symphony's reputation, hire renowned conductors, recruit fine musicians, locate outstanding instruments, and develop a musically astute audience. To handle financial issues and build a support staff, Ima hired Tom Johnson, the young manager of the struggling Austin Symphony Orchestra, to serve as business manager, effective in January 1948. Ima and the search committee invited several guest conductors to cover the 1947–1948 season, among them Carlos Chavez, whose work Ima had enjoyed while visiting Mexico City; the youthful Leonard Bernstein, who conducted and played the piano solo in January 1948; and Efrem Kurtz (1900–1995), who performed successfully in January 1947 and March 1948. Ima was charmed by Bernstein's vigor, and she tried to lure him from New York, but in the end, board members offered Kurtz a three-year contract to become resident conductor. Born and trained in Russia, the tall, elegant, and cosmopolitan Kurtz had toured widely with the Ballet Russe de Monte Carlo from 1932 to 1942. He served as music director of the Kansas City Philharmonic Orchestra from 1943 to 1948 before settling in Houston. His tenure began well, with high expectations and plans for expansion. Kurtz attracted "king of the keyboard" Arthur Rubinstein and a roster of top guest artists; patrons were turned away from sold-out concerts; and as the second season closed in 1950, no less a celebrity than conductor and impresario Sir Thomas Beecham[214] pronounced Houston's orchestra, previously "virtually unknown and on the verge of collapse," to be "one of the very best in the country."[215] Kurtz hired fresh talent, garnered national attention, and in 1950–1951 produced 103 performances, including forty on tour and twenty-six radio broadcasts. Spurred by success, the Houston Symphony Society board discussed the need for a new orchestra hall and a permanent endowment fund, and Ima led a committee to city hall in 1952 to negotiate a plan to redesign the music hall and the coliseum. By Kurtz's third season, however, Ima knew the conductor's repertoire was musically unchallenging, and ticket sales began to flag. Although not enthusiastic, the executive committee renewed the conductor's contract for two more years, but when the fifth season ended, new Chairman Warren S. Bellows told Kurtz his contract would not be renewed; the symphony would rely on guest conductors and on Kurtz as needed for the next year. While publicly citing musical stagnation, in fact, Ima and others were concerned about possible scandal resulting from the Kurtzes' pending divorce—caused by the conductor's affair with pathbreaking principal flutist Elaine Shaffer, who resigned in August 1953 and later married Kurtz.

Among the guest conductors in 1953–1954 was thirty-nine-year-old Hungarian Ferenc Fricsay, a European star whose "gymnastic baton style" and "magnificent masculinity" electrified his audience in November 1953. Ima and her committee began negotiations at once for a one-year, sixteen-concert residency. Implicit in the agreement announced January 15, 1954, was the promise of a longer contract if the Fricsays liked Houston well enough to make it their permanent home and if local audiences continued to admire the maestro's spirited style. Ima and her board wanted their leader to become part of the community and to spend his time upgrading the orchestra's skills, adding to its repertoire, and enhancing its reputation. Letters among Ima, business manager Johnson, Fricsay, and his agent Andrew Schulhof, sent before Fricsay arrived in Houston, suggested trouble ahead. The excitable maestro ignored efforts by Johnson and Schulhof to "orient" the Hungarian, "not only to our situation, but to the psychology of the American public" and to explain how orchestras in the United States were "dependent upon private enterprise and not state subsidy." Fricsay also dismissed Ima's program suggestions, made after she and Johnson reviewed the current repertoire. Yet, the fall 1954 concerts began well. Ima welcomed Fricsay and his wife to Bayou Bend; musicians appreciated the conductor's vigorous style; and audiences applauded his "stunning" performances.[216]

By December the honeymoon was over. Fricsay denounced the Music Hall acoustics as deplorable, and he submitted a long-range plan that included a new music hall designed solely for symphonic performance, extensive touring in the United States and Europe, better instruments, higher salaries, and a large house for himself. Board members, many of whom had paid for the recent Music Hall renovations, gasped. Although they "commended his desire to look to the future and visualize a superior orchestra for Houston," finance committee members stated flatly that Fricsay's demands could not be met. Unfortunately, Fricsay took his case to the press, explaining that his requests were not demands but merely ideas for an ideal symphony of the future. Business Manager Tom Johnson fed his friend and longtime *Houston Post* critic Hubert Roussel an expurgated version of the board position and ignored recently hired *Houston Chronicle* critic Ann Holmes. Faced with cascading rumors, Holmes hired an interpreter and interviewed Fricsay. The inevitable firestorm of conflicting stories made Ima and Chairman Harmon Whittington believe Fricsay "endeavored to disrupt the morale of the musical employees of the Society" when he talked to the press. By January 1955 Fricsay was gone. The Houston Symphony Society's public statement announced that the board had "learned with regret" that the conductor would not return, owing to "a serious rheumatic condition." The fracas made music lovers take sides and distressed Ima, whose friends reassured her that "Mr. Fricsay was not for us, and it is just as well . . . that we found that out early." Happily, Sir Thomas Beecham, seventy-six, agreed to abandon his semiretirement and finish the 1954–1955 season. The year 1955 proved musically thrilling. Elva Lobit founded the Houston Grand Opera; a group of ballet lovers announced formation of the Houston Ballet Foundation to support creation of a ballet school and resident company; and Leopold Stokowski accepted the call to raise his baton in Houston. Ima had followed the celebrated maestro's career since 1920 when she attended concerts while recuperating in Philadelphia. Though now seventy-three, Stokowski's willingness to sign a three-year contract suggested the Houston Symphony had at last found widespread recognition.[217]

During her decade as activist president of the Houston Symphony Society, Ima participated in all aspects of the orchestra's life. She befriended conductors and their families; she entertained musicians and board members at her home; she attended rehearsals and multiple performances of each program; she purchased instruments to improve the orchestra's sound; and she fought to achieve international recognition. With Women's Committee support, Ima developed "Music for Everybody" as the Houston Symphony Society slogan to articulate her inclusive vision that classical music should be available and enjoyable to every Houstonian. Under her watchful eye, the orchestra offered its formal subscription season, "Summer Symphonies" in the parks, radio broadcasts on Saturday evenings, and pops concerts featuring big band conductors Benny Goodman and Morton Gould. Ima believed arts organizations should cooperate, and in March 1948 she convened the Symphony Society, the Museum of Fine Arts, the Houston Public Library, Houston's Little Theatre, and the River Oaks Garden Club for the first Creative Arts Festival, an event that ran for several years and allowed Houstonians to enjoy an azalea trail of gardens, art exhibits, concerts, and plays. Ima also encouraged local talent and, as a "silent benefactress," organized the Texas Composers Commission to provide moral and financial support for young performing artists.[218]

Ima was particularly proud of the student concerts, given "for every child in Harris county's . . . schools to learn to love and listen to the greatest music of the age." She befriended Mildred Sage, head of the school district's music department, and organized concerts separately for elementary, high school, and African American students. Every year, Ima underwrote the cost of tickets for students and teachers, placed explanatory articles in the symphony programs, and made concerts for young people a top priority of her audience-building efforts. Ima and volunteer Josie Tomforde began a student competition to identify talented young artists whose winning performances earned them the right to play with the orchestra at student concerts. Ima asked a teenage friend, Francita Stuart, to write contemporaries and invite them to inaugurate a Junior Patrons group that would nurture future symphony supporters. In 1952 she announced a "Painting to Music" program and prizes for art inspired by student performances.[219]

In 1951 Ima launched the Houston Symphony Endowment Fund, to which she made large annual gifts. From 1953 until the end of her life, she placed Christmas messages in the Houston Symphony Society concert programs to thank donors, explain programs, laud sold-out concerts, extol the "wonderful spirit" of the musicians and staff, and urge Santas to remember symphony wish lists. In May 1956 Ima retired from her post as president, leaving her beloved Symphony Society in the capable hands of new President Maurice Hirsch and new Conductor Leopold Stokowski. "When I say that I have gained more than I have given, I am not being humble," she wrote to her board. "Association through so many years with hundreds and hundreds of men and women who are workers for something beyond themselves has given me a glow of love for Houston beyond measure." In response, Maurice and Winifred Hirsch endowed the Ima Hogg Scholarship Fund in her honor, Stokowski dedicated his opening program to her, and she graciously accepted president emerita status. She did not withdraw but instead agreed to chair the Advisory Committee of the Women's Committee.[220]

Ima Hogg presenting awards to Houston Symphony Fund Drive captains, 1950s, left to right: Mary Lou (Mrs. John) Margraves, Ima Hogg, and Selma (Mrs. Alfred) Neumann. Tom Colburn, *Houston Chronicle*. MS 21–059–001, Ima Hogg Papers, Museum of Fine Arts, Houston Archives.

Preparing Her Legacy: The 1950s

Often perceived by strangers as shy or reserved, Ima had long maintained a treasured circle of friends who delighted in music and art. While handling Houston Symphony Society crises and triumphs, Ima lost two of her concert devotees—in 1945 when college friend and frequent traveling companion Julia Ideson succumbed unexpectedly to a heart attack, and again in 1953 when Katherine Blunt Parker died on November 14. Only the year before, the founding president of the Symphony Association had accompanied Ima to the season's opening concert. Symphony enthusiasts Walter Walne, Gus Wortham, Maurice Hirsch, and their wives shared Ima's sense of civic duty, and Annette (Nettie) Lewis Jones, the music-loving wife of attorney Albert P. Jones became a cherished confidante and served as chairman of the Women's Committee in 1949. Even after the couple moved to Austin in 1962, beloved Nettie frequently attended concerts with Ima. A young friend recalled Ima's ability to motivate young women as a "major contribution."[221] Ima encouraged youthful companions to volunteer with the Women's Committee and invited them and their husbands to join her for small, preconcert dinners at Bayou Bend. As expected, many of these women became civic leaders. In the postwar years, Ima expanded her musical acquaintance when in 1946 she began attending the annual summer music festival of the Boston Symphony Orchestra at Tanglewood in Lenox, Massachusetts.

In the 1950s Ima formed a close bond with several collectors who were conserving America's heritage and shared her views about artistic expression. Dubbed the "antiquees" by Maxim Karolik, they included Henry Francis du Pont, who first invited Ima to visit Winterthur in 1948; Henry and Helen Flynt, who were restoring Historic Deerfield, Massachusetts; Ralph and Cynthia Carpenter, who led restoration efforts in Newport, Rhode Island; major Americana collectors Edgar and Bernice Chrysler Garbisch; and chief Williamsburg curator John Graham. Ima grew particularly close to Electra Havemayer Webb, who was gathering structures for an outdoor museum in Shelburne, Vermont, and to Katharine Prentis Murphy, whom she met while motoring through New England in the fall of 1951 in search of antiques. Although Ima lost her way to Murphy's country home and arrived after her hostess had dismissed the cook, the two collectors laughed away the confusion and soon were chatting on Sundays by telephone. Ima also found Maxim Karolik particularly congenial; an immigrant Russian tenor married to a much older, extremely wealthy woman, he shared Ima's musical tastes and formed collections of little-noticed folk art and overlooked nineteenth-century American landscape painting. "The Group," as Henry Flynt called these collectors, corresponded supportively and met occasionally at house parties to examine and appreciate each other's efforts to preserve period buildings and material culture.

Ima also enjoyed members of the extensive Stinson and Hogg families and remained close to her brothers' widows, Alice and Margaret. After Tom's death, the three women simplified their holdings and reduced office expenses further. In the late 1940s, Claud B. Hamill acquired the properties of Hogg Oil, with the family retaining certain royalty interests, and in June 1952, the University of Texas purchased all remaining assets of Varner Company, paid out to Ima and her sisters-in-law over two years. Alice, who had been briefly married to her former neighbor Harry Clay Hanszen from March 10, 1948, until his death in Kerrville on August 26, 1950, continued to work with William B. Ferguson, who oversaw her properties, a large stock portfolio, and a trust for her mother, sister, and niece. After Hanszen's death, the warmhearted, beautiful widow sold her home on Lazy Lane and moved to the Warwick apartment hotel but spent many months each year with family and friends at her Lazy Lane Ranch in Kerrville. Margaret enjoyed her sisters-in-law and managed her own business affairs. Following a brief marriage to childhood friend Norbert W. Markus of Philadelphia, the twice-widowed Margaret moved to Houston's Inwood Manor in January 1973, where she died four years later.

From July 1, 1952, until her death, Ima managed her business affairs from home with the help of legal adviser Leon Jaworski and private secretary Jane Zivley (1902–2003). A native of Mineral Wells, Texas, Zivley was working as a bookkeeper when she learned from a neighbor that Ima Hogg needed a secretary. Shortly before leaving for Europe, Ima interviewed Zivley, was immediately impressed by her ladylike demeanor and strong work ethic, and hired her part-time to pay bills and household employees that summer. Zivley put Ima's ill-kept books in order and was named full-time executive secretary when Ima returned in the fall. The employer-employee relationship soon developed into an effective partnership and strong friendship. Zivley paid the bills, carried on correspondence with dealers and scholars, researched provenance of many purchases, and devised a recordkeeping catalogue system to register every object in the collection. For twenty-three years, Zivley was Ima's "companion, advocate, confident, and friend" who gave her employer advice and urged the modest philanthropist to stress the "importance of the collection" when explaining her "extremely magnanimous" gift of Bayou Bend to the Museum of Fine Arts, Houston. Zivley appreciated her employer's generosity—a good salary and handsome gifts of jewelry, real estate, and antiques—and boldly defended the value of Ima's gift to Museum Board President Frank Coates. As coexecutor of Ima's estate, Zivley faithfully organized funeral arrangements, distributed bequests and gifts to the museum, and placed Ima's private papers, letters, and family memorabilia in archival repositories.[222]

Ima's exhilarating tenure as Houston Symphony Society president energized her imagination, and in the 1950s she began to think creatively about her stewardship of Bayou Bend and Varner Plantation. Mid-March announcements of the 1951 Azalea Trail promised a new delight: Ima Hogg was opening her "Texas Room" and "Blue Room" for the first time to Azalea Trail visitors and experimenting with ways she could use her Americana collections to illuminate the story of the United States. She had arranged the Texas Room with "shaper tiles on the floor," an early Texas dining table, a large open fireplace with iron pots, and collections of Texian Campaigne ceramics, historic glass flasks, and old maps. In the Blue Room, visitors found her mid-nineteenth-century Rococo Revival parlor suite and Sarah Stinson Hogg's square piano, on which little Ima had taken her first lessons from her musical mother. In January 1953 Katharine Prentis Murphy invited her Texas friend to join fellow collectors, dealers, scholars, museum curators, and Americana devotees at the Colonial Williamsburg Antiques Forum, an eye-opening experience Ima would repeat almost every year for the next two decades. In the summer of 1954, Ima joined a house party in Newport hosted by Maxim Karolik and attended by Katharine Murphy, Electra Webb, the Garbisches, and the Flynts. There Ima viewed the restoration work of Ralph Carpenter, who had recently saved the colonial period Hunter House from demolition. The next summer, while puttering about New England with Katharine Murphy, the two "antiquees" visited Henry and Helen Flynt at Deerfield, where they toured the Flynts' ongoing restoration of the town's colonial structures. Debating the demands of restoring old buildings and exhibiting Americana kindled Ima's desire to share Varner Plantation and Bayou Bend with the public.

In 1955 Ima and Museum of Fine Arts Director Lee Malone organized a Houston arts forum that Malone hoped would encourage participants to appreciate the culture and heritage of the Southwest and would become an annual event. Ima had loaned several important pieces of her collection to Malone's ambitious 1954 exhibit *George Washington's World*, which drew on local and national collections, and she was eager to pursue Texas-East Coast ties that would promote her goal of building bridges between East and West, North and South through deeper understanding of America's unifying heritage. She suggested forum speakers and made a guest list of collectors and dealers she hoped would participate. The three-day "American Heritage and the Southwest" forum began on Friday, March 9, 1956, with a dinner and keynote address by Metropolitan Museum of Art Editor Marshall Davidson, who had recently published his two-volume *Life in America* treatise. Ima's "antiquees," with the exception of Maxim Karolik, attended. Katharine Murphy and Electra Webb were daring and flew to Houston, where they stayed at Bayou Bend. Henry and Ruth du Pont motored, via New Orleans, from their winter home in Boca Grande, Florida, to the Shamrock Hotel, since 1949 Houston's glamor accommodation. Henry Flynt contributed an analysis of his experience "Restoring a New England Village," and Ralph Carpenter spoke on the subject, "Regional Characteristics, Texas and Rhode Island," placing Texas on the national map of decorative arts importance. Ima arranged for the du Ponts to visit Houston's premier gardens, and she welcomed the couple to Bayou Bend at a large cocktail party given in their honor. Thirty years before, du Pont was rushing to New York by train to examine a settee and matching side chairs from Massachusetts, but Will and Ima purchased the set before he arrived. Collectors never forget; when he saw the settee, in situ at Bayou Bend, he remarked, "There's my settee," or so he claimed a decade later. Although du Pont recalled encouraging Ima to create an independent house museum, the forum audience, which included her longtime friend Sadie Campbell Blaffer and dealer Albert Sack, enthusiastically supported her tentative plan to team with the Museum of Fine Arts. Participants were suitably impressed by the "memorable" symposium and the "sheer beauty of Bayou Bend." Alice Winchester, editor of *The Magazine Antiques*, thanked Ima for a "wonderful genial weekend" and hoped she was "as gratified and content with the forum as you well deserve."[223]

While meeting new friends and visiting collections and conservation projects on the East Coast, Ima completed historic preservation schemes related to family properties in Texas. As early as the 1920s, Will, Ima, and Mike linked the Hogg family's experience to the national drama and emphasized that successful families lay at the heart of a thriving nation. They assisted widowed and orphaned relatives, memorialized the governor's accomplishments, and maintained the trees planted at his grave, making sure the annual pecan harvest was shared with fellow Texans. Will and Mike corresponded about transferring their grandfather Joseph Lewis Hogg's remains to Texas from the battle site in Corinth, Mississippi. For decades the family retreated to Varner to celebrate their father's March 24 birthday. In 1935 Ima compiled and transcribed "Family Letters," written by the four children, their parents, and Aunt Fannie, as

Ima Hogg presenting a portrait of Governor James Stephen Hogg to Governor Alan Shivers, 1952. E-enr-111 Prints and Photographs Collection, Dolph Briscoe Center for American History, University of Texas at Austin.

Christmas gifts for Mike and Tom . In 1939 the Hogg siblings helped purchase 26.7 acres in Quitman for a city park to commemorate their parents, and they moved Honeymoon Cottage, where Will was born, to the site. Two years later Ima, Mike, and Tom purchased nearly 178 acres near Rusk, including some of the original Mountain Home land and a family graveyard, and they gave the property to the City of Rusk for a park.

In the late 1940s Ima hired the University of Texas archivist to transcribe her father's personal papers and underwrote publication of his speeches and state papers. After interviewing potential biographers, Ima selected Robert C. Cotner, a professor in the University of Texas Department of History, to prepare her father's authorized biography. As so often happened with her projects, Ima found outside support and persuaded her friend Estelle Sharp to defray the cost of Cotner's research by making a Sharp grant to Rice Institute, which was happy to assist the biographer. In gratitude for the institute's collaboration, Ima placed a complete copy of her father's transcribed and printed documents in the Rice Institute archives, and she underwrote a lecture at the institute's Fondren Library on March 18, 1951, to celebrate her father's one hundredth birthday. Cotner's diplomatic skills equaled his research capabilities, and the industrious historian provided serious analysis that satisfied academic critics while painting a sufficiently positive picture of the governor and his accomplishments to please his protagonist's exacting daughter. Ima threw herself into the project, spent hours finding documents, and took a critical interest in Cotner's product, which has remained the standard work since 1951.

To prepare for centennial celebrations of Governor Hogg's birth on March 24, 1951, Governor Beaufort Jester created the James Stephen Hogg Memorial Commission in 1949 and asked Ima to serve as chairwoman of the effort to develop a state park on the Quitman site where Honeymoon Cottage had been relocated. For fifteen months she cooperated with the State Parks Board to "secure appropriate mementos for the little house." She named an advisory committee to assure local support, met with architects to ensure authentic restoration, and used family or period objects to re-create the bedroom where Will was born. She placed her grandmother's piano in the parlor, which she furnished "so that the ladies of Quitman could use it for their club meetings." In the dining room, Ima displayed "a photographic history of father's career." In one small space, she memorialized her family and its Texas story, provided period authenticity, and made practical allowance for public activities. To observe the park's opening, she played the piano for guests. As she had done with her Museum of Fine Arts gifts, she provided funds for the project, applied her expertise to its execution, and remained interested in its management after she attended the Governor Hogg Memorial Park dedication on March 24, 1952.[224]

Ima's enthusiasm and hands-on participation did not go unnoticed. She had served on the board of the Governor's Mansion Restoration Committee since 1935 and had made generous gifts to mansion renovations in 1943. In September 1953 Governor Allan Shivers named her one of eighteen members on the newly created Texas State Historical Survey, an advisory committee to "survey the condition of the historical records of Texas" and make recommendations to the legislature concerning preservation and use. From the day in 1853 when Mount Vernon Ladies' Association founder Ann Pamela Cunningham of South Carolina challenged women to save George Washington's home and to preserve the past for contemporary audiences, women had played critical roles in historic preservation and would lead efforts in Texas. Ima's friend, the university archivist Winnie Allen, framed the commission's goals and specified that "records" meant documents, "historic buildings and museum artifacts."[225] Ima chaired the houses, sites, and landmarks subcommittee and, with members Mrs. Lane Taylor of San Antonio and Mrs. Mike Butler of Austin, gathered an advisory committee of experts to create the statewide marking and preservation protocol that remains the basis of preservation work for the successor Texas Historical Commission. By the time Ima delivered her final report in June 1954, her subcommittee had identified more than nine hundred historically significant buildings, a catalogue that still guides the marking program initiated in 1962.

Preparing Varner Plantation for public use challenged Ima. The house had been a "holy place" to the children, where the family spent happy hours relaxing and sharing ideas, but the remodeling Will ordered in the 1920s obliterated much of the antebellum structure. How could she "restore" the property as a house museum, and what interpretive theme would be appropriate? Ima had long assumed Varner would be given to the State of Texas and had thought about releasing the property after Mike died, but it was not until 1953, shortly after the Quitman dedication, that she wrote to the State Parks Board to announce that she wished to give Varner Plantation to the state. Finally, in August 1956, Ima met with the State Parks Board in Austin to explain that she would donate the house and about fifty acres of surrounding land to Texas, providing she could restore and furnish the house at her own expense "to reflect the era in which it prospered and was outstanding."[226] Ima also promised a $35,000 endowment and agreed that the state could charge entrance fees. She explained that furnishings would include family heirlooms, firearms, and historical documents, and she would appoint an advisory committee to help with the interiors and to research Brazoria County history. By then an active supporter of the National Trust for Historic Preservation, Ima wrote its director for advice about preservation and restoration guidelines. In the end, Ima compromised: she kept the 1919–1920 exterior but restored the interiors to their antebellum condition as much as possible. During the winter of 1956–1957, her friend and fellow preservationist, legendary architect O'Neil Ford,[227] began work, but Ima's hands-on approach drove him to claim he was unable to meet her deadline. She turned to John Staub to supervise the West Columbia contractor L. D. Moore. Staub understood his client's zeal and completed the project to her exacting standards, on schedule for a dedication ceremony on the former governor's birthday, March 24, 1958.

Ima supervised the interpretation and furnishing of the interiors, insisting the work was not a restoration, since its 1920 exterior and 1850 interior did not adhere to preservationists' use of the term. Instead, Ima hoped to create

Varner-Hogg Plantation. Courtesy of Texas Historical Commission.

sympathetic rooms that would demonstrate how historic conservation helped visitors understand the past, would tell the story of the Hogg family, and would narrate the history of coastal Texas. She asked her advisory committee to study period inventories, wills, the role of enslaved people, contemporary books about household management, wall finishes, floor coverings, curtain materials, gardens, and objects made in Texas or purchased elsewhere—outlining the sources that scholars of material culture use today but were only beginning to enrich the research of social historians in the 1950s. Downstairs in the east bedroom, Ima evoked the first Anglo-American pioneers in Texas; upstairs, her west bedroom explained French influence and included pieces by New Orleans cabinetmaker Prudent Mallard. In the dining room, with its portrait of Zachary Taylor, Ima reviewed the 1846–1848 Mexican-American War; while the east bedroom upstairs, housing a grand bedstead made in Brazoria County, explored the antebellum experience. Ima placed a Rococo Revival suite in the parlor to represent the Confederacy and displayed the governor's desk and chair and framed documents relating to his administration in the upstairs hall.

Ima used the kitchen area for a museum of Brazoria County artifacts provided by the advisory committee. Ima's installation illuminated the lives of the plantation's owners through the power of objects and outlined the trajectory of the area's economic development from sugar production through cotton growing and ranching to oil exploration. Although Ima did not explicitly develop spaces explaining the lives of enslaved people, by preserving the property's plantation past, she encouraged scholars to explore the roots of black and white Texans. Later scholars have built on her guidelines to tell a fascinating story of white, enslaved, freedwoman, convict, and cowboy activities. Although never satisfied with her compromise restoration, Ima paved the way for ongoing education and understanding.

An Extraordinary Gift

Ima transferred Bayou Bend and its collections and gardens to the Museum of Fine Arts, Houston during a period of explosive growth for the museum. Following the death of her husband, Robert E. L. Blaffer, in 1942, Sarah Campbell Blaffer publicized her collection of European paintings and underwrote the 1952 completion of the museum's 1924 building design. Museum trustees sold donated property to fund renovation of interior space in 1950–1953 as the Sterling Galleries. In 1953 the board allowed Rice Institute professor and part-time museum Director James H. Chillman Jr. (1924–1953) to retire after twenty-nine years of service and hired the first full-time museum director, Yale-educated Lee H. B. Malone, who held the position from 1953 to 1959. The board established the Permanent Endowment Fund in January 1956, opened the Wiess and Jones Memorial Galleries in January 1958, and dedicated Cullinan Hall, the soaring addition designed by Mies van der Rohe and funded largely by Nina Cullinan as a memorial to her parents, in October 1958. In gratitude for superlative generosity, the museum board named its first life trustees in June 1956: Ima Hogg, Nina Cullinan, Sarah Campbell Blaffer, Camilla and John H. Blaffer, Olga (Mrs. Harry) Wiess, Carroll Sterling (Mrs. Harry) Masterson, and Mary Gibbs (Mrs. Jesse) Jones.

By the late 1940s, Ima and a small coterie of intimate friends understood that Bayou Bend was designated for the Museum of Fine Arts one day, but it was not until December 1953, after lengthy discussions, that the museum board made a "special exception" to its policy not to assure donors about future use of their gifts. The trustees reassured the nervous, skeptical benefactress that the

Clio Garden at Bayou Bend, 1940s. Camh-dob-012145, Ima Hogg Photographs, Dolph Briscoe Center for American History, University of Texas at Austin.

previous and prospective gifts from her "rare and distinguished collection of furniture and other art treasures" would be properly preserved and displayed. With the board's vote of support, negotiations, later described by Ima as an "awful time," began in earnest. Neighbors fearful of public intrusion were "ugly" and critical of her proposed generosity. The 1926 compact that established Homewoods as an enclave separate from the River Oaks subdivision included a provision that required 100 percent agreement if any Homewoods owner wished to make a change in his or her property's status. In 1954 Ima and Baker Botts lawyer and museum board President Francis Graham Coates drafted a letter to Homewoods homeowners to seek their compliance. Ima's lawyers Leon Jaworski and Judge John Freeman approved the draft and sent letters and consent forms to all Lazy Lane residents. For two years Ima explained why her collection was important to Houston and Texas and assured doubters that public access to the property would involve constructing a bridge from Bayou Bend's West Garden across the bayou to a new parking lot on land that had been donated to the city by the Hoggs three decades earlier. Within two years, all the neighbors complied, but Coates himself proved a challenge; he wanted

Ima to establish a large maintenance endowment fund. Ima was a wealthy woman, but she knew the Houston Symphony Society, the Hogg Foundation, and the Houston Child Guidance Center expected handsome bequests, and she wanted any substantial monetary gift to be matched by the museum.[228]

Frustrated that agreement had still not been reached in 1956, Ima sent a memorandum explaining her position to museum board members. The collection, she insisted, was important to Texas and the American South and would be placed in a museum in Texas one day; it would be "unfortunate," she concluded, "if the furnishings could not remain in Houston in their entirety." On September 17, 1956, the board accepted the terms of her gift: she would turn over ownership of Bayou Bend and its collections and gardens to the Museum of Fine Arts of Houston; she would establish a trust to cover operating costs, which would be matched by museum fundraising efforts, her portion to total $750,000; and if at any time the museum could not fulfill terms of the trust, the collection would revert to the University of Texas. In November 1956 Ima, Alice Hogg Hanszen, and Dixon Cain agreed to serve as trustees of the Varner-Bayou Bend Heritage Fund, an estate-planning tool that would allow transfer of property and stock to the Bayou Bend Endowment Trust and to other philanthropic projects. On December 30, 1956, the museum announced Ima's stunning generosity, declaring Bayou Bend "one of three leading collections of Americana anywhere in the world"—the others being the American Wing at the Metropolitan Museum of Art in New York and Winterthur Museum and Gardens in Delaware. Ima Hogg, the museum assured her delighted admirers, would remain at Bayou Bend to oversee the transformation of her home "for the purpose of opening the house and grounds to the public." In May 1957 the board resolved officially to accept the conveyance of Bayou Bend to the Museum of Fine Arts of Houston and to defend the gift against any legal action.[229]

Not everyone was happy with Ima's promises. Upon learning of the gift, the River Oaks Property Owners Association (ROPO) sued Ima and the Museum of Fine Arts, Houston to prevent its consummation. Fortunately, the Hogg-museum legal team, led by Board Chairman Coates, successfully argued that ROPO had no legal standing to sue because a 1926 agreement gave autonomy to the independent ninety-acre Homewoods enclave. On January 8, 1958, the Harris County District Court ruled in favor of Ima and the museum. Ima congratulated Coates for the favorable ruling and reminded him that it was time for the legal team to press the city about the promised bridge and parking lot, a process that took seven years of patient diplomacy as Ima slowly persuaded the mayor and city council of Bayou Bend's civic value. Two-time president of the museum board and architect S. I. Morris designed the bridge across the bayou and secured the road extension to a ninety-car parking area—improvements paid for by the city. The Parks Department retained ownership of the land, and the surrounding area was renamed the Hogg Bird Sanctuary. By December 1959 Ima was satisfied that legal and funding issues had been resolved. On January 26, 1960, the trustees "unanimously ratified" Ima's plan to establish a Bayou Bend Advisory Committee, which would serve as liaison between the donor and the museum and would oversee operations and changes to the house and property. The board affirmed Ima's position as "Curator of Bayou Bend," responsible to the director, a position she held from 1956 to 1966. It also approved her recommendations for the advisory committee to include Ima as chairwoman and members Katherine McGowan Bryan, Dorothy Dawes Chillman, Madeleine Louise Staub, Thomas D. Anderson, and Hugo V. Neuhaus Jr. Board Chairman Theodore E. Swigart appointed a group to present the museum's approval and appreciation to Ima in person. Ima held the inaugural meeting of the advisory committee on February 24, 1960, and the advisors soon established a friends' group tasked with raising funds to match Ima's endowment pledge.[230]

Varner-Hogg and Bayou Bend demanded most of Ima's imaginative energy during the 1950s, but the engaged philanthropist did not ignore politics, public education, or mental health-care issues. Ima voted for Republican candidate Dwight D. Eisenhower in 1951 because she believed Democrats had held the presidency for too long, and in January 1952, she joined two carloads of supporters on the train to Ike's inauguration. To preserve local history, Ima helped several civic leaders in 1954 organize the Harris County Heritage and Conservation Society with the immediate goal of saving the 1847 Kellum-Noble House from demolition. As a former member of the Houston Board of Education, Ima spoke out against the ultraconservative Minute Women[231] and in 1954 joined an informal group of leading citizens to combat the Red Scare tactics that were paralyzing the school board. In October she wrote a well-received letter to the editor of the *Houston Post*, listing qualifications needed for school board candidates: an "intellectually and emotionally mature personality, . . . an open mind"; integrity; an "understanding of . . . the board as a judicial policy-making body; a "sound philosophy of education"; and regard for "spiritual and cultural aspects of living." Two years later Ima made a "wonderful contribution" to an appreciative television audience when she appeared on a "Town Meetings on Public Education" program to promote the importance of public education "to equip our children . . . emotionally to live as useful and happy adults in a changing world."[232]

During these years, Ima also wrote legislators urging passage of bills related to mental illness and served a three-year term on the board of the Texas Society of Mental Health from 1954 to 1957. In 1953 Ima invited Nina Cullinan, Dr. Abe Hauser (one of Houston's three psychiatrists), and a few prominent citizens to organize the Mental Health Society of Houston and Harris County, and she participated on the board for several years to advocate for improved services and to educate the public about mental health. In the early 1950s, Ima served on the personnel, budget and bylaws, and building committees of the Houston Child Guidance Center. She was principal speaker at the center's January 27, 1950, annual meeting and brought Hogg Foundation Director Robert Sutherland to address the January 23, 1956, annual event. She was the center's delegate to the Texas Department of Health's yearly conference in February 1951, and she worked with board members to address the center's three persistent issues: inadequate space, inability to fund competitive salaries, and exploding demand for services. As the Hogg Foundation flourished, Ima and her sisters-in-law made financial transfers that doubled the organization's income, and Ima continued to counsel with Director Sutherland. In February 1956, Ima attended the foundation's annual two-day conference and soon afterward provided $29,000 for scholarships in psychiatry. In 1958 she met for three hours with the University of Texas president to review the Hogg Foundation's purpose and to discuss its future.

As had happened several times before, the intense pressure of her busy schedule and the anxious discussions about her legacy led to exhaustion, the physical pain of sciatica, and depression. In September 1958 Ima checked into the Silver Hill Inn, founded in 1931 in New Canaan, Connecticut, to treat patients suffering "nervous, depressed, anxious, or malingering" symptoms.[233] While recuperating, she met Dr. William B. Terhune and immediately persuaded Sutherland to invite Yale University's founding professor of psychiatry to speak at the annual conference of the Texas Association for Mental Health, whose March 1959 meeting would focus on family mental health. Her spirits lifted, and she indulged in an antiquing spree while spending a week or two in New York before returning to Houston, but by June 1959 Ima was hospitalized again with sciatica, an ailment that plagued her all summer.

Bayou Bend Transformed: 1958–1966

Ima Hogg reentered the antiques market slowly in the 1940s, but her renewed interest had an immediate impact on prices as she vied with Henry du Pont, Henry Flynt, and a small group seeking the finest Americana examples. By the mid-1950s Ima's purchases in New York, forays to Philadelphia environs, or wanderings along the byways of New England consumed her self-imposed $50,000 per annum budget and netted several hundred objects. Ima asked curators Charles Cornelius, Joseph Downs, and Vincent Andrus at the Metropolitan Museum of Art's American Wing for advice and deepened her professional friendships with dealers Bernard Levy, Israel Sack, and John Walton, purchasing important examples with their help. Numerous letters reveal the dealers and collectors were friendly competitors. Dealers represented Ima at auctions, alerted her to hidden treasures that might come to market, and roiled her competitive instincts by suggesting that her collection must have a certain object or by disclosing purchases by her primary rivals. Although an increasingly confident collector who had passed her seventieth birthday in July 1952, Ima still avoided auctions and tended to binge. She bought ceramics in large lots and added pewter, brass, and American-made silver to her collections. In 1953 she purchased the first painting specifically for her Americana collection, *Portrait of John Gerry* by Joseph Badger (1708–1765). Always one of her favorites, this image of a three-year-old boy in a red coat by a Massachusetts native was the first of several children to attract Ima's attention.

Ima admired the work of Luke Vincent Lockwood (1872–1951), scholar, collector, museum installer, and author of the 1901 book *Colonial Furniture in America*, and had seen objects she coveted when visiting his home. After Lockwood's death in 1951, she made unsuccessful overtures to his widow Alice, but only at the May 13–15, 1954, Lockwood Sale at Parke-Bernet, New York, could she purchase something from his collection. Knowing their client's dislike of bidding at auction, Israel Sack, Bernard Levy, and John Walton wrote Ima, hoping to represent her. She asked Walton if the three "good friends" could "maybe . . . all get together and make me a suggestion for your mutual benefit." Sack bowed out, but Walton and Levy agreed to divide prospective purchases. Walton bid successfully on a matching Massachusetts bureau table and chest-on-chest with its original gilding (1750–1800). Ima was a "little shocked to hear what had been bid for them" and asked Walton to reduce his commission from 10 to 5 percent; on his invoice, Walton noted her request was "perfectly satisfactory." Levy suggested she specify pieces of interest and set the highest bid for each. Ima sent him a list of seven objects, including a carved chest and two pastels by premier colonial period portraitist John Singleton Copley: *Elizabeth Byles Brown* (1737–1763) circa 1763 and *Sarah Henshaw Henshaw* (1736–1822) circa 1770. She instructed Levy to bid more than the stipulated $3,500 for *Sarah Henshaw* (lot 453) if he lost *Elizabeth Brown* (lot 452). Delighted with Levy's successful acquisition of two luscious pastels—a medium that complemented her works on paper collection—Ima was dismayed to learn that Henry Flynt had wanted the portrait of Sarah Henshaw, a distant ancestress. She wrote to express her discomfort and mentioned a pastel"not nearly as beautiful"—at Knoedler Gallery; if Flynt would purchase it, she would "make an even exchange," only for him, although she had "almost no American paintings and I really need them." Always a gallant gentleman, Flynt recognized her "graciousness," said he would have stopped bidding had he known *Sarah Henshaw* "has found such a good home," and was "quite happy with the outcome." Ima promptly wrote Levy that she was very pleased "as I had really wanted the painting," and asked him to ship it to Houston at once.[234]

While enjoying gentle sparring with her favorite dealers and collecting rivals, Ima indulged in several splurges, the shopping sprees in 1958 being among the most memorable. On August 9 she acquired about forty historical flasks and transfer-printed ceramics from Sam Laidacker in Bristol, Connecticut, and in late September she purchased over one hundred items from several dealers. In New York, Israel Sack sold her a "wing" or easy chair, a joint stool, an armchair, a corner chair, and a Rhode Island tea table on September 29 and a pair of Boston black walnut Queen Anne-style chairs on October 16. At Ginsburg and Levy on October 14, she purchased a candlestand, two tables, a pair of side chairs, and a Philadelphia rococo low chest, and she returned on October 20 for an armchair. Until the end of her life, Ima continued to collect, methodically purchasing hundreds of items on wish lists she prepared for each room.

Sometimes Ima bargained hard, not forgetting her famous "museum discount" technique; but sometimes she just could not resist an opportunity. Docents usually regale visitors with the stirring acquisition of Charles Willson Peale's *Self-Portrait with Angelica and Portrait of Rachel* (circa 1782–1785). Rudolph Wunderlich of Kennedy Galleries in New York had been tantalizing Ima with promises about a Peale, which his gallery was acquiring "directly from the descendants," and he gave her the "right of first refusal." In March 1960 Wunderlich sent a photograph and a sales price: $35,000, less a 10 percent "museum" discount, which was more than Ima had ever paid for one object. Wunderlich promised to bring the triple portrait to Bayou Bend no later than June 1. He flew to Houston and presented the painting to Ima the following morning. The great Picasso was removed from the wall, and the Peale placed in its stead; overcome by the picture's beauty, Ima knew she was unlikely to encounter another rare triple portrait of such power. Yet, she told Wunderlich she would have to consult her advisory committee. When the dealer returned at four o'clock to hear the verdict, Ima said her committee felt the painting was "too expensive" and regretfully relinquished the tempting portrait. After a sleepless night, Ima interrupted the dealer's early breakfast with a 7:00 a.m. telephone call: "Would you do an old lady a favor and hold that painting for a day or two?" On June 3, ignoring her advisory committee's dictum, Ima agreed to the price and purchased the glorious masterpiece by the new nation's greatest artist. No one since has questioned the wisdom of her emotional response.[235]

The East Wing, set aside for her brothers, had been little used since Will's death in 1930, and Ima began her reorganization project there. She asked John Staub to draw plans to remodel the downstairs tap room and kitchenette into a large gallery resembling the ballroom of a New England home or inn, where she would place her seventeenth-century and early baroque collections (circa 1650–1720). She retained the Blue Room's original structure and color to house Massachusetts examples from the Revolutionary era 1760–1785. Upstairs Ima envisioned turning her brothers' bedrooms and bath area into three rooms to display Southern, Texas, and Newport furnishings. Although Ima took full responsibility for the "one-man project, with me furnishing the maintenance fund for the house, as well as making all the alterations," she did build a team of advisers.[236]

Quite naturally, she turned to her dear friend Katharine Prentis Murphy for help with the first step of her grand experiment. Murphy's eccentric installation expertise focused on early New England furniture from 1650 to 1710, including the 1957 Prentis House installation for Electra Havemayer Webb at Shelburne Museum. Murphy was knowledgeable and generous, often donating entire displays. She favored paneled fireplace walls with inset cupboards, floors painted black and white to resemble squares of marble, and furniture clustered as if awaiting a friendly gathering for tea. This mid-twentieth-century sensibility has caused several of her installations to be dismantled, but the Bayou Bend display remains as a mark of the era's scholarship and as an "homage to one of the pioneers in American collecting, who is a great benefactress . . . and very dear friend." To Ima's embarrassment, Murphy kept surprising her with unusual pewter chargers, blue and white delft wares, early crystal wine glasses, an exceptional English wall clock, and a set of ivory dominos in an ivory box, while Electra Webb delighted her with a rare "Mr. and Mss. H" delft charger. Ima began planning in 1958 and by April 1959 was "anxious" to proceed as soon as Staub completed his drawings. Confined to her bedroom suite by painful sciatica during the spring and summer months, Ima wrote often to Murphy

Dedication of the Murphy Room at Bayou Bend, November 27, 1959. Left to right: Ima Hogg, architect John Staub, and friend and collector Katharine Prentis Murphy Brandt. Bert & Associates. MS 21–056–001, Ima Hogg Papers, Museum of Fine Arts, Houston Archives.

describing the hammering, messy plaster, and her excitement: "Everything about this room is intended to reflect your inspiration . . . and imagine it coming all the way to Texas! It gives me a real thrill." Still in pain when the renovation was completed, Ima asked John Graham II, the director of collections and curator at Colonial Williamsburg, to help with color choices and furniture placement. Ima's good health returned. She was "still in the clouds" about her team, "who performed miracles," and charmed when Murphy, Graham, and Staub joined her for the grand opening on November 26. Guests were uniformly enthusiastic. Ima felt a "great sense of relief" when the room was christened. The Murphy Room, she said, "is a great joy to me and to everyone who sees it." Reenergized, Ima immediately plunged ahead with Bayou Bend's transformation.[237]

Ima recognized the complex technical challenges of her plan—placing objects made between 1650 and 1850 in a building completed in 1928 and finding the best period examples to reconstruct what could only be an imagined past. John D. Rockefeller Jr. at Williamsburg and the Flynts at Deerfield salvaged and restored period buildings; Henry du Pont hunted for entire rooms that he removed from period buildings and placed in his much-expanded house museum. Ima was unable to find much authentic paneling or flooring and relied on John Staub to specify period details and provide "a harmonious setting for [her] collection of American furnishings." Winterthur Director Charles Montgomery and his wife, Florence, also an authority, paid Ima a short visit in 1961 and responded to her quandary. Montgomery told Ima to explain the "philosophy" behind her wish to "present Bayou Bend to the public"—to tell America's story through material objects. He advised her to develop a theme for each room, persuaded her to record her actions, and helped her develop worksheets and inventories for objects she needed to complete each room. Ima invited her "antiquee" friends to serve as an "honorary advisory committee"—Ralph Carpenter, Henry Francis du Pont, Helen and Henry Flynt, John Graham II, Maxim Karolik, Charles F. Montgomery, Katharine Prentis Murphy, Ford Museum's Donald Shelley, and Alice Winchester of *The Magazine Antiques*. Electra Havemayer Webb died in 1960 before she could advise her friend, but committee members responded to a detailed questionnaire with insightful suggestions and a few treasures for the collection.[238]

Following her Murphy Room success, Ima sought the "expert advice" and assistance "of her dear friend" Dorothy Dawes Chillman to help her decorate and arrange the furnishings in the other East Wing rooms. Downstairs Ima placed the rococo settee and eight matching chairs, the Boston bombé desk and bookcase, a rare "turret-top" Boston tea table, and the matching high chest and bureau table in the Blue Room to create a Massachusetts Room on the verge of revolution. She used small, tiered tables to display her "excellent collection of Whieldon" ceramics, important English wares used in colonial North America. Upstairs she placed her Newport treasures and her colonial period silver in Mike's old bedroom, remodeled in the summer of 1960 as a parlor resembling closely a room in Newport's restored Hunter House. Four cherubs adorned a paneled wall surrounding the fireplace, which was flanked by two inset, shell-crowned cupboards. Ima playfully named the cherub carvings Henry du Pont, Henry Flynt, Electra Webb, and Katharine Murphy. For Will's old bedroom, Ima planned a neoclassical Southern parlor, but she could not find enough Southern furnishings from the years of early nationhood to fill the modest space. Even the "Baltimore" sofa Bernard Levy thought he had found in March 1961—to complement a Baltimore card table Ima had purchased in 1921—proved to be from New York, upon further examination. When Ima discovered a circa-1801 Philadelphia mantel, attributed to ornamental plaster artist Robert Wellford, she installed dentiled crown molding that matched the mantel ornament and period pine floorboards to create a "Federal Parlor" reflecting the taste of the new nation, and she furnished the room with selections from the Eastern Seaboard. Five decades later, conservators discovered a Robert Wellford label on the mantel, verifying Ima's unmatched ability to recognize unsigned works by the finest craftsmen.[239]

To complete her East Wing reorganization, Ima glazed the sleeping porch that overlooked the East Garden and placed Windsor seating furniture from Will's large collection in the space, which she planned to use for meetings, small exhibits, and a rest area for touring guests. In the bath and dressing rooms shared by her brothers, Ima reworked the space to install her Texas Room. She created a dining room where she displayed her large collection of Texian Campaigne ceramics; her historic flasks, most of which depicted early national or Mexican-American War (1845–1846) heroes; and her "old prints from The Mexican War," including works by popular New York lithographers Nathaniel Currier (1813–1888), Napoleon Sarony (1821–1896), and Henry B. Major (active 1844–1854) . She reworked the space with cypress flooring and Gothic arched cedar paneling, based on paneling that had been removed from an 1850s East Texas house and reinstalled in the home of her neighbors Agnes and Haywood Nelms in the 1930s. She then wrote to Ted James, who had been collecting Texana since the 1930s, and asked for advice. He responded that Texas furniture examples were much prized by family heirs and suggested she purchase pieces that could be replaced when Texas examples were "offered for sale." Ima took this advice, moved Joseph Lewis Hogg's portrait from the drawing room, and placed it on the wall opposite her Texian Campaigne display. She found a Tennessee sideboard, a Kentucky sugar chest, and an eastern dining table to tell the story of people like her grandfather, who pioneered across the South to East Texas in the years before the Civil War. Finally, Ima turned a former storage space into the Staffordshire Hall, where she displayed blue and white transfer-printed earthenware ceramics made for export from England to the young United States, each piece depicting a scenic or historic landmark—Niagara Falls and Bulfinch's Boston State House—or a new mode of transportation—steam ships and railroads.[240]

Although Ima had insisted museum trustees promise to preserve and display her collection in perpetuity, she also realized that it could be improved and expanded. While making lists of objects she planned to place in each room, she also made wish lists of objects she hoped one day would be found for the collection. After Ima's death, curators moved the blue and white Staffordshire ceramics to the Glazed Porch and renamed the hallway display space the Pennsylvania German Hall, where they exhibited artifacts from the German communities of eastern Pennsylvania. In the twenty-first century, collector William J. Hill completed Ima's dream when he donated two collections of objects made or used in Central Texas: furniture crafted by mid-nineteenth-century German American settlers and storage jars made by freed African American potters. Hill's generous donation transformed the Texas Room and the display alcove, renamed Texas Hall."[241]

While finishing the East Wing, Ima also reworked the White Bedroom, located off the corridor to the West Wing and previously reserved for Mary Fuller when she visited. Workmen closed the door to an adjacent bathroom and remodeled that space as an office. For the bedroom, Ima ordered crown molding, a paneled dado, and a chair rail in the mid-eighteenth-century manner. She chose stone-colored paint for the woodwork and received permission from Colonial Williamsburg to duplicate red wool moreen hangings in the Brush-Everard House for the handsome bedstead she had purchased in 1928. The renamed Chippendale Bedroom housed an aesthetically charming desk and bookcase with sinuous bombé sides and serpentine drawer fronts, which had descended in the Thomas Dawes family until David Stockwell sold it to Ima in 1954. In the former West Wing guest suite, Ima retained examples from the Federal period for a Music Room and a renamed McIntire Bedroom, and in 1965 was contemplating converting the suite's dressing room and bath into a "Belter Parlor" or "Empire Room" at a later date. Her bedroom and sitting room, refigured as the Queen Anne Sitting Room and Queen Anne Bedroom, would have to await her departure and removal of the piano and other modern objects to be completed.

Downstairs, the entrance hall was rechristened the Philadelphia Hall to celebrate important rococo examples from that city. In the Drawing Room, Ima removed her grand piano and arranged the finest examples of rococo furniture made in colonial America's five major ports—Boston, Newport, New York, Philadelphia, and Charleston—to show how cabinetmakers adapted English designs in distinctive ways suited to regional colonial tastes and North American woods. In 1963 she told members of the River Oaks Garden Club that she found "comparing indigenous styles . . . with those of other countries and noting sources of influence" a "fascinating pastime." Ima retained the Dining Room's original wall covering and the sideboard purchased from Israel Sack in 1951, and she bought a set of two armchairs and six side chairs from Ginsburg and Levy in 1960. Four years later, Sack sold her four more chairs in the same square-back pattern taken from Thomas Sheraton's *Drawing-Book* and popular with early national cabinet makers like Duncan Phyfe of New York City. Ima did not replace the English dining table, the "one thing for which I have a truly sentimental feeling," because its presence reminded her of the celebrities, friends, and family members who had dined at Bayou Bend. In the Library, Ima removed her book collection but retained the shelves, which she covered with paneling like the paneling installed around the fireplace in 1928. She also removed the Windsor furniture, and hooked rugs to create the Pine Room, which features early eighteenth-century examples, including the distinctive Boston high chest (circa 1700–1725) that John Walton found in 1953 and the desk (circa 1700–1730) that she purchased in 1927—both displaying sophisticated cabinetmaking techniques using black walnut with burl walnut veneer.[242]

While carpenters were hammering and Ima was making her inventories and lists of needed additions, she began planning how the house and garden would be maintained and interpreted. In 1957, the year the Museum of Fine Arts officially accepted her donation of home, gardens, and house contents, the River Oaks Garden Club asked Ima to open her gardens for the annual Azalea Trail in March 1958. Feeling unequal to supervising and preparing the gardens without help, she proposed a choice: she would simply make a $1,000 donation and not show the gardens, or she would provide $2,000 to the club for plantings and labor if its members would appoint a committee to oversee and assist garden preparation and flower arrangements. On December 7, 1957, the club accepted her "opportunity" with "a feeling of great responsibility and gratitude,"[243] and it appointed collector and friendly rival Faith Bybee[244] chairwoman of the Bayou Bend preparations committee. Ima had planted a seed, and four years later, on May 17, 1961, she received a letter that undoubtedly did not surprise her. Members of the River Oaks Garden Club, "in gratitude and as a lasting tribute to you . . . would like to assume permanent supervision of your garden." Ima replied the same day. The club's resolution "moves me deeply," she wrote her young friend Virginia Lawhon, and "assurance that the gardens will have substantial and expert care in the future . . . relieves me of a burden."[245] Over time, the club developed cooperative procedures with the Museum of Fine Arts; the Azalea Trail became a major fundraiser for garden upkeep; and provisional club members fulfilled their volunteer obligation by assisting the head gardener—whose salary was defrayed by the club—and his staff of three. At the suggestion of new Curator David Warren, the club announced in 1967 that it would create historically accurate arrangements of fresh-cut flowers for the house. That year the club made a gift of $10,000 to establish a Garden

Endowment Fund managed by trustees named by the club and the museum. Now a major source of enduring support, the fund provides income to underwrite upkeep for fourteen acres of harmonious beauty in the center of Houston.

Although Ima ceded management of the gardens to the River Oaks Garden Club, she did not lose interest in their development. High winds, a terrific storm surge, and heavy rain accompanied Hurricane Carla's landfall at Port O'Connor, Texas, on September 11, 1961. The deluge opened a glade between the Euterpe and East gardens, and Ima decided to create a charming circular Carla Garden, surrounded by azaleas. A decade later she added brick paving and enclosed the sheltered space with boxwood hedges and azaleas. At the March 5, 1971, garden club meeting, members learned Ima had embellished the reworked garden with a carousel peacock. In the mid-1960s Ima designed and paid for the entry guard's octagonal, grillwork gazebo and turned Clio ninety degrees, so visitors would see the statue's profile, not her back, as they crossed the bridge. Ima terraced the area around the gazebo and blended the new landscaping with the long-established Clio Garden. In 1966 Ima replaced the annual borders of the East Garden with Japanese boxwood, clipped to mimic the scroll ironwork of the east porch. About the same time, she added pink Japanese magnolias east of the Diana Garden and a few years later pink crepe myrtle at the reflecting pool to extend the blooming period for her gardens. At the end of her life, Ima provided funds to build a much-needed greenhouse and to replant the Clio Garden.

While gently encouraging the River Oaks Garden Club to take responsibility for the care of her gardens, Ima was also considering the best way to interpret her collections. Although she had visited Winterthur to confer with Henry du Pont and its curator, Charles Montgomery, and had learned much from them, she did not emulate their hunt for entire rooms, and she emphatically preferred volunteer docents to paid staff as collection interpreters. Marshaling the power of volunteer women had long been central to her success, and building the Bayou Bend Docent Organization affirmed Hogg family belief that citizen involvement would transmit values and aspirations to future generations and strengthen communities. Jonathan Fairbanks first visited Bayou Bend in 1960 as a recent graduate of the University of Delaware's Winterthur Museum Program who was seeking a curatorial position. That year James Johnson Sweeney, a modernist, replaced Lee Malone as Houston's museum director, and his priorities did not include hiring a curator for Bayou Bend. Fairbanks joined the staff at Winterthur, and the next summer Ima invited him to come to Houston for a month. She and Faith Bybee, chairwoman of the Harris County Heritage

The north façade and gardens at Bayou Bend, sketched by Buck Schiwetz, 1954. Bayou Bend Buildings Collection, Museum of Fine Arts, Houston Archives.

Society, agreed to defray a $500 salary to cover teaching the first docent class three mornings a week and lecturing at the Heritage Society in the afternoon. Ima asked Ruth Pershing Uhler, manager of the successful Museum of Fine Arts, Houston docent program staffed by Junior League volunteers, to help her select twenty-two "charming ladies," who were introduced to the docent concept at a series of small luncheons at Bayou Bend. Many candidates were teachers Ima had met during her years on the school board or volunteers she knew from the Houston Symphony Association Women's Committee. Few could refuse a personal request from Miss Hogg, and all recognized the great honor bestowed upon them as the pioneer group who would carry on a great legacy.[246]

Fairbanks arrived in early July to study the rooms and map a realistic tour plan. On Monday, July 5, 1961, Ima welcomed the first class and attended every session thereafter. Museum Board Chairman S. I. Morris introduced the young instructor, who noted that serious collecting of American furniture for its beauty rather than for its historical associations was a relatively recent development. He spent the first morning discussing the "Role of the Docent"—"to protect and preserve the collection" by following strict rules of behavior and to interpret objects by helping guests understand their significance "in America's artistic, social, economic, and industrial development." Fairbanks recorded, transcribed, and edited all lectures, which were used by members of the first class to train provisional docents for the next three years. Fairbanks's method of lecture, room study, and research paper frames provisional training today, as does Ima's wish that docents would "learn for themselves." Class attendees consulted a library of furniture, art history, and American history books, catalogued and maintained by Eloise Helbig Chalmers for many years. They studied inventory books, placed in each room, that contained color-coded cards explaining each object, a system Jane Zivley introduced in 1955 that continued until replaced by digital technology in 2020. When the class ended, Ima asked Eugenia Tennant to serve as chairwoman, a position she held from 1961 to 1964, and to prepare the next classes. Tennant deputized Joan Fleming to write bylaws and regulations for the Bayou Bend Docent Organization, based closely on the bylaws of the Girls Musical Club. In 1962 Fairbanks revealed the glories of the Bayou Bend Collection to Williamsburg Forum attendees.[247]

By 1965 Ima had remodeled the gardener's cottage and four-car garage as a visitors' center with meeting rooms for the docents, who met monthly. To complete provisional training, each docent prepared a substantial talk for one of these meetings. Until her death Ima attended every meeting, sat in the front row in her chic suit and fashionable hat, and listened attentively to the novice speakers—long remembered as an unnerving experience. She befriended many docents, and on May 31, 1971, spoke to meeting attendees about the origins of her collection. "About 1920," she recalled, she had one of her "unaccountable compulsions to make an American collection for some Texas museum." "Collecting," she explained, "is a disease. I think I had it from childhood. In Austin the streets . . . were covered with beautiful pebbles. When wet they sparkled like jewels, and in the spring the ditches . . . were filled with . . . wild flowers which could be pressed." She could not remember when she "was not interested in old things with a history," and recalled her grandfather's home and the many people who helped her satisfy an insatiable curiosity and build her collection. "I love each object in Bayou Bend for each has a special meaning to me," she concluded. Her high standards and her overarching purpose to "bring Texas closer to the heart of an American heritage which unites us" continue to inspire and motivate docents, who reach out to the public and strive to fulfill her dream.[248]

Since the 1960s, guests have crossed the swinging bridge from the parking lot and entered the Winedale Cottage visitors' center to discover a friendly interior based on Texas-German architecture of rural Central Texas, with pale green plank walls, salmon pink dado, and dark brown trim. For years, Audubon prints and a large portrait of the Jones children of Galveston by Thomas Flintoff (1809–1892) were displayed on the walls, while tables and chairs, a Southern wall cupboard, and a desk on chest from Washington County, Texas, furnished the space. Today the cottage houses Bayou Bend's gift shop. Touring began before Ima left the house, and several times docents reported ascending the stairs to discover their mentor, only too happy to join the guests. After Ima's departure, docents offered regularly scheduled two-hour tours of up to four guests for many years. In 1970 docents began traveling to schools to present a slide talk to fifth graders that used images of objects in the collection to illustrate America's story, and in 1992 docents introduced house tours for school groups. As the organization grew, Ima chose an enamel butterfly pin she had discovered in Mexico to reward board service and, after 1969, to celebrate eight years of service. The tradition of butterfly awards continued after her death, and in 1989 former docent and artist Mariquita Masterson designed a silver butterfly pin to honor twenty years of service. Masterson's design incorporates the butterfly, symbol of long life and happiness, the lyre, recalling Ima's love of music, and the pineapple, in homage to the hospitality Ima extended to hundreds of Bayou Bend visitors. In subsequent decades, Masterson has tweaked her design to celebrate thirty, forty, and fifty years of active docent service.[249]

By the spring of 1964, Ima and her fellow Museum of Fine Arts trustees concluded that it was time to hire a curator for the collection and turned to Charles Montgomery for suggestions. He sent two promising second-year Winterthur Program students to meet with Ima in New York City, but neither young man wanted a Texas adventure. Montgomery then cajoled reluctant Princeton graduate and Delaware native David B. Warren, who was entering his second year of the Winterthur Program, to consider Bayou Bend and travel to Houston after Christmas 1964 for an interview. Docent Sandy Thompson met Warren at the airport and drove him to Bayou Bend, where the applicant was surprised to discover several "extremely well dressed ladies sitting about on the floor" with "large, fat notebooks," having their usual "study day"—and spying on the candidate. After settling into the guest suite and learning that Miss Hogg was "indisposed," Warren began wandering through the collection and was "stunned by what I saw—room after room of superb objects"—"just extraordinary furniture!" When Warren finally met his hostess, he was "struck by how pretty she was, belying her 82 years, with lovely white skin, vivid blue eyes, and sandy-colored hair." Undaunted by dinners with Alice Hogg Hanszen and other advisers, Warren was happy to accept the offer made to him in January 1965 by Board Chairman Edward Rotan—even though he had never met his titular boss, Director Sweeney. Ima, who had been ill for much of the winter, rallied after the curatorial choice was made and began final preparations for her move to the apartment being finished at Inwood Manor to her meticulous specifications. In August she thanked the Bayou Bend Docent Organization for its "handsome check," the first in a continuous line of generous gifts to the collection, and she told Rotan and members of the advisory committee, she "could not be more pleased . . . with the selection of David Warren. . . . I think he has great knowledge and intuitive sense which is very valuable, good taste and maturity. I feel that Bayou Bend is going into the right hands." Warren assumed his post in midsummer, immediately assisted Ima with her departure, and began preparing for his first docent training course. Ima attended the September docent meeting in the remodeled garage space and afterward allowed her chauffeur and general factotum Lucious Broadnax to drive her away to the next phase of her long career. Late that fall, she invited Albert Sack to appraise the furniture and silver and called on Bernard Levy to evaluate everything else. The experts agreed Bayou Bend's contents were worth a little more than $8 million; concerned the figure would sound inflated, Ima asked the museum to value her collections at $5 million instead. Today, docents tell curious visitors the collections are priceless.[250]

Ima did not visit Bayou Bend for two or three months, but she returned in time to plan the formal dedication of her gift with activities scheduled for March 4–6, 1966. Headlines that week announced the B-52 bombing of Saigon (now Ho Chi Minh City) and a plunging stock market, but Houston's devoted civic leaders joined connoisseurs and collectors from out of state and braved chilly weather to dedicate Bayou Bend as the decorative arts wing of the Museum of Fine Arts, Houston on Saturday, March 5, and to celebrate Ima's extraordinary vision and generosity. For Ima the ceremony was not a culmination but a pause to recall years of hard work and the fulfillment of her 1920 pledge to form collections for a museum in Texas. A month before her eighty-fifth birthday, Ima sat down for an interview with the *Dallas Morning News*. "She has a young mind," the reporter noted. "Talking with her is like talking to a vibrant, intelligent girl." Her "luminous quality" and "kind, blue-green eyes" shone as she remembered her childhood home, where "there were a few tears. There were also music and flowers and laughter."[251] During the last decade of her life, Ima continued her lifelong commitment to music and mental health and added to all her collections. She also created an outdoor museum at Winedale, preserved her Grandfather Stinson's home, supervised new installations at Bayou Bend, inspired a volume on Texas furniture, and dispersed family and personal papers to archival repositories.

Rural Restorations: 1961–1975

After Ima left the September 1965 Bayou Bend Docent Organization meeting, she seemed to disappear. In fact, she had turned her attention to the farming village of Winedale, where she met Wayne Bell, a young employee at the University of Texas in the Office of the Architect. Bell had agreed to complete Ima's latest enthusiasm—the holistic restoration of several nineteenth-century structures to create an outdoor community of buildings devoted to explaining the flora, fauna, and people of Central Texas. In 1961 Ima's friend, the antiques dealer and conservationist Hazel Ledbetter, introduced the collector to old Texas buildings in rural Fayette County, about seventy miles west of Houston. After Hurricane Carla, Ledbetter purchased a storm-battered two-story frame house built by Anglo-American Samuel Lewis in the 1840s and sold to German immigrant Joseph George Wagner in 1882. Ledbetter thought Ima might be interested in the building's interiors, which boasted an intricately painted parlor ceiling by German-born artist Rudolph Melchior.[252] Ima was, indeed, intrigued, but with her usual scholarly caution, she asked newly named director of the Harris County Heritage Society, James Nonemaker, to visit Winedale in July 1962 and evaluate the house and its attendant barns and outbuildings to see if any of the structures could be used at Bayou Bend. Nonemaker was impressed by the main house, which local residents thought had been used as an inn in the late nineteenth century. "There is no question," he stated firmly, "that the Stage Coach Inn should be completely restored to its original appearance. . . . [T]he question of taking one room or any part . . . and abandoning the rest is unthinkable and would constitute a great dis-service to the State of Texas. . . . The importance of the building and its existing outbuildings warrants that every effort be made to restore it to its original site."[253] Ima agreed and asked Houston renovation specialists Langwith, Wilson & King to visit the site, take complete measurements, and prepare drawings that established the condition of the building before restoration. When Ima was unable to convince Ledbetter to restore the building, she purchased the almost unaltered mid-nineteenth-century structure and 130 acres of the former Wagner farm from her friend in

August 1963 and plunged into a project she hoped would demonstrate proper preservation techniques, be a training ground for future experts, and illuminate the stories of nineteenth-century German and Bohemian settlers in the area.

In September 1963 Ima hired John Young, a recent graduate of the School of Architecture at Rice University to create a restoration plan and oversee local contractors. Unfortunately, Ima and her young protégé did not relate well, partly because no research had been done on the building, partly because Ima oversaw every aspect of the renovation, and partly because Young was inexperienced and overwhelmed by the intense interest of his highly engaged employer. Ima sent meticulous lists of instructions about everything from wood finishes to hand-forged nails, made frequent visits to the site, and demanded detailed daily reports and thorough financial records. Extensive correspondence between perfectionist patron and intimidated employee led to inevitable misunderstandings and a need to "decide just what constitutes the 'correct' restoration of the Inn." Early in 1964, Ima asked Henderson Shuffler, a professor who specialized in Texas history and culture at the Humanities Research Center of the University of Texas, to lead a research committee, and she named a local man to be general contractor. Young was able to stabilize the residence and small outbuildings, restore the property's small foursquare barn, and convert the large barn into a performance space, but his efforts ended awkwardly when he stopped sending reports and Ima realized he had enrolled as a graduate student in architecture at the University of Texas. She cancelled his signature at Round Top Bank and requested he return all floor plans and drawings in his possession.[254]

On October 2, 1964, Ima wrote University of Texas President Harry Ransom to tell him she wanted to see "some Texas educational institution develop an appropriate architectural, historical, fine arts, or decorative arts program" on her property at Winedale. Ransom replied on October 11 that the university would be "deeply honored" to execute her "great vision." After a series of letters, discussions, and appraisals, Ima and Ransom agreed to terms, including the creation of an endowment of $500,000 in trust as the Hogg Winedale Center Fund, collaboration with other institutions, an advisory committee, and a public announcement at the UT System Board of Regents meeting on March 12–14, 1965. With the transfer formally announced, Ima worked with Ransom to establish a Winedale Advisory Council, chaired by University of Texas School of Architecture Professor Drury B. Alexander, and to hire a project architect for Ima's restoration program.[255]

In November 1965 Ima and restoration architect Wayne Bell established a good working relationship and eventual friendship. Bell served as liaison between Ima and the university and devoted his Saturdays to on-site visits, where he frequently met his patron, who continued to fund preservation efforts. In 1965 Ima purchased the roomy Lauderdale farmhouse, which she moved to the site and restored as a dormitory for visiting scholars and students.[256] On Saturday, April 8, 1967, the board of regents and chancellor of the University of Texas invited friends and supporters to an "Old-Fashioned German Barbecue" honoring Ima and celebrating a two-day dedication of the Winedale Inn properties as "a laboratory for the revival and restoration of a way of life." Events included a band concert, a dedicatory address by Winterthur Director Charles van Ravenswaay, a one-act play and folk dancing staged by the university's Department of Drama, services at the Bethlehem Lutheran Church in Round Top, and guided tours of the property. First Lady Lady Bird Johnson, state officials, university dignitaries, Houston admirers, and Katharine Prentis Murphy, sporting a huge hat, attended the launch of Ima's outdoor experiment. Texas First Lady Nellie Connally, wife of Governor John B. Connally, presented a Texas Restoration Award to the state's renowned conservationist. In 1969 Hazel Ledbetter donated a Texas dogtrot house—a one-story building with rooms on either side of an open breezeway, all covered by a single roof. Renamed Hazel's Lone Oak Cottage, the small building was placed near the Lewis-Wagner house, barns, and dependencies. That year Ima moved the 1861 McGregor plantation house, a vernacular Greek Revival building with three richly painted formal rooms, to a wooded site within walking distance of the other buildings. Ima hired a curator in 1970, and the recently formed Friends of Winedale volunteer support group purchased the remaining Wagner farm and lake across the road, creating a 215-acre recreational space.[257]

Wayne Bell continued his liaison role at Winedale until the restoration work was completed. He and Ima worked so well together that she asked him to oversee restoration of her Grandfather Stinson's beloved East Texas antebellum house with its "mysterious attic" filled with trunks and the "romantic contents of Godey Lady's Book." Ima acquired the old Stinson house and moved it thirteen miles to the Governor Hogg Memorial Park site in Quitman. Working with the Wood County Historical Survey Committee, she began a six-year restoration project, and she also organized the small Ima Hogg Museum to explain the history of East Texas through artifacts made or used there. At the museum's dedication on Sunday, May 25, 1969, Ima thanked the guests for their support, recalled her happy childhood visits to her grandfather's experimental farm, and asked attendees to "imagine my joy when I see the Stinson home . . . in the Park so near the Honeymoon Cottage—all nestled together around this Museum. . . . Here is peace on earth. . . . I feel I am coming home!" Five years later, when the Stinson House was officially opened on November 2, 1974, speaker T. C. Chadick dedicated the house to early East Texans "who turned . . . wilderness into productive farms and graceful homes."[258]

Curator Lonn Taylor and his scholarly wife, Diane, arrived at Winedale late in September 1970 to meet the "legendary Miss Ima Hogg" and to discover "a collection of German . . . furniture . . . in the middle of the most beautiful country in Texas." The Taylors and their engaged patron made a good team. Lonn and Ima held lengthy discussions about her vision and the programs she hoped to sponsor, while Diane proved a meticulous registrar who made complete inventories of over four thousand objects, trained docents to lead guests around the property, and maintained native plantings appropriate to each structure. As Lonn recalled, Ima wanted to create an open-air museum where visitors walked into the houses, similar to the Oslo and Stockholm folk museums she had experienced with such excitement in 1929. She "was using the buildings as a setting to display . . . a collection of German-American furniture" that showed the transmission of craftsmanship from Germany to Pennsylvania, Missouri, and Texas. Ima espoused a complex vision that involved several departments at the University of Texas in a cooperative effort to explore the agriculture, native plants and animals, and way of life of an ethnic group. Ima coaxed many nearby families to place beloved objects on long-term loan at Winedale and worked hard to cement friendly ties with local residents while also encouraging academic departments to use the facility for cultural immersion experiences.[259]

Lonn soon learned that Ima loved to experiment and was "someone who really liked to share her knowledge," a "wonderful teacher" who combined a "marvelous aesthetic sense" with a deep understanding of how furniture was made. From 1968 to 1972, Winedale held two-day public workshops on preservation and restoration techniques in cooperation with the Texas State Historical Survey Committee. These annual events drew university faculty, survey staff, well-known experts, and local owners who were restoring old buildings. In 1971 the Shakespeare Program, sponsored by the university's English and Drama departments, began its continuing summer performances in the theater barn. Lonn Taylor was promoted to director in 1972 and collaborated with Ima, Wayne Bell, and the advisory committee to craft a master plan for the property. To lure guests, Ima and the Taylors tried a fall festival of antiques dealers, a

Christmas open house featuring period trees and food, and a spring festival arts and crafts show.[260]

Until the last months of her life, Ima continued to collect Texas objects for Winedale, Bayou Bend, Quitman, and Varner-Hogg, treating these public properties as if their contents still belonged to her. She often surprised the Taylors by arriving "in a big blue Ford station wagon" driven by Lucious Broadnax. She "would just unload stuff" and begin arranging it in the buildings. If one historic site was not displaying something, she removed the neglected object and placed it somewhere else. One museum curator sent Diane a list of "wandering candlesticks," and in despair on May 6, 1975, Bayou Bend Curator Barry Greenlaw wrote Lonn to say that Ima, who was about to depart for Europe, had insisted on taking some objects from a Bayou Bend closet out to Winedale. Greenlaw tried to explain the objects had been accessioned at Bayou Bend, and she could not take them away. Somewhat amused, Lonn responded, "Short of physically preventing her from moving them, there seems to be no way to deal with it." Untangling the record of Winedale's objects continued until the Taylors left Winedale in 1977.[261]

When Ima furnished the McGregor House in 1972, she drew on family information and estate inventories to find German-inspired Texas furniture for the restored building. Since 1961, when Ima was furnishing the Texas Room at Bayou Bend, her knowledge of Texas furniture had expanded greatly, and more objects were available because families realized their attics and barns contained treasures desired by collectors. Ima's work at Winedale led to her final obsession—creation of a book on Texas furniture. Ima said that Charles van Ravenswaay's 1967 visit to the Winedale dedication and his discovery of a table and chest of drawers based on central European Biedermeier designs inspired her to produce a book, and she told David Warren he should write a book about Texan furniture. Warren was preoccupied by activities at Bayou Bend, so Ima got busy. She secured a promise from the University of Texas Press to publish the projected compendium, developed a questionnaire, and sent letters around the state asking for pictures of and information about Texas-made furniture. She asked university archivist Chester Kielman to send her census lists, which she hoped would reveal the presence of unknown craftsmen. Her efforts produced extensive information and many images—which mysteriously disappeared. When Lonn Taylor arrived at Winedale in 1970, she prevailed upon him to research the topic, write background essays, and serve as editor in chief, while Warren traveled around the state analyzing examples and supervising photography. As Ima's ninetieth birthday loomed, she urged the team to finish. When she learned that collecting rival Faith Bybee was helping the Witte Museum in San Antonio organize a huge 1973 loan exhibition and catalogue of Texas furniture, a daring effort that seemed to duplicate her project, Ima grew anxious, but she soon recognized that the Witte exhibit had whetted appetites for more information. She persuaded the Museum of Fine Arts, Houston to cosponsor publication of her book and in the summer of 1974 wrote an introduction for *Texas Furniture: The Cabinetmakers and Their Work, 1840–1880*. That winter she read the completed manuscript. While in London in July 1975, Ima received the book's dust jacket.[262]

New Horizons: 1966–1975

Ima never forgot sleeping in a giant mid-nineteenth-century bed at the Texas Governor's Mansion when she was a little girl. She placed Victorian furnishings in her powder room and displayed Rococo Revival furniture she purchased in 1944 from dealer Carll Chace in Bayou Bend's Blue Room. As she transformed Bayou Bend, she imagined creating a Belter Parlor to celebrate the pathbreaking innovations of premiere New York craftsman John Henry Belter,[263] and she addressed the issue with David Warren in the spring of 1966. Warren did not dampen her enthusiasm for high-style Victorian furniture but did suggest they move in chronological order and begin by remodeling space to exhibit decorative arts of the earlier Empire period, made popular by Berry B. Tracy's pioneering exhibition and catalogue for the Newark Museum in 1963. *Classical America: 1815–1845* awakened public interest in Empire and Restoration furniture based on French styles of Napoleon's empire and English styles of the Prince of Wales's regency. Inspired by the beautiful catalogue, Warren's logic, and consultations with Dorothy Dawes Chillman, Ima began hunting for furniture. During her years as an interior designer, Chillman had studied the period, and she guided Ima's early planning but sadly died on September 30, 1968, before the project was completed. Ima expressed her gratitude by naming the suite for her longtime friend and frequent consultant.

In July 1966 contractors were completing their renovation of the garage as a visitors' center and meeting rooms, and it seemed like a good time to remodel the unused housekeeper's quarters adjacent to the kitchen in the West Wing. When Peter Hill, in Washington, DC, found a large tilt-top loo table (circa 1825–1835) from Philadelphia and an outstanding New York sideboard (circa 1815–1830), attributed to Joseph Meeks and Son (1797–1868), Ima was so excited she inspired her sister-in-law Alice Hogg Hanszen to finance their purchase. Both pieces displayed the attributes of late classical craftsmanship—grained mahogany veneers, ebonizing, gilding, and stenciling—and Ima decided to divide the West Wing space, in the style of Greek Revival double rooms, to create a parlor for the loo table and a "dining" area for the splendid sideboard. Happily, Peter Hill found six period valences stenciled and painted with imaginary scenes to embellish six window openings. Workmen created an access gallery between the new suite and the dining room by enclosing the connecting porch and piercing its west wall to fashion a doorway. While David Warren was writing to curators and dealers about suggestions for paintings, fabrics, and carpets, Ima hired Langwith, Wilson, and King, who were helping her at Winedale, to prepare architectural drawings for the converted space and new entry. The architects completed drawings by spring 1968; construction was finished by Christmas; and the Empire (1810–1830) and Restoration (1830–1850) furniture, paintings, silver, and lighting fixtures were installed for the room's dedication on March 21, 1969. David Warren publicized Bayou Bend's newest room setting with an illustrated article in the January 1970 issue of *The Magazine Antiques*.

By the 1960s Ima's good judgment, discerning taste, and fashion sense had become as legendary as her independent spirit and willingness to explore untested territory. Henry du Pont created room after room of furniture made before 1820 but only tiptoed toward late neoclassical and scorned later styles. Harold Sack found mid-nineteenth-century fashion "not my cup of tea," and when he failed to admire a recently purchased sofa from John Henry Belter's workshop in 1966, Ima "shook her head sadly, and said, 'Harold, there's the future. You'd better get with it!'" When she finally turned her attention to creating the long-desired Belter Parlor, only the Brooklyn Museum offered a Rococo Revival period room. Ima considered space in the upstairs West Wing, but when curator David Warren remarked that the location was too small, the ceilings too low, and the windows inadequate, she realized the introduction of Belter furniture would disrupt the flow of ideas generated by exploring the wing's two neoclassical rooms. Ima agreed that demolishing the coatroom, telephone room, powder room, and passage to the former breakfast room would yield an excellent space with long windows and high ceilings on the northwest end of the Philadelphia Hall. Langwith, Wilson, and King again supplied working drawings, and construction began.[264]

Ima and Warren wanted the installation to be as historically correct as possible. To that end, Warren provided a list of needs to his patron in January 1969, and in June he wrote to the Brooklyn Museum to request exact spacing measurements from the Robert Milligan House parlor that had been reinstalled there recently. While Ima hunted for furniture, Warren wrote numerous letters to interior designers, art galleries, and experts inquiring about fabrics, wall papers, draperies, paintings, and accessories of every kind. When they learned that the contents of the Corliss-Brackett House—built in 1875 by mechanical engineer George Henry Corliss (1817–1888) of Providence, Rhode Island, and redecorated in the 1920s with Rococo Revival furniture—would come on the market in 1970, it seemed as if many issues might be resolved. Lengthy negotiations proved successful, and Ima acquired several objects from the mansion: a carved marble mantel, a mirror to place over the mantel, two elaborately carved cornice boards, a handsome gas chandelier, Brussels carpet, and part of a rosewood Rococo Revival parlor set, consisting of one sofa, two armchairs, and two of six side chairs, at the time attributed to Alexander Roux of New York. With draperies based on originals at Lansdowne Plantation in Natchez and wallpaper created for the room from period samples at the Cooper Hewitt Museum, Ima was able to install her most historically accurate room setting and stimulate enthusiasm for the mid-Victorian era. In 1981, a rosewood parlor set (1855) from the shop of John Henry Belter, complete with bill of sale, which Ima had given to the Texas Governor's Mansion in 1974, reverted to Bayou Bend, because the mansion supervisors decided to refurnish the structure with earlier nineteenth-century pieces in keeping with the building's construction date and style.[265]

For her last project at Bayou Bend, Ima reworked the Maple Bedroom, formerly the Rose Room adjacent to her dressing and bathroom. She had previously moved the separating wall to enlarge the space and had added a fireplace and paneling to suggest a country home lived in by many generations of one family. During the renovation, Ima visited the room frequently and insisted that the three-hued fireplace wall be repainted until the colors satisfied her. Ima and her companion made curtains and bed hangings from old blankets and linen sheets collected in the 1960s. In July 1975, while visiting *Paul Revere's Boston, 1735–1818*, curated by Jonathan Fairbanks for the Boston Museum of Fine Arts, Ima visited Vose Galleries and placed a hold on the portrait of Dr. Mason Fitch Cogswell (1761–1830), painted and signed by Connecticut artist Ralph Earl (1751–1801) in 1791. Friends completed the purchase in Ima's memory, and the portrait has remained in the Maple Bedroom ever since. Dr. Cogswell studied mental health care, and he is depicted sitting in a writing Windsor similar to an example in the room. In 1977 Alice Hogg Hanszen remodeled Ima's bath and dressing area as a memorial room to celebrate the many philanthropic interests of her brilliant and beloved sister-in-law. In 2009 these mementos were moved to the Legacy Room in the newly constructed Lora Jean Kilroy Visitor and Education Center to make way for a display of folk art.[266]

Ima's enthusiasm for the Houston Symphony never waned. In the last decade of her life, she continued to "say with confidence that Houston could not prosper without such cultural necessities as the Orchestra" when urging municipal, corporate, and individual support. She consulted board members about conductors, all of whom she entertained at Bayou Bend, and she applauded musicians, volunteers, and donors. In 1963 Ima told reporters the old music hall/wrestling arena was inadequate. She promised to support a "proper wrestling arena" on city land and was thrilled by the "dream come true for many in Houston" when the Jesse H. Jones Hall for the Performing Arts opened on October 3, 1966. She thanked corporate sponsors for supporting the Young Artists Competition and the Cullen Foundation for its "magnificent gift" to the orchestra endowment to match the $2 million Ford Foundation Grant received in 1966. Writing an open letter of praise to Ray Fliegel when he relinquished the responsibilities of concertmaster, Ima remembered him as "a small lad in knickers," who soloed under Frank St. Leger and noted his "beautiful tone and playing." In June 1973 Ima arranged a dinner honoring Business Manager Tom Johnson and his wife and gave them a silver tray and bowl to mark her gratitude for Johnson's service. That year she extoled the "substantial endowment" bequest from Mrs. Perkins Shepherd that enabled Rice University to build the Shepherd School of Music, a "new and most welcome musical addition" led by the "eminent musicologist" Samuel Jones.[267]

By 1970 only one musical gesture remained—to commission a symphonic work. During frequent sojourns to Mexico in the 1930s and 1940s, Ima attended symphony concerts and became friendly with composer and conductor Carlos Chavez. In 1946 she praised his attainments to attendees at a chamber of commerce dinner in the maestro's honor when he was leading the symphony as guest conductor. Two years later she tried to persuade Chavez to accept the position of permanent conductor. While he would not leave his "beloved orchestra" in Mexico City, he did return to the Houston podium in 1963 and agreed to compose *Ode to Clio*, a symphonic poem Ima commissioned in the spring of 1969. Ima told Chavez in August that she had seen an article in *Life* magazine, which caused her to ponder Clio, who "since creation has worn two masks. One is hideous and frightening. The other is infinitely beautiful—her face aglow with enlightenment." Combining her love of history with her passion for music, Ima continued, "What an opportunity it is to declare the exaltation which has inspired men to great achievements." Chavez replied in kind on November 24, when he advised his patron that *Clio: Symphonic Ode* was finished. "I have always thought that the historic process of mankind is reflected by the development of music through the ages," he said. Despite the recent death of his daughter, Chavez premiered the work in Houston on March 23, 1970, and Ima told the composer that she was "completely satisfied" and "proud to have your work in our repertoire."[268]

Houston Child Guidance Center minutes and a May 1959 in-depth study committee report underlined the persistent struggle to fund programs, retain directors, and explain the center's significance during the 1950s and 1960s. Ima made several important donations, attended meetings periodically, and agreed to serve on the building committee during the 1950s, when the center searched doggedly for a permanent headquarters. She and other board members lobbied Texas Medical Center planners for space on the new campus. Turned down, they were fortunate to attract the attention of Pauline Dillingham and her brother Edwin, who donated their large family home on Austin Street to the center in July 1959. The board hired architects Preston Bolton and Howard Barnstone to convert the property into commodious headquarters. Ima made an impact on the fundraising effort "little short of electrifying," first with an anonymous inaugural construction gift of $10,000 and then with strong letters to Judge John H. Freeman, chairman of M. D. Anderson Foundation, and John T. Jones Jr. at Houston Endowment. Both had declined to participate, but they could not deny Ima's "genuine regret" at their refusals to support "desperately needed facilities." She mentioned her own "substantial" contribution to the building fund and noted that $40,000 was still needed. She was so excited when M. D. Anderson Foundation reconsidered and pledged $25,000 that she picked up the telephone to express her "thanks and appreciation." Houston Endowment quickly followed suit, and Alice Hogg Hanszen closed the campaign with a generous gift in October 1960. In 1961 Ima made another construction gift of $18,000 to underwrite build-out of the Hogg Brothers Memorial Wing; she also promised $8,000 to support operations if the center did not raise fees for service. Ima lobbied the Hogg Foundation to support pilot programs at the center, and for thirty years she made periodic gifts to the foundation to support grants it was making to the center—almost always anonymously—because she knew grants from the esteemed Hogg Foundation would stimulate additional donations. After Ima's death, the long-standing struggle to define the center's purpose continued until DePelchin Children's Center and the Houston Child Guidance Center merged in 1992. DePelchin's mission to help children and families in crisis reflects Ima's emphasis on prevention and public education.

During Ima's last years, the mayor and mental health groups in Houston and Harris County frequently sought her advice. As she explained in 1960, "It is not due to lack of interest" that she often declined requests, but "I am very limited in time and strength." She would express the same assurances to Hogg Foundation Director Robert Sutherland in 1967. "I want you to know that my interest in mental health is as sharp as it ever was. My trouble is that my heart is divided in several parts each one of which I think of as an implication toward mental health."[269]

In the 1960s Ima followed Hogg Foundation developments closely and continued to attend the annual conference in April and the National Advisory Board meeting in November. In 1963 she was asked to serve on a planning committee to review the foundation's approach to funding, policy analysis, research, education, and convening, and to prepare for a crucial milestone—a request to the Ford Foundation for major support that would profoundly expand the foundation's impact in Texas communities. Ima discussed the significant request several times with William Stewart, an endowment officer at the University of Texas, and shepherded efforts to a "thrilling" conclusion: starting in 1963, the Ford Foundation would grant $550,000 over five years to the Hogg Foundation to match gifts from other foundations for community mental health projects and to initiate mental health programs. In 1969 the Ford Foundation provided another $150,000 to establish a major library of materials related to philanthropic institutions, research, and programs at Hogg Foundation headquarters. Ima was gratified when the office of UT System Chancellor Harry H. Ransom assumed direct oversight of foundation assets and activities in 1967. Her strong partnership with Sutherland never faltered, and in February 1969 she successfully urged his promotion to president of the foundation. In the fall of 1970, shortly before Sutherland's retirement, Ima and Ransom hosted a fall barbecue lunch at Winedale to celebrate the founding director's long tenure. Ima's moving toast to her friend and colleague applauded his thirty years of unselfish and wise leadership. Sutherland had long admired his helpful patron and understood that Ima's "years of experience in educational and community endeavor make her counsel invaluable" while her support stimulated other donors. The founding director's replacement, Wayne Holtzman, had been research and associate director since 1955, so the transition to new leadership was smooth.[270]

Spurred by affirmation from the Ford Foundation, Ima decided it was time to fulfill her 1940 promise to make a substantial personal gift to the Hogg Foundation. In 1955 Alice Hogg Hanszen and the estates of Mike and Tom Hogg had made large gifts to the Hogg Foundation endowment, thereby doubling the operating income to expand research. On October 2, 1964, Ima incorporated the Ima Hogg Foundation with an initial gift of shares and property valued at $550,000–$600,000; at her death, "all real and personal property not specifically bequeathed" to other entities would be distributed to the Ima Hogg Foundation to help thousands of troubled children in Houston and Harris County through direct healthcare programs. Ima had considered making a large endowment to the Houston Child Guidance Center but felt the investment skills and stability of the University of Texas would better protect her gift. Instead, she requested that the Houston Child Guidance Center be the "centerpiece" of Ima Hogg Foundation grants, which would feature networking with local funding sources to target children at risk, minority children, and new approaches to mental health care. The Ima Hogg Foundation, activated on May 3, 1976, under the administrative aegis of the Hogg Foundation, distributed its first grants the following year.[271]

In the 1960s Ima and her sisters-in-law made several major gifts to the University of Texas. They established the Ima Hogg Scholarship for those training in psychiatric social work; the Mike Hogg Memorial Fund for Mental Health to train visiting teachers; and professorships in psychology and sociology to fund staff members of the Hogg Foundation. When Ima and Mike established the Hogg Foundation, Ima worried about using the Hogg name because she wanted others to support the endowment. Perhaps this concern was justified. Dear friends like Dot Thornton left modest bequests, but during Ima's lifetime most endowment funding did come from the Hogg family. By 1963 the Hogg Foundation had outgrown its office space, and Ima enthusiastically discussed renovation of the geology building as the Will C. Hogg Building, which would house the Hogg Foundation for many years. Although she and her sisters-in-law made generous donations to the remodeling project, Ima could not be present at the dedication on June 8, 1968, but sent a speech to be read to the attendees. At the end of the month, she thoroughly enjoyed a "personal tour" of the "beautiful" building and was delighted to learn that the ample space could accommodate a long-desired student counseling program.[272]

Final Passages

Eighty-four when she relinquished her greatest enterprise—the collections and gardens of Bayou Bend—to the Museum of Fine Arts of Houston, Ima entered a period of reflection. She had lived to accomplish her greatest dreams; she had established institutions she believed would enable all Texans to find fulfillment and lead wholesome lives. Now it was time for others to carry on the work she had begun and for her to enjoy her final projects and her friends. Photographs and portraits from Ima's adult years reveal a wistful sadness in her clear blue eyes that betrays the pain of family loss and the struggle to achieve a balanced life. Yet her last years were filled with happy celebrations and the company of youthful friends. As she had for decades, Ima hosted small dinner parties before each symphony performance. She became enamored of the Beatles and inveigled the teenage son of a young friend to take her to the rock musical *Godspell*. Ima found the space program fascinating and was "briefed on operations" of the Apollo docking facilities by astronaut William Anders at NASA on June 5, 1967. She promptly adopted Tang as a favored beverage, "because the astronauts drink it in space." Arbor Day, January 17, 1969, found Ima in Austin, planting yet another tree at her father's grave. Every March, Azalea Trail guests discovered Ima greeting guests on the North Terrace; dressed in her signature hat, gloves, and elegant suit, she dispensed wrapped candies from a large bowl, often admonishing young visitors to take only one piece. Lunch guests encountered Ima in her apartment, singing to herself as she applied makeup before entertaining. Following bouts of illness in 1968 and 1970, her doctors insisted she employ a nurse-companion. She resisted but sensibly complied, instructing the women to wear street clothes and be introduced as her friends. She did not allow her weakening heart to depress her enthusiasm for shopping, whether for high fashion at Houston's new Nieman Marcus department store or for items on her wish lists for Bayou Bend, Varner-Hogg, and Winedale. Nor did health concerns keep her at home, as she continued to visit old haunts in Europe and attend concerts and art exhibitions in Houston, Boston, and New York. Her insatiable curiosity and eagerness to learn kept her young.[273]

In the 1960s, as Ima transformed her home into room settings for her collections, she transferred dozens of brother Will's books to the University of Texas, donated hundreds of books and records to libraries at Rice University and Texas Southern University, made several gifts to the Austin Public Library, and gave valuable art books to Looscan Library, the public library branch nearest her high-rise home. Ima saved almost every program from the hundreds of recitals and concerts she attended for seventy years, and early in 1965 she gave boxes of scrapbooks containing this evidence of her lifetime passion to the University of Houston in honor of the Tuesday Musical Club. Alfred R. Neumann, dean of the College of Arts and Sciences, recognized their value to later historical research as "the basis for a future history of music performances." The Hogg family's large collection of Texana remained at Bayou Bend, and the books are now available for research at the Kitty King Powell Library. Ima spent years organizing her personal papers, a task completed by Jane Zivley almost a decade after their owner's death. Original papers and transcripts of Hogg family documents are now found in archival collections at the University of Texas's Dolph Briscoe Center for American History; the Museum of Fine Arts, Houston Archives; and Rice University's Woodson Research Center. After Will's death, Ima reviewed proposed changes to Memorial Park. When she no longer was able to inspect the site or veto plans herself in the 1970s, she created an advisory committee and secured promises from young conservationists that they would continue her oversight and maintain the park as a nature preserve to comply with the Hogg family's deeds of gift.[274]

While Ima organized her collections for the public's enjoyment, her many admirers began to recognize her invaluable work. In March 1954 Ima received a certificate of appreciation from the Texas Society of Mental Health, and on March 10, 1955, she graciously accepted the Brotherhood Award at the sixth annual Brotherhood Dinner sponsored by the National Conference of Christians and Jews. Amid Red Scare propaganda, she noted her affiliation "with some of the forces which unite us in our religious faith and civic loyalties," and the "unifying" symphony and educational institutions that will "train and guide" our children "to be better equipped . . . as useful, happy citizens." On May 13, 1956, the Texas Heritage Foundation named Ima its Texian Woman of the Year for "outstanding patriotic, philanthropic, and humanitarian contributions to the welfare of Texas," and in November 1958 the Texas Social Welfare Society awarded her its Certificate of Merit. In 1957, 1958, and 1959 Ima served on the board of the Harris County Heritage and Conservation Society, which was transferring early Harris County buildings to Sam Houston Park downtown. She made an "eloquent appeal" for information about historic homes in the area, spoke to the society in 1956, and provided a chest of drawers to help furnish the first historic restoration project. On May 26, 1959, the Texas Chapter of the American Institute of Decorators welcomed Ima as an honorary member, calling her "an extraordinary cultural force in the South," who "stimulated enthusiasm among others." That year *The Magazine Antiques* devoted most of its August issue to her story. In May 1960 the Museum of Fine Arts, Houston invited Ima's friends to celebrate "her remarkable contributions to the city's culture," noted on an engraved plaque. In September 1960 President Dwight Eisenhower welcomed Ima to the Advisory Committee on the Arts for the National Cultural Center being planned for Washington, DC, now the Kennedy Center. That winter Chairman Henry F. du Pont invited Ima to join the twelve-member Fine Arts Committee for White House acquisitions. For four years the committee and eighteen advisors, an illustrious group of historians, curators, and museum administrators, examined objects being offered as gifts to the White House.[275]

Honors continued to flow in the 1960s. In 1962 Jacqueline Kennedy asked Ima to participate on a White House advisory panel created to help the First Lady acquire historic furniture for her refurbishing project. Will Hogg's Ex-Students' Association honored five "distinguished" alumni at a homecoming banquet on October 25, 1963; Ima, the only alumna, was lauded as "philanthropist, civic and cultural leader" and was joined by three oil entrepreneurs and James I. McCord, president of Princeton Theological Seminary. Dear friend and accomplished pianist Nettie (Mrs. Albert P.) Jones "pleased [her] most of all honors" by establishing the Ima Hogg Scholarship for outstanding piano students at the University of Texas in 1965. In March 1966 Ima received an achievement award from the Houston Federation of Garden Clubs, and in October she flew to Philadelphia to attend the twentieth annual meeting of the National Trust for Historic Preservation and receive its seventh annual Louise du Pont Crowninshield Award for her "superlative achievement in the preservation and interpretation of sites, buildings and objects significant in American history and culture." The citation also listed her many triumphs and generous gifts. When Ima rose to thank the crowd on October 8, she repeated the words she had spoken at Bayou Bend's dedication—she hoped "in a modest way" that her preservation efforts would "serve as a bridge to bring us closer to the heart of an American heritage that unites us." In October 1967 the Texas State Historical Commission acclaimed her "meritorious service" to the State of Texas, and the next year, the Philadelphia University Hospital dedicated its annual Antiques Show to her.[276]

Ima was terribly disappointed that a recent long hospitalization made it impossible for her to accept the first Santa Rita Award, a handsome bronze medallion given irregularly to recognize "persons who have excelled in assisting advancement" of the University of Texas. At the June 8, 1968, ceremony, Jack S. Josey of Houston accepted on her behalf, and attorney Leon Jaworski read a message from the grateful recipient. Prior to the ceremony, guests had dedicated the Will C. Hogg Building as the new home of the Hogg Foundation. In March 1969 Ima wrote members of the Houston chapter of the Sigma Alpha Iota Music Fraternity to accept "most gratefully" the "significant recognition and commendation" of honorary membership, which made her "feel maybe I have given back something to the cause of music. It has always seemed to me

Ima Hogg celebrating her ninetieth birthday at Winedale, August 1972. E_enr_121, Prints and Photographs Collection, Dolph Briscoe Center for American History, University of Texas at Austin.

that I have received more than I have given." Ima received the Award of Merit from the American Association for State and Local History in 1970; the next year the Texas Society of Architects gave her a "Special Citation of Honor" for her restoration work; and in 1972 she received the prestigious Thomas Jefferson Award for outstanding contributions to America's cultural heritage from the National Society of Interior Decorators. On May 6, 1971, she was thrilled to receive an honorary degree from Southwestern University, conferred on the college dropout by her former piano protégé, artist in residence Drusilla Huffmaster. No one better expressed Ima's effectiveness than Edward Rotan, when the combined Rotary Clubs of Houston honored the city's great patron in 1969. Ima "demonstrated a quality of conviction which has enabled her to inspire others to follow her leadership, an exceptional combination of gracious firmness, insistence on seeking perfection, and impatience with obstacles or excuses, untainted by selfishness and all mellowed by unfailing wit and feminine charm. She is the hardest lady of my acquaintance to say 'No' to."[277]

In the summer of 1972, Ima was traveling in Europe, but she wrote Varner-Hogg Park Manager Joe Cariker from Southampton, England, to say she wanted to spend her ninetieth birthday—July 10—at Varner. "But don't tell anyone," she admonished him. Cariker recalled that Ima arrived the day before to prepare a quiet noon lunch on the porch. In October the University of Texas invited her statewide coterie of admirers to sip champagne under a giant party tent at Winedale, where sparklers, music, and expressions of gratitude greeted the smiling nonagenarian, gowned in long-sleeved soft silk. That December the Houston Symphony invited world-renowned pianist Arthur Rubenstein to star in a gala tribute to the woman, who, over seventy years, had been the orchestra's most devoted angel. Bayou Bend docent Virginia Lawhon hosted a preconcert supper for eight, and two chauffeurs, escorted by police, whisked the party downtown to Jones Hall. Greeted by Thomas Johnson, the symphony's manager, and accompanied by her beloved pupil Drusilla Huffmaster, Ima entered the concert hall beautifully coiffed and gowned for the formal event, which included Rubenstein's sublime performance of both piano concertos by Johannes Brahms and praise for the honoree. For the rousing coda, the audience stood, and each attendee raised a glass of champagne to toast the woman who had brought music of international acclaim to Houston. The Whitfield Marshalls hosted a gala postconcert dinner for the honoree, the pianist, and special friends. Glamorous hostess Maisie (Mary Jane Walne) Marshall was the daughter of former Symphony Society president Walter Walne and had married her lawyer husband in the Bayou Bend gardens at Ima's special request.[278]

In the final years of her life, Ima continued to outline improvements she wanted to make and new objects she wanted to display at Bayou Bend and at her Varner-Hogg and Winedale restorations. Unusual among collectors, she anticipated that her collections would continue to grow after her death, and she left wish lists to guide future expansion. She corresponded frequently with Lonn Taylor about the Texas furniture book and worked with a young docent to prepare for publication the collection of Hogg family letters she had organized for her brothers in 1935. In March 1975 Ima paid a nostalgic visit to Varner-Hogg on her father's birthday; in April, she wrote Leonard Bernstein, urging him to conduct in Houston during the following season; and on May 31, banker John Cater invited her to join the symphony's Long-Range Planning and Development Committee. In June 1975 Ima and nurse-companion Yvonne Coates began a journey to Boston, New York, London, and Bayreuth, perhaps a farewell tour of the places where she had found many treasures and listened with joy to the world's most glorious musical performances. On a rainy August day in London, Ima and Mrs. Coates ventured to Harrod's, always a favorite shopping haunt and a good spot for tea. At the end of their pleasurable visit, Ima was stepping into a cab on Brompton Road when the vehicle lurched, and she fell to the ground. The horrified cabbie and gathering crowd tried to make the fallen traveler comfortable as the rain worsened. Always modest and thoughtful, Ima reassured everyone that she was all right, before an ambulance rushed her to Westminster Hospital, where doctors diagnosed a broken hip. Although the required operation was successful, Ima's heart could not bear the strain, and she died peacefully on the night of August 19, 1975, from the arterial disease that had plagued her last years. Associated Press reporters wired news of her death around the world, and the American ambassador arranged for her body to be flown home to Houston.[279]

Rain also fell steadily at Bayou Bend on Friday, August 22, when 350 mourners crowded into the front hall, dining room, and drawing room and sat tearfully on the curving staircase. Wet chairs on the North Terrace stared sadly across the sodden lawn toward the Diana Garden, and dripping umbrellas rested against the south entrance. As she had planned her many civic projects, so Ima left clear instructions for her funeral: "I do not wish to subject my friends and relatives to prolonged eulogies or ceremonies or to require them to listen to music which we have so deeply loved and enjoyed during my lifetime on an occasion of this nature." As requested, the Reverend Maurice M. Benitez, rector of St. John the Divine Episcopal Church, celebrated the seventeen-minute Episcopal service with readings from Psalm 91, Romans 8:14, and the Gospel of John 14:1. Rector emeritus, the Reverend Thomas W. Sumners remarked, "Bayou Bend itself is [Miss Hogg's] eulogy." Young relatives, descendants of her parents' many siblings, escorted the magnolia-draped coffin, and attendees included faithful Gertrude Vaughn and Lucious Broadnax; her friend, assistant, and executrix Jane Zivley; Bayou Bend docents and symphony volunteers; cultural, business, and political leaders; and her successor as overseer of Bayou Bend, David B. Warren. Following the 3:00 p.m. memorial service, Ima left the home of her dreams to begin her final journey to Austin, where the "First Lady of Texas" would be reunited with her parents and brothers in Oakwood Cemetery as Austin and University of Texas flags flew at half-staff for two days of official mourning. Ima was a determined fighter; she had overcome the untimely deaths of beloved parents and brothers and the recurring battles with mental and physical health to blossom as a great visionary and generous philanthropist, a curious adventurer and fully engaged civic presence until the last day of her life. She also was a devoted comrade, remembering birthdays and important events in the lives of others, dispensing recipes and advice, grapefruit and gadgets, plants and pecans, and celebrating the births of her youngest friends with inscribed bibles. It seemed hard to believe that she would no longer be calling early in the morning, "I've been thinking . . ." she would say, as she announced a new idea to improve the lives of all Texans, who comprised her enduring family.[280]

Epilogue

"Philanthropy Means Social Justice and Opportunity" declared a *Houston Post* headline on March 16, 1919, to introduce a reprise of Dr. Robert Dennis's February lecture at Rice Institute. Alice Baker, Julia Ideson, and Ima Hogg may have attended the lecture sponsored by their dear and mutual friend Estelle Sharp. Certainly they agreed with the headline and with Dr. Dennis's remarks. For over seventy years, Alice, Julia, and Ima created opportunities so fellow Houstonians could experience social justice and lead productive, satisfying lives. Alice, Julia, and Ima knew Houston offered endless possibility but recognized that access to the city's cultural resources and economic riches was not readily available to all their neighbors. Their long, productive lives as social justice pioneers refute the persistent image of Houston as a "perennial 'boom town'" of brash entrepreneurs who believed in "the individual's right to promote, speculate, build, buy, and sell without outside restraint or control." Contemporary photographs and documents do strongly support a history "characterized by rapid growth, boosterism, and the constant presence of white, black and brown 'outsiders'" who sought their fortunes in the Bayou City, but these documents also reveal a parallel story of women and men who recognized that economic success presented unique options to build a vibrant, beautiful, and just community for everyone. Ima Hogg is reputed to have remarked that Houston was lucky—its first millionaires built hospitals and parks, universities and museums, orchestras and libraries—and the city has benefitted profoundly from the generosity and vision of early civic leaders and philanthropists who dared to imagine a "City of Destiny" rising on a flat prairie watered by several meandering bayous.[1]

Alice, Julia, and Ima traveled different paths to the public square, but they shared civic goals, personality traits, and leadership styles. Their contemporaries remembered the three activists as elegant, charming, and ladylike—Alice welcoming and warm, Julia tall and vibrant, Ima petite and determined—leaders who encouraged their many admirers to share the daring belief that all citizens could and should participate in civic life. This exceptional trio had grown up in homes where women were valued, and from childhood, each was encouraged to develop her talents, to respect others, and to aspire to the highest standards in every endeavor. Yet, each had known uncertainty: Alice's childhood shadowed by the death of her father when she was a toddler; Julia's home threatened by the storms and fires that destroyed her father's business; and Ima's life changed irreparably by the loss of her mother and the assumption of adult responsibilities when she was only thirteen years old. All three girls matured as forceful women, determined to make significant contributions to their community; all three defied convention to discover self-fulfillment as civic leaders. For them, domestic homelife was not sufficient, and they secured moral authority for their causes by demonstrating their enduring commitment to public service. Volunteers willingly followed Mrs. Baker's gracious example; voters did not want to disappoint Miss Ideson; and powerbrokers could not deny Miss Hogg.

Alice placed Christian devotion and family at the center of her world. She felt blessed that her affectionate but ambitious husband could provide many of life's luxuries for their multigenerational household; she loved the beauty of music, art, and flowers; she maintained exacting standards for herself, her family, and her community; and she was deeply devout. In all her dealings, Alice followed two simple rules: She treated everyone with the respect she hoped they would show to her, and she believed all Houstonians were her neighbors. As a steward of God's benevolence to her, she wished to share her good fortune with others, so she reached out to those who were struggling, showed them how to help themselves, and introduced them to activities she enjoyed—gardening, music, reading, and friendship. She was drawn to the plight of less fortunate Houstonians, and she recruited teams of volunteers from women's clubs and church groups to address social inequities and environmental degradations. Revered as a daughter, sister, wife, mother, and grandmother, she could have spent her days nurturing family and friends, but she found that working to improve the lives of all Houstonians brought personal joy and completed her life's purpose to make a significant contribution to her community. She took bold steps when she advocated for sanitary housing, parks, playgrounds, and quality schools in all areas of town. Her work was truly pathbreaking. Using the inspiring club model she and her female friends had adopted to enrich their lives, she taught people living in neglected neighborhoods how to cooperate and organize in similar collaborative groups; she tried to break down social and racial barriers by inviting her privileged associates to befriend and understand those who had no access to municipal amenities; she worked closely with African American women to create Bethlehem Settlement within the association family; and she inspired fellow Houstonians to build and nurture an enduring institution founded on principles of access and inclusion as the best means to achieve social justice for everyone.

Julia was driven by professional ambition and personal aspiration to place the Houston Public Library at the center of civic culture in her adopted hometown. She linked education and community building by making access for everyone the primary goal of her municipal library and by insisting that reading and lifetime learning were essential to character formation, civic responsibility, and a well-lived life. The role of a public library was contested when Julia assumed leadership of Houston's most beautiful public building. Spurred by Andrew Carnegie's philanthropy, libraries for the public were being built everywhere, and librarians were embracing new organizational technologies and debating the role of a municipal library. Should this public asset try to shape "good taste" by stressing the great classics of literature, or should it serve a utilitarian purpose that addressed popular demand? Should it be a book exchange or a great storehouse of knowledge? Active in these debates at state and national levels, Julia thought a successful public library should nurture all these purposes. With "her force of character, her perseverance, her intelligent planning, and her unswerving devotion," she built an archive of knowledge, provided information so readers could improve their daily lives, and expanded imaginations by offering the finest examples of the written word. "Because of her zeal and enthusiasm, the resources of the library became an integral part of the cultural and educational resources of the community." As a brilliant steward of Houston's public library and a powerful voice for woman suffrage, Julia demonstrated the value of female careers and expanded possibilities for all women.[2]

From childhood, Ima understood that every citizen should be prepared to act in the public square. When oil gushed from wells on family property, she recognized the significance and responsibility of great wealth—a gift of good fortune, not the result of her labor or invention—and she determined to invest her riches wisely, in ways that could benefit all Texans, while, admittedly, giving her much pleasure. Like her father and brothers, she believed strong individuals and healthy families sustained a great nation. In her search for life's meaning, she recognized that harmonious relations required good mental health, and she believed that mental healthiness rested on access to education, safe homes, good jobs, beautiful natural surroundings, and the joy of music, art, and reading. In every generous endeavor, Ima tenaciously pursued excellence and engaged individuals in "something beyond themselves."[3] A complicated, intense woman who struggled courageously to overcome physical and mental health challenges, Ima addressed the complexity of urban life by linking cultural, social, medical, and economic forces in a holistic vision for the wholesome community. She viewed history as a treasury of values that uphold democracy, mold civic identity, and unify Americans in a common heritage, and she admired the underlying humanity in all forms of visual art and musical expression. During seventy years of brilliant, pathbreaking civic work, Ima drove herself to implement her farsighted plans and compiled a list of firsts: She created the first professional symphony in Texas, the first decorative arts collection in the region, the first foundation in the nation to focus on mental health wellness for families, and the first works on paper and indigenous American art to enter the collections of the Museum of Fine Arts, Houston.

Alice, Julia, and Ima used similar methods to achieve their goals—teamwork, cooperation, and persuasion infused with fervent belief that their efforts to improve everyone's quality of life ensured Houston's continued growth and prosperity. As effective leaders, Alice, Julia, and Ima worked well with women and men and knew how to use womanpower to address contentious issues. Forward-looking and imaginative, these innovative women were committed to positive civic action as the best path to develop strong families and communities, overcome social injustice in a great city, and sustain a strong nation. Ideally, their twentieth-century wholesome community would offer opportunities to everyone; would encourage citizens to reach their full potential through lifetime learning and reading; would provide physical and mental healthcare facilities to anyone in need; would make fine music, art, and architecture available to all; and would guarantee safe neighborhoods with access to public parks, schools, utilities, and transportation. The social justice they embraced was predicated on inclusion. All Houstonians were Alice Baker's neighbors; everyone could enjoy Julia Ideson's university of the people at accessible branches of the public library; and no one was excluded from Ima

Hogg's symphony, art museum, mental health associations, or educational endeavors. These pioneering activists strengthened their community by sharing their ideas and good fortune, by involving hundreds of volunteers in their projects, by listening, and by nurturing collaborative teamwork that brought together individuals from all walks of life to solve problems.

Julia became librarian in 1903, Alice founded the Settlement Association in 1907, and Ima launched the Houston Symphony Association in 1913, years before women secured the vote and during a time when government at all levels was weak and seemingly disinterested in social justice or cultural enhancement. The three advocates understood that the levers of municipal power rested in the hands of businessmen, philanthropists, and vocal clubwomen, and all three women turned to these sources for financial, legal, and volunteer support when they began their advocacy. They also pushed local government to expand its responsibility to oversee quality of life issues, and each developed different approaches to the political sector. Alice Baker, the most traditional of these innovators, ironically advanced a revolutionary experiment. Persuaded by the reasoned arguments of her friends Estelle Sharp and Will Hogg, she decided to place the privately organized and supported Settlement Association under the umbrella of the newly formed municipal Social Service Bureau in 1918 and to serve as volunteer chairwoman of the bureau's Settlement and Social Service Department. Alice's expectation that the city would fully fund and successfully supervise the delivery of social services did not materialize, and she joined other association supporters to withdraw from the bureau and reestablish private management of the Settlement Association a decade later, but her experiment illustrated the importance of municipal involvement in social service advancement. As a city employee, Julia Ideson reported to the mayor and worked closely with the city council to wrest annual budget increases from a municipal body loath to tax its constituency. Julia recognized that she would have to find alternative funding for major improvements or additional collections, and she was able to secure private donations and passage of large bond issues for the 1926 library building because she had cooperated with the volunteer library board, had earned the public's trust, and had placed the library at the center of Houston's cultural life. The daughter of an activist governor, Ima Hogg disliked politicking but recognized the power of public-private partnerships to secure acceptance of and funding for her many enterprises. She believed local and state governments should understand social and cultural challenges and should make social service and cultural institutions accessible to every Texan, and she advocated fervently for fully funded public education from preschool through graduate study. However, she understood the critical role of philanthropy and private action—to promote new ideas like child guidance clinics, to support little understood causes like mental health or classical music, and to enhance the value of expensive amenities like art museums and historic sites. From her earliest adventures with the Houston Symphony Association to her publication of a book on Texas furniture, Ima convened businesspeople, academic leaders, officeholders, artists, citizens, volunteers, and philanthropists to build bridges of understanding and acceptance among the peoples of Texas and from the state she loved to the nation she revered.

In the early twenty-first century, we identify different pathways to social justice. We try to comprehend the sociopolitical world that existed in the early twentieth century, and we are often impatient with forebears whose lives were bounded by mores we now reject. When Alice, Julia, and Ima began their civic work, they sincerely believed that all Houstonians included every woman, man, or child regardless of race or religion, and they pushed the boundaries of their sociopolitical world to overcome prejudices, improve understanding, and provide services. Their pioneering efforts to include everyone gave Houstonians hope. The unintended consequences of their inclusive approach prodded later generations to redefine social justice goals and demand equity, equality, and inclusion. The institutions Alice, Julia, and Ima founded still frame Houston's destiny. The Settlement Association Alice established became Neighborhood Centers, Inc. and is today known as BakerRipley. The mission she advanced has never changed. Alice invested in people and community, and BakerRipley continues to "bring resources, education, and connection to emerging neighborhoods." Alice believed strong neighborhoods would build a strong city, and today the community builders at more than seventy service sites work with neighbors to make the Houston region a "place of opportunity for all." Today over five hundred thousand people "who want nothing more than a better life" enjoy Alice's legacy and benefit from her example.[4] Julia Ideson's Houston Public Library now serves 2.3 million city residents at forty-four public service units that "link people to the world"—today's mission statement—and provide rich municipal archives for ongoing research at the Metropolitan Research Center in the Ideson Building and at the African American Library at Gregory School. Ima Hogg's beloved symphony is acclaimed worldwide. Her pathbreaking efforts to build public understanding for mental health care still inform DePelchin Children's Center mission to "strengthen the lives of children" through mental health care and physical well-being.[5] Her Hogg Foundation for Mental Health still supports mental health wellness for families in

Texas communities. The museum she imagined now maintains about seventy thousand objects from six continents at its multiplex main campus and two satellite sites—Rienzi, and Bayou Bend Collection and Gardens. More than one thousand docents and volunteers welcome visitors every year, thereby fulfilling Ima's belief that art is for everyone.

More than a century after Alice Baker, Julia Ideson, and Ima Hogg entered the public square, Houston's population comprises residents who have come from all over the world to build the largest multiethnic city in North America. Houstonians still struggle with greed and intolerance, inadequate neighborhood facilities, and poverty of spirit, but they are also heirs to the legacy of these extraordinary women, who countered persistent social injustice through civic engagement and philanthropic generosity. Alice, Julia, and Ima awakened Houstonians to urban problems and introduced new solutions. They had faith that women and men can cooperate, collaborate, and network for civic action; that residents can build a community based on ever-increasing inclusion and ever-expanding access; that municipal institutions will be strong enough to overcome forces of exploitation, exclusion, anger, and fear; and that engaged citizens will convene for the common good. By reaching out to others, by demanding access for all, by trying to understand that "the most important business in the world . . . is the business of living," and by building enduring civic institutions, Alice, Julia, and Ima paved the way for others to perform.[6] The examples they set offer hope that the long arc of the moral universe will continue to bend toward social justice and continue to inspire coming generations of actors in the public square.

ACKNOWLEDGMENTS

Seeds for *Building Community in Houston* were sown in the early 1970s when as a young docent in my late twenties, I worked with Ima Hogg on a project that was not finished when the fascinating philanthropist died at age ninety-three. Miss Hogg's youthfulness struck me as her most endearing quality, and I felt she had captured the secret of growing older. Here was a woman in her nineties whose accomplishments were legendary but whose unquenched curiosity allowed her to imagine a new career as publisher of family letters. In the late 1990s I began to study the Hogg family and its far-reaching, visionary philanthropy. My findings led to the publication of two books, archival encounters with several important Houston civic leaders, including Alice Baker and Julia Ideson, and many new friendships. With gratitude I enumerate the team that encouraged me to complete this book.

John Boles, Margaret Culbertson, Caroline Baker Hurley, the late Betty Kyle Moore, and Evelyn Nolen read earlier versions of some parts of this book and made important suggestions. My daughter Anne C. Leader, PhD, performed miracles of extensive genealogical research, which filled many gaps about the sparsely documented Graham, Baker, and Ideson families. Members of the Baker family tolerated my efforts to illuminate the accomplishments of their forebears with good humor and enduring support, and I owe special thanks to James A. Baker III, Julie Baker, Stewart A. Baker, Virginia Meyers Chandler, and the late Preston Moore Jr. They withstood many interviews, provided access to private papers at the Baker Institute for Public Policy, shared family photographs, and made me laugh. Fellow Bayou Bend docent Jennifer Bene scoured newspapers for invaluable information, which added greatly to my understanding of Alice Baker and Julia Ideson, neither of whom left personal papers to assist historians. I am indebted to Bayou Bend docent associates Claire Baker, who shared information about her grandmother Jane Zivley with me, and Carolyn Crawford, who called my attention to the ongoing and greatly expanded work of the Girls' Settlement Club in Austin. Sandy Hatcher answered all my queries with prompt and much-appreciated attention. The late Raphael Fliegel (1918–2005), longtime Houston Symphony concertmaster, spoke to me at length (in a telephone interview on October 4, 2003) about Miss Hogg's impact on the Houston Symphony.

Archives make all historical reconstruction possible, and I enjoyed support from many individuals and libraries: Ingrid Grant and the archivists at the African American Library, Gregory School; archivists at the Houston Metropolitan Research Center, the Houston Public Library; Terry Brown, preserver of Houston Symphony records; Don Carleton, Margaret Schlankey, and the archival staff at the Dolph Briscoe Center for American History, the University of Texas at Austin; Margaret Culbertson and Helen Lueders at the Kitty King Powell Library, Bayou Bend Collection and Gardens, Museum of Fine Arts, Houston; Marie Wise and the archivists past and present at the Museum of Fine Arts, Houston; Lee Pecht, Amanda Foch, Rebecca Russell, and the archivists of the Woodson Research Center, Rice University; Cara Setsu Bertram, archives program officer at the American Library Association Archives, University of Illinois at Urbana-Champaign; Jacqueline Hahn, Lawrenceville School; Hannah Kubacak, Genealogy Library, Waco, McLennan County Library; Joann Mitchell, vice president of development and communication, DePelchin Children's Center, who in the late 1990s searched through long-term storage to discover the minutes of the Houston Child Guidance Center; Dawn Orsack, director of the Philosophical Society of Texas; Cathy Skitko, Hill School; and Elizabeth Spilenek, Adams County, Nebraska, records archivist.

Finally, I would like to thank my history-loving friends Elizabeth Hutcheson Carrell, Stephen Fox, the late Francita Stuart Ulmer, and Joanne Seale Wilson, who have over the years shared their vast knowledge of Houston and its families with me. Their friendship and love for Houston's early civic leaders has brightened my journey and spurred me on.

NOTES

A Note on Sources

Ima Hogg preserved extensive records, which are now divided among the Dolph Briscoe Center for American History at the University of Texas at Austin; the Museum of Fine Arts, Houston (in the Archives, Registrar's Office, and Bayou Bend Collection files); the University of Houston Special Collections, Program Collection; and the Woodson Research Center at Rice University. I began to research the Hogg family in the late 1990s, and since that time Virginia Bernhard has transcribed and published family letters for the years 1887–1919 in *The Hoggs of Texas: Letters and Memoirs of an Extraordinary Family, 1887–1906*; "A Texan in the Trenches: Mike Hogg's World War I Letters," *Southwestern Historical Quarterly* 117, no. 1 (July 2012) and no. 2 (October 2013); "Ima Hogg in Europe, 1914: A Texan Experiences the Beginning of the Great War," *Southwestern Historical Quarterly* 119, no. 3 (January 2016); *The Smell of War: Three Americans in the Trenches of World War I*; and *Grand Tours and the Great War: Ima Hogg's Diaries, 1907–1918*. These printed transcriptions make the correspondence available to a wide audience, and I have cited them where appropriate. I am greatly indebted to Professor Bernhard for her diligent preservation of these valuable papers. Museum of Fine Arts, Houston scholars David B. Warren, Michael Brown (deceased), and Emily Neff have written extensively about Hogg family members and collections, and results are listed in the bibliography. In contrast, Julia Ideson's contributions have been largely ignored, in part because her private papers and books were destroyed during a flooding event at her home on Buffalo Bayou. Her story is told in the extensive minutes and annual reports at the Houston Public Library and in press reports. Alice Baker and her husband destroyed most of their personal letters, but those that remain depict the couple as described here and in *Captain James A. Baker of Houston*, the biography

I prepared to celebrate the Rice University Centennial. There are very few extant archives pertaining to the Houston Settlement Association, now BakerRipley. Every day I am reminded that there is so much we could learn from these outstanding visionaries and civic activists, whose generosity of spirit touched every aspect of life in Houston.

Abbreviations

BC Dolph Briscoe Center for American History, University of Texas at Austin

BHOT Virginia Bernhard, *The Hoggs of Texas: Letters and Memoirs of an Extraordinary Family, 1887–1906*

BIPP James A. Baker III personal collection, Baker Institute for Public Policy, Rice University

DCC Minute books of the Child Guidance Center, DePelchin Children's Center, Houston

EOL Edgar Odell Lovett papers, Woodson Research Center

ER Early Rice records, Woodson Research Center

HFR Hogg Foundation records, Dolph Briscoe Center for American History

HLAB Houston Library Association board minutes, Houston Metropolitan Research Center

HLAR Houston Library Association annual reports, Houston Metropolitan Research Center

HMRC Houston Metropolitan Research Center, Ideson Building, Houston Public Library

HPL Houston Public Library

HPWRC Hogg Family papers, Woodson Research Center

IHPBC Ima Hogg papers, Dolph Briscoe Center for American History

IHPMFAH Ima Hogg papers, MS 21, Museum of Fine Arts Houston

IHPCUH Ima Hogg Program Collection, University of Houston Archives

JIP Julia Ideson papers, MS 32, Houston Metropolitan Research Center

JSHBC James Stephen Hogg papers, Dolph Briscoe Center for American History

MFAH Museum of Fine Arts, Houston, Archives

MS40 Baker Family papers, Woodson Research Center

MS487 Baker scrapbooks, Woodson Research Center

MS609 Kate S. Kirkland research materials for *Captain James A. Baker of Houston*, Woodson Research Center

WCHBC William Clifford Hogg papers, Dolph Briscoe Center for American History

VBSHQ Virginia Bernhard, "Ima Hogg in Europe, 1914," *Southwestern Historical Quarterly*

WRC Woodson Research Center, Rice University

Prologue

1. Alexis de Tocqueville, *Democracy in America*, Part II, Book II: 29, 198–99 (Americans, all). Sophonisba P. Breckenridge, *Women in the Twentieth Century: A Study of Their Political, Social and Economic Activities*, vii (women's). Anne Firor Scott, *Natural Allies: Women's Associations in American History*, 2 (organized, heart); Suzanne Lebsock (*The Free Women of Petersburg: Status and Culture in a Southern Town, 1789–1869*) describes *Natural Allies* as a "landmark" and notes the book's "sweep" in her contribution to the book's jacket statement; Mary Ritter Beard, *Woman's Work in the Municipalities*.

2. Bixel and Turner, *Galveston and the 1900 Storm: Catastrophe and Catalyst*, 5 (lifeblood); *Oil Investors' Journal*, May 4, 1902: 10 (Young Man's, hustling).

3. *Progressive Houston*, November 18, 1911 (rise). The official city booster magazine founded in May 1909, was distributed to train passengers arriving at the downtown station through 1913. Progressive ideas were advocated through the 1920s in *Progressive Houston*, the "official organ" of the Young Men's Business League, in *Civics for Houston*, published by Will Hogg in 1928–1929, and in the slick magazine, *Houston Gargoyle*, sponsored by philanthropist Estelle Sharp in 1928–1929.

4. Ima Hogg, remarks, IHPBC, 4W195:10 (men and women).

5. Ima Hogg, statement, Annual Report, May 16, 1956, 1 Programs 1948–1958, IHP-CUH (responsibility).

6. Putnam with Garrett, *The Upswing: How America Came Together a Century Ago and How We Can Do It Again*, 10, presents a comprehensive, data-driven analysis of how the United States, between 1890 and 1970, made "steady upward progress toward *greater* economic equality, *more* cooperation in the public square, a *stronger* social fabric, and a *growing* culture of solidarity" and of how that progress unraveled between 1970 and 2020.

Chapter One

1. Tsanoff, *Neighborhood Doorways*, 2–6, states that the neighborhood in 1910 was 60% Jewish, 20% "negro," and 20% German, Irish, Mexican, and "native American." Following the Mexican Revolution (1910–1917), the area housed primarily Mexican refugees and immigrants.

2. Maj. George Bernard Erath (January 1, 1813, Vienna, Austria–May 13, 1891, Waco), educated Polytechnic Institute, emigrated, landed New Orleans July 18, 1832; to Texas 1833; fought at Battle of San Jacinto; organized Ranger company; surveyor, farmer, topographic expert; Texas legislator (1840–1848), Texas Senate (2 terms).

3. Erath, "Reminiscences," 18 (nestled, hills), 12 (quotes), 11–12 (early lots), 17 (gushing, inducement). Town lots ranged from $1.25 to $5.00.

4. Thomas Hudson Barron (1796, Virginia–1874), followed Stephen F. Austin to Texas 1822, returned to Arkansas, settled in Texas permanently 1830; Ranger captain; founder Ft. Fisher on Brazos River; fathered twenty-two children by two wives. Texas historical marker, accessed July 2, 2018.

5. John G. Graham (circa 1712–January 4, 1793), married recent Scottish arrival Ann Gilliland (circa 1714–circa 1819) in 1740, raised ten children; youngest child Hugh (February 15, 1762–May 23, 1834) married Mary Wallace (December 19, 1766–May 8, 1822) on October 11, 1787, raised eight children; Robert (son of Hugh and Mary Wallace) and Roxana Winchell lost two sons and a daughter, who died as toddlers, and one son before his twenty-first birthday. Genealogical information MS 609, 4:7.

6. Snead partnership dissolved 1837; from late 1840s Grahamton Manufacturing Company owned and operated by Thomas Anderson and sons W. George and Orville until 1868; Archibald Robinson became stockholder and ran company until death in 1904. Grahamton Manufacturing Company Records, University of Kentucky, accessed July 1, 2018.

7. McLennan County Library Archivist Hannah Kubacak notes that Mary Augusta Graham did not collect her husband's Civil War pension but could provide no postwar information about the Graham family.

8. Probably, Alice was named for Frank Graham's youngest sibling, Alice Rachel Graham, born in 1842, and Eddie was named for Frank's brother, Col. Edwin Smith Graham, who co-founded Graham, TX, with a third brother, Gen. Gustavus Adolphus Graham, who married Edmonia Woolfolk in 1859. Genealogy materials in MS 609, box 4.

9. I am indebted to Anne Conyers Leader, PhD, who searched census records, marriage records, city directories, and probate records to discover what is currently known about James Taylor. Materials in MS 609.

10. Erath, "Reminiscences," 21.

11. Erath, 49 (churches).

12. Great-grandchild Virginia Meyers Watt Chandler in discussion with the author.

13. Erath, "Reminiscences," 56 (literary institution); 52 (Sisters of Namur).

14. *Catalogue of the Officers and Students of Waco University, 1879-1880*, 18, 27 (rules), 31 (moral and religious instruction); *A Directory of Ex-Students of the College of Arts and Sciences of Baylor*, 130, accessed July 20, 2018. Anna Mae, Alice, and Frankie are listed by name; there is also a Graham with no first name that probably is Eddie since the dates coincide with her school years.

15. *Waco Daily Examiner*, May 2, 1882, (fairest flower).

16. For more extensive information about the Baker family, see Kirkland, *Captain James A. Baker*; genealogical materials in MS 609.

17. Wartime and other correspondence in MS 40, 1: 2, 3. Rowena and James were also the parents of Beverly Crawford, a boy born on March 15, 1855, who died six months before their second son James was born.

18. Mary Sharp College (1850–1896), first women's college to offer degrees similar to those offered in men's colleges. Notre Dame of Maryland (1873–present), one of oldest degree-granting women's colleges in United States; originally Preparatory School and Collegiate Institute; became four-year, degree-granting college in 1895.

19. Rowena Baker to Jimmie Baker, October 11, 1876 (liquor); James Addison Baker to Jimmie Baker, Jan. 31, 1877 (Houston, reputation); Superintendent John G. James to James Addison Baker, March 16, 1877, MS 40, 1:7 (esteem).

20. Walter Browne Botts (September 7, 1835, Fredericksburg, Virginia–March 7, 1894, Houston), graduated from Virginia Military Institute 1854; read law, to Houston 1857; joined Hood's Brigade, wounded; resumed practice as personal lawyer for William Marsh Rice and other entrepreneurs; moral and legal advice greatly influenced Captain Baker's career and civic life.

21. Archival sources suggest that by 1900, James Jr. was universally recognized as Captain Baker. As an historical figure, this name distinguishes him from his father, the judge, and from his grandson, James A. Baker III, former secretary of the treasury and of state. Descendants speculate Captain Baker retained his rank in a display of wry humor. He was not a vain man—often photographed in rumpled clothes with ill-fitting hats and a cigar in his hand—but from childhood he was a commanding figure, and his much older mentors were a judge and a colonel. Harris County records and other sources supporting the 1881 date of Baker, Botts, & Baker are on file in the offices of Baker Botts LLP and in MS 609.

22. Mrs. Croft and Mrs. Crawford moved their households, which included enslaved families, to Texas during the Civil War; those slave families mingled with the enslaved people owned by Judge and Rowena Baker. Census records suggest that several families stayed with the large household after emancipation and came to Houston in 1876. Robert Lee Baker and Andrew Morgan Baker Jr. lived with Judge Baker until their early twenties and then moved on; neither married. Numbers changed in later years, but 204 was the house designation in 1870s and 1880s.

23. *Galveston Daily News*, November 21, 1885, p. 3 (Graham incident); Captain James A. Baker to Stewart Addison Baker (age two), December 18, 1940, MS 609, 2:19 (illness). I am indebted to Stewart Baker for sharing his copy of the touching letter Captain Baker wrote to each of his grandchildren, giving each a life insurance policy and explaining how "life insurance helps men and women help themselves in ways that far exceed their fondest hopes." Baker began setting aside sums early in his marriage and in 1891 noted in his ledger that he planned to make ten-dollar payments to each child's account each month (Captain James A. Baker, ledgers, 1897-1912, Baker Botts LLP library, ledger, April 1, 1891-April 1, 1909, 48, 67). The dollhouse was moved five times (San Jacinto to Main St. to Courtlandt Place to The Oaks to Bissonnet and through the hedge to Berthea) for the enjoyment of Captain Baker's daughters, granddaughters, and great-granddaughters. Since 2011, the Harris County Heritage Society has used the building to explain childhood customs in Houston.

24. Lavinia Chilton Abercrombie Lovett (February 14, 1863, Huntsville–November 18, 1928, New York), held founding meeting of Houston Public School Art League; moved to New York City in 1904 when husband, Robert Scott Lovett (1860–1932), joined E. H. Harriman railroad interests; only child, Robert Abercrombie Lovett (1895–1986), educated at the Hill, Harvard, and Yale; served as secretary of defense from 1951 to 1953), charged with oversight of Korean War.

25. Katherine (Kate) Blunt Parker (died 1954), well-trained pianist and choral performer, vital leader of Houston's music appreciation movement; moved to Washington, DC, during World War I, transferred patronage to that city; only son died young.

26. Cesar Maurice Lombardi (August 6, 1845, Tessin–January 23, 1919), Swiss émigré educated at Jesuit College, New Orleans; joined cotton broker William D. Cleveland & Company (1871–1899); married Caroline Gaston Ennis (1877), whose father an associate of William Marsh Rice and director of the Houston & Texas Central Railway; led Houston's school board (1886–1898); 1891 named by Rice to original board of directors for Rice Institute (until death in 1919); managed Belo interests for brother-in-law (1906–1913); member of American Academy of Political and Social Sciences, National Press Club, UCLA Faculty Club.

27. Kirkland, *The Hogg Family and Houston: Philanthropy and the Civic Ideal*, 162 (quote).

28. *Galveston Daily Post*, May 31, 1896, p. 4 (club meeting); *Houston Post*, June 28, 1899, p. 21 (dance). For more information about the Ladies' Reading Club and its drive to found a public library, see Part 2: "Julia Bedford Ideson."

29. Baptisms in First Presbyterian Church records, microfilm, HMRC, RG 18: Alice G. Baker (twelve), March 19, 1899; James A. Baker Jr. (fourteen), November 25, 1906; Walter Browne Baker (almost eleven), December 23, 1910; Ruth G. Baker (thirteen), April 8, 1917; Malcolm G. Baker (fifteen), March 24 or 27 (writing unclear), 1921.

30. *Houston Post* June 18, 1899, p. 21 (musicale).

31. Bayland Orphan Home established 1866, reorganized 1867; for orphaned children of Confederate veterans; located for many years on land along Goose Creek; moved to Woodland Heights, Houston, 1888; burned during World War I; reorganized 1916 with separate institutions for boys and for girls.

32. *Galveston Daily News*, January 23, 1893, p. 5 (to care).

33. *Galveston Daily News*, September 3, 1893, p. 3 (charter); *Houston Post*, March 7, 1897, p. 8 (zeal).

34. *Galveston Daily News*, August 16, p. 3 (Knights of Pythias hop).

35. Captain James A. Baker to Nettie Baker, March 25, 1881, Captain James A. Baker to Nettie Baker Duncan, January 4, 1897, BIPP (illness).

36. Research has not yet revealed Harriet Taylor's death date or place of burial. Baker ledgers show regular payments of one hundred dollars to Harriet Taylor from Estate of M. A. Graham, payments to St. Vincent's Hospital (New York, 1902), Dr. Briggs (New York, 1903), Providence Sanitarium (Waco, 1905–1906), Cincinnati Sanitorium (1906–1912).

37. Barry Scardino, "Development of Domestic Architecture," in *Houston's Forgotten Heritage: Landscape, Houses, Interiors*, 84; photo, 136.

38. For a detailed account of the legal problems attendant on Mrs. Rice's will, see Kirkland, *Captain James A. Baker*, 85-93, 131-134.

39. For a full account of Rice's murder and the subsequent criminal investigation and trial, see Kirkland, *Captain James A. Baker*, 82-85, 93, 110-116, 122-127; ER, boxes 6, 8, 9, 11-13, 15, 19, 25, 30, 36-39, 53, 68, 75-78, 80, 81.

40. *Houston Post*, September 8, 1901, p. 28 (all quotes).

41. Bowie, *The Master of the Hill*, 305 (condition, avert); *Houston Chronicle*, February 13, 1902, p. 1, 2 (out, idolized).

42. I am indebted to Cathy Skitko for citation from The Hill School yearbook.

43. Captain James A. Baker to James Byrne, February 21, 1902, ER, 80:7 (reasons); Stewart Addison Baker and the late Preston Moore Jr., interviews with author, 2009 (life-changing).

44. Tsanoff, *Neighborhood Doorways*, 3 (woman of charm). For the story of Baker's influence on and development of Rice Institute, now Rice University, see Kirkland, *Captain James A. Baker*, 128-176, 240-246, 250-256, 284-294, 328-335.

45. Federation of Women's Clubs, *Key to the City*, 58 (struggle), 59-60 (Sheltering Arms, St. Anthony's Home).

46. Paul Whitefield Horn (April 30, 1870, Missouri–April 13, 1932), always called Professor P. W. Horn, received MA degree from Central (Missouri) College at eighteen; taught in Tennessee, came to Texas 1892; led Houston public schools 1904–1921; ran American School Foundation in Mexico City (1921), president of Southwestern University (1922–1925), first president of Texas Technological College in Lubbock (1925–1932).

47. Houston Settlement Association, 12 (yard).

48. Tsanoff, *Neighborhood Doorways*, 2 (moral surroundings, strangers); Houston Settlement Association, *Year Book*, 12 (neighborhood). No correspondence survives from the 1890-1920 period to indicate how Alice became so interested in the settlement movement. Arnold Toynbee and Jane Addams had published information about Toynbee Hall and Hull House by 1907. It is also possible that during Alice's frequent visits to New York from 1900 to 1907, she had been able to visit University Settlement (1886) or Henry Street Settlement (1893) on the Lower East Side. Jane Addams's first publication, *Democracy and Social Ethics* (1902), may have been known to Baker or Campbell; by 1907 the example of Addams's work had spread far beyond Chicago to inspire reform across the country. Through her friendship with Estelle Sharp, Alice was probably aware of Neighborhood House, founded by the Dallas Free Kindergarten Training and Industrial Association in 1900, the earliest recorded Settlement Movement experiment in Texas.

49. Federation of Women's Clubs, *Key to the City*, 61 (purpose); original board included Helen (Mrs. J. Lewis) Thompson, vice president; Roxalee (Mrs. Frank) Andrews, treasurer; Mrs. D. C. Glenn, recording secretary; Mrs. J. Allen Kyle, corresponding secretary; and Emma Richardson Cherry and Sybil Campbell, press committee. By 1911 Mary (Mrs. Edgar Odell) Lovett was a board member; officers elected every year for one-year term. See Houston Settlement Association, *Year Book, 1909*, p. 3, 15, 16 for 1909, 1907, and 1908 officers and other members.

50. Estelle Boughton Sharp (June 19,1873–August 30,1965), one of Houston's most important civic leaders and philanthropists from 1904 until her death; attended Oberlin College, supported social service groups, advocated for world peace; worked closely with Julia Ideson; frequently traveled with Ima Hogg.

51. Walter Benona Sharp (December 18, 1879–November 28, 1912), inventor, began career drilling water wells; invented rock drill bit and other tools that revolutionized oil exploration; 1904 president of Producers Oil Company (working with Joseph Cullinan and Will Hogg), original partner of Howard Hughes (Sharp-Hughes Tool Company); gave generously to United Charities, helped feed the hungry, Houston delegate to first National Progressive Convention in Chicago's Coliseum, August 5–7, 1912; died tragically fighting huge oil well fire, left $400,000 and shares in tool company to wife, whom he named executrix.

52. Federation of Women's Clubs, *Key to the City*, 62 (subscribers).

53. *Houston Post*, November 17, 1908 (Settlement belongs); Federation of Women's Clubs, *Key to the City*, 63 (not a charity).

54. Houston Settlement Association, *Year Book, 1909*, p. 14 (commodious, delightful spot), 15 (supporters). Descriptions of the space vary; a photograph album in the 1907–1920 Neighborhood Centers binder notes the Settegast space housed a club room, poolroom, parlors, and a home for the resident worker.

55. Russell Sage Foundation established by Margaret Olivia Slocum Sage (1828, Syracuse–1918, New York City) with gift of $10 million on April 19, 1907; named for husband, Russell Sage, railroad executive and financier; first general-purpose foundation in US; Sage made gift for "improvement of social and living conditions in the United States" and hoped to fulfill mission through "research, publication, education, the establishment and maintenance of charitable or benevolent activities, agencies and institutions" by examining "difficult problems" and working to "secure co-operation and aid" in finding solutions; 1907 foundation funded first systematic effort to survey employment and living conditions of working class families in big cities. See Part III (Ima Hogg) for Sage Foundation support of mental health and child helping projects. Today the foundation prioritizes social science research into the most pressing social and economic concerns.

56. *Houston Gargoyle*, May 4, 1930, p. 15 (refractory, useful). Seabrook School served delinquent and abandoned boys until 1955.

57. Houston Settlement Association, *Year Book, 1909*, p. 15, says settlement was open until August in 1909. Tsanoff, *Neighborhood Doorways*, published 1958, states that 1910 was "first year" settlement was open in summer. I rely on the accuracy of the 1909 report, published in 1910. Tsanoff, writing nearly fifty years after the fact, says Kranz "edited and probably wrote" the report. He could not have done so without Alice Baker's direction and information. Most settlements maintained a Penny Provident Bank, which allowed participants to save their pennies and learn the benefits of accumulating savings. When the account reached five dollars, the saver was encouraged to open a savings account with a Houston bank willing to accommodate such modest clients.

58. Houston Settlement Association, *Year Book, 1909*, title page (purpose), 2-3 (staff and board), 5 (social work definition); 1909 board included: "Mrs. James A. Baker, *President*; Mrs. H. R. Akin, *Vice-President*; Mrs. John McClellan, *First Vice-President*; Mrs. D. C. Glenn, *Secretary*; Mrs. J. Lewis Thompson, *Treasurer*; Mrs. J. B. Mayberry, *Corresponding Secretary*." Other members of the board included Sybil Campbell, Roxalee Andrews, Marian Seward Holt, Estelle Sharp, Mrs. Joseph Gohlman, Mrs. James A. Radford, Mrs. Thornwell Fay, Mrs. Howard Smith, Mrs. J. Allen Kyle.

59. Houston Settlement Association, *Year Book, 1909*, 5–8 (social work manifesto).

60. Houston Settlement Association, *Year Book, 1909, 18–27* (clubs and activities).

61. Houston Settlement Association, *Year Book, 1909*, 10–12 (settlement goals).

62. Alexander Caswell Ellis (May 4, 1871–October 9, 1948) mentored Ima Hogg while a young lecturer at University of Texas; consultant, reformer, and professor of educational philosophy there from 1908 to 1926; studied in Berlin (1905–1907); tirelessly promoted public education and improved economic, social, and educational conditions in Texas (1897–1926); directed adult education at the university and from 1926 to 1941 at Cleveland College (adult studies section of Case Western Reserve University).

63. Tsanoff, *Neighborhood Doorways*, 5 ("socialized" school).

64. Tsanoff, 5–6 (Campbell report); Montgomery, *Houston as a Setting of the Jewel*, 37 (praise).

65. "The History of Captain Baker," MS 609, 2: 3 (comment on Bakers family).

66. *Houston Post*, January 2, 1899, clipping, MS 609 (everywhere at once).

67. "The Echo of the Ball," n.d., clipping in MS 609 (every detail).

68. "Elegant Reception," n.d., clipping in MS 609 (floral basket). Alice's guests were Virginia Dorrance (No-Tsu-Oh Festival's maid of honor), Libbie Rice, Louise Fitzgerald, Miss Thompson (cousin from Ft. Worth), and Miss Mountz of Pennsylvania. *Houston Post*, March 8, 1908, p. 33 (railroad car).

69. *Chautauqua Minute Book*, Chautauqua file, HMRC (promote).

70. Trimble, *Houston Country Club Centennial*, 29–34 (quotes). Alice's grandson Preston Moore Jr. spearheaded the effort to repurpose and preserve the original Houston Country Club Golf Course as the Gus Wortham Park Golf Course.

71. Joseph Chappell Hutcheson Jr. (1879–1973), Houston legal counsel (1913–1917), mayor (1917–1918), US district judge of the Southern District of Texas (1918–1931), judge of the Fifth Circuit Court of Appeals (1931–1973); advised President Hoover's committee on law enforcement; 1945 US chairman of British-American Committee on the Settlement of Jews in Palestine.

72. Letters, May 23, 1910, and May 25, 1910, suggest entire amount quickly pledged, to be paid over five years; First Presbyterian Church records, roll eleven, HMRC. While most couples made one gift to the church as a couple, the Bakers are listed as two separate prospects on congregation donor lists.

73. *Houston Post*, September 30, 1906 (best music). The Treble Clef Club was first organized in 1893 or 1896. The board of the Music Festival Association held its

meetings in the Chamber of Commerce headquarters. Board directors included Captain James A. Baker, Rabbi Henry Barnstein, newspaper publisher M. E. Foster, investor Jesse Jones, Rice Institute President Edgar O. Lovett, and school superintendent Prof. P. W. Horn.

74. Helena Lewyn (December 16, 1889, Houston–August 30, 1980, Grants Pass, OR, while on vacation), pianist, composer; father a dentist, German Jewish family; studied piano in Chicago and Berlin; 1909 concerts in Germany; 1910 debut in London; 1910–1912 with New York Symphony; 1922 based in Los Angeles, continued to perform; 1930s and 1940s piano studio; married 1928, divorced; 1910 set poem by Texan Judd Mortimer Lewis to music.

75. Laura Baker (Wille) Hutcheson (1856, Grimes County, Texas–1924, Houston), named for mother, given nickname Wille as child after father William C. Hutcheson killed in Civil War; educated Wesleyan Female Institute (Staunton, VA) and Sorbonne, Paris (1876); married J. E. C. Wilson of Houston; six children, five of whom died in childhood; bitter divorce in 1899; resumed maiden name and became cultural critic, *Houston Post* cultural reporter, lecturer in music, French, German; member Christ Church; insatiable reader and clubwoman; only female correspondent to *Musical America*; introduced Houston to international music scene; educated readers and built music audience. Information courtesy of Joanne Hutcheson Seale Wilson.

76. Carroll, *Standard History*, 378–79 (music festival quotes); *Houston Post*, September 30, 1906, p. 29 (Cunningham).

77. Corinne Afton Abercrombie Waldo (October 21, 1877, Walker County–April 1972, buried Oakwood Cemetery, Huntsville) graduated from Wellesley College in 1900, married Gentry Waldo in 1903, one son, one daughter, founder of Houston Art League, cofounder of Houston Symphony, served as delegate for Wellesley at the opening ceremonies for Rice Institute in 1912, member of committee to provide revenue for World War I, woman suffrage supporter, and pianist. She was living in Galveston during the formation of the Girls' Musical Club but spent much of her life in Houston.

78. Girls' Musical Club, *Yearbook*, 1912-1913, IHPMFAH (purpose, privileged). This yearbook and an early history differ on number of invitees/attendees. Perhaps forty young ladies were invited and twenty-five attended the founding meeting.

79. "In Society," *Houston Chronicle*, November 22, 1911, p. 11 (roses).

80. For details about Captain Baker's devotion to Rice Institute, see Kirkland, *Captain James A. Baker*, and ER, Opening Ceremony file. The stipulations that the institute live on endowment interest, not borrow, and recruit white boys and girls caused later financial and racial justice problems, not fully addressed until the 1960s.

81. Margaret (Maggie) Bell Culbertson Hunter Kinkaid (April 29, 1874, Houston–December 20, 1951, Houston, automobile accident), attended Clopper Institute, qualified as teacher; married William J. Kinkaid 1899; discovered married women could not teach in public schools; in September 1904 invited seven students to form first kindergarten class in home at San Jacinto and Elgin; added one class per year; 1924 agreed with parents to organize board to raise funds for larger facility at Richmond

and Graustark; late 1920s began to offer upper school courses; Christian Scientist; encouraged "enrichment experience"; asked son to become principal (1941–1951); named John H. Cooper her successor just before retirement in 1951. The Kinkaid School, since 1957 housed on a large property in Piney Point Village, is the oldest continually operating private, non-parochial school in Houston.

82. Edgar Odell Lovett to Captain James A. Baker, September 13, 1912, MS 487 (reveal).

83. *Progressive Houston*, Vol. IV, No. 6, p. 1 (quote).

84. Frederick William Gross (February 14, 1861, Marshall, TX–September 15, 1915, Dallas), attended Wiley College and Fisk University before receiving BA in 1885 from Bishop College, established in 1881; Gross second degree holder at Bishop and subsequently studied at University of Chicago before returning to Bishop to complete MA in 1902; began teaching in Victoria, TX, in 1887; 1901 chief administrator of Victoria Colored School for newly created Victoria Independent School District; 1907 called to Houston Industrial College, served as president until his death; exerted tremendous influence due to education; served ten years as president of Baptist Missionary and Educational Convention of Texas; grand secretary of United Brothers of Friendship in Texas for many years; returning from the 1915 National Baptist Convention (Chicago), when died in Dallas at age fifty-four. Gross genealogy courtesy of Anne Leader, May 11, 2021; Frederick W. Gross, "Find a Grave," accessed May 13, 2021; archives, HMRC, HPL eServices search; *Houston City Directory*, 1915.

85. *Houston Post*, April 19, 1914, p. 3 (use, effort).

86. *Red Book* authors use the term Afro-American, although research through the Houston Public Library has not determined the frequency or timespan of this usage.

87. Corinne Fonde (April 27, 1883, Mobile, AL–April 8, 1950, Houston), lost mother at age two; close to older sister Dora, stepmother Alice B. Fonde, four half siblings; pursued career in several Southern towns before moving to Houston; visited family members in Alabama and Tennessee; more than three decades with Houston's Settlement Association and Recreation Department.

88. Corinne Fonde, "Rusk School, First Social Center," *Houston Daily Post*, August 6, 1916, p. 27 (all quotes).

89. Jefferson Davis Hospital operated as medical facility 1924–1938; designed by city architect Wilkes Alfred Dowdy; placed on National Register of Historic Places November 2013; now subdivided as artists' loft/studios.

90. Brackenridge also referred to as North Side Settlement. Settlement movement in Texas little studied; 1900–1917 Dallas expanded Neighborhood House to include Clara Chaison Kindergarten for Russian Jewish families, opened Cotton Mill Kindergarten; 1912 El Paso Methodist Church founded Rose Gregory Houchen Settlement for Segundo Barrio; 1913 San Antonio Women's Board of Mission of Christian Church founded Inman Institute (now Inman Christian Center); 1916 in Austin, twelve women formed Girls' Settlement Club, opened Girls' Settlement Home on East 31st Street as day nursery "for impoverished working families."

91. Philanthropist Harriet Levy (September 13, 1862, Houston–October 9, 1937) and brothers Abraham M. (Abe) Levy (September 23, 1859–November 10, 1924) and Haskel Levy (1866–1926), lived in French-style "chateau" designed by architect Olle J. Lorehn at 2016 Main Street (1906–1938); house demolished after Harriet's death at her request; siblings never married but participated actively in civic life; 1887 Abe and Haskel founded Levy Brothers Drygoods Company, largest mercantile in the South; amassed fortune; Abe was president of United Jewish Charities and director of two banks; named "Merchant Prince of Houston" in 1924.

92. "Mrs. Walter B. Sharp Talks to Woman's Club," *Houston Chronicle*, March 26, 1916, clipping in Sharp Papers, 11:2 (splendid work, United Charities, social "illness"); *Austin Statesman*, clipping in Sharp Papers 11:4 ("charity" offensive); board of United Charities in 1912 and board of Social Service Federation in 1914 essentially the same.

93. At this time, there were two population classifications, "Negro" and "white."

94. Chamber of Commerce, City of Houston, *Illustrated City Book*, 1916, p. 549 (planned); Houston Welfare Finance Committee Report, James L. Autry Papers, MS 3, WRC, 22: 5 (promote).

95. "Playground Association of America," *The Play and Playground Encyclopedia*, accessed March 3, 2019 (necessity, democracy, job); "Value of City Playgrounds: Lecture at High School," *Houston Post*, November 18, 1911, clippings in Sharp Papers 11:4 (value, mischief).

96. *Houston Chronicle*, May 9, 1917, clipping, Scrapbooks, MS 40, 6 (pretty girl); Alice Baker to Bonner Means, July 24, 1915, MS 40, 2:1 (endeared); James A. Baker Jr. to Bonner Means Baker, August 21, 1918, MS 40, 3:2 (love of country).

97. Telegram, Bonner Means to James A. Baker Jr., July 2, 1917, BIPP #4 (quiet); newspaper clipping, MS 40, 6: clippings file; *Houston Post*, August 5, 1917, clipping MS 40, 6: scrapbooks (wedding).

98. Houstonians raised over $40 million for Liberty loans, prepared 1,511,528 surgical dressings, knitted 29,004 articles, and made 177,102 garments for hospital patients. Although Parker tried to fulfill his law firm responsibilities, he never returned to Houston and presided over postwar US Liquidation Commission and Mixed Claims Commission until his death in 1929 at age sixty-one. Benda, *Our Community War Service Memorial: Houston and Harris County* (copy in HMRC).

99. Letter, Captain James A. Baker to James A. Baker Jr., MS 40, 3:2 (birdcage); Captain James A. Baker to James A. Baker Jr., BIPP #21 (envelope and letter, road to happiness).

100. Captain James A. Baker to James A. Baker Jr., sent at 3:34 a.m., June 16, 1918, MS 40, 6: scrapbook (telegram).

101. James A. Baker Jr. to Bonner Means Baker, August 21, 1918, MS 40, 3:2; James A. Baker Jr. to Alice Baker, October 11, 1918, BIPP #18f; Captain James A. Baker to James A. Baker Jr., October 4, 1918, MS 40, 3:2; Captain James A. Baker to James A. Baker Jr., October 4, 1918, MS 40, 3:2; command of Company L, MS 40, 6 (letter quotes). Baker family worries were well-founded—on Meuse-Argonne front, 1.2

million Americans engaged; 26,277 died; 95,786 wounded, half casualties of war. Lengel, *To Conquer Hell*, 4.

102. Telegram, Jesse H. Jones to Captain James A. Baker, November 30, 1918, MS 40, 3: 2, confirms the reassignment to Company I; James A. Baker Jr. to Alice Baker Jones, BIPP, #20 A (strings); Captain James A. Baker to M. A. Mitaranga, c/o Zifarin Fils & cie., Marseille, France, November 5, 1919, February 10, 1919, BIPP (Christmas box); telegram, Captain James A. Baker to Gen. John J. Pershing, February 3, 1919, MS 40, 3:2; letter, Captain James A. Baker to Gen. John J. Pershing, February 3, 1919, MS 40, 6 (discharge request).

103. Bonner Means Baker to James A. Baker Jr., April 4, 1919, MS 40:6 (when can I see you).

104. Captain James A. Baker to Bonner Means Baker, September 25, 1918, MS 40, 2:1 (dear sweet).

105. Tsanoff, *Neighborhood Doorways*, 13-21 (quotes). Tsanoff comments about lack of documents in the 1910s and 1920s. Searches at BakerRipley do not provide much information for these years. Tsanoff became chairman of Rusk Settlement (1932–1933), president of the Houston Settlement Association (1935–1943), and Houston representative to the national settlement association board (1953–1961).

106. Tsanoff, *Neighborhood Doorways*, 12 (strike out).

107. *Civics for Houston*, November 1928, 5 (recreation, important).

108. *Houston Post*, October 26, 1924, p. 10 (vocalists).

109. Roscoe Wright, "What Price Play," *Houston Gargoyle*, March 1, 1931, p. 11 (practically); *Houston Gargoyle*, March 6, 1929, p. 2 (more). Shortly after Fonde's death in 1950, the city created Fonde Park in southeast Houston in her memory. In 1960 Houston architects Frederick James MacKie Jr. (1905–1984) and Karl Kamrath (1905–1984) designed Fonde Recreation Center on Memorial Drive near downtown to remember Houston's pioneering proselytizer of recreation.

110. William Ward Watkin (January 21, 1886, Boston–June 24, 1952, Houston), BA 1908 University of Pennsylvania; traveled in Europe 1909; joined Cram, Goodhue & Ferguson in Boston; sent to Houston to oversee construction of Rice Institute buildings; professor of architectural engineering; established private practice; designed Autry House, Field House, Chemistry Building, Cohen House for Rice; designed Miller Outdoor Theatre and Houston Public Library (now Julia Ideson Building); worked with Mies van der Rohe on Museum of Fine Arts, Houston additions and with Kenneth Franzheim and Charles D. Hull on various Houston projects.

111. Baker family scrapbook, MS 487 (millionaires). Millionaires included oil men (E. F. Woodward, Ross Sterling, Robert Lee Blaffer, R. A. Welch, Joseph S. Cullinan, Will Hogg, Underwood Nazro), real estate moguls (Joseph F. Meyer, Jesse H. Jones, J. J. Settegast, Ross Sterling, Will Hogg, James Baker), cotton brokers (W. L. Clayton, Ben Clayton, M. D. Anderson), public utilities (James Baker), lumber (John H. Kirby). Five women had over $1 million: Mrs. Daniel Ripley, Mrs. E. L. Neville, Mrs. James L. Autry, Estelle Sharp, Ima Hogg.

112. Elwood Street, "Solving the Charity Solicitation Problem," *Houston*, November 1922, p. 14 (solving, irritation); Community Chest Annual Report, 1930, foreword: 1 (privation), 2 (care), 3 (live and grow), Community Chest Files, HMRC. In 1928, the Bakers' gift of $2,500 was among seventy-five individuals and corporations who gave $1,000 and over. *The Community Chest: A Description of Nine Months' Working, with a Statement of Accounts and a List of Subscribers, with Amounts Pledged, 1928*, pamphlet, MS 609.

113. King, *Except the Lord Build*, 91–92 (beautiful). The cookbook committee comprised Alice Baker, Mary E. Mayo, Mrs. D. C. Glenn, Mrs. W. G. Smiley, Mrs. J. W. Scott, and Kate Leavell.

114. Adelaide Lovett to Captain James A. Baker, October 10, 1922, MS 40, 2:2 (each Fall Day).

115. Letters in MS 40, 2:2 (useless). Dr. Elliott Joslin, a pioneer in diabetes treatment with insulin, operated a clinic in Boston, but Baker's 1922 ledger and other documents do not reveal the name of the clinic he attended or of the doctor who treated him that summer. Phillips House is today the VIP section of Massachusetts General Hospital, so it is probable Baker was being treated at that venerable institution.

116. MS 40, 2: 2 (darling).

117. MS 40, 2: 2 (considerate, helpful).

118. Alice Graham Baker to Captain James A. Baker, November 5 (My darling), 21 (enough), 1922; Anna Graham Herring to Alice Graham Baker, November 1, 1922, MS 40, 2:2 (happiest).

119. Alice Baker to Captain James A. Baker, November 11, 1922, MS 40, 2:2 (dress suit); *Houston Chronicle*, December 24, 1922, "In Society" page (luminous).

120. Captain James A. Baker to Mrs. James A. Baker, Rockhaven Cottage, Grape Vine Road, East Gloucester, July 12, 1923, July 14, 1923, MS 487, 1:3: Scrapbooks (telegrams).

121. John Fanz Staub (September 12, 1892, Knoxville–April 13, 1981, Houston), studied at University of Tennessee and Massachusetts Institute of Technology; apprenticed with New York architect Harrie Thomas Lindeberg (famed for country houses); 1921 to Houston to supervise three Lindeberg designs; established own practice (1923–1942) before reorganizing as Staub and Rather (1942–1952) and Staub, Rather, and Howze (1952–1971); 1920s used romantic European vernacular styles then in vogue to design houses noted for harmonious proportions, elegant detail, and fine materials; 1924–1958 designed thirty-one houses in River Oaks and several in Broadacres and River Crest, Fort Worth; houses he designed in Houston, Beaumont, Dallas, and Memphis now hold museum collections.

122. Birdsall Parmenas Briscoe (June 10, 1876, Harrisburg, TX–September 18, 1971, Houston; buried in Oak Hill Cemetery, Goliad), descendant Harrisburg founder John R. Harris; educated San Antonio Academy, Texas Agricultural and Mechanical College, University of Texas; known for elegantly detailed houses in many historical architectural styles; designed finest examples of "stylish country houses in garden

suburban neighborhoods" for leading Houston citizens (1926–1940); independent practice (1912); partner Sam H. Dixon Jr. (1922–1926); shared office with Maurice J. Sullivan (1919–1955); district officer for South Texas of Historic American Buildings Survey (1934–1941); fellow of American Institute of Architecture (1949–1971). Briscoe's house for Alice Baker and Murray Jones was one of four he built on Courtlandt Place. Its symmetrical plan adapted mid-eighteenth-century houses, while its entrance hall, living room, and dining room paneled with tall dark-wood wainscot and beamed ceilings recalled arts and crafts interiors popular in the period. See Fox, *The Architecture of Birdsall P. Briscoe*, 1 (stylish).

123. *Galveston Daily News*, December 7, 1924, p. 12 (trip); Captain James A. Baker to Mrs. James A. Baker Jr., written September 20 at the Hotel du Lion d'Or, but mailed to The Savoy, Houston, from Reims, Marne, September 22, 1924, BIPP (letter); Mackin, *Suddenly We Didn't Want to Die*, 236, 241 (endless waves, hell, knife-edge).

124. *Houston Post Dispatch*, "In Society," October 24, 27, 1926 (bouquet); *Houston Chronicle*, October 24, 27, 1926 (flowers).

125. *Houston News: The Junior League of Houston* 4, Fall, Winter 1999 and Spring, Summer 2000, (flowers).

126. Malcolm Baker to Alice Baker, September 22, 1920 (Brooks Brothers), November 3, 1922 (wedding shower), MS 40, 2:2.

127. *Houston Chronicle* November 14 (impressive, statewide), 15 (exquisite, cascaded), 1929; *Houston Post-Dispatch*, November 15, 1929 (flowers).

128. Four more grandchildren were born after Alice's death: Graeme Baker Vickery (1935–1991) to Browne and Adelaide; James Harrison Moore (1941–2011) to Ruth and Preston; Malcolm Graham Baker Jr. (born 1936) and Stewart Addison Baker (born 1938) to Malcolm and Anita. Shirley Baker Pond died in 1993, Walter Brown Baker Jr. in 1994, Alice Jones Meyers in 2008, Lovett Baker in 2010, Bonner Baker Moffitt in 2015, and Preston Moore Jr. on December 27, 2015.

129. Captain James A. Baker to Edgar Odell Lovett, September 26, 1931, EOL 36:3 (address); notebook on death of Alice Graham Baker, MS 487 (hypertension).

130. Quotes MEFO, *Houston Press*, clipping, *Houston Press*, May 10–11, 1932, *Houston Chronicle*, May 10, 1932, *Houston Post*, May 11, May 13, 1932, MS 487; Alice Graham Baker, grave marker, Baker family plot, Glenwood Cemetery, Houston.

131. The Bakers probably chose the angel to guard over their son Graham, but records do not show when the statue was placed at the site. Also buried in the family plot are Captain Baker's younger, bachelor brother Robert Lee Baker (1867–1939), his bachelor cousin Andrew Gabriel Baker (1864–1924), and his daughter Alice Graham Baker Jones (1887–1978).

Chapter Two

1. *Houston Chronicle*, October 17, 1926 (finest library headline); October 18, 1926, clipping in William Ward Watkin Papers, WRC, 6:40 (coming out).

2. *Women's Viewpoint*, July 1, 1924, p. 17 (bright page).

3. *Biographical and Historical Memoirs: Adams, Clay, Hall and Hamilton Counties, Nebraska* (1890), 168 (windstorm), courtesy of the Adams County Historical Society. A. B. Ideson's house was moved twelve inches. Hastings was named for Col. D. T. Hastings, an officer of the St. Joseph & Grand Island Railroad, who built the railroad through Adams County.

4. Advertisement, General City Directory of Hastings, Nebraska, 1882, p. 76 (celebrated).

5. Julia Bedford Ideson was named for her maternal grandmother Julia Ann Bedford (1811–1872), who married Sylvester Wesley Baseman (1809–1886). Margaret was named for her paternal grandmother Margaret Castree (1820–1855). The Ideson brothers were descended from John William Ideson who settled in the Parish of St. James, Middlesex, Maryland, in May 1765. Alison Baptiste and Sophia Eleanor had two more children born in Oshkosh, Wisconsin (Eleanor Gertrude, 1894–1957, and Alison Baptiste Jr., 1898–1958).

6. *Hastings Journal*, June 17, 1880 (house); *Hastings Gazette Journal*, June 15, 1882 (wallpaper); Burton and Lewis, *Past and Present of Adams County, Nebraska*, 271 (friendship). Courtesy of Adams County Historical Society.

7. Hastings City Directory (advertisements), 1882–1883 (business listings); *Hastings Daily Gazette Journal*, June 4, 1887 (popular), June 15, 1882 (closing hours), June 22, 1882 (falling out of bed).

8. Eleven books and a sampler sewn by Julia Bedford, Julia Ideson's grandmother, are preserved in JIP, 3. Julia Ideson also owned a *History of Rome*, *Beginners' Greek*, and *Beginning French*, but when these books were purchased is not clear.

9. *Oshkosh Northwestern*, August 10, 1901, p. 7 (crazy party), August 31, 1901, p. 7 (moonlight party).

10. *Houston Chronicle*, October 28, 1901, (dairy), November 21, 1901, p. 7 (house), January 25, 1902, p. 5 (rice land), April 3, 1904, p. 7 (ads); clipping *Houston Chronicle and Herald*, December 19, 1904, p. 7 (MoPac immigration bureau meeting). John C. Ideson is variously listed as bookstore clerk, traveling salesman, and realtor, and the family is listed at six different addresses between 1892 and 1903, when it settled at 1508 McKinney Avenue (Houston City Directories, 1892–1906).

11. Joseph Chappell Hutcheson (1842–1924), graduate of University of Virginia Law School (1867); migrated to Anderson, Texas; assumed antebellum law practice of older brother who died in Civil War; known always as Captain; moved to Houston; leading lawyer; defended Black and white clients; while in Texas Legislature helped create University of Texas; as member of US Congress helped bring deepwater port to Houston; served on many civic boards; father of eight children.

12. *Houston Post*, August 25, 1906, p. 14 (obituary).

13. *Galveston Daily News*, July 19, 1896, p. 3 (merry party); *Houston Post*, August 13, 1899, p. 21 (hop), May 30, 1899, p. 10 (Shakespeare).

14. The 1901 *Cactus* lists 51 seniors, 84 juniors, 137 sophomores, and 156 freshmen, suggesting that many aspirants did not complete the four-year program.

Thirty-three men and eighteen women received degrees that year. The Ashbel Smith Literary Society was named to honor first Board of Regents President Ashbel Smith, M.D. (1805, Hartford, CT–1886, Harris County, TX); educated Yale University; founded Texas Medical Association.

15. Frank Alfred Swertz (August 31, 1886, Cork, Ireland–January 26, 1953, New York), chemical engineer, married Margaret Ideson Ladd, August 18, 1923; lived in Chile for some years before emigrating to US; naturalized citizen February 3, 1932; Swertzes lived in Manhattan, Brooklyn, Rockaway Point (1942–1953).

16. *Austin American- Statesman*, January 18, 1903, p. 2 (dance), December 7, 1902, p. 13 (literary magazine), January 25, 1903, p. 6 (sorority).

17. Catalogue of the University of Texas, 109 (library science class).

18. University records suggest that Julia never formally received the BA degree, although she seems to have completed all required courses. Instead, she began working at the library as soon as she had completed the library science course credentials (*Cactus* and various alumni listings, BC).

19. Elizabeth Fitzsimmons Ring (October 31, 1857, Houston–1941, Houston), educated at Miss Mary B. Brown's Young Ladies' Boarding and Day School; 1880 married attorney Henry Franklin Ring; 1887 joined Ladies' Reading Club; 1900 helped form City Federation of Women's Clubs; board of Houston Public Library (1900–1941); life member of board of Texas Federation of Women's Clubs; after 1915 trained as social worker at Texas School of Civics and Philanthropy organized by Estelle Sharp; secured legislation to create College of Industrial Arts for Women (now Texas Woman's University); lobbied for prison reform and minimum wage; July 1964 Elizabeth Ring Branch Library dedicated to memory in Spring Branch area.

20. JIP, 1:1, correspondence 1900–1919 (all letters).

21. Looscan, "Early Houston Society and Its Relation to Libraries." Lucius Bicknell, an immigrant to Texas from Philadelphia, made the first attempt to bring a reading and debating society to Houston in the spring of 1837 when he organized the Houston Franklin Debating Society, comprised of several lawyers and politicians. He died of fever on October 4, 1837, and thus did not participate in subsequent events concerning the Houston Public Library. The Long Row is now preserved as part of Houston's Heritage Society Museum in Sam Houston Park.

22. E.P. Walker, "'So Good and Necessary a Work'": The Public Library in South Carolina, 1698–1980," accessed July 27, 2020, p. 1–2 (encouraged); HPL reports, 1904–1951, p. 5 (diffuse knowledge); *Telegraph and Texas Register*, 6–7, JIP (nothing, flourishing); 1848 charter granted to Abner Cooke, Peter W. Gray, E. A. Palmer, James Walker, Thomas Bagby, T. B. J. Hadley.

23. Edward Hopkins Cushing (1829, Royalton, VT–1879, Houston), graduate Dartmouth College; 1856 to Texas to teach; 1858 to Houston with bride Matilda J. Burke (1839–1883); owner-editor *Telegraph and Texas Register* (1858–1871); sold paper; ran wholesale and retail book business (1871–1879); accomplished

horticulturist, nurtured two hundred varieties of plant material, some new to Houston, at Bohemia, his ten-acre homestead; lyceum purchased his 140-volume library.

24. Henry H. Dickson, "First Report and Resume of the History of the Houston Lyceum and Carnegie Library Association to the Mayor and the City Council, Houston, Texas, March 2, 1904," p. 7, JIP (several ladies); Hatch, *Lyceum to Library*, 29 (insure), note 20: "Depositories are the most favored of all institutions . . . receiving as they do . . . the Journals, the Executive and Miscellaneous documents and reports of Committees of the two Houses of Congress, embracing all documents, . . . amounting to 125 or more volumes per Congress."

25. Adele Briscoe Looscan (February 5, 1848–November 23, 1935), daughter of prominent Republic of Texas figures Andrew Briscoe and Mary Jane Harris Briscoe, whose father John R. Harris founded Harrisburg; 1866 graduate Miss Mary B. Brown's Young Ladies' School in Houston; September 13, 1881 married Irish immigrant and Confederate Maj. Michael Looscan, lawyer, member of Houston Light Guard, Houston Lyceum; Adele member of several patriotic groups, author of several Texas histories, lifelong supporter of public library; 1967 neighborhood library on Weslayan Street named Adele Looscan Branch Library in her honor.

26. Hatch, *Lyceum to Library*, 60 (club life); Gunter, *100-Year History*, 1 (solidarity); *River Oaks Magazine*, August 1992, 17–18 (purpose). Three presidents dominated Ladies' Reading Club leadership in the early years: Adele Briscoe Looscan (1885-1887, 1889-1891, 1893-1894), Caroline Ennis Lombardi (1887-1889, 1896-1898), and Elizabeth Fitzsimmons Ring (1898-1900, 1916-1918). Ladies Reading Club vertical file, H (Clubs & Organization), HPL.

27. Dickson report, HPL Reports 1904–1951; Ideson summary, 7, 8 (quotes).

28. Belle Sherman Kendall (April 27, 1847, Harrisburg, TX–March 19, 1919, Houston), daughter of Gen. Sidney Sherman, a commander at the Battle of San Jacinto; married Judge William E. Kendall of Galveston; resident of Houston 1873–1919; founder of Daughters of the Republic of Texas; devout Catholic; president of Woman's Club 1898–1899; May 3, 1901, named life member of Houston Lyceum and Carnegie Library Association.

29. Chapman, *100 Years–100 Stories*, 5 (copy of Carnegie letter).

30. Dickson Report, HPL Reports 1904–1951, p. 13 (all property). Original board appointments: S. H. Brashear, W. W. Barnett, Henry H. Dickson, Elizabeth Ring, Belle Kendall, Norman S. Meldrum, W. H. Clute, W. H. Wilson, A. S. Grant. The 1904 board comprised Henry Dickson, president, Mayor Orren T. Holt, ex officio, J. R. Browne, W. H. Clute, C. P. Shearn, T. M Kennerly, E. P. Hamblen, and the three leaders of Houston's women's clubs: Elizabeth Fitzsimmons Ring, Belle Sherman Kendall, and Louise Cohn Raphael.

31. The committee named to administer the Norma Meldrum Fund included civic leader and attorney Captain James A. Baker, bank president William B. Chew, attorney Joseph C. Hutcheson Jr., Norma's aunt Edith Meldrum, Elizabeth Ring, and art patron Lavinia Abercrombie Lovett. Blanche Higginbotham replaced Edith

Meldrum, and in 1928, Norman Meldrum asked Julia Ideson to serve on the committee, following the death of Lavinia Lovett (who had been living in New York City since 1905). Term of service seems to have been for life.

32. James Riely Gordon (August 2, 1863, Winchester, VA–March 16, 1937, Pelham Heights, NY), trained with engineer father and in office of supervising architect of US; worked in San Antonio (1884–1900) and Dallas (1900–1902) before moving to New York City in 1903; served thirteen terms as president New York Society of Architects; in Texas designed hundreds of fine residences and public buildings, including eighteen courthouses, the federal courthouse and post office in San Antonio, and the medal-winning Texas Building at the World's Columbian Exposition in Chicago; in Texas worked in Classical or Beaux-Arts style central to era's urban aesthetic. Bradley, *Improbable Metropolis*, 79–80 and n. 9 (Gordon).

33. *Houston Post*, March 3, 1904, p. 5 ("Amid a Blaze of Light Great Crowds Assembled to Inspect the Carnegie Building—Statue Unveiled—Felicitous Speeches Delivered," third line of headline "The Library Dedicated").

34. Henry Havelock Dickson (1861, Louisville, KY–1924), 1869 to Marshall, TX, where father built foundry; in railroad business; 1887 to Houston to assist father at Dickson Car Wheel Company; active in Houston's civic and charitable projects; 1900–1908, 1915–1924 Library Association president; oversaw construction of two major buildings; did not live to see 1926 Central Library building he long supported; replaced by attorney William A. Vinson, who was HLA president until 1951.

35. *Houston Post*, November 3, 1904, p. 5 (all quotes); Chapman, *100 Years*, photographs, 7, 14 (exterior); 8, 12 (interior).

36. HPL Reports, 1904–1951, 17 (commodious), 19 (brilliantly, abundant, absolutely); *Houston Post*, September 25, 1903, p. 13 (expensive).

37. *Houston Post*, October 8, 1904, p. 5 ("important factor"); Philosophical Society of Texas, *Proceedings*, p. 57 (Ideson tribute); "Julia Ideson: Houston's First Librarian," HMRC website, accessed September 23, 2019 (original staff); *Houston Chronicle*, May 1, 1925, JIP 2:1 (just young girl).

38. "First Report and Resume," 13, JIP (indispensable); *Houston Post*, October 8, 1904, p. 5 (rapid but substantial growth).

39. *Houston Post*, October 8, 1904, p. 5 (pride).

40. Library supporters who gathered in Philadelphia during the 1876 Centennial celebrations to found the American Library Association noted that in 1876 there were 188 public libraries (free municipal institutions supported by taxes) in eleven states, with Massachusetts boasting 127 public libraries and Iowa and Texas one each. Garrison, *Apostles of Culture*, 4.

41. *Houston Post*, November 19, 1904, p. 4 (topics), May 5, 1910, p. 13 (information), May 6, 1910, p. 16 (library work).

42. JIP, 1:5 (all quotes).

43. Minutes suggest the Baldwin Collection came to the library officially in 1905. Ideson remembers in a 1935 reprise of library activities that the stock was presented

at the time of the collection's sale in 1898. Hatch, Ideson, and the minutes are occasionally at odds, and in general, I have followed the minutes since they record contemporary actions. It is likely that the promise was made in 1898, but the gift was not completed until 1905, per Julia Ideson, "Houston Public Library and Early Library Development/Based on 1904 report of the Houston Lyceum and Carnegie Library Association and Review of Minutes, October 1935."

44. *Progressive Houston: A Monthly Publication for the Benefit of the Taxpayer and General Public*, II, 1 (May 1910), WRC (business principles).

45. Judd Mortimer Lewis (September 13, 1867, New York–July 25, 1945, Houston), schooled in Ohio; 1893 to Houston; 1900 joined *Houston Post*; named first Poet Laureate of Texas; 1920 DLitt from Baylor University; 1921 president of Press Association of Texas; president of American Folklore Society; found homes in Houston for orphaned children.

46. Eugene Field (September 2, 1859–November 4, 1895), journalist, humorist, essayist, and poet known as the "poet of childhood" in his day; attained national celebrity; several statues and elementary schools dedicated to his memory; remembered long after his death for "Wynken, Blynken, and Nod" and "Little Boy Blue."

47. *Houston Post*, September 8, 1909 (Field reading quotes). In the summer of 1911, the board discussed hiring a children's librarian and paying her to take special training in Pittsburgh before beginning work in the fall of 1912.

48. Garrison, *Apostles of Culture*, 58 (relations); *Houston Post*, January 21, 1906, p. 5 (significant).

49. HLAB, vol. 1, 1907 October (material), November (interested, convenient), December (preferably).

50. JIP, 2:7 (Married Ladies Social Club).

51. Edward Ollington Smith (July 4, 1885, Selma, AL–October 13, 1945, Houston), BA Fisk University; 1904 principal, Goliad, TX; 1905 to Houston, where principal Hollywood night school, Frances Harper Junior High, and first principal Phillis Wheatley High School (1927–1945); pioneer of equal rights, belonged to many civic organizations; lauded for building Wheatly to 2,600 with sixty teachers and thirty extracurricular activities to prepare his students for life experiences and give them job skills.

52. HLAB, vol. 1, June 9, 1908 (colored branch), August 1, 1908 (establish), September 15, 1908 (secure); *Houston Post*, October 29, 1908, p. 16 (called attention). Colored High School, the only senior high school for African Americans in Houston from 1893 to 1926, was located at 303 West Dallas. Jack Yates High School opened in 1926 and Phillis Wheatley High School in 1927. Photograph of Colored High School in *Red Book*, 14, 87. High school information provided by Ingrid Grant, Collection Development Librarian, African American Library, Gregory School.

53. William Sidney Pittman (April 21, 1875, Montgomery, AL–March 14, 1958, Dallas), 1907 married Booker T. Washington's daughter Portia, three children; many commissions included schools, college buildings, hotels, churches, Fairmount

Heights residential community planned for African Americans in suburban Maryland; 1928 separated from wife, who returned to Tuskegee to teach; gave up architecture; skilled carpenter; published controversial weekly newspaper, *The Brotherhood Eyes*, critical of elite black behavior.

54. *Houston Post*, June 30, 1909, p. 5 (all quotes).

55. *Houston Post*, November 4, 1906, p. 54 (civic improvement).

56. HLAB, vol. 1, 1907–1920, October 8, 1907, p. 1 (although, board).

57. HLAB, vol. 1, 1907–1920, February 13, 1912, p. 144 (financial aid), April 9, 1912, p. 151 (drama).

58. HLAB, vol. 1, November 3, 1907, p. 6 (stacks), December 14, 1909, p. 67 (readable books).

59. Louise C. Raphael to Julia Ideson, letter, January 13, 1909, JIP,1:1 (trying illness).

60. HLAB, vol. 1, April 18, 1909, p. 53 (sufficiently strong), April 11, 1911, p. 113 (impossible).

61. Lyceum board and staff to Julia Ideson, letter, December 3, 1913 (losing, privilege), Elizabeth Ring to Julia Ideson, December 2, 1913 (too big), JIP, 1:1; *Houston Post*, November 23, 1913, p. 60 (farewell), November 28, 1913, p. 12 (Cherry), November 30, 1913, p. 50 (friends).

62. Philosophical Society of Texas tribute, 57 (deep, maintained, unusual); *Galveston Daily News*, Sun. May 7, 1905, p. 9 (wedding); *Houston Post*, February 28, 1909, p. 8 (ladies of Houston).

63. *Houston Post*, September 10, 1908, p. 9 (*Post* necessity), June 11, 1913, June 15, 1913, p. 8 (*Candida*).

64. *Houston Post*, October 2, 1909, p. 7 (prominent, complete), June 20, 1910, p. 14 (indefinitely), October 30, 1910, p. 52 (College Women's Club). An article in the *Houston Post*, September 13, 1909, p. 4, reported an early September meeting at which the Houston Scientific Society had agreed to expand and rename the organization, seek a state charter of incorporation, and open the museum free to the public at least two days a week.

65. Annette Finnigan (1873, West Columbia, TX–July 17, 1940, New York; buried Glenwood, Houston), attended Houston public schools, Tilden Seminary in NH, Wellesley College (1889–1894), where she studied fine arts and athletics, Columbia University, where she studied philosophy; took over father's business operations at his death; with two sisters introduced equal suffrage leagues to Houston and Galveston; 1904–1906 launched and was president of Texas Woman Suffrage Association; 1913–1915 shared leadership of Texas Woman Suffrage Association with Mary Eleanor Brackenridge; January 1915 lobbied in Austin for woman suffrage; 1916 suffered paralysis; retired from business, athletic activities, and political organizing; 1920–1940 collected antiquities and rare books for Museum of Fine Arts, Houston and Houston Public Library; donated eighteen acres on Houston's northside for park catering to African American community; died of cancer and made bequests to Wellesley

College, American Foundation for the Blind, and American Commission for Mental Hygiene.

66. Annette Finnigan file, MFAH (Finnigan praise).

67. *Houston Post,* January 29, 1912, p. 13 (suffrage cause).

68. Mary Eleanor Brackenridge (March 7, 1837, Warwick County, IN–February 14, 1924, San Antonio), attended Anderson Female Seminary, New Albany, IN; 1855 moved to Jackson County, TX; 1866 she and widowed mother joined brother George in San Antonio, where siblings shared home until deaths; championed civic and social betterment; active member Texas Federation of Women's Clubs, Daughters of the American Revolution, Texas Mothers' Congress, Woman's Christian Temperance Union, Presbyterian Church; founded Woman's Club of San Antonio, president for seven years; 1911 wrote *The Legal Status of Texas Women*; founding president San Antonio Equal Franchise Society; 1913 organized Texas Woman Suffrage Association; 1918 first woman in Bexar County to register to vote; 1902 founded College of Industrial Arts (now Texas Woman's University), regent 1902–1924; assisted students financially, traveled widely, served on boards of two banks founded by her brother.

69. *Houston Post,* July 13, 1913, p. 8 (witty), July 16, 1913, p. 5 (largest).

70. *Houston Post,* November 2, 1914, p. 12 (all quotes).

71. *Houston Post,* August 30, 1914 (war description), November 2, 1914, p. 12 (best sight). Julia's passage from Liverpool appears on the ship's manifest, but Margaret sailed on the SS *Rochambeau* from Bordeaux in 1916 (ship manifests courtesy of Anne C. Leader).

72. Photographs in Houston Public Library photography collections; *Houston Post,* March 28, 1915, p. 7 (go backward).

73. *Houston Post,* January 20, 1916, p. 9 (pretty disappointed), June 16, 1915, p. 11 (tableaux).

74. *Houston Chronicle,* April 9 (first fair); *Houston Post,* October 13, 1915 (brilliant musical programs), October 3, 1915, p. 31 (illustrated overview), October 17, 1915, p. 15, (1915 fair).

75. Chicago School of Civics and Philanthropy originated in 1903 with Chicago Theological Seminary Professor Graham Taylor, offered unaffiliated, nonsectarian classes for students in practical courses for careers in social work; 1904–1905 course listed under the University of Chicago downtown extension program (later the Institute of Social Science and Arts); 1907 renamed Chicago Institute of Social Service; 1908 incorporated as Chicago School of Civics and Philanthropy, Taylor as president, board including Jane Addams; 1908 state charter objective "to promote, through instruction, training, investigation, the efficiency of civic, philanthropic and social work, and the improvement of living and working conditions." Williams and MacLean, *Settlement Sociology in the Progressive Years,* 178, 180.

76. Sophonisba Preston Breckinridge (April 1, 1866, Lexington, KY–July 30, 1948, Chicago), BA Wellesley College (1888), PhD (political science, University of Chicago, 1901), law degree (University of Chicago, 1904); taught University of Chicago Department of Household Administration, lived Hull House (1907–1920), developed

Chicago Institute of Social Studies into Graduate School of Social Service Administration (1920); through teaching and writing set standards for US social work education; advanced government involvement in social welfare programs; active in suffrage advocacy; helped organize Woman's Peace Party and Women's International League for Peace and Freedom; 1909 research noted newly arrived immigrants most likely exploited with high rents for poor housing; listed light, air space, toilet facilities, number of rooms per family to reinforce problems of overcrowding, poor ventilation, etc. Williams and MacLean, *Settlement Sociology*, 150.

77. *Houston Post*, October 1, 1916, p. 10 (public social); Williams and MacLean, *Settlement Sociology*, 150 (demoralizing).

78. EOL, 35:6 (donation correspondence); Sharp Papers, WRC, 5:22 (social workers).

79. *Houston Post*, March 21, 1915, p. 33 (unaccustomed), March 25, 1915, p. 7 (reception speakers).

80. *Houston Post*, April 1, 1915, p. 7 (Baker), May 23, 1915, p. 33 (Ideson).

81. Winegarten and McArthur, *Citizens at Last*, 148 (voice of the Suffragist); *Houston Post*, May 15, 1915, p. 7 (finale, ivy, clever, successful). Some historians have called Finnigan's illness a "stroke," but contemporaries spoke only of a serious, crippling disease.

82. Winegarten and McArthur, *Citizens at Last*, 153 (corrupt liquor governor).

83. Malcolm Glenn Wyer (1877, Concordia, KS–1965), BLS NY State Library School, DLibSci University of Nebraska; served many school and public libraries beginning 1900, including University of Minnesota, Colorado College, University of Iowa, University of Nebraska; 1917–1919 on leave as assistant director of American Library Association Library War Service, assigned to Camp Logan November 1917–February 5, 1918; 1918 DC to oversee library administration at forty-four war camps; 1924 Denver Public Library; Dean of Denver School of Librarianship; many honors including President ALA 1936–1937.

84. ALA Archives, Series 89/1/15, Box 3 vol. 17, 359–383 (first class, popular, enjoyable); HLAR (1904–1929), clippings, 1918 report, published February 2, 1919 (khaki uniform).

85. *Houston Post*, December 12, 1917, p. 8 (Ideson resolution); Minnie Fisher Cunningham to Carrie Chapman Catt, July 31, 1917, in Winegarten and McArthur, *Citizens at Last*, 159–160 ("opportune moment").

86. HMRC, MSS0032–040 and other images(posters).

87. HLAR, 1918 (all quotes).

88. *Houston Post*, April 18, 1918, p. 1 (all quotes).

89. ALA Archives, WWI Library War Service Personnel and Pay records, series 89/1/78, Box 1, folder I-K, Box 3 (expenses). Pay records show departure date as February 18.

90. Steer letter, March 3, 1919, series 8901005a, Box 6, vol. 31, p. 425 (all quotes).

91. Julia Ideson to Houston Library staff, from Brest, France, Hotel Continental, Care of American Library Association, n.d., JIP, Box 1 (cheery, jammed,

good friends); Brest Area Report, March 1919, written April 6, 1919, ALA Archives, 8901005a-003-vol. 31, p. 432 (70,000, 7,000, calls, lonesome). The ALA reported on April 6, 1919, that they had 8,673 volumes in operation.

92. *Houston Post*, February 29, 1920, p. 3 (vital influence); *Austin American*, May 16, 1920, p. 14 (all librarians).

93. *Galveston Daily News*, August 28, 1920, p. 3 (all quotes).

94. *Galveston Daily News*, October 19, 1920, p. 4 (forward looking); *Houston Post*, December 29, 1920, p. 6 (rapidly), January 4, 1921, p. 4 (happy).

95. Julia Ideson, "Houston Public Library and Early Library Development," review in HLAB, October 1935, p. 12 (time ripe); *Houston Post*, January 6, p. 1 (calling); *Galveston Daily News*, January 8, 1921, p. 1 (all friends); Board Minutes, vol. 2, 1921 (levy).

96. HLAB, vol. 2, annual report 1921, p. 15 (substantial progress, adequate); *Houston Post*, November 7, 1921, p. 2 (public, friends). Louise Franklin became librarian of North Branch, Elise Wilkinson and then Marguerite Bergener oversaw Houston Heights Branch, and Bessie Osborne continued her duties at Colored Carnegie Branch.

97. *Houston Post*, April 25, 1922, p. 5 (urgent conditions); HLAR, 1921 (quotes on conditions).

98. "Lyceum to Landmark," 4 (inside, fit into daily life). After leaving Detroit, Ideson spent the next month visiting New York, Chicago, St. Louis (Gilbert library), Cleveland, Buffalo, Utica, Albany, Providence (Tilton library), Newark, Wilmington (Tilton library), and Philadelphia.

99. "Miss Ideson and the New Library," *Woman's Viewpoint*, July 1, 1924, 17, 30 (quotes).

100. "Lyceum to Landmark," 7 (thoroughly Spanish).

101. *Houston Post*, June 4, 1924, p. 9 (unremittingly); *Woman's Viewpoint*, 17 (Miss Ideson disappointed).

102. HLAR, 1925 (beautiful trees).

103. Mary Hazelton Blanchard Wade (March 23, 1860, Charlestown, MA–1936), educated in high school and by private tutors; 1877 became teacher; 1882 married Louis Francis Wade; popular and prolific author of children's books, including comprehensive series "Our Little Cousin" books about childhood around the world; wrote children's biographies of George Washington, Benjamin Franklin, and U. S. Grant and several children's histories of settlement and nation-building in North America.

104. HLAR, 1925 (splendid, beautiful); Julia Ideson, "New Building Nearing Completion," *Houston Chronicle*, November 15, 1925, in HLAR (clippings).

105. *Houston Chronicle*, October 18, 1926 (coming out); HLAR, 1925 (reading opportunities, move); *Galveston Daily News*, October 3, 1925, p. 2; October 19, 1926, October 24, 1926, clippings (Ideson's remarks).

106. "An Address Delivered at the Dedication Ceremonies of the Houston Public Library, Monday, October 18, 1926, at 7:30 O'clock, by Edgar Odell Lovett, President

of the Rice Institute," Presidential Papers (Lovett) 1912–1945, Series 3, 51:31, WRC (opening oration). The compilers of *Lyceum to Landmark* place the opening ceremonies on Sunday, October 17, but newspaper reports, the program pamphlet, and the copy of Edgar Odell Lovett's address all record Monday, October 18, 1926, at 7:30 as the day, date, and time of the event. The crowd was somewhere in the three to five thousand range, according to various reports.

107. Program Pamphlet, 10 (collar of lace), 16 (whispering gallery).

108. Julia Ideson to Adele Looscan, December 3, 1915, Adele Looscan Papers MSS 0037, 1:3, HMRC (thank you letter).

109. HLAR, 1928 (not bad).

110. HLAR, 1925, p. 24 (HPL Summary of Years 1921–1925); HLAR, 1930, p. 2, 3 (historical museum, exhibits).

111. HLAR, 1928 (political questions).

112. HLAR, 1929 (world friendship, contact).

113. HPL reports 1904–1951, 1927, p. 3 (many visitors).

114. HLAR, 1929 (lack of funds).

115. "The Community Chest," 1928, pamphlet MS 609 (care for).

116. *Houston Post*, May 26, 1921, p. 4 (outing club)

117. *Houston Post*, October 2, 1921, p. 27 (merit).

118. *Houston Gargoyle*, November 8, 1931, p. 12 (voluntary), September 8, 1929 (Eastman), December 8, 1929, p. 8 (Thomas).

119. *Houston Gargoyle*, April 21, 1929, p. 11 (torch, slim); JIP, 2:9, clippings 1929, scrapbook (tablet); *Houston Post Dispatch*, May 1, 1929, p. 1 (aloft, distinguished).

120. HLAR, 1931 (quotes).

121. "High Points from the Annual Report of the Houston Public Library, 1933," cover page (fighting, promoting); Annual Report, 1932, president's letter, (Black volume) p. 2 (throngs, search); HLAR, 1931, p. 17 (chief, many).

122. HLAR, 1930, Librarian Report, p. 1 (problem), 1932 (resolution), 1937, p. 16 (reduced, economy). The annual reports appeared in different formats and the figures are not always exactly the same, especially in the year 1937, when expenditures, for example, are listed as $75,917.28 and $78,905.90 (taken from copies of printed reports). The gist is clear—never enough money to do everything Ideson wanted to do.

123. HLAR, 1931 (books), 1936 (family).

124. HLAR, 1931 (Finnigan gifts); *Houston Post*, July 18, 1940 (bequest).

125. HLAR, 1933 (majority).

126. HLAR, 1930 (instructions, smoothly).

127. HLAR, 1935 (made over), 1937 (training, real).

128. HPL Reports 1904–1951, 1938 (book gypsies, visualized), 1939 (work). Loans to children climbed to 361,443 books in 1937, but circulation at the main library dropped to half its 1931 number. The librarian concluded, "This is to be expected as the neighborhood ceases to be residential."

129. HLAR, 1939 (pulse), 1930 (comprehend, joy).

130. HLAR, 1936 (questions), 1939 (manufacturing).

131. HLAR 1939 (Christmas), 1938 (convenient).

132. HPL, Reports 1904–1951, 1938, 8 (Bandy report quotes); *Houston Informer*, July 11, 1931(joke), similar comments in January 14, 1933, September 7, 1935.

133. HLAR, 1939 (all quotes).

134. Julia Ideson to Editor, *Houston Labor Journal*, August 21, 1930, JIP, 1:5; *Houston Labor Journal*, "Our Home Town" column, reproduced in Annual Report, 1930, p. 16–18; *Houston Chronicle*, November 16, 1941, p. 42 (bastion of democracy).

135. HLAR, 1935 (handbook quotes), 1930, p. 37 (crisp and cool).

136. Carlos Antonio de Padua Chávez y Ramirez (June 13, 1899, Mexico City–August 2, 1978, Mexico City), composer, conductor, pianist, music theorist, journalist; founder and director of Mexican Symphonic Orchestra; 1916 started cultural journal *Gladios*; 1934 staff of *El Universal* in Mexico City; 1947 founder National Symphony Orchestra; wrote six symphonies, most popular *Sinfonia india* (Second) uses Yaqui percussion instruments; ballets on Aztec themes; international touring career; conducted Houston Symphony; composed *Clio* in 1969 for Ima Hogg, with debut in Houston.

137. JIP, clipping, 2: 13 (airplane bungalow quotes), 8 (sunset). Robert Southey (1774–1842) wrote "The Inchcape Rock" in 1802, which inspired the house name. Julia Ideson's postcard collection (HMRC, MSS 1039) comprises over nine thousand cards, mostly collected by her to trace her travels.

138. JIP, 2:7 (European trip); "A Fleeting Look at European Libraries," *Bulletin of the Texas Library Association*, 6–8 (August 1938), in JIP, 1:5 (published analysis). Stops on the cruise included Algiers, Palermo, Naples, Caffaro Bay, Venice, and Trieste.

139. HLAR, Summary of Statistics, December 31, 1940, p. 11 (tidal wave).

140. HLAR, 1940, 1942, p. 23 (storage quotes).

141. *Houston Chronicle*, clipping "Deposit Centers for Victory Book Drive Announced"; JIP, 1:6, *Look & Listen* program April 10, 1942 (steady stream).

142. HLAR, 1944, p. 20 (war-weary).

143. JIP, 2: 2, 3, brochure Texas Commission on Interracial Cooperation, October 1942, p. 3 (*Negro Labor News* quote).

144. HLAR, 1944 (all quotes).

145. HLAR, 1941 (valiant, pride).

146. HLAR, 1941, Resolutions of death (Vinson remarks); Philosophical Society of Texas tribute, 57 (force, all, few); *Houston Chronicle*, July 16, 1945 (nationally known), July 17, 1945 (valiant woman). Henry Barnstein/Barnston information in city directories and in letter of resignation, April 21, 1920, Congregation Beth Israel Collection, 5:1, HMRC. Many US citizens anglicized the spellings of their names during the xenophobic 1920s. A well-known, civically active rabbi for decades, Barnstein changed to Barnston about 1920.

147. *Houston Chronicle*, December 19, 1945, p. 28 (kindliness, quiet). Dickson married Mr. Reynolds shortly after becoming librarian and was known as Harriet

Dickson Reynolds thereafter. Ideson's will left her estate in trust to the Houston Library Association, but her sister Margaret Ladd Swertz was provided a life interest in the income from the estate. After Swertz's death on November 5, 1949, the assets were sold and the proceeds used to establish the funds for former and current HPL staff members, JIP, 2:13.

148. Vertical file, Philosophical Society of Texas, BC (continuous study). To honor Julia Ideson, a solid silver alms basin was dedicated at Christ Church (Cathedral since 1949) to her mother Rose Baseman Ideson on July 16, 1945, *Houston Chronicle*, July 16, 1945.

Chapter Three

1. *Houston Chronicle*, March 7, 1966, Ann Mohler, "Society Today," Ima Hogg Vertical file, BC (weekend). All dedicatory remarks in "Bayou Bend Collection of the Houston Museum of Fine Arts: On the Occasion of the Dedication, March 5, 1966," MFAH. The committee comprised: Thomas D. Anderson, chairman of the Museum Bayou Bend Committee; Harris Masterson, chairman of the special Dedication Committee; Eugenia Tennant, chairman of the Bayou Bend Committee of the River Oaks Garden Club; Mrs. John Hamman, chairman of the Flower Arrangements Committee of Bayou Bend; Sandy Thompson, chairman of the Bayou Bend Docents; David B. Warren, curator of Bayou Bend.

2. Ann Holmes, *Houston Chronicle*, March 6, 1966, sec. 1, p. 20 (first lady); Helen Anderson, *Houston Post*, March 6, 1966, sec. 1, p. 11 (orchid). In her remarks (reprinted in full, *Bridge* 40: 4, February–March 2016), Ima refers to Charles Montgomery, "lately Director of the monumental collection of Americana, Henry Francis du Pont Winterthur Museum."

3. James S. Hogg to John W. Hogg, July 13, 1882, IHPBC, 3B111 (cup of joy). Ima Hogg told me the story of her name and confided that she had many beaux when she was a young woman, during work sessions (1973–1975) on a project that we did not complete due to her death. In *Ima Hogg*, p. 13–14, David B. Warren provides a convincing analysis of the ties between James Stephen Hogg and his brother Thomas Elisha, who died of typhoid fever in 1880 at age thirty-eight. Despite disclaimers, Ima's name did haunt her; she kept a file of letters from women who wrote they had been named for her, corresponded with these namesakes, and even visited with several "impetuous" callers (IHPBC, 3B150:1).

4. Ima Hogg, Remarks to the River Oaks Garden Club, November 5, 1963, Docent Papers, MFAH (discriminating, fastidious); Ima Hogg, "Reminiscences of Life in the Texas Governor's Mansion," IHPBC, 3B168: 4 (mother, exquisite), 7 (confidante), 3B130: 3, 10; Ima Hogg to *Houston Chronicle*, letter to editor, August 18, 1934 (Hogg characteristics). Reminiscences appear in various places but have now been printed as a booklet, *Ima: Reminiscences of Life in the Texas Governor's Mansion*, introduced by Jerry D. Frazee, 10 (avid student).

5. Ima Hogg, preface in Thomas Elisha Hogg, *The Fate of Marvin* (compulsive writer of verse); Kathleen Sproul, "James Stephen Hogg: March 24, 1851–March 3, 1906," pamphlet printed on the occasion of the dedication of the Varner-Hogg State Park, West Columbia, March 24, 1958, p. 9.

6. Lillian J. "Lillie" Stinson (January 17, 1868, Wood County–August 29, 1954, Winnsboro, Wood County) married and divorced as a teenager; 1889 married David Louis Burkett (1867–1940), moved to Winnsboro. Talented pianist Clifford "Cliffie" (1870, Wood County–1888) died from black jaundice (hideous bacterial infection of the liver attributed to rats).

7. In a letter to his daughter Sallie, Stinson explained that his great-grandfather came from Donegal, Ireland, where he was an earl whose lands had been confiscated during a rebellion. This story is not borne out by dates relating to Irish rebellions or to the Irish earls of Donegal. A ship, the *Earl of Donegall*, did carry emigrants from Belfast to Charlestown, South Carolina, in August 1767. Digital typescript of letter from James A. Stinson to Sallie Hogg, August 27, 1894, BC. In 1874 Colonel Stinson also supervised the wedding of his step-daughter Penelope Jane (Pink) Jones to Dr. William Jackson Rogers, and Justice of the Peace Jim Hogg performed the ceremony.

8. According to marriage, death, draft registration, and passport documents, the youngest child born to James Stephen and Sallie Stinson Hogg was named Thomas Elijah. As an adult, Tom officially used the Elijah spelling, not the Elisha used in previous Hogg generations. Before the Hoggs could move into their new home, the new attorney general lived briefly at the Avenue Hotel, three blocks from the capitol and then at Mrs. M. L. Andrews's boardinghouse at 1010 Lavaca, across the street from the Texas Governor's Mansion, while the family was in Speer.

9. Austin population: 4,428 in 1870; 11,013 in 1880; 14,575 in 1890; and 22,258 in 1900.

10. Elizabeth "Lizzie" Nancy Stinson (June 8, 1833, Georgia–July 1, 1920, Speer, TX) married John P. Phillips (1825–1888) on August 1, 1878, in Troup, Georgia. The couple moved to Wood County, Texas, and after Phillips's death, Lizzie joined her brother's household near Speer and became Ima Hogg's occasional roommate and musical companion.

11. IHPMFAH, 2: 95 (formal portrait photograph of baby Tom with his unnamed elegantly dressed wet nurse and her baby, both babies beautifully dressed); Hogg, *Reminiscences*, 24 (Cliffie, trips, enchanting, paradise); Ima Hogg, Remarks to the River Oaks Garden Club (Aunt Lizzie). Mr. and Mrs. R. L. Hood pioneered schools in Austin from 1875 until the early twentieth century.

12. "Reminiscences," IHPBC, 3B168:4 (father, mother); James S. Hogg to William C. Hogg, June 1, 1891, BHOT, 69 (lonesome, proud).

13. "Reminiscences," BHOT, 59 (grounds, compete, playmates, tacks), 63 (beautiful, little visit); Hogg, *Reminiscences*, 35 (found time, seats).

14. Abner Hugh Cook (1814, Salisbury, NC–1884, Austin) apprenticed as carpenter, architect, contractor to local master builder and gentleman farmer Samuel

Lemly, who built brick temple with Roman portico for Salisbury's First Presbyterian Church; to Macon, Georgia, where several Greek Revival buildings in progress; to Nashville where studied Andrew Jackson's Greek Revival-style Hermitage; by 1839 in Austin where designed and built homes, purchased interest in Bastrop-area lumber mills, built brick kiln on Shoal Creek; used local brick for buildings and pine strips from Bastrop for columns. Elisha Marshall Pease (January 3, 1812, Enfield CT–August 26, 1883, Lampasas, TX, buried Austin), lawyer, helped write constitution for Republic of Texas, elected governor 1853 and 1855; Unionist, organized Republican Party; appointed governor 1867, resigned 1869.

15. "Reminiscences," BHOT, 57 (prepared, entirely, many, enormous, except, very large), 58 (southwest, southeast), 65 (Grace Bauer, ordeal, housekeeping); Hogg, *Reminiscences,* 6 (white man, negro man). On February 11, 1854, legislators appropriated $17,500 to build and furnish a suitable residence and outbuildings for the governor and authorized sale of city lots to provide funds. Pease named himself, the treasurer, and the controller a committee to oversee the project, and Cook designed three similar residences—the public governor's mansion, and houses for the controller and the treasurer.

16. BHOT, 45 (Sour Lake, no one), 67 (often ill, gave orders), 68 (not greatly), 92 (Mamma).

17. *Galveston Daily News,* June 15, 1892, p. 6 (all quotes).

18. BHOT, 99 (very amazing, usually), 100 (colored cook, great disappointment, lovely things, piano), 101 (cat, grand, refrigerator), 102 (pack of men); Hogg, *Reminis cences,* 47 (charming, great relief). Warren (*Ima Hogg,* 26) notes that while in Rhode Island, the former governor Herbert W. Ladd and his daughter Hope gave Ima a party (IHPBC 3 B127).

19. BHOT, 105 (Mother seems), 107 (my engagements), 108 (quiet solitude, my period of life), 109 (I am so glad, my sister).

20. BHOT 114, (made great many), 115 (twenty-two).

21. James S. Hogg to Sarah S. Hogg, May 1, 1895, Sarah S. Hogg to James S. Hogg, May 12, 1895, BHOT116, (Wherever), 118 (I was with, bronchitis), 119 (car so rough, you can't, has not).

22. BHOT, 127 (to Papa), 127–128 (My dear Ima, pleasure, confidence, god bless), 130 (I am going), 131 (about the 7th), 133 (Mother does not); *Austin American Statesman,* September 25, 1895 (committee).

23. William C. Hogg to Sallie S. Hogg, May 10, 1895, IHPBC, 3B118 (you are gone); James S. Hogg to Julia McDugald Ferguson, October 14, 1895, HPWRC, 14 (in all the storms); James A. Stinson to James S. Hogg, JSHBC, 2J214: Family Letters Received (Yours of sixteenth). Julia Ann Hogg McDugald Ferguson (1839–1896) married Dr. William Wallace McDugald in 1865, settled in Rusk, where sons Joseph Lewis and James born; McDugald died about 1871; Julia married attorney Henry Clay Ferguson, 1873; two sons, William Brownlee and Bismarck; Julia died February 22, 1896; governor and his children remained close to cousins and to Ferguson.

24. BHOT, 139 (Our Aunt); interview with Robert Sutherland, Round Top August 24, 1970, HFR, MAI9/U1: 12 (no end, most outgoing). Martha Frances Hogg Davis (1834–1920) married William Brownlee Davis, 1850 (not yet sixteen); first son, Daniel, died at birth; second son, William Brownlee Jr., born 1852, year his father died of tuberculosis; widow at seventeen, lost father, fiancé, youngest brother, mother during Civil War; head of household for younger siblings.

25. IHPCUH, 1896 (electrifying, to imitate).

26. Thomas Mitchell Campbell (April 22, 1856–April 1, 1923, Galveston), self-educated, read law; publisher and editor *Lampasas Leader*; 1891 named receiver for troubled International-Great Northern Railroad; moved to Palestine, took company out of bankruptcy, became manager of reorganized corporation (1892–1897); 1897 moved to Austin, began promoting Democratic Party candidates; shared Governor Hogg's reformist principles and Hogg urged him to run for governor; 1906 Campbell elected governor (1907–1911). His daughter Sarah was a childhood and lifelong friend of Ima Hogg.

27. James S. Hogg to Col. R. B. Levy, June 1, 1896, HPWRC: 14 (comfortable home); BHOT 146 (excellent neighborhood), 147 (plenty of ground, great barnyard, spend awhile), 149 (very large, sit, at one time), 150 (photograph), 147–148 (did her best, canary birds), 148 (disciplinarian, pinched).

28. Even in the last years of her life, Ima Hogg talked about Aunt Fannie's tuberculosis scare with her friends and with author.

29. "Family Reminiscences," IHPBC, 3B130: 4 (father).

30. Will Hogg to Ima Hogg, November 27, 1897, IHPBC, 3B130: Family Letters (four invitations, sign); James S. Hogg to Will Hogg, July 26, 1898 (you have never), April 3, 1899 (wield), June 26, 1899 (indulge), JSHBC, 2J418: Letters to Will C. Hogg April 19, 1892–October 7, 1899; Will Hogg to Ima Hogg, December 17, 1895, IHPBC, 3B111: William C. Hogg (so you); Will C. Hogg to Ima Hogg, January 18, 1899, IH-PBC, 3B118: 1 (jolly time).

31. James S. Hogg to John Hogg, March 24, 1897, HPWRC, 15 (dear little Ima); James S. Hogg to Ima Hogg, July 10, 1899, IHPBC, 3B126: 1 (seventeenth birthday).

32. James S. Hogg to Will C. Hogg, August 24, 1897–September 15, 1897, JSHBC, 2J418: Letters to Will C. Hogg (1897 trip quotes).

33. BHOT, 172 (trip quotes); James S. Hogg to Will Hogg, August 16, 1898 (great traveler, a little lazy), December 18, 1898 (studying) JSHB, 2J418: Letters to Will C. Hogg; "I would love to live here [Honolulu] next to Texas better than any place in the world," IHPBC, 3B153: Travel, 1898: 1; Ima Hogg to author, also in Warren, *Ima Hogg*, 31 (premonition story).

34. James S. Hogg to R. H. Moseley, June 1, 1899, to Will C. Hogg, June 6, 1899, HPWRC, 16 (to labor); James S. Hogg to Ima Hogg, September 26, 1899, IHPBC, 3B111 (no objections).

35. Ima Hogg to Mrs. A. Caswell Ellis, June 5, 1961, MFAH, MS 21, vol. 2:3 (ideal, warm).

36. Derthick Music-Literary Clubs were popular in the 1880s and 1890s with many in Texas, where over four hundred music clubs of various types were active during those decades. The Derthick System used flash cards to teach music theory, history, and biography. Wilber M. Derthick, a Chicago music critic, scholar, and author, and his wife, May, sent out "agents" to found local clubs, which used their method and cards.

37. IHPBC, 3B163: 10 (Derthick Club, program, March 3, 1900, Ima played *The Nightingale*); *Alcalde*, November/December 1975, 46–47 (Red-letter, beautiful, from that night)

38. *Alcalde*, clipping, n.d., Gretchen Roschs Goldsmith, '03, IHPMFAH, MS21, series 14, scrapbook 1, p. 8 (really, most, unaffected, cozy); BHOT, 188 (every Saturday), 189 (all other quotes).

39. Joseph Cullinan (December 31, 1860, Sharon, PA–1937, pneumonia), Pennsylvania oil fields at fourteen; 1882 joined John D. Rockefeller's Standard Oil and moved up corporate ladder; 1895 organized Petroleum Iron Works to build storage tanks and steam boilers; 1897 to Corsicana to form J. S. Cullinan Co., a general oil business; March 28, 1901, chartered Texas Fuel Company at Spindletop; with Hogg-Swayne and two investors organized Producers Oil Co. capitalized at $1.5 million, and in 1902 Texas Company, capitalized at $3 million; partnered with Will Hogg and Walter B. Sharp (president Producers Oil Co); reverses in 1911 and 1912 caused Cullinan and Will Hogg to resign from Texas Company, which moved to New York and became Texaco; major Houston civic leader, philanthropist; innovations included building first oil-fueled locomotive engine in Texas, providing natural gas to consumers for lighting, building first Texas refinery at Corsicana field, supporting bill to regulate oil, gas, and water wells (signed March 19, 1899). Tommy W. Stringer, "Joseph S. Cullinan: Pioneer in Texas Oil," *East Texas Historical Journal*, 19:8, accessed September 25, 2020; "Joseph S. Cullinan," *Handbook of Texas Online*, accessed September 25, 2020. The Texas Company received its charter on April 7, 1902, and made a formal announcement on May 15. The original Hogg-Swayne Syndicate raised $40,000; Cotner, *James Stephen Hogg: A Biography* 526, 544.

40. BHOT, 188 (joyous); James S. Hogg to William Davis, January 25, 1901, HPWRC, 16 (Will).

41. Martin Varner (March 3, 1775, Fayette County, PA–February 14, 1844, Wood County, TX), 1824 land grant, one league in Brazoria and one labor in San Felipe, Waller County; raised corn, livestock; built house on highest point to avoid flooding, catch breezes, and oversee operation; 1834–1836 fought Mexico including Battle of San Jacinto; awarded 640 acres in Wood County; amassed several thousand acres; raised one son, six daughters; died from gunshot wound after quarrel over land rights. 1834 Columbus Patton purchased property for father John S. Patton; sugar cane plantations worked by sixty to eighty enslaved people; two-story sugar house, barn, stables, smokehouse, slave quarters. James Hogg bought property from Patton heirs.

42. "Family Reminiscences," IHPBC, 3B130: 10 (joyous); James S. Hogg to Ima Hogg, January 26, 1902, JSHBC, 2J215: 1 (signs letter Jym). Carlyle moved the school to Arlington, but as late as February 16, 1903, it was still located in Hillsboro.

43. Josef Hofmann (1876, Poland–1957), toured briefly at age twelve; 1892 studied with Anton Rubinstein and made adult debut 1894; composed over one hundred works; US citizen 1925; first professor of piano at Philadelphia's Curtis Institute of Music and director there (1927–1938); last decade in Los Angeles where inventor; seventy patents, including pneumatic shock absorbers for cars and airplanes, piano improvements for Steinway Co.

44. Emanuel Rubin, "Jeannette Meyer Thurber (1850–1946): Music for a Democracy," in Locke and Barr, *Cultivating Music in America*, 134 (outstanding institution); "Family Reminiscences," IHPBC, 3B130: 10 (all other quotes).

45. Thurber's fascinating story is told in Rubin, "Jeannette Meyer Thurber" in Locke and Barr, *Cultivating Music in America*, 134–159 (all quotes).

46. Adele Margulies (1863, Vienna–July 6, 1949) premiered last two movements of second piano concerto in D minor by well-regarded nineteenth-century American composer Edward MacDowell (1860–1908); 1890–1892 trio with Leopold Lichtenberg and Leo Schulz. Ima took great pleasure in conserving the extensive collection of piano and violin and piano and cello sonatas and trios for piano, violin, and cello that Margulies assembled during her lifetime and in donating them to the Houston Public Library in her honor. Margulies died on June 6, just days after receiving the thoughtful letter to her describing the gift.

47. Rafael Joseffy (July 3, 1852, Hungary–June 25, 1915, New York City), studied in Hungary and Leipzig, with Franz Liszt at Weimar (summers 1870, 1871); New York debut 1879; taught at National Conservatory (1870–1906); authority on Chopin; introduced Brahms's piano music to US.

48. Bertie Lucy to Ima Hogg, December 1901, IHPBC, 4Zg78: Correspondence 1899–1904 (complete failure); "Family Reminiscences," IHPBC, 3B130: 10 (Joseffy audition, Margulies).

49. JSHBC, 2J215: 3 (vibrate, queer), 2 (Episcopal church).

50. Will Hogg to Ima Hogg, BHOT, 230 (prepare . . . rich woman), 231–232 (massive, twenty-five); Pearl Coburn (undated) and Ramona Lee (April) to Ima Hogg, IHPBC, 4Zg77 (so sad).

51. BHOT, 240 (rigged, Prof. Wilmer), 245–246, (Dear Mickie, at last, Papa). Lawrenceville School information and copies of the report cards and four letters written by Will Hogg to Headmaster Dr. Simon J. McPherson supplied by Jacqueline Hahn, archivist, letter to author June 29, 2007. Students at Lawrenceville were assigned to houses, where they ate, slept, and engaged in house team sports. The grade system (or forms) changed during the two years the Hogg brothers attended, but clearly, Mike and Tom were behind their peers in preparation. Ima later recalled that her father had gotten a commission for Mike, but there is no documentary evidence to support this memory ("Questions by Dr. Cotner," June 20, 1949, IHPBC, 3B116: 2).

52. William C. Hogg to Dr. Simon J. McPherson, March 8, 1904, copy in author's possession, courtesy of Jaqueline Hahn, Lawrenceville School Archivist (lagging, backwardness, Tom); BHOT, 250 (shift, will be, you boys).

53. BHOT, 252 (unexpectedly, courting, extent); 256 (red hot iron, magnificent necklace).

54. "Recital by Miss Hogg," *Galveston Daily News*, September 29, 1904, p. 4 (distinguished, impromptu). Baylor Hogg was the son of Thomas Elisha Hogg.

55. Simon McPherson to Will Hogg, courtesy of Hahn (backbone); *Houston Post*, January 13, 1905, p. 4 (attending); BHOT, 265 (very bad cold, Father), 267 (nag, receptions).

56. W. G. Jameson, chief surgeon International and Great Northern Railroad, to Dr. J. R. Moore, Galveston, December 4, 1905, W G. Jameson Letter File 197, WRC; BHOT, 267–268 (had to cut), 268 (bundled, invalid, Ima, Tom), 269 (my running mate).

57. BHOT, 272 (dandy, everybody).

58. BHOT, 276 (improve), 277 (each day). The Battle Creek Sanitarium, founded in 1866 as the Western Health Reform Institute health resort for invalid Civil War veterans; renamed and managed by Dr. John Harvey Kellogg (February 26, 1852–December 14, 1943) from 1876 until his death. The sprawling health and wellness complex included a resort, hospital, research facility, and nursing school. In 1906 it served 7,006 patients

59. Marcus Weems to Ima Hogg, March 12, 1906, MS 17, MFAH (vigor of mental strength); *McKinney Daily Courier*, March 5, 1906, p. 4 (Great Commoner, peacefully, death details); *Houston Chronicle*, March 3, 1906 (stricken), *Houston Post*, March 4, 1906 (Ima); *Cameron Herald*, March 8, 1906, p. 4, reprinted from *Houston Post* (train and casket). Dr. Weems had spoken to Governor Hogg the Sunday before his death.

60. *Houston Post*, March 6, 1906, p. 13 (funeral under headline: "Laid to Rest without Display or Ostentation"); *Austin American-Statesman*, March 4, 1890, p. 1 ("Rugged and Strong Natured Man" headline); Kirkland, *Hogg Family*, 23–24 (trees) from Sproul, pamphlet, "James Stephen Hogg." The admonition about trees is printed in several places with slight variations, but the sentiment remains unchanged. Last testament covered in Will of James Stephen Hogg, IHPBC, 3B111, signed October 16; *Bryan Eagle*, March 13, 1906, p. 1, says will signed October 18. Newspaper accounts incorrectly stated that Ima had been left $50,000 and that the estate was worth $100,000 or $150,000. The estate was finally settled five years later, following problems with Tom.

61. James S. Hogg to John Hogg, March 24, 1897, HPWRC, 15 (sunlight); *San Antonio Gazette*, March 3, 1906, p. 1 (guardian angel); James S. Hogg to Ima Hogg, IHPBC, June 12, 1904, 2J215: 5 (Dear Darling Daughter, splendid character), May 6, 1902, 3B111 (influence); February 7, 1903, 3B130 (proudly take), April 1, 1902, 2J215:2 (best friend).

62. Sarah (Sadie) Campbell Blaffer (August 27, 1885, Waxahachie, TX–May 13, 1975, Houston) and Robert E. Lee Blaffer (1876, New Orleans–1942, Toronto, buried Glenwood, Houston) married April 22, 1909, St. Mary's Episcopal Church, Lampasas; discovered pleasure of visual arts on wedding trip to Paris; Blaffer chartered Humble Oil Co. in 1911 with William Stamps Faris II and other investors; Sadie daughter of Texas Company (later Texaco) founder William Thomas Campbell; educated at Catholic convent in Lampasas and Boston Conservatory; over many decades acquired art collection ranging from fourteenth-century Old Masters to impressionist and expressionist works of late nineteenth and early twentieth centuries; donated works to Museum of Fine Arts, Houston; 1964 established Sarah Campbell Blaffer Foundation to bring visual arts to people throughout Texas through traveling collection of outstanding works, loaned free of charge to communities that lack extensive art collections; 1973 art museum at University of Houston named Blaffer Gallery in her honor.

63. William C. Hogg to Mike and Tom Hogg, April 6, 1906, IHPBC, 3B118 (all quotes).

64. Letters from male admirers in IHPBC, 4Zg73, 4Zg77, 4Zg78; BHOT, 255 (pedestal, incorrigible), 271 (sweetheart). David B. Warren delves convincingly into the tantalizing problems surrounding Ima Hogg's suitors (Warren, *Ima Hogg*, 44, 46–53). Virginia Bernhard speculates that Walter Renn may be the "Sweetheart" correspondent (email to author, July 19, 2021) since Renn was a young businessman staying at the Rice Hotel during this time period. Walter Betz Renn (February 4, 1879, Illinois–April 4, 1929, Houston), 1903 Harvard graduate; 1904 moved to Rice Hotel, Houston; career in real estate; married Alice Latreyte (1885–1967) April 1909, father of four children; 1920 founding president Harvard Club of Houston.

65. BHOT, 152 (change, heart, hermit, intellectuals, blossomed), 25 (perfect), 24 (blunderbuss); William C. Hogg to Ima Hogg, March 26, 1906, IHPBC, 3B118: 2 (Tom spending); William C. Hogg to Col. James A. Stinson, July 6, 1906, WCHBC, 2J327: 1 (still quite nervous).

66. *Houston Post*, Sun. September 9, 1906, p. 26 (horse races, autos); William C. Hogg to Ima Hogg, WCHBC, 2J327 (confidently expect); William C. Hogg to Mike Hogg, December 10, 1906, MFAH, 15: 2 (long distance).

67. Helen Kerr Thompson (c. 1875–August 20, 1965, Houston), lifelong friend of Ima Hogg; father John Kerr farmer and well-known East Texas horticulturist; when two sons grown wanted occupation, husband gave her twelve thousand acres of forest land in Trinity County; established model agricultural community in 1920s and 1930s; developed purebred Hereford, grew corn, cotton, sugar cane with system of crop rotation and diversification; built modern farm houses for workers; established cooperative marketing; federal government took over land in 1934 and created rehabilitation and relief project for farmers; property became Woodlake; Thompson established community house and park, served as postmaster; traces of experiment disappeared after World War II; last two decades in Houston.

68. MFAH, Weems correspondence, MS 17, Ima Hogg to Weems May 7, 23, June 14, 18, 1907, June 25, 1908. Weems married and raised a family, but he kept his letters from Ima Hogg; decades after his death in 1946, a descendant placed the letters in the Museum of Fine Arts, Houston, archives.

69. All trip information from IHPBC, 3B153: 1 (1907–1908 diaries), 2 (postcards Great Britain), 3, 4 (postcards Continent); *San Antonio Gazette*, August 10, 1907, p. 5. The July 1 entry explicitly mentions Thompson, Foster, and Scott as the three male members of the group.

70. Diary, IHPBC, 3B153:1 (all quotes).

71. Diary, IHPBC, 3B153 (trip until Germany). On September 5 Lewis Thompson received cables calling him back to Houston. Mrs. Thompson accompanied him to Paris and returned to the touring party when it reached Venice. The Thompson children remained with their governess in Wiesbaden and then in Paris.

72. Mary J. Cooper, probably Mary Juliette Boone Gross Cooper (February 1, 1853, Chicago–December 29, 1927, Chicago), lived in Houston at 1102 Elgin Street with son Boone (1875–1910) after second husband, Henry Miller Cooper (1841–1903) died; 1890 traveled in Germany after death of first husband, Jabez Henry Cushman Gross, (1842–1886); August 1907 staying in Munich; 1916 returned to Chicago; corresponding secretary Chicago Historical Society until death.

73. Diary, IHPBC, 3B153 (quotes, trip in Germany); fan in Kitty King Powell Library collection, image in *Inside/Out* (MFAH, Spring/Summer 2022), 9.

74. IHPBC, 3B153 (all quotes).

75. William C. Hogg to Ima Hogg, October 12, October 19, IHPBC, 3B118: 3 (stay awhile, study); IHPBC, 3B153, diary January 1 (direct, final moment). In 2022 Virginia Bernhard published the transcribed diary (hereafter referred to as CD) in *Grand Tours and the Great War: Ima Hoggs' Diaries, 1907–1918*, edited with commentary by Virginia Bernhard and Roswitha Wagner.

76. CD, 36 (lonesome), 38 (room), 42 (Jan. 4, came, hoped). Mrs. White's apartment was one of eight in a building owned by architect Roland Goetze, who lived there with his family. Other occupants were artists and composers.

77. CD, 43 (nice), 49 (outrageous, not deep), 44 (I can't), 45 (wicked), 47 (I am absolutely, old sweethearts), 53 (to Xaver).

78. CD, 59 (encouraged), 60 (real work), 61 (fine German teacher), 63 (astonished); *Houston Post*, July 12, 1908, p. 26 (through fresh).

79. Lewis Avery Jones to author, letter, February 10, 2001 (fell in love, serious relationship). The gay evenings with young musicians at the Fishers' home were conducive to romance, but Lewis Jones, son of Ima Hogg's close friend and confidante Nettie (Mrs. Albert) Jones, says the subject of an unhappy romance was "off limits for discussion," and no friend has revealed a secret romance since Ima's death. Lewis Avery Jones to author, email February 28, 2001, and subsequent conversations. See also, Warren, *Ima Hogg*, 57–60 (Weems account).

80. William C. Hogg to Mike Hogg, February 25, 1909 (contemplating), William C. Hogg to Thomas E. Hogg, March 1, 1909 (all we have), IHPBC, 3B118: 3.

81. Julian Paul Blitz (May 21, 1885, Ghent, Belgium–July 17, 1951, Dallas), cellist, conductor, teacher; son of violist and pianist; first professional conductor of Houston (1913–1916) and San Antonio (1917–1922) symphony orchestras; 1920 codirector San Antonio College of Music; traveled and performed with wife, Flora Emma Briggs (1894–1994) of San Antonio (married 1921); 1922 pair first instrumentalists to perform live on radio in Texas; 1930–1934 director music at Kidd-Key College, Sherman; 1934–1950 chair music department Texas Technological College, Lubbock.

82. Michael Hogg to William C. Hogg, July 19, 1910 (good sailor), August 6, 1910 (cut out foolishness, four or five), IHPBC, 3B124: 2; 1910 diary, IHPBC 4Zg86 (Memling, not to be missed, profuse, gay).

83. Michael Hogg to Ima Hogg, July 23, 1912, IHPBC, 3B124: 2 (very fine, great wedding, lucky dog, sensible).

84. IHPBC, 3B179: 3 (fortress, inspiring). Founding members Alice McFarland, Ruth Curtin, Mary Elizabeth Rouse, and Laura Franklin (recording secretary during Ima's presidency) traveled with Ima in Europe.

85. Edna Dee Woolford Saunders (August 31, 1880, Houston–December 21, 1963, Houston; buried Glenwood Cemetery), daughter of Mayor John Dunnock Woolford (1900–1902), studied piano and voice at Gardner School, New York; "for half century reigned as an Empress of the Arts"; 1913–1917, president Woman's Choral Club; 1910–1918 found touring artists for Choral Club and City Auditorium; 1918 began forty-five-year career as "Edna W. Saunders Presents," bringing finest music to Houston, including tenor Enrico Caruso, Ballet Russe de Monte Carlo, ballerinas Moira Shearer and Morgot Fonteyn, Metropolitan Opera Company, Marian Anderson; 1927 Torchbearer Award; offices in Beaumont and Galveston; life member First Presbyterian Church; Green Room at Jones Hall dedicated to her memory. For Anderson's first concert, Saunders got permission to divide City Auditorium's main floor equally between "Blacks" and "Whites" and sat with the Houston mayor and African American civic leaders on the "Black" side.

86. Wille Hutcheson, *Houston Post*, June 22, 1913 (all quotes).

87. Wille Hutcheson, *Houston Post*, December 13, 1913, p. 8 (people's orchestra); B. R. Forman, *Houston Chronicle*, December 20, 1913, p. 5 (galaxy). H. F. MacGregor became treasurer, Mrs. E. F. Lillard recording secretary, and Mary (Mrs. William) Abbey corresponding secretary.

88. Advertisement, Levy Brothers Dry Goods Co., December 18, 1913, IHPCUH, Scrapbook 3 clipping (for the good); William C. Hogg to Bassett Blakely, November 18, 1913, IHPBC, 3B118 (dare not refuse); clipping December 15, 1915, IHPCUH, Scrapbook 3 (capacity).

89. 1914 Diary, IHPBC, 4Zg86, edited and published by Virginia Bernhard, VBSHQ, 280 (fear).

90. Ruth Curtin (March 20, 1895, Houston–May 22, 1976, Houston) sailed with two older friends, Ima Hogg and Mary Elizabeth Rouse, with plans to study in Germany; returned from Liverpool October 24, 1914; married Philip Heckman Arbuckle (1882–1932) June 24, 1923; mother of three children. Mary Elizabeth Rouse (November 6, 1872, Brenham, TX–June 12, 1961, Houston) piano teacher and performer in Houston by 1907; managed her own music studio and wrote music criticism for the *Gargoyle* and other publications; never married but known as an art patron at her death. Both women were founding members of the Girls' Musical Club. Information based on birth and death certificates, city directories, and ship manifests, courtesy of Anne C. Leader, Ph.D.

91. VBSHQ, 275 (channel quotes), 279 (news . . . sunset).

92. VBSHQ, 285 (liberal, beauty, sympathies); Ima Hogg to William C. Hogg, August 4, IHPBC, 3B124:2 (heading, brilliant); William C. Hogg to Ima Hogg, August 17, 1914, IHPMFAH, 15: 3 (You depict); William C. Hogg to William Jennings Bryan, WCHBC, 2J295: 6 (passage home).

93. VBSHQ, 275 (rejoiced, Germans), 276 (big crowd, rattled), 278 (flocks of Germans), 277 (boat left); Ima Hogg to William C. Hogg, July 28, August 4, 1914, IHPMFAH, 15: 3 (terrible, tragedy, deepest distress).

94. VBSHQ, 279 (forty dollars), 282 (melting, lovely, sat), 283 (calmer), 287 (Teagle visit).

95. VBSHQ, 285 (papers, most refined, case against), 286 (silver goblet), 287 (really a dream), 288 (almost no women, nothing impressed); Ima Hogg to William C. Hogg, September 3, 1914, IHPMFAH, 15: 3 (cites for all Guild Hall speakers).

96. VBSHQ, 289 (idea of mixing, frightened), 290 (mob, so violent), 292 (whole world ferment), 293 (network, same self-respect,) 294 (charm and excitement).

97. Ima Hogg to William C. Hogg, September 23, IHPMFAH 15:3 (glad to be home).

98. *Houston Post*, December 20, 1914, p. 38 (dinner).

99. Bessie Alva Griffiths (1896–c. 1971) studied with Ima Hogg (1909–1918) and in Europe periodically (1912–1916), gave recitals, and taught piano from a studio in her Houston home. Eloise Helbig Chalmers (1900–1966) became a popular music teacher and a close friend of Ima Hogg, who recommended that she study with Adele Margulies in New York. Helbig married briefly but returned to Houston and retained her married name. Records show that Ima subsidized Helbig and Margulies for many years (IHPCUH). These former pupils and Mary Fuller are among the women who played the piano with Ima in her upstairs sitting room. Jacques Abram performed with the Houston Symphony on November 13, 1939, February 7, 1944, December 9, 1946, January 21, 1949, November 17, 1953, October 30–31, 1961 (Terry Brown, email).

100. Marcellus Elliot Foster (MEFO, 1870–1942), attended University of Texas (1891–1892); wrote first newspaper article at age fifteen; *Houston Post* 1895, managing editor 1899; 1901 founded *Houston Chronicle* with money from Spindletop investment; 1908 sold half interest in *Chronicle* to Jesse Jones to finance a *Chronicle*

building; fought Klan in 1920s; 1926 sold out to Jones; editor *Houston Press*, where attacked Texas prison system; retired 1937; wrote column until fatal heart attack.

101. Wille Hutcheson, *Musical America*, April 20, 1918, 52 (most flattering, investigating).

102. City Directory, 1920–1921, R. S. Sterling Investments advertisement (Houston's). Conflicting accounts about the lot Q option make It hard to know what happened. Will asked for an extension on the option. Cullinan said he felt such a move would be unfair to other interested investors, but any animosity (or explosion of Will's temper) must have been forgotten, since the men cooperated on other matters, and Will established a scholarship in honor of his former business partner in a last testament written a decade later.

103. Panorama photograph of derricks at Varner, Varner Collection (on view in the Legacy Room, Kilroy Visitors' Center, Bayou Bend Collection and Gardens, Houston); WCHBC, 2J399 (1918 diary), 2J335: 2 (Hogg, Dickson & Hogg liquidation proceedings, March 31, 1918–February 18, 1919). The West Columbia field yielded 186,350 barrels in 1918 and 5,611,000 in 1919. By 1921 production topped 12 million barrels, and as late as 1947 the wells still produced more than 2 million barrels per year (Cotner, *James Stephen Hogg*, 583).

104. William C. Hogg to Ima Hogg, May 3, 1918, IHPBC, 3B119: 1 (now); Mike Hogg war letters in MFAH, printed in Bernhard, "A Texan in the Trenches," 166 (lamb's wool), 168 (impossible to write).

105. Edward Prather to William C. Hogg, July 29, 1918 (suffering, much run down), IHPBC, 3B119: 1; Michael Hogg to Ima Hogg, September 23, 1918, MFAH: World War Letters 1914–1918, printed in Bernhard, *The Smell of War*, 79 (alive, flowers), 82 (wonderful chateau), 137 (beautiful little town, lounging, rich); Ima Hogg to William C. Hogg, November 2, 1918, IHPBC, 3B119: 1 (see some).

106. Frances Xavier Dercum (August 10, 1856, Philadelphia–April 24, 1931, Philadelphia), 1877 MD University of Pennsylvania; clinician, scientist, teacher; expert in neurological and mental disorders; 1883–1892 chief of Nervous Disease Clinic; 1887 staff Philadelphia General Hospital; 1892 chair of mental diseases at Jefferson Medical College; consultant many mental hospitals; 1884 founder Philadelphia Neurological Society; 1886 president American Neurological Association; fellow American College of Physicians; numerous honors in US and Europe; October 1919 diagnosed President Woodrow Wilson (advised him to stay in office to give him reason to recover); 1931 while president American Philosophical Society, died in Benjamin Franklin's chair; many journal articles and books; identified and researched Dercum's Disease (*Adiposis dolorosa*), complex affliction with painful fatty deposits on legs, arms, and trunks; sister Clara Dercum MD in gynecology, also practiced in Philadelphia

107. Francis Dercum to William C. Hogg, June 26, 1919, IHPBC, 3B119: 2 (splendid), 3B119:3 (pretty house); Ima Hogg to William C. Hogg, October 31, 1920, 3B119: 3 (sailed forth . . . matinee). Ima was in Atlantic City from July 6–8, 1920, and at the

Lake Placid Club, Tularosa Cottage, July 14–October 6, 1920. Ima heard Leopold Stokowski conduct the Philadelphia Orchestra in November and attended recitals at the Philadelphia Academy of Music twice in November. After Christmas, she attended performances in Carnegie Hall on December 28 and January 12 and heard Sergei Rachmaninoff solo with the New York Symphony on January 20 (IHPCUH).

108. Ima Hogg to William C. Hogg, September 22, 1920, IHPBC, 3B120 (all quotes). Will purchased the 290 Park Avenue apartment on August 23, 1921, for occupancy on October 4 after redecorating was completed. The Houston office building later accommodated the Pappas interests and the Great Southern Life Insurance Co.

109. Madeleine McDermott, *Houston Chronicle*, July 23, 1972, sec. 6, p. 8 (showplace).

110. Ima Hogg to William C. Hogg, January 21, 1921 (been thinking, buy, firm), William C. Hogg to Ima Hogg, January 22, 1921 (just as you want), January 29, 1921, (unavoidably detained), February 28, 1921 (mass, first experience), IHPBC, 3B119: 3. January correspondence shows Ima is not in New York, and Will is looking for a "Duncan Fyffe" table for her.

111. Ima Hogg to William C. Hogg, June 1, 1921 (disgusting).

112. Correspondence between Edgar Odell Lovett and Ima Hogg, 1922, 1923 regarding Music Lectureship, Edgar Odell Lovett Presidential Papers, WRC, 24: 1 (stimulate, elevate); programs in IHPCUH. Ima's ability to attract Nadia Boulanger to Houston suggests her prestige in the musical world. Boulanger was touring in the United States in January and February under Walter Damrosch's auspices.

113. Nadia Boulanger (September 16, 1887, Paris–October 22, 1979, Paris), Conservatoire National Supérieure de Musique et de Danse; conductor, composer, pianist, organist, great teacher who taught many leading composers and musicians of the twentieth century; member of musical family; first woman to conduct major orchestras, including Boston Symphony and Philadelphia Orchestra; taught in United States and United Kingdom; 1921 joined French Music School for Americans at Fontainebleau, professor of harmony, 1946 named director; 1930s, 1940–1945 tours in US; chapel-master to Prince of Monaco and organized music for wedding to actress Grace Kelly.

114. Austen Fox Riggs (December 12, 1876, Kassel, Germany to American parents–March 4, 1940, Stockbridge, MA), 1898 Harvard BA, 1902 Columbia College of Physicians and Surgeons MD, 1904 Johns Hopkins School of Medicine postdoc; 1907 New York internist recuperating from tuberculosis at home in Stockbridge, influenced by mental hygiene movement; c. 1907 founded Stockbridge Institute for the Study and Treatment of Psychoneuroses, July 1917 renamed Austen Riggs Center, 1919 Austen Riggs Foundation (Stockbridge), 1920 Riggs Clinic (Pittsfield); author *Intelligent Living, Play: Recreation in a Balanced Life*; treatment based on talk therapy combined with structured routine of daily activities balancing work, play, rest, and exercise with the goal of coming to terms with emotional suffering and facilitate personal capacity to work, play, love; during Ima Hogg's lifetime, center attracted preeminent

staff and made significant contributions to study of illness and treatment within context of family; married Alice McBurney, who died in 1970, and had three daughters.

115. Ima Hogg to Robert Sutherland, November 21, 1961, May 10, 13, 1967, interviews HFR, MAI9/U1:12 (must have purpose); *Galveston Daily News*, October 26, 1924, p. 9 (period of study). A letter from Mrs. Percy V. Pennybacker to Estelle Sharp (Sharp Papers, August 16, 1923) indicates Pennybacker was friendly with Ima Hogg and attributed "a great share" of Ima's ability to "emancipate herself" from depression to Estelle Sharp. Ruby Blake Williamson remarried after the death of her husband, and as Mrs. H. W. Hargrave, she established the Shabby Shop antique gallery. Ima Hogg made many purchases for her collection there. I am indebted to Collection Manager Remi Dyll for checking the Bayou Bend object files to discover Mrs. Williamson/Hargrave's full name—Ruby Blake Williamson Hargrave.

116. The inventory of Ima Hogg's extensive library does not appear to include Andrew Carnegie's 1889 essay on "Wealth," *North American Review*, vol. 158, no. 391 (June 1889), 653 (problem).

117. Lomax, *Will Hogg, Texan*, 31, (the government); Ima Hogg, penciled memo, Ima Hogg to Robert Sutherland, 1940, HFR, MAI9/U1: 1 (wholesome life). In later years, when asked her profession, she described herself as a philanthropist and on the Down Town Club roster (1928) as a "composer of music" (E. Richardson Cherry Papers, 1:17, HMRC). Will signed letters Bill and Bilog; Mike and Alice use Mikandi, Mikalis, and Mickie; Ima tried Imogene, and her college friends continued with Imie and E(I)rmie.

118. "William Clifford Hogg," *Alcalde* 19 (October 1930), 9 (vivid, deliberately).

119. Oscar Odd (O. O.) McIntyre (February 18, 1884, MO–February 14, 1938, Manhattan), sent word of New York City to 508 newspapers across America; dapper, folksy, thrived on celebrities; syndicated "New York Day by Day" (about eight hundred words every day); most highly paid newspaperman in 1920s and 1930s; good friend to Will and Mike Hogg. Irvin Shrewsbury Cobb (June 23, 1876, Paducah, KY–March 11, 1944, Manhattan) journalist, humorist with *New York World*; most highly paid staffer in US; close friend of Will and Mike Hogg; correspondence with Hoggs housed in MFAH.

120. Emma Ferdinand (Ferdie) Trichelle (1884–1954), journalist in Louisiana; 1903 to Houston; lived with relatives in Houston Heights; editor and proprietor of *The Railroad Echo* (for railroad employees); founder 1916–1917 of *The Neutral*, monthly periodical dedicated to "attack [on] evil wherever . . . our help is needed"; founded and managed Emma R. Newsboy's Home (1910–1919) for homeless orphan boys, secured support from Will Hogg and civic leaders; named juvenile probation officer by Houston Police Department; founded Tri-Fin Operators, for oil exploration with partner Alice Finfrock; founded grocery business.

121. Joseph Cullinan Papers, University of Houston, Special Collections 2006–2009, 59: 18: 2 (harbor and guide); Lomax, *Will Hogg, Texan*, 41–42 (little rascals).

122. Originally called the Organization for the Enlargement and Extension by the State of the University Plan of Higher Education in Texas; immediately shortened to Hogg Organization or Ex-Students' Association. The Hogg Organization (Texas Exes) subscription book and plan, WCHBC, 311: 1. Original $250 signers included Houstonians Edwin B. Parker, Captain James A. Baker, W. B. Sharp, Jesse Jones, and M. E. Foster, then publisher of the *Houston Chronicle*, as well as George W. Brackenridge of San Antonio, and E. W. Littlefield of Austin.

123. Lomax Papers, 3D205: 9, BC (splendid spirit); Ferguson, "Hogg Family Financial History," 98 (brilliant manager, level-headed, acted).

124. Hogg Brothers created several subsidiary companies. Varner Realty bought 2,894 Stude Association shares in 1921, 1922, and 1925, and the final 166 shares in 1927. Varner Company acquired Varner Realty Company in an income tax-free merger of all realty and other assets and assumed liabilities of Varner Realty in exchange for seven thousand shares of Varner Co. stock. Information on the companies in Ferguson, "Hogg Family Financial History," 33–49. These sturdy Norhill houses are valued real estate choices in the twenty-first century.

125. William C. Hogg to donors, April 11, 1924, WCHBC, 2J337 (coterie); William Ward Watkin Papers, 2:18, WRC (motto). 1913, Houston Public School Art League (founded 1900) received state charter to build municipal art museum; August 1916, Joseph and Lucie Halm Cullinan paid for land on league's behalf; 1920, Art League hired Ralph Adams Cram and William Ward Watkin to develop construction proposal; league approved $200,000 budget; year campaign raised $80,000; plan scaled back; Claytons pledged $25,000, Cullinans promised $20,000, most other gifts $5,000 or less.

126. Catherine Mary Taylor Emmott (March 6, 1862, London–May 16, 1949, Austin), married John Horatio Emmott (April 15, 1859, London–December 7, 1914, Houston), five children; strong proponent of equal suffrage; chaired committee to rally public opinion behind formation of Memorial Park in 1920s; Catherine and her husband buried in Glenwood Cemetery, Houston.

127. Emmott, *Memorial Park*, 23–27 (in memory); Ferguson, "Hogg Family Financial History," 59 (for park). Environmentalist Terry Hershey claimed that Ima convinced her brothers not to develop the Camp Logan property but to preserve it as a park (comment to author, May 28, 2004). Although the Hoggs and others immediately referred to the city's Memorial Park, the city actually had to make annual payments from 1924 through 1934 to complete the purchase from Varner Realty; each of the deeds specified that the land being transferred was to be used for park purposes only; if not so used, the land would revert to Hogg family heirs. The deeds are in the MFAH Archives (Sally J. Tyler to author, email April 9, 2007). Park improvements began in the mid-1930s using PWA funding.

128. Allen V. Peden, "Presentations," *Gargoyle*, April 10, 1928, 11 (why not/buy out). David Warren, *Ima Hogg*, 103, attributes the buy-out/make it big quote to Ima

Hogg's memory of a conversation with Will in which she makes the buy-out statement, but the widely disseminated attribution to Will appears in Lomax and several other sources, albeit with slight variations in wording. That said, Ima and Will were certainly in agreement. The original Country Club Estates investors were lawyer and politician Tom Ball, cotton broker Kenneth Womack, and oilman William Farish.

129. Pamphlet, "Living in River Oaks," *River Oaks Magazine* (anniversary edition), Houston Subdivision Division Collection, HMRC, MS 118:2. Gift of Julia Ideson (simply, way of living).

130. Edward Muegge "Buck" Schiwetz (August 24, 1898, Cuero, TX–February 2, 1984, Cuero), began sketching surroundings as teenager; trained architect; 1928 to Houston as art director and partner in advertising firm Franke, Wilkinson, and Schiwetz; clients included River Oaks Corporation, Humble Oil and Refining Company, and several other oil businesses; awards for sketches, watercolors, oils of picturesque buildings, oilfields, Texas landscapes; *Buck Schiwetz' Texas* (1960) brought wide interest to work and buildings recorded in collection; 1966 retired from advertising; continued to sketch, paint; 1977–1978 named "state artist of Texas"; rose at 5:00 a.m. to paint multimedia works for eight to ten hours every day until his death.

131. Pamphlet, "Living in River Oaks" (quotes). The city of Houston annexed River Oaks and surrounding properties (about 3,465 acres) in 1927.

132. Sproul, "James Stephen Hogg," 9 (ark of safety); Neff, "Will Hogg: Building Heritage in Texas," in *Frederic Remington*, 19 (fix up the old place, simpler). In a letter to Maj. Bert Briscoe, Will reveals his friend's nickname, William C. Hogg to Birdsall Briscoe, January 18, 1919, WCHBC, 2J335; 2.

133. Description based on fifty years working in the house as a Bayou Bend docent. John Staub insisted that Ima Hogg invented the term "Latin Colonial" (Barnstone, *Architecture of John F. Staub*, 28). David B. Warren attributes the term to John Staub, but Stephen Fox, in his definitive study of John Staub's work, points out that there is no documentation to identify either "as the author of this evocative term," although Fox leans toward the Ima Hogg attribution.

134. Ima Hogg to William C. Hogg, February 8, 1926, William C. Hogg to Ima Hogg, June 16, 1927, IHPBC, 3B119: 5 (Mr. Briscoe . . . delighted).

135. Ima Hogg to William C. Hogg, February 8, 1926, (maximum, minimum, stunning character); William C. Hogg to Ima Hogg, June 16, 1927, IHPBC, 3B119:5 (loveliness).

136. Charles Over Cornelius (1890–1937) joined the Metropolitan staff in 1917 and was associate curator of the American Wing at his death.

137. William Andrew Mackay (1876, Philadelphia–1939, New York City), best known for three murals to memorialize achievements of President Theodore Roosevelt for the Roosevelt Memorial Rotunda of the American Museum of Natural History, New York (1936); also completed mural projects for Minnesota House of Representatives and Library of Congress; less well-known but major role developing ship camouflage during World War I; 1919 patent for important camouflage proposal.

138. William Andrew Mackay to Ima Hogg, April 16, 1928, IHPMFAH, 1: 1 (handsome, reverse).

139. *Houston Chronicle*, February 18, 1927 (retiring disposition, endorsements), February 20 (landslide), clippings, WCHBC, 2J416. Mike Hogg served two terms in the Texas Legislature (1927–1931).

140. *A Garden Book for Houston*, 1950 ed., Foreword (simple, practical); "A Forum of Civics for Houston," pamphlet, May 15, 1926, River Oaks Garden Club Records, MFAH (organization designed); *Civics for Houston*, January 1928 (practical ideas).

141. *Report of the City Planning Commission of Houston* (Houston: Forum of Civics, 1929), accessed at HPL. Although "zoning sought to replace real estate volatility" with planned use, zoning measures were proposed, and failed, four times during Ima's lifetime—in 1929, 1938, 1948, and 1962.

142. Kirkland, *Hogg Family*, 166–167 (special benefits); program, benefit concert, IHPCUH, Scrapbook 5.

143. Josephine Boudreaux (May 28, 1898, Grand Coteau, St. Landry Parish, LA–August 11, 1993, Houston), to Houston at age seven; 1913–1918 played second violin Houston Symphony Orchestra; 1918–1921 played at movie house Isis; June 1921 to American Conservatory at Fontainebleau (founded 1921 by New York Symphony Orchestra conductor Walter Damrosch and French composer/conductor Francis Casadesus), in the first class that included Aaron Copland; 1921–1923 great success (Paris); two years study Budapest; two years study Czechoslovakia; 1926 Paris debut (called "remarkable talent"); 1927 Houston in August, debut March 1, 1928; 1929–1931 Houston Symphony Association sponsored recitals of quartet and KTRH aired radio concerts; 1931–1937 concertmaster with Houston Symphony Orchestra; last performance January 1937 under Ernst Hoffman; career ended by injury, accident or carpal tunnel syndrome; 1937–1950s private violin studio; taught Houston's legendary Fredell Lack (for fifty years a violin virtuoso and professor).

144. Ima Hogg to Robert Sutherland, March 8, 1962, interview, Bayou Bend, HFR, MAI9/U1: 12 (normal, unadjusted). The Pittsfield clinic opened January 4, 1924, and was operated by William B. Terhune. Books by Terhune and Riggs are listed on undated Bayou Bend book inventories (MFAH). George Stevenson later became medical director of the National Association for Mental Health.

145. Commonwealth Fund, private foundation founded by Anna Maria Richardson Harkness October 18, 1918, to "do something for the welfare of mankind"; today, endowment at $700 million, mission "to promote a high-performing healthcare system that achieves better access, improved quality, and greater efficiency." Harkness (October 25, 137, Dalton, Ohio–March 27, 1926, New York City), widow of Stephen V. Harkness, two sons; supported medical, social welfare, religious, educational, and cultural causes in Cleveland, New York City, elsewhere; 1866 to Cleveland, many endowments to Western Reserve University; 1888 husband died, leaving her estate of $50 million mostly in Standard Oil Co. stock; 1891 moved to New York City, gave $3.5 million to Yale University, donated heavily to Presbyterian Church; 1918 original

fund endowment $10 million, continued to make gifts to fund, donated part of estate to fund at death; son Edward first president of fund, donated twenty acres for medical center at Columbia University (1924).

146. Minutes of the organizing meeting, October 23, 1929, Minute Book, 1929, DCC (make the public); IHPBC, 4W235: 6 (clinic purpose memorandum November 11, 1930, protects and conserves). Meeting attendees were 12, lists members of the steering committee: C. W. Areson of Faith Home, Walter Whitson of the Family Service Bureau, Dr. John Willis Slaughter, Ima Hogg, Nina Cullinan, Dr. Fred Lummis, J.W. Mills (HISD), and others.

147. "The Guidance Center of Houston," pamphlet, Sharp Papers, 5: 33 (protects, diagnosis). A memorandum lists a $2,000 donation from Ima for 1929, but other evidence indicates that she might have pledged more. Bylaws in 1929 cash book 2.3225U514.

148. William C. Hogg to Governor Dan Moody, June 19, 1928, WCHBC, 2J345 (Jesse Jones comment). This letter was widely distributed, and the author has copies from the files of several Houstonians.

149. Frederick Henry Harvey (1835–1901), English-born railroad promoter established chain of restaurants and souvenir shops along the Atchison, Topeka, and Santa Fe Railroad to encourage tourism and travel to the Southwest. George Gustav Heye (1874–1957), engineer and investment banker; amassed largest collection of Native American artifacts in US in his era; housed for many years in his Manhattan apartment, objects moved to pioneering Museum of the American Indian, which Heye owned and directed (1916– 1956); 1989 Smithsonian absorbed collection, some of which repatriated, to form core of national collection of Native American art; 1897 Heye purchased first object; bought lavishly prior to World War I.

150. New Educational Fellowship (1921–1938), established by two Englishwomen, movement that connected lay enthusiasts for educational reform with major figures in developing disciplines of psychology and science of education, including American John Dewey; group held seven international conferences and fostered international understanding through travel and education.

151. Ima Hogg to Julia Ideson, August 23, 1929, JIP, 1: 2 (Russian experience). Following the Russian adventure, Eloise Helbig Chalmers returned to New York on August 29 aboard the *Frederik VIII* (information from ship manifests, courtesy of Anne C. Leader, PhD).

152. H. E. Brigham to Ima Hogg in Paris, August 5, 1929, IHPBC, 3B151: 1 (shock, Mr. Will). Alice Nicholson married Walter B. Fraser in 1923; they divorced in 1927–1928; and she married Mike Hogg on July 20, 1929.

153. Ima purchased the small Henri Matisse oil painting *Lorette* or *Meditation* either in New York or Paris either in May 1928 or 1929. Archival and registrar records are misleading and conflicting, but it is clear contemporary art was a strong interest for Ima in the late 1920s. The MFAH website stated in March 2024 that the painting was purchased in 1928 in New York at King-Parker Inc., which represented Galerie Paul

Guillaume, Paris. Valentine Dudensing and Pierre Matisse showed Joan Miró, Henri Matisse, Pablo Picasso, and cubists; Julien Levy Gallery carried surrealist works; and J. B. Newmann Gallery sold German expressionists

154. Ima added ten watercolors and lithographs to her collection on this trip. Siegfried Wagner (June 6, 1869, Lucerne–August 4, 1930, Bayreuth), son of Richard Wagner and grandson of Franz Liszt, was a conductor, composer, and artistic director of the Bayreuth Festival from 1908 to 1930.

155. O. O. McIntyre, "In pace Requiescat," *Austin American*, September 25, 1930, clipping in William Clifford Hogg, vertical file, BC (devastatingly vivid, few men); tributes in "William Clifford Hogg: He Was a Loyal Son of a Proud University," *Alcalde* 19 (October 1930), 8–11, 22 (all other quotes).

156. MFAH, MS 21 scrapbook 3, 57 ("fascinating"); Lomax Papers, 3D205: 3 (big heart), 3D168: 1, clipping Will C. Hogg to *Austin Statesman*, February 9, 1917 (putrid paws).

157. Gilley returned to New York with the coffin and boarded with the McIntyres until Ima adopted him in January 1931 and brought him to Houston, where he was soon joined by a son Gilley and other dogs that formed a long line of pets Ima treasured until her death in 1975.

158. *Houston Gargoyle*, December 14, 1930, p. 11 (keen, problem).

159. Leopold Meyer (June 21, 1892, Galveston–November 1, 1982, Houston), Tulane University (BA 1912); career with F. S. Levy, Foley Brothers Dry Goods, 1946 Meyer Brothers, Inc. (chairman); phenomenal fundraiser for Texas Children's Hospital, St. Luke's Episcopal Hospital, Muscular Dystrophy Telethon, Houston Pediatric Society, Texas Association for Retarded Children, Community Chest, Baylor University; director Houston Livestock Show and Rodeo, sponsor Pin Oak Charity Horse Show; president Congregation Beth Israel; donated proceeds from 1975 autobiography to charity.

160. Nina Cullinan (1899, Washington, PA– February 22, 1983, Houston), one of five children born to Joseph S. and Lucie Halm Cullinan; patron of arts, parks, mental health services, including founding member Contemporary Arts Museum, Society for Performing Arts, Houston Ballet Foundation; board member Museum of Fine Arts, Municipal Arts Commission, Fine Arts Advisory Council of the University of Texas, Child Guidance Center, Houston Mental Health Society, National Parks Commission; 1950s funded construction of Cullinan Hall, designed by Ludwig Mies van der Rohe for the Museum of Fine Arts; left $4 million bequest to the Houston Parks Board for development of new park spaces. Cullinan frequently made anonymous donations and placed few restrictions on her gifts.

161. Memorandum, November 11, 1930, IHPBC, 4W235: 1 (designed to act).

162. Edison E. Oberholtzer (May 6, 1880, Patricksburg, IN–June 18, 1954, Houston), educated Indiana State Normal School, University of Chicago (MA 1915), Columbia University (PhD 1934); taught in Indiana schools; 1913–1923 superintendent Tulsa schools; 1924–1945 superintendent Houston schools; established forerunners of

University of Houston and Texas Southern University; 1945–1951 president University of Houston; president emeritus until death.

163. Ima Hogg to Dr. George S. Stevenson, November 18, 1930, IHPBC, 4W235 (panic, struggling clinic).

164. Hubert Roussel, *Houston Gargoyle*, January 25, 1931, p. 8 (Nespoli).

165. Hubert Roussel, *Houston Gargoyle*, January 25, 1931, p. 8 (not heretofore), March 15, p. 8 (representative), p. 32 (strictly commercial); *Houston Gargoyle*, December 20, 1931 (wise). Dr. Mullen was the first ear, nose, and throat specialist in Houston and a civic-minded activist who advocated for public health.

166. IHPMFAH, symphony program, scrapbook 1, p. 21 (hastily gathered); Hubert Roussel, "Symphony Week," *Houston Gargoyle*, May 10, 1931, p. 18 (played with a fine fury); Memorandum from Joseph Mullen, October 1, 1931, IHPBC, 3B174: 1 (verdict, Houston).

167. Unsigned letter to Ima Hogg, November 22, 1931, IHPBC, 3B174:1 (meritorious).

168. Drusilla Virginia Huffmaster (October 12, 1917, Houston–April 29, 2011, Georgetown, TX), daughter of organist and choirmaster Hu T. Huffmaster and wife Nonie; father taught her piano; Ima her patron, supporting her as pupil of Adele Margulies and as student at Julliard School of Music (1936–1940); toured in New York and Europe; 1961 artist-in-residence Southwestern University, taught and performed until retired in 1988; married twice, two daughters.

169. *Houston Press*, May 30, 1932, clipping, IHPBC, 3B174: 1 (charming); Hugh Potter, "Our Symphony," excerpt from an address, Febuary 27, 1932, reprinted in Houston Symphony Orchestra program November 7, 1932.

170. Joseph Mullen to Ima Hogg, August 11, 1933 (hepatic, lazy, beat), Florence Hogue to Ima Hogg, August 30, 1933, IHPBC, 3B174:1 (the symphony).

171. H. E. Brigham to Ima Hogg, October 11, 1933, IHPBC, 3B151: 1 (piano); Michael Hogg to Ima Hogg, November 8, 1933 (long, intrigues, ins and outs, the usual), Julia Ideson to Ima Hogg, November 27, 1933 (loneliness), Alice Hogg to Ima Hogg, December 21, 1933 (happy, Mickey), Gertrude Anderson to Ima Hogg, January 12, 1934 (largest), IHPBC, 3B174: 1.

172. Ima Hogg to Joseph Smith, July 23, 27, IHBPC, 3B174: 2 (a man, already); newspaper clippings, scrapbook 7, IHPCUH (significant).

173. Walter Walne to Ima Hogg, November 6, 1930, IHPBC 3B174 (the orchestra).

174. Concertmaster Raphael Fliegel to author, telephone interview, October 4, 2003 (fine, great); Meyer, *The Days of My Years: Autobiographical Reflections*, 161–162 (pop concert, indoctrinate); Walter Walne, Report of City Council, January 31, 1938, Walter Walne to Dr. H. T. Parlin, February 1, 1937, IHPBC, 3B174: 4 (negroes). Raphael Fliegel (August 23, 1918, Chicago–July 25, 2002, Bellaire, TX), began cello at four, switched to violin at six, debut with Houston Symphony at thirteen; 1936 member of orchestra; 1946–1972 concertmaster; 1972–1995 principal second violin; five decades, professor of music Shepherd School of Music, Rice University; emeritus professor violin after 1995 retirement.

175. Mrs. Robert Stuart to her daughter Francita Stuart Koelsch Ulmer, who shared the comment with author. I am indebted to the late Francita Ulmer for access to her Houston Symphony program collection, which has now been placed in the Houston Symphony Society archives.

176. Clippings from *Houston Post* and *Houston Chronicle*, 1937, IHPCUH, scrapbook 7 (canine farewell). Campaign records indicate Ima underwrote secretarial costs of nearly $1,000 in 1938–1939 at $.40 per hour, IHPBC, 3B177: 1. The Music Hall and Coliseum, a project of the Works Progress Administration, seated 2,200 and was completed in November 1937. It was demolished in 1998 to make way for the Hobby Center for the Performing Arts.

177. "Introduction to Bayou Bend Gardens," privately printed for Bayou Bend Endowment, 1975, (love affair).

178. Ima Hogg, at Dogwoods, to Mr. and Mrs. Henry Marsh, December 9, 1935, Margaret Mebus collection, copy of note and envelope in author's possession (great disaster, completely swamped).

179. The Dogwoods property was subdivided in the 1980s and the beautiful Birdsall Briscoe house was demolished in 2005. Vera Baker Chinn and Ruth London were graduates of the venerable Lowthorpe School of Landscape Architecture and Horticulture for Women, established in Groton, Massachusetts, 1901. Ima Hogg made several donations to Houston Studio Gardens in 1931–1932, Sharp Papers, 7:10.

180. Edward Avery McIlhenny (March 29, 1872–August 8,1949), son of Tabasco brand pepper sauce patent-holder Edmund McIlhenny; explored Arctic; established wildlife refuge and bird sanctuary on Avery Island; introduced exotic and specimen plants to Jungle Gardens, 170 acres of semi-tropical gardens along Bayou Petite Anse on Avery Island (salt dome, mined for salt during Civil War and site of oil strike in 1942).

181. Ima Hogg to H. E. Brigham, IHPBC, 3B151: 1 (it is time).

182. *Houston Post*, March 22, 1936, quoted in Warren, *Bayou Bend Gardens*, 40 (wide banks); Ima Hogg to Mr. H. B. Marsh, November 16, 1936, letter in author's possession (completing). McIlhenny hired Studio Gardens horticulturist Mrs. Arthur Boice to manage the Jungle Gardens outlet.

183. Garden Club of Houston Records, MS 14, series 1, 1: 1, MFAH (purpose).

184. *Houston Chronicle*, January 29, 1939, p. 50 (most beautiful).

185. The green marble plinth arrived and was installed, but there is no record to explain why it was unsatisfactory or when it was replaced by a brick pedestal. Ima sent Frilli final payment of $766 in January.

186. Small payments to Ruth London suggest she may have helped with the summer 1937 changes, but payments to her cease in 1938. Studio Gardens closed in 1937, and Ruth London established an independent practice in Houston. Mike's operation may have been for a malignant tumor in his pelvis or for a gall bladder, which was still troubling him in November 1940 (Irvin Cobb to Mike Hogg, November 5, 1940, Mike and Alice Hogg Papers, 4: 5). Between September 1938 and his death in October 1941, Mike underwent procedures for gall bladder, cancer, and hernia,

and the cancer was declared inoperable after a summer 1941 visit to Johns Hopkins Hospital.

187. *Landscape Architecture Magazine* 29:4 (July 1939), 183–191 (magical, miracle); Warren, *Bayou Bend Gardens*, 53 (cries, dramatically).

188. Garden Club of America 1939 Program, Kitty King Powell Library, Bayou Bend Collection and Gardens (exquisite, extensive); *Landscape Architecture Magazine* 29:4 (July 1939), 183–191 (accomplishment); *Houston Chronicle*, February 19, 1939 (Houston garden clubs).

189. Louise Evelina duPont Crowninshield (August 3, 1877, Winterthur–July 11, 1958, Wilmington), historic preservationist, gardener, philanthropist, collector of Americana; 1949 charter member of National Trust for Historic Preservation; 1955 appointed by President Dwight D. Eisenhower to Boston National Historic Sites Commission; 1896 made debut New York; married Boston yachtsman Francis Boardman Crowninshield (1869–1950); no children; homes in Boston, Marblehead, MA, Boca Grande, FL, and at Eleutherian Mills, the original duPont home north of Wilmington, which she restored.

190. Last will and testament of William C. Hogg, signed March 7, 1928, filed October 4, 1930, probated December 6, 1930, WCHBC, 2J329, 2J330: 1, 2J313 (all quotes). The will included a provision to "care for" Lillie Stinson Burkett, Sara Stinson Hogg's half sister; student loan funding included $100,000 for the University of Texas; and $25,000 to every other Texas institution of higher learning, including Prairie View College for Negroes. All servants in Houston or New York who had worked for the Hogg family for one year were to receive $500 for each six-month period of employment. The scholarships included pure or applied mathematics in honor of Arthur Lefevre Sr.; petroleum geology in memory of Walter Benona Sharp; petroleum geology in honor of Joseph S. Cullinan; law in honor of James Lockhart Autry; domestic science or home economics in honor of Estelle Boughton Sharp; domestic science or home economics in honor of his sister, Ima.

191. HFR, MA19/U1, (field of interest); William C. Hogg, will and codicil, WCHBC, 2J330 (common good, proved learning); *Houston Post*, August 19, 1939, list of properties, scrapbook, WCHBC, 2J408 (about $1.25 million). In later life, Ima recalled reading her father's marked copy of Henry Maudsley's *Responsibility in Mental Illness* (1878), Cotner, *James Stephen Hogg*, 347. Hogg Brothers assets were divided $2.05 million to Will's estate, $1.266 million to Tom, $1.235 million to Mike, and $1.228 million to Ima (IHPMFAH, 1:8).

192. William Claire Menninger (October 15, 1899–September 6, 1966), graduate of Cornell University College of Medicine; with father Charles Frederick and brother Karl co-founded Menninger Clinic, Sanitorium, and Foundation in Topeka, KS, which specialized in the treatment and study of behavioral and mental diseases. The Menninger Clinic relocated to Houston in association with Baylor College of Medicine in 2003. "Condensed Notes," of Robert Sullivan interview with Ima Hogg, November 21, 1961, IHPBC, 4W241: 4 (Menninger).

193. D. B. Hardeman, "Whispers from the State Capitol," *Dallas Dispatch-Journal*, July 20, 1939, scrapbook, WHPBC, 2J408 (social significance, first, expected); Leopold Meyer to Ima Hogg, Ima Hogg to Leslie Waggener, chairman Board of Regents, IHPBC, 4W239 (stunned).

194. "In Memoriam," HFR, MAI9/U14: 1 (Sutherland attributes); Ima Hogg to Robert Sutherland, October 17, 1940 (lovely family), HFR, MAI9/U1: 1; *Houston Post*, November 19, 1940, clipping, WCHBC, 2J408: W. C. Hogg Memorial Fund Scrapbook (about two hundred, get complete).

195. Homer Rainey, remarks, February 11, 1941 (home, play), Ima Hogg to Robert Sutherland, February 18, 1941 (joy, graciously), HFR, MAI9/U25: planning folder. Speakers included Frank J. O'Brien, director of guidance clinics for New York City public schools; Daniel A. Prescott, director of the University of Chicago Collaboration Center on Child Development; George S. Stevenson, director of the National Committee for Mental Hygiene; and Dr. Muriel Brown, consultant on Family Life Education in the US Office of Education.

196. Mike and Alice Hogg Papers, 2: 3 (assure, who will), 2: 7 (wholehearted); Ima address, clipping, October 12, IHPMFAH, scrapbook 1, p. 27 (maiden, Dem-Rep, kick).

197. Irvin Cobb, correspondence, Mike and Alice Hogg Papers, 4: 5 (May 1, Alice, distressed), 4: 6 (October 11, 1941, oldest); Robert Sutherland to Mike Hogg, August 11, 1941, HFR, MAI/9U1: 8 (not feeling well); *Alcalde*, November 1941, 29–30 (death notice comments); Thomas E. Hogg to Ima Hogg, November 5, 1941, IHPBC, 3B126: 2; HFR, MAI9/U25 (ill, present, grateful, fortitude).

198. Ferguson, "Financial History," 103–112 (fill, may).

199. H. E. Brigham to Mike Hogg, February 8, 1935, Mike and Alice Hogg Papers, MS 19, MFAH (render, running, taking); Mike Hogg to Ima Hogg, September 16, 1936, IHPBC, 3B124: 3 (in one, Marie was); Margaret Hogg to Ima Hogg, July 22, 1942 (coffee service), IHPBC, 3B126: 2. Margaret Jane Wells (August 25, 1899, Quincy, Illinois–June 18, 1977, Houston), oldest of five children born to James Russell and Henrietta Eaton Wells; married George H. Reynolds in Quincy October 14, 1922; divorced 1930s; 1942 married Thomas Elijah Hogg, Quincy; 1949–1968 Yuma, San Antonio, and Houston; January 20, 1968, married Norbert Herman Markus (1896–1972), Alexandria, Virginia; Markus from Quincy but lived in Haverford, PA (died March 20, 1972); Margaret purchased apartment at 3711 San Felipe; remained there until death June 18, 1977; buried Woodlawn Mausoleum, Houston.

200. James A. Chillman Jr. to Ima Hogg, letter, July 31, 1939, Miss Ima Hogg Collection, Accessions File 39, Registrar's Office, MFAH (enriched, high). Records show eighteen watercolors, thirty-one lithographs, nineteen etchings, nine drawings, one block print, five woodcuts, and one color reproduction.

201. Deed of gift letter, Ima Hogg to John Bullington, August 16, 1943, Accessions Files, 44.4–485, Registrar's Office MFAH (North American Indian Collection). The collection comprised 168 ceramics, ninety-six jewelry items, five photographs,

eighty-one paintings, 123 Kachina dolls, seven musical instruments, and seven miscellaneous items. The registrar's records use the term North American Indian, but Ima's correspondence uses "southwest" to describe the collection

202. Many canvases needed new linings, but the collection was in "excellent condition"; Charles Muskovitch to Ima Hogg, January 19, 1942, IHPBC, 4W234. Will left *Cavalry Scrap* to Mike; Mike bequeathed the large painting (4′ 8″ x 11′ 4″) to the University of Texas, and it is now displayed at the Jack S. Blanton Museum of Art. The Remington Collection was reinstalled in the Audrey Jones Beck Building in March 2000. *Cotopaxi* is identified by accession number 74.58.

203. Ima Hogg to MFAH Board President S. I. Morris, August 16, 1960, IHPMFAH, 1: 9. Dudley's urging is repeated in remarks to the first docent class, July 5, 1961, p. 3, IHPMFAH, 5:15 ("Ray Dudley who first urged me") and in a personal report of Miss Ima Hogg to Charles Montgomery and S. I. Morris, August 16, 1960, IHPMFAH, Scrapbook 2, p. 2.

204. Ima Hogg to Joseph Downs, January 1946, Downs file, IHPMFAH (rusty); Ima Hogg to James H. Chillman Jr., September 10, 1946, Chillman Papers, RG 2:1, series 2, box 1, MFAH (museum collection). David Warren describes a nine-piece parlor set purchased from Carll S. Chase of New York (Warren, Brown, Coleman, and Neff, *American Decorative Arts and Paintings in the Bayou Bend Collection*, F233). In a letter to Ima Hogg, Chase refers to seven pieces that had been purchased "directly" from Belter and had never been shown for sale (Carll S. Chace, New York, to Ima Hogg, September 30, 1944, IHPBC, 4W256). The set was shipped to Bayou Bend in November 1944.

205. Roy Cullen to President-elect Joseph S. Smith, April 16, 1946 (worked), Ima Hogg to Hugh Roy Cullen, January 2, 1944 (leadership), IHPBC, 3B176: 1.

206. *Houston Post*, March 12, 1943, sec. 1, p. 3 (citizens, go on board, lively, brilliant); Daily Papers, 2.1, HMRC (very old, Russian born); *Houston Chronicle*, April 6, 1943, B1 (benefit).

207. *Houston Informer*, April 17, 1943, 1 (most inspiring); *Houston Chronicle*, May 3, 1943 (second emancipation). Colored High School, located at 303 W. Dallas, served all African American students from 1893 to 1926; Jack Yates became the second high school to serve African Americans in 1926; and Phillis Wheatley High School opened in 1927. Information provided by archivists at the African American Library at Gregory School.

208. *Houston Post*, March 30, 1944, sec. 2, p. 17 (baffling), October 16, 1944, sec. 1, p. 6 (city has). The bond issues were $7.5 million in 1944 and $25 million in 1947, which proved inadequate to the needs. In the 1940s, the average expenditure per pupil in the South was about fifty dollars; in the rest of the country, about one hundred dollars; and in Houston $103, for the record-breaking 1945 budget year. Figures Egerton, *Speak Now Against the Day*, 346. Date book, 1945, IHPBC, 3B165, reveals busy schedule; engagements that week included the school-related meetings and visits as well as a meeting with Robert Sutherland, a garden club meeting, lunch and dinner engagements, and an evening at the opera.

209. *Houston Press*, October 15, 1944, p. 5 (known to the police); Ima Hogg, speech to Houston Teachers' Association, typescript, IHPBC, 4W237:1 (aid and supplement).

210. Ima Hogg to Robert Sutherland, September 16, 1949, IHPBC, 4W237.

211. Margaret Patrick to Ima Hogg, April 27, 1949 (unique, solution), Ima Hogg to Margaret Patrick, April 30, 1949, (I don't think), IHPBC, 4W237: 5.

212. Philosophical Society of Texas, 1948 Proceedings, December 10–11, XIII (1949), 4–7 (all quotes).

213. Hugh Roy Cullen to Ima Hogg, May 18, 1946, IHPBC, 3B176: 1 (shocked). Roussel, *Houston Symphony*, 116 (painful, sweet, reasonable)

214. Sir Thomas Beecham (1879–1961), second Baronet; trained in composition; used fortune to improve orchestral and operatic music in Great Britain; founded Own Orchestra for his conducting debut (1905), New Orchestra (1905), London Philharmonic (1932), Royal Philharmonic (1946); produced operas after 1910; 1915 founded Beecham Opera Company; World War II conducted Seattle Symphony, Metropolitan Opera Company; maintained international conducting career until 1960.

215. *Christian Science Monitor*, May 20, 1950, WCHBC, 2J413 (Beecham virtually, one). Of 103 performances in 1950–1951, twenty were subscription, five free Henke and Pillot Saturday evening concerts, ten for students, twenty-six radio broadcasts, forty touring engagements, and two special events. Elaine Shaffer had been second flute in Kansas City and had come with Kurtz to Houston, where she was principal 1948–1953. She married Kurtz in 1955, had a successful solo career, and died of lung cancer in 1973.

216. Pamphlet, 4W194:6, IHPBC (gymnastic, magnificent); Tom Johnson to Andrew Schulhof, June 17, 1954, IHPBC, 3B180 (orient, not only, dependent).

217. Ima Hogg to Tom Johnson, December 4, 1953 (commended), Ima Hogg to Harmon Whittington, December 20, 1954 (endeavored), Houston Symphony Society statement (learned, serious), F. M. Law to Ima Hogg, January 20, 1955 (not for us), IHPBC, 4W194: 6. *Houston Chronicle* critic Ann Holmes said "Ima 'froze,' and soon she and Fricsay could agree on nothing" (Holmes to author May 1, 2003).

218. Houston Symphony Society programs: "Music for Everybody," November 17, 1947; Leopold Stokowski to Mrs. Albert Burrage, December 16, 1958, ROGC 4:3 (silent benefactress).

219. Houston Symphony Society program, March 22, 1948, p. 18 (for every child). Francita Ulmer, a longtime supporter of civic causes, remembers as a teenager writing letters to all her friends, asking them to join the Junior Patrons for a one-dollar annual fee (the late Francita Stuart Ulmer to author, interviews 2007, 2019).

220. Houston Symphony Society programs: Christmas greetings, December 14, 15, 1959, p. 23 (spirit); Statement, Annual Report, May 16, 1956, IHPCUH, 1: Programs 1948–1959 (When I say).

221. Gervais Bell, letter to author, March 20, 2010 (major contribution).

222. Claire Baker, "Mary Jane Beeler Zivley," typescript, 2013. I am indebted to docent Claire Baker, granddaughter of Jane Zivley, for sharing her essay, which is based on taped interviews with Jane Zivley (October 23, 1992) and docent Cyril Hosley (May 13, 2013), whose grandmother Velma Beasley was cook and housekeeper for Ima Hogg from the 1930s until 1971.

223. Warren, *Ima Hogg*, 187 (my settee); Elizabeth Morford to Ima Hogg, (memorable, sheer beauty), Alice Winchester to Ima Hogg, March 14 (wonderful, gratified), IHPBC, 3B154:1. Speakers included Alonzo Lamsford, director of Isaac Delgado Museum of Art, New Orleans and Americo Castro, University of Houston Spanish professor. Guests included dealers Lillian Cogan, J. A. Lloyd Hyde, Emily Manheim, Albert Sack, John Walton, and Rudolph Wunderlich. The executive committee of support included Ima Hogg, Adelaide Lovett Baker, Faith P. Bybee, and Carroll Masterson.

224. *Dallas Morning News*, March 23, 1952, IHPMFAH, scrapbook 1, p. 7 (all quotes). The 20.7-acre Quitman park is now administered as the Gov. Hogg Shrine Historic Site by the City of Quitman. The 178-acre purchase of land in Rusk County is now Jim Hogg State Historic Park. The city of Rusk conveyed the deed to the state and by House Bill No. 110, the state accepted the Hogg family gift and agreed to beautify the land as a park.

225. Letter of appointment, March 6, 1935, IHPBC, 4W264: Governor's Mansion correspondence, 1935–1972 (survey); "Report of Subcommittee on Historic Buildings, Sites, and Landmarks," March 6, 1954, IHPBC, 4W266: Texas State Historical Survey Committee (records, historic). Correspondence suggests Ima did not enjoy her service as a mansion supervisor in the 1940s because of political maneuvering, although she continued to provide family mementos to the collection there in the 1960s.

226. Taylor, "Ima Hogg and the Historic Preservation Movement in Texas, 1950–1975," 15–17 (all quotes). In August 1957, Ima drove from Houston to Lexington, Kentucky, for the National Trust meeting (Ima Hogg to Katharine Prentis Murphy, August 1, 1957, IHPBC, 3B135), and in October she attended a seminar on historic house maintenance organized by the New York State Historical Association in Cooperstown, New York, Ima Hogg to O'Neil Ford, October 7, 1957, IHPBC 3B134.

227. O'Neil Ford (December 3, 1905–July 20, 1982), known for sharp wit, outspoken opinion; Texas's most renowned architect of mid-twentieth century; modernism touched by sympathetic understanding of Indigenous Southwest cultures brought important commissions, including Skidmore College, Trinity College, University of Texas at San Antonio.

228. Resolution, December 23, 1953, IHPBC, 4W202 (special, rare); copy of resolution, dated December 16, 1953, in Board Minutes, folder 25, MFAH (same resolution, although dates differ, and trustees' copy indicates a vote taken December 16, 1953); Ima Hogg, interview, October 2, 1974, Oral History, HMRC (awful, ugly).

229. Ima Hogg to Francis G. Coates, September 4, 1956, in IHPBC, 4W:382 and in MFAH, 1: 5; Press release December 30, 1965, IHPBC, 4W202 (one of three, for the purpose).

230. Theodore E. Swigart, MFAH board president to Ima Hogg, February 2, 1960, Chillman Papers, 1: 17 (unanimously, curator).

231. Minute Women of the USA, founded 1949, reached fifty thousand members in 1950s and early 1960s; attracted anti-Communist housewives to organize letter-writing campaigns, heckle speakers, and swamp opponents with telephone calls; Houston's five hundred-member chapter took over the local board of education in 1952; bedrock supporters of McCarthyism, defended constitutional limits, exposed alleged communist subversives, opposed atheism, socialism, internationalism, and New Deal social welfare provisions. See Carleton, *Red Scare! Right-Wing Hysteria, Fifties Fanaticism, and Their Legacy in Texas.*

232. Letter to the editor, *Houston Post,* October 7, 1954 (printed October 17), IHPBC, 4W237 (intellectually, understanding, sound, spiritual); Speech April 16, 1956, IHPBC, 3B168: 5 (to equip). Original members of the Harris County Heritage Society included prime proselytizer and collector Faith Poorman Bybee and her banker husband Charles, Birdsall Briscoe, Marie Lee Phelps, artist Mary Ellen Shipnes, Maria Taylor Gregory, Mary Vandenberge Hills, Ellen Hamilton Wilkerson, architects Kenneth Franzheim and Harvin C. Moore, collector Alvin S. Romansky, and landscape architect C. C. Fleming, Fox, *Birdsall Briscoe,* 27.

233. Robert Sutherland to Dr. William B. Terhune, October 28, 1958, Silver Hill, Valley Road, New Canaan, IHPBC, 3B166 (nervous).

234. Ima Hogg to John Walton, April 13, 1954 (friendly, maybe), May 17, 1954 (shocked), Bayou Bend accession files B.69.357–358 (F141, 142); Ima Hogg to Henry Flynt, May 17, 1954 (not nearly, make an, almost), Henry Flynt to Ima Hogg, May 19, 1954 (graciousness, has found, quite happy), Ima Hogg to Bernard Levy, May 21, 1954 (really wanted), accessions file B.54.25. The Copleys were framed at the Knoedler's Gallery in May 1959. In fall 1954, Ima purchased seven Copley works: *Portrait of a Boy* (1758–1760) in September, *Mrs. Paul Richard* (1771) in October, study for William Murray, First Earl of Mansfield (1782–1783), studies for *The Siege of Gibraltar* (1791).

235. Rudolf G. Wunderlich to Ima Hogg, accessions file B.60.49 (directly, right); Brown, *America's Treasures at Bayou Bend,* no. 43, p. 76 (would you).

236. Ima Hogg to James V. McMullan, October 22, 1959, Bayou Bend accessions file B.60.47 (one-man project).

237. Ima Hogg, remarks to the River Oaks Garden Club, November 5, 1963, Bayou Bend Docent Organization collection, box A, MFAH (honor); Ima Hogg to Katharine Prentis Murphy, April 7 (anxious), July 3 (everything), October 6 (miracles), December 4 (relief, joy), 1959, IHPBC, 3B149: 3.

238. Ima Hogg to S. I. Morris, August 16, 1960, IHPMFAH, 1: 9 (all quotes). Ima wrote two letters reporting to then board chairmen—S.I . Morris in 1960 and Ed

Rotan on August 12, 1965—both in the MFAH archives, hereafter referred to as Morris Report and Rotan Report.

239. Correspondence among Bernard Levy, Ima Hogg, Jane Zivley, Bayou Bend accession file, B.61.13, November 21, 1960, May 6, 10, 22, April 6, 1961 (all quotes).

240. Correspondence with Ted James, August 4, December 10, 1960, IHPMFAH (offered).

241. In 2010 the storage cupboard and Pennsylvania German artifacts were moved to the Folk Art Room.

242. Ima Hogg, remarks to River Oaks Garden Club, November 5, 1963, Docent Box A, MFAH (comparing, fascinating). Ima gave the grand piano to the Houston Symphony, where it was used until destroyed by serious flooding of Jones Hall in the twenty-first century. When Ima purchased the desk, it was attributed to an unknown New York maker. In the 2010s extensive research at Yale University caused the outstanding example to be reattributed to craftsmen from Newport, Rhode Island. In a September 1961 memorandum, Ima noted that remodeling expenses at that point, when most work was complete, were $132,255.58.

243. Mrs. Wesley West to Ima Hogg, December 7, 1957, ROGC Papers, 2: 1957–58 (opportunity, feeling).

244. Faith Poorman (August 10, 1900, Illinois–October 26, 1996, Houston) and Charles Lewis Bybee (July 7, 1900, Willis–April 7, 1972, Round Top), 1940s began collecting American furniture; preserved Texas history and culture; in 1985–1986 donated 998 examples of American Colonial and early national furnishings to Dallas Museum of Art (acquisition and gift). Charles attended Heights High School, Rice Institute, University of Texas; banker, chairman of Houston Clearing House Association, vice president and treasurer Houston Symphony Society; restored homes and buildings; married Faith Poorman on June 25, 1924. Faith was president of the Texas Historical Foundation; 1954 founder Harris County Heritage Society with Harvin Moore and Marie Phelps to save Kellum-Noble House, moved collection of endangered Harris County houses to Sam Houston Park; restored thirty-five nineteenth-century buildings in Round Top and furnished with Texas-made objects.

245. Members to Ima Hogg (in gratitude), Ima Hogg to Virginia Lawhon (moves, assurance), May 17, 1961, minutes, ROGC Papers: 1960–1961 folder. Original Garden Endowment Board: ROGC appointed Mrs. J. C. Hutcheson III, chairman, Mark Crosswell, Mrs. Ray Dudley, John Mayor; MFAH appointed Curator David Warren, Alice Hogg Hanszen, Advisory Committee Chairman Thomas Anderson.

246. Martha Erwin, "History of the Bayou Bend Docent Organization, *The Bridge*, April/May 1997, 3, 6 (charming ladies).

247. IHPMFAH, 1: 7, 8 (role, America's), 4: 4, 8 (team); "The First Provisional Class" interview with Jonathan Fairbanks, *The Bridge*, October/November 1998, 1, 3, 8 (learn for themselves). In 1962, scholar Helen Comstock included forty-two objects from the Bayou Bend Collection in her influential *American Furniture: Seventeenth, Eighteenth, and Nineteenth Century Styles*, which remained the standard work for half a century, Correspondence, February–May 1960, IHPMFAH, Comstock file.

248. Reprint of "Miss Hogg's Remarks, Bayou Bend Docent Meeting, May 31, 1971," *The Bridge*, May 1991, (all quotes). For 1975 views of the room installations, see Warren, *Bayou Bend: Furniture, Paintings and Silver from the Bayou Bend Collection*, 2 (Pine), 5 (Murphy), 21 (Queen Anne Sitting Room), 22 (Queen Anne Bedroom), 38 (Drawing Room), 41 (Philadelphia Hall), 42 (Chippendale Bedroom), 43 (Newport Room), 44 (Massachusetts Room), 73 (Dining Room), 74 (McIntire Bedroom), 75 (Federal Parlor), 76 (Music Room), 111 (Maple Bedroom), 112 (Texas Room), 113 (Glazed Porch), 114 (Staffordshire Hall), 115 (Winedale Cottage).

249. Recollections of author and Margaret Erwin. The butterfly became the symbol of the docent newsletter, renamed the *Bayou Bend Docent Flyer*, in September 1977. The docent newsletter, now delivered in digital format, was renamed *The Bridge* in the late twentieth century (Margaret Culberson to the author, September 30, 2021).

250. "David Warren Looks Back," *The Intelligencer*, Winter 2003–2004, 4, 5 (extremely, large, study, how pretty); David B. Warren to Madeleine McDermott Hamm, *Houston Chronicle*, January 3, 2004, D1, D4 (stunned, extraordinary); entry August 25, 1965, IHPMFAH, scrapbook 2, p. 64 (handsome check); Ima Hogg to Edward Rotan, August 12, 1965, Rotan Report (could not). Lucious Broadnax (1916–1991) and Gertrude Vaughn (September 2, 1900–April 17, 1993, Houston) watched over Ima until she died. Gertrude was seventeen when she began working for the Hogg family and Lucious was a young man. Like family, they sent her Valentine's Day cards and helped her with her many projects.

251. *Dallas News*, June 4, 1967, clipping in HFR, MAI9/U1: 7 (all quotes).

252. Rudolf Melchior (1836, Burg, Prussia–January 14, 1868, Galveston), cofounded Latium, Washington County, TX; trained as artisan in Germany; 1853 migrated with parents to Galveston; settled near Winedale, where he painted until Civil War; fifer in Confederate Army; settled in Galveston; died of yellow fever at age thirty-two.

253. James Nonemaker, "Observations and Recommendations for the Stage Coach Inn," July 14, 1962, IHPBC, 4W243: 2 (no question). John Edmund (Ed) Langwith (August 31, 1925–September 19, 2012), graduate Rice University School of Architecture; practiced with Charles B. Wilson and Robert L. King for thirty-six years; in retirement joined wife Diane Aitken Langwith-McFall (1931–2019) as a docent at Bayou Bend.

254. John Young to Ima Hogg, October 8, 1964, IHPBC, 4W243 (decide just what).

255. Ima Hogg to Harry Ransom, October 2, 1964 (some), Harry Ransom to Ima Hogg, October 11 (honored, vision), IHPBC, 4W245: 2.

256. Unfortunately, this structure burned in 1981 but was replaced by new facilities to accommodate university classes in conservation and meeting space for public programs.

257. *Houston Chronicle*, April 12, 1967, clipping IHPMFAH, scrapbook 3: 35 (laboratory).

258. Ima Hogg Museum, IHPBC,4W263: 4 (imagine . . . home), 3 (turned wilderness). Today the Quitman Arboretum manages the Stinson House while the Governor Jim Hogg City Park administers the Honeymoon Cottage and the Ima Hogg

Museum, which still houses artifacts focusing on the Hoggs, famous Wood Country citizens, and life in East Texas. In the early 2000s, the buildings had been neglected, and many objects were removed to Varner-Hogg, but city officers began preserving the park center of their town and collecting appropriate artifacts in 2020–2021. Comments courtesy of Quitman city officials June 2021.

259. Diane Taylor to Dorothy and George Kupers, October 28, 1970, Winedale Files, BC (legendary, collection); Winedale Oral History Collection, BC Lonn Taylor, interviewed by Martha Norkunas, February 28, 1996 (was using).

260. Lonn Taylor to author, email December 5, 2002 (someone, wonderful, marvelous).

261. Lonn Taylor, oral history (big blue, unload stuff); 1975 correspondence among Barry Greenlaw, Diane Taylor, Lonn Taylor, Katherine Howe, Winedale Files, BC (wandering candlesticks) .

262. Ima frequently consulted Charles van Ravenswaay on her projects, knowing he had studied German settlement up the Mississippi Valley into Missouri. In 2012 Lonn Taylor and David Warren reprinted volume 1 and published volume 2 of *Texas Furniture*, much expanding understanding of the popular genre.

263. John Henry Belter (1804, Hilter, Germany–October 15, 1863, New York, tuberculosis), apprenticed in Stüttgart; 1833 to New York; 1839 American citizen; 1846–1854 shop J. H. Belter and Co. at 372 Broadway; 1854 built five-story factory in heart of New York City; preeminent among many German immigrant cabinetmakers in New York; widely copied in New York, Philadelphia, Boston, New Orleans; name synonymous with Arabasket style that combines hand carving with lamination and steam pressure; many patents on unusual method of cutting through laminated layers to achieve delicately curved and carved shapes without sacrificing strength; famous in his day with many wealthy clients; family tried to carry on but could not maintain his imaginative work product.

264. Harold Sack quoted in Michael K. Brown, *America's Treasures at Bayou Bend: Celebrating Fifty Years*, 136 (all quotes). See also Harold Sack and Max Wilk, *American Treasure Hunt: The Legacy of Israel Sack* (New York: Little Brown and Co: 1983), 183.

265. The Parlor Set (B.81.9.1–10, F232) had been sold to Green H. Jordan, a cotton planter in Georgia and was purchased by Ima from descendants in 1973, given to the Governor's Mansion to revert to Bayou Bend if the mansion could no longer use the set; reverted to Bayou Bend in 1981. The set includes two sofas, two armchairs, four side chairs, a center table, and an étagère (Warren et al, *Collection 1998*, F232, pp. 142–144).

266. Letters Elizabeth Stokes and Jane Zivley, June 1961, January 1964, IHPMFAH, 2:4 (blankets and linens); The author, who saw Ima Hogg in the room with the painter several times, has been an active docent since 1971, and this information comes from general touring knowledge.

267. Miss Ima Hogg, Women's Committee column, Houston Symphony Society programs December 13, 14, 1965, p. 25 (cultural necessities), December 8, 9, 10, 1974,

p. 27 (proper wrestling, dreams), December 19, 20, 1966, p. 33 (magnificent gift), December 13, 14, 1971, p. 23 (Fliegel), December 9, 10, 11, 1973, p. 23 (Shepherd School).

268. Carlos Chavez to Ima Hogg, April 27, 1948, IHPBC, 4W194: 2 (beloved orchestra); Ima Hogg to Carlos Chavez, August 18, 1969, 4W194:3 (since creation, what an opportunity); Carlos Chavez to Ima Hogg, November 24, 1969, 4W194: 3 (I have always); Ima Hogg to Carlos Chavez, March 23, 1970, 4W194:3 (completely, proud). Contract terms included satisfactory completion by December 31, 1969, and premier at her choice of time and place. Although Ima saw an official contract draft in April, final draft was not accepted by all parties until July, giving Chavez not even six months to compose.

269. Lovett Peters to Ima Hogg, June 15, 1959, IHPBC 4W235 (electrifying); Ima Hogg to John H. Freeman, June 14, 1960, IHPBC, 4W235: 1 (regret, desperately, substantial); Ima Hogg to John H. Freeman, June 27, 1960 (phone, thanks); Ima Hogg to Leopold Meyer, June 20, 1960, IHPBC, 4W235:1 (limited time); Ima Hogg to Robert Sutherland, April 27, 1967, HFR, MAI9/U1: 7 (I want you).

270. Robert Sutherland to William W. Steward, July 29, 1963, MAI/U14: 5 (thrilling); Robert Sutherland to Harry Ransom, no date but circa February 1969, HFR, MAI9/U14: 8 (invaluable). A 1969 summary noted that during the grant period (September 1964 through August 1968), forty-one Texas foundations assisted twenty-seven agencies to develop thirty-eight demonstration projects assisting children, youth, and families in the Southwest. In January 1969 Ima insisted that Sutherland be asked to remain for an additional year and be promoted to president (Ima Hogg to "My dear Sutherland" and to Harry Ransom, "I know of no one who has more unselfishly and wisely directed the course of any foundation," HFR, MAI9/U14: 9).

271. "Ima Hogg Foundation: Ima Hogg's Legacy to the Children of Houston," pamphlet (Austin: Hogg Foundation for Mental Health, 1990), (quotes).

272. Ima Hogg to Robert Sutherland, MAI9/U1: 7 (personal, beautiful).

273. Interview, Pat Prioleau with Mary Ann (Muffy) McClanahan, October 26, 2000, *The Bridge*, February/March, 13 (*Godspell*); author's reminiscences (briefed, because). The group at NASA included an MSC protocol officer, docent Betty Duson, Jane Zivley, Ima Hogg, and astronaut Anders.

274. Alfred R. Neumannn, dean of the College of Arts and Sciences, University of Houston, to Ima Hogg, February 25, 1967, IHPBC, 3B175: 5 (basis for history). Ima intended to exhibit books at Bayou Bend but did not collect enough period examples to make a comprehensive display. She gave 173 important or rare books to Looscan in 1962, another six boxes in 1963, and about 220 more volumes in 1965. Members of the Memorial Park Advisory Committee included conservationist Terry Hershey, Bayou Preservation Association President Frank C. Smith Jr., River Oaks Garden Club President Sadie Guin Blackburn, Houston Botanical Society President Dr. John D. Staub, and a member of the League of Women Voters Park Committee.

275. Acceptance remarks, National Conference of Christians and Jews Annual Brotherhood Dinner, March 10, 1955, IHPBC, 3B166: 1 (with some . . . citizens);

Austin American-Statesman, May 13, 1956, clipping, HFR, MAI9/U1: 3 (Texian Woman of the Year Award, outstanding); IHPMFAH, scrapbook 1: 64 (appeal), 89, 93 (decorators, extraordinary); scrapbook 2: 1 (remarkable).

276. *Daily Texan*, October 24, 1963 (distinguished); *Houston Post*, clipping "3 Houstonians to be Honored" (Ex-Students' Association Award); IMPMFAH, scrapbook 2, p. 103 (pleased); *Houston Chronicle*, October 9, 1966 (Louise duPont Crowninshield Award, superlative). For the first time, the Crowninshield Award went to two honorees, Ima and Mrs. Gordon Latham Kellenberger of Greensboro, NC., whose long acceptance speech compared unfavorably to Ima's brief but eloquent and gracious thank you.

277. *Houston Post*, June 9, 1968 (Santa Rita Award, persons); Ima Hogg to Mrs. E. J. Wheeler, March 19, 1969, IHPMFAH scrapbook 3: 71 (significant, feel); Philosophical Society of Texas Proceedings of the Annual Meeting, December 5–6, 1975, Ima Hogg Memorial (Rotary Club quote, demonstrated).

278. Joe Cariker, Varner Recollections, *The Bridge*, June/July 1996, from remarks made to the Bayou Bend docents April 15, 1996 (but don't tell). For her ninetieth birthday at Jones Hall, Lucious Broadnax and Nettie Jones's driver Johnny drove the group downtown in two cars. Photographs taken at the Lawhon's home identify the guests as Drusilla Huffmaster, Joyce Arce, James Dick, Ima Hogg, Wayne Bell, Virginia Lawhon, Griffith Lawhon, December 15, 1972. The Whitfield Marshalls' daughter Diana was also married at Bayou Bend shortly before Ima moved out.

279. As Kate Leader, I was the young docent working on the project completed in 2012 by historian Virginia Bernhard as *The Hoggs of Texas: Letters and Memoirs of an Extraordinary Family*. Before she left for Europe, Miss Hogg requested I return a box of papers I was working on at home; later I wondered if she felt she might not return. In 1974 she gave my newborn daughter Jennifer Leader an inscribed Bible.

280. Author's recollections; Memorial Service Leaflet, clippings from *New York Times*, August 21, 1975; "First Lady of Texas is dead", Houston *Chronicle*, August 23, 1975, p. 1, *Houston Post*, Miss Ima Hogg, Vertical File, MFAH; *Alcalde*, November-December 1975, 46, 47, *Alumni News*, "University Mourns Miss Ima: Death Claims Benefactress, Age 93."

Epilogue

1. *Houston Post*, March 16, 1919, clipping, Sharp Papers, WRC, 23:10, 11 (philanthropy); Don Carleton and Thomas H. Kreneck, "Houston, Back Where We Started," pamphlet produced by *Houston City Magazine*, 1979 (perennial, individuals, characterized); Ima Hogg, remarks dedicated to the members of the Women's Committee of the Houston Symphony Society, 1937–1962, IHPBC, 4W195: 10 (city of destiny).

2. Tribute to Julia Ideson, Philosophical Society of Texas *Proceedings*, 1945, p. 57 (all quotes).

3. Ima Hogg, statement, Annual Report, May 16, 1956, IHPCUH:1 (something).

4. BakerRipley website, accessed March 22, 2024 (bring, place, who want) .

5. DePelchin Children's Center website, mission statement, accessed Mar. 22, 2024 (strengthen).

6. "Houston's Greatest Need—Mother's and Children's Hospital," *Houston*, December 1919, p. 14 (most important).

WORKS CONSULTED

Archival Sources

Adams County (Nebraska) Historical Society, records

American Library Association, archives

Baker Botts LLP, library

  Baker, Captain James A., ledgers

DePelchin Children's Center

  Child Guidance Center board minute books

Dolph Briscoe Center for American History, University of Texas at Austin

  Board of Regents records, University of Texas at Austin

  Catalogue of the University of Texas, 1900–1901

  General Register of the Students

  Hogg, Ima papers, photography collection

  Hogg, James Stephen papers

  Hogg, William Clifford papers

  Hogg Foundation for Mental Health records

  Ideson, Julia vertical file

  John A. Lomax Family papers

  Winedale archives

  Winedale oral history collection

Houston Independent School District, Board of Education minutes, 1943–1949

Houston Metropolitan Research Center, Houston Public Library

  Chautauqua file

  Cherry, E. Richardson papers, MS 27

Committee on Inter-Racial Cooperation file
Community Chest files, 1928–1931
Congregation Beth Israel collection
Covington, Dr. Benjamin collection, MS 170
Daily, Ray K. papers, oral history
Downtown Club file
Federation of Women's Clubs file
First Presbyterian Church, Houston records, RG18
Hare and Hare collection
Hogg, Ima vertical file, oral history
Houston Light Guard file
Houston Library Association annual reports
Houston Library Association board minutes
Houston Library Association reports, 1904–1951
Houston Little Theatre file
Houston Open Forum records
Houston Social Service Bureau records, RGA-28
Houston Subdivision Collection
Ideson, Julia papers, MS32
Ladies' Reading Club vertical file
Milsaps, John E. T. collection, MS33
Ring, Elizabeth Fitzsimmons file
Tuesday Musical Club file
McLennan County, probate minutes
Museum of Fine Arts, Houston
Art League of Houston records
Art Museum Guild papers, 1939–1944
Bayou Bend Collection and Gardens, object files
Bayou Bend Docent Organization records, docent papers
Cherry, Emma Richardson vertical file
Chillman, James H. papers
Directors' records: James H. Chillman Jr, Lee Malone, James Johnson Sweeney
Exhibition files
Fall, Mrs. Henry B. (Florence K.) vertical file
Ferguson, William Booker, "Hogg Family Financial History," vertical file
Finnigan, Annette vertical file
Garden Club of Houston papers, MS14
Hanszen, Mrs. Harry C. vertical file
Hogg, Ima papers, vertical file
Hogg, Mike and Alice papers
Hogg, William Clifford vertical file

Hogg Brothers Collection records
Hogg Family personal papers
Registrar's Files
River Oaks Garden Club records
Trustee records
Nebraska Historical Society
Place Makers of Nebraska, digital version
University of Houston Special Collections
Cullinan, Joseph Stephen papers
Ima Hogg Program Collection, 1900–1978
University of Kentucky
Grahamton Manufacturing Company Records, digital version
Woodson Research Center, Rice University
Baker, James A. scrapbooks, MS 487
Baker Family Papers, MS 40
BakerRipley Foundation records, centennial records
Barnes, Marguerite Johnston personal papers MS491, oral histories MS455
Captain James A. Baker of Houston, 1857–1941, biography research materials, MS 609
Early Rice Institute records, UA-1
Hogg Family papers, MS 8
Lovett, Edgar Odell, personal papers
Presidential Office records, Edgar Odell Lovett, 1912–1945
Rice Institute, opening ceremony files
Sharp, Walter B. and Estelle B. papers, 1861–1978
Shurtleff, Stella Hope research and manuscript, MS 237
Tsanoff, Radoslav A., information file
Watkin, William Ward papers, MS 352

Newspapers, Magazines, Journals

Alcalde
Austin American
Austin American Statesman
The Bridge
Bryan Eagle
Bulletin of the Texas Library Association
Civics for Houston
Daily Southerner (Tarboro, NC)
Dallas Dispatch-Journal
El Paso Herald
Fort Worth Star-Telegram
Galveston Daily News

Galveston Daily Post
Hastings Gazette Journal
Hastings Journal
Houston Chronicle
Houston Chronicle and Herald
Houston Gargoyle
Houston Labor Journal
Houston Post
Houston Post-Dispatch
Houston Press
Houston Symphony Society programs
The Intelligencer
Landscape Architecture Magazine
McKinney Daily Courier
Missions: American Baptist International Magazine
Musical America
National Tribune (Washington, DC)
Oshkosh Northwestern
Philosophical Society of Texas Proceedings
Progressive Houston: A Monthly Publication for the Benefit of the Taxpayer and General Public
River Oaks Magazine
Round Top Register
San Antonio Express
San Antonio Gazette
Waco Daily Examiner
Waco Morning News
Waco News Tribune
Winnsboro News
Woman's Viewpoint

Published Sources

Americans at Home: The Bayou Bend Collection of American Decorative Arts." Brochure. Houston: Museum of Fine Arts, 1997.

Andrews, F. Emerson. *Philanthropic Foundations*. New York: Russell Sage Foundation, 1956.

Aulbach, Louis F. *Buffalo Bayou: An Echo of Houston's Wilderness Beginnings*. Houston: Louis F. Aulbach, 2012.

———, Linda C. Gorski, and Robbie Morin. *Camp Logan: Houston, Texas, 1917–1919: A World War I Emergency Training Center*. Houston: Louis F. Aulbach, 2014.

Baines, May Harper. *Houston's Part in the World War*. Houston: Author, 1919.

Banttari, Sally Robert. "The Evolution of the Bayou Bend Gardens, Houston, Texas (1926–1989)." Master of Landscape Architecture thesis, Louisiana State University, Baton Rouge, 1975.

Barnstone, Howard, Stephen Fox, Jerome Iowa, and David Courtwright. *The Architecture of John F. Staub: Houston and the South*. Austin: University of Texas Press, 1979.

Beard, Mary Ritter. *Woman's Work in the Municipalities*. New York: D. Appleton and Company, 1915.

Benda, Ilona B. *Our Community War Service Memorial: Houston and Harris County*. 1919.

Bernhard, Virginia, ed. *Grand Tours and the Great War: Ima Hogg's Diaries, 1907–1918*. With commentary by Virginia Bernhard and Roswitha Wagner. College Station: Texas A&M University Press, 2022.

———. *The Hoggs of Texas: Letters and Memoirs of an Extraordinary Family, 1887–1906*. Denton: Texas State Historical Association, 2013.

———. "Ima Hogg in Europe, 1914," *Southwestern Historical Quarterly*, 119 (January 2016).

———. *The Smell of War*. College Station: Texas A&M University Press, 2018.

———. "A Texan in the Trenches: Mike Hogg's World War I Letters," *Southwestern Historical Quarterly*, 117 (July, October 2013).

Bixel, Patricia Bellis, and Elizabeth Hayes Turner. *Galveston and the 1900 Storm: Catastrophe and Catalyst*. Austin: University of Texas Press, 2000.

Blair, Karen J. *The Torchbearers: Women and Their Amateur Arts Associations in America, 1890–1930*. Bloomington: Indiana University Press, 1994.

Bobick, Ruth. *Six Remarkable Hull-House Women*. Portsmouth, NH: Peter E. Randall Publisher, 2015.

Boles, John B. *University Builder: Edgar Odell Lovett and the Founding of Rice Institute*. Baton Rouge: Louisiana State University Press, 2007.

Bowie, Walter Russell. *The Master of the Hill: A Biography of John Meigs*. New York: Dodd Mead and Company, 1917.

Bradley, Barrie Scardino. *Improbable Metropolis: Houston's Architectural and Urban History*. Austin: University of Texas Press, 2020.

Breckenridge, Sophonisba P. *Women in the Twentieth Century: A Study of Their Political, Social and Economic Activities*. New York: McGraw-Hill Book Company, Inc., 1933; reprint, New York: Arno Press, 1972.

Brooks, David. *The Second Mountain: The Quest for a Moral Life*. New York: Random House, 2019.

Brown, Michael K. *America's Treasures at Bayou Bend: Celebrating Fifty Years*. Museum of Fine Arts, Houston: Scala Publishers, 2007.

Bullard, Robert D. *Invisible Houston: The Black Experience in Boom and Bust*. College Station: Texas A&M University Press, 1987.

Burlingame, Dwight F., ed. *The Responsibilities of Wealth*. Bloomington: Indiana University Press, 1992.

Burton, William R. and David J. Lewis. *Past and Present of Adams County, Nebraska*, 2 vols. Chicago: The S. J. Clarke Publishing Company, 1916.

Cactus, University of Texas, 1898–1903.

Carleton, Don E. *Red Scare! Right-Wing Hysteria, Fifties Fanaticism, and Their Legacy in Texas*. Austin: Texas Monthly Press, 1985.

Carnegie, Andrew. "Wealth," *North American Review* 158, no. 398 (June 1889).

Carroll, B. H. *Standard History of Houston, Texas: From a Study of the Original Sources*. Knoxville: H. W. Crew, 1912.

Chapman, Betty. *Houston Women: Invisible Threads in the Tapestry*. Virginia Beach: Donning Company Publishers, 2000.

———. "Julia Bedford Ideson: A Woman for All Seasons," *Houston History* 6, no. 2 (Spring 2009).

———. *100 Years–100 Stories: Houston Public Library, 1904–2004*. Houston: Houston Public Library, 2004.

———. "100 Years of the Chautauqua Study Club," *Houston History* 7, no. 2 (Spring 2010).

Chernow, Ron. *Titan: The Life of John D. Rockefeller, Sr.* New York: Random House, 1998.

Cotner, Robert C. *James Stephen Hogg: A Biography*. Austin: University of Texas Press, 1959.

Cummins, Light Townsend. *Emily Austin of Texas, 1795–1851*. Fort Worth: Center for Texas Studies at Texas Christian University, 2009.

Davidson, Judge Mark. "The Making of a Judge: 1862, Electing a Judge during the Civil War," *The Houston Lawyer*, September/October 1998.

Directory of Ex-Students of the College of Arts and Sciences of Baylor. Digitized version.

Downs, Fane, and Nancy Baker Jones. Keynote Essay by Elizabeth Fox-Genovese. *Women and Texas History: Selected Essays*. Austin: Texas Historical Association, 1993.

Edward, Laura F. *Scarlett Doesn't Live Here Anymore: Southern Women in the Civil War Era*. Urbana: University of Illinois Press, 2000.

Egerton, John. *Speak Now Against the Day: The Generation before the Civil Rights Movement in the South*. New York: Alfred A. Knopf, 1994.

Ehrenberg, John. *Civil Society: The Critical History of an Idea*. New York: New York University Press, 1999.

Ellis, A. Caswell, and Hugo Kuehne. "School Buildings," *Bulletin of the University of Texas*, Series no. 13, June 15, 1905.

Ely, Glen Sample. *Murder in Montague: Frontier Justice and Retribution in Texas*. Norman: University of Oklahoma, 2020.

Emerson, Jon, and Associates. "A Plan for the Preservation, Management, and Interpretation of Bayou Bend Gardens, Houston, Texas: A Property of the Museum of Fine Arts, Houston." Baton Rouge. Courtesy of Susan Keeton, River Oaks Garden Club.

Emmott, Sarah. *Memorial Park: A Priceless Legacy.* Houston: Herring Press, 1992.

Erath, George B. "Reminiscences," *Waco City Directory, 1878.* Baylor University, The Texas Collection, Waco City Directories, digital version.

Faust, Drew Gilpin. *Mothers of Invention: Women of the Slaveholding South in the American Civil War.* Chapel Hill: University of North Carolina Press, 2000.

Federation of Women's Clubs. *The Key to the City of Houston.* Houston: State Printing Company, 1908.

Fenberg, Steven. *Unprecedented Power: Jesse Jones, Capitalism, and the Common Good.* College Station: Texas A&M University Press, 2011.

Fox, Stephen. *The Architecture of Birdsall P. Briscoe.* Photography by Paul Hester. College Station: Texas A&M University Press, 2023.

———. *The Country Houses of John F. Staub.* College Station: Texas A&M University Press, 2007.

Freeman, J. H. *The People of Baker Botts.* Houston: Baker & Botts, 1992.

A Garden Book for Houston. Houston: Forum of Civics, 1929; River Oaks Garden Club, 1945.

Garrison, Dee. *Apostles of Culture: The Public Librarian and American Society, 1876–1920.* New York: The Free Press, 1979.

Ginzberg, Lori D. *Women and the Work of Benevolence: Morality, Politics, and Class in the Nineteenth-Century United States.* New Haven, CT: Yale University Press, 1990.

Glenn, John M., Lilian Brandt, and F. Emerson Andrews. *Russell Sage Foundation, 1907–1946.* New York: Russell Sage Foundation, 1947.

Goodwin, Doris Kearns. *The Bully Pulpit: Theodore Roosevelt, William Howard Taft, and the Golden Age of Journalism.* New York: Simon & Schuster, 2013.

Gould, Lewis L. *Progressives and Prohibitionists: Texas Democrats in the Wilson Era.* Austin: University of Texas Press, 1973.

———. "The University Becomes Politicized: The War with Jim Ferguson, 1915–1918," *Southwestern Historical Quarterly,* 86 (October 1982).

Gray, E. Berry. *Victorian County Courthouses and County History in Post Cards.* Durham, NC: Lulu Press, Inc., 2017.

Gunter, Jewel Boone Hamilton. *Committed: The Official 100-Year History of the Women's Clubs of Houston, 1893–1993.* Houston: Woman's Club, 1995.

Hall, Peter Dobkin. *Inventing the Nonprofit Sector and Other Essays on Philanthropy, Voluntarism, and Nonprofit Organizations.* Baltimore: Johns Hopkins University Press, 1992.

Hall, Randal, ed. *William M. Rice and His Institute: The Centennial Edition*. College Station: Texas A&M University Press, 2012.

Hallas, James H. *Squandered Victory: The American First Army at St. Mihiel*. Westport, CT: Praeger, 1995.

Handbook of Texas Online (Texas State Historical Association).

Hastings City Directory.

Hatch, Orin Walker. *Lyceum to Library: A Chapter in the Cultural History of Houston*. Texas Gulf Coast Historical Association, 1965.

Haynes, Robert V. *A Night of Violence: The Houston Riot of 1917*. Baton Rouge: Louisiana State University Press, 1976.

Henderson, Archie. "City Planning in Houston, 1920–1930," *Houston Review*, IX:3, 1987, p. 107–136.

Hogan, Margaret A., and C. James Taylor, eds. *Letters of Abigail and John Adams*. Cambridge: Harvard University Press, 2007.

Hogg, Ima. *Reminiscences of Life in the Texas Governor's Mansion*. With an Introduction by Jerry D. Frazee. Austin: Paragon Printing, 2013.

Hogg, Thomas Elisha. *The Fate of Marvin*. Reprint: Press of Premier, September 1973.

Horn, Margo. *Before It's Too Late: The Child Guidance Movement in the United States, 1922–1945*. Philadelphia: Temple University Press, 1989.

Horowitz, Helen Lefkowitz. *Culture & The City: Cultural Philanthropy in Chicago from the 1880s to 1917*. Chicago: University of Chicago Press, 1989.

Houghton, Dorothy Knox Howe, Barry M. Scardino, Sadie Gwin Blackburn, and Katherine S. Howe. *Houston's Forgotten Heritage: Landscape, Houses, Interiors, 1824–1914*. Houston: Rice University Press, 1991.

Houston Artist Cooperatives in the 1930s. Essays by Randolph K. Tibbits, Kelly Montana, Scott Grant Barker. San Angelo, TX: Center for the Advancement and Study of Early Texas Art, 2017.

Houston City Directories.

Houston Foundation. *The Community: Review of Philanthropic Thought and Social Effort* 1, no. 1, May 1919.

Houston Settlement Association. *Year Book, 1909*. Houston: Settlement Association, 1910.

"Houston Women in Texas and U.S. History," *The Houston Review of History and Culture* 1, no. 1, 1–70.

Ilchman, Warren F., Stanley N. Katz, and Edward L. Queen II. *Philanthropy in the World's Traditions*. Bloomington: Indiana University Press, 1998.

Johnson, Joan Marie. *Southern Ladies, New Women: Race, Region, and Clubwomen in South Carolina, 1890–1930*. Gainesville: University Press of Florida, 2004.

Jones, Howard. *The Red Diary: A Chronological History of Black Americans in Houston and Some Neighboring Harris County Communities—112 Years Later*. Austin: Nortex Press, 1991.

Kellar, William H. "Alive with a Vengeance: Houston's Black Teachers and Their Fight for Equal Pay," *Houston Review: History and Culture of the Gulf Coast* 18, no. 2 (1996), 89–99.

Kerber, Linda. *Women of the Republic: Intellect and Ideology in Revolutionary America.* Chapel Hill: University of North Carolina Press, 1980.

Kiger, Joseph C. *Philanthropic Foundations in the Twentieth Century.* Westport, CT: Greenwood Press, 2000.

King, Judy. *Except the Lord Build . . . The Sesquicentennial History of First Presbyterian Church, Houston, Texas 1839–1989.* Houston: The Church, 1989.

Kirkland, Kate Sayen. *Captain James A. Baker of Houston, 1857–1941.* College Station: Texas A&M University Press, 2012.

———. "For All Houston's Children: Ima Hogg and the Board of Education, 1943–1949," *Southwestern Historical Quarterly* 101 (April 1998).

———. *The Hogg Family and Houston: Philanthropy and the Civic Ideal.* Austin: University of Texas Press, 2009.

———. "A Wholesome Life: Ima Hogg's Vision for Mental Health Care," *Southwestern Historical Quarterly* 104 (January 2001).

Kiser, Clyde V. *The Milbank Memorial Fund: Its Leaders and Its Work, 1905–1974.* New York: Milbank Memorial Fund, 1975.

Klineberg, Stephen L. *Prophetic City: Houston on the Cusp of a Changing America.* With Amy Hertz. New York: Avid Reader Press, 2020.

Koen, Karleen. "Bayou Bend," *Houston Home & Garden,* March 1975.

Lagemann, Ellen Condliffe. *Philanthropic Foundations: New Scholarship, New Possibilities.* Bloomington: Indiana University Press, 1999.

Lengel, Edward G. *To Conquer Hell: The Meuse-Argonne, 1918.* New York: Henry Holt and Company, 2008.

Levitsky, Steven, and Daniel Ziblatt. *How Democracies Die.* New York: Crown, 2018.

Locke, Ralph P., and Cyrilla Barr, eds. *Cultivating Music in America: Women Patrons and Activists since 1860.* Berkeley: University of California Press, 1997.

Lomax, John A. *Will Hogg, Texan.* Austin: University of Texas Press, 1956.

Looscan, Mrs. A. B. "Early Houston Society and Its Relation to Libraries," *Houston Public Library Annual Report for 1926.* Houston: Houston Public Library, 1927.

Looser, Donald William. "A Musical Renaissance: The Growth of Cultural Institutions in Houston, 1929–1936," *Houston Review: History and Culture of the Gulf Coast* 6:3 (1984), 135–155.

———. "Music in Houston, 1930–1971," with annotated index. PhD diss., Florida State University, 1972; revised and updated, 2020. Digital Version.

Lundberg, Dr. Robert H. *Bass Rocks Golf Club, 1896–1996.* Author, 1995.

"Lyceum to Landmark: The Julia Ideson Building of the Houston Public Library." Houston: School of Architecture, Rice University and Friends of the Houston Public Library, 1979.

Mackin, Elton E. *Suddenly We Didn't Want to Die: Memoirs of a World War I Marine.* Introduction and annotation by George B. Clark. Novato, CA: Presidio Press, 1993.

Maxwell, W. J., and John A. Lomax. *General Register of the Students and Former Students of the University of Texas.* Austin: 1917.

McGerr, Michael. *A Fierce Discontent: The Rise and Fall of the Progressive Movement in America, 1870–1920.* New York: Free Press, 2003.

McSwain, Mary Brown. "Julia Bedford Ideson: Houston Librarian, 1880–1945." Master's thesis, Library Science, University of Texas, 1966.

McWhorter, Thomas. "Trailblazers in Houston's East End: The Impact of Ripley House and the Settlement Association on Houston's Hispanic Population." *Houston History* 9:1 (Fall 2011), 9–13.

Meyer, Leopold. *The Days of My Years: Autobiographical Reflections.* Houston: Universal Printer, 1975.

Montgomery, Julia Cameron. *Houston as a Setting of the Jewel: The Rice Institute.* Houston: Julia Cameron Montgomery, 1913; Republished by Rice Historical Society, 2002.

Muensterberger, Werner. *Collecting: An Unruly Passion; Psychological Perspective.* Princeton: Princeton Legacy Press, 1994.

Muir, Andrew Forest. "Intellectual Climate of Houston during the Period of the Republic." *Southwestern Historical Quarterly* 62:3 (January 1959), 312–321.

Muncy, Robyn. *Creating a Female Dominion in American Reform, 1890–1935.* New York: Oxford University Press, 1991.

Neff, Emily. *Frederic Remington: The Hogg Brothers Collection at the Museum of Fine Arts, Houston.* Princeton: Princeton University Press, 2000.

Neighborhood Centers, Inc. *An Enduring Promise: 100 Years.* Bellaire, Texas: Neighborhood Centers, Inc., 2007.

———. *Heart of Gold Yearbook.* Houston: Neighborhood Centers, Inc., 1997.

Norton, Mary Beth. *Liberty's Daughters: The Revolutionary Experience of American Women, 1750–1800.* Ithaca: Cornell University Press, 1980.

Ostrower, Francie. *Why the Wealthy Give: The Culture of Elite Philanthropy.* Princeton: Princeton University Press, 1998.

"Our Story/First Presbyterian Church Timeline." Digital version.

Philanthropy in the Southwest: Foundations Cooperate in Community Programs, A Résumé of the Years 1966–1968. Austin: Hogg Foundation for Mental Health, University of Texas, 1969.

Play and Playground Encyclopedia Online.

Putnam, Robert D., and Shaylyn Romney Garrett. *The Upswing: How America Came Together a Century Ago and How We Can Do It Again.* New York: Simon & Schuster, 2020.

The Red Book of Houston: A Compendium of Social, Professional, Religious, Educational and Industrial Interests of Houston's Colored Population. Houston: SOTEX Publishing Company, 1915. Reproduced by Forgotten Books, 2018.

Report of the City Planning Commission of Houston. Houston: Forum of Civics, 1929.

Roussel, Hubert. *The Houston Symphony Orchestra, 1913–1971*. Austin: University of Texas Press, 1972.

Sanborn Maps, Hastings, Nebraska, 1880s; Houston, Texas, 1890s–1940s.

Scott, Anne Firor. *Natural Allies: Women's Associations in American History*. Urbana: University of Illinois Press, 1991.

———. *The Southern Lady: From Pedestal to Politics, 1830–1930*. Chicago: University of Chicago Press, 1970.

Scott, Janelle D. "Local Leadership in the Woman Suffrage Movement: Houston's Campaign for the Vote 1917–1918." *Houston Review* 12 (1990).

Sealander, Judith. *Private Wealth & Public Life: Foundation Philanthropy and the Reshaping of American Social Policy from the Progressive Era to the New Deal*. Baltimore: The Johns Hopkins University Press, 1997.

Shields, Patricia, ed. *Jane Addams: Progressive Pioneer of Peace, Philanthropy, Sociology, Social Work, and Public Administration*. New York: Spring International Publishing, 2017.

Sloan, Anne. "Altering the Fine Edge of Respectability: Business Women in Houston, 1880–1920," *Houston Review* 1:1 (Fall 2003), 37–46.

SoRelle, James Martin. "The Darker Side of 'Heaven': The Black Community in Houston, Texas, 1917–1945." PhD diss., Kent State University, 1980.

Spilenek, Elizabeth H. *Hastings: Then and Now*. Charleston, SC: Arcadia, 2009.

Sproul, Kathleen. "James Stephen Hogg: March 24, 1851–March 3, 1906." Pamphlet. West Columbia, TX: Author, March 24, 1958.

Stillinger, Elizabeth. *The Antiquers: The Lives and Careers, the Deals, the Finds, the Collections of the Men and Women Who Were Responsible for the Changing Taste in American Antiques, 1850–1930*. New York: Alfred A. Knopf, 1980.

Stringer, Tommy W. "Joseph S. Cullinan: Pioneer in Texas Oil." *East Texas Historical Journal*, 19:2 (1981).

Taylor, Lonn. "Ima Hogg and the Historic Preservation Movement in Texas, 1950–1975," *Southwestern Historical Quarterly* 117 (2015).

———, and David B. Warren. *Texas Furniture: The Cabinetmakers and Their Work, 1840–1880*, vol. 1, rev. ed. Foreword by Ima Hogg. vol. 2, foreword by Don Carleton. Austin: University of Texas Press, 2012.

Texas Cook Book, The: A Thorough Treatise on the Art of Cookery. Houston: Ladies' Association of the First Presbyterian Church, 1883.

Texas Historical Markers, digital version.

Toqueville, Alexis de. *Democracy in America*. Edited by Richard D. Heffner. New York: Penguin Group, Menton, 1956.

Trimble, Frances G. *Houston Country Club Centennial, 1908–2008*. Houston: Houston Country Club, 2008.

Tsanoff, Corrinne S. *Neighborhood Doorways*. Houston: Neighborhood Centers Association of Houston and Harris County, 1958.

Turner, Elizabeth Hayes. *Women, Culture, and Community: Religion and Reform in Galveston, 1880–1920*. New York: Oxford University Press, 1997.

US Census, 1850–1970.

Waco City Directories.

Waco History. Digital version.

Warren, David B. *Bayou Bend: American Furniture, Paintings and Silver from the Bayou Bend Collection*, foreword by Ima Hogg. New York Graphic Society: Museum of Fine Arts, Houston, 1975.

———. *The Bayou Bend Gardens: A Southern Oasis*. London: Scala Publishers, 2006.

———. *Ima Hogg: The Extraordinary Cultural Patron behind the Unusual Name*. Houston: Museum of Fine Arts, Houston, 2016.

———, Michael K. Brown, Elizabeth Ann Coleman, and Emily Ballew Neff. *American Decorative Arts and Paintings in the Bayou Bend Collection*. Princeton: Museum of Fine Arts, Houston in association with Princeton University Press, 1998.

White, Lonnie J. *The 90th Division in World War I: The Texas-Oklahoma Draft Division in the Great War*. Manhattan, KS: Sunflower University Press, 1996.

Williams, Joyce E., and Vicky M. MacLean. *Settlement Sociology in the Progressive Years: Faith, Science, and Reform*. Leiden/Boston: Brill, 2015.

Winegarten, Ruthe, and Judith N. McArthur, eds. *Citizens at Last: The Woman Suffrage Movement in Texas*. College Station: Texas A&M University Press, 2015.

Wythe, George. *A History of the 90th Division*. The 90th Division Association, 1920.

INDEX